The Chronicle of United States Theater Since 1920

Best Plays Theater Yearbook

Founded by Burns Mantle

THE BEST PLAYS OF 2000–2001

Jeffrey Eric Jenkins
Editor

EDITORIAL BOARD
Robert Brustein
Tish Dace
Christine Dolen
Mel Gussow
Robert Hurwitt
John Istel
Chris Jones
Julius Novick
Michael Phillips
Christopher Rawson
Alisa Solomon
Jeffrey Sweet
Linda Winer
Charles Wright

PAST EDITORS
(1919-2000)
Burns Mantle
John Chapman
Louis Kronenberger
Henry Hewes
Otis L. Guernsey Jr.

CONSULTING EDITOR
Henry Hewes

ASSISTANT EDITORS
Rue E. Canvin, Joshua Crouthamel, Vivian Cary Jenkins

THE BEST PLAYS
THEATER YEARBOOK

THE BEST PLAYS OF 2000–2001

EDITED BY JEFFREY ERIC JENKINS

Illustrated with photographs and with drawings by HIRSCHFELD

LIMELIGHT EDITIONS

ISBN: 0-87910-968-8

ISSN: 1071-6971

Printed in the United States of America

Al Hirschfeld is represented exclusively by the Margo Feiden Galleries, New York City.

For nearly four decades, one man nurtured and strengthened the *Best Plays* series through all manner of challenges in the theater and in publishing. It is largely due to his efforts that we have this continuing record of theater in the United States.

The Best Plays of 2000–2001
is dedicated to the memory of
Otis L. Guernsey Jr.
1918–2001

INTRODUCTION

AS THIS 82ND EDITION of the *Best Plays* series goes to press, Americans everywhere grieve for the loss of thousands of innocent lives in the terrorist attacks of September 11, 2001. Although *Best Plays* traditionally focuses solely on the events of the theater season it covers—in this volume from June 1, 2000 to May 31, 2001—it seems appropriate to acknowledge the circumstances in which we now find ourselves.

For those of us who make our homes in New York, the occasional glance toward where the World Trade Center towers once stood, casting their looming shadows over large portions of downtown, serves as a painful reminder of those tragic events. Because the skyline of this great city is filled with so many distinctive outlines, some may find it difficult to locate precisely where that massive pair of landmarks once stood. When darkness falls, however, the lights from the recovery site emit a brilliant, eerie glow that fills the evening sky.

In the blocks beyond the immediate work area, downtown theaters Off and Off Off Broadway have begun to see their audiences return after weeks when several of the smaller institutions tottered on the brink of collapse. Drama students, their teachers and theater artists ask themselves, "Why theater?" at this time of difficulty, when the drumbeat of war sets the rhythm of political life. The question, of course, underpins part of the crisis facing the arts in the United States. It is a question born of the view that theater is mere entertainment, diversion, frivolity. But the view from this corner is more expansive.

Unlike other performance-oriented media such as film and television with their flat, hypermediated imagery, theater forges an immediate, human connection that is increasingly important in our technology-driven society. It is the power of this connection that encourages us to join others—as spectators and performers—for a few evanescent moments of shared experience. Entertainment often follows, but so too does a deeper understanding of ourselves, of others and of our relationships to one another.

Why theater, then? Because it is a candle that shines in the gathering darkness of confusion, despair and terror.

As we move forward with our ongoing chronicle of theater in the United States, we pause to think of those who were lost and to honor their sacrifice by reporting on those points of human communion wherever we may find them.

* * *

GROWING UP as a New York Yankees fan in Kansas, I was more obsessed with Mickey Mantle than I was with Burns Mantle. While researching a musical comedy at the new public library in Wichita, though, I discovered a treasure trove of theater music in Broadway cast albums. Using the library's mid-1960s state-of-the-art listening stations, I could don a headset and be transported to the Great White Way of yore.

Rodgers and Hammerstein, Lerner and Loewe, Rodgers and Hart, Cole Porter, Irving Berlin and others filled those hours when I could steal away from my father's shoe repair, where I worked after school and on weekends. (Trips to the library were always allowed; if only he knew how I often spent the time.)

At some point early on, I found the album covers and liner notes lacking the information I craved to get a fuller sense of the live Broadway musical experience. A helpful librarian pointed me to the *Best Plays* series, founded by Burns Mantle in 1920, and I began to work my way through excerpts, indices, seasons, statistics. Along the way, I fell under the spell not just of musicals, but of all aspects of drama and theater. Until the recent past, when low-cost air travel and long runs for hit shows became the norm—not to mention the rapid expansion of the resident theater movement across the country—the *Best Plays* series was the armchair view of the theater season upon which many Americans relied.

As we now launch the series into a new era, a time when millions more Americans have access to quality professional theater, we have made important changes to the structure of the *Best Plays* book that reflect the growth of theater and theater education throughout the country. In the place of the play excerpts, which once allowed those in the hinterlands to get a literary approximation of the theater experience, we now have critical appreciations of the Best Plays in essays by prominent critics from around the country.

This new approach to celebrating the finest theater writing in the United States accomplishes several things at once. At their best, the excerpts were a poor substitute for the experience of hearing a text spoken by living actors. They were, however, elegantly rendered by past editors right up to and including (especially) my predecessor, Otis L. Guernsey Jr. But they were, as the saying goes, "neither fish nor fowl." A scholar wishing to study the textual mysteries of a play would need to look somewhere besides our redacted collection. Acting students seeking a scene to study for a class would likewise turn to other sources. Budding playwrights looking for inspiration or understanding of structure might find it in part, but there would remain the play editor's subjective imprint on another's creative work.

As play publishing and production in this country continued to grow, it became clear to Mr. Guernsey, and his longtime collaborator, Jonathan Dodd, that theater culture had outgrown the excerpt format. When I was asked to keep this series going as the sixth editor, it was clear we needed to make a change that would better reflect theater today. Over the course of the 20th century there was exciting growth in programs of theater and theater studies in higher education. At the beginning of that century there were no formal programs of study, but by its end there were nearly 1,200 theater and theater studies programs throughout the United States. Theater publishing of the past decades has likewise seen a strong upward surge in critical writing as a variety of perspectives are sought by teachers and students alike. When combined with our long tradition of providing comprehensive reference information on play productions in New York and throughout the country, we believe that the *Best Plays* essays provide an important overview of United States theater to theater lovers, librarians, historians, critics, students and scholars.

II

WHEN THE GOLDEN ERA of the American musical began in 1943 with the premiere of *Oklahoma!*, Mr. Mantle was in his 24th season as editor of the series. Until that 1942–43 volume, only three musicals had been deemed worthy of *Best Plays* honors; an average of about one every eight years. For the 1942–43 edition, though, the editor departed "from routine" and included the groundbreaking *Oklahoma!* among the Best Plays. Since that watershed season, 71 musicals have been honored in these pages—averaging a little more than one per year, still a small percentage of the total—under Mr. Mantle's leadership and that of his successors: John Chapman, Louis Kronenberger, Henry Hewes and Mr. Guernsey.

The inclusion of musicals in lists of Best Plays leads us to two thorny questions about dramatic works: "What is a play?" and "What is a Best Play?" The latter question is somewhat easier to address, given the book's track record and the changes we are making with this edition. But the former query carries with it the biases of generations of theater people, critics and audiences.

Since the mid-19th century, the Scribean formula of the *pièce bien faite*—better known as the "well-made" play—has held sway over Anglo-European dramatic discourse. The "well-made" play consists of familiar storytelling techniques that include a pattern of increasing tension, a seesaw battle between two forces, corresponding low and high points for the hero, and a credible, satisfying resolution to the tale. There are other elements of lesser importance that comprise this type of drama, but the careful reader of *Best Plays* past will find that the "well-made" has constituted a substantial proportion of our past honorees.

Partly in response to developments outside the theatrical mainstream, United States theater practitioners and scholars of the past two generations have begun to think more deeply and broadly about the phenomenon of performance as it relates to text and vice versa. Even as early as 1920, though, Mr. Mantle ruminated on these issues:

> As frequently has been pointed out, there are many plays that read well which do not "act," as the players phrase the description, and many a success that "acts," usually by reason of the popularity and skill of the players engaged, becomes the sheerest piffle when submitted to the test of type.

The founding editor argued for a "sanely considered compromise," and yet we find "well-mades" dominating the *Best Plays* honors for more than four-score years. To look at the list of honored plays at the back of this book is to bear witness to a graveyard of 20th-century dramatic aspiration. How is it possible, we might ask, that Sam Shepard has been honored but once—for his relatively late-career *Fool For Love*—and Zoë Akins was honored twice?

Ms. Akins was a popular scenarist in the early 20th century, but she is best known for winning the 1935 Pulitzer Prize in Drama for *The Old Maid*. New York drama critics were so outraged at the choice that they formed the New York Drama Critics Circle and began giving awards to balance—some might say "to counter"—the Pulitzer. By honoring 10 works, *The Best Plays of 1934–35* was able to celebrate Ms. Akins and not overlook Clifford Odets's *Awake and Sing*, Lillian Hellman's *The Children's Hour*, Robert E. Sherwood's *The Petrified Forest*, Maxwell Anderson's *Valley Forge*, George S. Kaufman and Moss Hart's *Merrily We Roll Along* and others.

Mr. Shepard, a Pulitzer winner for *Buried Child*, began his career in the coffee shops of Off Off Broadway experimenting with language that had a rock-and-roll sensibility laced with the iconography of the Old West (as defined by the myth machine of Hollywood). His plays about family and identity locate him as a prime theatrical interpreter of the late 20th century zeitgeist. Indeed, one might draw a straight line between Eugene O'Neill's estranged brothers in *Beyond the Horizon* (1920) and Mr. Shepard's not dissimilar pair in the popular *True West* (1981). Even though we might suppose there was room on a slate of 10 for one of Mr. Shepard's plays at several times in his theater-writing career, it happened only once.

The reasons for inclusion or exclusion in *Best Plays* lie, of course, in the tastes of editors and editors are shaped by (even as they hope to help shape) the cultural tastes of their times. A look at the most honored playwrights in the *Best Plays* series is illustrative. Maxwell Anderson, rarely produced in recent decades, was honored 19 times for his own plays and for his collaborations with Kurt Weill (*Lost in the Stars*) and Laurence Stallings (*What Price Glory?*). A cursory glance at *Best Plays*'s most honored playwrights is an otherwise familiar litany: George S. Kaufman (17 times), Neil Simon (15), Mr. O'Neill (12), Moss Hart (11), Terrence McNally (11), Tennessee Williams (11), Philip Barry (10), S.N. Behrman (9), Lillian Hellman (9) and Robert E. Sherwood (9).

This list is interesting because it represents not only the 10 top honorees, but is also a history of early 20th century commercial theater in the United States. The prolific Neil Simon and the versatile Terrence McNally are still among us, but the rest of the group are a generation or more removed from new production. To be fair to more recent dramatists, the next group of 10 includes Arthur Miller (8), Stephen Sondheim (8), August Wilson (8), Edward Albee (7), Athol Fugard (7), Tom Stoppard (7), Brian Friel (6) and David Mamet (6)—all of whom are still productive. As the 20th century unfolded, writers who once focused on theater began to drift to the West Coast and more lucrative forms of employment in film and television. Nowadays it is more and more common for a playwright to have an Off Broadway success followed by a job as a writer or producer on a television program—and playwriting takes a backseat to what television producer Steven Bochco once called "the script monster."

III

WHEN MR. MANTLE began this series with an appreciation of the 1919–20 New York theater season, he wrote,

> The intention frankly has been to compromise between the popular success, as representing the choice of the people who support the theater, and the success with sufficient claim to literary distinction of text or theme to justify its publication.

Over the decades, the standards declared by the founding editor varied slightly from time to time and from editor to editor. But as Mr. Mantle also wrote in that first volume, "no more is claimed than that [these plays] represent the best judgment of the editor, variously confirmed by the public's indorsement."

In the interest of greater representation, I asked a group of distinguished critics and theater writers from around the United States to join an editorial board to consider the list of finalists for *Best Plays* honors, to make certain that worthy dramatic works are not overlooked and to contribute essays to the book. Although the final choices remain the purview of the editor, these dedicated editorial board members—who are listed elsewhere in the front matter—provide an important service to the series and to theater in the United States.

Even though theater in this country has increasingly decentralized and the resident theater movement has taken root in cities large and small, *Best Plays* has clung, in the past, to the notion that the finest works emanate from New York. As a result, the Best Play choices have been limited to New York. Indeed, through much of the 20th century, new plays often toiled in pre-New York engagements meant to develop those works' potential. But New York was the goal and the New York production was the yardstick by which new plays would be measured.

As Mr. Mantle wrote in his introduction to that first volume:

> We feel, therefore, that every drama entitled to inclusion in this record is shown in New York some months ahead of the time it is ready to be submitted to the country at large, and it is the theater followers of the country at large whom we seek to serve.

The notion embedded in Mr. Mantle's statement is that New York production—essentially, Broadway—conferred legitimacy on a dramatic work. It was, perhaps, his version of "If you can make it there. . . ."

As the decades passed, *Best Plays* editors expanded the book's reach to include Off Broadway. Former editor and now consulting editor Henry Hewes points out, though, that O'Neill's *The Emperor Jones* was honored for its far-off Broadway production in 1920 at Greenwich Village's Provincetown Playhouse, although it soon moved to Broadway. Off Off Broadway, which sprang to life in the early 1960s, has traditionally been considered "developmental." In the *Best Plays* tradition of the past few decades, Off Off Broadway scripts were not considered "frozen" or "locked" into a particular textual form. In recent years, however, even playwrights such as Mr. Albee and Mr. Shepard have chosen to revise their important works long after they were expected to be in a permanent form.

Beginning with this edition, Off Off Broadway productions of new plays will also be eligible for Best Plays consideration. Indeed, my predecessor, Mr. Guernsey, occasionally conferred "special citations" on Off Off Broadway productions such as Wallace Shawn's *The Designated Mourner* (1999–2000).

The lively theater that thrives beyond the boundaries of the Hudson River continues to be represented in our expanding USA section and by essays covering the American Theatre Critics Association's Steinberg New Play Award and Citations. The membership of ATCA and its honors, which are funded by the Harold and Mimi Steinberg Charitable Trust, help the editors of *Best Plays* track the finest in new works for theater in this country.

IV

IT WAS AN HONOR for me to be invited to join Mr. Guernsey as an associate on his final volume as editor. That experience was compounded when I was asked to succeed him, the longest-serving editor of this important record of theater. When Mr. Guernsey died after a brief illness on May 2, it was a shock to many of us who knew him as an impassioned writer, patient editor, gentlemanly mentor and honest friend.

There have been many times over the past months when I have wanted to call my friend on the telephone to ask a question or seek his counsel only to have that familiar pang of sorrow return. Despite that great loss, it has been my good fortune to have the support and consultation of Mr. Dodd, the longtime publisher of the *Best Plays* series, Henry Hewes, former editor of this series and my invaluable consulting editor, and Melvyn B. Zerman, publisher of Limelight Editions. As we managed the transfer of files and coordinated the continuation of the series, Dorianne D. Guernsey, David LeVine and Noel Silverman were of great assistance.

The collection of data for a volume such as this relies on the labors of many people. I have had the benefit of Camille Dee's many years as associate editor to Mr. Guernsey and the continued support of longtime contributors such as Rue E. Canvin—who deserves some sort of medal for nearly 40 years of work on the series—Jeffrey Finn Productions (Cast Replacements and Touring Productions), and Mel Gussow for his continuing fine coverage of the Off Off Broadway theater.

The current editorial team of *Best Plays* has spent the past eight months attempting to complete a process that usually takes more than a year. I am deeply indebted to all of the press representatives who assisted in the gathering of information for this volume, but I particularly want to acknowledge Adrian Bryan-Brown and Chris Boneau of Boneau/Bryan-

Brown for their support of the series and its editors. My former student, Joshua Crouthamel, has served as my able assistant for two editions of the series and has begun to develop the United States theater section into an even more valuable resource to scholars and statisticians. Bob Kamp, a wizard of all things graphic and digital, is responsible for the handsome new *Best Plays* logo and for many of the improvements to our photographic imagery.

Thanks also are due to the members of the *Best Plays* editorial board, who give their imprimatur to our work by their presence on the masthead. Among that group, I particularly want to thank Robert Brustein for his generous support of and contribution to this volume. Thanks as well to those who have offered and provided extra support and assistance to this edition: Charles Wright, John Istel, Christopher Rawson, Tish Dace (Hewes Design Awards), Caldwell Titcomb (Elliot Norton Awards), David A. Rosenberg (Connecticut Critics Circle Awards), Lawrence Bommer (American Theatre Critics/Steinberg New Play Award and Citations), Edwin Wilson (Susan Smith Blackburn Prize), Michael Kuchwara (New York Drama Critics Circle Awards), Henry Hewes (Theater Hall of Fame Awards) and Ralph Newman of the Drama Book Shop.

We congratulate and thank all of the *Best Plays* honorees who made the 2000–01 season so invigorating to contemplate. Edward Albee, David Auburn, Mel Brooks, Complicite, Rebecca Gilman, Greg Kotis, Mark Hollmann, Kenneth Lonergan, Thomas Meehan, Adam Rapp, Tom Stoppard and August Wilson all enriched our lives during the season under review and their respective essayists tell us why. The photographers who capture theatrical images on film and help keep those ephemeral moments alive are also due thanks for their contributions to the greater body of theatrical work. This year we have included credits with each photograph and indexed the photographers' names for easier reference. Similarly, we have added biographical information about each of this volume's essayists and editors in a brief section at the back of the book. And a tradition that started in the 1950s continues with illustrations from the incomparable Al Hirschfeld, who has a longer relationship with *Best Plays* than anyone except our former publisher, Mr. Dodd. Thanks to Mr. Hirschfeld and his representative, Margo Feiden.

For most of the past year, my wife, Vivian Cary Jenkins, has put much of her own life on hold while we assembled, collated and checked the information contained in this reference work. In addition to her superb editorial work on the book, she has also been my sounding board, my partner and my best friend. Without her work and sacrifice, in addition to those mentioned above, there would be no *Best Plays* this year. She, and they, have my deepest gratitude.

As for that other thorny question raised above, "What is a play?" there are many answers. They lie in the essays that follow and the volumes to come.

JEFFREY ERIC JENKINS
NEW YORK

Contents

THE SEASON ON AND OFF BROADWAY

THE SEASON: BROADWAY AND OFF BROADWAY

○○○○○ *By Jeffrey Eric Jenkins* ○○○○○

IT IS FAIRLY TYPICAL for the New York theater season to begin with a whimper and end with a bang, but no one (except, perhaps, the untamed ego that drives Mel Brooks) could have predicted a year like the one we cover in this edition.

By the time that the American Theatre Wing's Tony Awards are given—for good or ill, the capstone of every season—the new theater season has already begun. When those small trophies honoring the memory of Antoinette Perry are doled out each year, the editors of *Best Plays* are busily tracking the next season of theater work in New York and around the country.

On the morning following the whirl of events surrounding the ceremony, everyone in New York theater slows a notch. Come that Monday "the party's over," as Faith Prince sang in *Bells Are Ringing* at the Plymouth Theatre this season, but instead of calling it a day, theater folk begin planning for the build to the frenzy of the next awards season: Pulitzer Prize, New York Drama Critics Circle Awards, Outer Critics Circle Awards, Drama Desk Awards and Tony Awards. (And, in enlightened self-interest, let's not forget the *Best Plays* honors, which are second only to the Pulitzers in longevity.)

It's no surprise, then, that the summer brings a bit of down time as locals begin to escape the city for holidays abroad or weekends in the Hamptons and the Berkshires. As the tourist crowds began to fill theaters in June—a 1999–2000 League of American Theatres and Producers survey found that 56 percent of Broadway audiences came from beyond New York City and its suburbs—a pair of Broadway veterans returned with mixed results in classic plays. Kelsey Grammer, who enjoyed success as Cassio in the 1982 James Earl Jones and Christopher Plummer production of *Othello*, before becoming one of television history's most popular sitcom characters in *Cheers* and *Frasier*, landed with a thud in the title role of *Macbeth* at the Music Box.

BROADWAY SEASON 2000–2001

Productions in a continuing run on May 31, 2001 in bold
Productions honored as Best Plays *selections in italics*

NEW PLAYS (6)

The Dinner Party
Proof
The Tale of the Allergist's Wife
Judgment at Nuremberg (National Actors Theatre)
King Hedley II
The Gathering

NEW MUSICALS (6)

The Full Monty
Seussical
Jane Eyre
A Class Act
The Producers
The Adventures of Tom Sawyer

PLAY REVIVALS (6)

Macbeth
The Man Who Came to Dinner (Roundabout)
Gore Vidal's The Best Man
Betrayal (Roundabout)
Design for Living (Roundabout)

PLAY REVIVALS (*cont'd*)

One Flew Over the Cuckoo's Nest

MUSICAL REVIVALS (4)

The Rocky Horror Show
Follies (Roundabout)
Bells Are Ringing
42nd Street

SOLO PERFORMANCES (3)

Patti LuPone "Matters of the Heart" (Lincoln Center Theater)
The Search for Signs of Intelligent Life in the Universe
George Gershwin Alone

FOREIGN PLAYS (2)

The Invention of Love (Lincoln Center Theater)
Stones in His Pockets

SPECIALTIES (1)

Blast!

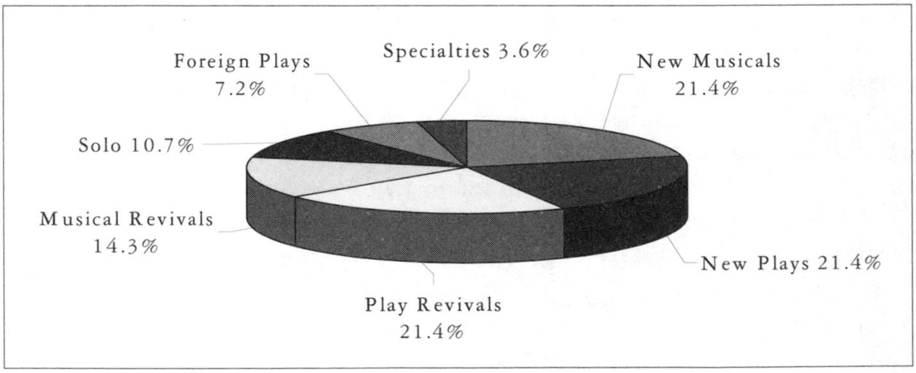

Grammer got no slack from critics for his portrayal of Shakespeare's Scottish usurper, which seemed to arrive on 45th Street by way of Elsinore. Darkly designed with an emphasis on designer-director Terry Hands's lighting to set the mood, the production's starkness didn't help audiences warm to the character's (or the actor's) tragic plight. Cloaked in fitted black trousers and shirt, Grammer's ponderous, internal delivery appeared better suited to the Prince of Denmark—or to a television camera. There were glimmers of the Shakespearean that lay beneath the layers of laugh track, but even Grammer's Lady Macbeth (Diane Venora) lacked the sexual fire needed to ignite Macbeth's ambition.

It probably didn't help matters that Grammer came to New York with the millstone of Boston critical rejection around his neck. (Where's the gang from Cheers when you need them?) In backstage comments at the 2000 Tony Awards, according to Robert Hofler in *Variety*, Grammer said, "We were savaged by the ignorant," going on to call the offending critics "those two butt-heads from Boston" before acknowledging his anxiety at facing New York critics. After suffering the cruelties of the New Yorkers (this one included), we can only wonder what epithets were hurled when the show closed after an unlucky 13 performances.

Nathan Lane's return to Broadway gave the star a needed lift after misfortune in his own television sitcom. Lane, interestingly, made comments similar to Grammer's about critics and anatomy in an interview with the *New York Observer*'s Mike Batistick. The story ran just before George S. Kaufman and Moss Hart's *The Man Who Came to Dinner* (1939) was revived by the Roundabout Theatre Company at its sumptuous new American Airlines Theatre—the Selwyn before its recent restoration. Gearing up for his turn as the obnoxious arbiter of taste, Sheridan Whiteside (based on critic Alexander Woollcott), Lane complained about the worst reviews he had received in the past and went on to proclaim the diminutive qualities of critical gentalia.

His shot across the bow may have worked because critical praise abounded for the limited-run production. The nagging exception was Ben Brantley's insightful review in the *New York Times*, which called the production "soggy" and reserved praise for Lewis J. Stadlen and Byron Jennings in small supporting roles. The *Times* aside (a nice trick, if you can manage it), the Roundabout production completed a respectable run, was broadcast on public television and gave Lane a nice career bounce before his smashing spring success in *The Producers*.

As summer turned into the fall election season, Broadway producers continued to mine the past with a production of Gore Vidal's 1960 election drama, *The Best Man*. Coming after eight years of scandalous revelations about President Clinton and his family, Vidal's political tale of leaked psychiatric reports and hidden homosexuality seemed relatively tame. (Of course, Vidal was somewhat prescient: *The Best Man* first appeared 12 years before reports about Thomas Eagleton's mental health history forced him to relinquish his place as George McGovern's candidate for Vice President.)

The new production of *Gore Vidal's The Best Man*, as it was retitled, tottered onto the stage with reports of shaky acting. The company included Spalding Gray and Chris Noth as the political combatants, with Elizabeth Ashley, Charles Durning, Christine Ebersole and Michael Learned leading the cheers from the sidelines. Walter Cronkite made a cameo vocal appearance as a news commentator. The show closed at year's end as originally planned, but the raging post-election controversy over tainted results between George W. Bush and Al Gore caused a kind of "election fatigue" that gradually siphoned away interest. In the production's own Virginia Theatre polling booths, where audience members were encouraged to vote, Gore beat Bush by a landslide—so much for verisimilitude.

Something New: American Plays

BY OCTOBER, THE PROSPECTS FOR AMERICAN PLAYWRIGHTS seemed to brighten on Broadway. After years of domination by authors from abroad, the fall saw openings of three new plays by American writers, one of whom was truly a new voice on the scene. David Auburn's *Proof* transferred from Off Broadway's Manhattan Theatre Club to the Walter Kerr Theatre with Mary-Louise Parker leading the terrific cast of Larry Bryggman, Ben Shenkman and Johanna Day.

Although the play lost a bit of its intimacy and emotional impact in the shift to the larger space, Daniel Sullivan's steady direction—which won a long-overdue Tony Award—and John Lee Beatty's evocative set kept the focus on Auburn's well-honed text. Auburn made a clean sweep of all of the major awards (Pulitzer, Tony, New York Drama Critics Circle, Lortel, Outer Critics Circle, Drama League, Drama Desk, etc.). An essay by Bruce Weber in the next section celebrates *Proof* as a *Best Plays* honoree.

Charles Busch wrote a play for an *actual* woman—a notion, of course, that is politically contested in an era of transgendered identities—and took it uptown after years of drag roles in his creations such as *Vampire Lesbians of Sodom*. It's possible, of course, that he wrote the play for himself and later decided to tack toward the mainstream by having Manhattan Theatre Club stage the play with Linda Lavin as the neurotic middle-age Jewish

Six is a party: Penny Fuller, John Ritter, Henry Winkler, Len Cariou, Veanne Cox and Jan Maxwell in The Dinner Party. *Illustration: Hirschfeld*

wife of a successful physician. Lynne Meadow's expert comic direction helped make the play—a pleasure, if a guilty one—an instant hit Off Broadway in the 1999–2000 season and the splendid cast (Lavin, Tony Roberts, Michele Lee, Anil Kumar and Shirl Bernheim) made a seamless transfer to the Ethel Barrymore Theatre in November 2000.

Before the end of the season, two other rookies would bring new plays to Broadway, but neither could be considered new voices—and both would concern themselves with Holocaust topics. Longtime television producer Abby Mann, best known for the *Kojak* series, brought his 1961 Academy Award-winning script of *Judgment at Nuremberg* (itself based on a televised version), to the Longacre Theatre in a National Actors Theatre production featuring Maximilian Schell, George Grizzard, Marthe Keller, Michael Hayden and Robert Foxworth. The production, which focused on trials of members of the Nazi judiciary, garnered generally respectful notices and ran just less than two months before closing in May. The best result of John Tillinger's directing was the clear, honest acting—especially that of Schell, whose smoldering silence spoke emotive volumes. Ultimately, though, the play was too true to its television roots in its equivocation between German and American points of view. What made for searing broadcast drama 40 years earlier, lacked a dramatic edge in the new millennium.

Arje Shaw's *The Gathering*, which ran for less than a month at the Cort Theatre, had worked its way from Off Off Broadway to Off Broadway's Jewish Repertory Theatre. It might have done better to avoid Broadway, where its sentimental pap and unbelievable situations weren't likely to get a favorable hearing (although it *has* happened). Hal Linden starred as a Jewish grandfather who reveres Muhammad Ali (such a *mensch*!) and disrespects his son's work for President Reagan and Pat Buchanan (think William Safire, Ben Stein and others who have crossed traditional Jewish political lines). Unlike Mann's *Judgment*, Shaw's play makes it all too clear—far in advance—what the writer thinks and where he is going.

The other two new American plays of the season returned seasoned veterans to the Broadway spotlight. Neil Simon brought a relationship comedy (what else?) to the Music Box for a mixed critical reception, but a positive bottom line, according to *Variety*, before the season ended. Audiences, apparently well trained by decades of television sitcoms, chortled on cue. But the humor in this play, about a group of Parisians who have their troubled emotional lives sorted in a mysterious fashion, is the timeworn sort that has one uncomfortable character crack that his tuxedo "has to be back by ten." Does anyone need to hear that line or its tired siblings again? Many apparently do, because *The Dinner Party* kept John Ritter, Henry Winkler, Len Cariou, Penny Fuller, Jan Maxwell and Veanne Cox busy for the better part of the season and the run extended into the summer.

August Wilson brought the eighth of his 10-play cycle on African-American life in the 20th century, *King Hedley II*, to the Virginia Theatre in May. Starring Brian Stokes Mitchell in the title role and Leslie Uggams as his estranged mother, the play was a sprawling, ambitious spoken opera that finally got tangled in its own text. Although chosen as a *Best Play* and celebrated in an essay by Christopher Rawson in the section that follows, *Hedley* is perhaps the greatest of Wilson's works in aspiration and the least in execution. After a long development process in resident theatres that saw the play whittled from four hours to about three, there remained elaborate textual details and unnecessary exposition that kept the piece from truly soaring.

Director Marion McClinton, who staged Wilson's *Jitney* with a deft touch in the prior season, seemed a bit out of his depth with the rambling poetry of *King Hedley II*. In a case of critical "emperor's new clothes," the reviews that appeared weren't enthusiastic, but were less than openly critical. Wilson was praised more for his body of work than the specific play under review. An exception was Clive Barnes of the *New York Post* who called *King Hedley II*, "probably Wilson's best." Howard Kissel of the *Daily News* paid obeisance to Wilson's lyricism by writing that, as in opera, "it's more important to discuss the music than the plot," but later admitted that the playwright had "written tauter, deeper plays than this." *Variety*'s Charles Isherwood called it "a disappointing entry in this ongoing literary landmark," and the *Times*'s Ben Brantley concurred, writing that it "takes much concentration and several leaps of faith for the audience to unravel" the story. Linda Winer at *Newsday* also noted the play's unruliness, but captured the feeling of most critics and theater lovers when she wrote of the installments yet to come, "We wait with dread, anticipation, and, more definitely, awe." It is worth noting here, as it is in Christopher Rawson's essay, that *Hedley* marked the first time the New York Drama Critics Circle chose not to honor a new Wilson play.

From Across the Pond

PART OF THE REASON THAT *HEDLEY* was denied the New York Drama Critics Circle Award had to do with the competition from new plays on Broadway and off (see the Awards section of this book for details of the voting), which included *Proof*, *The Play About the Baby*, *Lobby Hero* and *Boy Gets Girl*—all *Best Plays* honorees. Each of these plays received more first-ballot votes than *Hedley*, but it was Tom Stoppard's *The Invention of Love*

Math maven: Mary-Louise Parker in Proof. *Illustration: Hirschfeld*

that was chosen best play. (*Proof* eventually won best American play and *The Producers* easily won best musical.) So even though American plays experienced a resurgence this season, the offshore presence was still felt. Indeed, Irish playwright Marie Jones's *Stones in His Pockets* followed *Invention* to Broadway by just a few days.

The Jones play scooped up numerous awards in its runs in Ireland and England (including the 2001 Olivier Award and the 2000 *Evening Standard* Award in London) before popping into the John Golden Theatre—just in time for Tony Award consideration. In *Stones*, a pair of Irishmen interact with Hollywood types when they work as extras on a film shot near their home. Seán Campion and Conleth Hill portrayed all of the many characters in carefully nuanced performances that, while very funny, drew an unsettling picture of rural Irish folk into sharp relief. The success of the stage-Irish, rural-peasant imagery of Martin McDonagh (and others) in recent years is ironic when we consider that Ireland has evolved into a modern country with a burgeoning economy. And yet some writers insist on excavating imagery more associated with J.M. Synge's 1907 *The Playboy of the Western World*. In *Stones*, though, Ian McElhinney's direction of two actors playing many roles encourages the audience to think—as they laugh—about how stereotypes are perpetuated in media and myth.

Conor McPherson, another Irish writer who often trades in types, was represented Off Broadway by a 1994 monologue, *The Good Thief*, in which a professional thug (played by the superb Brian d'Arcy James) confesses the misdeeds of his life. Originally titled *The Light of Jesus*, the monologue is a modern version of the tale of the thief who obtained forgiveness when he repented while hanging on a cross near Jesus. Running a little under 90 minutes (at 45 Bleecker after transferring from an Off Off Broadway run at the Jose Quintero Theatre), *The Good Thief* was a riveting exercise that demonstrated the power of an innocuous text in the hands of a fine actor.

Over at the Brooklyn Academy of Music, Joseph V. Melillo and Karen Brooks Hopkins continued to build on the traditions of their mentor, Harvey Lichtenstein, with five Off Broadway productions of classic plays from abroad. (All BAM Next Wave offerings are considered Off Off Broadway for *Best Plays* purposes.) The Almeida Theatre Company brought its Ralph Fiennes-starring productions of *Richard II* and *Coriolanus* to the BAM Harvey Theater (formerly the BAM Majestic). These productions originated at the Almeida's cavernous Shoreditch performance space in Islington, North London, where the audiences had a similar perspective to those at the BAM Harvey: decidely unposh bench seating that looks down on the action, stadium-style.

It was fitting in that Bush-Gore election season to see a pair of leaders whose weaknesses overshadowed their strengths. Directed by Almeida's Jonathan Kent, Fiennes's fey Richard grew to understand, too late, how he had misused his kingly powers and misjudged his opposition. Similarly, Coriolanus sets up his own fall when he refuses to understand that the voice of the people must be heeded and that a true leader responds not only to his singular ego but also to the needs of those around him. At the time, more than a month before the post-election chaos in Florida, it was easy to see each of the major presidential candidates through the timeless Shakespearean lens.

Later in the season, Gale Edwards, who directed the Broadway revival of *Jesus Christ Superstar* and BAM's *Don Carlos* last season, returned to BAM with a flashy Sidney Theatre Company production of John Webster's *The White Devil.* But the high point of the BAM theater season was Peter Brook's *The Tragedy of Hamlet* with Adrian Lester playing an impish, charming Dane. Beginning and ending with Hamlet's Boswell, Horatio (Scott Handy), saying, "Who's there?" we were instantly reminded that the character's narrative keeps Hamlet "alive" as the tale is reinscribed on our consciousness. Brook, a master of theatrical essence, laid bare Shakespeare's tale in an intermissionless performance of more than two hours. In playing a dozen or so roles, the eight performers made the piece fresh and immediate so that it never felt like the "greatest hits" of *Hamlet.*

In the waning days of the season, Simon Russell Beale headed a cast from the Royal National Theatre in a touring production of *Hamlet* directed by John Caird, who also co-wrote and co-directed Broadway's murky *Jane Eyre* this season. Beale portrayed a Hamlet in middle-age, wracked by his neuroses and grown soft from his scholarship. Presented on a Gothic-looking cathedral setting in BAM's Howard Gilman Opera House, its impenetrably dark lighting appropriately manifested its lack of wit and life.

It was Tom Stoppard's *The Invention of Love*, though, presented by Lincoln Center Theater at Broadway's Lyceum Theatre, that made the biggest impression among plays from abroad. As essayist Charles Wright points out in the section to follow, *Invention* wasn't exactly a new play when it opened here: the London production had played four years earlier. However dense Stoppard's increasingly demanding plays become, there are always moments of sublime pleasure in their playing. In *Invention*, an aged pedant, as he is about to cross the River Styx, confronts his younger self and sifts through memories of opportunities won and lost. After a long life spent pursuing the thoughts and feelings of the ancients, while virtually ignoring his own, he gazes on his younger self and says, wistfully, "I'm not as young as I once was, whereas you are." There is poetry and sadness in that moment as he knows (and we suspect) what is to come in the young man's life.

Beyond the tale of poet A.E. Housman's unrequited love there is an interwoven narrative that relates to life and to the life of the mind. It is a story about how ideas and information are passed (or translated) from one generation to the next—whether those generations are separated by a few years or many centuries. Although the production, directed with clarity by Jack O'Brien and featuring lovely scenic and lighting designs by Bob Crowley and Brian MacDevitt, survived the end of the season, the play's historical and literary allusions were tough slogging for theater audiences and signaled doom for the play's exemplary run. Still, Robert Sean Leonard and Richard Easton received Tony Awards for best supporting actor and best actor in their roles as Housman, young and old.

Musical Numbers

SIX NEW AMERICAN PLAYS (and two imports) signaled a rebound for the spoken word on Broadway, but they also marked the first time since the mid-1990s that new plays outnumbered new musicals. Sheer numbers of productions, of course, are not the measure of a season's artistic success (a different set of numbers—in dollars—is the measure with which most producers concern themselves). But even though the early part of the 2000–01 season evolved as a breath of fresh air in American playwriting, new musicals discouraged some observers.

After development at San Diego's Old Globe Theatre, Terrence McNally (book) and David Yazbek (music and lyrics) brought their adaptation of a working-class English film, *The Full Monty*, to the Eugene O'Neill Theatre. Relocating the unemployed steelworkers of the film from Sheffield to Buffalo, New York—so they needn't replicate the movie's dialect?—the creative team kept the conceit that a group of down-on-their-luck guys would turn to stripping in a desperate move to earn some money. Where the film's silent, hulking smokestacks and empty steelyards provide a poignant contrast to the intimate story of men with nowhere to turn, the musical's brassy razzle-dazzle and self-conscious, feel-good energy eviscerate the story. We're left with a show that's only real hook is the audience's knowledge that the men will strip completely (the Full Monty) and spectators will have a chance (very slim) to see the actors' personal equipment.

McNally's book is surprisingly hollow and Yazbek's jazzy pop-inflected score, which won a Drama Desk Award, is the kind of inoffensive work that brings to mind the opening titles of a television talk show (think David Letterman, Jay Leno, Conan O'Brien). The best thing about *Full Monty* was

Buff boys: Patrick Wilson and company in The Full Monty. *Illustration: Hirschfeld*

the appearance of veteran actor Kathleen Freeman, at age 77, on the Broadway stage. As the wise-cracking pianist who helps the boys get their act together, she could always be relied on to light up a scene (and steal it). Freeman stayed with the show through the end of the season—she was nominated for Drama Desk and Tony Awards—and into the summer. She gave her final performances a few days before she died on August 23, 2001.

The Full Monty received puzzlingly positive notices from New York critics. *Variety*'s Charles Isherwood admitted that, "Challenging or interesting it isn't [. . .] musically or otherwise," but only after he asserted that it was "funny, earthy and appealingly performed." Ben Brantley at the *New York Times* wrote that it was "that rare aggressive crowd pleaser that you don't have to apologize for liking"—and he didn't. The *Times* even offered a line that producers usually only dream about (particularly from that muscular gatekeeper of the arts): "The Eugene O'Neill Theatre won't have to look for a new tenant for a long, long time." The sensible Linda Winer, at least, reported in *Newsday* that there were "insufficient charms and infrequent bursts of wit." The show received a healthy 10 Tony Award nominations, but was shut out by *The Producers* steamroller, which won a record 12 Tony Awards.

OFF BROADWAY SEASON 2000–2001

Productions in a continuing run on May 31, 2001 in bold

Productions honored as Best Plays *selections in italics*

NEW PLAYS (38)

Current Events (MTC)
Neil Simon's Hotel Suite (Roundabout)
Spinning Into Butter (Lincoln Center)
Avow
High Infidelity
The Butterfly Collection (Playwrights)
Tallulah Hallelujah!
The Unexpected Man
Tabletop
Alice in Bed (NYTW)
Cobb
Strictly Personal
End of the World Party
Maybe Baby, It's You
Comic Potential (MTC)
Down the Garden Paths
Kit Marlowe (Public/NYSF)
Jesus Hopped the "A" Train
Old Money (Lincoln Center)
The Bitter Tears of Petra Van Kant
The Wax (Playwrights)
Resident Alien (NYTW)
The Play About the Baby
Cellini (Second Stage)
Boy Gets Girl (MTC)
A Skull in Connemara (Roundabout)
Dogeaters (Public/NYSF)
If It Was Easy . . .
Ten Unknowns (Lincoln Center)
Mnemonic
Up Against the Wind (NYTW)
References to Salvador Dalí Make Me Hot (Public/NYSF)
Madame Melville
Lobby Hero (Playwrights/Transfer)
Six Goumbas and a Wannabe
Nocturne (NYTW)
Blur (MTC)
Glimmer, Glimmer and Shine (MTC)

NEW MUSICALS (12)

The Bubbly Black Girl Sheds Her Chameleon Skin (Playwrights)
Imperfect Chemistry
The Gorey Details
A Class Act (MTC)
Fermat's Last Tango (York)
Pete 'n' Keely
Time and Again (MTC)

NEW MUSICALS *(cont'd)*

Suburb (York)
Bat Boy: The Musical
Love, Janis
The IT Girl (York)
Urinetown

MUSICAL REVIVALS (1)

Godspell

PLAY REVIVALS (7)

The Winter's Tale (Public/NYSF)
Julius Caesar (Public/NYSF)
Juno and the Paycock (Roundabout)
Tiny Alice (Second Stage)
Passion Play
Crimes of the Heart (Second Stage)
Uncle Bob

SOLO (5)

The Syringa Tree
Shakespeare's Villains: A Masterclass in Evil (Public/NYSF)
In Dreams and Gimpel
The Good Thief
Lackawanna Blues (Public/NYSF)

SPECIALTIES (9)

Penn & Teller
Arsenic and Old Lace (Voices!)
Book of the Dead (Second Avenue) (Public/NYSF)
Little Murders (Voices!)
A Connecticut Yankee (Encores!)
The Devil and Daniel Webster (Voices!)
Bloomer Girl (Encores!)
Hair (Encores!)
Cinderella

REVUES (5)

Berlin to Broadway With Kurt Weill
4 Guys Named José . . . and Una Mujer Named Maria!
American Rhapsody: A New Musical Revue
Forbidden Broadway 2001: A Spoof Odyssey
Newyorkers (MTC)

FOREIGN PLAYS (5)

Richard II (BAM)
Coriolanus (BAM)
The White Devil (BAM)
The Tragedy of Hamlet (BAM)
Hamlet (BAM)

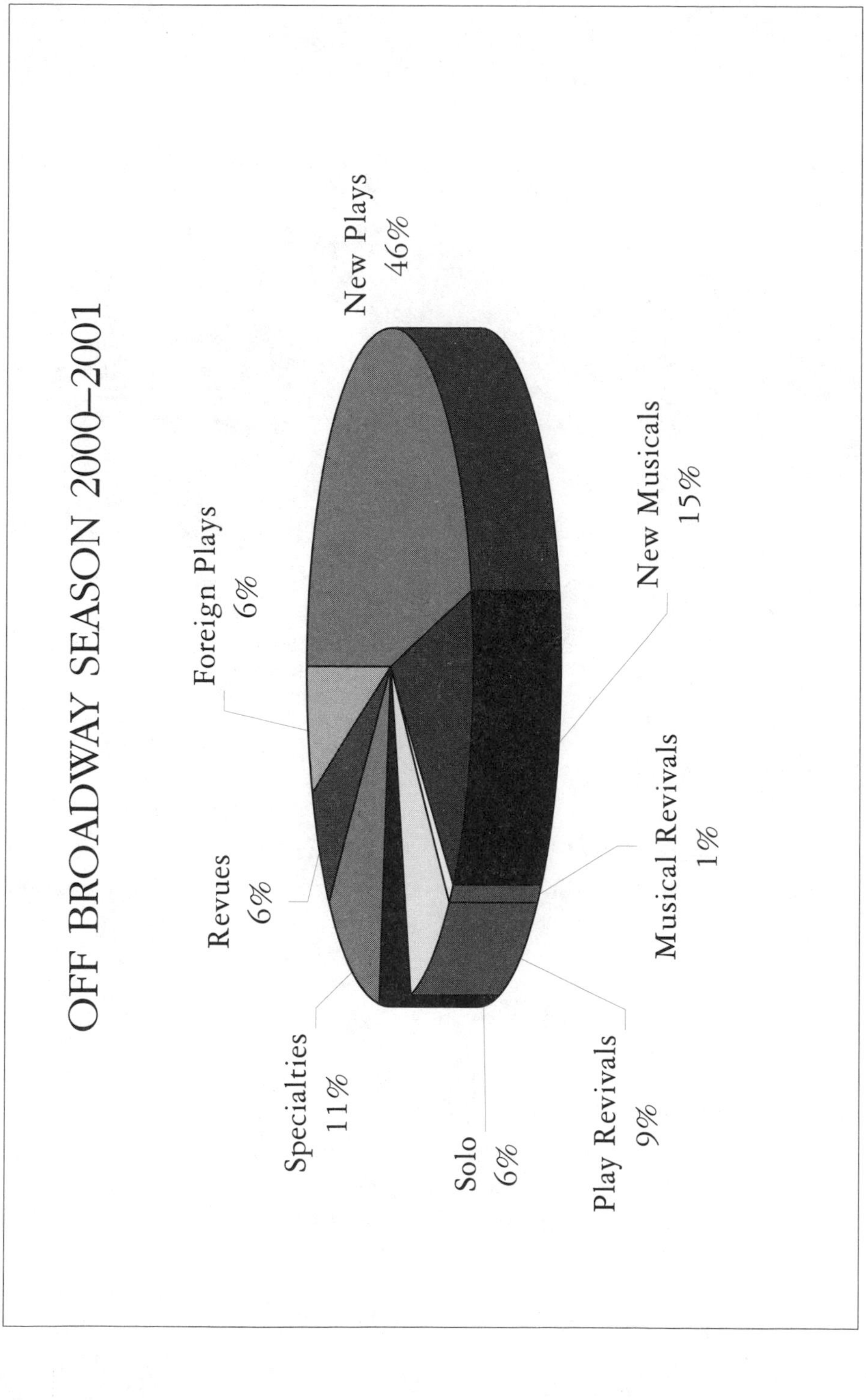
OFF BROADWAY SEASON 2000–2001
New Plays
46%
Foreign Plays
6%
New Musicals
15%
Revues
6%
Musical Revivals
1%
Specialties
11%
Solo
6%
Play Revivals
9%

Seams straight? Dick Cavett, Joan Jett, Tom Hewitt and Daphne Rubin-Vega in The Rocky Horror Show. *Illustration: Hirschfeld*

Compared to what happened with *Seussical*, though, *The Full Monty* was a happy story. Beset by problems almost from its conception, the Lynn Ahrens and Stephen Flaherty musical, based on the works of Theodor Geisel (Dr. Seuss), started as a project of Garth Drabinsky's Livent back in the free-spending days of that company's existence. Originally conceived by Ahrens, Flaherty and comedian Eric Idle, the musical developed in a series of readings and workshops that raised expectations for an exciting finished product from a Tony-winning team. Ahrens and Flaherty won Tonys for *Ragtime*, director Frank Galati won two for *The Grapes of Wrath* (he also adapted the John Steinbeck story) and scene designer Eugene Lee was a winner for *Candide* (1974) and *Sweeney Todd* (1979).

On the musical's trek from New York to Toronto to Boston, while preparing for its Broadway bow, it shed key members of the creative team and took on new ones. In a *New York Times* postmortem, Robin Pogrebin quoted producer Marty Bell, who had been involved with the piece in its infancy at Livent, "We were looking to do *The Fantasticks*, it was a show about the words." But, Bell told the *Times*, "the show that was done was Ringling Brothers." By all appearances, the three-ring circus wasn't confined to the stage.

The composer-lyricist team of Flaherty and Ahrens jettisoned Idle, who had been commisioned by Drabinsky to write the book, because, the comedian told the *Times*, they wanted to write the book themselves. In a conversation with *Best Plays*, though, Ahrens disagreed with Idle's assertion in the *Times* article, "Eric turned in a treatment that was deemed unworkable by everyone who read it," she said. "He then became unavailable due to other commitments." As the Livent bankruptcy imbroglio took on a life of its own, the creative team realized that for the show ever to see production, Ahrens said, "We needed to take it forward on our own and hope for the best." Of course, moving ahead with something in the theater is rarely done on one's own, as the *Seussical* creators soon discovered. While the Livent fiasco unfolded, Ahrens and Flaherty found themselves working with a string of producers that began with Drabinsky and ended with Barry and Fran Weissler (those in-between included Roy Furman, Todd Haimes, Miles Wilkin and Gary Gunas). With all of those hand-offs, the creators may have felt like batons in a long-distance relay race.

Unfortunately for the talented writing team, the lack of a coherent book was one of the main critical complaints about the show—that and its overstimulated production elements. Although internet gossip was blamed for some of the production's troubles, it couldn't have helped when the director and designers also got caught in the show's revolving door and were replaced amid tryouts. Director Galati was succeeded by Rob Marshall, whose sister Kathleen Marshall was the show's choreographer. Scene designer Eugene Lee gave way to Tony Walton and costume designer Catherine Zuber stepped aside for William Ivey Long. Of the three, only Long supplanted Zuber in the show's credits; Galati and Lee remained director and scene designer of record. Former Monty Pythoner Idle, who played the Cat in the Hat in an early New York reading, remained a co-conceiver of record.

A pastiche of lively songs that had the stitched-together quality of a revue (without the requisite comic edge), *Seussical* bounced along after its uninspired opening at the Richard Rodgers Theatre. Clown David Shiner, who played the Cat in the Hat, found himself nudged out of the picture by a series of guest stars that included Rosie O'Donnell and Cathy Rigby. Losing its entire $10.5 million investment (and receiving only one Tony nomination), *Seussical* folded on May 20 and everyone involved went away to lick their wounds. Back in February, though, Ahrens and Flaherty gamely appeared at a luncheon of the American Theatre Critics Association. Still in the midst of the Broadway hurly-burly at the time, Ahrens answered a question, posed earlier, through an Seussian poem. The question was, "What would you change about Broadway today?"

How would I change Broadway?
I pondered and puzzled.
Hmm. Can't shoot the producers
Or keep critics muzzled!
So I thought and I thought
And then this came to mind—
I'll invent a new way
To make everyone kind!
We'll send only kind thoughts
To new shows in the works,
We will hope for the best
And won't gossip like jerks!
And a thousand producers—
(Well, at least eight or nine)
Will love art just as much
As that darned bottom line.
We'll be kind to new writers,
Won't bludgeon or slay 'em,
We'll support their attempts—
Why, we might even pay 'em!
We'll praise worthy failures,
Forgive dreadful messes,
And celebrate all of each other's
Successes.
We'll be just kind enough
To give all shows a chance,
And we'll outlaw all minds
Made up months in advance.
No knives, and no venom.
That's it, I thought! Yup!
That's how I'll change Broadway!
And then,
I woke up. (© 2001 Lynn Ahrens)

Although the cast album was nominated for a Grammy and awaited the awards ceremony at press time, perhaps the big winner on *Seussical* was the Target department store chain, which underwrote part of the production as a presenter. The company's logo of red-and-white concentric circles was incorporated into the design of set pieces and costumes throughout. It was a bit of subliminal advertising that put Hollywood's product-placement schemes to shame.

As the days grew shorter in December, the next Broadway musical made the nights seem especially long. *Jane Eyre*, the John Caird and Paul Gordon musical based on Charlotte Brontë's novel, took a long and winding road to Broadway that started in Wichita, Kansas. During the five-year trip to New York the show passed through Canada (Toronto) and California (La Jolla). But the flood of recent adaptations of Victorian novels—in all performance media—may have drained audiences of the patience necessary to enjoy Jane's dour trip up the social scale. Although Marla Schaffel received a Drama Desk Award for her work as plain Jane, that was just another cruel trick of fate encouraging producers to hang on for the Tony Awards (nominated for five, it earned none).

The first half of the season also saw producer Jordan Roth's raucous revival of *The Rocky Horror Show*, directed by Christopher Ashley, installed at Circle in the Square. The terrific cast included Tom Hewitt, Jarrod Emick and Alice Ripley, with Raúl Esparza, rocker Joan Jett, stage siren Daphne Rubin-Vega and comedian Lea DeLaria providing support. David Rockwell's versatile setting—theater seats rotated offstage through the floor and a la-BOR-a-tory flew in from overhead—helped provide a theatrical edge that attracted younger audiences, which is always good news. For the fogies (young and old) in the crowd, the quick-witted Dick Cavett provided a stream of tongue-in-cheek commentary.

As has become the trend in recent years, though, most of the season's musicals (new and revivals) opened just before the Tony deadline to keep shows fresh in the minds of prospective voters and to minimize the financial impact if reviews and awards don't match producers' fantasies. *A Class Act*, which played a brief run at Off Broadway's Manhattan Theatre Club before transferring to the Ambassador Theatre, got the spring musical season started. Based on the life and death of Edward Kleban, whose professional apex may have been his collaboration with Marvin Hamlisch on *A Chorus Line*, the show used its subject's music and lyrics wrapped inside a book by Linda Kline and Lonny Price. Serving also as director and leading man (he played Kleban), Price wore three hats in this production.

It was pleasant to be reminded of Kleban's talents and sad that the theater lost him too soon, which—the production practically shouted—was *not* to AIDS. Finally, though, the move to Broadway must be viewed as an act of faith on the part of producers and artists who loved Kleban. The tissue-thin book is the telling of Kleban's life story set against the backdrop of a memorial service in which he is a ghostly presence. The treacly first scene and the sentimental tone throughout caused a few critical cringes, but Kleban's delightful songs made the performance pass felicitously.

The Roundabout Theatre Company production of Stephen Sondheim and James Goodman's *Follies* (at the Belasco Theatre) suffered a critical backlash, it seemed, for not being the 1998 Paper Mill Playhouse production. Back then, Ben Brantley wrote in a *New York Times* review of the New Jersey production, "There should be an audience of baby boomers ready to find their own faces in the mirrors of this *Follies* if it moves to Broadway, which it definitely should." Producers sped through tunnels and over bridges in anticipation of a hit show with a rave *Times* review waiting. But it never happened. Producers later lamented that the show was too costly to mount.

Fast forward to the 2001 Roundabout production headlined by Blythe Danner, Gregory Harrison, Treat Williams and Judith Ivey. Matthew Warchus's icy direction (more about that later) and the insecure singing of the stars left critics—that is, *the* critic—in the lurch. "The beauty we fell in love with 30 years ago isn't looking so good these days," Brantley wrote, and he went on to compare it poorly with the Paper Mill version. It lacked, as another daily critic said privately, "the glitz and the glamour" of the 1998 production; without those qualities, one might argue, it's just one midlife song after another about wrong turns and missed chances. The main exception in the Roundabout production was the star turn of Polly Bergen singing "I'm Still Here" with a committed gusto that gave audiences a genuine, old-school Broadway thrill.

Follies is also a celebratory dirge for the great American musical theater, so it's ironic that the next show out of the gate celebrated a musical rebirth of sorts. *The Producers* arrived from Chicago like a late spring blizzard when it opened at the St. James Theatre April 19. Who could have imagined the excitement and hype that would surround yet another film adaptation? After a string of movie-to-stage flops—*Big*, *Footloose* and *Saturday Night Fever* among them—the reports of soldout houses in Chicago were puzzling. Mel Brooks wrote the music? Who were they kidding? No one, it turned out (except, perhaps, Adolph Hitler).

The Producers opened to a string of glowing reviews for its unrelenting, occasionally disturbing humor and the wizardly direction and choreography of Susan Stroman. Nathan Lane and Matthew Broderick, both of whom had suffered poor notices in recent times, were hailed as the conquering heroes of the Broadway musical. And the producers of *The Producers*—in a move destined to be compared to Max Bialystok and Leo Bloom, the thieving shlockmeisters portrayed in the musical—began grabbing money hand over fist, raising the top ticket price to $100 the morning after the opening. When the price increase went into effect, it was too late for critics to consider for their reviews. Before this book went to press, the producers also announced a new luxury rate of ticket prices available to patrons who didn't want to wait a year to see the show. The price? A mere $480 each. Thus was the Broadway musical reborn into a familiar mold: not making a living, making a killing. A *Best Plays* honoree, the Mel Brooks and Thomas Meehan musical is discussed by Julius Novick in the section that follows.

The last of the new musicals to open in the 2000–01 season, *The Adventures of Tom Sawyer*, came and went quickly, playing just 21 performances from its opening night. Based on incidents taken from Mark Twain's classic book, the show tried to appeal both to adults and their children, succeeding on neither end of the spectrum. The humor was cornpone, the drama was television trite and the music was more Branson, Missouri, than Broadway. On the positive side, it gave a group of exciting young newcomers (such as Kristen Bell and Joshua Park) a taste for the big stage and brought another of Heidi Ettinger's suggestive, cartoonlike sets to an appreciative public.

The two final musical revivals, *Bells Are Ringing* and *42nd Street*, met with surprisingly different results. *Bells*, the Betty Comden, Adolph Green and Jule Styne musical, had a cool, distant feel that we don't expect in a

Five faces of Lil': Lily Tomlin in The Search for Signs of Intelligent Life in the Universe. *Illustration: Hirschfeld*

show starring Faith Prince and Marc Kudisch. A few of the songs have survived the years, but Tina Landau's cardboard cutout staging and Jeff Calhoun's listless choreography seemed merely to mark time.

The opening of *42nd Street* brought the total of musical revivals to four, which made for a tidy Tony category. The big question about *42nd Street*, though, was, "Do we need a revival already?" The original production, which ran for 3,486 performances, closed in 1989—a mere 12 years earlier. But the hyperamplified tapping of "those dancin' feet" overcame the reluctance of the doubters and *42nd Street* won the Tony Award for best musical revival (Christine Ebersole won the best actress in a musical Tony for her part as Dorothy Brock, a musical star who has crested the hill).

There was another kind of musical revival on Broadway, but it didn't come with the opening of a new production. Nearly two years after it opened on Broadway, the revival of Irving Berlin's *Annie Get Your Gun* got a jolt at the box office when country music star Reba McEntire joined the cast in the title role. Sporting one of the finest musical theater scores, *Annie*'s battle of the sexes story struck many as too creaky for the end of the 20th century. Peter Stone's updating of the Herbert and Dorothy Fields book didn't add much and the show still creaked and groaned under the burden of gender and ethnic stereotypes when Bernadette Peters opened as Annie in 1999.

After Peters left the show, television stars Susan Lucci and Cheryl Ladd passed through the title role (with Peters making a return appearance in between). Then along came Reba. With her open face and big eyes, McEntire lit up the stage and melted the hardest critical hearts. Her cow-country, aw-shucks delivery—she's originally from Oklahoma—was just plain adorable. And that voice! Her soaring dramatic delivery of Berlin's songs put us in mind of the great Patsy Cline. McEntire was terrific, but not enough to rescue the show, which remained an unfocused mess (although some baby boomers enjoyed seeing Larry Storch, from the old *F Troop* television show, as Sitting Bull).

Immodest Proposals

A THEME THAT CONTINUED TO EVOLVE in the 2000–01 season—apart from the shift in emphasis from new American plays to all *Producers*, all of the time—was the chill beginning to form in theater directing. As the next generation of directors takes root in the theater, a restive detachment accompanies the work of some of the most promising of the group. It is as though this rising crop of artists has been trained or encouraged to focus so intently on "the theatrical" that visceral human connections are stunted.

Baby talk: Brian Murray, Kathleen Early, David Burtka and Marian Seldes in The Play About the Baby. *Illustration: Hirschfeld*

Potent visual imagery and emotional depth are not mutually exclusive—the original works of Chicago's Mary Zimmerman and others amply demonstrate that. But when the look or style of a production is all that touches the audience, the theater experience shifts away from the spirit to focus on the intellect. It's a perfectly valid artistic choice, but it is also one that alienates audiences—even, one might add, intellectuals.

Perhaps it is a Brechtian notion of alienation that leads artists down this chilly path. Those of us who teach have coaxed and prodded our budding artists to think beyond the box of realism, to make the audience consider its social situation and resist the seductions of a world onstage that merely replicates the details of life. But even as we analyze and criticize the world around us there remains a primal need for the emotional connections that sustain us—for the open and sincere acting that gives theater its life. Harold Clurman put it best when he wrote in *On Directing*, "all theatre is real, but not all theatre is 'realistic.' [. . .] It is important to remember that style in the theatre is not chiefly a matter of décor, costumes and the like, but of acting."

Since Daniel Sullivan left the Seattle Repertory Theatre in 1997, he has kept busy as a director here in New York and there have been snide comments such as: "Aren't there any other directors in town?" Of course there are, but producers and artistic directors can count on Sullivan's actors to be intimately connected to the text, to one another onstage and to the audience. Even the antic direction of Anne Bogart—which overflows with the arcana of theatrical imagery—is always deeply rooted in a profoundly human (that word again) experience filled with truth and a bit of perplexity.

In the 2000–01 season, Matthew Warchus's direction of *Follies* at the Belasco was exhibit two in an argument for why the adept British director seems adrift with American texts and themes. The director had indicated that he would focus more attention on the acting in the musical, making some wonder, in advance, if that was because the actors couldn't sing. And yet, for all of the talk about acting, there was a lack of cohesion, of ensemble, among a group of theater folk playing theater folk. Exhibit one of Warchus's directorial dissociation was his Broadway production of Sam Shepard's *True West* in the 1999–2000 season with Philip Seymour Hoffman and John C. Reilly. In that production, the work of one of the great poets of the American stage had all of the subtlety of a match for the World Wrestling Federation (which, by the way, has a theater in Times Square these days).

Warchus has shown his directing skill to its best effect in productions of Yasmina Reza's *Art* (Broadway) and *The Unexpected Man* (Off Broadway at the Promenade Theatre), and with *Hamlet* at BAM (for the Royal Shakespeare Company). But even this season's *Unexpected Man*, with Alan Bates and Eileen Atkins as strangers on a train, kept the audience at some remove, which makes even the most engaged theatergoer think, "Who cares?" This isn't a campaign against Matthew Warchus, Tina Landau (*Bells Are Ringing*), Brian Kulick—the director of *Kit Marlowe* and *The Wax* this season who has become known for his stylish, if disengaged productions of the classics—or any of the other up-and-coming directors who skim emotional surfaces. These directors may feel compelled to reinvent theater, to react to the drain of theater audiences in the direction of film and television, to do what *only* theater can do. First, though, these artists must remember that people go to the theater to be part of a live experience, an ephemeral experience, an experience that can never be had sitting before a screen—whether it is 27 inches diagonally or 40 feet wide. The plea from this corner is for theater artists to dig deeper, to plumb the depths of texts—whether classics or spanking new—and to shine a light on the honest, human connections that lie there.

Play it Again

SPEAKING OF A FROSTY MUG OF EMOTION, the Roundabout Theatre Company had a challenging season with the Broadway outings in its new home. The company was responsible for half of the play revivals on Broadway this season, including *The Man Who Came to Dinner*, Harold Pinter's *Betrayal* (with Juliette Binoche, Liev Schreiber and John Slattery) and Noël Coward's *Design for Living* (with Jennifer Ehle, Dominic West and Alan Cumming in the leads). The latter two, directed by the usually reliable David Leveaux and Joe Mantello, seemed to beg us to ask, "Why?" Why were these plays done? How do they reflect our lives?

Most clearly reflected in the Roundabout Broadway productions from this season are the excruciating demands placed on not-for-profit theater companies working in the Broadway realm. Although a commercial Broadway producer can announce a show's closing midweek for the coming weekend, the nonprofit arena relies on a combination of subscribers and single-ticket buyers in a prescribed run. Quick closures are not feasible and failures generally run their slated time. Although the Roundabout retains much of the mission of its founder, Gene Feist, it has been brilliantly reinvented by Todd Haimes as the company has expanded in the past decade. But the move to a fancy 42nd Street address created a subtle shift in perception for the company. The plush seats and elegant setting of the former Selwyn Theatre may eventually give the company less room to

Welcome to New York: Reba McEntire in Annie Get Your Gun. *Illustration: Hirschfeld*

Music man: Randy Graff, Lonny Price and company in A Class Act. *Illustration: Hirschfeld*

maneuver when it comes to perceived success or failure, whether financial or artistic.

In the cases of both *Betrayal* and *Design for Living* there was a museum-piece essence to the productions. The work was competent, but nothing much stood out to mark the plays as material to our cultural or social discourse. Joe Mantello managed to unearth a homosexual *frisson* in *Design for Living*—but it's Coward, how submerged could it have been? Juliette Binoche was her lovely self in *Betrayal*, although the camera better captures the nuances of her acting. There was nothing really wrong with the acting in these shows, except for a reiteration of the chill that passes for style these days. One wonders if in the new, somewhat more introspective world of post-September 11, 2001, actors' edges will soften and the maximum cool will warm.

The last of the play revivals on Broadway was the Steppenwolf Theatre Company production of Dale Wasserman's adaptation of the Ken Kesey novel *One Flew Over the Cuckoo's Nest*. Featuring Gary Sinise as the edgy rebel, Randle P. McMurphy, who cons his way into a psychiatric hospital in lieu of jail time, the Terry Kinney-directed production failed to enthrall the critics. The play's theme of rebellion against bourgeois values by a slightly diverse group of inmates, who resemble members of Eisenhower-era "organization man" society, was a bit creaky for the 21st century. But audiences were happy to see film star Sinise in a role made famous by another leading man (Jack Nicholson) and the production won the best play revival Tony Award.

Of the 11 revivals on Broadway this season (6 plays, 4 musicals, 1 solo performance), the one that succeeded best in an artistic sense was *The Rocky Horror Show*. Alive, crazed and a little sexy, it awakened audiences from whatever torpor marked their daily lives and encouraged a bit of tongue-in-cheek (and harmless) bacchanalic fun. Most of the other revivals seemed merely to fill theater space as producers continually searched for that elusive cash cow: Something like *Oh! Calcutta!*, *Grease* or, more recently, *Chicago*—the three longest-running revivals in Broadway history.

City Center's Encores! series of musicals in concert version has become the place where producers troll for product that can be easily transferred—as was *Chicago* in 1996. Originally created to revivify overlooked musicals of the past, the installation of producer Jack Viertel as the new artistic director may signal an increasing emphasis on the development of future transfers. The 2000–01 season's concerts of *A Connecticut Yankee*, *Bloomer Girl* and *Hair* were joined by a concert reading series devised by City Center board member Alec Baldwin. Called Voices!, the series aims to bring disused plays of the past to a new audience. It's hard to say, though, just how "overlooked" a play such as Joseph Kesselring's *Arsenic and Old Lace* might be considered. It surely must compete with Thornton Wilder's *Our Town* for the title of most-produced drama by high schools and community theaters. The series also revisited *Little Murders*, with stage directions read by author Jules Feiffer, and an adaptation of Stephen Vincent Benét's *The Devil and Daniel Webster*. If Baldwin and company are really interested in rescuing underproduced American plays from another era, how about something by Clyde Fitch, Rachel Crothers or Maxwell Anderson?

Solo Shots

LILY TOMLIN RETURNED TO BROADWAY with her one-woman 1985 show, *The Search for Signs of Intelligent Life in the Universe*. At a luncheon of the American Theatre Critics Association, Tomlin found herself the object of admiration of a dozen or so other actors on hand, many of whom testified to Tomlin's artistic influence on their lives and careers. Although it could be said that little new was to be found in Tomlin's characters (as written by longtime collaborator Jane Wagner), there was a certain delight in seeing the versatile actor-comedian flex her creative muscles at the Booth Theatre.

Broadway diva Patti LuPone returned after a too-long absence in a limited-run musical revue, *Patti LuPone "Matters of the Heart,"* at the Vivian Beaumont Theater. But the real head-scratcher of the season was Hershey Felder's *George Gershwin Alone*, starring Felder as George Gershwin at the Helen Hayes Theatre. Other than his facial profile, which was used for program publicity, Felder had little in common with the composer whom he impersonated with mawkish stories and less-than-inspired stabs at playing *Rhapsody in Blue*. In the performance we attended, the sole moment of dramatic interest occurred when a cell phone erupted and the flustered performer worked to regain his composure, which he accomplished admirably. (And a pox on all who allow their cell phones to ring in the theater!)

Uptown at the Triad Theatre, the effervescent Mark Nadler and KT Sullivan performed *American Rhapsody: A New Musical Revue* to much livelier effect. But even they left the listener longing for an evening of Michael Feinstein working his way through the Gershwin repertoire.

Elsewhere Off Broadway, Pamela Gien created a stir with her one-woman performance of a white child's life in apartheid-era South Africa. Gien assumed a variety of characters that ranged from her parents—who seemed straight out of the Victorian era—to her kindly black nanny. *The*

Faded glories: Gregory Harrison (with glass), Treat Williams, Polly Bergen (above center), Blythe Danner, Judith Ivey and company in Follies. *Illustration: Hirschfeld*

Syringa Tree is a story of colonial/postcolonial pain and reconciliation that divided audience opinion. While we found the piece weakly structured and acted to simpering effect—notably when Gien played herself as an adorable child—the actor got enough support from theater writers to receive the Drama Desk Award for solo performance.

Steven Berkoff, a vital force in theatrical innovation for several decades (and a well-known film actor), performed *Shakespeare's Villains: A Masterclass in Evil* at Joe's Pub at the Joseph Papp Public Theater and reopened it later in the Public's Anspacher Theater. The masterly actor Berkoff, who is especially satisfying as an evil genius, kept audiences in his thrall for nearly 90 minutes before sending them away with a deeper appreciation of the actor's craft and of Shakespeare's enduring relevance.

Elsewhere at the Public, Ruben Santiago-Hudson shared his experiences and the characters of his childhood in *Lackawanna Blues*. Ably accompanied by musician Bill Sims Jr., Santiago-Hudson spun a web of tales that played like a finely nuanced blues song with Loretta Greco providing a focused, seamless directorial hand. The pain, suffering and (occasional) violence of a community's marginal existence were balanced by the small wonders that a child experiences when he is loved and nurtured by a strong female figure. A Broadway veteran of *Jelly's Last Jam* and August Wilson's *Seven Guitars*, Santiago-Hudson is a powerful presence we should see more often.

Off Broadway: Home of the Best Plays . . .

IT WAS A GOOD YEAR for playwriting Off Broadway. Six of the 10 *Best Plays* honorees came from those venues, further confirming Off Broadway as the place where exciting new works get done. (The quality of the writing and the increasing willingness of stars to work Off Broadway was part of the reasoning behind the price increase of some tickets to a high of $65—which, as *Variety*'s Robert Hofler pointed out, put those seats on a par with some Broadway shows.) The best of the best all opened in the latter half of the season when Edward Albee continued his exploration of identity and generational conflict with *The Play About the Baby* at the Century Center for the Performing Arts. Directed by David Esbjornson, with a cast that included the superb Brian Murray and the inimitable Marian Seldes, this addition to the Albee *oeuvre* was an animated, stimulating experience that prodded the intellect even as it pressed emotional buttons. Christine Dolen's essay on this Best Play takes its measure in the following section.

Rebecca Gilman landed on the "A" list of playwrights in the 2000–01 season with Off Broadway productions of *Spinning Into Butter* at Lincoln

Center Theater and *Boy Gets Girl* at Manhattan Theatre Club. *Spinning* seemed a too-contrived tale of a college dean's self-confessed racism and her confusion over today's racial politics. Some who saw the Lincoln Center production and Chicago's Goodman Theatre production, though, felt that Chicago's Mary Beth Fisher as the doubting dean gave a clearer sense of her character's dilemma and dawning consciousness. In the New York production, however, these same observers said that Hope Davis seemed to accept her predicament too easily, which left the drama flat.

Boy Gets Girl replicated Michael Maggio's Chicago direction in a production supervised by Manhattan Theatre Club's Lynne Meadow. Maggio's staging—the director died of post-transplant lymphoma in August 2000—brought Mary Beth Fisher to New York as beleaguered magazine writer Theresa Bedell, whose blind date begins to stalk her and turns her life into a nightmare. Gilman's play is a taut, poignant reminder of the objectification (and vulnerability) with which women still struggle, even though so much has been accomplished to help redress gender inequities. Chris Jones's essay on this Best Play follows in the next section.

People who don't quite understand how they got where they are in life are a frequent topic in the plays and screenwriting of Kenneth Lonergan. The writer's clueless losers generally find some sort of connection with another person before his narratives end, but in the world according to Lonergan, it is the journey that matters most. The Playwrights Horizons production of *Lobby Hero* showed a night watchman (played by Glenn Fitzgerald) trying to untangle the mess of his life when a woman cop (Heather Burns) turns his head and (maybe) changes his life. As directed by Mark Brokaw, Lonergan's characters stumbled forward, retreated quickly, yet somehow managed to progress. In the section to follow, Tish Dace discusses the ethos of Lonergan and his characters in her essay on this Best Play.

With *Mnemonic* by Complicite, the group formerly known as Theatre de Complicite, we see a shift in the *Best Plays* dynamic about what constitutes a play. As John Istel points out in his essay about this Best Play, *Mnemonic* awakens the senses and makes the audience think about the role of memory in cognition and in the creation of identity. The work, as directed by Simon McBurney, may be best described as sui generis, perhaps rendering our choice of it questionable. To any questions, though, our reply is another: Does this play help us to better understand and appreciate the human condition? That, finally, is the salient question we ask when considering a work's importance to our theatrical culture. Here, the answer is, "Yes."

When Robert Brustein called our attention to playwright Adam Rapp's *Nocturne*, the promising young writer was already on our radar screen. A

Yes-s-s-s-s-s-s-s-s! Roger Bart in The Producers. *Illustration: Hirschfeld*

Dancin' fool: Matthew Broderick in The Producers. *Illustration: Hirschfeld*

gifted novelist and former playwriting fellow at Juilliard, Rapp creates a dramatic poetry that sings to its audience even as it sends the reader/listener on a journey of self-consciousness. Although criticized by some for being too literary, *Nocturne* awakens us to the still small voice reminding us of the choices we make, the paths we take and the paths we leave behind. His near-monologue about a pianist who accidentally kills his younger sister was directed to pitch perfection by Marcus Stern. And no one who saw it will ever hear Steely Dan's "Hey Nineteen" or think about driving quite the same again. Brustein assesses this Best Play in the next section.

Urinetown took many of us in New York by surprise, not least by its unappetizing title. But it was ultimately a pleasant distraction as the clever musical made its way from the New York International Fringe Festival to Off Broadway. Dripping with irony from top to bottom, this Best Play quotes the musical styles and thematic structures of several substantial predecessors. The satirical edge created by authors Greg Kotis and Mark Hollmann, in a story about a place where people must pay to use the bathroom, celebrates musicals even as it lampoons them. Jeffrey Sweet discusses the influences on *Urinetown* in his essay in the next section.

With 38 new plays opening Off Broadway—which *Best Plays* defines as productions playing 8 performances per week in a venue that seats fewer than 500—there were a number of plays to celebrate in the 2000–01 season. Stephen Adly Guirgis's *Jesus Hopped the "A" Train* brought the gritty realism of New York City's corrections system to the East 13th Street Theatre with fine performances by John Ortiz, David Zayas, Elizabeth Canavan, Salvatore Inzerilo and Ron Cephas Jones. Directed with a fierce intensity by Philip Seymour Hoffman—who acted in the lamented *True West* of last season—the play reminded cable-television viewers of the HBO program *Oz*. (In an peculiar twist, Zayas, who plays an inmate on *Oz*, played a cruel guard in *Jesus*.) The chief difference between the two is that while the television show vividly demonstrates the physical violence of the corrections system, Guirgis's play sparks the imagination, which can be infinitely more resonant and horrifying than the "reality" of television.

Jessica Hagedorn's sprawling play about the Philippines at the end of the Marcos era, *Dogeaters*, played in Martinson Hall at the Joseph Papp Public Theater. Crisply directed by Michael Greif, the play poked fun at the icons and stereotypes of life in the Philippines—Imelda Marcos (and her shoes), sexual tourism, a corrupt military, terrorized politicians—as it tried (futilely) to peel away the layers of colonial influence. Framed by a pair of smiling television hosts, the humor of the story carried a tragic undertone that implied, "As long as we keep dancing, we can never drop." What we cannot tell from our distance—geographical and cultural—is if the dance continues, and how.

Also at the Public, which enjoyed a rewarding year in its new-play programming, José Rivera's poetic *References to Salvador Dalí Make Me*

Hot, played in the Shiva Theater starring John Ortiz, Rosie Perez and Carlo Alban. Perez played the lonely wife of a serviceman who finds herself speaking to the moon (Michael Lombard) and conversing with a cat (Kristine Nielsen) and a coyote (Kevin Jackson). Alban played the boy next door who dreams of the older woman's warm embrace. Just when it seems she will be swept away by her desert reveries, her soldier husband (Ortiz) returns from the field and wants life back to normal—now. The play lost its ethereal allure when the playwright shifted away from the early poetic fantasies and embraced a kind of kitchen-table realism. The scenes between Ortiz and Perez were taut and dramatic, but the stylistic shift caused a psychic disconnect and made the piece appear to be two distinct plays. Part of the difficulty lay with Perez's discomfort in the less naturalistic scenes. In the early going, her unease showed on the stage when the text required that she fly with Rivera's poetry, but she seemed reluctant to spread her wings.

Twain meet: Kristen Bell (smiling, above), Jim Poulos and Joshua Park in The Adventures of Tom Sawyer. *Illustration: Hirschfeld*

Up at Lincoln Center, a pair of well-known playwrights displayed their wares for Mitzi Newhouse Theater audiences. (Since the opening of the Tony-winning *Contact* at the Vivian Beaumont, that theater has been home only to the musical and to special events on Sunday and Monday evenings.) Wendy Wasserstein opened her latest, *Old Money*, in December. Directed by Mark Brokaw, the play was a quirky meditation on the parallels between those who legally fleece the public of their money and those who get rich the old-fashioned way: inheritance. Going off in several directions at once—with near-hallucinatory shifts back and forth in time—Wasserstein mulls over what she wants to say about capital and its acquistion, and then seems to murmur, "Never mind."

Jon Robin Baitz made a splash with his celebrity-stocked production of *Ten Unknowns* at the Newhouse. Directed by longtime collaborator, Daniel Sullivan, *Ten Unknowns* featured superb performances by Donald Sutherland and Julianna Margulies as an aging expatriate artist and a beautiful young scientist who encounter one another in southern Mexico. At stake in Baitz's engaging discussion, are issues of art, commerce, authenticity and possession (of art, land, culture, work). Lively and funny in its repartee, *Ten Unknowns* unravels before the end of the first act—when it becomes clear that the artist's assistant (played by Justin Kirk) is doing more work than simply cleaning brushes and stretching canvas. Only partly explored by the playwright are how notions of "art" and "ownership" evolve over time. Veering away from this discourse, Baitz allows his story to unwind in a rather perfunctory—and altogether too ennobling—manner. The play was optioned for Broadway, but scheduling difficulties caused delays and it now seems unlikely to land with the star cast intact.

Other new plays of note Off Broadway included Alan Ayckbourn's futuristic comedy about android actors, *Comic Potential* (Manhattan Theatre Club), which provided a showcase for Janie Dee as a robot who begins to feel. Lee Blessing's *Cobb* about the great, but reviled baseball player, Ty Cobb, managed a three-month run at the Lucille Lortel Theatre after Kevin Spacey took a producing interest in the Melting Pot Theatre Company production. *Tabletop* moved up in stages from Off Off Broadway's Dance Theatre Workshop to the Off Broadway's American Place Theatre. The Rob Ackerman play centered on the stresses and strains that face advertising people whose job it is to make products look appealing. *Six Goumbas and a Wannabe* by Vincent M. Gogliormella also made the jump from Off Off by capitalizing on *The Sopranos* craze.

Martin McDonagh's *A Skull in Connemara*, the second part of his Leenane trilogy, opened at the Roundabout Theatre Company's Gramercy

Theatre space—nearly intact—after a run at Seattle's A Contemporary Theatre. Gordon Edelstein provided a steady directorial hand for Kevin Tighe, Zoaunne LeRoy, Christopher Carley and Christopher Evan Welch. By now, though, the quaint stereotypes of McDonagh's rural Irish are beginning to wear thin. What's clear to anyone who's seen more than one of the trilogy is that those imagined folks of Leenane are a bloody lot.

Macaulay Culkin and Joely Richardson brought Richard Nelson's adolescent fantasy about a teenage boy and his sexy, worldly teacher, *Madame Melville*, to the Promenade Theatre. Except for the presence of the multitalented Nelson as writer and director, it could well have been event theater: "Come see the kid from the *Home Alone* movie in a live, sexy role." In the event, though, Culkin was hardly sexy and barely seemed alive—his acting technique may make the camera love him, but the stage asks for more—and we were left to wonder at the teacher's attraction to the bland, blond boy.

Manhattan Theatre Club ended the season with a pair of new plays, which opened a few days apart. Melanie Marnich's *Blur* charts a young woman's discovery of love in odd friendships just as a rare condition robs her eyesight. The play, directed by Lynne Meadow, with Polly Draper as the girl's mother, is a bit thin in its plot and story, but coupled with Marnich's *Quake*, which debuted at the Humana Festival of New American Plays in Louisville, Kentucky, an interesting new voice appears to be developing. Warren Leight's *Glimmer, Glimmer and Shine* continues the playwright's affair with jazz music and its players. John Spencer and Brian Kerwin played a pair of brothers who traveled different paths—one embraced music and its marginal lifestyle, the other rejected them—and reunite just before the musician brother dies. Lacking the raw emotional core of Leight's *Side Man*, *Glimmer* winds itself into a neat dramaturgical bundle by its end.

A handful of Off Broadway play revivals bear note. Roundabout Theatre Company's *Juno and the Paycock*, a 1924 play by Sean O'Casey, provided an interesting lead-in for the McDonagh play mentioned above. Where McDonagh's characters are all avarice and mean spirit, O'Casey's poverty-stricken family is more a victim of a society in chaos (or "chassis" as Jack Boyle calls it). To be sure, O'Casey's women are beset by men who exploit them and abandon them, but McDonagh's women are as selfish and unpleasant as the men (perhaps it's the playwright's idea of equal rights).

Second Stage Theatre presented Mark Lamos's staging of Edward Albee's *Tiny Alice* featuring Richard Thomas and Laila Robins as Brother Julian and Miss Alice. Originally produced at Hartford Stage in 1998, this production resuscitated Albee's 1964 play after decades of neglect. The

Hoofer's dream: Christine Ebersole, Michael Cumpsty and Kate Levering in 42nd Street. *Illustration: Hirschfeld*

reason that the play has stayed tucked safely away in the library is that critics and audiences have had a devil of a time figuring out what it means. Ultimately, it must be seen as the playwright's rumination on the relationship of the world of the spirit to the world of the material, of the flesh. Albee seems to ask (and answer) "What is the price of a man's immortal soul?" In the playwright's construct, organized religion (i.e., the Catholic Church) is all too prepared to assign a value and to make the trade. Although Albee's murky religious allusions seem less obscure in the 21st century, his mysteries are still a wonder to behold.

The company also staged Beth Henley's 1981 Pulitzer Prize-winning *Crimes of the Heart*. These days, the frustrated women who populate this tale of burgeoning southern womanhood seem a bit too familiar. Director Garry Hynes, the first woman to receive a play-directing Tony Award (for *The Beauty Queen of Leenane*), offers no new insights when giving life to the Mississippi women in Henley's play. Enid Graham, Amy Ryan and Mary Catherine Garrison played the three sisters, with Julia Murney as their ditsy, competitive cousin.

Peter Nichols's 1983 *Passion Play* came and went quickly in a commercial production at the Minetta Lane Theatre. Maureen Anderman and Simon Jones were fine as a married couple who struggle to keep their relationship together in the face of infidelity—even as the husband hopes to keep his newfound randiness intact. The couple's younger selves appear on the scene to comment, to argue and to describe the feelings that the older pair have learned to keep under wraps. Although the story may sound somewhat contrived, the production was poignant and affecting. Some critics were disappointed that Elinor Renfield's staging hadn't quite the intensity of a Donmar Warehouse revival in London the prior year—and that sentiment probably kept the show from enjoying a longer run.

Austin Pendleton's weird little play, *Uncle Bob*, was revived at the Soho Playhouse with George Morfogen reprising his role as an angry semi-closeted gay man who is dying of AIDS. Originally produced by the Mint Theater Company in 1995, the play is an incessant rant about Bob's miserable life. Into his life comes his homophobic nephew Josh (played by Showtime's *Queer as Folk* co-star, Gale Harold), who himself comes out of the closet and insists on getting infected so that he can be of comfort to his Uncle Bob. Pendleton was quoted as saying that he wrote the play at a time when he was experiencing a lot of loss from friends dying of AIDS. But since it plays like an overlong suicide note, one suspects it would be unlikely ever to see a stage were it not for its author's relative celebrity and the willingness of similarly well-known actors to play the roles.

. . . If Not the Best Musicals

ALTHOUGH OFF BROADWAY NEW-MUSICAL PRODUCTION surged ahead of last year by 25 percent, there wasn't a lot to celebrate. But Kirsten Childs's *The Bubbly Black Girl Sheds Her Chameleon Skin* got the season off to a good start. Charting the journey of a bright, young African-American dancer, the musical was patterned after the author, who is a former Broadway dancer. With a pocketful of grants and awards to sustain it, *Bubbly* enjoyed a buzz-filled, month-long run at Playwrights Horizons that seemed to mark the show for a future life Off Broadway. Alas, it was not to be, partly because the subject matter of a woman-child's loss of innocence as she discovers the impact of racism makes better fodder for children's theater or afterschool television programming. But Childs's clever way with music and lyrics bodes well for her next project.

The York Theatre Company continued its search for new musicals to offer its loyal audiences with productions of *Fermat's Last Tango*, *Suburb* and *The IT Girl*. *Fermat*, by Joanne Sydney Lessner and Joshua Rosenblum, brought the scintillating topic of mathematic theorems to life, which probably might not be surprising in a season that saw *Proof* rise to the top of the heap—and who can forget last season's snob hit, *Copenhagen*? Try as they might, though, the creators of *Fermat* made math neither fun nor sexy. In David Javerbaum and Robert S. Cohen's *Suburb*, a couple decides to start a family and leave the city for safer, friendlier environs. It was a strange choice at a time when the term "suburban sprawl" had mostly negative connotations and many people were opting for the cultural advantages of raising families in urban settings. Why, one wonders, didn't they present this piece in some New Jersey bedroom community?

Of the three York offerings, *The IT Girl*, by Paul McKibbins, Michael Small and BT McNicholl, seemed most ready for prime time—if prime time means the Depression era when escapist musicals showed the possibility of rising to wealth with nothing to show but a shapely pair of legs. (Yes, we know the original film was made *before* the Depression. But the filmmakers didn't know it was coming and we know it happened—making the stereotypes of *The IT Girl* all the more difficult to appreciate and enjoy. Context is everything.) *The IT Girl* attracted 20 investors whose names appeared above the title, as if it were being prepared for a move to another venue, but the show closed after three weeks. Television star Jean Louisa Kelly (*Yes, Dear*) made a tempting IT Girl, but the entire project was a dated (not to mention politically discomfitting) enterprise.

Manhattan Theatre Club tried its hand at musical works with a Jack Viertel adaptation of the popular Jack Finney novel, *Time and Again*. Although it boasted a topnotch cast that included Laura Benanti and Julia Murney, the page to stage transition was a bumpy one as the show developed during the past decade. *Time* lasted a mere three weeks. *Newyorkers*, a musical revue, did marginally better with the critics, but lasted only 16 performances.

Other revues included the revival of *Berlin to Broadway With Kurt Weill*, based on the great composer's collaborations with a variety of writers. *Berlin* ran for 121 performances at the Triad Theatre uptown. The long-run champ among revues, of course, is *Forbidden Broadway*. During the 2000–01 season, creator Gerard Alessandrini premiered an updated version, *Forbidden Broadway 2001: A Spoof Odyssey*. The new show was cited by the Drama Desk Awards in its May 2001 ceremony. David Coffman and Dolores Prida adapted Prida's work to create *4 Guys Named José . . . and Una Mujer Named Maria!* In *4 Guys* a group of Latino men put on a midwinter show in Omaha. Employing an anthology of popular Latin songs to help propel the story, the show ran for much of the season (191 performances), before embarking on a reported tour.

The tragic rock star Janis Joplin's letters to her mother were adapted by Randal Myler in the musical *Love, Janis*, which featured a pair of actors

Bon vivant: Vincent Canby, film and theater critic of the New York Times. *Illustration: Hirschfeld*

playing Janis the person (Catherine Curtin) and Janis the performer (alternating Andra Mitrovich and Cathy Richardson). Using Joplin's own songs to help punctuate the story, Myler's production concept had significant runs in Denver (where it began in 1994) and Chicago (1999) on the road to Off Broadway. Playing at the Village Theater, the production continued into the summer.

In addition to *Urinetown*, which was clearly destined for greater things, the big news on the Off Broadway musical front was the opening of *Bat Boy: The Musical*. Based on a "story" from a supermarket tabloid, the *Weekly World News*, which was listed in the program as a licensor, the musical is a tacky tour of small minds in a small town—perhaps made that way through inbreeding—that also touches on themes of bestiality and anthropomorphism. With its loud, rockish music and terminally hip ironies, the musical almost seems like a backwoods version of *Little Shop of Horrors*. But where *Little Shop* tempered its satirical point with a sweet love story, *Bat Boy* employs a festive scene of bestiality in a forest that is neither very funny, nor imaginative. And yet, it is different; and in a culture addicted to the new, oddity often reigns supreme.

A Season for Renewal

THE SEASO4N THAT STARTED FEEBLY ended with a *Blast!* as a genuine marching band took the stage of the Broadway Theatre, made possible by the departure of the long-running *Miss Saigon* after 4,097 performances. Why a marching band and flag twirlers were on a Broadway stage was anyone's guess, but come Tony time a special award was announced for the show—which amused some and outraged others. But the big Tony topic, in a season that started with an exciting burst of new American plays, was *The Producers* sweeping away the competition and setting a new record when it won 12 Tonys. (When Daniel Sullivan received his Tony for best direction of a play for *Proof*, he said, "There must be some mistake, I had nothing to do with *The Producers*.") The show had been nominated for a record 15 awards, but there was some overlap when three *Producers*' men were nominated for best featured actor (Gary Beach won) and Nathan Lane and Matthew Broderick went head-to-head for best actor (Lane won).

When the season ended, *Variety* reported that it was another record year for Broadway theater with nearly 12 million theatergoers in attendance (11,937,962) and receipts of more than $665 million. Average ticket prices continued to rise to nearly $56 each, an increase over the previous season of about 5 percent. Business was booming and competition was intense for theater space on Broadway and off—where top tickets ($65) were higher than the Broadway average. And *The Lion King*'s 1997 single-day ticket sales record was shattered when the reviews of *The Producers* appeared and nearly $3 million in advance tickets were sold on that day.

As an old-fashioned book musical rejuvenated Broadway near the season's end, the 2000–01 season also marked the closure of one of the shows that shifted creative energies toward the musical theater spectacles (mostly British) that dominated in the 1980s and 1990s. *Cats*, the longest-running show in Broadway history closed on September 10, 2000. With the end of *Cats* and *Miss Saigon*, the media asked if we were entering a new age of musical theater. It's a tough call to make—although many tried—but it's interesting that it took members of the so-called "Greatest Generation" to breathe new life into American musical theater.

We lost two valuable friends of theater and film during the season with the deaths of our colleagues Otis L. Guernsey Jr., former editor of *Best Plays* and longtime critic for the *New York Herald Tribune*, and Vincent Canby, film and theater critic for the *New York Times* and, earlier, for *Variety*. Guernsey served at the *Herald Tribune* as a writer, critic and editor for 19 years before leaving the newspaper to explore other opportunities. He later served as film critic for *Show Magazine* and consulted at CBS to help bring dramatic programming from the stage to the television screen.

Guernsey loved words and he loved the performing arts, so he was a perfect audience member. But he also had a creative spirit that was aroused when he read a news story about State Department employees who, on a lark, "invented" a spy complete with phony dossiers. Guernsey thought it would make a great idea for a movie if a tourist were to be mistaken for this "spy" and decided to present it to Alfred Hitchcock through a mutual friend. Hitchcock then had Ernest Lehman write the script for what became *North by Northwest*. At the time, Guernsey didn't want credit for the story because he was a working journalist and he wanted to avoid any impropriety. Years later he read a speech given by Hitchcock in which the filmmaker referred to "Otis Guernsey's idea for *North by Northwest*." Only then, several decades after the film had been made, did he openly take credit for the idea.

Whenever Guernsey was in New York—he lived for many years in Woodstock, Vermont—he stayed at his beloved Yale Club, where a martini with lunch was his ritual. For the last 36 years of his life, he shepherded the *Best Plays* series through all manner of challenges and helped to support the craft of playwriting in many ways. He was a gentleman of the old school, a mentor and a friend. The theater is the poorer without him. He is survived by his wife of many years, Dorianne D. Guernsey.

Vincent Canby joined the staff of *Variety* in 1959 and worked as a film and theater reporter for the trade newspaper until 1965 when he joined the *New York Times*. From 1969 to 1993 he was the senior film critic for the *Times*, advocating for the work of such diverse filmmakers as Woody Allen, Rainer Werner Fassbinder and Spike Lee. Beginning in 1993, Canby joined the theater beat at the *Times* as the Sunday columnist. For a brief time, in 1994, he served as chief theater critic before returning to his Sunday post.

In addition to his support and encouragement of three generations of performing artists, Canby also wrote novels and plays. In his final years, he used the Sunday *Times* column as a bully pulpit from which to champion plays and productions that he believed deserved another, more sympathetic perspective.

The beauty of a theater season is that it mimics the seasons of life. There is the hope of new beginnings, which can come in June or in February. There are days (and performances) that seem without end and others that leave us panting for more—more laughter, more tears, more time, more life. As this book goes to press, the new season is well underway and many wonder how theaters will weather the challenges experienced by a country at war. At the same time, the New York and national economic situations look bleak due to political, social and cultural repercussions following terrorist attacks on American soil.

Theater leaders, though, look hopefully toward the future. The answers to the questions posed by our current uncertainty will come soon enough. But people will always seek the connection, the human communion of theater. It will happen whenever an actor stands in a darkened room, rays of light across his face and says, "Who's there?"

THE BEST PLAYS OF 2000–2001

2000–2001 Best Play

BOY GETS GIRL

By Rebecca Gilman

○○○○○

Essay by Chris Jones

> THERESA: Maybe being a woman, to me, meant tolerating a lot of shit. And maybe I never learned otherwise. I still tolerate shit, but I do it now as a reporter, so it just seems like part of the job. But maybe it's really still me thinking that's what I'm supposed to do, as a woman. Sit and listen to some asshole go on and on about himself, and then reward him for it. So maybe that's why I told Tony that it was entirely me, when that wasn't the truth. It was entirely him.

WHEN REBECCA GILMAN'S MANUSCRIPT for *Boy Gets Girl* first started circulating around the Goodman Theatre towards the end of 1999, staffers began quietly referring to it as "the stalker play."

This was, of course, away from the ears of the public. The Goodman has a reputation for occupying the upper echelons of the theatrical food chain, and it's certainly not known for pandering to thematic concerns of the moment. This is a theater historically more comfortable with reviving the works, say, of Lorraine Hansberry or Luis Valdez than with appropriating territory more associated with Hollywood or a television network's movie of the week.

But Gilman was already a special case at the Goodman long before *Boy Gets Girl.*

A modest and unassuming woman in her mid-thirties, Gilman came to Chicago from Trussville, Alabama. After initially collecting fistfuls of rejection letters from Chicago theater companies, Gilman's big break came when a tiny Chicago-area theater company called the Circle Theatre in Forest Park produced one of her early plays, *The Glory of Living*. Favorable reviews reached the ears of the Goodman Theatre's literary manager, Susan V. Booth—now the artistic director of the Alliance Theatre in Atlanta—and Gilman quickly became the Goodman's favorite daughter. One would have to go back to David Mamet to find a locally based scribe that this theater has sponsored with such largesse.

Breast theory: Howard Witt and Mary Beth Fisher in Rebecca Gilman's Boy Gets Girl. *Photo: Liz Lauren*

The Goodman produced Gilman's *Spinning Into Butter*, a play that deals with white liberal racism, during its 1998–99 season. Set on a fictional college campus, the play follows the reaction of white administrators to the news that an African-American freshman has been receiving threatening and anonymous letters. In the second act, a stressed-out dean snaps in front of a colleague and unleashes a monologue in which she confesses her own racism. Since the character is hitherto empathetic—and the racism is expressed with the language and logic usually favored by liberals—the monologue garnered the play strong media attention and a subsequent production at Lincoln Center in New York.

Roughly simultaneously, Gilman began to rack up various international awards, including the American Theatre Critics Association's M. Elizabeth Osborn Award, various Joseph Jefferson Awards in Chicago, and London's *Evening Standard* Award for Most Promising Playwright (Gilman was the first American writer to win).

But prior to *Boy Gets Girl*, Gilman's aesthetic universe was still difficult to pin down.

The Glory of Living, which deals with the youngest woman ever to be sentenced to death in Alabama, is a gritty, violent play set amid the rural underclass. *Spinning Into Butter* is set in the more rarified world of academia. Although there is a mystery at the base of its narrative, *Spinning* is a play organized more along thematic lines than around a narrative hook.

Boy Gets Girl, which subsequently moved to Off Broadway's Manhattan Theatre Club, is something entirely different. As she was working on the play, Gilman said in an interview that she was trying to write a play "about how people have incorporated cultural attitudes into their own make-up." Word quickly went around that Gilman was working on a contemporary thriller about the relationship between the genders.

Even the title caused some early controversy. Originally entitled *Boy Meets Girl*, it ran afoul of the copyrighted play of the same name by Sam and Bella Spewack—who also wrote the libretto for *Kiss Me, Kate*, among other works. Gilman was forced to change her drama to *Boy Gets Girl*, which seemed to fit the final version of the play all the better.

Boy Gets Girl was also beset by a very sad event. Michael Maggio, the much-beloved associate artistic director of the Goodman Theatre and a nine-year survivor of a lung transplant, died shortly after his premiere production had closed at the Goodman.

Before his death, a deal had already been struck for Maggio's production of *Boy Gets Girl* to move to New York and no one wanted to change that. So in a highly unusual move, Manhattan Theatre Club artistic director Lynne Meadow set about recreating Maggio's production with the help of Goodman's Booth. The cast and creative teams remained the same, although Gilman made some minor changes to the script before the New York production. Thus the credit "directed by Michael Maggio" remained attached to the play. Since Gilman has said that Maggio had a great deal to do with the genesis of the play, this was entirely reflective of her wishes.

Boy Gets Girl is a tense contemporary drama about the aftermath of the blind date from hell. In the play, a fictional journalist named Theresa Bedell (played by Mary Beth Fisher) has a couple of beers with a seemingly eligible guy who then begins to completely destroy her life. Since almost anyone who has ever gone on a date with a total stranger has worried about a spurned romantic partner becoming a threat to one's ongoing career or happiness, it's unsurprising that Gilman's drama resonated so strongly with the urban audiences in both New York and Chicago.

Theresa is a single, thirtysomething woman who works for a Manhattan publishing company. Thanks to one of her friends, she finds herself on a casual blind date with a fellow named Tony (Ian Lithgow). At first, he seems like a charming, self-deprecating sort who works in computing. She even agrees to see him again.

But the clingy Tony proves inappropriately enthusiastic and, sensing a weird vibe, Theresa decides to gently ditch him before there is anything beyond a couple of casual meetings. But Tony does not go quietly. First, flowers arrive at Theresa's office. Then he shows up in person. Even though Theresa tells him never to come back, he keeps calling—and calling, and calling.

Even as Theresa has to deal with Tony, she's also coping with a thorny assignment at work. Her genial, fatherly boss, Howard (Matt DeCaro), has insisted that she interview a notorious pulp moviemaker known for exploiting women's bodies in his films. Based on the real-life character of Russ Meyer, Gilman's fictional Les Kennkat (Howard Witt) is a cheerful, unrepentant sexist who argues that there's nothing wrong with his life's work of fetishizing women's breasts. Even as Theresa finds herself more and more repulsed by his work, she also finds herself liking this honest, shameless fellow.

Meanwhile Tony's obsession progressively becomes criminal harassment. To Theresa's horror, she comes to understand that a preening,

Mister Lonely: Ian Lithgow and Mary Beth Fisher in Rebecca Gilman's Boy Gets Girl. *Photo: Liz Lauren*

twentysomething assistant, Harriet (Shayna Ferm), has been ignoring her instructions and has given Tony her home number and other personal information. Harriet gets fired—but Tony still won't be shaken off.

Increasingly desperate (and without living parents or other family connections), Theresa turns to the seemingly sympathetic figure of Mercer (David Adkins), a fellow writer. But beneath his non-sexist platitudes, Mercer embodies—in a latent fashion—many of the undesirable aspects of Tony's personality. To Theresa's horror, he announces that he wants to write a story for the magazine about her troubles with Tony. Mercer argues that it will do some good—but Theresa feels it's a violation.

By now, Theresa has called the police. A hard-nosed female officer (Ora Jones) shows up to say there's not much the police can do until the creep commits a violent crime. Gradually and inevitably, the terrified Theresa is robbed of her identity.

Tony ransacks her apartment and destroys her possessions. In the play's intense climax, Tony comes to Theresa's house—where Mercer and Howard are helping Theresa pack. We never see Tony again—but we do see Theresa leave for a new job in Denver under an assumed name.

On one level, of course, *Boy Gets Girl* functions as a suspense drama in the tried-and-true Hollywood fashion of, say, *Single White Female*. Since so much contemporary theater eschews this kind of urban realism (perhaps for fear of unfavorable comparisons with film and television), this type of plot-driven urban nightmare has become more distinctive of late. Much of the broad appeal of this play with audiences doubtless rests on the universality—especially among women—of Theresa's dilemma.

But Gilman did not merely write a pulp thriller that happened to tap into the urban nightmare *du jour*. Unlike the Hollywood genre-movie, this avowedly feminist play takes great pains to note that Tony's inappropriate behavior results not from his being an aberrant "other" in the traditional thriller style. On the contrary, Gilman suggests that Tony's aggression is, to a large degree, an outgrowth and intensification of more latent forms of sexist behavior.

One of the main points of the play is that reasonable men need to understand this connection if they are going to get past it. By the second act, the hitherto smug Mercer is beginning to get the point:

> MERCER: You know, I was wondering, did I ever do anything to scare a woman before? Not intentionally, but did I ever do anything that came off as scary. And I know, when I was in college, I had a girlfriend who dumped me for another guy and I would call her dorm room, just to see if she was there, or walk out of my way to see

> if her light was on. But just a couple of times, you know. I didn't make a career of it.
>
> HOWARD: Everybody's done something like that.
>
> MERCER: I know. I think that's my point. It's not exactly abnormal behavior. But it's on the same continuum.

The presence of Theresa's vapid assistant, Harriet, allows Gilman to show the culpability of women in their own objectification. A wealthy young woman, Harriet tries to use her mother's credit card to give Theresa "a treat" from Saks, but she fails to understand that "cute" Tony is a danger to women—and she fails at sisterhood.

Even Theresa has to understand her own role in her victimization. Beck, the savvy police officer, explains that she should have dumped Tony far more firmly, so the stalker did not keep believing he had a chance. After initial resistance, Theresa tries to understand what she did:

> THERESA: Okay. When I was a freshman in college, I dated a guy who was a bartender. I would go and sit at the bar and wait for him to get off work. And there was this old man there who was always drinking alone. And one night, he started talking to me, telling me all about his life and how he had lost his wife and how his children didn't speak to him any more and I felt really sorry for him and I told

Caller ID: David Adkins and Mary Beth Fisher in Rebecca Gilman's Boy Gets Girl. *Photo: Liz Lauren*

> him so and he told me it would make him feel better to kiss a pretty girl. So I let him kiss me. On the mouth. (*Beat*) I didn't want to at all. He was an old drunk and it made me sick. But I did it anyway because it's what I thought I was supposed to do. I was supposed to be nice.

Finally, Theresa begins to appreciate that by politely blaming herself for her wish not to continue the relationship, she was actually doing damage both to herself and to women in general. And yet regardless of the validity of the sexual-political issues that it dissects with such power, *Boy Gets Girl* badly needs the sexist filmmaker Les Kennkat. Without him, it would be a polemic. And it would not have worked.

By the end of the play, Theresa and Les become unlikely friends, but Gilman does not suggest that the filmmaker's breast-obsessed films are without moral culpability. One senses that the author was comfortable in turning a professional sexist into a sympathetic figure largely because he is old, sick and can do no further damage to women. Still, the scenes between Theresa and Les are probably the strongest in the play.

In all of Gilman's work, she exhibits a darkly satiric sense of humor, which usually bubbles just below the surface of her plays. It's most evident when Les justifies his sleazy art form:

> LES: These women just want to show off their breasts. They know they have colossal tits. It's no secret to them. So I just give them the opportunity to do that. And by that, I like to think I do them a service. And I do the guys who want to see these tremendous breasts a service, because I give them a good story and a good deal of expert camera work for really showing off these breasts in optimum conditions. What I do is, I shoot the breasts from down here, you know, low down with maybe a blue sky in the background. Maybe just a touch of treetops and a blue sky with clouds as a back drop for these beautiful supple breasts. To me, there's nothing more breathtaking than a gorgeous pair of tits just sort of floating in the treetops.

Aside from having some fun (and perhaps avoiding charges of political correctness in advance), Gilman is also arguing that the cultural depiction of breasts, like most things in life, is always more complex than it first appears.

That's what gives this play some necessary ambiguity. Still, the great strength of *Boy Gets Girl* is that it engages the mind in the complexities of male-female communication styles, even as it quickens the pulse with the compelling and credible tale of a woman whose life is ruined by a man.

This time around, Gilman's frame of reference was very different from dirt-poor folks in Alabama (*The Glory of Living*) or collegiate racism

(*Spinning Into Butter*), but this Best Play had more in common with Gilman's previous work than might first meet the eye.

It's theme may be the dating game, but *Boy Gets Girl* is also unflinching in its attack on the prejudices, objectification and amorality that simmer just below the polite surface of contemporary society.

2000–2001 Best Play

THE INVENTION OF LOVE

By Tom Stoppard

○○○○○

Essay by Charles Wright

> POLLARD: Like everything else, like clocks and trousers and algebra, the love poem had to be invented. (Act I)

> WILDE: In the mirror of invention, love discovered itself. Then we saw what we had made—the piece of ice in the fist you cannot hold or let go. (Act II)

THE INVENTION OF LOVE wouldn't have landed in the commercial universe of Broadway but for an expensive gamble by a major non-profit producing organization. Back in 1997, when British newspapers raved about Tom Stoppard's fantasia on the life of an obscure poet, classical scholar and teacher, several New York impresarios rushed to London to catch Richard Eyre's production at the Royal National Theatre. According to reports at the time, producers dismissed the play as a sure-fire loser, believing Yankees wouldn't sit still for Stoppard's abstruse historical and literary allusions. Yet during the four years before Lincoln Center Theater put its money on *Invention*, the play proved engaging to American audiences—albeit in limited runs—in San Francisco, Philadelphia, Minneapolis and Chicago.

A.E. Housman, hugely famous in his own day for the 63 brief, lapidary lyrics published as *A Shropshire Lad*, is an unlikely choice as protagonist of a Broadway play. His name cropped up previously as a prominent reference in the dialogue of another Stoppard play, *Indian Ink*. In that 1995 drama, not yet seen in New York, a character recalls Housman (his classics tutor at Cambridge) saying that "[w]hen it comes to love, . . . you're either an Ovid man or a Virgil man." Virgil's position is that "you can't win against love." Housman, according to *Indian Ink*, "was an Ovid man," adamant that "[l]ove won't win against me!" In *The Invention of Love* Stoppard portrays the Victorian poet as a man for whom amorous defeat is the sine qua non of scholarly and poetic achievement.

Wilde company: Daniel Davis and Richard Easton in Tom Stoppard's The Invention of Love. *Photo: Paul Kolnik*

Jack O'Brien directed the Broadway production of Stoppard's ambitious script with cinematic fluidity and deliberate pacing that gave sweep and dignity to the proceedings but extended the running time to almost three hours. Working harmoniously with lighting designer Brian MacDevitt, Bob Crowley provided painterly scenic designs in Turneresque colors—autumnal sunset and twilight, leafy vistas, quaint bridges and, inevitably for the sequences in Oxford, "dreaming spires."

The 22-member cast featured Richard Easton and Robert Sean Leonard in accomplished portrayals of Housman, in age and youth respectively, along with notable performances by David Harbour and Michael Stuhlbarg as Housman's closest friends and Daniel Davis as a portly, blooming Oscar Wilde. Mark Nelson, playing a slightly camp colleague of Housman's, offered a brief comic turn, remarkably touching but largely overlooked by reviewers. Critical responses were generally enthusiastic, with particularly strong notices from the New York dailies. At season's end, Easton and Leonard won Tony Awards and Outer Critics Circle Awards; and Easton received a Drama Desk Award. O'Brien got Drama Desk and Outer Critics Circle citations for direction of a play, and Crowley received the Drama Desk Award for set design of a play. The New York Drama Critics Circle named *The Invention of Love* best play of the season.

Housman's was a life marked by contrasts. Having failed final examinations for the bachelor of arts at Oxford, he pursued independent research and ended up a professor at Cambridge. He was outwardly self-effacing, but his writings on classical subjects have a high sheen of arrogance. In flourishes that W.H. Auden (in the sonnet, "A.E. Housman") termed "savage foot-notes on unjust editions," Housman let rip with colorful invective against scholars who didn't share his views. On the other hand, his English verse is gentle and rueful, dealing with comradeship, unrequited love, suicide and wartime casualties. Intensely private, he nonetheless wrote a few poems—bold for the era and published posthumously—which have been widely interpreted as lamentations on his sexual rejection by another man, Moses Jackson (played by Harbour).

With two actors embodying Housman, one from ages 18 to 26 and the other in old age, Stoppard fashions facts from the poet-scholar's life into a saga of emotional concealment that follows the dramatic arc of Auden's sonnet: "Heart-injured in North London, he became / The Latin Scholar of his generation." But, with its rambling, whimsical dramaturgy, reflecting the associative nature of dreams, and with frequent fanciful incursions by figures from history and myth, *Invention* is no common-and-garden biographical drama. Reviewing the play in *New York*, John Simon commented that, while "plot and characterization are not completely lacking," they are "minimal in importance."

Ever since *Rosencrantz and Guildenstern Are Dead* premiered in 1966, Stoppard has been celebrated for the complex, scintillating language of his dramas, which include puns, jokes, double entendre, verbal jousting and virtuosic flourishes. In *Invention* he takes linguistic prestidigitation to new heights, with references sly, subtle and multivalent to classical languages, myth, religion, historical events and literature. Overall, the play has the compression and many-layered allusiveness of a long poem. It arguably bears more resemblance to T.S. Eliot's *The Waste Land* and Ezra Pound's *Cantos* than to any recent Broadway play. The elegiac final beats of the second act, with characters speaking to the audience out of Stygian gloom, illustrate the lyrical, complexly evocative nature of the script. First, Jackson repeats a rhetorical question from earlier dialogue:

> JACKSON: What will become of you, Hous?

The younger manifestation of Housman quotes a fragment of Theocritus in Greek (a fragment that has also appeared previously in dialogue), then renders the same verse in English:

> HOUSMAN: When thou art kind I spend the day like a god; when thy face is turned aside, it is very dark with me [. . . .]

And then Wilde's voice rings out from Charon's boat (the Irishman is being poled across the Styx) with three epigrammatic lines:

> WILDE: Wickedness is a myth invented by good people to account for the curious attractiveness of others.
>
> One should always be a little improbable.
>
> Nothing that actually occurs is of the smallest importance.

After that, the curtain falls on a dulcet speech from the older Housman, which piles reference upon reference to cultural allusions that have appeared previously in the play.

In his review, Simon remarked that *Invention* is "not really a play, if by *play* we mean something that can be followed by an audience with a standard education and average intelligence." Simon added, "[b]y *followed* I do not mean getting the general drift, but catching at least a good part of the allusions, quotations, parodistic references, word play and other fine points, for fine points are Stoppard's stock-in-trade."

As in most of Stoppard's dramatic writing, *Invention* is vividly disputatious. In the tissue of satire that weaves in and out of the principal story, a group of tendentious academics—Jowett of Balliol, Pattison of Lincoln, Ellis of Trinity, Pater of Brasenose and Oxford's Slade Professor of

Oxford fellows: Robert Sean Leonard, David Harbour, Richard Easton (standing), Michael Stuhlbarg, Jeff Weiss (also standing) in The Invention of Love. *Photo: Paul Kolnik*

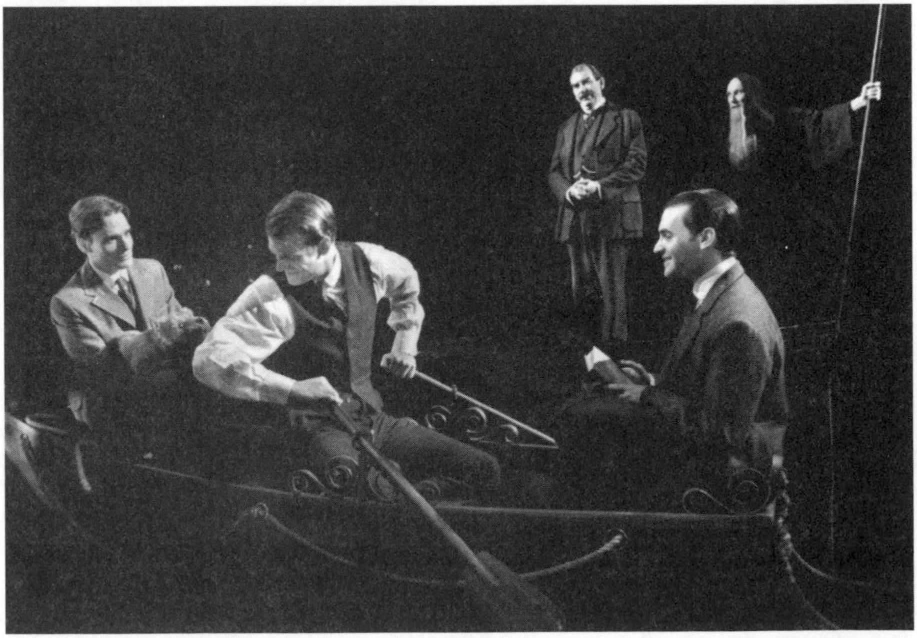

Art, John Ruskin—mime croquet while knocking about issues of 19th-century philosophy, just as they might knock about croquet balls.

RUSKIN: I have announced the meaning of life in my lectures. There is nothing beautiful which is not good, and nothing good which has no moral purpose. [. . .]

JOWETT: I was eighteen when I came up to Oxford. That was in 1835, and [. . . e]ducation rarely interfered with the life of the University. Learning was carried on in nooks and corners, like Papism in an Elizabethan manor house. [. . .]

PATTISON: The great reform made us into a cramming shop. The railway brings in the fools and takes them away with their tickets punched for the world outside.

JOWETT: The modern university exists by consent of the world outside. We must send out men fitted for that world. What better example can we show them than classical antiquity? Nowhere was the ideal of morality, art and social order realized more harmoniously than in Greece in the age of the great philosophers.

RUSKIN: Buggery apart.

JOWETT: Buggery apart.

In Act II, the dons are replaced by establishment tastemakers—Henry Labouchère, MP, Frank Harris of the *Evening News* and W.T. Stead of the *Pall Mall Gazette*—who puff ideas at each other like smoke from their after-dinner cigars.

STEAD: The *Pall Mall Gazette* is testament enough that the Lord is at my elbow, and was there today when I—yes, I!—forced Parliament to pass the Criminal Law Amendment Act [pertaining to sexual acts between males]. [. . .]

HARRIS: When I took over the *Evening News* I edited the paper with the best in me at twenty-eight. The circulation wouldn't budge. So, I edited the paper as a boy of fourteen. The circulation started to rise and never looked back.

STEAD: No, by heavens, Harris! In the right hands the editor's pen is the sceptre of power! [. . .]—we journalists have a divine mission to be the tribunes of the people. [. . .]

LABOUCHÈRE: I'm a Member of Parliament, I don't have to be a journalist to be a tribune of the people. [. . .] The Criminal Law Amendment is badly drawn up and will do more harm than good, as I said in my paper. [. . .] (*to Stead*) The bill should have been referred to a Select Committee, and would have been but for the government being stampeded by your disgusting articles. [. . .]

STEAD: When I came down from Darlington to join the Gazette [. . .] it never sold more than 13,000 copies and never deserved to—it

> kept the reader out. [. . .] I introduced the crosshead in '81, the illustration in '82, the interview in '83, the personal note, the signed article—[. . .] I invented the New Journalism!

Stoppard's dons and powerbrokers reinforce and amplify themes introduced in the Housman scenes, provide historical commentary and, most of all, protect the proceedings from getting bogged down in the sentimentality of the love story. *Invention* is indebted to the chipper spirit of works by W.S. Gilbert and Jerome K. Jerome—and to the structure of Aristophanes's *The Frogs*—in much the way that Stoppard's *Travesties* is indebted to Wilde's *The Importance of Being Earnest*. As is often the case in Stoppard's writing, there's an unmistakable seriousness about the puns and word play, the ideological pugilism and the quicksilver shifts from the sublime to the silly, all of which work together to create an intricate, highly theatrical picture of Victorian Britain.

Invention closes with a *coup de théâtre* in which a wildly fictionalized Oscar Wilde, exuberant despite the hard knocks of scandal, prison and exile, materializes to serve as foil to Housman. For Housman the repressed textual critic, facts are a stock-in-trade, pursued for their intrinsic value and as clues for scientific recovery of ancient texts. Wilde, on the other hand, pooh-poohs "facts" as nothing more than elements of "biography," which is the "mesh through which our real life escapes." Truth, a "work of the imagination" to Wilde, is whatever gloss one puts on brute facts. The melancholy Housman calls Wilde's life "a terrible thing" and laments that the Irishman—and, by implication, he himself—didn't live "in Megara when Theognis . . . made his lover a song sung unto all posterity." But Wilde ridicules this saccharine fantasy of a more tolerant classical past. For Wilde, the truth about his life isn't "terrible." "I lived at the turning point of the world where everything was waking up new," he proclaims; and his famously deceitful lover, Lord Alfred Douglas, is "Hyacinth when Apollo loved him, . . . the only one who understands me."

Wilde's appearance in *Invention* is, essentially, an extended Stoppardian aria challenging Housman's belief that one can attain knowledge apart from interpretation or perceive "facts" except through a filter imposed by the categories of one's psychological structure and particular time in history. In a chilling moment, Stoppard's Wilde remarks: "We would never love anybody if we could see past our invention."

Housman never met Wilde ("the most dangerous product of modern civilization," according to 25-year-old André Gide); but it was, perhaps, inevitable that the epigrammatic Irishman should materialize in Stoppard's

Wise words: Robert Sean Leonard and Richard Easton share a moment in Tom Stoppard's The Invention of Love. *Photo: Paul Kolnik*

Victorian play. Eighty years ago, when Lytton Strachey, in *Eminent Victorians*, took the first significant steps in Britain's reassessment of the Victorians, he focused on the era's stiff upper lips. In succeeding decades, as Sigmund Freud's influence concentrated attention increasingly on the libido, a vast array of scholars and artists has celebrated Wilde as social iconoclast and pioneering "gay" public figure. As a result, Wilde's story imposes a remarkable imprint on the public imagination.

The Wilde of *Invention* is an imperfect foil to Housman because he runs away with the play—or he did in the New York production. Were the character not so compelling, his disquisition on "truth" might serve merely as a clever warning that, living in time as fish swim in water, we cannot avoid imposing a 21st-century consciousness on the facts of Housman's biography. But from the moment of his appearance, late in the play, there's no question that Stoppard's brash version of Wilde will be the play's usurping central image by the time the final curtain descends.

Stoppard's protagonist, whose "life is marked by long silences," is reticent in the face of Wilde's braggadocio—and the Irishman rides roughshod over him. Had Stoppard chosen to write an "obligatory scene" in which Housman could face down Wilde and articulate the value or disadvantage of the inventions with which he has made his own life bearable, the spectator might assess whether Housman has developed as a character between his college days and his deathbed. Without such a confrontation, the spectator is in the dark.

Even more curious, in a play about the era in which the term "homosexual" was emerging in Euro-American discourse and the heterosexual/homosexual distinction registering with at least part of the population, Stoppard leaves his audience wondering precisely what this paradigm shift means for the protagonist. This is to say that, though *Invention* offers two actors playing the principal character (and though the playwright arranges things so that the old and young Housman may converse with each other), the dramatist never penetrates the poet's façade. As a result, Stoppard settles for a theatrical concoction that's pleasing and tasty but, like an underdone pudding, lacks the dramatic heft and emotional impact playgoers are entitled to expect from this gifted dramatist in his maturity. For all its intellectually lustrous qualities, *Invention* falls short because its protagonist is as much a mystery at the end as at the outset.

2000–2001 Best Play
2001 ATCA/Steinberg Citation
KING HEDLEY II
By August Wilson

○○○○○

Essay by Christopher Rawson

> KING: It was alright when they ain't had to pay you. They had plenty of work for you back then. Now that they got to pay you there ain't no work for you. I used to be worth twelve hundred dollars during slavery. Now I'm worth $3.35 an hour. I'm going backwards. Everyone else moving forward.

AUGUST WILSON'S *KING HEDLEY II* is as accidental as a roll of the dice and as inevitable as weather. As massive as a megalith, it is a tragedy of throttled honor and dreams set against a long history of killings—a tale that is dark, bitter and uncomfortably true. The eighth in Wilson's astonishing series of plays, each set in a different decade of the 20th century, *Hedley* brings his robust epic of African-America to the 1980s of drive-by death and failed economic trickle. It's the craggiest of Wilson's eight major works and the most deserving of the Shakespearean echo of its title.

That title is partly a joke. The central character was named King after his supposed father, whose own name derived from a desire similar to Red Carter's in Wilson's *Seven Guitars*, who named his son Mister "so the white man have to call him Mister." King Hedley II is the hero's name, not his title. But a name is also a title, just as for a Shakespearean king, a title is also a name. (See *Richard II* for particulars.) And the presumably joking Shakespearean sound of this title turns out to be amply justified by the play's big themes, which are those of Shakespeare's tragic histories: inheritance, honor and power in both the family and the larger world.

This is Wilson's darkest play so far. A tragedy without the final uplift of *Fences*, it is grimmer even than *Ma Rainey's Black Bottom*, which has more humor, or *Seven Guitars*, which bookends tragedy with hopeful apotheosis. Although it contains robust humor, its foreboding darkness and length (a shade under three hours on Broadway; up to 40 minutes more in its evolving earlier versions), together with Wilson's typically meandering,

King and queen: Brian Stokes Mitchell and Viola Davis in August Wilson's King Hedley II. *Photo: Joan Marcus*

layered plot and character development, all make it hard going for some audiences. In many ways, it is the least audience-friendly of Wilson's plays. But *Long Day's Journey into Night* is no picnic, either, or *King Lear* or *The Oresteia*. These are the company *King Hedley* keeps, all centered on the search for responsibility, guilt and identity in the most painful, intimate place—the family.

Over time, Wilson's work has matured—or our familiarity with it has deepened—so that his words now easily reverberate both in their tawdry present and down the dusty track of history. "Everything done got broke up," says King, and "this the only dirt I got." "If they had some barbed wire you could cut through it," says Mister. They speak about the specific now but we hear the eternal then, as well. Measured against Shakespeare and the Greeks, the language is not grandly eloquent, but it is articulate with passion, history and life.

If you were going to prep for *King Hedley*, you'd do best to re-read the story of Abraham, Isaac and the demanding God of the Old Testament. The God of *King Hedley* is a grim patriarch, "one bad motherfucker," as the backyard seer, Stool Pigeon, admiringly calls him. That sounds sacrilegious, but how else to make sense of a world in which survival seems random and hard and the killing claims children? Taking place in 1985, *King Hedley* is the most recent of Wilson's plays both in setting and creation, which partially explains its dark bite: there is no historical distance to drape these characters with understanding or nostalgia, as in the earlier installments in Wilson's century-long epic.

The tale is of blood, ancient and modern. At its center is King, a sacrificial lamb, duly anointed by Stool Pigeon (telling name), the truth-teller, and by Aunt Ester, the unseen sibyl. The tale's constant dialectic is between aspiration and defeat. On the one hand are such homey desires as a shop of one's own and a family that stays together, along with such abstract necessities as respect and honor. On the other is everything that militates against them. There is a pitiable distance between the high aspirations of these characters and this playwright and the everyday means available to express them: shooting craps for one's soul, a few green leaves to signal the future, a bedraggled black cat for resurrection. But just as the characters turn everyday dreams into grails, so Wilson turns them all into tragedy of operatic size. That *Hedley* tends toward the melodramatic is the measure of the height to which it aspires.

The action takes place on a poor patch of dirt, but as King says, "This is me, right here."

> KING: Ruby tell me my dirt ain't worth nothing. It's mine. It's worth it to have. I ain't gonna let nobody take it. Talking about I need some good dirt. Like my dirt ain't worth nothing. A seed is a seed. A seed will grow in dirt.

So he plants his seed—literally (twice over) and figuratively. Gradually the dusty ground becomes the arena for issues of honor, a place of primal ritual like the scruffy palace yards where Greek chieftains settled blood feuds in the aftermath of the Trojan War.

We have met these characters before in Wilson. The angry young man with dreams, the phlegmatic friend, feisty wife, wise elder, inspired neighborhood fool—variants of them have appeared in his other plays, echoing their dreams down the century. But we also have a head start on knowing these specific characters because, for the first time, Wilson has picked up characters from a previous play—*Seven Guitars*, set in 1948 in a similar back yard in Pittsburgh's Hill District (the scene of all Wilson's major plays except *Ma Rainey*). *Seven Guitars* ends with its hero, Floyd Barton, dead, killed by the crazed Caribbean prophet, Hedley. One of Floyd's friends, Canewell, knows the truth of the murder; another, Red Carter, has named his baby Mister. And young Ruby, made pregnant down South by either Leroy or Elmore, has decided to marry Hedley and let her child inherit his name.

Flash forward 37 years to 1985. That child is King, an angry adult searching for his kingdom after doing time in the penitentiary for killing a man to avenge a 112-stitch scar on his face. Mister has grown into King's best friend. King's new wife, Tonya, has an office job, an angry teen-age daughter and a baby on the way. Sharing their house is King's selfish but charming mother, Ruby, recently returned from years on the road as a singer, having abandoned King long ago to be raised by his aunt. Next door lives Stool Pigeon, the Bible-spouting shaman who hoards newspapers in an attempt to capture history.

Defiant one: Brian Stokes Mitchell in August Wilson's King Hedley II. *Photo: Joan Marcus*

Slowly, almost accidentally, because these characters do not arrange and narrate history in an organized, linear way (who does?), we realize that Stool Pigeon is Canewell, his nickname given him because he had informed on Hedley for murdering Floyd Barton. Though Ruby and Stool Pigeon are continuing characters, you don't need to know *Seven Guitars* any more than you need to have seen Oedipus kill the stranger at the crossroads. The necessary information is included. Gradual revelation is used to build the pyre of tragedy.

King claims to know his worth:

> I can dance all night if the music's right. Ain't nothing I can't do. I could build a railroad if I had the steel and a gang of men to drive the spikes. I ain't limited to nothing. I can go down there and do Mellon's job. I know how to count money. [. . .] I ain't got no limits. I know right from wrong. I know which way the wind blow too. It don't blow my way. Mellon got six houses. I ain't got none. But that don't mean he six times a better man than me.

But in this scruffy backyard we discover King and Mister hustling a buck selling hot refrigerators. Their dream is a video store, but first there are simpler necessities. Soon they escalate to a feckless plan to rob a jewelry store. Elmore arrives, the stylish gambler from Ruby's past, now dying, seeking Ruby and determined to tell King the truth about his father. The blood of the past is reflected in the present: Elmore and King have done time for killings, both mesmerizingly described. King also grieves for his first wife, Neesi, and throughout the play there's developing news of a woman avenging the shooting of her child.

The past is constantly present. Twice King remembers powerful anecdotes from the third grade. "The people need to know the story, see how they fit into it," says Stool Pigeon, piling up newspapers against the coming apocalypse. And how far back does history go? For starters, there's Aunt Ester, the ancient personal adviser who is heard of in several other Wilson plays. When she dies in the course of *King Hedley*, Stool Pigeon says she's 366 years old. This takes her back to 1619, the year the first shipment of African slaves arrived in the Virginia colony. The Houses of Lancaster and Atreus have nothing on Wilson's black America.

There's also Shakespearean size in Wilson's monologues, great towers of talk in which Elmore, King and Tonya, especially, search past and present for pattern. To Tonya, confronted with a pregnant 17-year-old daughter, the issue is clear.

> TONYA: I'm thirty-five years old. Don't seem like there's nothing left. I'm through with babies. I ain't raising no more. Ain't raising no

> grandkids. [. . .] I ain't raising no kid to have somebody shoot him. To have his friends shoot him. To have the police shoot him. Why I want to bring another life into this world that don't respect life? I don't want to raise no more babies when you got to fight to keep them alive.

In trying to understand why young people are killing each other in apparently accidental drive-bys, Wilson discovers a repeating legacy of killing for respect. The killings line up in telling parallel, each revealed to have its own accident—or fate. There's ironic juxtaposition of the jewelry store robbery, Stool Pigeon's mugging by kids and King's insistence that "this business depends on trust." As the play's climax approaches, calm precedes the storm on every front. King sides with Elmore in his final story, sharpening his own dilemma unawares—King doesn't know that the play's subcutaneous theme is the search for true parentage, a variant of the search for roots and identity always central to Wilson. When Elmore climactically tells King his father was the man he (Elmore) killed, a tragic end seems assured.

But first, a glimpse of something better. The prophetic Stool Pigeon waxes explicit that King must seek the "key to the kingdom," the only thing that will end the cycle of blood. This key, we learn, is the ability to forgive. In a wrenching moment of growth, King makes that leap and grasps that key—but tragedy (or fate or accident) is already wound too tight to be denied. In trying to defend her son, Ruby accidentally kills him. It seems the play's most random killing, but surely it is fated, too. Stool Pigeon thinks so: "In the land of plenty, I want your best," his Old Testament God declares. The final killing is shock, accident and ritual. As the myth has it, the king must die.

Hedley makes explicit the religious underpinning of Wilson's work, where each play is a station of agony or reflection on a journey both backwards to recover a painful past and onward into an uncertain future. But for all its tragic sacrifice, *Hedley* suggests some hope. King does find the key; the cycle of blood can someday end. As the final catastrophe gathers force, he embodies his new knowledge in a ritual gesture of peace. But history and that implacable God can't be so easily swayed.

As with his other plays, Wilson developed *King Hedley* through a series of independent productions in regional theaters before bringing it to Broadway. Starting with a co-production between the Pittsburgh Public Theater and Seattle Repertory Theatre—a fitting collaboration between Wilson's native city and his current home—*Hedley* went on to Boston's Huntington Theatre, Los Angeles's Mark Taper Forum, Chicago's Goodman Theatre and Washington's Kennedy Center. As it went, it kept shedding and gaining text. (*Hedley* should contribute richly to the volume of "outtakes" that Wilson has said he will someday publish.) As it went, its cast of six also changed. Eventually, only Charles Brown (Elmore) made the entire journey from Pittsburgh to Broadway—along with David Gallo's resolutely unsentimental row of ramshackle Hill District houses and Donald Holder's often painterly lighting, a vivid assertion that Wilson's theater has an emblematic dimension beyond backyard naturalism.

Throughout the play's journey, the director remained Marion McClinton. In helping to shape this massive work, McClinton became the first director other than Wilson's original mentor and collaborator, Lloyd Richards, to

Cozy couple: Leslie Uggams and Charles Brown in King Hedley II. *Photo: Joan Marcus*

bring a Wilson play to Broadway. While forging this collaborative bond, McClinton clearly drew on his own experience as a playwright. He also directed Wilson's 1970s play, *Jitney*. Though written before even *Ma Rainey*, *Jitney* started its full professional life at the Pittsburgh Public only in 1996, then took an even longer tour through regional theaters to its eventual triumph Off Broadway, making it the first and so far only major Wilson play not to appear on Broadway. Although *Hedley* returned Wilson to

Broadway, it broke another string—it is the first of the eight plays not to be honored by the New York Drama Critics Circle Award.

In its successive pre-Broadway versions, *Hedley* changed mainly in telling its story more clearly by clarifying events and motivations. The characters and their typically rich language were there from the start, with more than a half-dozen massive monologues that were eventually whittled down. When it reached Broadway, *Hedley* was still a big play, but it had become relatively crisper. Stool Pigeon became more explicit about the "key to the kingdom" King must seek. The final version is less rough-hewn and more wiry, as reflected in the portrayal of King by Brian Stokes Mitchell. The initial King, Tony Todd, seemed more doomed from the start. In spite of his charismatic stage presence, Mitchell dominated less, a smaller hero fighting an implacable enemy that is only partly within himself. If his King still seemed unsympathetic, the same is true of Macbeth or Othello. Like them, King climbs the mountain of self-knowledge. Brandishing his machete, he is a flawed heroic warrior—it's just that his visible dragons have dwindled into a surly clerk at Sears.

As Broadway's Ruby, Leslie Uggams shone with a willful heat that linked her perfectly to the young sexpot Ruby of *Seven Guitars*. She was a beautiful opportunist who revealed her heart slowly. Her dance in Act II may have been an acknowledgement of Uggams' stardom, but it fit Ruby, too. Brown's vibrant, forceful Elmore was a stout fashion plate all the more steely for his dapper surface. Though he lost some of Elmore's hefty, set-piece monologues, Brown developed greater desperation, making him more threatening. Stephen McKinley Henderson was a bulldog Stool Pigeon, anchoring prophecy firmly in gritty realism, although finding the right balance between grit and spirit in Stool Pigeon seems to have been as hard for Wilson as it was with his shamanistic predecessor, Hedley in *Seven Guitars*. Viola Davis's Tonya had a dead-on intensity which, when she launched into her great aria about parenthood and death, swept all before it. As Mister, Monté Russell had a quiet strength and a believable bond with King—and the Pittsburgh native knew to say "Picksburg," too.

Hedley survived for only 72 performances. Though a short run for a serious play on Broadway is a disappointment, it is no surprise, and it hardly matters in the long run, since, like all Wilson's plays, its home will be in the true national theater—America's resident companies. Strategically, *Hedley* may have suffered from arriving in New York right on the heels of *Jitney*, which would have been the better bet for Broadway; although it is hardly a comedy, it is a lighter, easier experience for the audience.

Wilson took the early closing of *Hedley* philosophically. "You can only close if you opened," he said. "We were there. You're not going to stay open forever." (He showed the same acceptance when asked if he was disappointed that *Hedley* was passed over for the Pulitzer Prize: "My attitude is, I got two.") Asked after the closing how he'd characterize his accomplishment in *Hedley*, he said: "I like the size of it. I was able to layer this other story [the mystery of 366-year-old Aunt Ester] over the realistic aspects. I tried to model it after Greek tragedy and I was at least 80 percent successful. I'd do a few things different, now, but I learned a lot that will help on my next two plays." Then he told a story of a painter, 96 years old, who said, "I think I'm finally getting the hang of this drawing stuff."

The two plays still to come will be the bookends to the sequence, set in the first and last decades of the century. Working on them in tandem, Wilson hopes to provide a consciously enveloping shape to the many parallels and connections with which the eight plays are already interwoven. And in the first of the two, we may actually meet Aunt Ester.

2000–2001 Best Play

LOBBY HERO

By Kenneth Lonergan

○○○○○

Essay by Tish Dace

> DAWN: I gotta be the worst judge of character in the history of Earth. . . . Three days ago I'm practically in love with the guy and now he's tellin' me— Well, that is not gonna happen. I don't know what's gonna happen when it doesn't, but that is not happening. Let him get me kicked off the Force. Let him try. . . . I'm not gonna be one of those, "Oh yeah, I let him rape me because I didn't know what else to do. . . ." I'd rather be dead, OK?

KENNETH LONERGAN ESTABLISHED both his playwriting and screenwriting reputations by creating typical turn-of-the-century slackers who drift, devoid of focus or purpose. The young men who populate *This Is Our Youth* (1996) and the loser brother in the Oscar-nominated film *You Can Count on Me* (2000) prefigure Jeff—the title character in this season's *Lobby Hero*—who lacks even the requisite motivation to read a self-help book.

The dramatist creates in taskmaster William, Jeff's boss, the perfect foil to this young security guard working the graveyard shift. William lectures his protégé ad nauseam about responsibility and rectitude, until we just know Lonergan must be setting up the supervisor for a fall.

> WILLIAM: [I]f you stick to the rules, then you never have to have a discussion about whether or not you were justified not sticking to the rules.

In an era when the whole world knows about our previous president's sexual peccadilloes and speculates about our present president's failure to win election, Lonergan zeroes in on the ethics—or lack thereof—of ordinary, uniformed blue-collar workers: two security guards and two police officers, all four sworn to protect us and uphold rules and/or laws.

Although Lonergan's reputation rests on his funny dialogue and quirky characters, he also constructs his plot skillfully, which both confirms and contradicts William's principle. He articulates it three minutes into the play, while Jeff stands at his post in a Manhattan Upper East Side high rise's

Riot act: Glenn Fitzgerald and Dion Graham in Kenneth Lonergan's Lobby Hero. *Photo: Joan Marcus*

lobby—tackily authentic in its modernism thanks to designer Allen Moyer—and receives a dressing down from his straight-arrow boss for failing to require a visitor to sign the book and for the mess in his desk drawers. We watch Glenn Fitzgerald's fidgety, gawky portrayal of the charming loser Jeff as he resists the uptight African-American William's (Dion Graham) efforts to shape him into a conscientious guard and doorman.

The play has barely begun when, amid casual conversation, the duo explicitly delineate their initial viewpoints. Lonergan foreshadows how the men's relationship will develop when the supervisor recalls an incident when he felt compelled to enforce his rules.

> WILLIAM: Any man on my command who can't straighten out and fly right is gonna get busted, man.
>
> JEFF: That certainly was terrific how you fired that skinny old man right before he was supposed to retire.

The playwright soon adds information that the police have arrested William's brother, which sets in motion the reversal we already expect. As people do, William expresses contradictory impulses—to wash his hands of his brother and, much later, to save him from an unjust criminal justice system.

We wait a long time, however, before William begins to experience such temptation. Indeed, we almost forget the signals the playwright provides as to what propels this plot. The supervisor continues to hassle his charge about frittering away his life and confides his own ambition to move into management. Jeff acknowledges he was booted out of the Navy after getting caught smoking pot while on duty. We recall this later as we watch the male cop, Bill (Tate Donovan)—so convincingly played we forget he's an actor—break the rules while on duty, even while he, in other respects, mentors his rookie female partner and provides her a role model of a savvy foot patrolman.

What viewers most remember, however, involves not such structurally important parallels and contrasts, but the amusing, rambling dialogue, especially Jeff's slacker wisecracks and his convolutedly hilarious exposition. His ineptitude resembles that of David Mamet's petty crooks in *American Buffalo*, as he describes the months leading up to William hiring and thus rescuing him:

> JEFF: —I try to work up a little stake playing poker, I turn around, I got the Goddamn loansharks comin' after me. I gotta borrow five thousand dollars from my brother so I don't get my legs broken. I date this girl, it turns out she's still a prostitute only now she only does it "on the side" whatever that means. I break up with her, I'm scared I'm gonna get AIDS, I can't meet anybody—

Lonergan begins and ends this speech in mid-sentence, which helps to give Jeff his characteristically stream-of-consciousness effect. The playwright builds the rhythms right into the language, so actor and director know exactly how to phrase the thoughts all in a rush of four arcs, one per "sentence" if we stop only at the periods. Jeff soon thanks William for turning around his life by hiring him. Later we recall his gratitude—"I owe it all to you"—when, with typical Lonergan irony, he betrays his supervisor by adopting the man's own moral rigidity.

Lonergan introduces Dawn, a probationary cop, as the catalyst to motivate Jeff's change of heart. A stand-out among four bravura performances, Heather Burns adopts a working-class regional accent and frequent abrupt tempo shifts—from lingering on vowels, to clipping phonemes—to characterize this young rookie smitten with (and sleeping with) her partner. It is she who will summon the courage to turn on her partner when he violates her values, the police force's rules and the ethical imperatives that Lonergan champions even as he engenders sympathy for more flexible and ego-driven codes. When Jeff spills the beans to her that her lover nips upstairs for a quickie with a hooker—while she cools her heels in the lobby each evening—she refuses to believe the story.

We have already heard William discourage Jeff's attraction to Dawn because "you're just an imitation cop" whereas she's the real McCoy. Lonergan then rapidly tosses into the mix several plot points: Jeff asks what charge the cops have brought against William's brother, but his boss refuses to confide in him. We learn from Bill and Dawn that he must testify she did not use inappropriate force against an attacker. Bill refuses to sign the visitors' book when he heads upstairs, and Jeff blurts out his love for Dawn.

So when Jeff informs Dawn of her partner's real reason for visiting apartment 22J, she first denies it, then defends him, but rapidly progresses to displacing her anger onto Jeff.

> DAWN: I don't need to get hit on by the night doorman while he's upstairs gettin' his rocks off with some fuckin' whore.

The emotional range that the playwright provides Dawn continues to make possible the play's powerhouse punches and ultimately its most touching moments.

Bad cop, good cop: Tate Donovan and Heather Burns in Kenneth Lonergan's Lobby Hero. *Photo: Joan Marcus*

After Dawn denounces Jeff, Lonergan returns to desultory dialogue between characters inching their way towards romance. The dramatist doesn't permit them quite to reach that destination by play's end, as a writer of more plot-driven drama would doubtless do. Yet he doesn't imply, say, the ineffectuality of Lopakhin and Varya in Chekov's *The Cherry Orchard* either. We believe the next time Jeff asks her out Dawn will say, "Yes." Although he doesn't respond favorably, she even suggests he take her to his friend's wedding.

First, however, Lonergan must dispose of Bill and show up William's hypocrisy. (Although Lonergan wrote the characters as more complex men than their names suggest, he began by giving them the formal and diminutive of an appellation that has meant *power* since 1066.) This requires more exposition concerning a pending Civilian Complaint Review Board charge of police brutality against Dawn and her efforts to win the male cops' respect. Jeff tries to date Dawn, and William asks Jeff's advice: Should he provide a false alibi for his brother who has been charged with murdering a nurse who saw a drug robbery?

Initially William plans to tell the truth, while Jeff suggests perjury. But then William does lie. After informing William that the nurse who died had three children, Bill decides to believe William's false alibi—his claim that his brother had accompanied him to the movies at the time of the murder. We infer that Bill acts partly out of self-interest, to discourage William from reporting him for dereliction of duty. This sets up his subsequently throwing his weight around, when he vouches for William's veracity with the detectives investigating the murder. Bill also lies to Dawn, until she finds out the truth; thereafter, he intimidates and threatens her.

Lonergan also mocks the NYPD by having Jeff wonder what would happen if, during Bill's visits to 22J, "a major outbreak of crime" occurs on their beat. Dawn demonstrates a concept of her on-duty obligations superior to her partner's in one of the play's best lines: "I can't be cryin' on duty," which Jeff tops with another satiric crack about how cops operate: "You'll drive around, you'll shoot some perpetrators, you'll feel better."

The playwright ends his first act on a suspenseful note. Dawn refuses to cover for Bill with their dispatcher: "I signed up to be a cop, not lookout patrol at the whorehouse." He orders her to cover for him, saying cops support each other, but she rightly queries "They help each other get laid?" They exchange threats: he offers to make her job miserable, she counters by saying she'll tell the lieutenant what he's been doing, and he announces he'll lie at her hearing. During intermission, we wonder if Dawn will lose her job because she has stood up to bully Bill.

Early in Act II, Lonergan gives William his chance to rationalize his lying to the cops. This fellow who plays by the rules makes excuses about his brother never having had a chance in life, and he describes the defense attorney as so inept he doesn't even know which case his brother figures in. William says he's lying to help his brother receive a fair trial, yet he continues to insist "My whole life I've told the truth, I always tell the truth." Just after William asks Jeff not to tell anyone, Bill brings the news that he has vouched for William's credibility with the detectives and the assistant district attorney.

The next time Bill leaves Dawn in the lobby and heads upstairs, Dawn suggests to Jeff the sort of big trouble Bill would land in if she turned him in. As we anticipate her doing just that, Lonergan reminds us how much she needs Bill to back up her story about why she hit the guy who now is "gonna lose his eye." The dramatist sets up one of his parallel situations here, employing contrasting details. Dawn needs Bill to tell the truth, but she has motivated him to lie. William wants to tell the truth, but circumstances and family loyalty have prompted him to lie. Then the couple grow more comfortable as they chat, and Jeff confides his abhorrence of machismo, "the way men behave in a group." Dawn responds, "You'd love the police force."

Although the playwright strives to make all four characters somewhat sympathetic, by this juncture he has tipped our affections squarely toward Jeff and Dawn. Then Jeff's conscience bothers him, so he begins a long "hypothetical" question concerning somebody providing a false alibi. He keeps up the fiction for a while, but finally her desire to see justice done and his attraction to her enable her to worm the truth from him. She only asks him to uphold the principle William has drummed into him, the one he believes his boss should have adhered to. The fact that she can now stop Bill from raping her might, of course, taint her motives, but we cheer her on.

Lobby Hero's major moral choices convey themes of dishonesty, control and betrayal. William lies about his brother attending a movie with him during the time when the nurse was killed. Bill lies about the nature of his nightly visits to apartment 22J and lies again in order to prompt William to fire Jeff. Jeff lies to Dawn when he claims to know nothing about William's brother's alibi. Control freak Bill makes both African-American William and female Dawn depend on his putting in a good word for them with, respectively, the detectives and the Civilian Complaint Review Board. Then, in a retaliatory move, he nearly wrecks Jeff's chance at renting his own apartment. All four characters commit acts of betrayal: Jeff betrays William's

Boy meets cop: Glenn Fitzgerald and Heather Burns in Kenneth Lonergan's Lobby Hero. *Photo: Joan Marcus*

confidence when he tells Dawn that his boss has provided a false alibi; Bill threatens to lie at his partner's inquiry and then turns her precinct against her; and Dawn betrays her partner, albeit to protect herself. As for William, he betrays Bill's trust by not warning him to mind his own business, he betrays his own principles and he starts to fire Jeff in order to retaliate for his subordinate's blabbing his secret.

These choices characterize those who make them; they tell us the stuff of which they're made. Yet Jeff, Dawn and William redeem themselves by taking the high road toward the play's end. Jeff decides to tell Dawn the truth, even though we suspect he does it to win points with the woman he loves. Dawn demonstrates courage in seeing that justice will be done, even though she may lose her job and will suffer should she remain in her precinct—never mind that she protects herself as well. And William quickly changes his mind about firing Jeff, recognizing his own motive as retaliatory. He even rebukes himself for confiding in Jeff and for hitting him.

Who, then, qualifies as the title lobby hero? Given all the mixed motives, does anyone deserve such a designation? Lonergan's penchant for irony suggests he may intend an ironic interpretation. Clearly Bill, who shacks up with a hooker while he should patrol his beat, who plans to rape Dawn, who lies and manipulates and self-aggrandizes nearly nonstop, doesn't qualify. Yet if we assume all human actions stem from mixed motives and all potentially heroic actions could be interpreted as suspect, perhaps the efforts Jeff, Dawn and William make to do the right thing count as much as any such efforts could. Dawn especially exhibits laudable courage and true dedication to seeing justice done. Perhaps she, like the sister in Lonergan's Oscar-nominated film, can be counted on, whereas the playwright again captures his male characters in their less dependable moments.

Despite its carefully constructed plot packed with an offstage murder and onstage bad behavior, *Lobby Hero* will turn up often on regional stages because directors and actors will relish, not its pyrotechnics, but its small moment-to-moment personal interactions and the way its characters lob lines back and forth like tennis balls only to meander off into amusingly laconic exchanges.

2000–2001 Best Play

MNEMONIC

By Complicite

○○○○○

Essay by John Istel

> SIMON: Anyway, our job, the job of remembering is to *reassemble*, to literally re-member, put the relevant members back together. But what I am getting at is that re-membering is essentially not only an act of retrieval but a creative thing, it happens in the moment, it's an act, an act . . . of the imagination.

COMPLICITE'S PRODUCTION OF *MNEMONIC* is a surprising, provocative and haunting experience, not unlike those times when a cherished memory of the past suddenly gurgles to mind. The play's program cover in New York and the published script (Metheun, 2001) include the definition of the title word as a subtitle: "mnemonic (ni'mon'ik) adj. 1 assisting or intending to assist the memory; 2 of memory." And true to the suggestion, the play's cinematic form—with scenes leaping creatively from one narrative into another—attempts to be a mnemonic device, goading us into an investigation of our relation to our pasts, personal and shared. Meanwhile, the work's narrative content fulfills definition number two by being about memory and how we construct individual and communal history.

Mnemonic, on a more obvious level, also reminds audiences that the British troupe Théâtre de Complicite is a world-class ensemble of theater artists dedicated to rigorously physical productions in which the actors' bodies, imaginatively employed, are the central scenic element. The acclaimed company, led by co-founder and director Simon McBurney, makes spectacular theater, filled with stunning transformations in which actors' movement, inspired stagecraft and simple props alter and transmute the stage reality before our eyes. In the genetics of the last century's theater, Complicite's chromosomes include genes spliced from a variety of the world's branches. The seven-member cast's training is proof: credits include stints at *L'Ecole Jacques Lecoq* and the Royal Academy of Dramatic Art, while some members have worked previously with Bread & Puppet Theatre, Ariane Mnouchkine, Peter Brook and others.

Re-call: Simon McBurney in Complicite's Mnemonic. *Photo: Alastair Muir*

In a previous New York visit, Complicite brought John Berger's own adaptation of his tale of a French peasant woman, *The Three Lives of Lucie Cabrol.* In that production actors portrayed not only a village full of idiosyncratic, highly defined friends and neighbors, but also furniture and berry bushes as well. In its theatricalization of Bruno Schulz's hallucinatory Nazi-era memoir, *The Street of Crocodiles,* Complicite made the stage abound in eye-popping, surreal imagery: a man walked down the rear wall of the theater, parallel to the ground, and a library of books suddenly took flight as a flock of birds, flying across the stage in the actors' hands.

Solely as a text, however, *Mnemonic* is a departure. Unlike many of Complicite's shows, including the two just mentioned, or *The Chairs,* which McBurney brought to Broadway the previous season, it doesn't sprout from a single pre-existing root. Instead, *Mnemonic* interweaves a multiplicity of concerns, themes and sources into a 30-odd scene, two-hour whirlwind theatrical adventure. Originally produced both at the Salzburg Festival and in London, the play focuses on two central narrative threads. One concerns a woman auspiciously named Alice, who abandons her lover, Virgil, to search for her father through Europe in 1998. The other story documents the discovery of the 5,200-year-old "Iceman" and the subsequent controversies over its origin and provenance, as well as the competing theories surrounding the circumstances that originally led to his death.

Don't let the title and its double dictionary definition of a subtitle fool you: *Mnemonic* is not your typical memory play. No mournful, soulful narrator appears onstage to step back into his nostalgia-laden memories after waxing lyrical about them (*The Glass Menagerie*, *Side Man* and *Dancing at Lughnasa* are three diverse examples). Instead, *Mnemonic* is a play about memory itself, and the play's fragmentary structure of interlocking scenes that morph into one another mirrors the way our memories mutate, bubble up, digress, and float away—dividing us from, or connecting us to, one another. You get the sense that we're listening to a friend's fascinating dream. Like such an experience, it can be either engrossing or enervating, depending on your fondness for the dreamer.

Mnemonic specifically deals with these ideas in context of contemporary European history. The play at its foundation explores what it means to be European at a time when nationalist, regionalist, linguistic and ethnic differences seem to no longer work as identity defining features, especially as these countries have adopted a single currency and their borders have become increasingly porous and meaningless. In the course of the play, the seven-member ensemble takes on more than two dozen characters who speak a polyglot of languages, including English, French, German, Greek and Polish.

The opening scene of *Mnemonic* is three or four times as long as the other 30 or so scenes, and it's an incredible tour de force. It serves the play much like an overture does an opera, setting themes and offering specific dialogue to be repeated later, like melodic fragments. The scene encompasses direct address by McBurney, who plays Simon; metatheatrical references such as when Virgil answers a cell phone as if in a theater and describes the play he's been watching, which turns out to be the same one we are; documentary voiceover about time capsule technology from a television; and the fictional narrative of which Virgil becomes a major part as he tries to reconnect with his lover, Alice, who has suddenly disappeared.

It begins as an audacious variation on the standard memory play in that a narrator steps forth to deliver a long introductory monologue. The "character" is essentially that of Simon McBurney, who conceived and directed the piece, and who plays a central role in performance. He introduces himself with a vaudevillian joke:

> SIMON: Good evening, ladies and gentlemen. Before we start the show I'd like to say one or two words about memory. Yesterday somebody asked me why are you doing a show about memory and I was trying to remember. . . .

And with that twisted stab at humor, we're thrust into an engaging lecture on new neurological theories of memory. Simon, our genial guide, is personable and intimate as well as professorial. He deliberately draws attention to the fact that we're watching theater, as Complicite does in so much of its work, while explaining how memories "sprout" and leap from one thing to the next until we're confronted with the fundamental nature of our identity.

> SIMON: As I stand here trying to remember my text for some reason my father is coming to mind. Why is that? Probably it's to do with this thing about origins, because he was an archaeologist and so was fascinated by origins . . . he died twenty years ago, actually and he was American, if we are talking about origins, and my mother is Irish, well, part Irish, part Scottish, part Welsh, part English, which I suppose makes me British.

After several minutes, the lecture swerves from title definition number two to number one, from being about memory to being a show determined to make its audience commit acts of remembering. That's accomplished when Simon asks the audience to open a plastic pouch that we had discovered on our seats when we entered the auditorium. In the packet is a sleep mask and a tree leaf. We're asked to don the masks, and once

Alice through the glass: Katrin Cartlidge and Simon McBurney in Mnemonic. *Photo: Alastair Muir*

masked, Simon asks the audience to hold the leaf. He leads the audience in a visualization exercise that asks us to imagine our parents, grandparents and great-grandparents standing in rows behind us. The farther back we go in time, the larger the numbers.

> SIMON: At the beginning of the eighteenth century, assuming there are no kinship ties, there is a line of 4,064. . . . And a thousand years ago, if there really were no kinship ties, that line would be longer than all people who have ever been born. Which, of course, is not possible . . . but it means that you are related to everyone sitting in this theatre.

We're part of the same tree, in other words, born from different veins or lines—as on a leaf.

The way people are connected to each other—physically and invisibly—quickly becomes a concern as the play from here turns to an investigation of origins and identity. When we take off our masks, we realize Simon's voice emanates from the sound system and that McBurney is another character. That's when the cell phone goes off—our modern form of connection—and the actor, playing Virgil, becomes our guide not into paradise or purgatory as in Dante, but into the past and the way it shapes the present.

Virgil's relationship with Alice is defined completely by cell phone conversations and answering machine voiceovers. She's gone; he wants to find her. He replays her final message: "You have to wait now and this time follow me." Alice, it turns out, has discovered at her mother's funeral that the father she never met might actually be alive. Like her Lewis Carroll namesake, she sets out across the dark wonderland of Europe, a character in search of an identity, a past. She has the following conversation with a cab driver, which is pretty much an adaptation of an anecdote Simon has relayed in his opening set piece about a cab ride he had on the way to the theater:

> ALICE: Where are you from?
>
> SIMONIDES: Me? I am from Islington.
>
> ALICE: No, no . . . I mean originally.
>
> SIMONIDES: Oh, Greece.

Although seemingly innocuous, by that scene—about two-thirds through the approximately three dozen scenes—we've been primed to understand how the ambiguity of identity surfaces constantly in contemporary life, and where one comes from "originally" is a loaded question.

That's because *Mnemonic* has another parallel story to tell: intercut with Alice's search is the discovery of the Iceman in the Alps that occurred in 1991. It's presented documentary style, starting in the third scene, with voiceovers relating how hikers one sunny day came across a body sticking out from a glacier. Onstage, the Complicite ensemble enacts the events via the sound system. From the third scene forward, the cast never leaves the stage completely, instead gliding effortlessly into a succession of characters, scenes and tableaux. A signature bit of stage business occurs as the Iceman is discovered: the ensemble creates the mountain weather by simply putting their hands in pockets of raincoats and windbreakers, and making them flap stiffly as if these mountaineers were being buffeted by a strong, cold wind.

In fact, the scenic elements, as in most Complicite productions, are few. A table becomes a mountain top in one scene, a dissection table in the next. A chair, which Simon presented in the monologue, comes apart and transforms into the Iceman's skeleton and is animated like a puppet. A small, metal square frame held by the actors becomes the window of the Iceman's refrigeration unit. A two-way mirror now reflects a character's image, now merges the reflection with another character. A heavy gauge plastic scrim serves as backdrop, but with sophisticated lighting and a clear square cut in the plastic it becomes a window on the train that speeds Alice through Europe. As in previous works, though, the primary scenic device is the actor's body. McBurney is exhibit one. Naked much of the play, he morphs from nervous jilted lover into the frozen prehistoric hunter who died one day in the Alps, making physical the metaphorical connection between the Iceman and modern man.

At least a third of the play is devoted to the discovery of and research into the Iceman. One of the primary sources credited in a program note is the book *The Man in the Ice* by Konrad Spindler, and in fact Spindler is a character, sometimes lecturing on the discoveries about the Iceman, sometimes providing details via voiceover. Clearly, *Mnemonic* presents the Iceman as a kind of ur-father; and the scientists' attempts to figure out the identity, habits and cultural traits are juxtaposed in obvious ways to Alice's attempt to discover similar facts about her father. After being robbed in Berlin, she ends up in Warsaw, at the home of her father's sister-in-law. She is handed a box of ordinary possessions—a shoe, a lighter, a scarf—that belonged to her father. And she tries to decipher his personality through these objects just as the scientists studying the Iceman catalog the 17 different kinds of wood he carried or try to piece together the remnants of a hunting bow.

Eventually, Alice meets a character called BBC Man, on a train, and they have a brief affair. He informs Alice that the scarf is really a tallith, a Jewish prayer shawl. He's a Jew himself and in one of the more touching scenes in the play, teaches her an old Yiddish drinking song he learned from his grandfather. "It's the only cultural baggage I've got," he says. As they sing, the whole ensemble joins them and they cross the stage as if in a mass migration, transitioning into the next scene. The moment echoes a line Virgil repeats several times in the play as he wonders about the Iceman's identity: "How many songs did he know? Had he yet heard the story of the flood?"

After stops in Riga, Galicia and Kiev, Alice finally meets her father, she tells Virgil via phone, but improbably doesn't remember the encounter. She apparently had a sudden urge to flee and finds herself in Balzano, Italy, which (coincidentally, of course) is home of the Iceman's remains. This ending isn't completely satisfying. The play tries to force the issue, assuming we're as fascinated with the Iceman and his story and how it connects to the fictional Alice as the play is. As the ensemble gathers around the tiny window of the refrigerated unit holding the Iceman, one member slips under the window frame and literally lies in the Iceman's place on the table as McBurney slips off. One by one, each cast member repeats the action, suggesting that everyone is inescapably drawn and connected to the 5,200 year old ancestor. The ensemble gathers in a line as a montage of voices for the umpteenth time enumerates the objects the neolithic hunter had in his possession at his death: "A broken stick. Splinters of wood. Scraps of leather . . ." The lights fade to black.

Although fascinating in many more ways than much of contemporary theater, the piece has its ponderous side and McBurney's constant presence as Simon, Virgil and the Iceman, comes across as a bit indulgent. He's naked for much of the play as the Iceman and in scenes that seem to occur in Virgil's memory, imagination or dreams as he tosses about in his bedroom. Another repeated line—"What does nakedness remind us of?"—doesn't work as justification. The suggestion is that a naked body is also a mnemonic device: it reminds us of our own body. But watching a naked body of an actor onstage, I find, rarely does that. Instead, it makes me wonder about the theater's temperature or sets me wondering whether the performer showers before or after the performance or both. But it's an example of the many threads and themes woven into the play, all of which can't be detailed here.

Finally, because the play was "written by"—and credit and copyright go to—"Complicite," as the ensemble seems to prefer being known, the "play" is inextricably bound to its production by the company. *Mnemonic*, like so many experimental projects, remains a work in flux, unfixed, an evolving experiment. As McBurney writes in a program note: "Like all Theatre de Complicite shows this is a new departure. We are searching for another form to tell our stories. It is not finished. It represents a point of departure rather than a destination."

It's difficult to imagine the text of this production staged or revived by a theater group other than Complicite, whose virtuosic theatricality imbues every project it takes on. Just as it's hard to envision a regional theater staging of the Living Theatre's *Paradise Now* or the Wooster Group's adaptation of Chekhov, *Brace Up!*, in all likelihood *Mnemonic* will rarely be seen anywhere other than in the Complicite repertoire. Nevertheless, thanks to McBurney and the ensemble's virtuosity, the play will live on, most appropriately, in the memories of those who experienced this production.

2000–2001 Best Play

NOCTURNE

By Adam Rapp

○○○○○

Essay by Robert Brustein

> THE SON: I can change the order of the words. My sister I killed fifteen years ago. I, fifteen years ago, killed my sister. Sister my killed I years ago fifteen. [. . .] There's a finality in a fact. Something medical, almost. A fact is crafted. Vaguely industrial. It has permanence. It's a stain or a smudge. A botch or a spot or a blemish. A fact is a flaw. It's made of wood and left to fossilize; to gather minerals and geologically imprint itself on the side of a mountain.

NOCTURNE IS UNLIKE ANY OTHER PLAY yet produced by the young Adam Rapp, whose output, despite his relatively tender age (34), has thus far been extraordinarily prolific. First of all, the play is written on a much smaller canvas than is usual with this dramatist. It is in the form of a long monologue, 42 pages in manuscript length, originally intended to be performed by a single actor. In the play's first production, it is true, Rapp was persuaded to add four more cast members, but two of these are mute, and the remaining two are provided with only minimal dialogue. *Nocturne* is a tour-de-force for a single actor that requires maximal memory and multiple performance skills.

The second way this play differs from Rapp's other work is in its style and characters. Rapp, who trained at Juilliard under the tutorship of Marsha Norman and Christopher Durang, usually writes in a tradition of magic realism, showing the influence not only of his two Juilliard mentors but also of Sam Shepard, Harold Pinter, Craig Lucas, David Mamet and other theatrical fantasists of that kidney. His recent play, *Animals and Plants*, for example, seems like a hybrid of Shepard's *True West* and Harold Pinter's *The Dumbwaiter*, being about two losers in a motel room in the middle of a blizzard, waiting to make a drug deal (one of them will walk out naked into the snowstorm after having been betrayed by the other and after receiving mysterious phone calls from a menacing heavy breather). And his recent two-hander, *Blackbird*, shows some of the influence of Shepard and David Rabe in its telling of the brutally tender relationship between a teenage hooker/addict and an older crippled Vietnam veteran.

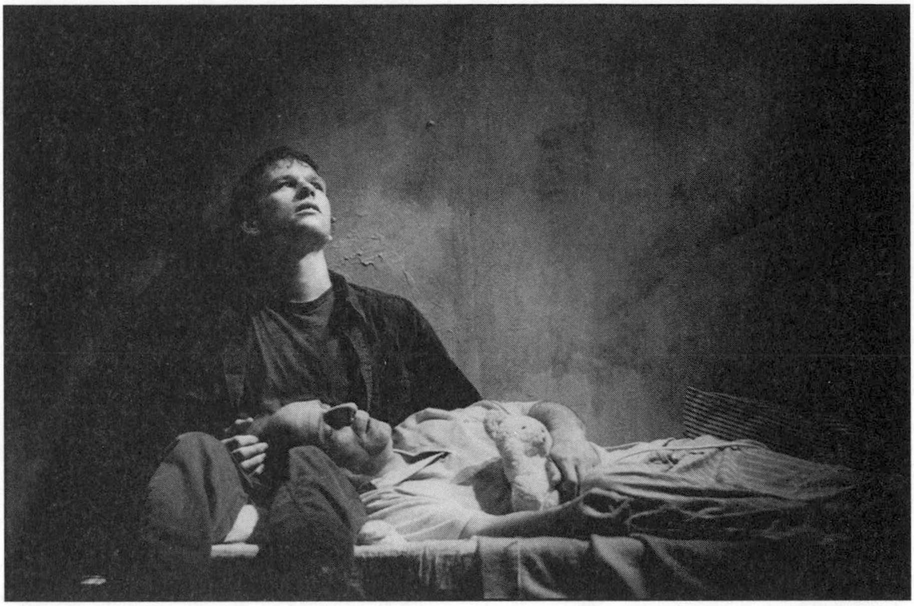

Pietá Papa: Dallas Roberts and Will LeBow in Adam Rapp's Nocturne. *Photo: Joan Marcus*

By contrast with Rapp's usual *dramatis personae* of inarticulate or prolix working-class characters in extreme situations, *Nocturne* is a much more self-conscious work with a much better-educated, even middle-class hero. Many of Rapp's characters are without families, or have families that are absent. The Son (as his name suggests) is almost wholly defined by his relationship to his mother, father and sister. Even his mild teenage rebelliousness is related to the surrounding domesticity. On the hood of the family piano, for example, there are family photos: his father "holding a rather bored looking bass," his parents "clutching each other at the altar looking like they're about to walk into a meat locker." And among the less appealing bougeois features of his house is its "infinite Formica. . . . There's so much Formica it's as if it was archaeologically excavated and the house was built around it in honor of its laminated magnificence. I sometimes think the color of my skin is not white but Formica."

But as this passage suggests, the major difference between *Nocturne* and Rapp's other work is its total fascination with language. The Son's shocking first line—"Fifteen years ago I killed my sister"—is immediately followed by a long declension of the verb "to kill," before the text returns to that tragic, inexorable fact of an accidental event that radically changes the life of the protagonist. "I am obsessed with language," Rapp said in a recent interview. "People can't control their government, taxes, life spans or whom they date. But we can control how we construct language. It's a kind of government that we consciously create."

Despite Rapp's preoccupation with the government of language, however, the literary quality of *Nocturne* is not only grammatical, and not merely expressed in the mournful verbal arpeggios that reverberate throughout the text. Rapp is highly conscious of, indeed he virtually advertises, how indebted he is to the tradition of the 20th-century western novel (he has written four novels himself). After the Son moves to New York and starts working in a bookstore, he begins to collect books, which he reads voraciously before turning them into "literary furniture," as the building blocks of a table or a credenza. These include works by Hemingway, Salinger, Wharton, Baldwin, Nabokov, Joyce and Don De Lillo, among others, and he intones the names of these authors ("The names alone," he says, "are a kind of escape") with the same hypnotic and obsessed fascination that he reads their books. Chief among these names is that of William Faulkner and chief among the novels is *The Wild Palms*, Faulkner's lugubrious tale of another man who commits an accidental homicide against a person he loves, with even more desperate consequences.

There is, in fact, a line in *The Wild Palms* that, although not quoted in the play, could very well be its epigraph. When Faulkner's hero is imprisoned for having killed his mistress through a mismanaged abortion, he considers suicide for a moment, then decides against it, saying "Between grief and nothing I will take grief." Consciousness, even in its most despairing form, is to be preferred above nonbeing, where memory cannot even evoke the shades of past experience.

The Son has a very similar existential crisis, having to decide whether to be or not to be after he has not only decapitated his sister in an automobile accident, but plunged his mother into an incurable depression and destroyed the hopes of his despairing father. The Father, as a result, tries to kill him. That terrible action, which shadows the ending of the first part of the play, is what impels the Son onto his spiritual journey and geographical odyssey—and presumably initiates his love affair with the English language.

His other related love is music, particularly as played on the piano, a love that invades Rapp's approach to literature ("When I read a poem or a novel," he has said, "I always see it as a kind of musical arrangement"). A few other dramatists, most notably August Strindberg in such works as *The Ghost Sonata*, have tried to turn drama into music, not in Strindberg's case because he valued words but rather because he considered music to be purer than language.

Like *The Ghost Sonata* (which has a classical sonata form based on Beethoven's *Ghost Trio*), the very title of Rapp's play is from a musical piece, not the Steely Dan number the Son is listening to on the car radio the moment before the fatal accident, but one that vividly contrasts with it, notably Edvard Grieg's *Nocturne*. A nocturne is a lullaby or a musical piece appropriate for evening—and so is the play named after it.

Perhaps this is the piece that the Son has practiced three hours a day for seven years on the family's 1942 Steinway. Whatever the case, this highly polished black instrument enjoys the gift of the author's full descriptive powers, virtually becoming another character in the play:

> THE SON: The piano doesn't sing. It sobs. It aches without release. Like a word that can't wrench itself from the throat. Like an alkaline trapped in the liver. A C-sharp. The death of a small bird. An F. A stranded car's horn bleating for help on the highway. [. . .] The final movement of a sonata. An almost human tragedy. Slow, brutal heart failure. Coronary thrombosis.

The metaphors and similes that stud this passage are the stylistic signature of the play. Rapp virtually challenges you to call him "literary," or "self-conscious," or to accuse him of indulging in "fine writing," and a number of critics have been eager to oblige him with these obloquies. But he is clearly taking a large risk with this play in trying to bring the American drama into the wider nexus of American literature from which it has so long been divorced.

That he succeeds so well with *Nocturne* puts him in a class with a very small number of American playwrights—preeminently Tennessee Williams and Tony Kushner, perhaps Edward Albee, marginally David Mamet—whose plays read as well as they perform (however powerful the plays of Eugene O'Neill and Arthur Miller, they do not fit into the category of literary works). In the second part of *Nocturne*, an Underwood typewriter takes the stage away from the Steinway piano, as the Son—like the writer who created him—attempts to redeem his past through literary acts. It is the only human area in which the Son remains potent. His attempt to make love to "the red-headed girl with gray-green eyes" ends in failure, and he becomes, as a result, more and more reclusive.

But by turning his own life story into fiction, the Son achieves a modicum of self-confidence that permits him to go on, especially when his novel is published and enjoys modest sales (2,000 copies). But ultimately even this small reservoir of comfort will dry up. "The books turn into years. The years into books. The Underwood stops calling to him."

And then he receives a message from his father. Significantly, it comes to him in literary form, however crude. It is a short story, written many years before, entitled "The Story of My Life," which the Father has been encouraged to share with the Son, after having read his novel. Rough and primitive as his father's writing is, this literary artifact is the beginning of a reconciliation between the two men. Having been diagnosed with testicular cancer, the Father is signaling his son to come to his death bed.

Their reunion in Joliet is one of the most moving scenes in recent drama. In Marcus Stern's production at the American Repertory Theatre (and later at the New York Theatre Workshop), this poignancy was heightened by a physical feeling of claustrophobia. The ceiling in Christine Jones's set for this scene was so low that the Son was unable to stand upright. Bending towards his father, who lies in bed being fed morphine intravenously, he achieves the kind of bonding that Stephen Daedalus enjoyed with Leopold Bloom—the union of two similar spirits if unlike sensibilities. Having been separated for fifteen years, they share stories, trivial and important. And after the Father, weeping, persuades the Son to stay the night, he dies before morning, his fingers curled around his Son's hand.

"Grief does not expire like a candle or a beacon on a lighthouse," reflects the Son in a lyrical coda. "It simply changes temperature. It becomes a kind of personal weather system. [. . .] The heart fills with warm rain that turns to mist and evaporates through a colder artery." All of the dead remnants of his family are calling to him, his sister, his mother, his father. So is the Underwood. He will try again with the redheaded girl: "Even the greatest sleeping sea can be awakened by the tide."

When I first read *Nocturne*, I felt the hairs rise on the back of my neck, for me the most convincing sign that I was experiencing something unique. Only one other play had affected me this way in the reading, namely Marsha Norman's *'night Mother*, another account of a character in desperate circumstances, written with tenderness and forgiveness. My wife called me to dinner. I rudely told her to wait until I had finished reading this engrossing work.

It is so rare when the act of reading a play can be as fulfilling as the act of seeing it. This was one of those occasions, and the experience was only enhanced when we found ourselves in a position to stage it. Those who had a chance to see Dallas Roberts's performance as the Son, pulsing with lyricism and pain, and Will LeBow as the suffering Father, pushed beyond his good nature to an act of violence, or Nicole Pasquale as the mute, wide-eyed, empathic Sister, or Candice Brown and Marin Ireland as the Mother and the Redheaded Girl with the Green Eyes, had the opportunity to unite with a stage experience that has done that rare thing—shed some light on the darkness of the human condition.

2000–2001 Best Play

THE PLAY ABOUT THE BABY

By Edward Albee

○○○○○

Essay by Christine Dolen

> MAN: Have you seen the baby? Cute, no? They love it, don't they—the baby. They really love it. I wonder how much they love it? How much they need it? Perhaps we should find out. As the lady said, stay tuned.

YES, VIRGINIA WOOLF, THERE REALLY *IS* A BABY in three-time Pulitzer Prize-winner Edward Albee's latest work, aptly titled *The Play About the Baby*. In Albee's 1962 masterpiece *Who's Afraid of Virginia Woolf?*, sparring spouses George and Martha move through a long, emotional brutalizing night from the fiction of a baby to the acceptance of truth, of childlessness. In *The Play About the Baby*, a Girl and a Boy journey from nurturing their real infant to doubting whether they were ever parents at all.

But of course, Albee's more recent play is about much more than a baby, real then denied. (When asked what this or any of his plays is about, Albee—loath to explain his art—is apt to reply, "It's about two hours long.")

The Play About the Baby is an allegorical piece in which one of America's greatest playwrights mines familiar thematic territory anew. It premiered at London's Almeida Theatre in 1998 in a production directed by Howard Davies and was subsequently staged at Houston's Alley Theatre in April 2000, with direction by Albee himself. The Off Broadway production opened at the Century Center for the Performing Arts in March 2001, with David Esbjornson directing. Memory, self-deception, illusion, loss, truth, lies: themes that give tensile strength to such Albee plays as *A Delicate Balance* and *Who's Afraid of Virginia Woolf?* are carefully, amusingly, terrifyingly woven through *The Play About the Baby*.

As in *Virginia Woolf*, the play pairs an older couple playing an eviscerating game with a younger one. These four characters, however, are symbolic abstractions, closer to *commedia dell'arte* figures than to the biographically detailed George and Martha and Honey and Nick.

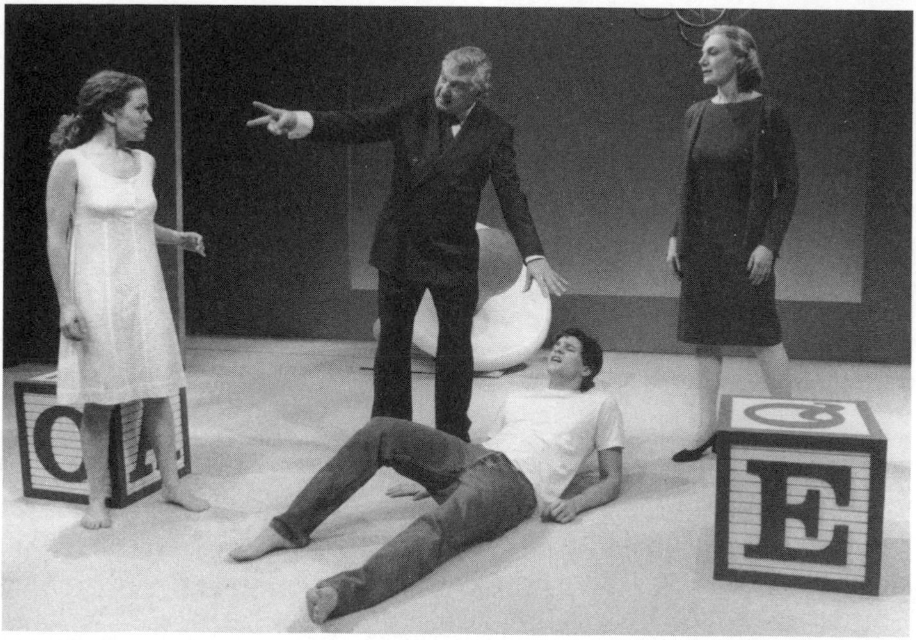

Baby talk: Kathleen Early, Brian Murray, David Burtka (floor), Marian Seldes in Edward Albee's The Play About the Baby. *Photo: Carol Rosegg*

In *The Play About the Baby*, Girl and Boy (Kathleen Early and David Burtka in the New York production) serve to remind us of Edenic innocence, of the beginning of life when everything seems to be joyful, abundant possibility. The elder pair, Man and Woman, are polished, amusing, worldly wise—and up to no good. They exist to "educate" the innocents, to wound them, toughen them, give them the scars that will make future joy ephemeral.

Done in a presentational space—at the Century Center, on John Arnone's visually witty and deceptively soothing pastel-colored set with two oversized baby blocks, a carriage, a rocking horse and a giant pacifier—the play gets right down to business with the "hugely pregnant" Girl's first line: "I'm going to have the baby now." She exits, moans and screams. A slap. We hear the baby cry. And she's back, slender again, vaguely remembering her pain.

As she talks with her boy-husband, in language simple yet erotically charged, it becomes clear that she has two babies, really: the infant and its father, the young man who took her virginity and gave her his, who wants (and, discomfitingly for some in the audience, takes) his turn at her breast, whose defining "tragedy" to date was the breaking of his arm by some concert-crashers he unwisely confronted.

When they exit for more extensive physical consolation, the mesmerizing Man (in New York, Brian Murray, radiating mordant charm) enters to play the proper, demonically beguiling host. A storyteller of vaudevillian ease, given to seeming digressions (usually far more pointed than they initially seem), he ignores the fourth wall to share tales from Albee's oeuvre/imagination/experience: his bemused chagrin at not remembering that this "tall, older woman" next to him at a party was his mother; the unreliability and malleability of memory; a warning that he will deceive others, us included.

His partner in crime, Woman (opposite Murray, the reedy and brilliantly theatrical Albee veteran, Marian Seldes), offers her own digressive set pieces, about her disagreeable former husband and the arrogance of creative types (not to mention the annoyance that dilettantes such as she can cause them). As she carries on "vamping" (*The Play About the Baby* makes much of its own theatrical artifice), the Boy and Girl scamper nude across the stage, Adam and Eve at play in Eden. But not for long.

The younger couple's romantic recollections and acknowledgements of lust become tainted by fear. They talk of gypsies, predictions, tricks; the harm a gypsy could do them by taking their baby. (Kidnapping was one of the great childhood fears of Albee himself, who thought that what happened to the Lindbergh baby might happen to him. It wasn't an irrational fantasy: as the adopted son of those now famously cold WASPs, Reed and Frances Albee, whose considerable fortune derived from the Keith-Albee vaudeville houses, he might have been an attractive target.) The Boy pleads, in a speech that will recur in Act II, to be allowed to hold on to joy, happiness, youth. He has, of course, no chance.

After another hilariously digressive story by the Woman—about her possibly real, definitely embroidered long-ago affair with a much-older painter—the Boy gets around to asking Man what he wants. At first, Man offers some cosmic sidestepping:

> MAN: What do we *want*. Well, I would imagine we want what almost everybody wants—eternal life, in great health, no older than we are when we want it; easy money, with enough self-deception to make us feel we've earned it, are worthy people; a government that lets us do whatever we want, serves our private interests and lets us feel we're doing all we can for . . . how do they call it—the less fortunate?; a bigger dick, a more muscular vagina; a baby, perhaps?

Then, a partial confession that seems to detonate:

> MAN: What do we want. Well, it's really very simple. We've come to take the baby.

And, when the panicked Girl checks to find the infant gone, re-entering with a hysterical query—"WHERE'S THE BABY?! WHAT HAVE YOU DONE WITH THE BABY?!"—Man and Woman acknowledge their real purpose.

MAN: *What* baby?

WOMAN: Yes; *what* baby?

Naked innocence: David Burtka and Kathleen Early in The Play About the Baby. *Photo: Carol Rosegg*

Easing the audience back into the play—into the theater itself—Man begins Act II with a monologue on the habits of theatergoers—post-intermission stragglers, smokers, drinkers, coffee drinkers, women who stand in long lines to use too-few bathroom stalls. Then he guides us thematically back toward the pre-intermission tragedy he and Woman set up—"We can't take glory because it shows us the abyss," he observes—and orchestrates the repetition of the disturbing scene we so recently witnessed.

They continue, probing for soft spots, opening wounds, making them deeper. Man feints and threatens, warning the younger couple that if they hope to see their baby again, they'd better cooperate. He responds to Woman's ironic compliment about his "way with children" by claiming to be the father of six: " . . . two black, two white, one green, and the other . . . well, I'm not certain, or I've lost track, or whatever." Back and forth he goes, from fantastic fiction to bullying, purposefully observing: "If you have no wounds how can you know if you're alive? If you have no scar, how do you know who you are? Have been?"

On the subject of wounding, Man and Woman are battle-scarred, elegant experts. Albee makes their carving of the innocents progressively more difficult to watch. Jealousy becomes a cutting tool. Man suggests that the lusty, lovely memories we've heard really belong to himself and Boy, not Girl and Boy. Woman behaves as though she's had both of the young partners. Man, speaking to the increasingly distraught pair, piles it on: "I'd like to know, for example, why you took up with this young woman, when you obviously despise her."

The amusing touches, though receding, continue. Woman does some hilarious faux signing for the hearing impaired. Man waxes philosophical. But the damage has been done.

> BOY: [. . .] Have you come to hurt us? Beyond salvation? Hurt us to the point that...if you want to do this to us, hurt us so, ask *why*! Ask what we've *done*. I can take pain and loss and all the rest *later*; I *think* I can—*we* can—when it comes as natural as . . . sleep? But . . . now? Not now. We're happy; we love each other; I'm hard all the time; we have a baby; we don't even understand each other yet. So . . . give us some time. Please?
>
> (Pause)
>
> MAN: Time's up.

And after a bit more flim-flam and sleight-of-hand, Boy and Girl come, albeit erroneously, to the same conclusion as George and Martha: there never really was a baby at all.

Albee's disquieting, blazingly theatrical chamber piece lets the snakes into Eden to amuse, then terrify. For all of the engaging, amusing speeches Man and Woman have lobbed our way—Albee, both on the page and off the stage, is a playwright adept at dry wit—when the play ends, we feel as wrung out as the lost innocents. Laughter wed to tears: Such is *The Play About the Baby*. Such is an Albee play. Such is life.

2000–2001 Best Play

THE PRODUCERS

Book by Mel Brooks and Thomas Meehan
Music and lyrics by Mel Brooks

○○○○○

Essay by Julius Novick

I wanna be a producer
With a big show on Broadway.
I wanna be a producer,
Lunch at Sardi's every day. [. . .]
I'm gonna be a producer,
Sound the horn and beat the drum. [. . .]
I'm gonna be a producer,
Look out Broadway, here I come!!

EVEN BEFORE ITS OUT-OF-TOWN TRYOUT in Chicago, *The Producers* was generating buzz, and when it opened at the St. James Theatre in New York, the buzz became a roar. Ben Brantley in the *New York Times* called it "sublimely ridiculous . . . a big Broadway book musical that is so ecstatically drunk on its powers to entertain that it leaves you delirious, too." *Time*'s Richard Zoglin said it was "a gift from the show-biz gods." To Charles Isherwood at *Variety* it was "a rip-roaring, gut-busting, rib-tickling, knee-slapping, aisle-rolling (insert your own compound adjective here) good time." The bedazzled John Heilpern of the *New York Observer* pronounced it simply, "the best show ever."

As soon as the opening-night reviews came out, the producers raised the top ticket price to $100, enabling the show to gross a cool million dollars a week. Undaunted by this blatant profiteering, eager theatergoers bought three million dollars worth of tickets the next day—a record. (Outside the St. James Theatre a few weeks later, someone was offering $500 a ticket—for a Wednesday matinee!) *The Producers* was nominated for 15 Tony Awards in 12 categories, another record, and it won in every category. Accepting his Tony for best direction of a play (for staging *Proof* by David Auburn), Daniel Sullivan said, "There must be some mistake—I had nothing to do with *The Producers*."

Double trouble: Nathan Lane and Matthew Broderick in The Producers. *Photo: Paul Kolnik*

Of course, nothing could possibly be as wonderful as *The Producers* is said (and screamed, and assumed) to be. The show is a lot of fun, but it is, after all, yet another movie recycled into a musical—after *Beauty and the Beast*, *The Lion King*, *Big*, *Footloose*, *Saturday Night Fever*, *The Full Monty* and other hits and flops. It is a pre-sold product, very close in outline and often in detail to the cult-classic film that Mel Brooks wrote and directed in 1968. And no one denies its essential conventionality. What then made it, in *Variety*'s words, such a "headline-making megahit?" The short answer is that Broadway was ready for the antic, sometimes frantic, yet deeply traditional sensibility of Mel Brooks, who wrote the book for the megahit (with Thomas Meehan), the lyrics (by himself), and the music (plinking out the tunes on a piano and humming them into a tape recorder, to be arranged by Glen Kelly and orchestrated by Doug Besterman). And Mel Brooks, age 74, was ready for Broadway—ready, that is, to channel his comic imagination through the Broadway professionalism of his collaborators, most notably his director-choreographer, Susan Stroman.

As everybody knows, the big musicals of recent decades have tended to be solemn affairs: *The Phantom of the Opera*, *Les Misérables*, *Miss Saigon*. Old-fashioned Broadway musical *comedy* has seemed to be a thing of the past. But many people still hungered for it, as evidenced by the successful revivals of shows like *Guys and Dolls* and *A Funny Thing Happened on the Way to the Forum* (both starring Nathan Lane). And then along came this new yet strangely familiar show (again starring Nathan Lane) devoted heart and soul to comedy.

There is a widespread feeling that Broadway has seen better days, and that *The Producers* evokes them: that it is, in the words of the *New York Post*'s Clive Barnes, "a cast-iron, copper-bottomed, super-duper mammoth old-time Broadway hit." Thomas Viertel, one of its producers, told *Time*, "It's as if this is that one last musical from the 1950s, and everybody forgot to produce it. And now here it is." Moreover, *The Producers* is not just an old-fashioned musical comedy. It is an old-fashioned musical comedy about the making of an old-fashioned musical comedy, an episode in Broadway's long-running love affair with its own past. (While *The Producers* was raking in all possible Tonys, the award for best revival of a musical went to *42nd Street,* another musical comedy about the making of a musical comedy. *Follies*, with its evocation of *The Ziegfeld Follies*, was a runner-up.) Mel Brooks has spent most of his career working in television and films, but by his own account, he has been in love with Broadway musical comedy since he saw *Anything Goes* at the age of nine. Unlike the movie, the show is infused with that love. Broadway adores *The Producers*, in part, because *The Producers* adores Broadway.

The overture begins with a drumroll, and then the brasses blare out the first notes of the big tune: *Da*-dum, da-*da*-dum, da-*da*-da-dum—sounding like every other musical-comedy overture, only more so. There have been plenty of musicals in which every song sounds as if you've heard it before—but this time it's on purpose. Nearly every moment of this show is an affectionate parody, burlesque, pastiche, reminiscence or plain knockoff of some musical (or many musicals) gone by. It is not done subtly—nothing in *The Producers* is done subtly—but it is part of the fun.

For all its immersion in the good old days, the show is never saccharine or precious. As Susan Stroman, the director-choreographer, said while accepting one of her Tonys, "In the world of Mel Brooks, there is a sense of freedom to try comic ideas that might in normal circumstances seem outrageous." Accepting her other Tony, she quoted a Brooksian precept: "Don't tap the bell, *ring* the bell." The world of *The Producers* is the world of broad comedy, low comedy, farce comedy: a wish-fulfillment fantasy world; a crazy world of preposterous dangers and preposterous rescues; a world where chasing, fleeing, hiding, grabbing, hitting, kicking, rolling on the floor all release joyous energies; a world of intoxicating freedom. Where the movie is wild but darkly misanthropic, and held down by the inherent naturalism of cinema, the show is ebullient, liberated by the open artifice of musical theater. Under Stroman's direction, the acting has its own outrageousness, its own kind of freedom: uninhibited, physical, *italicized*, stylized almost to the point of kabuki, with silent arias of mugging: always on the edge of too much, yet disciplined and focused; eruptive yet smooth.

The traditions within which the show operates with such authority and zest are ultimately the traditions of comedy itself, traceable as far back

Squeeze me, fleece me: Madeleine Doherty and Nathan Lane in The Producers. *Photo: Paul Kolnik*

as comedy goes; Brooks seems to have taken them in with his mother's milk. Ever since *The Birds* of Aristophanes, in which a scheming, fast-talking Athenian manages to make himself king of the universe, comedy has been about breaking the rules, fooling the fools, and *getting away with it*—as Max Bialystock and Leopold Bloom do in *The Producers*. In the movie, they were merely incorrigible; in the show, they are triumphant.

Max and Leo form a highly traditional comic duo: the enterprising leader and the hesitant, bewildered follower: think Laurel and Hardy, Didi and Gogo or, for that matter, Pisthetairos and Euelpides in *The Birds*. Max is a Broadway producer, a scheming, fast-talking con man; Leo is a mousy, downtrodden accountant who secretly wants to be a producer himself. (Brooks himself pointed out another ancient theme, in an interview with *Time*: "It's the story of a caterpillar who became a butterfly—that's Leo Bloom. And that's me. A little kid from Brooklyn who finally made it across the vast East River to Manhattan, to Broadway.") Pudgy, expansive, plaintively bellowing Nathan Lane as Max, and clenched, tic-ridden Matthew Broderick as Leo, visibly torn between fear and desire, play off each other splendidly. The movie is darkened by the magnificent monstrosity of Zero Mostel as Max; Lane's Broadway geniality helps keep the musical bright.

Like the hero of *The Birds* and his sad-sack sidekick, Max and Leo have a wild idea. It occurs to Leo that "under the right circumstances, a producer could make more money with a flop than he could with a hit." Max, who has had a succession of flops, is fascinated. The idea is simple: raise more money than the show costs, and when it flops, pocket the difference. (If it doesn't flop, they go to jail for selling 25,000 percent of their show.) Max summarizes:

> MAX: Step One: We find the worst play ever written. Step Two: We hire the worst director in town. Step Three: I raise *two* million dollars—
>
> LEO: Two?
>
> MAX: Yes! One for me, one for you. There's a lot of little old ladies out there. Step Four: We hire the worst actors in New York and open on Broadway. And before you can say Step Five we close on Broadway, take our two million, and go to Rio.

In carrying out this scheme, Max and Leo encounter a succession of characters even more off-the-wall and over-the-top than they are: a spectacular succession of zanies. "The worst play ever written" turns out to be *Springtime for Hitler*, subtitled *A Gay Romp with Adolf and Eva at Berchtesgaden*. Franz Liebkind, its author (played by Brad Oscar), is a pixilated Nazi in lederhosen and a German army helmet, whose beloved pigeons sing hilarious backup as he warbles about "old Bavaria." His broad German accent is very traditional: for English speakers, there is something intrinsically funny about the sound of German. "Dutch comics" were a staple of the vaudeville stage, and Brooks himself wrote classic German-accented sketches for Sid Caesar to perform on television.

The next stop for Max and Leo is the elegant townhouse of Roger De Bris (Gary Beach), "the worst director in town," who makes his stately entrance in an evening gown. Roger and his entourage are homosexual stereotypes so exaggerated as to be parodies of homosexual stereotypes. Roger envisions *Springtime for Hitler* as a musical:

> ROGER: I see German soldiers dancing through France,
> Played by chorus boys in very tight pants.

Back in their office, the producers audition another stereotype, but Ulla Inga Hansen Bensen Yonsen Tallen-Hallen Svaden-Svanson (Cady Huffman) is not just another tall, sexy, available blonde. She refers to herself in the third person—"You vant Ulla make audition?"—like Elmo, the cuddly little monster on *Sesame Street*, and what her Swedish accent can do to the letter "u" has to be heard to be believed. She provides what little romance there is in this briskly unsentimental show by seducing Leo. It is another traditional comic gambit: the seduction of a shy, frightened male virgin by an enticing, experienced woman.

Max goes on to Step Three, raising money by seducing randy old ladies. This takes place in "Little Old Lady Land," an *hommage* to the "Loveland" sequence in Stephen Sondheim's *Follies*, which in turn is an *hommage* to *The Ziegfeld Follies*. But Little Old Lady Land is populated by identically dressed biddies with names like "Lick Me-Bite Me," "Hold Me-Touch Me," and "Kiss Me-Feel Me." This sequence features the now-famous tap number, performed by the old ladies, in which the tapping sounds are provided by their walkers—less gross than perhaps it sounds, since the old ladies are obviously being played by healthy young chorus girls—and boys.

The surprise plot-twist of *The Producers* (though many will have seen it coming) is that *Springtime for Hitler* turns out to be a huge hit. Threatened with jail, Leo takes off for Rio with Ulla, but Max is arrested and tried. Just as he is about to be sentenced, Leo bursts into the courtroom to plead for his friend—and the judge sends them both to jail. (Folded inside this raucous parody of a sentimental rescue scene is just a touch of the real thing.) Incarcerated but incorrigible, the boys produce a musical called *Prisoners of Love*, and are pardoned because they have "brought joy and laughter into the hearts of every murderer, rapist and sex maniac in Sing Sing." *Prisoners of Love* becomes a hit on Broadway, and Max and Leo live happily ever after.

The most famous, most controversial number in the show is the title tune from *Springtime for Hitler*. It begins as another *Ziegfield Follies* takeoff: German-themed showgirls parade down a staircase while a syrupy tenor sings:

> Springtime for Hitler and Germany
> Deutschland is happy and gay!

Haute couture: *Gary Beach, Matthew Broderick, Nathan Lane and Roger Bart in* The Producers. *Photo: Paul Kolnik*

We're marching to a faster pace
Look out, here comes the master race!

Dancing storm troopers strut their stuff, and then the star of Franz Liebkind's *magnum opus* appears at the top of the staircase, replying to a volley of "Heil Hitler"'s with

Heil myself,
Heil to me,
I'm the Kraut who's out to change our history!
Heil myself,
Raise your hand,
There's no greater dictator in the land!
Everything I do, I do for you!
If you're looking for a war, here's World War Two!
Heil myself,
Raise your beer
Ev'ry hotsy-totsy Nazi stand and cheer!

And the number ends with the hotsy-totsy Nazis in a great big Busby Berkeley finish!

Not everyone thinks this is funny. Freud explains that laughter comes from the release of psychic tension, and Hitler, God knows, still generates plenty of that. But where the tension is too strong to be released, there is no laughter. And so there were indignant letters in the newspapers, and one man even took out an ad in the *New York Times* to register his "pain and dismay":

> I was horrified by the trivialization of Adolph Hitler, Nazi uniforms and swastikas. [. . .] Laughter may sometimes be the "best medicine," but it becomes poison when it desecrates the memory of millions who were brutally slaughtered.

But it is not their memory, but Hitler's, that is desecrated. (Imagine what *he* would have thought of *The Producers*.)

Mel Brooks, who fought the Nazis in World War II, is a Jew working here in a Jewish tradition of gallows humor, a characteristically Jewish response to Jewish history. As a non-indignant letter to the *Times* points out,

> This kind of humor derives from synagogue Purim plays in which the would-be genocidal Vizier Haman, is usually portrayed by a child in oversized but portentous clothes and Chaplinesque shoes, topped by Haman's death-signifying tricorn hat. The murderous villain is reduced to a clown who makes us laugh, and his mythic importance is deflated.

By portraying someone, you exercise control over him. For the moment, he is what you make him. Of course Hitler was not in fact a silly song-and-dance man. But *The Producers* is a fantasy, not a documentary. The joke *depends* on Hitler's evil power; without it, there would be no tension to discharge. But "Springtime for Hitler" is a comic song of triumph over that power.

"Springtime for Hitler" is what everybody remembers best about the movie, and about the musical. But *The Producers* is not really about Hitler. As he himself sings at one point,

> The thing you gotta know is,
>
> Everything is show biz.

The Producers is about Max Bialystock and Leo Bloom, the producers, and their joyful Cloud-Cuckoo-Land of show business.

2000–2001 Best Play

PROOF

By David Auburn

○○○○○

Essay by Bruce Weber

CATHERINE: I didn't find it.

HAL: Yes you did.

CATHERINE: No.

CLAIRE: Well, did you find it or did Hal find it?

HAL: I didn't find it.

CATHERINE: I didn't find it. I wrote it.

THE DIALOGUE ABOVE, which brings down the first act curtain in *Proof*, is a moment of revelation that leaves audience members gasping with surprise. It takes place on the evening before the funeral of Robert, a world-class mathematician at the University of Chicago who was plagued by mental illness in the latter half of his life. Hal, his protégé and former student, has been going through his dozens of unexamined notebooks to determine if, amid the voluminous ramblings of a madman, any of them contain valuable work. And Robert's older daughter, Claire, has returned from New York to attend the funeral and to persuade her sister Catherine, who has aborted her own education to live with and care for their father, to move back with her.

Catherine, at 25, has already shown us she is quick-witted and both sexually provocative and provokable. She's also depressed, lonely and defensive, leaning toward paranoid. She is most calmly herself with the ghost of her father, who is consoling in the visit her imagination has conjured up. Indeed, her erratic behavior has made us suspect she may have inherited his mental illness. But as the first act ends she also lays claim to his genius—the "it" in the dialogue above is an original and important work of mathematics—and the question that leaps to mind is: Could this be possible?

This is the representative moment of *Proof*, the surprise critical and popular hit of the 2000–01 season that, with a kind of head-shaking respect for and appreciative amusement at their knotty inexplicability, examines

Math-minded: Mary-Louise Parker in David Auburn's Proof. *Photo: Joan Marcus*

parallel mysteries—the natures of genius and love. The revelatory curtain line before intermission is, for one thing, perfectly indicative of the play's tone, both serious and playful, intellectually piquing and show-bizzy, respectful of the audience and mindful of the playwright's duty to entertain.

It is, after all, an effective dramatic tactic, setting up the second act as, among other things, a whodunit (well, a whowroteit). And it raises an issue—whether qualities of mind can be inherited or more generally whether mental gifts and afflictions descend on people by fateful decree or as if mysteriously bequeathed—that is irresistibly ponderable.

Proof is a particularly tantalizing contribution to dramatic literature because the issue of suddenly emergent creativity is in many ways applicable to the play itself. Many critics, myself included, were left wondering the same thing about the playwright, David Auburn, as we were about his compelling protagonist. Auburn, after all, was just 31 when *Proof* was presented by the Manhattan Theatre Club, moved to Broadway and went on to win the Pulitzer Prize for drama and the Tony Award for best play. The odds that a writer so young and inexperienced—he had only one previously produced play to his credit—could have created *Proof* seemed as long as those of a largely untrained young woman solving a centuries-old problem in mathematics. Where does such acumen come from?

Not that it's so unusual for literary talent to surface early, but *Proof* has none of the earmarks of precocious playwriting. The language isn't particularly lyrical or idiosyncratic, the most frequently attention-grabbing characteristic of a new voice. The characters are not shockingly antisocial, generationally distinct, living on the societal fringe, prone to violence or even rebellious. And though the world of the play is a bit arcane—it's about people who pursue abstruse intellectual goals, after all—the play itself is not. Auburn, who has said that the high point of his own mathematical history was a B– in first-year calculus, isn't exactly bringing an exotic perspective to the table.

Indeed, the setting, the Hyde Park neighborhood of Chicago, and the set, the slightly ramshackle back porch of a weatherbeaten brick house, testifies to the very familiar tweed-and-flannel atmosphere of a college town. (John Lee Beatty's set for the original production was sensationally evocative and location-specific. Anyone who's ever lived in Chicago felt immediately at home.)

And certainly part of the appeal of the play is that even though three of the four characters are part of the distinct subculture that is fluent in the abstractions of number theory (Claire, who seems to have inherited none of her father's more troublesome characteristics, is the exception), contrary to stereotype they live in the same emotional universe as the rest of us. Mathematicians, it turns out, are people too. Consider the following speech by Catherine, an eloquently mundane expression of entirely comprehensible exasperation with her sister:

> CATHERINE: *Okay?* I really don't need this, Claire. I'm fine, you know, I'm totally fine, and then you swoop in here with these questions, and "Are you okay?" and your soothing tone of voice and "Oh the poor policemen"—I think the police can handle themselves!—and bagels and bananas and jojoba and "Come to New York" and vegetarian *chili*. I mean it really pisses me off so just *save* it."

The point is that the accomplishment of *Proof* is not of the sort that abashes critics and audiences with the revelation of something new in the theatrical universe. Rather, the play is most impressive for an evident mastery of stage convention that is rare enough among all playwrights—"well-made" is not a frequently applied adjective to "play" in this day and age—but particularly so among young playwrights because it is generally garnered only by experience. In *Proof*'s neat, economical and potent narrative structure, in its astute appropriation from hoary genres like the detective story and the psychological thriller, in its reliance on characters who are defined not by their manner of speaking but their manner of thinking and behaving—these people are, in other words, credibly organic—Auburn has displayed an assuredness with craft that is well beyond his years.

Sister act: Johanna Day and Mary-Louise Parker in David Auburn's Proof. *Photo: Joan Marcus*

Much of this is apparent in the first act finale, the scene that culminates in the excerpt above. Beyond the clever manipulation of the dialogue to set up the beautifully timed curtain line—you're either completely surprised by Catherine's revelation or you see it coming only in the instant before she makes it—the scene provides a clearcut swiveling point for the play at intermission.

It brings to an abrupt and decisive close an opening act that seems to meander—it doesn't, really; it's far cagier than that—in its introduction of the four characters. And it immediately focuses our expectations for the second act on a single dramatic question: Who wrote the proof? Catherine or Robert? The result is that the plot takes on a whole new momentum. In spite of the touching flashback scenes, which fill in our knowledge of Catherine's relationship with her father and the history of his disease, the play moves irresistibly forward. The structure is terrifically skillful, as though at its midpoint the play had crested a hill and was suddenly pointed downward and home.

In the first act, of course, Auburn's aim is foreshadowing, and what is especially impressive about *Proof* is how much literary work gets done without our knowing it.

The wry beginning, in which Robert offers Catherine a birthday bottle of bad champagne, gives off just a whiff of something not being quite right in Robert's perspective on his daughter's life.

"Kid, I've seen you," he says. "You sleep till noon, you eat junk, you don't work, the dishes pile up in the sink."

Why does it seem as though he's emerging from the ether, as though he's been watching her and not living with her? Because he's dead, of course, because he's a figment of Catherine's desperate imagination. Not long afterward, when Robert bluntly acknowledges as much, Catherine is brought back to herself instantly.

"You died a week ago," she says dully. It's a moment full of meaning, suggesting at once that Catherine's bond with her father was intellectually and emotionally profound, that released from worry about him she's now worried about herself, that her sanity might very well be fragile. It informs the audience of the playwright's ease with stage artifice—using ghosts can be a hokey and thus dicey business—and it also puts us on notice that Auburn is a deft planter of seeds. Virtually every moment of the first act comes back to resonate in the second.

Perhaps the most subtle example of this is Catherine's conversation with Hal in which she tells him about Sophie Germain, the young female mathematician in 18th-century France who corresponded with Gauss, pretending to be a man.

> CATHERINE: The French Revolution was going on, the Terror. She had to stay inside for safety and she passed the time reading in her father's study. The Greeks . . . Later she tried to get a real education but the schools didn't allow women. So she wrote letters. She wrote to Gauss. She used a man's name. Uh — Antoine-August Le Blanc. She sent him some proofs involving a certain kind of prime number, important work. He was delighted to correspond with such a brilliant young man. Dad gave me a book about her.

It's an anomalous episode in the play, reliant on specific historic research and a kind of specialized erudition. (Auburn uses only one slightly arcane mathematical term in all of *Proof*, which represents the square root of negative one, an "imaginary" number, and that only to indulge a very good joke.) For that reason it is a striking moment but a puzzling one; in any case, it passes quickly, almost an extraneous diversion. Its significance surfaces only much later.

Catherine is no ardent feminist, but she is acutely aware of the paucity of female mathematicians and the prejudice against them. As it turns out she was using the story not only to flirt with Hal but to test him. Does he think as most men do, she wonders, that math is a men's-only game? Or is he as accepting as Gauss and her father?

That she judges Hal to have passed the test is one reason Catherine sleeps with him, and more importantly, one reason she entrusts to him the crucial notebook. This is not just simple plotting. The play would track without the Germain story; Catherine is hungry for affection, after all, reason enough for her to take Hal to bed, and taking him to bed is reason enough for her to want to reveal to him her secret.

Yet without our understanding of Catherine's attachment to Germain, her second-act breakdown would feel awfully prosaic, the result simply of romantic disappointment. She flips when Hal expresses what really is a very understandable skepticism about Catherine's claim to the authorship of the proof, but it isn't merely that she feels betrayed by a man whose trust she feels she's earned with bedroom intimacy. In addition, it's that what she fears most has been proven so; that who she believes she is, a mathematician, will always be denied. Catherine is possessed of a familiar kind of female frailty, yes. But at stake for her also is her grasp on a unique and deeply felt identity.

This adds a stratum of depth to Catherine that is essentially the difference between a contrived, easy-to-digest character and a believably

Best medicine: Mary-Louise Parker and Larry Bryggman share a laugh in David Auburn's Proof. *Photo: Joan Marcus*

rounded one. And appreciating the distinction is one essential difference between being a green playwright and a seasoned one.

Indeed, given by Auburn the capability and penchant for self-scrutiny, the other characters are similarly layered. Claire is not merely the self-satisfied and unsympathetic yuppie conformist that might satisfy a less gifted playwright; not only is she saddled with guilt for leaving the care of her father to Catherine, and disappointment for being the least intellectually gifted member of the family, she's also decent enough to acknowledge these things. Hal's role is written both to illustrate and debunk the stereotype of the socially inept math geek. And even in Robert's episodes of madness, he knows he owns brilliance; it's also true that in his brilliance he knows the other thing, the twisted tumult, is in him.

All of this—the unflashy, conversational language, the crafty structure that makes the story feel uncontrived, the characters who seem able to look at themselves independently of the playwright's puppeteering—is a gift, most of all, to the director and the performers.

One of the paradoxes of the playwright's art is that the more complete it appears, the more the writer seems to have thought of everything, the more it leaves depths and boundaries to be explored.

A well-made play with a consistent voice allows the director—in the case of the original production of *Proof*, Daniel Sullivan—to concentrate on narrative enhancement and deepening the colors of character more than dramaturgical troubleshooting. It calls, in other words, for creative work rather than repairs.

By the same token, a beautifully put together, well-rounded character is one that is *not* prescriptive, and anyone who was seen more than one performance of Mary-Louise Parker's virtuosic work in *Proof* will notice that her Catherine became more aggressive, tougher to impress, more resistant to sympathy as the play's run continued.

It was terrifically interesting and probing work on her part, and as the character changed, so the others in the cast—Ben Shenkman, Larry Bryggman and Johanna Day—responded in kind. A spinier Catherine made the rest of them necessarily more defensive. The play changed, became tenser—not better or worse, but different. It's a mark of a play's solidity that it encourages such continued actorly exploration, and though Ms. Parker has put an indelible stamp on the role, I write this as Jennifer Jason Leigh is about to replace her on Broadway—and my confidence in the play is strong enough that I will return to it eagerly to see the hidden strains of character that Ms. Leigh will unearth in Catherine.

This is, once again, the kind of thing one might say about the playwright as well as his creation. It's exciting to contemplate the strains of his talent that are—keep your fingers crossed—shortly to emerge.

2000–2001 Best Play

URINETOWN

Music and lyrics by Mark Hollmann
Book and lyrics by Greg Kotis

○○○○○

Essay by Jeffrey Sweet

OFFICER LOCKSTOCK: You're too young to understand it now, but nothing can kill a show like too much exposition.

LITTLE SALLY: How about bad subject matter?

OFFICER LOCKSTOCK: Well —

LITTLE SALLY: Or a bad title, even? That could kill a show pretty good.

URINETOWN IS INDEED A TITLE TO MAKE YOU CRINGE. The story is off-putting, too. The setting is a city where, because of a long-term drought and water shortage, the residents are legally compelled to go to privately owned toilets for relief. What's more, they have to pay for the privilege, a situation engineered by the corrupt Urine Good Company and its head, the contemptible Caldwell B. Cladwell. Between the hold Cladwell has on the legislature and Officer Lockstock's brutal police, few dare protest. Those who do challenge the system or try to avoid payment by relieving themselves in the bushes are dragged off to Urinetown and a fate unknown but undoubtedly unpleasant. (Urinetown, as narrator Lockstock informs us, is not where the story is set. It's a "mythical" location. And, oh yes, we should keep our eyes open for symbolism.)

The hero of the piece is Bobby Strong, who, as the show begins, is a lowly assistant at an amenity that caters to the poorest and most wretched members of society. His boss at the facility is a hard-boiled woman named Penelope Pennywise. No matter how desperately her customers plead, she won't allow a free pass, not even to Bobby's father. When Old Man Strong pees without authorization, Officer Lockstock and his associate, Officer Barrel, whisk him away to Urinetown.

Also on this day, Bobby meets Hope, a beautiful and well-to-do young woman home from a fancy college to begin a job faxing and copying in her father's office. Plot complication: her father is the evil Cladwell. (At this

Officer friendly: Jeff McCarthy and Spencer Kayden in Urinetown. *Photo: Joan Marcus*

point, of course, Hope is unaware of the evil her father does.) Strolling together at night, Bobby confides to Hope that he reproaches himself for not taking action when the authorities dragged away his father. Hope tells Bobby the best way to decide what to do is to listen to his heart.

Bobby's heart urges him to revolt against Urine Good Company. The next day, he commandeers the amenity, offering free relief to all. When Cladwell sends Lockstock and his minions to arrest Bobby and his followers, the rebels escape, taking Hope hostage.

Lured to Urine Good Company's headquarters by the prospect of negotiating a settlement with Cladwell, Bobby is seized and sent to Urinetown (this turns out to mean being thrown from the top of a tall building to his death). Hearing the news, a politically galvanized Hope persuades the rebels to shift her status from hostage to leader in Bobby's place. Together with her mother (oh yes, Penelope has revealed to Hope that she had an affair with Cladwell and Hope was the product of their passion), Hope leads an assault on her father and the privileged classes, who are themselves sent to Urinetown. The downtrodden having won, we are primed for a triumphant ending . . . and don't get it. But more on that later.

As I expect is apparent by now, *Urinetown* is a satire. The first clues are in the opening phrases of the overture—a strident marching theme reminiscent of Kurt Weill and Marc Blitzstein blasted out by trombone, clarinet, piano and drums as if to announce, "We're going to be brave and uncompromising and show you the truth, as ugly as it may be." The work of co-authors Mark Hollmann (music and lyrics) and Greg Kotis (book and lyrics) specifically refers to Blitzstein's *The Cradle Will Rock* and the Bertolt Brecht-Kurt Weill collaboration *The Rise and Fall of the City of Mahagonny*—both of which also introduce fictional corrupt cities to dramatize the evils of capitalism and give central roles to heroes who become martyrs by challenging the system.

If Hollmann and Kotis had restricted themselves to lampooning *Cradle* and *Mahagonny*, the show would have limited appeal. How many in the audience, after all, are likely to have sufficient familiarity with either of these pieces to enjoy a full evening of jokes at their expense? Rather, Hollmann and Kotis target the whole range of earnest musicals (good and bad) that embrace two contrary impulses—to proselytize and to entertain. On the one hand, the creators of such works as *Sweeney Todd*, *Les Misérables*, *Grand Hotel*, *Chicago* and *West Side Story* want to rouse the audience to the world's ills. On the other, they want to elicit laughs and applause.

Part of the problem with the "serious" musical lies in this contradiction. A mature political work is a call to the intellect. It asks that the audience engage its analytical skills, comparing and contrasting the philosophies and actions of the various characters. A musical, on the other hand, generally doesn't make a call to the part of the mind favoring the coolness of analysis, but to the part that responds giddily and uncritically to the delight of the senses.

A prime example of these impulses at cross purposes is found in Alain Boublil and Claude-Michel Schönberg's *Miss Saigon*. Pleading the pitiable circumstances of the abandoned illegitimate offspring of Asian women and American soldiers, an American veteran of the Vietnam war sobs as he sings a wrenching song called "Bui-Doi." As he sings, on a screen behind him is projected documentary footage featuring the haunting images of the real children. At the end of the number, what is one supposed to do—applaud the skillful histrionics of the actor playing the veteran or sit in silent respect for the innocent victims of war?

Hollmann and Kotis understand that this bind makes the Boublil-Schönberg school of writing an appropriate target of satire. Putting up a musical about peeing and representing it as social commentary is as appalling as exploiting footage of abandoned children for a round of applause. The difference, of course, is that Boublil and Schönberg are dead serious, and Hollmann and Kotis aren't.

Another difference, to my taste anyway, is that Mark Hollmann is a better composer than the soupy Schönberg. Even though the score consists of a series of parodies of song forms found in traditional musicals, an original melodic impulse bubbles under many of the numbers. The lyric of the song Hope sings to inspire Bobby, "Follow Your Heart," may be intentionally sappy ("We all want a world/Filled with peace and with joy/With plenty of justice/For each girl and boy. . . ."), but the tune is genuinely haunting. A choral declaration of police brutality ("Cop Song") builds to a percussive clatter that is as rhythmically infectious as a passage from *Stomp*.

Snuff her!: Jennifer Laura Thompson and the cast of Urinetown. *Photo: Joan Marcus*

The structure of the score also highlights the split nature of the form. When Hope is held prisoner by the rebels in their hideaway, her captors work themselves into a vengeful frenzy in Bobby's absence and spit out a tense number:

Look at us here
In a hole, on the lam
With our hearts full of fear
What a rip! What a sham!
Cops will be here
Bustin' heads mighty quick
But we'll beat them to the punch
When we snuff out that chick.

The cast then explodes into jazzy modern dance menacing Hope with contortions out of Bob Fosse and Jerome Robbins (at one point the ensemble, shoulders hunched in hostility, charges downstage in a quotation of *West Side Story*'s "Cool").

At the end of the number, Bobby Strong returns in time to save his beloved from destruction, changing the mood by launching into an inspirational song called, "Run, Freedom, Run." Within seconds, what had been a lynch mob turns into a hand-clapping gospel choir. In the script, "Snuff That Girl" ends on the bottom of page 69 and "Run, Freedom, Run" begins on the top of page 72. Is the transition remotely credible? Only in a musical. But Hollmann and Kotis have made their subversive point: both lynch mob and gospel choir can only occur when a group of people surrender their individual identities to group-think. Which, come to think of it, describes an audience, too. (Who has not found themselves swept up in a standing ovation for an undeserving show?)

And yes, the audience is also in the sights of the authors. After all, a critique of a popular form is necessarily a critique of the audience that, by embracing the form, makes it popular. In his script, Kotis explores the dynamic between an audience and a show in a series of dialogues between the narrator, Office Lockstock, and Little Sally. Little Sally is a comic summation of all of the innocents and orphans (think *Annie*, *Oliver!* and *Les Misérables*) who naively ask the simple questions that cut to the heart of the matter.

LITTLE SALLY: Say, Officer Lockstock, I was thinkin'. We don't spend much time on hydraulics, do we?

OFFICER LOCKSTOCK: Hydraulics?

LITTLE SALLY: You know, hydraulics. Hydration. Irrigation. Or just plain old laundry. Seems to me that with all the talk of water shortage

> and drought and what-not we might spend some time on those things, too. After all, a dry-spell would effect hydraulics too, you know.
>
> OFFICER LOCKSTOCK: Why, sure it would, Little Sally. But . . . how shall I put it. Sometimes—in a musical—it's better to focus on one big thing rather than a lot of little things. The audience tends to be happier that way. And it's easier to write.

A look at the authors' biographies suggests the roots of the work. Kotis took a BA in political science from the University of Chicago, moved into Chicago's lively improvisational theater scene, and worked with a troupe called the Neo-Futurists—which specialized in short, frequently satiric sketches. Hollmann lists among his credits a stint playing piano for Second City, Chicago's flagship improvisational theatre, also known for sketches. Parody is a common device of sketch humor, often employed to attack the cant and easy sentimentality that are the underpinning of a great deal of popular culture. In a society in which much of what people think they know about the world around them is gleaned from entertainment (e.g., people who watch *The Sopranos* and fancy themselves in the know about the workings of the mob in New Jersey), it is wise to be wary of the alleged information propelled our way from stages, screens and speaker systems. Hollmann and Kotis use parody to not only identify the weaknesses in what popular culture feeds us but the weaknesses in the audience that keeps swallowing these offerings without questioning their underlying assumptions.

Urinetown wouldn't work as well as it does if it weren't itself a highly accomplished piece of stage craft. After the disappointment of Neil Simon's *The Dinner Party*, it is refreshing to see director John Rando working at the peak of form. John Carrafa's choreography and musical staging are funny and fluid in themselves—even funnier if you can identify the specific paraphrases of and references to memorable numbers from the last 50 years of musical theater. Orchestrator Bruce Coughlin works magic similar to that he did with *Floyd Collins*, getting a wide variety of textures out of a four-piece band.

The cast is fully up to the challenges. In some cases, knowledge of their past credits enhances the experience. John Cullum, the hero of a fair number of landmark musicals, is the villain Cladwell; the man who once sang of optimism and human potential in *On a Clear Day You Can See Forever* here sings of social Darwinism and warns us "Don't Be the Bunny." Ken Jennings, the innocent Toby who went mad and dispatched the title character in the original production of *Sweeney Todd*, ratchets the madness up a notch or two as Hot Blades Harry, the most unbalanced of the rebels. Hunter Foster (a veteran of two Boublil-Schönberg epics) and Jennifer Laura

Money, not the bunny: John Cullum in Urinetown. *Photo: Joan Marcus*

Thompson have every lip-quivering moment to perfection as the doomed romantic leads, and Nancy Opel expertly calls to mind all the hard-luck musical theater dames from Lotte Lenya and Georgia Brown on.

The team that comes close to hijacking the evening are Jeff McCarthy as Lockstock and Spencer Kayden (another veteran of the Chicago improv scene) as Little Sally, but then they have the benefit of some of the evening's sharpest material. It is left to their characters to wrap up the story. As Lockstock informs us, Hope takes over Urine Good Company and indeed makes its facilities available to all for free. But in so doing, prone to sentimentality and the desire to be liked, she leads the community to ecological disaster. "What kind of musical is this?!" Little Sally protests. "The good guys finally take over and everything falls apart!" Hope eventually meets her father's fate, and the residents slide back into lives of desperation.

> LITTLE SALLY: I don't think many people are going to come see this musical, Officer Lockstock.
>
> OFFICER LOCKSTOCK: Why do you say that, Little Sally? Don't you think people want to be told that their way of life is unsustainable?
>
> LITTLE SALLY: That, and the title's awful.
>
> OFFICER LOCKSTOCK: I suppose you're right, Little Sally. I do suppose you're right.

LITTLE SALLY: Can't we do a happy musical next time?

OFFICER LOCKSTOCK: If there is a next time I'm sure we can.

In 1985, Neil Postman published a critique of popular culture's baleful influence on our ability to deal maturely with public issues called *Amusing Ourselves to Death*. It could well be the subtitle of *Urinetown*.

PLAYS PRODUCED IN NEW YORK

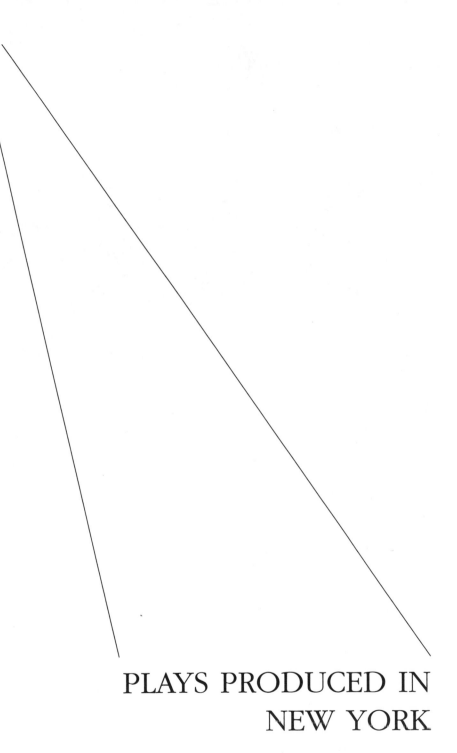

PLAYS PRODUCED ON BROADWAY

○○○○○

FIGURES IN PARENTHESES following a play's title give the number of performances. These figures do not include previews or extra nonprofit performances. In the case of a transfer, the Off Broadway run is noted but not added to the figure in parentheses.

Plays marked with an asterisk (*) were still in a projected run June 1, 2001. Their number of performances is figured through May 31, 2001.

In a listing of a show's numbers—dances, sketches, musical scenes, etc.—the titles of songs are identified wherever possible by their appearance in quotation marks (").

HOLDOVERS FROM PREVIOUS SEASONS

BROADWAY SHOWS THAT WERE RUNNING on June 1, 2000 are listed below. More detailed information about them appears in previous *Best Plays* volumes of the years in which they opened. Important cast changes since opening night are recorded in the Cast Replacements section of this volume.

Cats (7,485; longest-running show in Broadway history). Musical based on *Old Possum's Book of Practical Cats* by T.S. Eliot; music by Andrew Lloyd Webber; additional lyrics by Trevor Nunn and Richard Stilgoe. Opened October 7, 1982. (Closed September 10, 2000)

***Les Misérables** (5,859). Musical based on the novel by Victor Hugo; book by Alain Boublil and Claude-Michel Schönberg; lyrics by Herbert Kretzmer; original French text by Alain Boublil and Jean-Marc Natel; additional material by James Fenton. Opened March 12, 1987.

***The Phantom of the Opera** (5,570). Musical adapted from the novel by Gaston Leroux; book by Richard Stilgoe and Andrew Lloyd Webber; music by Andrew Lloyd Webber; lyrics by Charles Hart; additional lyrics by Richard Stilgoe. Opened January 26, 1988.

Miss Saigon (4,097). Musical with book by Alain Boublil and Claude-Michel Schönberg; music by Claude-Michel Schönberg; lyrics by Richard Maltby Jr. and Alain Boublil; additional material by Richard Maltby Jr. Opened April 11, 1991. (Closed January 28, 2001)

***Beauty and the Beast** (2,891). Musical with book by Linda Woolverton; music by Alan Menken; lyrics by Howard Ashman and Tim Rice. Opened April 18, 1994.

***Rent** (2,125). Transfer from Off Broadway of the musical with book, music and lyrics by Jonathan Larson. Opened Off Off Broadway January 26, 1996 and Off Broadway

February 13, 1996 where it played 56 performances through March 31, 1996; transferred to Broadway April 29, 1996.

***Chicago** (1,894). Revival of the musical based on the play by Maurine Dallas Watkins; book by Fred Ebb and Bob Fosse; music by John Kander; lyrics by Fred Ebb; original production directed and choreographed by Bob Fosse. Opened November 14, 1996.

Jekyll & Hyde (1,543). Musical based on the novella *The Strange Case of Dr. Jekyll and Mr. Hyde* by Robert Louis Stevenson; conceived by Steve Cuden and Frank Wildhorn; book and lyrics by Leslie Bricusse; music by Frank Wildhorn. Opened April 28, 1997. (Closed January 7, 2001)

***The Lion King** (1,482). Musical adapted from the screenplay by Irene Mecchi, Jonathan Roberts and Linda Woolverton; book by Roger Allers and Irene Mecchi; music by Elton John; lyrics by Tim Rice; additional music and lyrics by Lebo M, Mark Mancina, Jay Rifkin, Julie Taymor and Hans Zimmer. Opened November 13, 1997.

***Cabaret** (1,292). Revival of the musical based on the play by John Van Druten and stories by Christopher Isherwood; book by Joe Masteroff; music by John Kander; lyrics by Fred Ebb. Opened March 19, 1998.

Footloose (708). Musical based on the original screenplay by Dean Pitchford; adapted by Dean Pitchford and Walter Bobbie; music by Tom Snow; lyrics by Dean Pitchford. Opened October 22, 1998. (Closed July 2, 2000)

***Fosse** (1,001). Dance revue with choreography by Bob Fosse; conceived by Richard Maltby Jr., Chet Walker and Ann Reinking; artistic advisor, Gwen Verdon. Opened January 14, 1999.

***Annie Get Your Gun** (938). Revival of the musical with book by Herbert and Dorothy Fields as revised by Peter Stone; music and lyrics by Irving Berlin. Opened March 4, 1999.

Dame Edna: The Royal Tour (297). Solo performance piece by Barry Humphries; devised and written by Barry Humphries; additional material by Ian Davidson. Opened October 17, 1999. (Closed July 2, 2000)

Saturday Night Fever (502). Musical based on the Paramount/RSO picture based on a story by Nik Cohn, screenplay by Norman Wexler; stage adaptation by Nan Knighton in collaboration with Arlene Phillips, Paul Nicholas and Robert Stigwood; songs by the Bee Gees (B. R. and M. Gibb). Opened October 21, 1999. (Closed December 31, 2000)

***Kiss Me, Kate** (640). Revival of the musical with book by Sam and Bella Spewack, music and lyrics by Cole Porter. Opened November 18, 1999.

Swing! (461). Musical revue by various authors (see 1999-2000 *Best Plays*). Opened December 9, 1999. (Closed January 14, 2001)

Much Ado About Everything (183). Solo performance by Jackie Mason; written by Jackie Mason. Opened December 30, 1999. (Closed July 30, 2000)

True West (154). Revival of the play by Sam Shepard. Opened March 9, 2000. (Closed July 29, 2000)

***Riverdance on Broadway** (515). Return engagement of the dance and music revue with music and lyrics by Bill Whelan. Opened March 16, 2000.

A Moon for the Misbegotten (120). Revival of the play by Eugene O'Neill. Opened March 19, 2000. (Closed July 2, 2000)

***Aida** (496). Musical suggested by the Giuseppe Verdi opera; book by Linda Woolverton, Robert Falls and David Henry Hwang; music by Elton John, lyrics by Tim Rice. Opened March 23, 2000.

***Lincoln Center Theater** production of ***Contact** (489). Dance play by Susan Stroman and John Weidman; written by John Weidman. Opened March 30, 2000.

The Ride Down Mt. Morgan (120). Revival of the play by Arthur Miller. Opened April 9, 2000. (Closed July 23, 2000)

Copenhagen (326). By Michael Frayn. Opened April 11, 2000. (January 21, 2001)

The Wild Party (68). Musical based on the poem by Joseph Moncure March; book by Michael John LaChiusa and George C. Wolfe; music and lyrics by Michael John LaChiusa. Opened April 13, 2000. (Closed June 11, 2001)

Jesus Christ Superstar (161). Revival of the musical by Andrew Lloyd Webber, lyrics by Tim Rice. Opened April 16, 2000. (Closed September 3, 2000)

The Real Thing (136). Revival of the play by Tom Stoppard. Opened April 17, 2000. (Closed August 13, 2000)

The Green Bird (56). By Carlo Gozzi; translated by Albert Bermel and Ted Emery; original music, Elliot Goldenthal. Opened April 18, 2000. (Closed June 4, 2000)

Taller Than a Dwarf (56). By Elaine May. Opened April 24, 2000. (Closed June 11, 2000)

***Meredith Willson's The Music Man** (454). Revival of the musical with book, music and lyrics by Meredith Willson; story by Meredith Willson and Franklin Lacey. Opened April 27, 2000.

Roundabout Theatre Company production of **Uncle Vanya** (49). Revival of the play by Anton Chekhov. Opened April 30, 2000. (Closed June 11, 2000)

Dirty Blonde (352). By Claudia Shear; conceived by Claudia Shear and James Lapine. Opened May 1, 2000. (Closed March 4, 2001)

PLAYS PRODUCED JUNE 1, 2000–MAY 31, 2001

Macbeth (13). Revival of the tragedy by William Shakespeare. Produced by SFX Theatrical Group and Emanuel Azenberg at the Music Box. Opened June 15, 2000. (Closed June 25, 2000)

Seyton ... Peter Gerety
Witches ... Myra Lucretia Taylor, Starla Benford, Kelly Hutchinson
Duncan ... Peter Michael Goetz
Malcolm ... Sam Breslin Wright
Ross ... Michael Gross
Macbeth ... Kelsey Grammer
Banquo ... Stephen Markle
Lennox ... Ty Burrell
Lady Macbeth ... Diane Venora
Fleance ... Jacob Pitts
A Porter ... Peter Gerety
Macduff ... Bruce A. Young
Donalbain ... Austin Lysy
An Old Man ... Peter Michael Goetz
Murderers ... John Ahlin, Mark Mineart
Lady Macduff ... Kate Forbes
Her Son ... Grant Rosenmeyer

Her Daughter .... Parris Nicole Cisco
An English Doctor .... Peter Michael Goetz
A Scottish Doctor .... John Ahlin
Gentlewoman .... Kelly Hutchinson
A Servant .... Jacob Pitts
Young Siward .... Austin Lysy
Siward .... Peter Michael Goetz

Understudies: Miss Venora—Kate Forbes; Mr. Wright—John Ahlin; Mr. Markle—Mark Mineart; Miss Forbes—Starla Benford; Mr. Gerety—John Ahlin; Mr. Goetz—John Ahlin; Mr. Young—Ty Burrell; Misses Taylor, Benford, Hutchinson—Starla Benford, Kate Forbes; Mr. Burrell—Mark Mineart; Mr. Lysy—Jacob Pitts; Mr. Pitts—Austin Lysy; Mr. Wright—Austin Lysy, Jacob Pitts.

Directed by Terry Hands; original music, Colin Towns; set and costume design, Timothy O'Brien; lighting, Mr. Hands; sound, Tom Morse; fight direction, B.H. Barry; executive producers, Lynn Landis, SFX Theatrical Group; associate producer, Ginger Montel; casting, Jay Binder; production stage manager, John M. Galo; stage manager, Jenny Dewar; press, John Barlow, Michael Hartman, Wayne Wolfe.

Revival of Shakespeare's "Scottish play" about a married couple with designs on the crown. The last major New York revival featured Alec Baldwin and Angela Bassett in a Joseph Papp Public Theater/New York Shakespeare Festival engagement that opened 3/15/98 for 17 performances.

Roundabout Theatre Company production of **The Man Who Came to Dinner** (85). Revival of the comedy by Moss Hart and George S. Kaufman. Todd Haimes artistic director, Ellen Richard managing director, Julia C. Levy executive director of external affairs, at the American Airlines Theatre. Opened July 27, 2000. (Closed October 8, 2000)

Mrs. Stanley .... Linda Stephens
Miss Preen .... Mary Catherine Wright
Richard Stanley .... Zach Shaffer
John .... Jeffrey Hayenga
June Stanley .... Mary Catherine Garrison
Sarah .... Julie Boyd
Mrs. Dexter .... Kit Flanagan
Mrs. McCutcheon .... Julie Halston
Mr. Stanley .... Terry Beaver
Maggie Cutler .... Harriet Harris
Dr. Bradley .... William Duell
Sheridan Whiteside .... Nathan Lane
Harriet Stanley .... Ruby Holbrook
Bert Jefferson .... Hank Stratton
Professor Metz .... Stephen DeRosa
Prison Guard .... Hans Hoffman
Prisoners .... Michael Bakkensen, Ian Blackman, André Steve Thompson
Expressmen (Act II) .... Michael Bakkensen, Ian Blackman
Sandy .... Ryan Shively
Lorraine Sheldon .... Jean Smart
Beverly Carlton .... Byron Jennings
Mr. Westcott .... Ian Blackman
Radio Technicians .... Hans Hoffman, André Steve Thompson
Choir Boys .... Jack Arendt, Zachary Eden Bernhard, Jozef Fahey, Brandon Perry, Matthew Salvatore, Ryan Torino
Banjo .... Lewis J. Stadlen
Deputies .... Michael Bakkensen, Hans Hoffman
Police Officer .... Ian Blackman
Expressmen (Act III) .... Ian Blackman, André Steve Thompson

Standbys: Mr. Lane—Robert Ari. Understudies: Messrs. Beaver, DeRosa—Ian Blackman; Miss Harris—Julie Boyd; Mr. Stadlen—Stephen DeRosa; Misses Garrison, Holbrook—Kit Flanagan; Misses Wright, Smart—Julie Halston; Mr. Shaffer—Jeffrey Hayenga; Messrs. Duell, Stratton, Jennings—Michael McKenzie; Misses Boyd, Flanagan, Halston—Kathleen McKiernan; Mr. Shively—Michael Bakkensen; Mr. Blackman—Hans Hoffman; Miss Garrison—Amelia Nickles; Messrs. Shaffer, Bakkensen, Blackman, Thompson, Hoffman—Brian Schreier.

Directed by Jerry Zaks; scenery, Tony Walton; costumes, William Ivey Long; lighting, Paul Gallo; sound, Peter Fitzgerald; casting, Jim Carnahan; production stage manager, Andrea J. Testani; press, Boneau/Bryan-Brown.

Time: The Christmas holiday season in the 1930s. Place: The home of Mr. and Mrs. Stanley, in a small Ohio town. Presented in three parts.

A noisome celebrity disturbs the peace of a midwestern family in this comic revival. A *Best Plays* choice in 1939–40, it first opened on Broadway at the Music Box 10/16/39 for 739 performances.

Gore Vidal's The Best Man (121). Revival of the play by Gore Vidal. Produced by Jeffrey Richards, Michael B. Rothfeld, Raymond J. Greenwald, Jerry Frankel, Darren Bagert at the Virginia Theatre. Opened September 17, 2000. (Closed December 31, 2000)

The Candidates
Secretary William Russell .... Spalding Gray
Alice Russell, his wife .... Michael Learned
Dick Jensen,
his campaign manager .... Mark Blum
Catherine,
a campaign aide .... Kate Hampton
Senator Joseph Cantwell .... Chris Noth
Mabel Cantwell,
his wife .... Christine Ebersole
Don Blades,
his campaign manager ....Jordan Lage

The Party
Ex-President
Arthur Hockstader .... Charles Durning
Mrs. Sue-Ellen Gamadge,
Chairman of the Women's
Division .... Elizabeth Ashley

Senator Clyde Carlin .... Ed Dixon
Delegates ....Joseph Culliton,
Joseph Costa, Patricia Hodges,
C.J. Wilson, Lee Mark Nelson

The Visitors
Dr. Artinian,
a psychiatrist ....Michael Rudko
Sheldon Marcus .... Jonathan Hadary

The Press
First Reporter .... Joseph Culliton
Second Reporter ....Joseph Costa
Third Reporter .... Patricia Hodges
Fourth Reporter .... C.J. Wilson
Fifth Reporter .... Lee Mark Nelson
Additional Reporters
and Hotel Staff .... Kate Hampton,
Michael Rudko
News Commentator .... Walter Cronkite

Standbys: Mr. Gray—Joseph Culliton; Mr. Noth—C.J. Wilson; Mr. Durning—Ed Dixon; Ms. Learned—Patricia Hodges; Ms. Ebersole—Kate Hampton, Patricia Hodges; Mr. Blum—Joseph Costa, Lee Mark Nelson; Mr. Lage—Lee Mark Nelson, C.J. Wilson; Miss Ashley—Patricia Hodges; Mr. Dixon—Joseph Costa; Mr. Rudko—Joseph Costa, Joseph Culliton; Mr. Hadary—Michael Rudko; Misses Hampton, Hodges—Carol Halstead; Messrs. Culliton, Costa, Wilson, Nelson—Carol Halstead.

Directed by Ethan McSweeny; scenery, John Arnone; costumes, Theoni V. Aldredge; lighting, Howell Binkley; original music and sound, David Van Tieghem; associate producers, Francis Finlay,

Odd trio: John Ritter, Henry Winkler and Len Cariou in Neil Simon's The Dinner Party. *Photo: Carol Rosegg*

Numerical attraction: Ben Shenkman and Mary-Louise Parker in David Auburn's Proof. *Photo: Joan Marcus*

Norma Langworthy, Louise Levathes; casting, Stuart Howard, Amy Schecter, Howard Meltzer; production stage manager, Jane Grey; stage manager, Matthew Farrell; press, Jeffrey Richards Associates, John Michael Moreno, Chloe Taylor.

Time: July 1960. Place: Philadelphia. The play was presented in two parts.

Election-time revival about backroom maneuvering by political candidates and their handlers in the heat of a national convention. A *Best Plays* choice in 1959–60, the first Broadway production opened at the Morosco Theatre 3/31/60 for 520 performances.

***The Dinner Party** (256). By Neil Simon. Produced by Emanuel Azenberg, Ira Pittelman, Eric Krebs, Scott Nederlander, ShowOnDemand.com and Center Theatre Group, Mark Taper Forum, Gordon Davidson at the Music Box. Opened October 19, 2000.

Claude Pichon	John Ritter	Mariette Levieux	Jan Maxwell
Albert Donay	Henry Winkler	Yvonne Fouchet	Veanne Cox
Andre Bouville	Len Cariou	Gabrielle Buonocelli	Penny Fuller

Understudies: Messrs. Ritter, Cariou—John Boyle; Misses Fuller, Maxwell—Jennifer Harmon; Miss Cox—Susie Spear.

Directed by John Rando; scenery, John Lee Beatty; costumes, Jane Greenwood; lighting, Brian MacDevitt; sound, Jon Gottlieb; associate producers, Ginger Montel, Marcia Roberts; casting, Jay Binder, Amy Lieberman; production stage manager, David O'Brien; stage manager, Lisa J. Snodgrass; press, Bill Evans and Associates, Jim Randolph, Jonathan Schwartz.

Time: The present. Place: A private dining room in a first-rate restaurant in Paris. Performed without an intermission.

A round-robin of relationship humor among three Parisian couples.

***Proof** (252). Transfer from Off Broadway of a play by David Auburn. Produced by Manhattan Theatre Club, Lynne Meadow artistic director, Barry Grove executive producer; Roger Berlind, Carole Shorenstein Hays, Jujamcyn Theaters, Ostar Enterprises, Daryl Roth, Stuart Thompson at the Walter Kerr Theatre. Opened October 24, 2000.

Robert .... Larry Bryggman
Catherine .... Mary-Louise Parker
Hal .... Ben Shenkman
Claire .... Johanna Day

Standbys: Misses Parker, Day—Caroline Bootle; Mr. Shenkman—Adam Dannheisser; Mr. Bryggman—Ron Parady.

Directed by Daniel Sullivan; scenery, John Lee Beatty; costumes, Jess Goldstein; lighting, Pat Collins; original music and sound, John Gromada; casting, Nancy Piccione, David Caparelliotis; production stage manager, James Harker; stage manager, Heather Cousens; press, Boneau/Bryan-Brown, Chris Boneau, Steven Padla, Rachel Applegate.

Time: The present. Place: The Chicago home of a mathematics genius and his daughter. The play was presented in two parts.

A young woman comes to terms with the loss of her father as she discovers the depth of her own talents and finds a potential mate. Transferred from Off Broadway's Manhattan Theatre Club (see Plays Produced Off Broadway section). A 2000–01 *Best Plays* choice (see essay by Bruce Weber in this volume); recipient of the Pulitzer Prize in Drama and the Tony Award for Best Play.

***The Full Monty** (249). Musical with book by Terrence McNally; music and lyrics by David Yazbek. Produced by Fox Searchlight Pictures, Lindsay Law, Thomas Hall at the Eugene O'Neill Theatre. Opened October 26, 2000.

Georgie Bukatinsky .... Annie Golden
Buddy "Keno" Walsh .... Denis Jones
Reg Willoughby .... Todd Weeks
Jerry Lukowski .... Patrick Wilson
Dave Bukatinsky .... John Ellison Conlee
Malcolm MacGregor .... Jason Danieley
Ethan Girard .... Romain Frugé
Nathan Lukowski (Tues., Wed. mat., Fri., Sat. mat.) .... Thomas Michael Fiss
Nathan Lukowski (Wed. eve, Thur., Sat. eve, Sun.) .... Nicholas Cutro
Susan Hershey .... Laura Marie Duncan
Joanie Lish .... Jannie Jones
Estelle Genovese .... Liz McConahay
Pam Lukowski .... Lisa Datz
Teddy Slaughter .... Angelo Fraboni
Molly MacGregor .... Patti Perkins
Harold Nichols .... Marcus Neville

Struttin' it: The men of The Full Monty. *Photo: Craig Schwartz*

Vicki Nichols .... Emily Skinner
Jeanette Burmeister .... Kathleen Freeman
Noah "Horse" T. Simmons .... André De Shields
Police Sergeant .... C.E. Smith
Minister ....Jay Douglas
Tony Giordano ....Jimmy Smagula

Orchestra: Kimberly Grigsby conductor; Zane Mark associate conductor, keyboard; Ronald Sell music coordinator; Lino Gomez, Paul Vercesi reeds; Bob Millikan, Kevin Batchelor trumpet; Michael Boschen, Herb Besson trombone; Dan Lipton piano; Steve Bargonetti guitar; Chris Smylie bass; Dean Sharenow drums; Howard Joines percussion.

Swings: Sue-Anne Morrow, Jason Opsahl, Matthew Stocke, Ronald Wyche.

Understudies: Ms. Golden—Laura Marie Duncan, Jannie Jones, Sue-Anne Morrow; Mr. Jones—Angelo Fraboni; Mr. Wilson—Jay Douglas, Matthew Stocke; Mr. Conlee—Jimmy Smagula; Mr. Neville—Todd Weeks; Mr. Danieley—Jay Douglas, Jason Opsahl; Mr. Frugé—Denis Jones, Jason Opsahl; Miss McConahay—Laura Marie Duncan, Sue-Anne Morrow; Ms. Datz—Laura Marie Duncan, Sue-Anne Morrow; Ms. Skinner—Liz McConahay, Laura Marie Duncan; Ms. Freeman—Patti Perkins; Mr. De Shields—C.E. Smith, Ronald Wyche.

Directed by Jack O'Brien; choreography, Jerry Mitchell; music direction, vocal and incidental music arrangements, Ted Sperling; scenery, John Arnone; costumes, Robert Morgan; lighting, Howell Binkley; sound, Tom Clark; orchestrations, Harold Wheeler; dance music arrangements, Zane Mark; casting, Liz Woodman; production stage manager, Nancy Harrington; stage manager, Judy Baldauff; press, Barlow-Hartman Public Relations, Michael Hartman, John Barlow, Wayne Wolfe.

Time: The present. Place: Buffalo, New York. The play was presented in two parts.

Musical adaptation of British film about down-on-their-luck factory workers who decide that stripping is a good way to earn some extra cash. First performed at San Diego's Old Globe Theatre on May 23, 2000.

ACT I

Overture .... Orchestra
"Scrap" .... Jerry, Dave, Malcolm, Ethan, Reg and the Men
"It's A Woman's World" .... Georgie, Susan, Joanie and Estelle
"Man" .... Jerry and Dave
"Big-Ass Rock" .... Jerry, Dave and Malcolm
"Life With Harold" .... Vicki
"Big Black Man" .... Horse and the Guys
"You Rule My World" .... Dave and Harold
"Michael Jordan's Ball" .... The Guys

ACT II

Entr'acte .... Orchestra
"Jeanette's Showbiz Number" .... Jeanette and the Guys
"Breeze Off the River" ....Jerry
"The Goods" .... The Guys and the Women
"You Walk with Me" .... Malcolm and Ethan
"You Rule My World" (Reprise) .... Georgie and Vicki
"Let it Go" .... The Guys and the Company

***The Tale of the Allergist's Wife** (240). Transfer from Off Broadway of a play by Charles Busch. Produced by Manhattan Theatre Club, Lynne Meadow artistic director, Barry Grove executive producer; Carole Shorenstein Hays, Daryl Roth, Stuart Thompson and Douglas S. Cramer at the Ethel Barrymore Theatre. Opened November 2, 2000.

Mohammed ....Anil Kumar
Marjorie .... Linda Lavin
Ira ....Tony Roberts
Frieda ....Shirl Bernheim
Lee ....Michele Lee

Understudies: Mr. Roberts—Jamie Ross; Mr. Kumar—Deep Katdare; Miss Bernheim—Rose Arrick; Misses Lavin, Lee—Jana Robbins.

Directed by Lynne Meadow; scenery, Santo Loquasto; costumes, Ann Roth; lighting, Christopher Akerlind; sound, Bruce Ellman, Brian Ronan; casting, Nancy Piccione, David Caparelliotis; production

Cocktails á trois*: Tony Roberts, Linda Lavin and Michele Lee in Charles Busch's* The Tale of the Allergist's Wife. *Photo: Joan Marcus*

stage manager, William Joseph Barnes; stage manager, Laurie Goldfeder; press, Boneau/Bryan-Brown, Chris Boneau, Jackie Green, Rachel Applegate.

Time: The present. Place: New York City. The play was presented in two parts.

Comedy about the paths to fulfillment explored by a middle-age New York woman. First presented at Manhattan Theatre Club on 2/29/00 for 56 performances.

Lincoln Center Theater production of **Patti LuPone "Matters of the Heart"** (19). André Bishop artistic director, Bernard Gersten executive producer, at the Vivian Beaumont Theater. Opened November 13, 2000. (Closed December 17, 2000.)

Featuring Patti LuPone and the Matters of the Heart Orchestra. Dick Gallagher piano; Rick Dolan first violin; Rob Taylor second violin; Richard Brice viola; Arthur Fiocco cello.

Conceived and directed by Scott Wittman; musical direction and arrangements, Dick Gallagher; costumes, Oscar de la Renta; additional dialogue, John Weidman; lighting, John Hastings; sound, Mark Fiore, production supervisor, Richard Hester; press, Philip Rinaldi.

The production was presented in two parts.

Limited run musical revue.

Roundabout Theatre Company production of **Betrayal** (90) Revival of the play by Harold Pinter. Todd Haimes artistic director, Ellen Richard managing director, Julia C. Levy executive director of external affairs, at the American Airlines Theatre. Opened November 14, 2000. (Closed February 4, 2001)

Emma	Juliette Binoche	Robert	John Slattery
Jerry	Liev Schreiber	Waiter	Mark Lotito

Understudies: Miss Binoche—Melissa Bowen; Messrs. Schreiber, Slattery, Lotito—Ray Virta.

Directed by David Leveaux; sets and costumes, Rob Howell; lighting, David Weiner; sound, Donald DiNicola; casting, Jim Carnahan; production stage manager, Arthur Gaffin; press, Boneau/Bryan-Brown. Adrian Bryan-Brown, Amy Jacobs.

Love's gaze: Juliette Binoche and Liev Schreiber in Harold Pinter's Betrayal. *Photo: Joan Marcus*

Setting: Scene 1—Pub. Scene 2—Later, Jerry's house. Study. Scene 3—Two years earlier. Flat. Winter. Scene 4—One year earlier. Robert and Emma's house. Autumn. Scene 5—One year earlier. Venice. Summer. Scene 6—Later. Flat. Scene 7—Later. Restaurant. Scene 8—Two years earlier. Flat. Summer. Scene 9—Three years earlier. Robert and Emma's house. Winter. The play was presented without intermission.

Revival of a tale of broken vows told in reverse order. A *Best Plays* choice in 1979–80, it first opened on Broadway at the Trafalgar Theatre1/5/80 for 170 performances.

***The Rocky Horror Show** (226). Book, music and lyrics by Richard O'Brien. Produced by Jordan Roth by arrangement with Christopher Malcolm, Howard Panter, Richard O'Brien at the Circle in the Square. Opened November 15, 2000.

Usherette .... Daphne Rubin-Vega
Usherette .... Joan Jett
Janet Weiss .... Alice Ripley
Brad Majors .... Jarrod Emick
Narrator .... Dick Cavett
Riff Raff .... Raúl Esparza
Magenta .... Daphne Rubin-Vega
Columbia .... Joan Jett
Frank 'N' Furter .... Tom Hewitt
Rocky .... Sebastian LaCause
Eddie .... Lea DeLaria
Dr. Scott .... Lea DeLaria
Phantoms .... Kevin Cahoon, Deidre Goodwin, Aiko Nakasone, Mark Price, Jonathan Sharp, James Stovall

Orchestra: Henry Aronson conductor, keyboard; John Korba associate conductor, synthesizer; Clint de Ganon drums; Irio O'Farrill electric bass; John Benthal guitar.

Understudies: Mr. Emick—John Jeffrey Martin, Jonathan Sharp; Ms. Ripley—Kristen Lee Kelly, Aiko Nakasone; Mr. Hewitt—Kevin Cahoon, James Stovall; Ms. Rubin-Vega—Deidre Goodwin,

---

Rocky madness: (opposite page, clockwise from top left) Jarrod Emick, Tom Hewitt, Alice Ripley, Dick Cavett, Raúl Esparza, Sebastian LaCause, Daphne Rubin-Vega, Joan Jett, Lea DeLaria in The Rocky Horror Show. *Original photos: Ari Mintz/© 2000 Newsday, Inc. Photo collage: Bob Kamp*

Aiko Nakasone; Ms. Jett—Kristen Lee Kelly, Aiko Nakasone; Mr. Esparza—Mark Price, John Jeffrey Martin; Mr. LaCause—Jonathan Sharp, John Jeffrey Martin; Ms. Delaria—James Stovall, Mark Price; Mr. Cavett—James Stovall, Kevin Cahoon.

Swings: John Jeffrey Martin, Kristen Lee Kelly.

Directed by Christopher Ashley; choreography, Jerry Mitchell; scenery, David Rockwell; costumes, David C. Woolard; lighting, Paul Gallo; sound design, T. Richard Fitzgerald, Domonic Sack; video design, Batwin and Robin Productions; musical direction, vocal arrangements, Henry Aronson; new orchestrations, Doug Katsaros; music coordinator, John Miller; original orchestration, Richard Hartley; original costumes, Sue Blane; sets and effects, Showmotion Inc.; assistant director, Jules Ochoa; assistant choreographer, Angie L. Schworer; casting, Bernard Telsey; production stage manager, Brian Meister; stage manager, Brendan Smith, Marisha Ploski; press, the Jacksina Company, Judy Jacksina, Heather Prince, Maribel Aguitar.

Time: Then and now. Place: Here and there. The production was presented in two parts.

Revival of a risqué musical spoof of horror films. The original Broadway production opened at the Belasco Theatre 3/10/75 for 32 performances.

ACT I

"Science Fiction Double Feature" .... Usherettes, Phantoms
"Damn It, Janet" .... Brad, Janet, Phantoms
"Over at the Frankenstein Place" .... Brad, Janet, Riff Raff, Phantoms
"The Time Warp" .... Riff Raff, Magenta, Columbia, Narrator and the Company
"Sweet Transvestite" .... Frank 'N' Furter, Brad, Riff Raff, Magenta, Columbia, Phantoms
"The Sword of Damocles" .... Rocky, Narrator and the Company
"I Can Make You a Man" .... Frank 'N' Furter and the Company
"Hot Patootie" .... Eddie and The Company
"I Can Make You a Man" (Reprise) .... Frank 'N' Furter and the Company

ACT II

"Touch-A-Touch-A-Touch Me" .... Janet, Magenta, Columbia, Phantoms
"Once in a While" .... Brad, Phantoms
"Eddie's Teddy" .... Dr. Scott, Narrator, Columbia, Frank 'N' Furter and the Company
"Planet Schmanet—Wise Up Janet Weiss" .... Frank 'N' Furter and the Company
"Floor Show/Rose Tint My World" .... Columbia, Rocky, Brad, Janet, Frank 'N' Furter and the Company
"I'm Going Home" .... Frank 'N' Furter and the Company
"Super Heroes" .... Brad, Janet, Narrator, Phantoms
"Science Fiction Double Feature" .... Usherette, Phantoms

The Search for Signs of Intelligent Life in the Universe (185). Revival of the one-woman performance piece by Jane Wagner. Produced by Lily Tomlin, Tomlin and Wagner Theatricalz in association with the Seattle Repertory Theatre and McCarter Theatre Center at the Booth Theatre. Opened November 16, 2000. (Closed May 20, 2001)

Featuring Lily Tomlin. Directed by Jane Wagner; scenery, Klara Zieglerova; lighting, Ken Billington; sound, Tom Clark, Mark Bennett; co-producer, Janet Beroza; stage manager, Ilyse Bosch; press, Barlow-Hartman Public Relations, John Barlow, Michael Hartman, Wayne Wolfe.

Time: The present. Place: Various locations. Presented in two parts.

Revival of one-woman show. The original Broadway production opened at the Plymouth Theatre 9/26/85 for 398 performances.

ACT I

Lily .... Booth Theatre–New York City
Trudy .... 49th and Broadway–New York City
Lily .... Booth Theare–New York City
Trudy .... 49th and Broadway–New York City

Li'l celebration: Lily Tomlin in the revival of Jane Wagner's The Search for Signs of Intelligent Life in the Universe. *Photo: Annie Leibovitz*

Agnus Angst	Anti Club–Indianapolis
Trudy	49th and Broadway–New York City
Chrissy	A Health Club–Los Angeles
Kate	A Beauty Salon–New York City
Paul	A Health Club–Los Angeles
Agnus	International House of Pancakes–Indianapolis
Lud and Marie	Suburban Home–Greenwood, Indiana
Trudy	A Pocket Park–New York City
Tina	A Pocket Park–New York City
Lud and Marie	Suburban Home–Greenwood, Indiana
Agnus	Anti Club–Indianapolis

ACT II

Trudy	A Pocket Park–New York City
Brandi and Tina	49th and Broadway–New York City
Trudy	Howard Johnson's–49th and Broadway
Lyn	A Backyard–California
Edie and Marge	Lyn's Reminiscence
Trudy	Outside Carnegie Hall–New York City
Kate	A Cocktail Lounge–New York City
Trudy	Outside the Booth Theatre

Seussical (197). Musical based on the works of Theodor Geisel (Dr. Seuss); book by Lynn Ahrens and Stephen Flaherty; music by Mr. Flaherty; lyrics by Ms. Ahrens; concept by Ms. Ahrens, Mr. Flaherty and Eric Idle. Produced by SFX Theatrical Group, Barry and Fran Weissler and Universal Studios at the Richard Rodgers Theatre. Opened November 30, 2000. (Closed May 20, 2001)

The Cat in the Hat .... David Shiner
Horton the Elephant .... Kevin Chamberlin
Gertrude McFuzz .... Janine LaManna
Mayzie LaBird .... Michele Pawk
JoJo .... Anthony Blair Hall
JoJo (Wed. eve.,
Sat. mat.) .... Andrew Keenan-Bolger
Sour Kangaroo .... Sharon Wilkins
The Mayor of Whoville .... Stuart Zagnit
Mrs. Mayor .... Alice Playten
Cat's Helpers .... Joyce Chittick,
Jennifer Cody, Justin Greer,
Mary Ann Lamb, Darren Lee, Jerome Vivona
General Genghis Kahn
Schmitz .... Erick Devine
Bird Girls .... Natascia Diaz,
Sara Gettelfinger,
Catrice Joseph
Wickersham Brothers .... David Engel,
Tom Plotkin,
Eric Jordan Young
The Grinch .... William Ryall
Vlad Vladikoff .... Darren Lee
Judge Yertle the Turtle .... Devin Richards
Marshal of the Court .... Ann Harada

Citizens of the Jungle of Nool, Whos, Mayor's Aids, Fish, Cadets, Hunters, Circus McGurkus Animals and Performers: Joyce Chittick, Jennifer Cody, Erick Devine, Natascia Diaz, David Engel, Sara Gettelfinger, Justin Greer, Ann Harada, Catrice Joseph, Eddie Korbich, Mary Ann Lamb, Darren Lee, Monique L. Midgette, Casey Nicholaw, Tom Plotkin, Devin Richards, William Ryall, Jerome Vivona, Sharon Wilkins, Eric Jordan Young.

Horton hearing: Kevin Chamberlin in Seussical.
Photo: David LaChapelle

Orchestra: David Holcenberg conductor; Steve Marzullo associate conductor, keyboard; Naomi Katz concertmaster; Karl Kawahara violin; Maxine Roach viola; Stephanie Cummins cello; Paul Sundfor, Dan Willis, John Winder woodwinds; Brian O'Flaherty, John Reid trumpet; Larry Farrell trombone; Jeffrey Lee Campbell, Jack Cavari guitar; Francisco Centeno electric bass; Warren Odze drums; Charles Descarfino percussion; Philip Fortenberry keyboard.

Understudies: Mr. Shiner—Eric Jordan Young; Mr. Chamberlin—Casey Nicholaw; Miss Pawk—Sara Gettelfinger; Miss LaManna—Jenny Hill; Miss Wilkins—Catrice Joseph, Monique L. Midgette; Mr. Zagnit—Casey Nicholaw; Miss Playten—Ann Harada; Mr. Devine—William Ryall; Misses Diaz, Gettelfinger, Joseph—Jenny Hill, Michelle Kittrell; Messrs. Engel, Plotkin, Young—Shaun Amyot, David Lowenstein; Misses Chittick, Cody, Greer, Lamb, Lee, Vivona—Shaun Amyot, Jenny Hill, Michelle Kittrell, David Lowenstein; Mr. Ryall—David Lowenstein; Mr. Lee—Shaun Amyot; Mr. Richards—David Lowenstein; Miss Harada—Jenny Hill.

Standby for The Cat in the Hat—Bryan Batt.

Swings: Shaun Amyot, Jenny Hill, Michelle Kittrell, David Lowenstein.

Directed by Frank Galati; choreography, Kathleen Marshall; scenery, Eugene Lee; costumes, William Ivey Long; lighting, Natasha Katz; sound, Jonathan Dean; vocal arranger, Stephen Flaherty; orchestrator, Doug Besterman; music director, David Holcenberg; music coordinator, John Miller; dance arranger, David Chase; associate director, Stafford Arima; associate choreographers, Rob Ashford, Joey Pizzi; executive producers, Gary Gunas, Alecia Parker; casting, Jay Binder, Sherry Dayton; stage managers, Andrew Fenton, Joshua Halperin; press, Barlow-Hartman Public Relations, John Barlow, Michael Hartman, Ash Curtis.

Musical based on the characters and situations in children's books by Theodor Geisel (Dr. Seuss).

ACT I

"Oh, The Thinks You Can Think!" .... The Cat in the Hat and the Company
"Horton Hears A Who" .... Bird Girls, Horton and Citizens of the Jungle of Nool
"Biggest Blame Fool" .... Sour Kangaroo, Horton, Wickersham Brothers, Bird Girls, Gertrude McFuzz, Mayzie LaBird, Citizens of the Jungle of Nool and the Cat
"Here On Who" .... Mayor of Whoville, Mrs. Mayor, the Grinch, Whos, Horton
"A Day for The Cat in The Hat" .... The Cat, JoJo and Cat's Helpers
"It's Possible" (McElligot's Pool) .... JoJo, the Cat and Fish
"How To Raise A Child" .... Mayor and Mrs. Mayor
"The Military" .... Gen. Genghis Kahn Schmiz, Mayor, Mrs. Mayor, JoJo and Cadets
"Alone In The Universe" .... Horton and JoJo
"The One Feather Tail of Miss Gertrude McFuzz" .... Gertrude
"Amayzing Mayzie" .... Mayzie, Gertrude and Bird Girls
"Amazing Gertrude" .... Gertrude, the Cat and Bird Girls
"Monkey Around" .... Wickersham Brothers
"Chasing The Whos" .... Horton, Sour Kangaroo, Bird Girls,
.... Wickersham Brothers, the Cat,
.... Vlad Vladikoff and Whos
"How Lucky You Are" .... The Cat
"Notice Me, Horton" .... Gertrude and Horton
"How Lucky You Are" (Reprise) .... Mayzie, Horton and the Cat
Act I Finale .... Full Company

ACT II

"How Lucky You Are" (Reprise) .... The Cat
"Egg, Nest, and Tree" .... Sour Kangaroo, Bird Girls, Wickersham Brothers, the Cat, Cat's Helpers and Hunters
"The Circus McGurkus" .... The Cat, Horton and the Circus McGurkus Animals and Performers
"The Circus on Tour" .... Horton
"Mayzie in Palm Beach" .... Mayzie, the Cat and Horton
"Solla Sollew" .... Horton, Animals and Performers, Mayor, Mrs. Mayor and JoJo
"The Whos' Christmas Pageant" .... The Grinch and Whos
"A Message From The Front" .... Gen. Schmitz, Mayor, Mrs. Mayor and Cadets
"Havin' a Hunch" .... The Cat, JoJo and Cat's Helpers
"All For You" .... Gertrude and Bird Girls
"The People Versus Horton the Elephant" .... Horton, Sour Kangaroo, Wickersham Brothers, Marshal, Judge Yertle the Turtle, Bird Girls, Gertrude, Mayor, Mrs. Mayor, JoJo, Whos and the Cat
"Finale"/ "Oh, The Thinks You Can Think!" .... Full Company

***Jane Eyre** (197). Musical with book by John Caird; music and lyrics by Paul Gordon; additional lyrics by John Caird. Based on the novel by Charlotte Brontë. Produced by Annette Niemtzow, Janet Robinson, Pamela Koslow, Margaret McFeeley Golden in association with Jennifer Manocherian, Carolyn Kim McCarthy at the Brooks Atkinson Theatre. Opened December 10, 2000.

Jane Eyre .... Marla Schaffel
Young Jane .... Lisa Musser
Young John Reed .... Lee Zarrett
Mrs. Reed .... Gina Ferrall
Mr. Brocklehurst .... Don Richard
Miss Scatcherd .... Marguerite MacIntyre
Marigold .... Mary Stout
Helen Burns .... Jayne Paterson
Schoolgirls .... Nell Balaban, Andrea Bowen, Elizabeth DeGrazia, Bonnie Gleicher, Rita Glynn, Gina Lamparella
Mrs. Fairfax .... Mary Stout
Robert .... Bruce Dow
Adele .... Andrea Bowen
Grace Poole .... Nell Balaban
Edward Fairfax Rochester .... James Barbour
Bertha .... Marguerite MacIntyre
Blanche Ingram .... Elizabeth DeGrazia
Lady Ingram .... Gina Ferrall
Mary Ingram .... Jayne Paterson
Young Lord Ingram .... Lee Zarrett
Mr. Eshton .... Stephen R. Buntrock
Amy Eshton .... Nell Balaban
Louisa Eshton .... Gina Lamparella
Colonel Dent .... Don Richard
Mrs. Dent .... Marguerite MacIntyre
Richard Mason .... Bill Nolte
The Gypsy .... Marje Bubrosa
Vicar .... Don Richard
St. John Rivers .... Stephen R. Buntrock

Dark lady: Marla Schaffel in Jane Eyre. *Photo: Joan Marcus*

Orchestra: Steven Tyler conductor; David Gursky associate conductor, keyboard; Antony Geralis assistant conductor, keyboard; Regis Iandiorio concertmaster; Rebekah J. Johnson, Mineko Yajima violin; Leo Grinhauz cello; Mark Vanderpoel bass; Helen Campo winds; John J. Moses clarinet, bass clarinet; Brian Greene oboe, English horn; Jerry W. Peel, French horn; Thomas Hoyt trumpet, flugelhorn; William Hayes percussion; Steven Withers keyboard.

Understudies: Miss Schaffel—Jayne Paterson, Gina Lamparella; Mr. Barbour—Stephen R. Buntrock, Bradley Dean; Miss Stout—Sandy Binion; Miss Ferrall—Sandy Binion, Erica Schroeder; Mr. Richard—Bradley Dean, Bruce Dow; Miss Paterson—Gina Lamparella, Erica Schroeder; Mr. Dow—Lee Zarrett, Bradley Dean; Miss Bowen—Rita Glynn, Bonnie Gleicher; Miss Balaban—Erica Schroeder, Sandy Binion; Miss MacIntyre—Sandy Binion; Miss DeGrazia—Gina Lamparella, Nell Balaban; Miss Lamparella—Erica Schroeder, Sandy Binion; Mr. Nolte—Bruce Dow, Don Richard; Miss Musser—Bonnie Gleicher, Rita Glynn; Mr. Zarrett—Bonnie Gleicher, Rita Glynn.

Swings: Sandy Binion, Bradley Dean, Erica Schroeder.

Directed by John Caird and Scott Schwartz; scenery, John Napier; costumes, Andreane Neofitou; lighting, Jules Fisher, Peggy Eisenhauer; sound, Mark Menard, Tom Clark; music contractor, Eugene Bianco; orchestration, Larry Hochman; music director and arranger, Steven Tyler; projections, John Napier, Lisa Podgur Cuscuna, Jules Fisher, Peggy Eisenhauer; associate scenic designer, Keith Gonzales; associate producer, Alison Farquhar; casting, Johnson-Liff Associates, Tara Rubin; production stage manager, Lori M. Doyle; stage manager, Debra A. Acquavella; press, the Publicity Office, Bob Fennell, Marc Thibodeau, Candi Adams, Michael S. Borowski.

Time: 1840's Place: Various locations in England. The play was presented in two parts.

Musical adaptation of the Brontë novel about a plain Jane who becomes a lady of the manor.

ACT I

"The Orphan" .... Jane
"Children of God" .... School Girls, Brocklehurst, Mrs. Reed, Scatcherd, Ensemble
"Forgiveness" .... Helen, Young Jane, Jane
"The Graveyard" .... Jane, Young Jane, Ensemble
"Sweet Liberty" .... Jane, Ensemble
"Perfectly Nice" .... Mrs. Fairfax, Adele, Jane
"As Good As You" .... Rochester
"Secret Soul" .... Jane, Rochester
"The Finer Thngs" .... Blanche
"Oh, How You Look In the Light" .... Rochester, Blanche, Ensemble
"The Pledge" .... Jane, Rochester
"Sirens" .... Rochester, Jane, Bertha

ACT II

"Things Beyond this Earth" .... Ensemble
"Painting Her Portrait" .... Jane
"In the Light of the Virgin Morning" .... Jane, Blanche
"The Gypsy" .... Gypsy
"The Proposal" .... Jane, Rochester
"Slip of a Girl" .... Mrs. Fairfax, Jane, Robert, Adele
"The Wedding" .... Ensemble
"Wild Boy" .... Rochester, Jane, Bertha, Ensemble
"Sirens" (Reprise) .... Jane, Rochester
"Farewell Good Angel" .... Rochester
"Forgiveness" (Reprise) .... Mrs. Reed, Jane, Ensemble
"The Voice Across the Moors" .... St. John, Jane, Rochester
"Poor Master" .... Mrs. Fairfax, Jane
"Brave Enough For Love" .... Jane, Rochester, Ensemble

***A Class Act** (115). Musical with book by Linda Kline and Lonny Price; music and lyrics by Edward Kleban. Produced by Marty Bell, Chase Mishkin and Arielle Tepper, in association with Manhattan Theatre Club, at the Ambassador Theatre. Opened March 11, 2001.

Lucy .... Donna Bullock
Bobby et al. .... David Hibbard
Ed .... Lonny Price
Felicia .... Sara Ramirez
Lehman .... Patrick Quinn
Charley et al. .... Jeff Blumenkrantz

Mona .... Nancy Anderson Sophie .... Randy Graff

Orchestra: David Loud conductor, keyboards; Dan Riddle associate conductor, keyboards; Eddie Salkin, William Sneddon woodwinds; Hollis Burridge, Matthew Peterson trumpet; Patrick Hallaran trombone; Peter Grant drums; Ray Kilday bass.

Standbys: Messrs. Price, Quinn—Danny Burstein; Messrs. Quinn, Hibbard, Blumenkrantz—Jonathan Hadley; Miss Anderson—Jamie Chandler-Torns; Misses Bullock, Graff, Ramirez—Ann Van Cleave.

Directed by Mr. Price; choreography, Marguerite Derricks; musical direction, additional arrangements, Mr. Loud; scenery, James Noone; costumes, Carrie Robbins; lighting, Kevin Adams; sound, Acme Sound Partners; orchestrations, Larry Hochman; music coordinator, John Miller; executive producer, East Egg Entertainment; associate producers, Robyn Goodman, Tokyo Broadcasting System/Kumiko Yoshii; casting, Jay Binder; production stage manager, Jeffrey M. Markowitz; stage manager, Heather Fields; press, Richard Kornberg, Tom D'Ambrosio, Don Summa.

Time: 1958–88. Place: The stage of the Shubert Theatre and other locations. The production was presented in two parts.

A celebration of the life and work of composer and lyricist Edward Kleban. Originally produced Off Broadway by the Manhattan Theatre Club 11/9/00 for 29 performances; previously developed by Musical Theatre Works.

Bye Bye Eddie: Members of the Broadway company of A Class Act. *Photo: Joan Marcus*

ACT I

Scene 1: Shubert Theatre, 1988
"Light on My Feet"* .... Ed and Company
Scene 2: Hillside Hospital, 1958
"The Fountain in the Garden" .... Company
"One More Beautiful Song" .... Ed and Sophie
Scene 3: Shubert Theatre, 1988
Scene 4: BMI Musical Theatre Workshop, 1966
"Fridays at Four" .... Company
"Bobby's Song" .... Bobby
"Charm Song" .... Lehman and Company
"Paris Through the Window"** .... Ed, Bobby, Charley
Scene 5: Ed's Apartment, 1966
"Mona" .... Mona

Scene 6: Recording Studio/Columbia Records, 1966–71
"Under Separate Cover" .... Lucy, Ed, Sophie
"Don't Do It Again" .... Felicia and Ed
"Gauguin's Shoes" .... Ed and Company
"Don't Do It Again" (Reprise) .... Lehman
Scene 7: Outside the Royal Alexandra Theatre, Toronto, 1972
"Follow Your Star" .... Sophie and Ed

* Additional lyrics by Brian Stein

** Additional lyrics by Glenn Slater

ACT II

Scene I: Shubert Theatre, 1988; Manhattan, 1973
"Better"† .... Ed and Company
Scene 2: Sophie's Laboratory, 1973
"Scintillating Sophie" .... Ed
"The Next Best Thing to Love" .... Sophie
Scene 3: Central Park, 1973
Scene 4: Michael Bennett's Studio, 1973
"Broadway Boogie Woogie" .... Lucy
Scene 5: The Public Theater, 1974–75
A Chorus Line excerpts§ .... Company
Scene 6: Manhattan, 1975–85
"Better" (Reprise)† .... Ed and Company
"I Choose You" .... Ed and Lucy
"The Nightmare" .... Ed
Scene 7: Sophie's Laboratory, 1985
"Say Something Funny" .... Company
Scene 8: BMI Musical Theatre Workshop, 1986
"I Won't Be There" .... Ed
Scene 9: St. Vincent's Hospital, 1987
"Self Portrait" .... Ed
Scene 10: Shubert Theatre, 1988
"Self Portrait" (Reprise) .... Company

† "Better" used with permission of the Kleban Foundation, Inc.

§ From *A Chorus Line*, conceived, choreographed and directed by Michael Bennett, book by James Kirkwood and Nicholas Dante, music by Marvin Hamlisch, lyrics by Edward Kleban.

Roundabout Theatre Company production of **Design for Living** (69). Revival of the comedy by Noël Coward. Todd Haimes artistic director, Ellen Richard managing director, Julia C. Levy executive director of external affairs, at the American Airlines Theatre. Opened March 15, 2001. (Closed May 13, 2001)

Gilda .... Jennifer Ehle
Ernest .... John Cunningham
Otto .... Alan Cumming
Leo .... Dominic West
Miss Hodge .... Jenny Sterlin
Mr. Birbeck .... Saxon Palmer
Grace .... Marisa Berensen
Henry .... T. Scott Cunningham
Helen .... Jessica Stone

Understudies: Misses Ehle, Stone, Mr. Palmer—Tina Benko; Messrs. Cumming, Cunningham—Saxon Palmer.

Standby Misses Sterlin, Berenson—Patricia Hodges.

Directed by Joe Mantello; scenery, Robert Brill; costumes, Bruce Pask; lighting, James Vermeulen; original music and sound, Douglas J. Cuomo; casting, Jim Carnahan, Amy Christopher; production stage manager, Andrea J. Testani; stage manager, Bradley McCormick; press, Boneau/Bryan-Brown, Adrian Bryan-Brown, Matt Polk, Kel Christofferson.

Time: 1930s. Place: Apartments in Paris, London and New York. The play was presented in two parts.

A crowd?: Dominic West, Jennifer Ehle and Alan Cumming in Noël Coward's Design for Living. *Photo: Joan Marcus*

Revival of the brittle tale of a love triangle between three members of the artsy Bohemian set. A *Best Plays* choice in 1932–33, it first opened on Broadway at the Ethel Barrymore Theatre 1/24/33 for 135 performances.

Judgment at Nuremberg (56). By Abby Mann. Produced by the National Actors Theatre, Tony Randall founder and artistic director, in association with Earle I. Mack at the Longacre Theatre. Opened March 26, 2001. (Closed May 13, 2001)

Narrator	Philip LeStrange
Colonel Parker	Robert Foxworth
Judge Haywood	George Grizzard
General Merrin	Jack Davidson
Captain Byers	Peter Francis James
Court Interpreter 1	Peter Hermann
Emil Hahn	Peter Maloney
Court Interpreter 2	Jurian Hughes
Fredrich Hoffstetter	Philip LeStrange
Werner Lammpe	Reno Roop
Oscar Rolfe	Michael Hayden
Ernst Janning	Maximilian Schell
Judge Norris	Henry Strozier
Judge Ives	Fred Burrell
Guard	Ty Jones
Dr. Wickert	Joseph Wiseman
Mrs. Habelstadt	Patricia Conolly
Mme. Bertholt	Marthe Keller
Rudolf Peterson	Michael Mastro
Geuter	Peter Kybart
Maria Wallner	Heather Randall
Thea	Kellie Overbey
Waiter	Peter Hermann
Elsa Lindnow	Susan Kellermann

Understudies: Mr. Schell—Peter Maloney; Mr. Grizzard—Jack Davidson; Messrs. Hayden, James, Mastro—Peter Hermann; Mr. Foxworth—Philip LeStrange; Messrs. Strozier, Burrell, Kybart—Reno Roop; Messrs. James, Hermann, Hughes—Ty Jones; Messrs. Wiseman, Davidson, Hermann—Peter Kybart; Misses Randall, Kellermann, Conolly—Jurian Hughes; Messrs. Maloney, Roop, LeStrange—Mitch Erickson.

Directed by John Tillinger; scenery, James Noone; costumes, Jess Goldstein; lighting, Brian MacDevitt; original music and sound, David Van Tieghem; projections, Elaine J. McCarthy; executive producer, Manny Kladitis; managing director, Fred Walker; casting, Jay Binder; production stage manager, Anita Ross; press, Springer/Chicoine Public Relations, Gary Springer, Joe Trentacosta, Susan Chicoine, Ann Guzzi, Michelle Moretta.

Time: 1947. Place: Nuremberg, Germany. The play was presented in two parts.

Stage adaptation of 1961 Academy Award-winning film about the human toll of war and crimes against humanity.

***Lincoln Center Theater** production of ***The Invention of Love** (73). By Tom Stoppard. André Bishop artistic director, Bernard Gersten executive producer, at the Lyceum Theatre. Opened March 29, 2001.

A.E. Housman, aged 77 .... Richard Easton
Charon .... Jeff Weiss
A.E. Housman,
aged 18–26 .... Robert Sean Leonard
Alfred Wiliam Pollard .... Michael Stuhlbarg
Moses John Jackson .... David Harbour
Mark Pattison;
W.T. Stead .... Peter McRobbie
Walter Pater;
Frank Harris .... Martin Rayner
John Ruskin;
Jerome K. Jerome .... Paul Hecht
Benjamin Jowett;
Henry Labouchère .... Byron Jennings
Robinson Ellis;
John Percival Postgate .... Guy Paul
Katherine Housman .... Mireille Enos
Chamberlain .... Mark Nelson
Chairman
of Selection Committee ...... Andrew McGinn
Oscar Wilde;
Bunthorne .... Daniel Davis

Ensemble: Neal Dodson, Brian Hutchison, Andrew McGinn, Matthew Floyd Miller, Peter A. Smith, David Turner.

Understudies: Mr. Easton—Martin Rayner; Mr. Leonard—Matthew Floyd Miller; Mr. Nelson—Peter A. Smith; Mr. Stuhlbarg—David Turner; Mr. Harbour—Brian Hutchison; Messers. Weiss, McGinn—Julian Gamble; Mr. McRobbie—Andrew McGinn; Mr. Rayner—Guy Paul; Mr. Hecht—Julian Gamble; Mr. Jennings—Guy Paul; Mr. Paul—Andrew McGinn; Miss Enos—Caitlin Muelder; Mr. Nelson—Peter A. Smith; Mr. Davis (Oscar Wilde)—Julian Gamble; Mr. Davis (Bunthorne)—Andrew McGinn; Ensemble—Aaron Krohn.

Directed by Jack O'Brien; scenery and costumes, Bob Crowley; lighting, Brian MacDevitt; sound, Scott Lehrer; original music, Bob James; assistant director, Matt August; casting, Daniel Swee; stage manager, Susie Cordon; press, Philip Rinaldi.

Execution of justice: Maximilian Schell and George Grizzard in Abby Mann's Judgment at Nuremberg. *Photo: Joan Marcus*

Time: Various dates in the Victorian era. Place: England and the netherworld. The play was presented in two parts.

The imagined story of A.E. Housman's passion for language, poetry, the meaning of meaning, and a man. A 2000–01 *Best Plays* choice (see essay by Charles Wright in this volume), it also received the New York Drama Critics Circle Award for best play.

***Stones in His Pockets** (80). By Marie Jones. Produced by Paul Elliott, Adam Kenwright, Pat Moylan, Ed and David Mirvish, and Azenberg/Pittelman, at the John Golden Theatre. Opened April 1, 2001.

Charlie Conlon .... Conleth Hill
Jake Quinn .... Seán Campion

Celluloid hopefuls: Conleth Hill and Seán Campion in Marie Jones's Stones in His Pockets. *Photo: Joan Marcus*

Standby for Mr. Hill—Declan Mooney; Mr. Campion—Stevie Ray Dallimore.

Directed by Ian McElhinney; scenery, Jack Kirwan, lighting, James McFetridge; executive producers, David Bownes, Ginger Montel; casting, Jay Binder; production stage manager, David O'Brien; press, Boneau/Bryan-Brown, Adrian Bryan-Brown, Jackie Green, Jim Byk, Martine Sainvil.

Time: The present. Place: Ireland. The play was presented in two parts.

Filmmaker's invasion of Ireland provides ample opportunities to spoof the American dreams of the Irish and to lampoon Hollywood egos and mores.

***Roundabout Theatre Company** production of ***Follies** (64) Revival of the musical with book by James Goodman; music and lyrics by Stephen Sondheim. Todd Haimes artistic director, Ellen Richard managing director, Julia C. Levy executive director of external affairs, at the Belasco Theatre. Opened April 5, 2001.

Dimitri Weismann .... Louis Zorich
Showgirls .... Jessica Leigh Brown, Colleen Dunn, Amy Heggins, Wendy Waring
Sally Durant Plummer .... Judith Ivey
Sandra Crane .... Nancy Ringham
Dee Dee West .... Dorothy Stanley
Stella Deems .... Carol Woods
Sam Deems .... Peter Cormican
Solange La Fitte .... Jane White
Roscoe .... Larry Raiken
Heidi Schiller .... Joan Roberts
Emily Whitman .... Marge Champion
Theodore Whitman .... Donald Saddler
Carlotta Campion .... Polly Bergen
Hattie Walker .... Betty Garrett

Song in their hearts: Judith Ivey, Treat Williams, Blythe Danner and Gregory Harrison in Stephen Sondheim's Follies. *Photo: Joan Marcus*

Phyllis Rogers Stone	Blythe Danner
Benjamin Stone	Gregory Harrison
Buddy Plummer	Treat Williams
Young Phyllis	Erin Dilly
Young Sally	Lauren Ward
Young Dee Dee	Roxane Barlow
Young Emily	Carol Bentley
Young Carlotta	Sally Mae Dunn
Young Sandra	Dottie Earle
Young Solange	Jacqueline Hendy
Young Heidi	Brooke Sunny Moriber
Young Hattie	Kelli O'Hara
Young Stella	Allyson Tucker
Young Roscoe	Aldrin Gonzalez
Young Ben	Richard Roland
Young Buddy	Joey Sorge
Young Theodore	Rod McCune
Kevin	Stephen Campanella
"Margie"	Roxane Barlow
"Sally"	Jessica Leigh Brown

Ensemble: Roxane Barlow, Carol Bentley, Jessica Leigh Brown, Stephen Campanella, Colleen Dunn, Sally Mae Dunn, Dottie Earle, Aldrin Gonzalez, Amy Heggins, Jacqueline Hendy, Rod McCune, Kelli O'Hara, T. Oliver Reid, Alex Sanchez, Allyson Tucker, Matt Wall, Wendy Waring.

Orchestra: Eric Stern conductor, piano; Martin Agee concertmaster; Cenovia Cummins second violin; Debra Shufelt viola; Roger Shell cello; Brian Cassier bass; Les Scott, Rick Heckman, John Campo woodwinds; Bob Millikan, Jon Owens trumpet; Randy Andos trombone; Billy Miller percussion; Beth Robinson harp.

Standbys and Understudies: Messrs. Harrison, Williams, Saddler—Don Correia; Misses Roberts, Ringham, Stanley—Joan Barber; Misses Danner, Campion, Woods, Bergen—Dorothy Stanley; Misses Ivey, Garrett, White—Nancy Ringham; Misses Dilly, Ward, Barlow—Kelli O'Hara; Messrs. Roland, Sorge—Matt Wall; Messrs. Zorich, Raiken—Peter Cormican.

Swings: Nadine Isenegger, Parisa Ross, Jeffrey Hankinson.

Directed by Matthew Warchus; choreography, Kathleen Marshall; scenery, Mark Thompson; costumes, Theoni V. Aldredge; lighting, Hugh Vanstone; sound, Jonathan Deans; original dance music, John Berkman; additional dance music, David Chase; orchestrations, Jonathan Tunick; music direction, Eric Stern; executive producer, Frank P. Scardino; music coordinator, John Miller; associate director, Thomas Caruso; associate choreographer, Joey Pizzi; casting, Jim Carnahan; production stage manager, Peter Hanson; stage manager, Karen Moore; press, the Publicity Office, Bob Fennell, Marc Thibodeau, Candi Adams, Michael S. Borowski.

Time: 1970 and earlier. Place: The stage home of the *Weismann Follies.*

Revival of the musical that mourns the passing of musical theater's Golden Era as well as the loss of innocence that comes with middle age. A *Best Plays* choice in 1970–71, it first opened on Broadway at the Winter Garden Theatre 4/4/71 for 521 performances.

ACT I

Prologue/Overture	Company
"Beautiful Girls"	Roscoe and Company
"Don't Look at Me"	Sally and Ben
"Waiting for the Girls Upstairs"	Buddy, Ben, Phyllis, Sally, Young Buddy, Young Ben, Young Phyllis, Young Sally
"Rain on the Roof"	Emily and Theodore
"Ah, Paris!"	Solange
"Broadway Baby"	Hattie
"The Road You Didn't Take"	Ben
"Danse d'Amour"	Emily, Theodore, Young Emily, Young Theodore
"In Buddy's Eyes"	Sally
"Who's That Woman?"	Stella and Ladies
"I'm Still Here"	Carlotta
"Too Many Mornings"	Ben and Sally

ACT II

"The Right Girl"	Buddy
"One More Kiss"	Heidi and Young Heidi
"Could I Leave You?"	Phyllis

The Follies: The Folly of Love

"Loveland"	Ensemble

The Folly of Youth

"You're Gonna Love Tomorrow"	Young Phyllis and Young Ben
"Love Will See Us Through"	Young Sally and Young Buddy

Buddy's Folly

"The God-Why-Don't-You-Love-Me Blues"	Buddy, "Margie," "Sally"

Sally's Folly

"Losing My Mind"	Sally

Phyllis's Folly

"The Story of Lucy and Jessie"	Phyllis and Men

Ben's Folly

"Live, Laugh, Love"	Ben and Ensemble

Flying low: Eric Johner, Gary Sinise, K. Todd Freeman and Amy Morton in Dale Wasserman's adaptation of One Flew Over the Cuckoo's Nest. *Photo: Tristam Kenton*

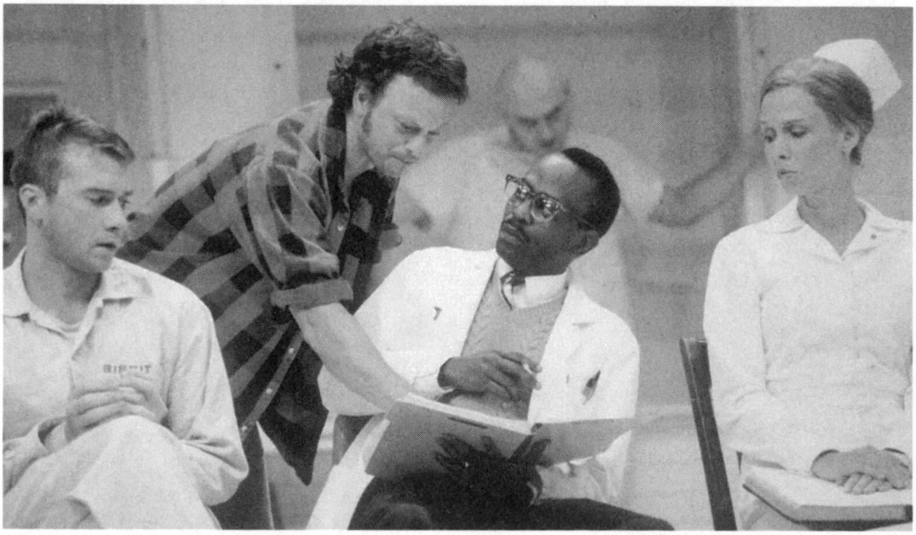

***One Flew Over the Cuckoo's Nest** (57). Revival of the play by Dale Wasserman; based on the novel by Ken Kesey. Produced by Michael Leavitt, Fox Theatricals, Anita Waxman, Elizabeth Williams, in association with John York Noble, Randall L. Wreghitt, Dori Bernstein, at the Royale Theatre. Opened April 8, 2001.

Chief Bromden .... Tim Sampson
Aide Warren .... Ron OJ Parson
Aide Williams .... Afram Bill Williams
Nurse Ratched .... Amy Morton
Nurse Flinn .... Stephanie Childers
Dale Harding .... Ross Lehman
Billy Bibbit .... Eric Johner
Scanlon .... Alan Wilder
Cheswick .... Rick Snyder
Martini .... Danton Stone
Ruckley .... Misha Kuznetsov
Colonel Matterson .... Bill Noble
Patient #1 .... Bruce McCarty
Patient #2 .... Steven Marcus
Randle P. McMurphy .... Gary Sinise
Dr. Spivey .... K. Todd Freeman
Aide Turkle .... John Watson Sr.
Candy Starr .... Mariann Mayberry
Technician #1 .... Bruce McCarty
Technician #2 .... Jeanine Morick
Sandra .... Sarah Charipar

Understudies: Messrs. Sinise, Lehman—Bruce McCarty; Misses Morton, Charipar—Jeanine Morick; Mr. Johner—K. Todd Freeman; Misses Mayberry, Childers—Sarah Charipar; Mr. Freeman—Misha Kuznetsov; Messrs. Wilder, Snyder, Stone, Noble—Steven Marcus; Mr. Watson—Afram Bill Williams; Messrs. Sampson, Williams, Parson, Kuznetsov, Marcus—Michael Nichols.

Directed by Terry Kinney; scenery, Robert Brill; costumes, Laura Bauer; lighting, Kevin Rigdon; original music and sound, Rob Milburn, Michael Bodeen; projection design, Sage Marie Carter; fight choreographer, Robin H. McFarquhar; casting, Phyllis Schuringa, Pat McCorkle; executive producer, Kristin Caskey; associate producers, Mike Isaacson, Doug Teitelbaum, Lynne Peyser, D. Harris/B. Smith, Robert Cole; production stage manager, Robert H. Satterlee; stage manager, Michele A. Kay; press, Richard Kornberg and Associates, Richard Kornberg, Don Summa, Tom D'Ambrosio.

Time: 1960s. Place: The day room in a ward of a state mental hospital somewhere in the Pacific Northwest. The play was presented in two parts.

Revival of an adaptation about a free spirit who sparks emotional liberation in a group of timid, troubled men. It first opened on Broadway at the Cort Theatre 11/13/63 for 82 performances.

Love on the hoof: Faith Prince and Marc Kudisch in Bells Are Ringing. *Photo: Carol Rosegg*

***Bells Are Ringing** (57). Revival of the musical with book and lyrics by Betty Comden and Adolph Green; music by Jule Styne. Produced by Mitchell Maxwell, Mark Balsam, Victoria Maxwell, Robert Barnades, Mark Goldberg, Anthony R. Russo, James L. Simon, in association with Fred H. Krones, Allen M. Shore and Momentum Productions, Inc., at the Plymouth Theatre. Opened April 12, 2001.

TV Announcer .... Shane Kirkpatrick
Telephone Girls .... Caitlin Carter, Joan Hess, Emily Hsu, Alice Rietveld
Sue .... Beth Fowler
Gwynne .... Angela Robinson
Ella Peterson .... Faith Prince
Carl .... Julio Agustin
Inspector Barnes .... Robert Ari
Francis .... Jeffrey Bean
Sandor .... David Garrison
Jeff Moss .... Marc Kudisch
Larry Hastings .... David Brummel
Louie .... Greg Reuter
Ludwig Smiley .... Lawrence Clayton
Dr. Kitchell .... Martin Moran
Blake Barton .... Darren Ritchie
Joey .... Shane Kirkpatrick
Paddy, the Street Sweeper .... Roy Harcourt
Mrs. Simms .... Joan Hess
Olga .... Caitlin Carter
Corvello Mob Men .... David Brummel, Greg Reuter
Mrs. Mallet .... Joan Hess
Maid .... Linda Romoff
Paul Arnold .... Lawrence Clayton
Bridgette .... Joan Hess
Man on Street .... Josh Rhodes
Madame Grimaldi .... Joanne Baum

Ensemble: Julio Agustin, Joanne Baum, David Brummel, Caitlin Carter, Lawrence Clayton, Roy Harcourt, Joan Hess, Emily Hsu, Shane Kirkpatrick, Greg Reuter, Josh Rhodes, Alice Rietveld, Darren Ritchie, Angela Robinson, Linda Romoff.

Dancers: Caitlin Carter, Roy Harcourt, Joan Hess, Emily Hsu, Shane Kirkpatrick, Greg Reuter, Josh Rhodes.

Orchestra: David Evans conductor; Joseph Baker associate conductor, keyboards; Robert Lawrence, Maura Giannini violin; Jill Jaffe viola; Scott Ballantyne cello; Steven Kenyon, Kenneth Dybisz, Daniel Block, Ronald Jannelli woodwinds; Stu Satalof, Bruce Staelens trumpet; Clinton Sharman trombone; Peter Gordon, French horn; Louis Bruno bass; Richard Rosenzweig percussion.

Understudies: Miss Prince—Linda Romoff, Joan Hess; Miss Fowler—Joanne Baum, Joan Hess; Mr. Kudisch—Josh Rhodes; Mr. Garrison—David Brummel; Mr. Moran—Greg Reuter; Mr. Ari—Lawrence Clayton; Mr. Bean—Shane Kirkpatrick; Mr. Agustin—Roy Harcourt, Marc Oka, James Hadley; Miss Robinson—Stacey Harris, Kelly Sullivan; Mr. Ritchie—James Hadley, Marc Oka, Shane Kirkpatrick; Mr. Brummel—Lawrence Clayton, James Hadley, Marc Oka; Mr. Clayton—James Hadley, Marc Oka; Miss Carter—Stacey Harris, Kelly Sullivan.

Swings: James Hadley, Stacey Harris, Marc Oka, Kelly Sullivan.

Directed by Tina Landau; choreography, Jeff Calhoun; scenery, Riccardo Hernandez; costumes, David C. Woolard; lighting, Donald Holder; sound, Acme Sound Partners; musical direction and vocal arrangements, David Evans; orchestrations, Don Sebesky; incidental music, David Evans, Mark Hummel; dance music arrangements, Mark Hummel; video, Batwin and Robin Productions; music coordinator, Seymour Red Press; associate choreographer, Patti D'Beck; associate producers, Alan S. Kopit, Richard Berger; casting, Stephanie Klapper; production stage manager, Erica Schwartz; stage manager, James Latus; press, Barlow-Hartman Public Relations, Michael Hartman, John Barlow, Ash Curtis, Jeremy Shaffer.

Time: Spring, the late 1950s. Place: New York City. Presented in two parts.

Revival of a musical about an answering service operator who finds love on the wire. First produced at the Shubert Theatre 11/29/56 for 924 performances.

ACT I

Overture .... Orchestra
"Bells Are Ringing" .... Telephone Girls
"It's a Perfect Relationship" .... Ella
"Independent" .... Jeff and Dancers
"You've Got To Do It" .... Jeff
"It's A Simple Little System" .... Sandor and Ensemble
"Better Than A Dream" .... Ella and Jeff

"Hello, Hello There" .... Ludwig Smiley, Ella, Jeff and Ensemble
"I Met A Girl" .... Jeff and Ensemble
"Is It A Crime?" .... Ella, Barnes and Frances
"Long Before I Knew You" .... Jeff and Ella

ACT II

Entr'acte .... Orchestra
"Mu-Cha-Cha" .... Carl, Ella, Gwynne and Dancers
"Just in Time" .... Jeff, Ella and Ensemble
(Original Dance Arrangment by John Morris)
"Drop That Name" .... Ensemble with Ella
"The Party's Over" .... Ella
"Salzberg" .... Sue and Sandor
"The Midas Touch" .... Dr. Kitchell and Dancers
"I'm Going Back" .... Ella
Finale .... Company

***Blast!** (49). Marching band musical entertainment with music by various authors. Produced by Cook Group Incorporated and Star of India at the Broadway Theatre. Opened April 17, 2001.

Cast: Trey Alligood III, Rachel J. Anderson, Nicholas E. Angelis, Matthew A. Banks, Kimberly Beth Baron, Wesley Bullock, Mark Burroughs, Jesus Cantu Jr., Jodina Rosario Carey, Robert Carmical, Alan "Otto" Compton, Dayne Delahoussaye, Karen Duggan, John Elrod, Brandon J. Epperson, Kenneth Frisby, J. Derek Gipson, Trevor Lee Gooch, Casey Marshall Gooding, Bradley Kerr Green, Benjamin Taber Griffin, Benjamin Raymond Handel, Benjamin W. Harloff, Joe Haworth, Darren M. Haslett, Tim Heasley, Freddy Hernandez Jr., George Hester, Jeremiah Todd Huber, Martin A. Hughes, Naoki Ishikawa, Stacy J. Johnson, Sanford R. Jones, Anthony F. Leps, Ray Linkous, Jean Marie Mallicoat, Jack Mansager, Brian Mayle, Dave Millen, Jim Moore, Westley Morehead, David Nash, Jeffrey A. Queen, Douglas Raines, Chris Rasmussen, Joseph J. Reinhart, Jamie L. Roscoe, Jennifer Ross, Christopher Eric Rutt, Christopher J. Schletter, Andrew Schnieders, Jonathan L. Schwartz, Greg Seale, Andy Smart, Radiah Y. Stewart, Bryan Anthony Sutton, Sean Terrell, Andrew James Toth, Joni Paige Viertel, Kristin Whiting.

Directed by James Mason; choreography, Jim Moore, George Pinney, John Vanderkolff; scenery, costumes, Mark Thompson; lighting, Hugh Vanstone; sound, Mark Hood, Bobby Aitken, Tom Morse; orchestrations, James Prime; executive producer, Dodger Management Group; associate producer, Donnie Vandoren; production stage manager, William Coiner; stage manager, Victor Lukas; press, Boneau/Bryan-Brown, Adrian Bryan-Brown, Susanne Tighe, Jackie Green, Amy Jacobs, Adriana Douzos.

The production was presented in two parts.

Marching band music and choreography on a Broadway stage.

ACT I

"Bolero" .... M. Ravel
"Color Wheel" .... J. Lee
"Split Complimentaries" .... J. Talbott
"Everybody Loves the Blues" .... M. Ferguson, N. Lane
"Loss" .... D. Ellis
"Simple Gifts," "Appalachian Spring" .... A. Copland
"Battery Battle" .... T. Hannum, J. Lee, P. Rennick
"Medea" .... S. Barber
"The Promise of Living" .... A. Copland

ACT II

"Color Wheel Too" .... John Vanderkolff
"Gee, Officer Krupke" .... L. Bernstein, S. Sondheim
"Lemontech" .... J. Vanderkolff
"Tangerinamadidge" .... J. Mason, J. Vanderkolff

"Land of Make Believe" .... C. Mangione
"Spiritual of the Earth: Marimba Spiritual" .... M. Miki
"Earth Beat" .... M. Spiro
"Malaguena" .... E. Lecuona

***The Producers** (47). Musical with book by Mel Brooks and Thomas Meehan; music and lyrics by Mel Brooks. Produced by Rocco Landesman, SFX Theatrical Group, the Frankel-Baruch-Viertel-Routh Group, Bob and Harvey Weinstein, Rick Steiner, Robert F.X. Sillerman, Mel Brooks, in association with James D. Stern/Douglas Meyer, by special arrangememt with Studio Canal, at the St. James Theatre. Opened April 19, 2001.

The Usherettes .... Bryn Dowling, Jennifer Smith
Max Bialystock .... Nathan Lane
Leo Bloom .... Matthew Broderick
Hold-me Touch-me .... Madeleine Doherty
Mr. Marks .... Ray Wills
Franz Liebkind .... Brad Oscar
Carmen Ghia .... Roger Bart
Roger De Bris .... Gary Beach
Bryan .... Peter Marinos
Kevin .... Ray Wills
Scott .... Jeffry Denman
Shirley .... Kathy Fitzgerald
Ulla .... Cady Huffman
Lick-me Bite-me .... Jennifer Smith
Kiss-me Feel-me .... Kathy Fitzgerald
Jack Lepidus .... Peter Marinos
Donald Dinsmore .... Jeffry Denman
Jason Green .... Ray Wills
Lead Tenor .... Eric Gunhus
Sergeant .... Ray Wills
O'Rourke .... Abe Sylvia
O'Riley .... Matt Loehr
O'Houllihan .... Robert H. Fowler
Guard .... Jeffry Denman
Bailiff .... Abe Sylvia
Judge .... Peter Marinos
Foreman of Jury .... Kathy Fitzgerald
Trustee .... Ray Wills

Ensemble: Jeffry Denman, Madeleine Doherty, Bryn Dowling, Kathy Fitzgerald, Robert H. Fowler, Ida Gilliams, Eric Gunhus, Kimberly Hester, Naomi Kakuk, Matt Loehr, Peter Marinos, Angie L. Schworer, Jennifer Smith, Abe Sylvia, Tracy Terstriep, Ray Wills.

Orchestra: Patrick S. Brady conductor; Phil Reno associate conductor, keyboard; Rick Dolan concertmaster; Ashley D. Horne, Louise Owen, Karen M. Karlsrud, Helen Kim violin; Laura Bontrager

Ulla-la-la: Matthew Broderick and Cady Huffman in The Producers. *Photo: Joan Marcus*

cello; Robert Renino string bass; Vincent Della Rocca, Steven J. Greenfield, Jay Hassler, Alva F. Hunt, Frank Santagata woodwinds; David Rogers, Rick Marchione, Frank Greene trumpet; Dan Levine, Tim Sessions tenor trombone; Chris Olness bass trombone; Jill Williamson, French horn; Cubby O'Brien drums; Benjamin Herman percussion; Anna Reinersman harp.

Understudies: Mr. Lane—Ray Wills, Brad Oscar; Mr. Broderick—Jamie LaVerdiere, Jeffry Denman; Mr.Oscar—Jim Borstelmann, Jeffry Denman; Mr. Bart—Jamie LaVerdiere, Brad Musgrove; Mr. Beach—Brad Oscar, Jim Borstelmann, Brad Musgove; Miss Huffman—Ida Gilliams, Angie L. Schworer.

Swings: Jim Borstelmann, Adrienne Gibbons, Jamie LaVerdiere, Brad Musgrove, Christina Marie Norrup.

Directed and choreographed by Susan Stroman; scenery, Robin Wagner; costumes, William Ivey Long; lighting, Peter Kaczorowski; sound, Steve C. Kennedy; orchestrations, Doug Besterman; music direction and vocal arrangements, Patrick S. Brady; musical arrangements and supervision, Glen Kelly; music coordinator, John Miller; production stage manager, Steven Zweigbaum; associate choreographer, Warren Carlyle; assistant choreographer, Lisa Shriver; associate producers, Frederic H. and Rhoda Mayerson, Lynn Landis; casting, Johnson-Liff Associates; press, Barlow-Hartman Public Relations, John Barlow, Michael Hartman, Bill Coyle.

Time: 1959. Place: New York City. Presented in two parts.

Musical version of Mel Brooks's 1968 cult film about a pair of producers who hatch a scheme to become rich with a Broadway flop. A 2000–01 *Best Plays* choice (see essay by Julius Novick in this volume) and record-setting Tony Award-winner.

ACT I

Scene 1: Shubert Alley
"Opening Night" .... The Ensemble
"The King of Broadway" .... Max and Ensemble
Scene 2: Max's office, June 16, 1959
"We Can Do It" .... Max and Leo
Scene 3: The Chambers Street offices of Whitehall and Marks
"I Wanna Be A Producer" .... Leo and the Accountants
Scene 4: Max's Office
"We Can Do It" (Reprise) .... Max and Leo
Scene 5: The rooftop of a Greenwich Village apartment building
"In Old Bavaria" .... Franz
"Der Guten Tag Hop Clop" .... Franz, Max, Leo
Scene 6: The living room of renowned theatrical director Roger Debris' elegant Upper East Side townhouse on a sunny Tuesday afternoon in June
"Keep It Gay" .... Roger, Carmen, Bryan, Kevin, Scott, Shirley, Max, Leo
Scene 7: Max's office
"When You Got It, Flaunt It" .... Ulla
Scene 8: Little Old Lady Land
"Along Came Bialy" .... Max, Little Old Ladies
"Act One Finale"Max, Leo, Franz, Ulla, Roger, Carmen, Bryan, Kevin, Scott, Shirley, Ensemble.

ACT II

Scene 1: Max's office, late morning, a few weeks later
"That Face" .... Leo, Ulla, Max
Scene 2: The bare stage of a Broadway theater
"Haben Sie Gehoert Das Deutsche Band?" .... Jason Franz
Scene 3: Shubert Alley
"Opening Night" (Reprise) .... The Usherettes
"You Never Say 'Good Luck' on Opening Night" .... Roger, Max, Carmen, Franz, Leo
Scene 4:The stage of the Shubert Theatre
"Springtime For Hitler" .... Lead Tenor, Roger, Ulla, Ensemble
Scene 5: Max's Office, later that night
"Where Did We Go Right?" .... Max, Leo
Scene 6: The holding cell of a New York courthouse, ten days later
"Betrayed" .... Max

Scene 7: A New York courtroom
"'Til Him" .... Leo, Max
Scene 8: Sing Sing
"Prisoners Of Love" .... The Convicts
Scene 9: The stage of the Shubert Theatre
"Prisoners Of Love" (Reprise) .... Roger, Ulla, the Ensemble
Scene 10: Shubert Alley
"Leo and Max" .... Leo, Max
Curtain Call
"Goodbye!" .... The Company

The Gathering (24). By Arje Shaw. Produced by Martin Markinson, Lawrence S. Toppall, Bruce Lazarus, Daniel S. Wise, Martha R. Gasparian, Steve Alpert, Robert Massimi, in association with Diaspora Productions, at the Cort Theatre. Opened April 24, 2001. (Closed May 13, 2001)

Mensch *on a mission: Hal Linden and Max Dworin in Arje Shaw's* The Gathering. *Photo: Carol Rosegg*

Gabe .... Hal Linden
Michael .... Max Dworin
Diane .... Deirdre Lovejoy
Stuart .... Sam Guncler
Egon .... Coleman Zeigen

Standbys and Understudies: Mr. Linden—Ben Hammer; Mr. Dworin—Ricky Ashley; Miss Lovejoy—Ru Flynn; Messrs. Guncler, Zeigen—Myk Watford.

Directed by Rebecca Taylor; scenery, Michael Anania; costumes, Susan Soetaert; lighting, Scott Clyve; sound, T. Richard Fitzgerald; music, Andy Stein; associate producers, Michael H. Goldsmith, Elsa Daspin Haft, Esther Shaw; casting, Laurie Smith; production stage manager, Dom Ruggiero; stage manager, Betsy Herst; press, Keith Sherman and Associates, Brett Oberman, Miller Wright, Dan Fortune, Peter Kindlon.

Time: 1985. Place: New York and Bitburg, Germany.

Domestic drama centering on an elderly Jewish man's protest of President Reagan's visit to a German World War II cemetery.

The Adventures of Tom Sawyer (21). Musical based on the novel by Mark Twain; book by Ken Ludwig; music and lyrics by Don Schlitz. Produced by James M. Nederlander, James L. Nederlander and Watt/Dobie Productions at the Minskoff Theatre. Opened April 26, 2001. (Closed May 13, 2001)

Tom Sawyer	Joshua Park	Aunt Polly	Linda Purl
Ben Rogers	Tommar Wilson	Sid Sawyer	Marshall Pailet
George Bellamy	Joe Gallagher	Doc Robinson	Stephen Lee Anderson
Lyle Bellamy	Blake Hackler	Reverend Sprague	Tommy Hollis
Joe Harper	Erik J. McCormack	Lanyard Bellamy	Richard Poe
Alfred Temple	Pierce Cravens	Gideon Temple	Ric Stoneback
Amy Lawrence	Ann Whitlow Brown	Lemuel Dobbins	John Christopher Jones
Lucy Harper	Mekenzie Rosen-Stone	Muff Potter	Tom Aldredge
Susie Rogers	Élan	Huckleberry Finn	Jim Poulos
Sabina Temple	Nikki M. James	Injun Joe	Kevin Durand
Sally Bellamy	Stacia Fernandez	Judge Thatcher	John Dossett
Sereny Harper	Donna Lee Marshall	Becky Thatcher	Kristen Bell
Lucinda Rogers	Amy Jo Phillips	Widow Douglas	Jane Connell
Naomi Temple	Sally Wilfert	Pap	Stephen Lee Anderson

Orchestra: Paul Gemignani conductor; Nicholas Archer associate conductor, synthesizer; Marilyn Reynolds concertmaster, violin; Andrea Andros, Jonathan Kass, violins Shelly Holland-Moritz viola; Deborah Assaael cello; Blake Hackler fiddle; Scott Shachter, Martha Hyde, Kelly Peral, Thomas Sefcovic woodwinds; Lawrence DiBello, French horn; Hiro Noguchi, Phil Granger trumpet; Dean Plank trombone; Paul Ford piano; Andrew Schwartz, Gregory Utzig, Gordon Titcomb guitar; Erik J. McCormack dulcimer; Kermit Driscoll bass; Larry Lelli drums; Charles Descarfino percussion.

Understudies: Mr. Park—Blake Hackler, Erik J. McCormack; Mr. Poulos—Joe Gallagher, Tommar Wilson; Miss Bell—Nikki M. James, Kate Reinders; Miss Purl—Stacia Fernandez, Sally Wilfert; Mr.

Birth of a salesman: Joshua Park and company in The Adventures of Tom Sawyer. *Photo: Joan Marcus*

Dossett—Richard Poe, Patrick Boll; Mr. Durand—Patrick Boll; Mr. Aldredge—John Herrera; Miss Connell—Stacia Fernandez, Amy Jo Phillips; Mr. Pailet—Pierce Cravens; Mr. Jones—Stephen Lee Anderson, John Herrera; Mr. Hollis—Stephen Lee Anderson, John Herrera; Mr. Poe—Patrick Boll, John Herrera; Mr. Stoneback—Patrick Boll, John Herrera; Mr. Anderson—Patrick Boll, John Herrera; Miss Brown—Kate Reinders; Mr. Wilson—Michael Burton; Mr. McCormack—Michael Burton.

Swings: Patrick Boll, Michael Burton, John Herrera, Kate Reinders, Elise Santora.

Directed by Scott Ellis; choreography, David Marques; scenery, Heidi Ettinger; costumes, Anthony Powell; lighting, Kenneth Posner; sound, Lew Mead; fight direction, Rick Sordelet; musical direction, Paul Gemignani; orchestrations, Michael Starobin; dance and incidental music, David Krane; Ronald Sell, music coordinator; associate choreographer, Rommy Sandhu; additional choreography, Jodi Moccia; casting, Jim Carnahan, J.V. Mercanti, Todd Lundquist; press, Boneau/Bryan-Brown, Adrian Bryan-Brown, Amy Jacobs.

Time: 1844. Place: St. Petersburg, Missouri. The production was presented in two parts.

Musical adaptation of stories about Mark Twain's most famous character.

ACT I

Scene 1: A meadow and the town of St. Petersburg
"Hey, Tom Sawyer" .... The Boys, Tom, Aunt Polly, Dobbins, Sprague and the People of St. Petersburg
Scene 2: The fence in front of Tom's house
"Here's My Plan" .... Tom
"Smart Like That" .... Tom, Huck and the Boys
Scene 3: The graveyard
"Hands All Clean" .... Injun Joe
"The Vow" .... Tom, Huck
Scene 4: On the way to church
"Ain't Life Fine" .... The People of St. Petersburg
Scene 5: Outside the schoolhouse
"It Just Ain't Me" .... Huck
Scene 6: Inside the schoolhouse
"To Hear You Say My Name" .... Tom, Becky
Scene 7: The alley behind the jail
"Murrel's Gold" .... Injun Joe, Muff, Tom, Huck
Scene 8: Inside the courthouse
"The Testimony" .... Tom and the People of St. Petersburg

ACT II

Scene 1: The school and the town
"Ain't Life Fine" (Reprise) .... The Boys and Girls
Scene 2: Tom's bedroom
"This Time Tomorrow" .... Aunt Polly
Scene 3: Widow Douglas's front porch
"I Can Read" .... Huck, Widow Douglas
Scene 4: The picnic grounds, Cardiff Hill
"You Can't Can't Dance" .... Judge Thatcher, Aunt Polly, the People of St. Petersburg
"Murrel's Gold" (Reprise) .... Injun Joe
Scene 5: McDougal's Cave
"Angels Lost" .... Aunt Polly, Judge Thatcher, the People of St. Petersburg
"Light" .... Tom
"Angels Lost" (Reprise) .... Becky
Scene 6: Inside and outside the church
"Light" (Reprise) .... The People of St. Petersburg
Finale .... Tom, Huck, Becky, Boys, Girls

***George Gershwin Alone** (52). One-man performance piece on the life of George Gershwin. Book by Hershey Felder; music and lyrics by George Gershwin and Ira

Gershwin. Produced by Richard Willis, Martin Markinson, HTG Productions, at the Helen Hayes Theatre. Opened April 30, 2001.

George Gershwin .... Hershey Felder

Directed by Joel Zwick; scenery, Yael Pardess; lighting, James F. Ingalls; sound, Jon Gottlieb; production stage manager, Arthur Gaffin; press, Keith Sherman and Associates, Brett Oberman, Miller Wright, Dan Fortune, Peter Kindlon.

Setting: In the mind and memory of George Gershwin. Performed without an intermission.

One-man performance piece on the life of George Gershwin.

***King Hedley II** (36). By August Wilson. Produced by Sageworks, Benjamin Mordecai, Jujamcyn Theaters, 52nd Street Productions, Spring Sirkin, Peggy Hill, and Manhattan Theatre Club, in association with Kardana-Swinsky Productions, at the Virginia Theatre. Opened May 1, 2001.

Generations behind fences: Leslie Uggams, Charles Brown, Brian Stokes Mitchell and Viola Davis in King Hedley II. *Photo: Joan Marcus*

Stool Pigeon ...... Stephen McKinley Henderson
King .... Brian Stokes Mitchell
Ruby .... Leslie Uggams
Mister .... Monté Russell
Tonya .... Viola Davis
Elmore .... Charles Brown

Standbys: Miss Davis—Yvette Ganier; Ms. Uggams—Lynda Gravátt; Messrs. Mitchell, Russell—Keith Randolph Smith.

Directed by Marion McClinton; scenery, David Gallo; costumes, Toni-Leslie James; lighting, Donald Holder; sound, Rob Milburn; waltz choreography, Dianne McIntyre; fight direction, David S. Leong; casting, Barry Moss; production stage manager, Diane DiVita; stage manager, Cynthia Kocher; press, Barlow-Hartman Public Relations, John Barlow, Michael Hartman, Wayne Wolfe.

Time: 1985. Place: The Hill District in Pittsburgh, Pennsylvania.

The eighth installment in Wilson's ten-play cycle about 20th-century African-American life focuses on the destruction of black men by white society and other black men. First performed at Pittsburgh Public Theater in December 1999. A 2000–01 *Best Plays* choice (see essay by Christopher Rawson in this volume) and 2001 American Theatre Critics/Steinberg New Play Citation honoree.

***42nd Street** (33). Revival of the musical based on the novel by Bradford Ropes and the 1933 movie; book by Michael Stewart and Mark Bramble; music by Harry Warren; lyrics by Al Dubin. Produced by Dodger Theatricals, Joop van den Ende and Stage Holding at the Ford Center for the Performing Arts. Opened May 2, 2001.

Andy Lee .... Michael Arnold
Maggie Jones .... Mary Testa
Bert Barry .... Jonathan Freeman
Mac .... Allen Fitzpatrick
Phyllis .... Catherine Wreford
Lorraine .... Megan Sikora
Diane .... Tamlyn Brooke Shusterman
Annie .... Mylinda Hull

A star is made: Kate Levering and company in 42nd Street. *Photo: Joan Marcus*

Ethel .... Amy Dolan
Billy Lawlor .... David Elder
Peggy Sawyer .... Kate Levering
Oscar .... Billy Stritch
Julian Marsh .... Michael Cumpsty
Dorothy Brock .... Christine Ebersole
Abner Dillon .... Michael McCarty
Pat Denning .... Richard Muenz
Waiters .... Brad Aspel, Mike Warshaw, Shonn Wiley
Thugs .... Allen Fitzpatrick, Jerry Tellier
Doctor .... Allen Fitzpatrick

Ensemble: Brad Aspel, Becky Berstler, Randy Bobish, Chris Clay, Michael Clowers, Maryam Myika Day, Alexander deJong, Amy Dolan, Isabelle Flachsmann, Jennifer Jones, Dontee Kiehn, Renée Klapmeyer, Jessica Kostival, Keirsten Kupiec, Todd Lattimore, Melissa Rae Mahon, Michael Malone, Jennifer Marquardt, Meredith Patterson, Darin Phelps, Wendy Rosoff, Megan Schenck, Kelly Sheehan, Tamlyn Brooke Shusterman, Megan Sikora, Jennifer Stetor, Erin Stoddard, Yasuko Tamaki, Jonathan Taylor, Jerry Tellier, Elisa Van Duyne, Erika Vaughn, Mike Warshaw, Merrill West, Shonn Wiley, Catherine Wreford.

Orchestra: Todd Ellison conductor; Fred Lassen associate conductor, piano; Michael Migliore, Ken Hitchcock, Dave Pietro, Tom Christensen, Roger Rosenberg, Andrew Drelles, Tim Ries woodwinds; Joe Mosello, Ravi Best, Barry Danielian, Dave Ballou, trumpet; Mark Patterson, Steve Armour, Mike Christianson, trombone; Theresa MacDonnell, Leise Anscheutz, Michael Ishii, French horn; John Arbo bass; Scott Kuney guitar; Victoria Drake harp; Tony Tedesco drums; Kory Grossman percussion.

Standby for Misses Ebersole, Testa—Beth Leavel.

Understudies: Miss Ebersole—Jessica Kostival; Mr. Cumpsty—Richard Muenz, Jerry Tellier; Miss Levering—Meredith Patterson, Erin Stoddard; Miss Testa—Amy Dolan; Mr. Freeman—Brad Aspel; Mr. Elder—Shonn Wiley; Mr. Muenz—Allen Fitzpatrick, Jerry Tellier; Mr. McCarty—Allen Fitzpatrick; Mr. Arnold—Brad Aspel, Randy Bobish; Miss Hull—Becky Berstler, Amy Dolan; Miss Sikora—Erin Stoddard; Miss Wreford—Elisa Van Duyne; Mr. Fitzpatrick—Darin Phelps, Luke Walrath; Miss Shusterman—Renée Klapmeyer.

Swings: Kelli Barclay, Melissa Giattino, Brian J. Marcum, Luke Walrath.

Partial Swings: Becky Berstler, Isabelle Flachsmann, Jerry Tellier, Elisa Van Duyne, Merrill West.

Directed by Mark Bramble, based on original direction and dances by Gower Champion; musical staging and new choreography, Randy Skinner; scenery, Douglas W. Schmidt; costumes, Roger Kirk; lighting, Paul Gallo; sound, Peter Fitzgerald; orchestrations, Philip J. Lang; musical direction, Todd Ellison; additional orchestrations, Donald Johnston; music coordinator, John Miller; additional lyrics, Johnny Mercer, Mort Dixon; assistant choreographer, Kelli Barclay; executive producer, Dodger Management Group; casting, Jay Binder; production stage manager, Frank Hartenstein; stage manager, Karen Armstrong; press, Boneau/Bryan-Brown, Adrian Bryan-Brown, Susanne Tighe, Amy Jacobs, Jim Byk, Adriana Douzos.

Time: 1933. Place: The action takes place in New York City and Philadelphia.

A hoofer with stars in her eyes goes onstage a nobody and becomes a star. A *Best Plays* choice in 1980–81, it first opened on Broadway at the Winter Garden Theatre 8/25/80. It moved twice, to the Majestic and St. James Theatres, running for a total of 3,486 performances.

ACT I

Overture .... Orchestra
Scene 1: Stage of the 42nd Street Theatre, New York City
"Audition" .... Andy Lee and Ensemble
"Young and Healthy" .... Billy Lawlor and Peggy Sawyer
"Shadow Waltz" .... Maggie Jones, Dorothy Brock and Ensemble
Scene 2: The Gypsy Tea Kettle Restaurant
"Go Into Your Dance" .... Maggie, Annie, Peggy, Phyllis, Lorraine and Andy
Scene 3: Stage of the 42nd Street Theatre
"You're Getting To Be A Habit With Me" .... Dorothy, Billy, Peggy and Ensemble
Scene 4: Dorothy Brock's Dressing Room
Scene 5: Stage of the 42nd Street Theatre
"Getting Out of Town" .... Full Company
Scene 6: The Arch Street Theatre, Philadelphia
"Dames" .... Billy and Men
"Keep Young and Beautiful" .... Maggie, Bert Barry and Girls
"Dames" (Continued) .... Full Company
Scene 7: Regency Club and Dorothy Brock's Hotel Suite
"I Only Have Eyes for You" .... Dorothy
Scene 8: Opening Night of *Pretty Lady* at the Arch Street Theatre, Philadelphia
"I Only Have Eyes for You" (Reprise) .... Bill and Girls
"We're in the Money" .... Annie, Peggy, Lorraine, Phyllis, Billy and Ensemble
Act One Finale .... Dorothy and Company

ACT II

Entr'acte .... Orchestra
Scene 1: A Backstage Corridor at the Arch Street Theatre, Philadelphia. Fifteen minutes later.
Scene 2: Dressing Rooms at the Arch Street Theatre
"Sunny Side to Every Situation" .... Annie and Ensemble
Scene 3: Backstage Corridor at the Arch Street Theatre
Scene 4: Broad Street Station, Philadelphia
"Lullaby of Broadway" .... Julian Marsh and Full Company
"Getting Out of Town" (Reprise) .... Bert, Maggie and Full Company

Scene 5: Stage of the 42nd Street Theatre, New York City
"Montage" .... Julian, Andy, Peggy and Ensemble
Scene 6: Peggy's Dressing Room
"About a Quarter to Nine" .... Dorothy and Peggy
Scene 7: The Opening Night of *Pretty Lady*
Overture .... Orchestra
"With Plenty of Money and You" .... Peggy and Men
"Shuffle Off to Buffalo" .... Bert, Maggie, Annie and Girls
"42nd Street" .... Peggy, Billy and Ensemble
Scene 8: Stage of the 42nd Street Theatre
"42nd Street" (Reprise) .... Julian
Finale .... Full Company

PLAYS PRODUCED OFF BROADWAY

○○○○○

DISTINCTIONS BETWEEN OFF BROADWAY AND BROADWAY productions at one end of the scale and Off Off Broadway productions at the other end have continued to blur in the New York theater. For the purposes of *Best Plays* listing, the term "Off Broadway" signifies a show that opened for general audiences in a mid-Manhattan theater seating 499 or fewer and 1) employed an Equity cast, 2) planned a regular schedule of 8 performances a week in an open-ended run (7 a week for solo shows and some other exceptions) and 3) offered itself to public comment by critics after a designated opening performance.

Occasional exceptions of inclusion (never of exclusion) are made to take in visiting troupes, borderline "showcase" presentations and nonqualifying productions that readers might expect to find in this list because they appear under an Off Broadway heading in other major sources of record.

Figures in parentheses following a play's title give number of performances. These numbers do not include previews or extra non-profit performances.

Plays marked with an asterisk (*) were still in a projected run on June 1, 2001. Their number of performances is figured from press opening through May 31, 2001.

In a listing of a show's numbers—dances, sketches, musical scenes, etc.—the titles of songs are identified wherever possible by their appearance in quotation marks (").

HOLDOVERS FROM PREVIOUS SEASONS

OFF BROADWAY SHOWS that were running on June 1, 2000 are listed below. More detailed information about them appears in previous *Best Plays* volumes of appropriate date. Important cast changes since opening night are recorded in the Cast Replacements section of this volume.

***The Fantasticks** (16,907; longest continuous run of record in the American theater). Musical suggested by the play *Les Romanesques* by Edmond Rostand; book and lyrics by Tom Jones; music by Harvey Schmidt. Opened May 3, 1960.

***Perfect Crime** (5,837). By Warren Manzi. Opened October 16, 1987.

***Tony 'n' Tina's Wedding** (4,168). By Artificial Intelligence. Opened February 6, 1988.

***Blue Man Group (Tubes)** (4,621). Performance piece by and with Blue Man Group. Opened November 17, 1991.

***Stomp** (3,048). Percussion performance piece created by Luke Cresswell and Steve McNicholas. Opened February 27, 1994.

***I Love You, You're Perfect, Now Change** (2,032). Musical revue with book and lyrics by Joe DiPietro; music by Jimmy Roberts. Opened August 1, 1996.

***Late Nite Catechism** (962). By Vicki Quade and Maripat Donovan. Opened October 3, 1996.

***De La Guarda** (1,144). Spectacle devised by De La Guarda (Pichon Baldinu, Diqui James, Gabriel Kerpel, Fabio D'Aquila, Tomas James, Alejandro Garcia, Gabriella Baldini). Opened June 16, 1998.

Over the River and Through the Woods (800). By Joe DiPietro. Opened October 5, 1998. (Closed September 3, 2000)

Forbidden Broadway Cleans Up Its Act! (754). Musical revue created and written by Gerard Alessandrini. Opened November 16, 1998. (Closed August 30, 2000)

***Naked Boys Singing!** (792). Musical revue conceived by Robert Schrock; written by various authors. Opened July 22, 1999.

The Countess (618). By Gregory Murphy. Opened September 28, 1999. (Closed December 30, 2000)

***The Vagina Monologues** (687). By Eve Ensler. Opened October 3, 1999.

Proof (79). By David Auburn. Opened May 23, 2000. (Closed July 30, 2000) Transferred to Broadway where it reopened 10/24/00; see the Plays Produced on Broadway section.

Dinner With Friends (654). By Donald Margulies. Opened November 4, 1999. (Closed May 27, 2001)

Bomb-itty of Errors (216). By Jordan Allen-Dutton, Jason Catalano, G.Q. and Erik Weiner; music by J.A.Q. Opened December 12, 1999. (Closed June 18, 2000)

Fully Committed (675). By Becky Mode; based on characters created by Becky Mode and Mark Setlock. Opened December 14, 1999. (Closed May 27, 2001)

***Our Sinatra** (613). Musical revue conceived by Eric Comstock, Christopher Gines and Hilary Kole; music and lyrics by various authors. Opened December 19, 1999.

Jitney (311). By August Wilson. Opened April 25, 2000. (Closed January 28, 2001)

Wake Up and Smell the Coffee (45). Solo performance by Eric Bogosian; written by Eric Bogosian. Opened May 4, 2000. (Closed June 11, 2000)

The Laramie Project (126). By Moisés Kaufman and members of the Tectonic Theater Project. Opened May 18, 2000. (Closed September 2, 2000)

PLAYS PRODUCED JUNE 1, 2000–MAY 31, 2001

Penn & Teller (8). At the Beacon Theater. Opened June 6, 2000. (Closed June 11, 2000)

WITH: Penn Jillette and Teller.

Sound, Rex Harris; music, Gary Stockdale; stage manager, Robert P. Libbon.

Manhattan Theatre Club production of **Current Events** (40). By David Marshall Grant. Lynne Meadow artistic director, Barry Grove executive director at City Center Stage II. Opened June 13, 2000. (Closed July 16, 2000)

Ethan .... John Gallagher Jr.
Danny .... Seth Kirschner
Diana .... Christine Ebersole
Adam .... Jon Tenney
Jamie .... Jeremy Hollingsworth
Eleanor .... Barbara Barrie

Directed by David Petrarca; scenery, Derek McLane; costumes, Jane Greenwood; lighting, Brian MacDevitt; sound, Bruce Ellman; original music, Jason Robert Brown; production stage manager, Jason Scott Eagan.

Presented in two parts.

Family secrets and gay coming-out drama played, with a sense of humor, against a backdrop of national politics.

Roundabout Theatre Company production of **Neil Simon's Hotel Suite** (102). By Neil Simon. Todd Haimes artistic director, Ellen Richard managing director, Julia C. Levy executive director, external affairs, at the Gramercy Theatre. Opened June 15, 2000. (Closed September 10, 2000)

Diana .... Helen Carey
Sidney .... Leigh Lawson
Millie .... Randy Graff
Marvin .... Ron Orbach
Borden; Bellhop .... Charlie McWade
Grace; Mimsey;
Women in Bed .... Amanda Serkasevich

Standbys and Understudies: Miss Carey—Francesca Faridany; Mr. Lawson—Ian Stuart; Ms. Graff—Ellen Ratner; Mr. Orbach—Richard Ziman; Mr. McWade—Matt Opatrny; Miss Serkasevich—Sandy Rustin.

Directed by John Tillinger; scenery, James Noone; costumes, Theoni V. Aldredge; lighting, Kevin Adams; sound, G. Thomas Clark; casting, Jay Binder, Jim Carnahan; production stage manager, Jay Adler; stage manager, Bradley McCormick; press, Boneau/Bryan-Brown, Adrian Bryan-Brown, Erin Dunn, Johnny Woodnal.

Presented in two parts.

Four playlets that echo other Neil Simon suites dealing with the farcical (and sentimental) frustrations of families under stress.

Playwrights Horizons production of **The Bubbly Black Girl Sheds Her Chameleon Skin** (32). Musical by Kirsten Childs. Tim Sanford artistic director, Leslie Marcus managing director, William Russo general manager, in association with Wind Dancer Theater, at Playwrights Horizons. Opened June 20, 2000. (Closed July 16, 2000)

Viveca .... LaChanze
Miss Pain; Harriet Tubman;
Secretary; Tallulah;
Granny .... Cheryl Alexander
Emily; Nilda; Sandra ... Natalie Venetia Belcon
Larry; Keith .... Duane Boutte
Gregory .... Darius de Haas
Chitty Chatty Pal 1; Secretary;
Ballet Teacher; Sophia .... Angel Desai
Jazz Teacher;
Dance Captain; Lucas .... Jerry Dixon
Prince; Cosmic; Policeman;
Director Bob .... Jonathan Dokuchitz
Chitty Chatty Pal 2; Secretary;
Modern Teacher; Scarlett .... Felicia Finley
Daddy; Policeman .... Robert Jason Jackson
Mommy; Yolanda; Delilah ... Debra M. Walton

Directed by Wilfredo Medina; choreography, A.C. Ciulla; scenery, David Gallo; costumes, David C. Woolard; lighting, Michael Lincoln; sound, Jon Weston; musical director, Fred Carl; orchestrations, Joe Baker; associate producer, Ira Weitzman; production stage manager, Alexis Shorter; press, the Publicity Office.

Presented without intermission.

The musical journey of a female African-American Broadway dancer from childhood to adulthood. Partially developed during the 1998 National Music Theater Conference at the Eugene O'Neill Theater Center.

The Joseph Papp Public Theater/New York Shakespeare Festival production of **The Winter's Tale** (10). Revival of the play by William Shakespeare. George C. Wolfe producer, Rosemarie Tichler artistic producer, Mark Litvin managing director, at the Delacorte Theater. Opened July 6, 2000. (Closed July 16, 2000)

Time; Clown	Michael Stuhlbarg
Archidamus	Gareth Saxe
Camillo	Henry Stram
Polixenes	Graham Winton
Leontes	Keith David
Hermione	Aunjanue Ellis
Mamillius	Paul W. Tiesler
Emilia; Mopsa	Emma Bowers
Second Lady; Dorcas	Kena Tangi Dorsey
First Lord	Francis Jue
Antigonus	Jonathan Hadary
Polina	Randy Danson
Jailer	Wayne Kasserman
First Attendant; Florizel	Jesse Pennington
Servant; Mariner	Michael Traynor
First Officer	Daniel G. Pino
Old Shepherd	Bill Buell
Autolycus	Bronson Pinchot
Perdita	Erica N. Tazel

WITH: Lucia Brawley, Phyllis Johnson, Jenny Sandler.

Directed by Brian Kulick; choreography, Naomi Goldberg; scenery, Riccardo Hernandez; costumes, Anita Yavich; lighting, Kenneth Posner; sound, Ken Travis; original music, Mark Bennett; associate producers, Wiley Hausam, Bonnie Metzgar; casting, Jordan Thaler, Heidi Griffiths; production stage manager, James Latus; press, Carol Fineman, Tom Naro.

Presented in two parts.

A king destroys his family in this Shakespearean romance about the effects of jealous rage. First noted performance at the Globe Theatre on May 15, 1611.

Lincoln Center Theater production of **Spinning Into Butter** (61). By Rebecca Gilman. André Bishop artistic director, Bernard Gersten executive producer, produced in association with Lincoln Center Festival 2000, at the Mitzi E. Newhouse Theater. Opened July 26, 2000. (Closed September 16, 2000)

Sarah Daniels	Hope Davis
Patrick Chibas	Jai Rodriguez
Ross Collins	Daniel Jenkins
Dean Burton Strauss	Henry Strozier
Dean Catherine Kenney	Brenda Wehle
Mr. Meyers	Matt DeCaro
Greg Sullivan	Steven Pasquale

Understudies: Miss Davis—René Augesen; Mr. Rodriguez—Michael Ray Escamilla; Mr. Jenkins—Karl Kenzler; Messrs. Strozier, DeCaro—Traber Burns; Miss Wehle—Pat Nesbit; Mr. Pasquale—Johnathan F. McClain.

Directed by Daniel Sullivan; scenery, John Lee Beatty; costumes, Jess Goldstein; lighting, Brian MacDevitt; original music and sound, Dan Moses Schreier; casting, Daniel Swee; stage manager, Michael Brunner; press, Philip Rinaldi Publicity.

Time: The present. Place: Belmont College in Vermont. Presented in two parts.

A college dean confronts her own attitudes toward race and racism amid expanding diversity in higher education. Originally produced by Chicago's Goodman Theatre in 1999.

Avow (29). By Bill C. Davis. Produced by Janet Robinson, MJM Productions, Leonard Soloway and Steven M. Levy, at Century Center for the Performing Arts. Opened July 27, 2000. (Closed August 20, 2001)

Tom	Scott Ferrara
Brian	Christopher Sieber
Father Raymond	Alan Campbell
Irene	Sarah Knowlton
Julie	Kathleen Doyle
Rose	Jane Powell
Father Nash	Reathel Bean

Understudy: Miss Powell—Kathleen Doyle.

Directed by Jack Hofsiss; scenery, David Jenkins; costumes, Julie Weiss; lighting, Ken Billington; sound, Peter Fitzgerald; associate producers, Jeff Blumenkrantz, Jeffrey Kent; casting, Julie Hughes, Barry Moss; production stage manager, Lee J. Kahrs; press, Cromarty and Company.

Time: The present. Place: An American city.

A gay couple seeks to be married by a Catholic priest, who then becomes enamored of the pregnant sister of one of the men. Originally presented in New York by the Directors Company.

Godspell (77). Revival of musical based on the Gospel according to St. Matthew; book by John-Michael Tebelak; music and new lyrics by Stephen Schwartz. Produced by NET Theatrical Productions at the Theatre at St. Peter's Church. Opened August 2, 2000. (Closed October 7, 2000)

CAST: Shoshana Bean, Tim Cain, Catherine Carpenter, Will Erat, Barrett Foa, Lucia Giannetta, Capathia Jenkins, Chad Kimball, Leslie Kritzer, Eliseo Roman.

Directed by Shawn Rozsa and RJ Tolan; choreography, Ovi Vargas; scenery, Kevin Lock; costumes, William Ivey Long, Bernard Grenier; lighting, Herrick Goldman; musical direction, Dan Schachner; production stage manager, Samuel-Moses Jones; press, Keith Sherman and Associates, Tom Chiodo.

Fervent, flower-child inflected retelling of the Gospel according to St. Matthew in musical form. Originally opened at the Cherry Lane Theatre 5/15/71. Transferred to Off Broadway's Promenade Theatre where it ran for 2,124 performances before a 527 performance Broadway run at the Broadhurst.

Berlin to Broadway With Kurt Weill (121). Revival of the musical revue drawn from the work of Kurt Weill. Lyrics by Maxwell Anderson, Marc Blitzstein, Bertolt Brecht, Jacques Deval, Michael Feingold, Ira Gershwin, Paul Green, Langston Hughes, Alan Jay Lerner, Ogden Nash, George Tabori, Arnold Weinstein. Text and format by Gene Lerner. Produced by Laura Heller, Carol Ostrow and Edwin W. Schloss at the Triad Theatre. Opened August 19, 2000. (Closed December 2, 2001)

Mezzo .... Lorinda Lisitza
Soprano .... Veronica Mittenzwei
Baritone .... Björn Olsson
Tenor .... Michael Winther
Pianist .... Eric Stern

Understudies: Messrs. Winther, Olsson—Richard Todd Adams; Misses Lisitza, Mittenzwei—Cristin J. Hubbard; Mr.Stern—Benjamin Toth.

Directed and choreographed by Hal Simons; scenery, William Barclay; lighting, Phil Monat; costumes, Suzy Benzinger; musical direction, arrangements, Eric Stern; production stage manager, Richard Costabile; press, Media Blitz, Beck Lee.

Presented in two parts.

A musical collage covering the shows and songs to which Kurt Weill contributed his versatile talents. Originally produced at Off Broadway's Theatre de Lys 10/1/72 for 152 performances.

ACT I

"How to Survive" .... Cast
"Barbara Song" .... Lorinda
"Useless Song" .... Michael
"Jealousy Duet" .... Lorinda and Veronica
"Pirate Jenny" .... Veronica
"Mack the Knife" .... Björn and Cast
"March Ahead"/"Don't Be Afraid" .... Veronica
"Surabaya Johnny" .... Lorinda
"Bilbao Song"/"Mandalay Song" .... Björn and Michael
"Alabama Song" .... Veronica and Cast
"Deep in Alaska" .... Michael and Cast
"As You Make Your Bed" .... Cast
"I Wait for a Ship" .... Veronica and Men
"Sailor's Tango" .... Björn and Cast

ACT II

"How Can You Tell An American?" .... Cast
"Hymn To Peace" .... Cast
"Johnny's Song" .... Michael
"September Song" .... Björn
"It Never Was You" .... Lorinda
"Saga of Jenny" Lorinda and Men
"My Ship" .... Veronica
"Speak Low" .... Cast
"That's Him" .... Veronica
"Progress" .... Björn and Michael
"Ain't It Awful, the Heat?" .... Cast
"Lonely House" .... Michael
"Train to Johannesburg" .... Michael and Cast
"Cry, the Beloved Country" .... Veronica and Cast
"Lost in the Stars" .... Björn and Cast
"Love Song" .... Cast

The Joseph Papp Public Theater/New York Shakespeare Festival production of **Julius Caesar** (13). Revival of the play by William Shakespeare. George C. Wolfe producer, Rosemarie Tichler artistic producer, Mark Litvin managing director, at the Delacorte Theater. Opened August 20, 2000. (Closed September 3, 2000)

Julius Caesar .... David McCallum
Marcus Brutus .... Jamey Sheridan
Caius Cassius .... Dennis Boutsikaris
Casca; Titinius .... Ritchie Coster
Decius Brutus;
Messala .... Peter Jay Fernandez
Cinna; Lucilius .... James Shanklin
Metellus .... Cimber Ezra Knight
Trebonius; Strato .... Curt Hostetter
Caius Ligarius;
Volumnius .... Larry Paulsen
Marc Antony .... Jeffrey Wright
Octavius Caesar .... Sean McNall
Lepidus; Cicero .... Clement Fowler
Publius .... Neal Lerner
Popilius Lena .... Jonathan Earl Peck
Calphurnia .... Judith Hawking
Portia .... Colette Kilroy
Soothsayer .... Ching Valdes-Aran
Artemidorus .... Nadia Bowers
Clitus .... Keldrik Crowder
Dardanius .... Richard Frankfather
A Cobbler .... Pablo T. Schreiber
Lucius .... Wayne Kasserman
Servant to Antony .... Robert K. Wu
Cinna, the poet .... Jason Howard

WITH: Sila Agavale, Dylan Carusona, Lizzy Davis, Holly Natwora, Lloyd C. Porter, Charles Daniel Sandoval, Christopher Sheller.

Directed by Barry Edelstein; scenery, Narelle Sissons; costumes, Angela Wendt; lighting, Donald Holder; sound, Ken Travis, fight direction, J. Steven White; original music, John Gromada; associate producers, Wiley Hausam, Bonnie Metzgar; casting, Jordan Thaler, Heidi Griffiths; production stage manager, Martha Donaldson; press, Carol Fineman, Tom Naro.

Shakespeare's story of the conflict between political ambition and jealousy played in ancient Rome. It was the play with which Orson Welles and John Houseman, in a Fascist-inspired interpretation, introduced their Mercury Theatre (at the former Comedy) 11/11/37 for 157 performances. First noted performance at the Globe Theatre on September 21, 1599.

High Infidelity (38). By John Dooley. Produced by Jennifer Smith Rockwood at the Promenade Theatre. Opened August 23, 2000. (Closed September 24, 2000)

Jane McAlpin .... Jennifer Roszell
Dr. Edward Finger .... Neil Maffin
Bill Brennan .... Daniel Ziskie
Charles Gordon .... John Davidson
Ellen Gordon .... Morgan Fairchild

Directed by Luke Yankee; scenery, Harrison Williams; costumes, Carrie Robbins; lighting, Jack Mehler; sound, Catherine D. Mardis; production stage manager, Christine Catti; press, Keith Sherman and Associates.

Presented in two parts.

Comedy about a philandering politician and his long-suffering wife.

Imperfect Chemistry (46). Musical with story and music by Albert Tapper; book and lyrics by James Racheff. Produced by Back to Back Productions at the Minetta Lane Theatre. Opened August 24, 2000. (Closed October 1, 2000)

Dr. Goodman; Dr. Bubinski .... John Jellison
Harry Lizzarde .... Brooks Ashmanskas
Dr. Alvin Rivers .... Ken Barnett
Dr. Elizabeth Gibbs .... Amanda Watkins
Ensemble .... Joel Carlton, Michael Greenwood, Deirdre Lovejoy, Sara Schmidt

Orchestra: August Eriksmoen conductor, keyboard; Matt Beck electric guitar, classical guitar, banjo; Jay Brandford flute, clarinet, alto and tenor saxophone; Nicolas D'Amato double bass, electric bass; Ray Franks clarinet, bass clarinet, tenor and baritone saxophone; Brad Mason trumpet; Michael C. Surprenant drums.

Understudies: Mr. Barnett—Joel Carlton; Messrs. Jellison, Ashmanskas—Michael Greenwood; Miss Watkins—Sara Schmidt.

Swings: Sunita Param, Jonathan Stewart.

Directed and choreographed by John Ruocco; scenery, Rob Odorisio; costumes, Curtis Hay; lighting, John-Paul Szczepanski; sound, Robert Kaplowitz; musical direction, vocal arrangements, orchestrations, August Eriksmoen; executive producer, Peter Press; casting, Cindi Rush; production stage manager, Renée Rimland; press, the Pete Sanders Group.

Presented in two parts.

Love and science pair in a comedy about a cure for baldness that has devolutionary side effects and unscrupulous drug marketers.

ACT I

A lecture hall: the Avalon compound
"Avalon" .... Full Company
Rivers and Gibbs's lab at Avalon
"Dream Come True" .... Rivers and Gibbs
Bubinski's basement office next to his cyclotron
"Serious Business" .... Bubinski, Lizzarde and Ensemble
Goodman's tower office
"Dreams Come True" (Reprise) .... Rivers and Gibbs
Bubinski's office
Rivers and Gibbs's lab
"It's All Written In Your Genes" .... Rivers and Gibbs
"Ahhhh" .... Gibbs
On a golf course fairway
"St. Andrew" .... Goodman and Ensemble
In the lab, late at night
"Leave Your Fate to Fate" .... Lizzarde
Goodman's office, late at night
"Ahhhh" (Reprise) .... Rivers, Gibbs
In the lab, the morning after
Goodman's office, the same day
"Hell to Pay" .... Goodman and Ensemble
Outside the gates of Avalon
"Dream Come True"; "Avalon" (Reprise) .... Rivers and Gibbs

ACT II

In limbo with Bubinski and Lizzarde
"Loxagane (Avalon)" .... Company
A television studio shoot for an informercial
"Loxagane (Avalon)" .... Company
Backstage at the studio
"Big Hair" .... Lizzarde and Ensemble

A hotel room in Tokyo/A hotel room in Rio
"E-Mail Love Notes" .... Rivers/Gibbs
A steambath
"Bub's Song" .... Bubinski, Lizzarde and Ensemble
New York City Street
"Chaos Ballet" .... Company
In the cockpit of a small airplane
A tropical island
"Avalon" (Reprise) .... Company

Brooklyn Academy of Music presentation of an **Almeida Theatre Company** production of **Richard II** (14). Revival of the play by William Shakespeare. Bruce C. Ratner chairman of the board, Karen Brooks Hopkins president, Joseph V. Melillo executive producer, at the BAM Harvey Theater. Opened September 7, 2000. (Closed October 1, 2000)

King Richard the Second .... Ralph Fiennes
John of Gaunt .... David Burke
Edmund, Duke of York .... Oliver Ford Davies
Henry Bolingbroke .... Linus Roache
Duke of Aumerle .... Oliver Ryan
Thomas Mowbray .... Paul Moriarty
Queen Isabel .... Emilia Fox
Lady .... Danielle King
Duchess of York .... Barbara Jefford
Duchess of Gloucester .... Angela Down
Lord Marshal .... Ian Barritt
First Herald .... Damian O'Hare
Second Herald .... Stephen Campbell Moore
Salisbury;
Abbot of Westminster .... Roger Swaine
Bagot .... Sean Baker
Bushy .... David Fahm
Green .... Ed Waters
Bishop of Carlisle .... Bernard Gallagher
Captain of the Welsh army .... Alan David
Henry Percy .... Robert Swann
Harry Percy .... Stephen Campbell Moore
Lord Ross;
Duke of Surrey .... Philip Dunbar
Lord Willoughby;
Lord Fitzwater .... Stephen Finegold
Exton .... John Bennett
Exton's Man .... David Fahm
Gardener .... Alan David
First Gardener's Man;
York's Man .... Damian O'Hare
Second Gardener's Man .... Ed Waters
Keeper of the prison .... Paul Benzing
Groom to King Richard .... Philip Dunbar
Attendants .... Paul Benzing, David Salter, Alex Sims, Marc Small

Directed by Jonathan Kent; scenery and costumes, Paul Brown; lighting, Mark Henderson; sound, John A. Leonard; fight direction, Paul Benzing; music, Jonathan Dove; assistant director, David Salter; press, Elena Park, Susan Yung, Amy Hughes, Kila Packett.

Presented in two parts.

Shakepeare's history play in which an inept ruler rises to some stature, but too late.

This production originally was presented March–August 2000 at the Almeida's Shoreditch perfomance space in Islington, North London. The first noted performance was at the Globe Theatre on February 7, 1601, the eve of the Earl of Essex's planned (and failed) rebellion against Queen Elizabeth.

Brooklyn Academy of Music presentation of an **Almeida Theatre Company** production of **Coriolanus** (12). Revival of the play by William Shakespeare. Bruce C. Ratner chairman of the board, Karen Brooks Hopkins president, Joseph V. Melillo executive producer, at the BAM Harvey Theater. Opened September 9, 2000. (Closed September 30, 2000)

Romans
Caius Martius (Coriolanus) .... Ralph Fiennes
Titus Lartius .... Robert Swann
Cominius .... David Burke
Menenius Agrippa .... Oliver Ford Davies
Volumnia .... Barbara Jefford
Virgilia .... Emilia Fox
Valeria .... Angela Down
Gentlewoman .... Danielle King
Young Martius .... Gregg Prentice, Rowland Stirling

First Roman Senator .... Philip Dunbar
Second Roman Senator .... Roger Swaine
Sicinius Velutus .... Alan David
Junius Brutus .... Bernard Gallagher
1st Citizen .... Paul Moriarty
2nd Citizen .... Sean Baker
3rd Citizen .... Damian O'Hare
4th Citizen .... Stephen Finegold
5th Citizen .... Ed Waters
6th Citizen .... Paul Benzing
7th Citizen .... Marc Small
Messenger .... Oliver Ryan

Volscians
Tullus Aufidius Linus Roache
1st Volsci Senator .... John Bennett
2nd Volsci Senator .... Ian Barritt
1st Volsci .... Stephen Campbell Moore
2nd Volsci .... David Fahm
3rd Volsci .... Oliver Ryan

Directed by Jonathan Kent; scenery and costumes, Paul Brown; lighting, Mark Henderson; sound, John A. Leonard; fight direction, William Hobbs; music, Jonathan Dove; assistant director, David Salter; press, Elena Park, Susan Yung, Amy Hughes, Kila Packett.

Presented in two parts.

A Shakespearean warning that pride goes before the fall as Coriolanus refuses to acknowledge the importance of listening to the masses. This production originally was presented March–August 2000 at the Almeida's Shoreditch perfomance space in Islington, North London. The first performance of the play was probably around 1609.

***The Syringa Tree** (297). By Pamela Gien. Produced by Matt Salinger at Playhouse 91. Opened September 14, 2000.

Performed by Pamela Gien.

Directed by Larry Moss; scenery, Kenneth Foy; costumes, William Ivey Long; lighting, Jason Kantrowitz; sound, Tony Suraci; production stage manager, Fredric H. Orner; press, Bill Evans and Associates, Jim Randolph.

Cinco amigos: Ricardo Puente, Henry Gainza, Lissette Gonzalez, Philip Anthony and Allen Hidalgo in 4 Guys Named José . . . and Una Mujer Named Maria! *Photo: Carol Rosegg*

Time: Various times, past and present, beginning in 1963. Place: Johannesburg, South Africa. Performed without intermission.

A young woman grapples with the many ripples spread by South African apartheid. First produced at Seattle's A Contemporary Theatre.

4 Guys Named José . . . and Una Mujer Named Maria! (191). Musical revue by David Coffman and Dolores Prida, book by Miss Prida. Produced by Enrique Iglesias and Dasha Epstein at the Blue Angel Theatre. Opened September 18, 2000. (Closed March 4, 2001)

CAST: Philip Anthony, Henry Gainza, Lissette Gonzalez, Allen Hidalgo, Ricardo Puente.

Directed by Susana Tubert; choreography, Maria Torres; scenery, Mary Houston; costumes, Tania Bass; lighting, Aaron Spivey; sound, T. Richard Fitzgerald; musical supervision and arrangments, Oscar Hernandez; production stage manager, Joe Witt; press, Keith Sherman and Associates, Dan Fortune.

Anthology of popular Latin songs wrapped around a story of four Latino men who put on a show in midwinter Omaha.

Playwrights Horizons production of **The Butterfly Collection** (16). By Theresa Rebeck. Tim Sanford artistic director, Leslie Marcus managing director, William Russo general manager, at Playwrights Horizons. Opened October 3, 2000. (Closed October 15, 2000)

Sophie	Maggie Lacey	Laurie	Betsy Aidem
Frank	Reed Birney	Ethan	James Colby
Margaret	Marian Seldes	Paul	Brian Murray

Directed by Bartlett Sher; scenery, Andrew Jackness; costumes, Ann Hould-Ward; lighting, Christopher Akerlind; sound, Kurt B. Kellenberger; production stage manager, Roy Harris; press, the Publicity Office.

Presented in two parts.

No flitting: Marian Seldes and Brian Murray in Theresa Rebeck's The Butterfly Collection. *Photo: Joan Marcus*

The men in an artistically inclined, dysfunctional Connecticut family compete for the attentions of a young woman who is the literary assistant to one of them.

Tallulah Hallelujah! (97). By Tovah Feldshuh, with additional material by Larry Amoros and Linda Selman. Produced by Eric Krebs and Chase Mishkin at the Douglas Fairbanks Theatre. Opened October 10, 2000. (Closed December 31, 2000)

Tallulah .... Tovah Feldshuh
Meredith Willson .... Bob Goldstone
Corporal Chapman .... Mark Deklin

Directed by William Wesbrooks; scenery, Michael Schweikardt; costumes, Carrie Robbins; lighting, Jeff Croiter; sound, Jill B.C. DuBoff; musical direction, arrangements, Bob Goldstone; production stage manager, Babette Roberts; press, KPM Associates, Kevin P. McAnarney, Grant Lindsey.

Presented without intermission.

Tallulah Bankhead giving an impromptu performance at a USO show on the evening following a controversial 1956 opening as Blanche DuBois in *A Streetcar Named Desire*.

The Gorey Details (65). Musical by Edward Gorey, music by Peter Matz. Produced by Ken Hoyt and Kevin McDermott, in association with Brent Peek, at Century Center for the Performing Arts. Opened October 16, 2000. (Closed December 10, 2000)

CAST: Alison Crowley, Allison DeSalvo, Matt Kuehl, Daniel C. Levine, Kevin McDermott, Ben Nordstrom, Liza Shaller, Clare Stollak, Christopher Youngsman.

Directed and choreographed by Daniel Levans; scenery, Jesse Poleshuck; costumes, Martha Bromelmeier; lighting, Craig Kennedy; sound, Johnna Doty; orchestrations, Peter Matz; musical direction, Bruce W. Coyle; production stage manager, Thom Schilling; press, Keith Sherman and Associates, Brett Oberman.

Presented in two parts.

Sketches with songs inspired by the artist-writer's macabre work.

Roundabout Theatre Company production of **Juno and the Paycock** (77). Revival of the play by Sean O'Casey. Todd Haimes artistic director, Ellen Richard managing director, Julia C. Levy executive director, external affairs, at the Gramercy Theatre. Opened October 19, 2000. (Closed December 24, 2000)

Johnny Boyle .... Jason Butler Harner
Mary Boyle .... Gretchen Cleevely
Juno Boyle .... Dearbhla Molloy
Jerry Devine .... Norbert Leo Butz
Captain Jack Boyle .... Jim Norton
Joxer Daly .... Thomas Jay Ryan
Sewing Machine Man ... Edward James Hyland
Coal Vendor .... John Keating
Charles Bentham .... Liam Craig
Maisie Madigan .... Cynthia Darlow
Mrs. Tancred .... Roberta Maxwell
Needle Nugent .... Edward James Hyland
Neighbor .... Kelly Mares
Mobilizer .... George Heslin
Furniture Man .... John Keating
Irregular .... Michael LiDondici
Policeman .... John Keating

Understudies: Miss Molloy—Cynthia Darlow; Messrs. Norton, Ryan—Claywood Sempliner; Miss Cleevely—Kelly Mares; Misses Maxwell, Darlow—Barbara Sims; Messrs. Butz, Hyland—George Heslin; Messrs. Craig, Heslin—John Keating; Messrs. Harner, Keating—Michael LiDondici.

Directed by John Crowley; scenery and costumes, Rae Smith; lighting, Brian MacDevitt; original music and sound, Donald DiNicola; casting, Amy Christopher; production stage manager, Jay Adler; stage manager, Marienne Chapman; press, Boneau/Bryan-Brown, Adrian Bryan-Brown, Matt Polk, Orlando Veras.

Time: August and November, 1922. Place: The Boyle family apartment in a Dublin tenement. Presented in two parts.

An impoverished Irish family of incapacitated men and victimized women attempts to rebuild in the wake of civil war. This production was a restaging of a 1999 version directed by Mr. Crowley, featuring Miss Molloy, for the Donmar Warehouse, London.

The Unexpected Man (111). By Yasmina Reza, translated by Christopher Hampton. Produced by Julian Schlossberg, Ben Sprecher, Ted Tulchin, William P. Miller, in association with Aaron Levy and Morton Wolkowitz, at the Promenade Theatre. Opened October 24, 2000. (Closed January 28, 2001)

The Man .... Alan Bates
The Woman .... Eileen Atkins

Standbys: Mr. Bates—Jack Davidson; Miss Atkins—Jennifer Sternberg.

Directed by Matthew Warchus; scenery and costumes, Mark Thompson; lighting, Hugh Vanstone; sound, Mic Pool, David Bullard; original music, Gary Yershon; associate producer, Sonny Everett; casting, Stephanie Klapper; production stage manager, Michael Brunner; press, Jeffrey Richards Associates, John Michael Moreno, Chloe Taylor, Sid King.

Presented without intermission.

A French man and woman fantasize about what each might say to the other as they travel on a train from Paris to Frankfurt. Originally produced in the Pit Theatre, London, by the Royal Shakespeare Company.

Tabletop (72). By Rob Ackerman. Produced by Amy Danis, Richard Firestone, Mark Johannes, Joan D. Firestone and Ellen M. Krass, in association with Karen Davidov, at the American Place Theatre. Opened October 30, 2001. (Closed December 31, 2000)

Oscar .... Harvy Blanks
Ron .... Jeremy Webb
Jeffrey .... Dean Nolen
Dave .... Jack Koenig
Andrea .... Elizabeth Hanly Rice
Marcus .... Rob Bartlett

Understudy: Miss Rice—Edelen McWilliams.

Directed by Constance Grappo; scenery, Dean Taucher; costumes, Ilona Somogyi; lighting, Jack Mehler; casting, Jerry Beaver; production stage manager, Donald Fried; press, Cromarty and Company, Peter Cromarty, Alice Cromarty, Sherri Jean Katz.

Don't ask Alice: Joan MacIntosh and Jeroen Krabbe (top) in Susan Sontag's Alice in Bed. *Photo: Chris Van der Burght*

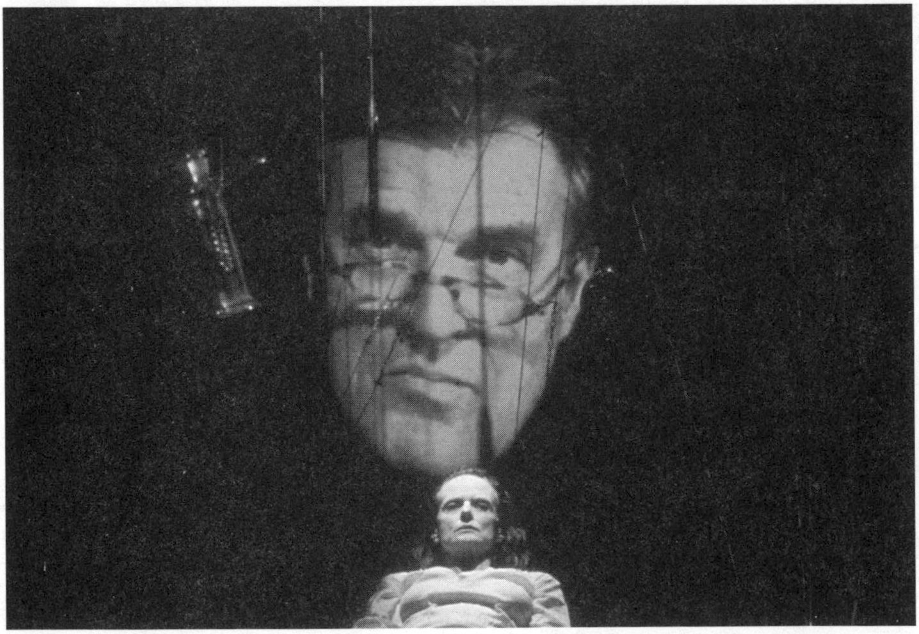

Time: Now. Place: Studio of Marcus Gordon. Presented without intermission.

The comic stresses, strains and ego negotiations in a television-commercial studio. Originally produced by the Working Theatre at Dance Theatre Workshop.

New York Theatre Workshop production of **Alice in Bed** (39). By Susan Sontag. James C. Nicola artistic director, Lynn Moffat managing director, in association with Het Zuidelijk Tonnel and Holland Festival. Opened November 5, 2000. (Closed December 9, 2000)

Alice .... Joan MacIntosh
Young Man .... Jorre Vandenbussche
Father .... Jeroen Krabbe
Harry, Her Brother .... Paul Rudd
Mother .... Valda Setterfield
Margaret Fuller .... Elizabeth Marvel
Emily Dickinson .... Arija Bareikis
Kundry .... Constance Hauman
Myrtha .... Aurelia Schaefer

Directed by Ivo van Hove; scenery, Jan Versweyveld; costumes, A.F. Vandevorst; videography, Runa Islam; production stage manager, Martha Donaldson; press, Richard Kornberg and Associates, Don Summa.

Presented without intermission.

Technology-driven exploration of the frustrated life of famous sister Alice James, whose siblings included novelist Henry and philosopher William.

Cobb (93). By Lee Blessing. Produced by Melting Pot Theatre Company, Larry Hirschhorn artistic director, Darren Press managing director, by arrangement with Kevin Spacey and Trigger Street Productions, at the Lucille Lortel Theatre. Opened November 8, 2000. (Closed February 11, 2001)

Mr. Cobb .... Michael Cullen
The Peach .... Matthew Mabe
Ty .... Michael Sabatino
Oscar Charleston .... Clark Jackson

Directed by Joe Brancato; scenery, Matthew Maraffi; costumes, Daryl A. Stone; lighting, Jeff Nellis; sound, Jerry M. Yager, One Dream Sound; production stage manager, Richard A. Hodge; press, Barlow-Hartman Public Relations.

Presented without intermission.

A great baseball player confronts his younger self and the demons that drive him.

Strictly Personal (150). By Jake Feinberg. Produced by Strictly Productions at the Soho Playhouse. Opened November 8, 2000. (Closed March 11, 2001)

Darlene .... Angela Roberts
Dan .... Daniel Cantor
James .... Hayden Adams
Freddie .... Steven Arvanites
Mike .... Angela Roberts
Mom .... Lucy Martin
Billie .... Kimberly Farrell
Louise .... Anne Newhall
Lori .... Anne Bobby

Standbys: Misses Roberts, Martin, Farrell, Newhall, Bobby—Stacey Scotte; Messrs. Cantor, Adams, Arvanites—Chris Tomaino.

Directed by Donna Drake; scenery, George Xenos, Robert Bissinger; costumes, Caroline Birks; lighting, Michael Gilliam; casting, Jessica Gilburne, Ed Urban; production stage manager, Brian Klevan Schneider; press, Origlio Public Relations, Tony Origlio, Emily Lowe, Lawrence Kern.

Time: Today. Place: New York City. Presented in two parts.

A romantic comedy about two people who re-enter the dating game after failed marriages.

Manhattan Theatre Club production of **A Class Act** (29). Musical with music and lyrics by Edward Kleban; book by Linda Kline and Lonny Price. Lynne Meadow artistic director, Barry Grove executive producer, in association with Musical Theatre Works, at City Center Stage II. Opened November 9, 2000. (Closed December 3, 2000)

Just Marvy (and me): Lonny Price and Ray Wills in the Off Broadway production of A Class Act. *Photo: Joan Marcus*

Mona .... Nancy Anderson
Lucy .... Carolee Carmello
Lehman .... Jonathan Freeman
Sophie .... Randy Graff
Bobby .... David Hibbard
Felicia .... Julia Murney
Ed .... Lonny Price
Charley .... Ray Wills

Directed by Lonny Price; choreography, Scott Wise; scenery, James Noone; costumes, Carrie Robbins; lighting, Kevin Adams; sound, Mark Menard, Geoff Zink; orchestrations, Larry Hochman; musical direction, vocal arrangements, dance music, Todd Ellison; music coordinator, John Miller; additional choreography, Marguerite Derricks; production stage manager, Heather Fields; press, Boneau/Bryan-Brown, Chris Boneau, Steven Padla, Rachel Applegate.

Celebration of the life of Edward Kleban told through his own music and lyrics. Transferred to Broadway where it opened 3/11/01; see Plays Produced on Broadway section for complete listing.

End of the World Party (108). By Chuck Ranberg. Produced by Kings Road Entertainment, in association with Tim Ranney, at the 47th Street Theatre. Opened November 9, 2000. (Closed February 25, 2001)

Hunter .... Jim J. Bullock
Roger .... Christopher Durham
Phil .... Brian Cooper
Will .... Anthony Barrile
Travis .... David Drake
Nick .... Russell Scott Lewis
Chip .... Adam Simmons

Understudies: Messrs. Bullock, Barrile—Curtis Harwell; Messrs. Cooper, Simmons—Michael Seelbach; Messrs. Drake, Durham, Lewis—Steven Guy.

Directed by Matthew Lombardo; scenery, Christopher Pickart; costumes, Raymond Dragon; lighting, Michael Gilliam; sound, original music, Michael Sottile; production stage manager, Megan Smith; press, David Gersten and Associates.

Time: Last Summer. Place: Beach house on Fire Island in the pines and environs. Presented in two parts.

Gay men gather at Fire Island in the summer to talk about life and love.

***Maybe Baby, It's You** (145). By Charlie Shanian and Shari Simpson. Produced by Entertainment Events at the Theater at St. Luke's. Opened November 9, 2000.

CAST: Charlie Shanian, Shari Simpson.

Directed by Peter Webb; costumes, Emily Straka; lighting, Jim Hultquist; design consultant, Christopher Goumas; press, David Gersten and Associates.

Series of sketches about romantic relationships. Restaging of a production that played at the Currican Theater and Soho Playhouse.

American Rhapsody: A New Musical Revue (231). Songs by George Gershwin and Ira Gershwin. Text by Ruth Leon, KT Sullivan and Mark Nadler. Produced by Louise Westergaard, Stephen Downey, Jay Harris and Peter Martin, in association with Linda Wassong, at the Triad Theatre. Opened November 10, 2000. (Closed May 27, 2001)

CAST: Mark Nadler, KT Sullivan.

Directed by Ruth Leon; musical staging, Donald Saddler; scenery, William Barclay; costumes, Roz Goldberg; lighting, Phil Monat, John Tees III; musical arrangements, Mark Nadler, KT Sullivan; production stage manager, Claude E. Sloan Jr.; press, the Pete Sanders Group, Pete Sanders, Jim Mannino, Glenna Freedman.

Presented in two parts.

Revue featuring songs by George Gershwin and Ira Gershwin.

City Center Voices! presentation of **Arsenic and Old Lace** (1). Staged reading of the play by Joseph Kesselring. Judith E. Daykin president and executive director, Alec Baldwin producer, Steve Lawson artistic director, at City Center. Opened November 11, 2000. (Closed November 11, 2000)

Beach boys: Jim J. Bullock, Christopher Durham, Brian Cooper, Russell Scott Lewis and Adam Simmons (overalls) in Chuck Ranberg's End of the World Party. *Photo: David Morgan*

Abby Brewster .... Celeste Holm
Rev. Dr. Harper .... Edmond Genest
Teddy Brewster .... Tuck Milligan
Officer Brophy .... John Hines
Officer Klein .... John Rothman
Martha Brewster .... Joanne Woodward
Elaine Harper .... Jennifer Van Dyck
Mortimer Brewster .... Alec Baldwin
Mr. Gibbs .... William Duell
Jonathan Brewster .... Terrence Mann
Dr. Einstein .... Lee Wilkof
Officer O'Hara .... Joe Grifasi
Lieutenant Rooney .... Edmond Genest
Mr. Witherspoon .... William Duell
Stage Directions .... Ethan Sandler

Directed by Steve Lawson; lighting, Tricia Toliver; sound, Scott Lehrer; production stage manager, Casey Aileen Rafter; press, Philip Rinaldi Publicity.

Time: September in the early 1940s. Place: Living room of the Brewster home in Brooklyn. Presented in three parts.

Original Broadway production by Howard Lindsay and Russel Crouse. *Arsenic and Old Lace* was a 1940–41 *Best Plays* choice, opening 1/10/41 for 1,444 performances.

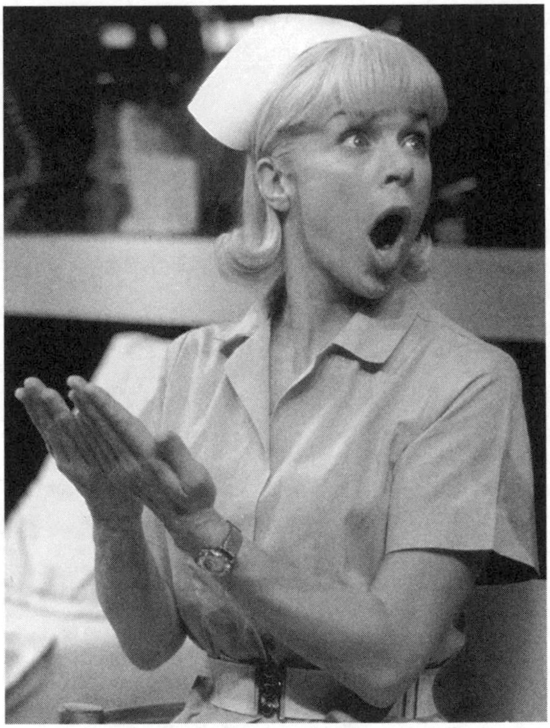

Dee-licious: Janie Dee in Alan Ayckbourn's Comic Potential. *Photo: Joan Marcus*

Manhattan Theatre Club production of **Comic Potential** (62). By Alan Ayckbourn. Lynne Meadow artistic director, Barry Grove executive producer, by special arrangement Michael Codron, at City Center Stage I. Opened November 16, 2000. (Closed January 7, 2001)

Adam Trainsmith .... Alexander Chaplin
Doctor; Farmer;
Man in Dress Shop;
Turkey .... John Curless
Jacie Triplethree .... Janie Dee
Lester Trainsmith;
Hotel Desk Clerk;
Hotel Waiter .... MacIntyre Dixon

Son; Marmion;
Hotel Waiter;
Technician .... Carson Elrod
Chandler Tate .... Peter Michael Goetz
Trudi Floote;
Girl in Dress Shop .... Mercedes Herrero
Carla Pepperbloom .... Kristine Nielsen
Prim Spring .... Kellie Overbey
Mother; Farmer's Wife;
Dress Shop Assistant;
Prostitute .... Rose Stockton

Understudies: Misses Nielsen, Stockton, Herrero—Claudia Fielding; Misses Dee, Overbey—Tertia Lynch; Messrs. Goetz, Curless, Dixon—Joel Rooks.

Directed by John Tillinger; choreography, Jeff Calhoun; scenery, John Lee Beatty; costumes, Jane Greenwood; lighting, Brian MacDevitt; sound, Bruce Ellman; fight direction, Rick Sordelet; original music, John Pattison; casting, Nancy Piccione, David Caparelliotis; production stage manager, Susie Cordon; press, Boneau/Bryan-Brown, Chris Boneau, Steven Padla, Jackie Green, Rachel Applegate.

Presented in two parts.

Comic fantasy set in a future when television actors are replaced by robots, one of which begins to have human feelings.

***Forbidden Broadway 2001: A Spoof Odyssey** (220). Musical revue created and written by Gerard Alessandrini. Produced by John Freedson, Harriet Yellin and Jon B. Platt in association with Steve McGraw, Nancy McCall, Peter Martin, Gary Hoffman, Jerry Kravat and Masakazu Shibaoka at the Stardust Theatre. Opened November 18, 2000.

CAST: Felicia Finley, Danny Gurwin, Tony Nation, Christine Pedi.

Directed by Phillip George and Gerard Alessandrini; choreography, Phillip George, scenery, Bradley Kaye; costumes, Alvin Colt; musical director, Brad Ellis; musical coordinator, W. Brent Sawyer; production stage manager, Jim Griffith; press, the Pete Sanders Group, Glenna Freedman.

Latest version of the perennial satire of theater in song. Transferred to the Douglas Fairbanks May 8, 2001 with no break in performance schedule..

Down the Garden Paths (65). By Anne Meara. Produced by Elliot Martin, Max Cooper, Ron Shapiro, Sharon Karmazin at the Minetta Lane Theatre. Opened November 19, 2000. (Closed January 14, 2001)

Professor Cramer .... Angela Pietropinto
Arthur Garden .... John Shea
Stella Dempsey Garden .... Anne Jackson
Sid Garden .... Eli Wallach
Liz Garden .... Leslie Lyles
Max Garden .... Adam Grupper
Sharon Garden;
Jody Garden .... Amy Stiller
Claire Shayne;
Claire Garden .... Roberta Wallach
Special Video Apearance .... Jerry Stiller

Directed by David Saint; scenery, James Youmans; costumes, David Murin; lighting, Michael Lincoln; sound, Chris Bailey; associate producer, Marjorie Martin; casting, Pat McCorkle; production stage manager, Thomas Clewell; press, Jeffrey Richards Associates.

Presented without intermission.

Comedy about how choices made by one man (and their parallel possibilities) affect the lives led by his family.

The Joseph Papp Public Theater/New York Shakespeare Festival production of **Kit Marlowe** (17). By David Grimm. George C. Wolfe producer, Rosemarie Tichler artistic producer, Mark Litvin managing director, in the Newman Theater. Opened November 19, 2000. (Closed December 3, 2000)

Thomas Walsingham .... Sam Trammell
Ingram Frizer .... Martin Rayner
Nicholas Skeres .... Bostin Christopher
Kit Marlowe .... Christian Camargo
Edward Alleyn .... Richard Ziman
Sir Francis Walsingham .... Jon DeVries

Anthony Babington .... Richard Ziman
Robert Poley .... David Patrick Kelly
A French Merchant .... Chris Kipiniak
Brother Auguste .... Craig Bockhorn
Robert Deveraux,
Earl of Essex .... Robert Sella
A Musician .... Chris Kipiniak
Sir Walter Raleigh .... Keith David
A Young Actor .... Ned Stresen-Reuter
Henry Percy,
Earl of Northumberland .... Richard Ziman
Thomas Harriot .... Craig Bockhorn

Revelers at a bear-baiting, attendants, monks, huntsmen, actors, wedding guests: Craig Bockhorn, Bostin Christopher, Chris Kipiniak, Martin Rayner, Robert Sella, Ned Stresen-Reuter.

Directed by Brian Kulick; scenery, Narelle Sissons; costumes, Anita Yavich; lighting, Mimi Jordan Sherin, D.M. Wood; sound, Kurt B. Kellenberger; fight direction, Normand Beauregard; original music, Mark Bennett; associate producer, Bonnie Metzgar; casting, Jordan Thaler, Heidi Griffiths; production stage manager, Buzz Cohen; stage manager, Elizabeth Moreau; press, Carol Fineman, Tom Naro.

Time: 1586 to 1593. Place: England and France. Presented in two parts.

History-based drama that speculates on the tumultuous life and violent death of the Elizabethan writer, Christopher Marlowe.

Deadheads: Patricia R. Floyd, Theo Bleckmann and Drue Williams in John Moran's Book of the Dead (Second Avenue). *Photo: Michal Daniel*

The Joseph Papp Public Theater/New York Shakespeare Festival production of **Book of the Dead (Second Avenue)** (32). Music theater piece conceived by John Moran. George C. Wolfe producer, Rosemarie Tichler artistic producer, Mark Litvin managing director, in Martinson Hall. Opened November 20, 2000. (Closed December 17, 2000)

CAST: Theo Bleckmann, Patricia R. Floyd, Darryl Gibson, Anthony Henderson, Michael Huston, John Moran, Laine Satterfield, Cabell Tomlinson, David West and M. Drue Williams. Recorded narration by Uma Thurman.

Directed by John Moran; scenery, projections, Mr. Moran; costumes, James Schuette; lighting, Jonathan Spencer; sound, Andrew Keister; assistant director, mask and puppet designs, Cabell Tomlinson; stage manager, Renee Lutz; press, Carol Fineman, Tom Naro.

Presented without intermission.

Pre-recorded multimedia opera that explores the nature and reach of human consciousness.

Jesus Hopped the "A" Train (38). By Stephen Adly Guirgis. Produced by Ron Kastner, Roy Gabay and John Gould Rubin in association with Labyrinth Theater Company at the East 13th Street Theater. Opened November 29, 2000. (Closed December 31, 2000)

Angel Cruz .... John Ortiz
Valdez .... David Zayas
Mary Jane Hanrahan .... Elizabeth Canavan
D'Amico .... Salvatore Inzerilo
Lucius Jenkins .... Ron Cephas Jones

Directed by Philip Seymour Hoffman; scenery, Narelle Sissons; costumes, Mimi O'Donnell; lighting, Sarah Sidman; sound, original music, Eric DeArmon; associate producer, Marie Therese Guirgis; production stage manager, Babette Roberts; press, Erin Dunn Public Relations.

Place: New York City correctional system, largely at Riker's Island. Presented in two parts.

Jailhouse drama about the way the criminal justice system destroys its inmates.

Second Stage Theatre production of **Tiny Alice** (40). Revival of the play by Edward Albee. Carole Rothman artistic director, Mark Linn-Baker 2001 season artistic director, Carol Fishman managing director, Alexander Fraser executive director. Opened December 5, 2000. (Closed January 7, 2001)

Lawyer .... Stephen Rowe
Cardinal .... Tom Lacy
Brother Julian .... Richard Thomas
Butler .... John Michael Higgins
Miss Alice .... Laila Robins

Directed by Mark Lamos; scenery, John Arnone; costumes, Constance Hoffman; lighting, Donald Holder; sound, David Budries; fight direction, B.H. Barry; casting, Bernard Telsey; production stage manager, Lloyd Davis Jr.; stage manager, Amy Patricia Stern; press, Richard Kornberg and Associates, Don Summa, Tom D'Ambrosio, Rick Miramontez, Jim Byk.

Presented in two parts.

A religious man is fatally seduced by the possibilities of lust, love and money. Originally produced at Broadway's Billy Rose Theatre 12/29/64 for 167 performances. A 1964–65 *Best Plays* honoree.

Doll house: John Michael Higgins, Stephen Rowe, Richard Thomas and Laila Robins in Edward Albee's Tiny Alice. *Photo: T. Charles Erickson*

York Theatre Company production of **Fermat's Last Tango** (30). Musical with book by Joanne Sydney Lessner; music by Joshua Rosenblum; lyrics by Miss Lessner and Mr. Rosenblum. James Morgan artistic director, at the Theatre at Saint Peter's. Opened December 6, 2000. (Closed December 31, 2000)

Carl Friedrich Gauss;
Reporter .... Gilles Chiasson
Anna Keane .... Edwardyne Cowan
Pythagoras; Reporter .... Mitchell Kantor
Pierre de Fermat .... Jonathan Rabb
Daniel Keane .... Chris Thompson
Euclid; Reporter .... Christianne Tisdale
Sir Isaac Newton;
Reporter .... Carrie Wilshusen

Orchestra: Milton Granger conductor, piano; Chip Prince keyboard; Nina Evthuhov, violin; Ed Matthew woodwinds; Barbara Merjan drums, percussion.

Understudies: Misses Cowan, Tisdale, Wilshusen—Wendy Baila; Messrs. Thompson, Rabb, Chiasson, Kantor—Neal Young.

Directed by Mel Marvin; scenery, James Morgan; costumes, Lynn Bowling; lighting, John Michael Deegan; orchestrations, Joshua Rosenblum; music direction, Milton Granger; musical staging, Janet Watson; casting, Norman Meranus; production stage manager, Peggy R. Samuels; stage manager, Joanna P. Zischang; press, Keith Sherman and Associates, Dan Fortune.

Time: 1993–94. Place: A conference hall, Keane's attic and points heavenward. Performed without an intermission.

Musical inspired by the work of a math professor who offered a proof in 1993 to a particularly prickly 300-year-old theorem.

A Conference Hall
"Prologue" .... Reporters, Fermat
"Press Conference I" .... Reporters, Keane
Keane's Attic
"You're a Hero Now" .... Anna, Keane
"The Beauty of Numbers" .... Keane
"Tell Me Your Secret" .... Keane, Fermat
The AfterMath
"Sing We to Symmetry" .... Mathematicians
"Welcome to the AfterMath" .... Mathematicians, Keane, Fermat
"Your Proof Contains a Hole" .... Mathematicians, Fermat, Keane
Keane's Attic
"I Dreamed" .... Keane, Anna
"Press Conference II" .... Keane, Anna, Reporters
"My Name" .... Fermat
Keane's Attic ....
"All I Want For My Birthday" .... Anna, Keane
"The Game Show" .... Fermat, Keane, Mathematicians
"Math Widow" .... Anna
"I'll Always Be There" (Fermat's Last Tango) .... Fermat, Keane, Anna
The AfterMath
"The Relay Race" .... Mathematicians
Keane's Attic
"I'm Stumbling" .... Keane
"Oh, It's You" .... Keane, Pythagoras
"The Beauty of Numbers" (Reprise) .... Keane, Anna
A Conference Hall
"Press Conference III" .... Reporters, Keane, Fermat

Lincoln Center Theater production of **Old Money** (45). By Wendy Wasserstein. André Bishop artistic director, Bernard Gersten executive producer, at the Mitzi E. Newhouse. Opened December 7, 2000. (Closed January 14, 2001)

Ovid Walpole Bernstein;
Tobias Pfeiffer II .... Charlie Hofheimer
Jeffrey Bernstein;
Arnold Strauss .... Mark Harelik

Flinty McGee;
Florence DeRoot .... Kathryn Meisle
Tobias Vivian Pfeiffer III;
Schuyler Lynch .... John Cullum
Sid Nercessian;
Tobias Pfeiffer .... Dan Butler
Penny Nercessian;
Betina Brevoort .... Jodi Long
Mary Gallagher;
Caroline Nercessian .... Emily Bergl
Saulina Webb;
Sally Webster .... Mary Beth Hurt

Robber barons and eccentrics: Mary Beth Hurt and Mark Harelik in Wendy Wasserstein's Old Money. *Photo: Joan Marcus*

Understudies: Mr. Hofheimer—Charles Socarides; Mr. Harelik—Peter Samuel; Miss Meisle—Carol Linnea Johnson; Mr. Butler—Tony Campisi; Miss Long—Sonnie Brown; Miss Bergl—Autumn Dornfeld; Miss Hurt—Laura Hicks.

Directed by Mark Brokaw; choreography, John Carrafa; scenery, Thomas Lynch; costumes, Jane Greenwood; lighting, Mark McCullough; sound, Janet Kalas; original music, Lewis Flinn; casting, Daniel Swee; stage manager, James FitzSimmons; press, Philip Rinaldi Publicity, Brian Rubin.

Time: A Saturday night in August; now and rhen. Place: The private home of Jeffrey Bernstein on Manhattan's Upper East Side. Presented in two parts.

The parallels and contrasts between the moneyed classes from two eras in American history.

The Bitter Tears of Petra Van Kant (32). By Rainer Werner Fassbinder. Translated by Denis Calandra; adapted by Barbara Sauermann and Ian Belton. Produced by David Henderson and P. Jennifer Dana at the Henry Miller Theatre. Opened December 11, 2000. (Closed January 7, 2001)

Petra .... Rebecca Wisocky
Marlene .... Anita Durst
Sidonie .... Rosalyn Coleman
Karin; Gabi .... Tami Dixon
Valerie .... Joy Franz

Directed by Mr. Belton; scenery, Jeff Cowie; costumes, Greco; lighting, Rick Martin; sound, Darron L. West; stage manager, Marjorie Horne; press, Richard Kornberg and Associates, Richard Kornberg, Jim Byk.

Presented without intermission.

A study in desire, submission, domination and the boundaries of sexual power.

Pete 'n' Keely (96). Musical by James Hindman; music and lyrics by Patrick S. Brady and Mark Waldrop. Produced by Steve Asher, David W. Unger and Avalon Entertainment at the John Houseman Theater. Opened December 14, 2000. (Closed March 11, 2001)

Pete .... George Dvorsky Keely .... Sally Mayes

Understudies: Miss Mayes—Allison Briner; Mr. Dvorsky—Robert McCormick.

Musicians: Patrick S. Brady piano; Robert Renino bass; Brad Flickinger drums.

Directed by Mr. Waldrop; choreography, Keith Cromwell; scenery, Ray Klausen; costumes, Bob Mackie; lighting, F. Mitchell Dana; sound, Jon Weston; musical direction, arrangements, Mr. Brady; associate producer, Joel C. Cohen; production stage manager, Julia P. Jones; press, the Pete Sanders Group, Pete Sanders, Jim Mannino, Glenna Freedman, Clint Bond Jr.

Time: 1968. Place: A television studio. Presented in two parts.

Married show-business couple perform a variety show on live television while bickering and cooing.

Playwrights Horizons production of **The Wax** (17). By Kathleen Tolan. Tim Sanford artistic director, Leslie Marcus managing director, William Russo general manager, at Playwrights Horizons. Opened January 7, 2001. (Closed January 21, 2001)

Chris .... Frank Wood
Maureen .... Laura Esterman
Angie .... Mary Testa
Hal .... Robert Dorfman
Ben .... David Greenspan
Lily .... Lola Pashalinki
Bert .... Gareth Saxe
Amelia .... Mary Shultz
Kate .... Karen Young

Directed by Brian Kulick; scenery, Walt Spangler; costumes, Elizabeth Hope Clancy; lighting, Kevin Adams; sound, Jill B.C. DuBoff; production stage manager, Pamela Edington; press, the Publicity Office.

Presented without intermission.

A wedding sets the stage for a group of friends to reunite, couple and uncouple in a series of farcical interludes.

The Joseph Papp Public Theater/New York Shakespeare Festival production of **Shakespeare's Villains: A Masterclass in Evil** (29). Solo performance of highlights from the works of William Shakespeare; adapted by Steven Berkoff. George C. Wolfe producer, Fran Reiter executive director, at the Anspacher Theater. Opened January 10, 2001. (Closed February 11, 2001)

Performed by Steven Berkoff.

A one-man survey of the heights and depths of Shakespeare's great villains. Reopened after a limited run at Joe's Pub earlier in the season.

Brooklyn Academy of Music presentation of a **Sydney Theatre Company** production of **The White Devil** (7). Revival of the play by John Webster. Bruce C. Ratner chairman of the board, Karen Brooks Hopkins president, Joseph V. Melillo executive producer, at the BAM Howard Gilman Opera House. Opened January 13, 2001. (Closed January 20, 2001)

Brachiano .... Marcus Graham
Vittoria Corombona .... Angie Milliken
Flamineo .... Jeremy Sims
Marcello .... Matthew Newton
Cornelia .... Julia Blake
Zanche .... Paula Arundell
The Duke of Florence .... Michael Siberry
Isabella .... Jacqueline McKenzie
Monticelso .... John Gaden
Camillo .... Bruce Spence

Lodovico .... William Zappa
Antonelli .... Tony Poli
Gasparo .... Mark Pegler
Doctor Julio .... Keith Robinson
Hortensio .... Brian Green
Jaques .... Joseph Manning
Gaoler .... Bruce Spence
Lawyer .... Mark Pegler
Giovanni .... Ryan Ottey

Understudies: Male—Kyle Rowling; Female—Genevieve O'Reilly.

Adapted and directed by Gale Edwards; scenery, Brian Thomson; costumes, Roger Kirk; lighting, Trudy Dalgleish; sound, Paul Tilley; fight choreography, Steve Douglas-Craig; music, Max Lambert, Martin Armiger; assistant director, Carlton Lamb; fight captain, Kyle Rowling; stage manager, R. Michael Blanco; press, Elena Park, Melissa Cusick, Amy Hughes, Tamara McCaw, Kila Packett.

Time: 1500s. Place Italy. Presented in two parts.

Passion, adultery, politics and revenge fuel the tragedy of this Jacobean drama written in 1611–12.

Civil tongue: Bette Bourne in Tim Fountain's Resident Alien. *Photo: Joan Marcus*

New York Theatre Workshop production of **Resident Alien** (45). By Tim Fountain. James C. Nicola artistic director, Lynn Moffat managing director. Opened January 18, 2001. (Closed February 25, 2001)

Quentin Crisp .... Bette Bourne

Directed by Mike Bradwell; scenery and costumes, Neil Patel; lighting, Brian MacDevitt; sound, Jerry M. Yager; production stage manager, Charles Means; press, Richard Kornberg and Associates, Richard Kornberg, Don Summa.

Presented in two parts.

Collection of thoughts, musings and utterances of the homosexual writer made famous by his autobiography, *The Naked Civil Servant*.

Good times: Laura Benanti and Lewis Cleale in Time and Again. *Photo: Joan Marcus*

Manhattan Theatre Club production of **Time and Again** (24). Musical based on the book by Jack Finney; book by Jack Viertel; music and lyrics by Walter Edgar Kennon; additional story material by James Hart. Lynne Meadow artistic director, Barry Grove executive producer, at City Center Stage II. Opened January 30, 2001. (Closed February 18, 2001)

Bessie et al. .... Melissa Rain Anderson
Mrs. Carmody et al. .... Ann Arvia
Julia .... Laura Benanti
Si Morley .... Lewis Cleale
Felix et al. ....Jeff Edgerton
Mr. Carmody et al. ....Eric Michael Gillett
Young Dr. Danziger et al. .... Gregg Goodbrod
Jake Pickering et al. .... Christopher Innvar
Aunt Evie et al. .... Patricia Kilgarriff
Trolleyman et al. .... Joseph Kolinski
Harriman et al. ....George Masswohl
Dr. Danziger et al.................. David McCallum
Kate et al. .... Julia Murney
Clarissa et al. .... Amy Walsh
Emily et al. .... Lauren Ward

Directed by Susan H. Schulman; choreography, Rob Ashford; scenery, Derek McLane; costumes, Catherine Zuber; lighting, Ken Billington; sound, Brian Ronan; fight direction, Rick Sordelet; music director, Kevin Stites; casting, Jay Binder; production stage manager, Peggy Peterson; press, Boneau/Bryan-Brown, Chris Boneau, Steven Padla, Jackie Green, Martine Sainvil.

Presented in two parts.

Based on popular 1970 novel about an artist who travels back in time to seek his muse. Developed in readings at the 1993 National Theater Conference at the Eugene O'Neill Theater Center. World premiere at the Old Globe Theatre in San Diego, Calif in 1995.

City Center Voices! presentation of **Little Murders** (1). Staged reading of the play by Jules Feiffer. Judith E. Daykin president and executive director, Alec Baldwin producer, Steve Lawson artistic director, at City Center. Opened January 30, 2001. (Closed January 30, 2001)

Marjorie Newquist .... Blythe Danner
Kenny Newquist .... Christopher Fitzgerald
Carol Newquist .... Joel Grey
Patsy Newquist .... Polly Draper
Alfred Chamberlain .... Patrick Breen
The Judge .... Louis Zorich

Rev. Henry Dupas .... Mark McKinney
Lt. Miles Practice .... Joe Morton
Stage Directions .... Jules Feiffer

Directed by Steve Lawson; lighting, Tricia Toliver; sound, Scott Lehrer; projections, Jules Feiffer; production stage manager, Kimberly Russell; press, Philip Rinaldi Publicity.

Place: The Newquist apartment. Presented in two parts.

First produced by Alexander H. Cohen at Broadway's Broadhurst Theatre 4/25/67 for 7 performances. It was revived by Circle in the Square 1/5/69 for 400 performances.

***The Play About the Baby** (137). By Edward Albee. Produced by Elizabeth Ireland McCann, Daryl Roth, Terry Allen Kramer, 52nd Street Productions, Robert Bartner, Stanley Kaufelt, in association with the Alley Theatre, at the Century Center for the Performing Arts. Opened February 2, 2001.

Girl .... Kathleen Early
Boy .... David Burtka
Man .... Brian Murray
Woman .... Marian Seldes

Understudies: Miss Seldes—Kathleen Butler; Miss Early—Hillary Keegin; Mr. Burtka—Curtis Billings.

Directed by David Esbjornson; scenery, John Arnone; costumes, Michael Krass; lighting, Kenneth Posner; sound, Donald DiNicola; associate producer, Franci Neely Crane; casting, Jerry Beaver; production stage manager, Mark Wright; press, Shirley Herz Associates, Shirley Herz, Sam Rudy, Kevin P. McAnarney, Nancy Khuu.

Presented in two parts.

An elliptical exploration of the role of children—lost and found—within the family dynamic. A 2000–01 *Best Plays* honoree (see essay by Christine Dolen in this volume). World premiere in 1998 at London's Almeida Theatre; US premiere in 2000 at Houston's Alley Theatre, directed by Mr. Albee.

Who's the baby?: Brian Murray, Marian Seldes, Kathleen Early and David Burtka in Edward Albee's The Play About the Baby. *Photo: Carol Rosegg*

City Center Encores! presentation of **A Connecticut Yankee** (5). Concert version of the musical adapted from *A Connecticut Yankee in King Arthur's Court* by Mark Twain. Music by Richard Rodgers; lyrics by Lorenz Hart; book by Herbert Fields. Judith E. Daykin president and executive director, Jack Viertel artistic director, Rob Fisher musical director, Kathleen Marshall director-in-residence, at City Center. Opened February 8, 2001. (Closed February 11, 2001)

Arthur Pendragos;
later King Arthur .... Henry Gibson
Gerald Gareth;
Sir Galahad .... Seán Martin Hingston
Martin Barrett
(The Yankee) .... Steven Sutcliffe
Albert Kay;
Sir Kay .... Mark Lotito
Fay Morgan;
Morgan LeFay .... Christine Ebersole

Evelyn Lane;
Dame Evelyn .... Nancy Lemenager
Alice Carter;
Alisande (Sandy) .... Judith Blazer
Angela; Maid;
Angela .... Megan Sikora
Henry Merle;
Merlin .... Peter Bartlett
Sir Launcelot .... Ron Leibman
Guinevere .... Jessica Walter

Dancers: Robert M. Armitage, Vance Avery, David Eggers, Anika Ellis, Matt Lashey, Elizabeth Mills, Aixa M. Rosario Medina, Megan Sikora.

Singers: Anne Allgood, Kate Baldwin, Tony Capone, Julie Connors, John Halmi, Chris Hoch, Robert Osborne, Frank Ream, Keith Spencer, Rebecca Spencer, J.D. Webster, Mimi Wyche.

Orchestra: Rob Fisher conductor; Suzanne Ornstein concertmistress, violin; Seymour Red Press flute, piccolo, clarinet; Rob Ingliss oboe, English horn; Dennis Anderson clarinet, bass clarinet, English horn; John Campo bassoon, clarinet, tenor sax, flute, bass clarinet; Russ Rizner, French horn; John Frosk, Glenn Drewes, Kamau Adilifu trumpet; Jack Gale trombone; Leslie Stifelman piano; David Silliman drums; Erik Charlston percussion; Belinda Whitney, Maura Giannini, Mineko Yajima, Christoph Franzgrote, Lisa Matricardi, Eric De Gioia, Robert Lawrence violin; Jill Jaffe, Richard Brice, David Blinn, Crystal Garner viola; Clay Ruede, Jeanne LeBlanc cello; John Beal acoustic bass.

Directed by Susan H. Schulman; choreography, Rob Ashford; scenery, John Lee Beatty; costumes, Toni-Leslie James; lighting, Natasha Katz; sound, Scott Lehrer; original orchestrations, Don Walker; musical coordinator, Seymour Red Press; casting, Jay Binder; production stage manager, Bonnie L. Becker; press, Philip Rinaldi Publicity.

Presented in two parts.

Originally produced at the Vanderbilt Theatre 11/3/27 for 418 performances. It was revived at the Martin Beck Theatre 11/17/43 for 135 performances.

ACT I

For Encores! presentations song performances are listed by the actors' names.

Overture .... Orchestra
Scene 1: The grand ballroom of a hotel in Hartford, Connecticut, 1927
"Here's Martin the Groom" .... Henry Gibson, Steven Sutcliffe, and Men
"This is My Night to Howl" .... Christine Ebersole, Tony Capone, John Halmi, Chris Hoch and J.D. Webster
"My Heart Stood Still" .... Steven Sutcliffe and Judith Blazer
Scene 2: On the road to Camelot in the year 528 AD
"I Blush" .... Judith Blazer, Nancy Lemenager and Ladies
"Thou Swell" .... Steven Sutcliffe and Judith Blazer
Scene 3: Courtyard of the castle of King Arthur
"At the Round Table" .... Chris Hoch, Peter Bartlett and Company
"On a Desert Island with Thee!" .... Seán Martin Hingston and Nancy Lemenager
"To Keep My Love Alive" .... Christine Ebersole
Finale Act I .... Steven Sutcliffe, Peter Bartlett and Company

ACT II

Entr'acte .... Orchestra
Scene 1: A corridor of a royal factory, three months later.
"Ye Lunchtime Follies" .... Seán Martin Hingston and Company

"To Keep My Love Alive" (Reprise) .... Christine Ebersole
"Thou Swell" (Reprise) .... Steven Sutcliffe and Judith Blazer
"I Feel at Home with You" .... Seán Martin Hingston and Nancy Lemenager
Scene 2: On the road to Camelot
"The Sandwich Men" .... Men
"You Always Love the Same Girl" .... Henry Gibson and Steven Sutcliffe
Scene 3: The palace of Queen Morgan Le Fay
"The Camelot Samba" .... Anne Allgood, Kate Baldwin, Rebecca Spencer, Mimi Wyche and Dancers
"Can't You Do a Friend a Favor?" .... Christine Ebersole and Steven Sutcliffe
"My Heart Stood Still" (Reprise) .... Steven Sutcliffe and Judith Blazer
Epilogue: Hartford
Finale Ultimo .... Entire Company

Second Stage Theatre production of **Cellini** (24). By John Patrick Shanley. Carole Rothman artistic director, Mark Linn-Baker 2001 season artistic director. Opened February 12, 2001. (Closed March 4, 2001)

Boy; Workman; Bernard; Giacamo .... Lucas Papaelias
Cellini .... Reg Rogers
Duke of Florence; Judge; Merchant .... Daniel Oreskes
Duchess; Gambetta; Serving Maid .... Lisa Bansavage
Pope; Paolo; Riccio; King Francois; Workman .... Richard Russell Ramos
Caterina; Mona Fiore .... Jennifer Roszell
Tasso; Judge .... Gary Perez
Bandinello; Cardinal Cornaro; Workman; Judge .... John Gould Rubin
Pope Clement; Bargello; Gorini; French Treasurer .... David Chandler

Directed by John Patrick Shanley; scenery, Adrianne Lobel; costumes, Martin Pakledinaz; lighting, Brian Nason; sound, David Van Tieghem; fight director, B.H. Barry; stage manager, Ramona S. Collier; press, Richard Kornberg and Associates, Richard Kornberg, Tom D'Ambrosio.

Time: 1558. Place: Florence. Presented in two parts.

A great artist struggles with passions base and exalted, in a work based on his life story.

Trouble on the line: Mary Beth Fisher in Rebecca Gilman's Boy Gets Girl. *Photo: Liz Lauren*

Manhattan Theatre Club production of **Boy Gets Girl** (56). By Rebecca Gilman. Lynne Meadow artistic director, Barry Grove executive producer, in association with the Goodman Theatre, at City Center Stage I. Opened February 20, 2001. (Closed April 8, 2001)

Mercer Stevens .... David Adkins
Howard Siegel .... Matt DeCaro
Harriet .... Shayna Ferm
Theresa Bedell .... Mary Beth Fisher
Madeline Beck .... Ora Jones
Tony .... Ian Lithgow
Les Kennkat .... Howard Witt

Understudies: Messrs. DeCaro,Witt—Michael Arkin; Misses Ferm, Jones—Nicole E. Lewis; Messrs. Adkins, Lithgow—Jeff Parker; Miss Fisher—Henny Russell.

Directed by Michael Maggio; scenery, Michael Philippi; costumes, Nan Cibula-Jenkins; lighting, John Culbert; sound, original music, Rob Milburn, Michael Bodeen; production stage manager, Ed Fitzgerald; press, Boneau/Bryan-Brown, Chris Boneau, Steven Padla, Jackie Green, Martine Sainvil.

Time: The present. Place: Various locales in New York City. Presented in two parts.

A blind date turns into a woman's ongoing nightmare. A 2000–01 *Best Plays* honoree (see essay by Chris Jones in this volume). Original production at Chicago's Goodman Theatre in 2000, directed by Mr. Maggio. The New York production was billed as directed by Mr. Maggio, who died August 19, 2000. The staging for New York was recreated by Ms. Meadow.

Diggers plot: Kevin Tighe, Zoaunne LeRoy and Christopher Carley in A Skull in Connemara. *Photo: Joan Marcus*

Roundabout Theatre Company production of **A Skull in Connemara** (101). By Martin McDonagh. Todd Haimes artistic director, Ellen Richard managing director, Julia C. Levy executive director, external affairs, at the Gramercy Theatre. Opened February 22, 2001. (Closed May 20, 2001)

Mick Dowd .... Kevin Tighe
Maryjohnny Rafferty .... Zoaunne LeRoy
Mairtin Hanlon .... Christopher Carley
Thomas Hanlon .... Christopher Evan Welch

Standbys: Mr. Tighe—James Doerr; Miss LeRoy—Lucille Patton; Messrs. Carley, Welch—Austin Jones.

Directed by Gordon Edelstein; scenery, David Gallo; costumes, Susan Hilferty; lighting, Michael Chybowski; sound, Stephen LeGrand; original music, Martin Hayes; fight director, J. Steven White; casting, Amy Christopher, Laura Richin; production stage manager, Jay Adler; press, Boneau/ Bryan-Brown, Adrian Bryan-Brown, Matt Polk, Kel Christofferson, Cindy Valk.

Place: Rural Galway. Presented in two parts.

The second part of a trilogy of Irish country-peasant life in which murder and mayhem always lurk beneath the surface. The others in the Leenane trilogy are *The Beauty Queen of Leenane* and *The Lonesome West*. Originally produced in 1997 by Galway's Druid Theatre and London's Royal Court Theatre. The 2000 US premiere was produced by Seattle's A Contemporary Theatre, with Mr. Edelstein directing.

York Theatre Company production of **Suburb** (29). Musical with book by David Javerbaum and Robert S. Cohen; music, Mr. Cohen; lyrics, Mr. Javerbaum. James Morgan artisic director, in association with Jennifer M. Sanchez and Roberta Plutzik Baldwin, at the Theatre at Saint Peter's. Opened March 1, 2001. (Closed March 25, 2001)

Alison .... Jacquelyn Piro
Stuart .... James Ludwig
Tom .... Dennis Kelly
Rhoda .... Alix Korey

Ensemble: Adinah Alexander, Ron Butler, Jennie Eisenhower, James Sasser.

Musicians: Jeffrey R. Smith piano; Phil Chester reeds; Dennis Christians bass; Ann Gerschefski synthesizer; Glenn Rhian percussion.

Understudies: Miss Piro—Jennie Eisenhower; Mr. Ludwig—James Sasser; Mr. Kelly—Ron Butler; Miss Korey—Adinah Alexander; Messrs.Butler, Sasser—Rob Lorey; Misses Eisenhower, Alexander—Jessica Wright.

Directed by Jennifer Uphoff Gray; choreography, John Carrafa; scenery, Kris Stone; costumes, Jan Finnell; lighting, John Michael Deegan; orchestrations, Larry Hochman; Jeffrey R. Smith, musical director; music supervision, Steven Tyler; assistant director, Nancy S. Chu; assistant choreographer, Rachel Bress; casting, Norman Meranus; production stage manager, Peggy R. Samuels; press, Keith Sherman and Associates, Dan Fortune.

Presented in two parts.

A young couple struggles with the idea of departing the city for suburban life. Originally developed by Musical Theatre Works. Winner of the 2000 Richard Rodgers Development Award.

ACT I

Prologue
"Directions" .... Company
Rhoda's Office
"Mow" .... Stuart, Alison, Ensemble
Tom's Basement
"Do It Yourself" .... Tom
Suburb, Main Street
"Suburb" .... Ensemble
Tom's Living Room
"Not Me" .... Alison
The Neighbors' Backyard
"Barbecue" .... Ensemble
Rhoda's Office
"The Girl Next Door" .... Rhoda, James, Ron, Stuart
Alison and Stuart's Apartment
Ahmed's World of Nuts/Tom's Basement
"Ready Or Not" .... Stuart, Tom
Suburb Train Station
"Commute" .... Company

ACT II

Suburb Mall
"Mall" .... Company

Alison and Stuart's Apartment
"Duet" .... Alison, Stuart
Rhoda's House
"Handy" .... Rhoda, Tom
Suburb Community Park
"Walkin' to School" .... Ensemble
Bagels 4 U
"Bagel-Shop Quartet" .... Ensemble
"Trio for Four" .... Tom, Stuart, Alison
Tom's House
"Everything Must Go" .... Ensemble
Alison and Stuart's House/Rhoda's House
"Someday" .... Alison, Stuart, Tom, Rhoda

The Joseph Papp Public Theater/New York Shakespeare Festival production of **Dogeaters** (25). By Jessica Hagedorn. George C. Wolfe producer, Fran Reiter executive director, Rosemarie Tichler artistic producer, in Martinson Hall. Opened March 4, 2001. (Closed March 25, 2001)

Nestor Noralez .... Ralph B. Peña
Barbara Villanueva .... Mia Katigbak
Joey Sands .... Hill Harper
Daisy Avila .... Rona Figueroa
Leonor Ledsma, the Penitent .... Ching Valdes-Aran
Rio Gonzaga .... Kate Rigg
Father Jean Mallat .... Christopher Donahue
Pucha Gonzaga .... Eileen Rivera
Freddie Gonzaga .... Raul Aranas
Uncle .... Joel Torre
Santos Tirador .... Arthur Acuña
Senator Domingo Avila .... Joel Torre
Romeo Rosales .... Jonathan Lopez
Lolita Luna .... Christine Jugueta
Trinidad Gamboa .... Eileen Rivera
The Kasama .... JoJo Gonzalez
The Waiter .... JoJo Gonzalez
Chiquiting Moreno .... Ralph B. Peña
Andres "Perlita" Alacran .... Alec Mapa
Pedro .... JoJo Gonzalez
Rainer Fassbinder .... Christopher Donahue
Imelda Marcos .... Ching Valdes-Aran
General Nicasio Ledesma .... JoJo Gonzalez

Imelda's true love: Ching Valdes-Aran in Jessica Hagedorn's Dogeaters. *Photo: Michal Daniel*

Lt. Pepe Carreon .... Arthur Acuña
Severo Alacran .... Raul Aranas
Dolores Gonzaga .... Christine Jugueta
Lola Narcisa .... Ching Valdes-Aran
Tito Alvarez .... Arthur Acuña
Steve Jacobs .... Alec Mapa
Bob Stone .... Christopher Donahue
Ka Lydia .... Mia Katigbak
Ka Pablo .... Jonathan Lopez
Ka Edgar .... Raul Aranas

Directed by Michael Greif; scenery, David Gallo; costumes, Brandin Barón; lighting, Michael Chybowski; sound, Mark Bennett, Michael Creason; projection design, John Woo; associate producers, Bonnie Metzgar, John Dias; casting, Jordan Thaler, Heidi Griffiths; production stage manager, Lee J. Kahrs; press, Carol Fineman, Tom Naro.

Time: 1982. Place: Manila, the Philippines. Presented in two parts.

A comic and dramatic whirlwind set amid the political and social unrest of the Philippines in the 1980s. Originally produced in 1998 by San Diego's La Jolla Playhouse.

If It Was Easy . . . (30). By Stewart F. Lane and Ward Morehouse III. Produced by James M. Nederlander and Stellar Productions Intl., Inc., at the Douglas Fairbanks Theatre. Opened March 7, 2000. (Closed April 1, 2001)

Randi Lester .... Bonnie Comley
Steve Gallop .... John Jellison
Lucy Handover .... Vicki Van Tassel
Joey Fingers ....William Marshall Miller
Charlie .... Brad Bellamy
Wilbur; Waiter .... Gustave Johnson
Lars; Mailman .... Christian Kauffmann
Papa .... Martin LaPlatney

Directed by Mr. Lane; scenery, Michael Anania; costumes, Steven Epstein; lighting, Phil Monat; sound, Peter Fitzgerald; production stage manager, Alan Fox; press, Keith Sherman and Associates, Keith Sherman, Brett Oberman.

Presented in two parts.

Tale of a producer and a journalist who decide to create a Broadway musical based on the life of Frank Sinatra.

Lincoln Center Theater production of **Ten Unknowns** (45). By Jon Robin Baitz. André Bishop artistic director, Bernard Gersten executive producer, at the Mitzi E. Newhouse Theater. Opened March 8, 2001. (Closed April 15, 2001)

Trevor Fabricant .... Denis O'Hare
Malcolm Raphelson .... Donald Sutherland
Judd Sturgess .... Justin Kirk
Julia Bryant ....Julianna Margulies

Understudies: Mr. O'Hare—James Joseph O'Neil; Mr. Sutherland—Barry Snider; Mr. Kirk—Ebon Moss-Bachrach; Miss Margulies—Eliza Foss.

Directed by Daniel Sullivan; scenery, Ralph Funicello; costumes, Jess Goldstein; lighting, Pat Collins; sound, Janet Kalas; original music, Robert Waldman; casting, Daniel Swee; production manager, Jeff Hamlin; stage manager, Roy Harris; press, Philip Rinaldi, Brian Rubin.

Time: 1992. Place: Near a town in South Mexico. Presented in two parts.

Reclusive painter and his dissolute assistant engage in a battle over talent, aesthetics and authenticity.

Playwrights Horizons production of **Lobby Hero** (40). By Kenneth Lonergan. Tim Sanford artistic director, Leslie Marcus managing director, William Russo general manager, at Playwrights Horizons. Opened March 13, 2001. (Closed April 15, 2001)

Jeff .... Glenn Fitzgerald
William .... Dion Graham
Dawn .... Heather Burns
Bill .... Tate Donovan

Understudies: Miss Burns—Mia Barron; Mr. Graham—Rafael Cabrera; Messrs. Fitzgerald, Donovan—David Paluck.

Directed by Mark Brokaw; scenery, Allen Moyer; costumes, Michael Krass; lighting, Mark McCullough; sound, Janet Kalas; casting, James Calleri; production manager, Christopher Boll, production stage manager, James FitzSimmons; press, the Publicity Office, Bob Fennell, Marc Thibodeau, Michael S. Borowski, Candi Adams.

Time: The present. Place: The lobby of a high-rise apartment building in Manhattan. Presented in two parts.

Victims and victimizers clash in this modern exploration of ethics, truth and criminal justice. A 2000–01 *Best Plays* honoree (see essay by Tish Dace in this volume). Transferred to a commercial Off Broadway run; see May 8, 2001 listing for more information.

Officer unfriendly: Glenn Fitzgerald and Tate Donovan in Kenneth Lonergan's Lobby Hero. *Photo: Joan Marcus*

City Center Voices! presentation of **The Devil and Daniel Webster** (1). Staged reading based on the short story by Stephen Vincent Benét. Judith E. Daykin president and executive director, Alec Baldwin producer, Steve Lawson artistic director, at City Center. Opened March 13, 2001. (Closed March 13, 2001)

Jabez Stone .... James Naughton
Mary Stone .... Jennifer Van Dyck
Daniel Webster .... Harris Yulin
Mr. Scratch .... Eric Bogosian
Fiddler; Clerk .... William Duell
Wedding Guest;
 Justice Hathorne .... Nick Wyman
Wedding Guest;
 Simon Girty .... Nick Brooks
Wedding Guest;
 Walter Butler .... Chris Hoch
Wedding Guest;
 King Philip .... Stephen Mendillo
Wedding Guest;
 Blackbeard Teach ....James Matthew Ryan
Violin .... Julie Lyonn Lieberman

Directed by Steve Lawson; lighting, Tricia Toliver; production stage manager, Jill Cordle; press, Philip Rinaldi Publicity.

Time: 1841. Place: The New England farmhouse of Jabez Stone on his wedding night. Presented in two parts.

Tale loosely based on Goethe's *Faust* in which a farmer sells his soul to the devil, reneges on the deal and is defended by orator Daniel Webster.

In Dreams and Gimpel (31). Based on "In Dreams Begin Responsibilities" by Delmore Schwartz and "Gimpel the Fool" by Isaac Bashevis Singer, translated by Saul Bellow. Produced by Eric Krebs at the Maverick Theater. Opened March 19, 2000. (Closed April 13, 2000)

Performed by David Margulies.

Directed by David Margulies with Fay Simpson; scenery, Valerie Green; costumes, Tina Haworth; lighting, Richard Latta; production stage manager, David Mead; press, Cohn Davis Associates, Helene Davis, Lois Cohn.

Presented in two parts.

The cycle of life mined from two perspectives, in adaptations of contrasting short stories.

Only in NYC: Stephen DeRosa, Jesse Tyler Ferguson and Jerry Dixon in Newyorkers. *Photo: Joan Marcus*

Manhattan Theatre Club production of **Newyorkers** (16). Music revue with music by Stephen Weiner; lyrics by Glenn Slater. Lynne Meadow artisic director, Barry Grove executive producer, at City Center Stage II. Opened March 27, 2001. (Closed April 8, 2001)

Stephen	Stephen DeRosa	Pamela	Pamela Isaacs
Jerry	Jerry Dixon	Liz	Liz Larsen
Jesse	Jesse Tyler Ferguson	Priscilla	Priscilla Lopez

Orchestra: Robert Billig conductor, keyboard; Richard Kriska woodwinds; Douglas Romoff bass; Keith Crupi percussion.

Directed by Christopher Ashley; choreography, Daniel Pelzig; scenery, Derek McLane; costumes, David C. Woolard; lighting, Ken Billington; sound, Brian Ronan; orchestrations, Robby Merkin; music direction,vocal arrangements, Robert Billig; casting, Nancy Piccione, David Caparelliotis; production stage manager, Kate Broderick; press, Boneau/Bryan-Brown, Chris Boneau, Steven Padla, Jackie Green, Martine Sainvil.

Performed without an intermission.

Archetypical tales of life in present day New York City, told in song.

***Bat Boy: The Musical** (82). Musical with story and book by Keythe Farley and Brian Flemming; music and lyrics by Laurence O'Keefe; licensed under agreement with *Weekly World News*. Produced by Nancy Nagel Gibbs, Riot Entertainment, Robyn Goodman, Michael Alden, Jean Doumanian and the Producing Office, at Union Square Theatre. Opened March 21, 2001.

Bat Boy .... Deven May
Ruthie Taylor .... Daria Hardeman
Rick Taylor .... Doug Storm
Ron Taylor .... Kathy Brier
Sheriff Reynolds .... Richard Pruitt
Bud .... Jim Price
Clem .... Kathy Brier
Mr. Dillon .... Doug Storm
Daisy .... Jim Price
Maggie .... Kathy Brier
Lorraine .... Doug Storm
Shelley Parker .... Kerry Butler
Meredith Parker .... Kaitlin Hopkins
Roy .... Trent Armand Kendall
Ned .... Daria Hardeman
Dr. Thomas Parker .... Sean McCourt
Mrs. Taylor .... Trent Armand Kendall
Reverend Hightower .... Trent Armand Kendall
King of the Forest .... Jim Price
Institute Man .... Trent Armand Kendall
Storytellers,
Townspeople, Animals .... Full Company

Blood brother: Kerry Butler and Deven May in Bat Boy: The Musical. *Photo: Joan Marcus*

Orchestra: Alex Lacamoire conductor, piano; Jason DeBord keyboard; Ed Fast drums; Matt Rubano bass; Greg Skaff guitar.

Understudies: Mr. May—J.P. Potter; Miss Hopkins—Stephanie Kurtzuba; Miss Butler—Daria Hardeman, Stephanie Kurtzuba; Mr. McCourt—John Treacy Egan, Jim Price.

Swings: John Treacy Egan, Stephanie Kurtzuba, J.P. Potter.

Directed by Scott Schwartz; scenery, Richard Hoover, Bryan Johnson; costumes, Fabio Toblini; lighting, Howell Binkley; sound, Sunil Rajan; arrangements and orchestrations, Laurence O'Keefe,

Alex Lacamoire; musical staging, Christopher Gattelli; casting, Dave Clemmons; production stage manager, Renee Lutz; press, the Karpel Group, Bridget Klapinski.

Time: Today. Place: Hope Falls, West Virginia. Presented in two parts.

Story of a blood-craving mutant boy who wants only to love and be loved. Originally produced at Los Angeles's Actors' Gang.

ACT I

Prologue
“Hold Me, Bat Boy” .... Full Company
Scene 1: Parker Home, Living Room
“Christian Charity” .... Sheriff, Meredith, Shelley
“Ugly Boy” .... Shelley
“Watcha Wanna Do?” .... Rick, Shelley
“A Home For You” .... Meredith, Bat Boy
Scene 2: Hope Falls Slaughterhouse
“Another Dead Cow” .... Townsfolk
Scene 3: Parker Home, Living room
“Dance With Me, Darling” .... Parker
Scene 4: Hospital Room
“Ruthie's Lullaby” .... Mrs. Taylor
Scene 5: Parker Home, Living Room
“Show You a Thing or Two” .... Full Company
Scene 6: Hope Falls Town Council ....
“Christian Charity” (Reprise) .... Sheriff, Parker, Townsfolk
Scene 7: Parker Home, Living Room
“A Home for You” (Reprise) Bat Boy
“Comfort and Joy” Full Company

ACT II

Scene 1: The Revival Tent ....
“A Joyful Noise” .... Rev. Hightower, Congregation
“Let Me Walk Among You” .... Bat Boy
Scene 2: The Woods
“Three Bedroom House” .... Meredith, Shelley
Scene 3: A Clearing in the Woods
“Children, Children” .... King of the Forest, Company
Scene 4: Hope Falls Slaughterhouse
“More Blood” .... Parker
Scene 5: A Clearing in the Woods
“Inside Your Heart” .... Shelley, Bat Boy
Scene 6: The Darkest Part of the Woods
“Apology to a Cow” .... Bat Boy
“Revelations” .... Meredith, Parker
Finale: “I Imagine You're Upset” .... Full Company
“Hold Me, Bat Boy” (Reprise) .... Full Company

City Center Encores! presentation of **Bloomer Girl** (5). Concert version of the musical based on a play by Dan and Lilith James; book by Sig Herzig and Fred Saidy; music by Harold Arlen; lyrics by E.Y. Harburg. Judith E. Daykin president and executive director, Jack Viertel artistic director, Rob Fisher musical director, Kathleen Marshall director-in-residence, at City Center. Opened March 22, 2001. (Closed March 25, 2001)

Serena Applegate .... Anita Gillette
Her Daughters
Octavia .... Michele Ragusa
Lydia .... Joy Hermalyn
Julia .... Ann Kittredge
Phoebe .... Teri Hansen
Delia .... Gay Willis
Daisy .... Donna Lynne Champlin
Horatio Applegate .... Philip Bosco
Gus .... Ned Eisenberg
Evelina Applegate .... Kate Jennings Grant
The Applegate Sons-In-Law
Joshua Dingle .... Joe Cassidy
Herman Brasher .... David de Jong

Ebenezer Mimms .... Eddie Korbich
Wilfred Thrush .... Tim Salamandyk
Hiram Crump .... Roger DeWitt
Dolly Bloomer .... Kathleen Chalfant
Jeff Calhoun .... Michael Park
Pompey .... Jubilant Sykes
Sheriff Quimby .... Mike Hartman
Hamilton Calhoun .... Herndon Lackey
Augustus .... Todd Hunter
Alexander .... Everett Bradley
Governor's Aide .... Carson Church
Governor Newton .... Merwin Goldsmith

Ballet soloists: Karine Plantadit-Bageot, Nina Goldman, Robert Wersinger, Todd Hunter.

Suffragettes, sheriff's deputies, parade followers and citizens of Cicero Falls: Deborah Allton, Kate Baldwin, Joe Cassidy, Carson Church, David de Jong, Susan Derry, Roger DeWitt, Donna Dunmire, John Halmi, Teri Hansen, Joy Hermalyn, Cherylyn Jones, Ann Kittredge, Eddie Korbich, Jason Lacayo, Mary Kate Law, Lori MacPherson, Michele Ragusa, Vale Rideout, Tim Salamandyk, Gay Willis.

Orchestra: Rob Fisher conductor; Suzanne Ornstein concertmistress, violin; Elizabeth Mann, Seymour Red Press flute, piccolo; Melanie Field oboe, English horn; Lawrence Feldman clarinet; Lino Gomez clarinet, bass clarinet; John Winder bassoon; John Frosk, Glenn Drewes trumpet; Jack Gale, Bruce Bonvissuto trombone; Russ Rizner, French horn; Leslie Stifelman piano; Belinda Whitney, Christoph Franzgrote, Ronald Oakland, Laura Seaton-Finn, Mia Wu, Paul Woodiel, Lisa Matricardi, Robert Zubrycki violin; Ken Burward-Hoy, David Blinn, Crystal Garner viola; Clay Ruede, Lanny Paykin cello; John Beal bass; Susan Jolles harp; Jay Berliner guitar, banjo; Eric Kivnick percussion; John Redsecker drums.

Directed by Brad Rouse; choreography, Rob Ashford; scenery, John Lee Beatty; costumes, Toni-Leslie James; lighting, Ken Billington; sound, Scott Lehrer; original orchestration, Robert Russell Bennett; musical coordinator, Seymour Red Press; ballet music arrangement, Trude Rittman; casting, Jay Binder; production stage manager, Bonnie L. Becker; press, Philip Rinaldi Publicity.

The original production of *Bloomer Girl* opened in New York on 10/5/44 for 654 performances at the Shubert Theatre.

ACT I

For Encores! presentations song performances are listed by the actors' names.

Overture .... Orchestra
Scene 1: The Applegate Mansion, spring of 1861
"When the Boys Come Home" .... Daughters and Sons-in-Law
"Evelina" .... Michael Park and Kate Jennings Grant
"Welcome Hinges" .... Anita Gillette, Philip Bosco, Kate Jennings Grant, Michael Park, Daughters and Sons-in-Law
Scene 2: The Smoking Room
"The Farmer's Daughter" .... Sons-in-Law
Scene 3: A former bordello, now the offices of "The Lily"
"Good Enough for Grandma" .... Kate Jennings Grant, Donna Lynne Champlin, Kathleen Chalfant and the Suffragettes
"The Eagle and Me" .... Jubilant Sykes and Ensemble
"Right as the Rain" .... Michael Park and Kate Jennings Grant
Scene 4: Outside the Applegate Estate
"T'morra, T'morra" .... Donna Lynne Champlin
Scene 5: The Buyers' Pavilion
"The Rakish Young Man in the Whiskers" .... Kate Jennings Grant and Ensemble
"Pretty as a Picture" .... Men

ACT II

Entr'acte .... Orchestra
Scene 1: The Village Green
"Sunday in Cicero Falls" Company
Scene 2: The Cicero Falls Town Jail
"I Got a Song" .... Everett Bradley, Jubilant Sykes, Todd Hunter and Ensemble
"Lullaby" .... Kate Jennings Grant
"I Got a Song" (Reprise) .... Everett Bradley, Todd Hunter and Ensemble

Scene 3: The Town Hall
"Liza Crossing the Ice" .... Teri Hansen and Ensemble
"Never Was Born" .... Donna Lynne Champlin
"Man for Sale" .... Jubilant Sykes
Ballet .... Karine Plantadit-Bageot, Nina Goldman, Robert Wersinger, Todd Hunter, Deborah Allton, Donna Dunmire, Cherylyn Jones, Jason Lacayo and Lori MacPherson
"The Eagle and Me" (Reprise) .... Company
Scene 4: The Applegate Mansion
Finale: "When the Boys Come Home" .... Entire Company

Mnemonic (67). By Complicite. Produced by Thomas Viertel, Steven Baruch, Marc Routh, Richard Frankel, Dede Harris/Lorie Cowen Levy, Timothy Childs, Herb Goldsmith, Libby Adler Mages/Mari Glick, Margo Lion, at John Jay College Theater. Opened March 28, 2001. (Closed May 24, 2001)

CAST: Katrin Cartlidge, Simon McBurney, Tim McMullan, Eric Mallett, Kostas Philippoglou, Catherine Schaub Abkarian, Daniel Wahl.

Directed by Simon McBurney; scenery, Michael Levine; costumes, Christina Cunningham; lighting, Paul Anderson; sound, Christopher Shutt; puppet design, Simon Auton; production stage manager, Arabella Powell, press, Philip Rinaldi Publicity, Barbara Carroll.

Presented without intermission.

Exploration of the role memory plays in the development of identity and culture. A 2000–01 *Best Plays* honoree (see essay by John Istel in this volume).

Out, brief candle: Anthony Mackie in Michael Develle Winn's Up Against the Wind. *Photo: Joan Marcus*

New York Theatre Workshop production of **Up Against the Wind** (15). By Michael Develle Winn. James C. Nicola artistic director, Lynn Moffat managing director. Opened April 2, 2001. (Closed April 14, 2001)

The Girl, LeeLee, etc. .... Olubunmi Banjoko
Record Store Clerk, etc. .... David Brown Jr.
Suge Knight .... Kevin Daniels
Afeni Shakur .... Hazelle Goodman
Ed Gordon, etc. .... J.D. Jackson
Booker, etc. .... Nashawn Kearse

LaDonna, etc. .... Tracey A. Leigh
Tupac Shakur .... Anthony Mackie
Jerome Perez .... Jesse J. Perez
Prison Guard, etc. .... Christopher Rivera
Jimmy Iovine ....Joseph Siravo
Sekiywa Shakur .... Tracie Thoms
Lt. Dan ....Isiah Whitlock Jr.

Directed by Rosemary K. Andress; scenery, Narelle Sissons; costumes, Olu-Orondava Mumford; lighting, Peter West; sound, Jerry M. Yager; original music, Jonathan Sanborn; production stage manager, Jason Scott Eagan; press, Richard Kornberg and Associates, Don Summa.

Presented in two parts.

The short life and violent death of Tupac Shakur. First presented in 1999 at the Juilliard School of Drama.

The Good Thief (54). Transfer of the play by Conor McPherson. Produced by the Culture Project at 45 Bleecker, Nicholas S.G. Stern, Allan Buchman, in association with Keen Theater Company, Niclas Nagler and Wayne Williams, at 45 Bleecker. Opened April 4, 2000. (Closed May 26, 2001)

Performed by Brian d'Arcy James.

Directed by Carl Forsman; scenery, Nathan Heverin; costumes, Theresa Squire; lighting, Josh Bradford; sound, Stefan Jacobs; associate producer, Savitri Durkee; casting, Jennifer Sauer; production stage manager, Kara Bain; press, Karen Greco Entertainment.

Presented without intermission.

A professional thug unburdens himself in a matter-of-fact manner that offers a bit of repentance and a dollop of remorse. Transferred from an Off Off Broadway run at the Jose Quintero Theatre where it opened 3/11/01 for 11 performances. First performed in 1994 as *The Light of Jesus* at Dublin's City Arts Centre.

Passion Play (38). Revival of the play by Peter Nichols. Produced by Louise and Stephen Kornfeld, Kardana-Swinsky Productions, Karen Adler, Teri Solomon Mitze, in association with Roy Gabay, Lawrence Roman, at the Minetta Lane Theatre. Opened April 4, 2001. (Closed May 6, 2001)

Kate ....Natacha Roi
James .... Simon Jones
Eleanor .... Maureen Anderman
Agnes .... Lucy Martin
Jim ....John Curless
Nell .... Leslie Lyles

WITH: Peter Bradbury, Rosemarie DeWitt, Cynthia Hood, Claywood Sempliner.

Understudies: Miss Roi—Rosemarie DeWitt; Misses Anderman, Martin, Lyles—Cynthia Hood; Messrs. Jones, Curless—Claywood Sempliner.

Directed by Elinor Renfield; scenery, Narelle Sissons; costumes, Christine Field; lighting Jeff Croiter; sound, Ken Travis; casting, Ilene Starger; production stage manager, Allison Sommers; press, Richard Kornberg and Associates.

Time: The present. Place: London. Presented in two parts.

A married couple's inner (and outer) selves struggle with the fallout from one partner's sexual dalliance with a family friend.

The Joseph Papp Public Theater/New York Shakespeare Festival production of **References to Salvador Dalí Make Me Hot** (24). By José Rivera. George C. Wolfe producer, Fran Reiter executive producer, Rosemarie Tichler artistic producer, in the Shiva Theater. Opened April 9, 2001. (Closed April 29, 2001)

Coyote .... Kevin Jackson
Cat .... Kristine Nielsen
Moon .... Michael Lombard
Martin .... Carlo Alban
Gabriela .... Rosie Perez
Benito .... John Ortiz

Directed by Jo Bonney; scenery, Neil Patel; costumes, Clint E.B. Ramos; lighting, David Weiner; sound, Donald DiNicola, Obadiah Eaves; original music, Carlos Valdez; associate producers, Bonnie

Metzgar, John Dias; casting, Jordan Thaler, Heidi Griffiths, production stage manager, Mike Schleifer; press, Carol Fineman, Tom Naro.

Time: A few months after the Persian Gulf War. Place: Barstow, California. Presented in two parts.

The dream-world of a lonely serviceman's wife threatens to overtake her life. Originally produced by South Coast Repertory, Costa Mesa, Calif.

Dream girl: Carlo Alban and Rosie Perez in José Rivera's References to Salvador Dalí Make Me Hot. *Photo: Michal Daniel*

The Joseph Papp Public Theater/New York Shakespeare Festival production of **Lackawanna Blues** (44). By Ruben Santiago-Hudson. George C. Wolfe producer, Fran Reiter executive director, Rosemarie Tichler artistic producer, in LuEsther Hall. Opened April 14, 2001. (Closed May 27, 2001)

CAST: Ruben Santiago-Hudson with musician Bill Sims Jr.

Characters: Narrator; Miss Rachel Crosby (Nanny); Lady; Ol' Po' Carl; Ricky; Lottie; Junior; Mr. Lemuel Taylor; Numb Finger Pete; Small Paul; Freddie Cobb; Melvin Earthman; Norma and Gerald; Norma's Mom; Jimmy Lee and Pauline; Saul; Dick Johnson; Bill; Sweet Tooth Sam; Mr. Lucious

Directed by Loretta Greco; scenery, costumes, Myung Hee Cho; lighting, James Vermeulen; original music, Bill Sims Jr.; associate producers, Bonnie Metzgar, John Dias; casting, Jordan Thaler, Heidi Griffiths; production stage manager, Buzz Cohen; press, Carol Fineman.

Time: Then and now. Place: Lackawanna, N.Y. Presented without intermission.

Santiago-Hudson's one-man narrative about of growing up in and around Lackawanna, N.Y.

Second Stage Theatre production of **Crimes of the Heart** (32). Revival of the play by Beth Henley. Carole Rothman artistic director, Mark Linn-Baker 2001 season artistic director, Carol Fishman managing director, Alexander Fraser executive director. Opened April 16, 2001. (Closed May 13, 2001)

Chick .... Julia Murney
Lenny .... Enid Graham
Doc .... Talmadge Lowe
Meg .... Amy Ryan
Babe .... Mary Catherine Garrison
Barnett .... Jason Butler Harner

Directed by Garry Hynes; scenery, Thomas Lynch; costumes, Susan Hilferty; lighting, Rui Rita; sound, original music, Donald DiNicola; casting, Johnson-Liff Associates; production stage manager, Kelley Kirkpatrick; stage manager, Amy Patricia Stern; press, Richard Kornberg and Associates, Don Summa, Tom D'Ambrosio.

Time: Five years after hurricane Camille. Place: Hazlehurst, Mississippi. Presented in two parts.

Three sisters deal with the vicissitudes of modern Southern existence. A 1980–81 *Best Plays* honoree, it later opened at Broadway's John Golden Theatre on 11/4/81 for 535 performances.

***Love, Janis** (44). Musical based on the book by Laura Joplin; adapted and directed by Randal Myler. Produced by Jennifer Dumas, Jack Cullen, Patricia Watt and Jeff Rosen, in association with Laura Joplin and Michael Joplin, at the Village Theater. Opened April 22, 2001.

Janis .... Catherine Curtin
Janis Joplin .... Andra Mitrovich
Cathy Richardson (alternating)
Interviewer .... Seth Jones

Directed by Randal Myler; production design, Jules Fisher and Peggy Eisenhauer; costumes, Robert Blackman; sound, Tony Meola; projections, Bo Eriksson; musical direction, arrangements, Sam Andrew; co-producers, Jay and Cindy Gutterman; associate producers, Jennifer Taylor, Madelyn Bell Ewing, Robert Schreiber, Jamie Cesa, Carl D. White, Tom Smedes, Scooter Weintraub; casting, Jessica Gilburne, Ed Urban; production stage manager, Jack Gianino; press, Springer/Chicoine Public Relations.

Presented in two parts.

Adaptation of the singer's letters to her mother performed by two women who represent Ms. Joplin in, respectively, spoken word and song. Originally produced at the Denver Center Theatre Company.

Bob's your uncle: Gale Harold and George Morfogen in Austin Pendleton's Uncle Bob. *Photo: Yasuyuki Takagi*

***Uncle Bob** (43). Revival of the play by Austin Pendleton. Produced by Rebellion Theatre Company, LLC at the Soho Playhouse. Opened April 23, 2001.

Bob .... George Morfogen
Josh .... Gale Harold

Understudy: Mr. Morfogen—T.R. Shields.

Directed by Courtney Moorehead; scenery, Matt Corsover, Andrew Sendor; costumes, Pamela Snider; lighting, Jason A. Cina; sound, Jared Coseglia; fight direction, Lee Willet; production stage manager, Jason Sutton; press, Origlio Public Relations, Tony Origlio, Emily Lowe, Richard Hillman, Joel Treick.

Time: The present. Place: Bob's brownstone apartment in the West Village.

Presented in two parts.

An angry old man, dying of AIDS, is confronted by his nephew, a younger version of himself. Originally produced by the Mint Theater Company in 1995.

Brooklyn Academy of Music production of **The Tragedy of Hamlet** (12). Revival of the play by William Shakespeare; adapted by Peter Brook. Bruce C. Ratner chairman of the board, Karen Brooks Hopkins president, Joseph V. Melillo executive producer. Co-produced with the C.I.C.T/Théâtre des Bouffes du Nord, Wiener Festwochen, Festival d'Automne à Paris at the BAM Harvey Theater. Opened April 24, 2001. (Closed May 6, 2001)

Horatio .... Scott Handy
Claudius; The Ghost .... Jeffery Kissoon
Hamlet .... Adrian Lester
Polonius; Gravedigger .... Bruce Myers
Gertrude .... Natasha Parry
Rosencrantz;
First Player .... Naseeruddin Shah
Ophelia .... Shantala Shivalingappa
Guildenstern;
Second Player; Laertes .... Rohan Siva

Directed by Peter Brook; scenery, costumes, Chloé Obolensky; lighting, Philippe Vialatte; music, Toshi Tsuchitori; artistic collaboration, Marie-Hélène Estienne; stage managers, Jean-Paul Ouvrard, Kim Beringer; press, Elena Park, Melissa Cusick, Fateema Jones, Tamara McCaw, Kila Packett.

Presented with no intermission.

Mr. Brook's adaptation of Shakespeare's classic tragedy of usurpation and murder with a Dane who is more trickster than madman.

York Theatre Company production of **The IT Girl** (29). Musical based on the Paramount Picture *It*; book by Michael Small and BT McNicholl; music by Paul McKibbins; lyrics by BT McNicholl. James Morgan artistic director, in association with the It Girl Productions, LLC, at the Theatre at Saint Peter's. Opened May 3, 2001. (Closed May 27, 2001)

Betty Lou Spencer .... Jean Louisa Kelly
Mr. Notting; Barker;
Reporter; Sailor;
Trevor Pitstop .... Monte Wheeler
Jane; Mrs. Sullivan;
Mrs. Van Norman;
Snake Charmer .... Danette Holden
Daisy; Molly;
Hootchie-Kootchie .... Susan M. Haefner
Dancer; Brearley Chapin;
Jonathan Waltham .... Jonathan Dokuchitz
Monty Montgomery .... Stephen DeRosa
Adela Van Norman .... Jessica Boevers

Musicians: Albin Konopka piano; Chris Miele reeds, clarinet, flute, saxophone; Amy Kimball violin; Ratso Harris bass; Ray Grappone drums, percussion.

Understudies: Female Understudy—Susan Owen; Male Understudy—Christopher Sutton.

Directed by BT McNicholl; choreography, Robert Bianca; scenery, Mark Nayden; costumes, Robin L. McGee; lighting, Jeff Nellis; projections, Elaine J. McCarthy; orchestrations, Paul McKibbins; dance music arrangements, Albin Konopka, Charles Eversole; music director, Albin Konopka; casting, Norman Meranus; production stage manager, Peggy R. Samuels; press, Keith Sherman and Associates, Dan Fortune.

Time: The late 1920s. Place: New York City. Presented in two parts.

Based on the 1927 Clara Bow film in which an aspiring shopgirl marries her boss.

ACT I

"Black and White World" .... Betty and Company

"Why Not?" .... Betty and Girls
"Stand Straight and Tall" .... Jonathan
"It" .... Monty and Company
"Mama's Arms" .... Molly
"What to Wear?" .... Betty, Molly, Adela, Mrs. Van Norman, Jonathan and Monty
"It" (Reprise) .... Jonathan
"A Perfect Plan" .... Adela
"Coney Island" .... Betty, Jonathan and Company
Act I Finale .... Adela and Company

Girl gets boy: Jean Louisa Kelly and Jonathan Dokuchitz in The IT Girl. *Photo: Carol Rosegg*

ACT II

"Woman and Waif" .... Company
"Stay With Me"/"Left-Hand Arrangement" .... Jonathan and Betty
"Step Into Their Shoes" .... Molly, Betty, Monty
"Out at Sea" .... Company
"How Do You Say?" .... Betty and Company
"Step Into Their Shoes" (Reprise) .... Betty
"You're the Best Thing that Ever Happened to Me" .... Betty and Jonathan
Finale .... Company

***Madame Melville** (33). By Richard Nelson. Produced by Madame Melville Producing Partners, in association with Sonny Everett, Ted Tulchin, Darren Bagert and Aaron Levy, at the Promenade Theatre. Opened May 3, 2001.

Carl .... Macaulay Culkin
Claudie Melville .... Joely Richardson
Ruth .... Robin Weigert

Understudies: Mr. Culkin—Zachary Knighton; Misses Richardson, Weigert—Yvonne Woods; Miss Weigert—Heather Goldenhersh.

Teen fantasy: Macaulay Culkin and Joely Richardson in Madame Melville. *Photo: Joan Marcus*

Directed by Richard Nelson; scenery, Thomas Lynch; costumes, Susan Hilferty; lighting, Jennifer Tipton; sound, Scott Myers; casting, Mark Bennett; production stage manager, Matthew Silver; press, the Publicity Office, Bob Fennell, Marc Thibodeau, Candi Adams, Michael S. Borowski.

Time: 1966. Place: Paris. Presented without an intermission.

Coming of age story of an American teenager seducing and being seduced by his lovely French teacher. Originally produced in London's West End.

City Center Encores! presentation of **Hair** (5). Concert version of the musical with book and lyrics by Gerome Ragni and James Rado; music by Galt MacDermot. Judith E. Daykin president and executive director, Jack Viertel artistic director, Rob Fisher musical director, Kathleen Marshall director-in-residence, at City Center. Opened May 3, 2001. (Closed May 7, 2001)

Claude .... Luther Creek
Berger .... Tom Plotkin
Woof .... Kevin Cahoon
Hud .... Michael McElroy
Sheila .... Idina Menzel
Jeanie .... Miriam Shor
Dionne .... Brandi Chavonne Massey
Crissy .... Jessica-Snow Wilson
Mother .... Sheri Sanders, Kathy Deitch, Eric Millegan
Father .... Kevin Cahoon, Gavin Creel, Miriam Shor
Principal .... Kevin Cahoon, Gavin Creel, Miriam Shor
Tourist Couple .... Jesse Tyler Ferguson, Billy Hartung
General Grant .... Jesse Tyler Ferguson
Abraham Lincoln .... Rosalind Brown
Buddhadalirama .... Miriam Shor
The Tribe .... Rosalind Brown, Bryant Carroll, E. Alyssa Claar, Gavin Creel, Kathy Deitch, Jessica Ferraro, Jesse Tyler Ferguson, Stephanie Fittro, Billy Hartung, Todd Hunter, Eric Millegan, Sean Jeremy Palmer, Sheri Sanders, Carolyn Saxon, Michael Seelbach, Yuka Takara

Orchestra: Rob Fisher conductor, keyboard; Galt MacDermot keyboard; Allen Won saxophone, flute, piccolo, clarinet; Jay Berliner, David Spinozza guitar; Wilbur Bascomb bass; John Frosk, Glenn Drewes, Chris Jaudes trumpet; Bernard Purdie drums; Erik Charlston percussion.

Directed and choreographed by Kathleen Marshall; scenery, John Lee Beatty; costumes, Martin Pakledinaz; lighting, Ken Billington; sound, Scott Lehrer; musical coordinator, Seymour Red Press; associate choreographer, Joey Pizzi; casting, Jay Binder; production stage manager, Bonnie L. Becker; press, Philip Rinaldi Publicity.

The original production of *Hair* opened at the Public Theater on 10/29/67. A revised version opened on Broadway at the Biltmore Theatre on 4/29/68 and played for 1,742 performances.

ACT I

For Encores! presentations song performances are listed by the actors' names.

"Aquarius" .... Eric Millegan and Company
"Donna" .... Tom Plotkin and Company
"Hashish" .... Company
"Sodomy" .... Kevin Cahoon and Company
"Colored Spade" .... Michael McElroy, Todd Hunter and Sean Jeremy Palmer
"Manchester England" .... Luther Creek and Company
"Ain't Got No" .... Kevin Cahoon, Michael McElroy, Brandi Chavonne Massey and Company
"Dead End" .... Rosalind Brown, Todd Hunter, Sean Jeremy Palmer and Carolyn Saxon
"I Believe in Love" .... Idina Menzel, E. Alyssa Claar, Kathy Deitch and Jessica Ferraro
"Ain't Got No" (Reprise) .... Company
"Air" .... Miriam Shor, Brandi Chavonne Massey and Jessica-Snow Wilson
"I Got Life" .... Luther Creek and Company
"Initials" .... Company
"Going Down" .... Tom Plotkin and Company
"Hair" .... Tom Plotkin, Luther Creek and Company
"My Conviction" .... Jesse Tyler Ferguson
"Easy To Be Hard" .... Idina Menzel
"Don't Put It Down" .... Kevin Cahoon, Bryant Carroll, Billy Hartung and Tom Plotkin
"Frank Mills" .... Jessica-Snow Wilson
"Be-In (Hare Krishna)" .... Company
"Where Do I Go" .... Luther Creek and Company

ACT II

"Electric Blues" .... Gavin Creel, Kathy Deitch, Jessica Ferraro and Michael Seelbach
"Oh Great God of Power" .... Company
"Black Boys" .... E. Alyssa Claar, Kathy Deitch, Sheri Sanders, Michael McElroy, Todd Hunter and Sean Jeremy Palmer
"White Boys" .... Brandi Chavonne Massey, Rosalind Brown and Carolyn Saxon
"Walking in Space" .... Brandi Chavonne Massey, Gavin Creel, Jessica-Snow Wilson, Idina Menzel, Miriam Shor and Company
"Abie Baby" .... Michael McElroy, Todd Hunter, Sean Jeremy Palmer and Rosalind Brown
"Three-Five-Zero-Zero" .... Company
"What a Piece of Work is Man" .... Sean Jeremy Palmer and Michael Seelbach
"Good Morning Starshine" .... Idina Menzel and Company
"The Bed" .... Company
"The Flesh Failures (Let the Sun Shine In)" .... Luther Creek, Idina Menzel, Brandi Chavonne Massey and Company

Cinderella (11). Musical with music by Richard Rodgers; book and lyrics by Oscar Hammerstein II; adapted for the stage by Tom Briggs, from the teleplay by Robert L. Freedman. Produced by Radio City Entertainment at the Theater at Madison Square Garden. Opened May 3, 2001. (Closed May 13, 2001)

Fairy Godmother .... Eartha Kitt
Cinderella .... Jamie-Lynn Sigler
Prince Christopher .... Paolo Montalban
Stepmother .... Everett Quinton
Grace .... NaTasha Yvette Williams
Joy .... Alexandra Kolb
Lionel .... Victor Trent Cook
Queen Constantina .... Leslie Becker
King Maximillian .... Ken Prymus

Directed by Gabriel Barre; choreography, Ken Roberson; scenery, James Youmans; costumes, Pamela Scofield; lighting, Tim Hunter; sound, Duncan Edwards; musical supervision, arrangements, Andrew Lippa; orchestrations, David Siegel; original orchestrations, Robert Russell Bennett; music director and conductor, John Mezzio; production stage manager, Daniel L. Bello.

***Urinetown** (28). Musical with book and lyrics by Greg Kotis; music and lyrics by Mark Hollmann. Produced by the Araca Group and Dodger Theatricals, in association with TheaterDreams, Inc., and Lauren Mitchell, at the American Theatre of Actors. Opened May 6, 2001.

Officer Lockstock .... Jeff McCarthy
Little Sally .... Spencer Kayden
Penelope Pennywise .... Nancy Opel
Bobby Strong .... Hunter Foster
Hope Cladwell ....Jennifer Laura Thompson
Mr. McQueen .... David Beach
Senator Fipp .... John Deyle
Old Man Strong;
  Hot Blades Harry .... Ken Jennings
Tiny Tom; Dr. Billeaux .... Rick Crom
Soupy Sue;
  Cladwell's Secretary .... Rachel Coloff
Little Becky Two Shoes;
  Mrs. Millennium .... Megan Lawrence
Robbie the Stockfish;
  Business Man #1 .... Victor W. Hawks
Billy Boy Bill;
  Business Man #2 .... Lawrence Street
Old Woman;
  Josephine Strong .... Kay Walbye
Officer Barrel .... Daniel Marcus
Caldwell B. Cladwell ....John Cullum

Orchestra: Ed Goldschneider conductor, piano; Paul Garment clarinet, bass clarinet, alto sax, soprano sax; Ben Herrington tenor trombone, euphonium; Tim McLafferty drums, percussion.

Understudies: Messrs. McCarthy, Foster, Marcus, Jennings—Victor W. Hawks; Miss Kayden—Megan Lawrence; Misses Thompson, Walbye—Rachel Coloff; Misses Opel, Lawrence—Kay Walbye; Mr. Cullum—Daniel Marcus; Messrs. Beach, Deyle—Rick Crom; Messrs. Hawks, Crom and Misses Coloff, Lawrence—Lawrence Street.

Directed by John Rando; musical staging, John Carrafa; scenery, Scott Pask; costumes, Jonathan Bixby, Gregory Gale; lighting, Brian MacDevitt; sound, Jeff Curtis; fight direction, Rick Sordelet; orchestrations, Bruce Coughlin; music coordinator, John Miller; music direction, Edward Strauss; casting, Jay Binder, Cindi Rush, Laura Stanczyk; production stage manager, Julia P. Jones; stage manager, Martha Donaldson; press, Boneau/Bryan-Brown, Adrian Bryan-Brown, Jim Byk, Amy Jacobs, Karalee Dawn, Rob Finn.

Presented in two parts.

A town with a water shortage finds itself paying dearly for one of the most basic human needs in this eco-satire and spoof of Broadway musicals. A 2000–01 *Best Plays* choice (see essay by Jeffrey Sweet in this volume). Originally presented as part of the 1999 New York International Fringe Festival.

ACT I

Overture .... Orchestra
"Urinetown" ....Lockstock and Company
"It's a Privilege to Pee" .... Pennywise and the Poor
"It's a Privilege to Pee" (Reprise) .... Lockstock and the Poor
"Mr. Cladwell" ....Cladwell and the UGC Staff
"Cop Song" .... Lockstock, Barrel and the Cops

"Follow Your Heart" .... Hope and Bobby
"Look at the Sky" .... Bobby and the Poor
"Don't Be the Bunny" .... Cladwell, Fipp, McQueen, Lockstock, Barrel and Pennywise
Act I Finale .... Full Company

Pennies from peeing: Nancy Opel in Urinetown. *Photo: Joan Marcus*

ACT II

"What is Urinetown?" .... Full Company
"Snuff that Girl" .... Hot Blades Harry, Little Becky Two Shoes and the Poor
"Run, Freedom, Run!" .... Bobby and the Poor
"Follow Your Heart" (Reprise) .... Hope
"Why Did I Listen to that Man?" .... Pennywise, Hope, Fipp, Lockstock, Barrel and Bobby
"Tell Her I Love Her" .... Little Sally, Bobby, and the Poor
"We're Not Sorry" .... Full Company
"We're Not Sorry" (Reprise) .... Cladwell and Pennywise
"I See A River" .... Hope, Little Becky Two Shoes, Josephine Strong and Company

***Lobby Hero** (27). Transfer of the play by Kenneth Lonergan. Produced by Jenny Wiener, Jon Steingart, Hal Luftig, in association with Playwrights Horizons, at the John Houseman Theatre. Opened May 8, 2001.

Understudies: Mr. Graham—Rafael Cabrera; Messrs. Fitzgerald, Donovan—David Paluck; Miss Burns—Nicole Alifante.

Production stage manager, Thea Bradshaw Gillies.

See March 13, 2001 listing for more information.

***Six Goumbas and a Wannabe** (25). By Vincent M. Gogliormella. Produced by Gardenia Productions at the Players Theatre. Opened May 10, 2001

Vinny Gugliotta .... Joe Maruzzo
Anna Gugliotta .... Kathrine Narducci
Danny Milito .... Dan Grimaldi
Rose DiVincenzo .... Sian Heder
Richie DiVincenzo .... Sal Petraccione
Tony Piscatelli .... Ernest Mingione
Jen Piscatelli .... Tara Kapoor
Cathy Milito .... Sian Heder

Tommy Gugliotta .... Joe Iacovino
Angela Gugliotta .... Tara Kapoor
Mike Ardito .... James Lorenzo
Charles Harris .... Charles E. Wallace
Wayne Morganstern .... Howard Spiegel
Hotel Clerk .... Joe Iacovino
Gina Price .... Annie McGovern
Sonny Rigatoni .... George Ramford

Understudies: Messrs. Grimaldi, Petraccione, Spiegel, Mingione—Joseph Tudisco; Mr. Lorenzo—David Cera; Misses Narducci, Kapoor—Terri Mintz.

Directed by Thomas G. Waites; scenery, lighting, Mark Bloom; costumes, Lorree True; sound, David A. Gilman; production stage manager, Duff Dugan; press, Media Blitz, Beck Lee.

Time: A weekend in September. Place: Various locations in New York and New Jersey. Presented in two parts.

Comic reunion of a bunch of Italian-American stereotypes whose escapades take them to Atlantic City. Transferred from CAP 21 Theater Off Off Broadway where it opened 3/27/01 for 35 performances.

***New York Theatre Workshop** production of ***Nocturne** (18). By Adam Rapp. James C. Nicola artistic director, Lynn Moffat managing director, in collaboration with the American Repertory Theatre, Robert Brustein artistic director, Robert J. Orchard managing director. Opened May 16, 2001.

The Mother .... Candice Brown
The Red-Headed Girl
with the Gray-Green Eyes .... Marin Ireland
The Father .... Will LeBow
The Sister .... Nicole Pasquale
The Son .... Dallas Roberts

Directed by Marcus Stern; scenery, Christine Jones; costumes, Viola Mackenthun; lighting, John Ambrosone; sound, Marcus Stern, David Remedios; production stage manager, Jennifer Rae Moore; press, Richard Kornberg and Associates. Presented in two parts.

A young man is haunted by his responsibility for the accidental death of his sister and the repercussions his family suffers. A 2000–01 *Best Plays* honoree (see essay by Robert Brustein in this volume). Originally produced in 2000 at American Repertory Theatre in Cambridge, Mass.

Happy horn player: John Spencer in Warren Leight's Glimmer, Glimmer and Shine. *Photo: Joan Marcus*

***Manhattan Theatre Club** production of ***Blur** (17). By Melanie Marnich. Lynne Meadow artistic director, Barry Grove executive producer at City Center Stage II. Opened May 17, 2001.

Mom .... Polly Draper
Dot DiPrima .... Angela Goethals
Doctor; Student; Voices .... Ken Marks
Joey D'Amico .... Chris Messina
Francis Butane .... Susan Pourfar
Father O'Hara .... Bill Raymond

Understudies: Misses Goethals, Pourfar—Bridget Barkan; Messrs. Raymond, Marks—Tony Carlin; Mr. Messina—Johnny Giacalone; Miss Draper—Margo Skinner.

Directed by Lynne Meadow; scenery, Santo Loquasto; costumes, James Schuette; lighting, Brian MacDevitt; original music, sound design, David Van Tieghem; fight direction, Rick Sordelet; casting, Nancy Piccione, David Caparelliotis; production stage manager, Harold Goldfaden; press, Boneau/Bryan-Brown, Chris Boneau, Jackie Green, Steven Padla, Martine Sainvil.

A young woman finds love and quirky friendships as she suffers from a rare condition that destroys her eyesight.

***Manhattan Theatre Club** production of ***Glimmer, Glimmer and Shine** (9). By Warren Leight. Lynne Meadow artistic director, Barry Grove executive producer, in association with the Mark Taper Forum, at City Center Stage I. Opened May 24, 2001.

Jordon .... Scott Cohen
Daniel .... Brian Kerwin
Delia .... Seana Kofoed
Martin .... John Spencer

Understudies: Messrs. Spencer, Kerwin—Ray Virta.

Directed by Evan Yionoulis; scenery, Neil Patel; costumes, Candice Donnelly; lighting, Donald Holder; sound, Jon Gottlieb; original music, Evan Lurie; casting, Nancy Piccione, David Caparelliotis; production stage manager, Richard Hester; press, Boneau/Bryan-Brown, Chris Boneau, Jackie Green, Steven Padla, Martine Sainvil.

Time: 1990. Place: New York City and Greenwich, Conn. Presented in two parts.

Jazz-playing brothers who chose different life paths reunite when one falls on hard times. Originally produced by Penguin Repertory Company in Stony Point, N.Y. Later produced by the Center Theatre Group at the Mark Taper Forum in Los Angeles for its 2000–01 season.

***Brooklyn Academy of Music** presentation of a **Royal National Theatre** production of **Hamlet** (2). Revival of the play by William Shakespeare. Bruce C. Ratner chairman of the board, Karen Brooks Hopkins president, Joseph V. Melillo executive producer, at the BAM Howard Gilman Opera House. Opened May 30, 2000.

Horatio .... Simon Day
Hamlet .... Simon Russell Beale
Hamlet's Ghost;
Player King .... Sylvester Morand
Claudius .... Peter McEnery
Gertrude .... Sara Kestelman
Polonius; Gravedigger .... Peter Blythe
Laertes .... Guy Lankester
Ophelia .... Cathryn Bradshaw
Reynaldo; Francisco .... Edward Gower
Rosencrantz .... Christopher Staines
Guildenstern .... Paul Bazely
Player Queen .... Janet Spencer-Turner
Other Player .... Chloe Angharad
Barnardo; Priest .... Ken Oxtoby
Marcellus .... Martin Chamberlain
Osric; Other Player .... Michael Wildman

Directed by John Caird, scenery, costumes, Tim Hatley; lighting, Paul Pyant; music, John Cameron; sound, Christopher Shutt; fight director, Terry King; press, Elena Park, Melissa Cusick, Fateema Jones, Tamara McCaw, Kila Packett.

Presented in two parts.

The second of two highly anticipated versions of *Hamlet*, both presented by BAM.

CAST REPLACEMENTS AND TOURING COMPANIES

○○○○○

Compiled by Jeffrey Finn Productions

THE FOLLOWING IS A LIST of the major cast replacements of record in productions that opened in previous years, but were still playing in New York during a substantial part of the 2000–01 season; and other New York shows that were on a first-class tour in 2000–01.

The name of each major role is listed in *italics* beneath the title of the play in the first column. In the second column directly opposite appears the name of the actor who created the role in the original New York production (whose opening date appears in *italics* at the top of the column). In shows of the past five years, indented immediately beneath the original actor's name are the names of subsequent New York replacements, together with the date of replacement when available. In shows that have run longer than five years, only the more recent cast replacements are listed under the names of the original cast members.

The third column gives information about first-class touring companies. When there is more than one roadshow company, #1, #2, etc., appear before the name of the performer who created the role in each company (and the city and date of each company's first performance appears in *italics* at the top of the column). Their subsequent replacements are also listed beneath their names in the same manner as the New York companies, with dates when available.

AIDA

	New York 3/23/00	*Minneapolis, MN 4/6/01*
Aida	Heather Headley	Simone
Radames	Adam Pascal	Patrick Cassidy
Amneri	Sheri René Scott Taylor Dayne	Kelli Fournier
Mereb	Damian Perkins	Jacen R.Wilkerson
Zoser	John Hickok	Neal Benari

ANNIE GET YOUR GUN

	New York 3/4/99	*Dallas, TX 07/25/00*

Buffalo Bill	Ron Holgate
	  Christopher Councill 9/99
	  Dennis Kelly 1/00
	  Conrad John Schuck
		George McDaniel

Frank Butler	Tom Wopat	Rex Smith
	↳ Brent Barrett	↳ Tom Wopat 10/31/00
Dolly Tate	Valerie Wright	Susann Fletcher
	↳ Michelle Blakely	↳ Julia Fowler 5/8/01
	↳ Valerie Wright	
	↳ Kerry O'Malley	
Tommy Keeler	Andrew Palermo	Eric Sciotto
	↳ Randy Donaldson	↳ Randy Donaldson 1/9/01
	↳ Eric Sciotto	↳ Sean Michael McKnight 4/3/00
Winnie Tate	Nicole Ruth Snelson	Claci Miller
	↳ Claci Miller	↳ Carolyn Ockert 12/27/00
Charlie Davenport	Peter Marx	Joe Hart
Annie Oakley	Bernadette Peters	Marilu Henner
	↳ Susan Lucci	↳ Karyn Quackenbush 4/3/01
	↳ Bernadette Peters 1/18/00	
	↳ Cheryl Ladd	
	↳ Reba McEntire	

BEAUTY AND THE BEAST

	New York 4/18/94	*Minneapolis 11/7/95* *Closed 3/7/99* *#3 Tulsa 9/7/99*
Beast	Terrence Mann	Fred Inkley
	↳ Jeff McCarthy	↳ Roger Befeler
	↳ Chuck Wagner	#3 Grant Norman
	↳ James Barbour	
	↳ Steve Blanchard	
Belle	Susan Egan	Kim Huber
	↳ Sarah Uriarte	↳ Erin Dilly 2/11/98
	↳ Christianne Tisdale	#3 Susan Owen
	↳ Kerry Butler	↳ Danyelle Bossardet
	↳ Deborah Gibson	
	↳ Kim Huber	
	↳ Toni Braxton	
	↳ Andrea McArdle	
	↳ Sara Litzsinger	
Lefou	Kenny Raskin	Dan Sklar
	↳ Harrison Beal	↳ Jeffrey Howard Schecter
	↳ Jamie Torcellini	↳ Aldrin Gonzalez
	↳ Jeffrey Howard Schecter	#3 Michael Raine
	↳ Jay Brian Winnick 11/12/99	↳ Brad Aspel
	↳ Gerard McIsaac	
Gaston	Burke Moses	Tony Lawson
	↳ Marc Kudisch	#3 Chris Hoch
	↳ Steve Blanchard	↳ Edward Staudenmayer
	↳ Patrick Ryan Sullivan	
	↳ Christopher Seiber	
Maurice	Tom Bosley	Grant Cowan
	↳ MacIntyre Dixon	#3 Ron Lee Savin
	↳ Tom Bosley	

	Kurt Knudson Tim Jerome J.B. Adams 11/12/99	
Cogsworth	Heath Lamberts Peter Bartlett Gibby Brand John Christopher Jones Jeff Brooke 11/12/99	Jeff Brooks #3 John Alban Coughlan Ron Bagden
Lumiere	Gary Beach Lee Roy Reams Patrick Quinn Gary Beach Meshach Taylor Patrick Page Paul Schoeffler Patrick Page	Patrick Page David DeVries Gary Beach David DeVries #3 Ron Wisniski Jay Russell
Babette	Stacey Logan Pamela Winslow Leslie Castay Pam Klinger Louisa Kendrick	Leslie Castay Mindy Paige Davis 2/15/97 Heather Lee #3 Jennifer Shrader
Mrs. Potts	Beth Fowler Cass Morgan Beth Fowler Barbara Marineu 11/12/99	Betsy Joslyn Barbara Marineu 7/2/97 #3 Janet MacEwen

CABARET

	New York 3/19/98	*Los Angeles 2/99*
Emcee	Alan Cumming Robert Sella 9/17/98 Alan Cumming 12/1/98 Michael Hall 6/8/99 Matt McGrath10/17/01	Norbert Leo Butz Jon Peterson 1/2/00
Sally Bowles	Natasha Richardson Jennifer Jason Leigh 8/20/98 Mary McCormack 3/2/99 Susan Egan 6/17/99 Joely Fisher 6/2/00 Lea Thompson 8/2/00 Katie Finneran 11/21/00 Gina Gershon 1/19/01	Teri Hatcher Joely Fisher 9/4/99 Lea Thompson 3/19/00 Kate Shindle 7/11/00 Andrea McArdle 1/23/01
Clifford Bradshaw	John Benjamin Hickey Boyd Gaines 3/2/99 Michael Hayden 8/3/99 Matthew Greer 1/19/01	Rick Holmes Jay Goede 10/16/99 Hank Stratton 1/23/01
Ernst Ludwig	Denis O'Hare Michael Stuhlbarg 5/4/99 Martin Moran 11/9/99 Peter Benson 1/19/01	Andy Taylor Drew McVety 10/16/99

Fraulein Schneider	Mary Louise Wilson Blair Brown 8/20/98 Carole Shelley 5/4/99	Barbara Andres Alma Cuervo 9/4/99 Barbara Andres 6/08/01
Fraulein Kost	Michele Pawk Victoria Clark 5/4/99 Candy Buckley	Jeanine Morick Lenora Nemetz 2/20/00
Herr Schultz	Ron Rifkin Laurence Luckinbill 5/4/99 Dick Latessa 11/9/99 Larry Keith	Dick Latessa Hal Robinson 9/4/99

CATS

	New York 10/7/82
Alonzo	Hector Jaime Mercado Hans Kriefall 4/24/95 Lenny Daniel 11/1/99
Bustopher	Stephan Hanan Richard Poole 12/12/94 Michael Brian Daniel Eli Friedman 4/14/97 Michael Brian 6/8/98 John Dewar 8/21/99
Bombalurina	Donna King Marlene Danielle 1/9/84
Cassandra	Rene Ceballos Ida Gilliams 5/22/95 Meg Gillentine Lynne Calamia 7/5/99 Melissa Rae Mahon 3/10/00
Demeter	Wendy Edmead Mercedes Perez 6/17/94 Mamie Duncan Gibbs Emily Hsu Amanda Watkins Celina Carvajal 5/17/99 Gayle Holsman 6/10/00
Grizabella	Betty Buckley Liz Callaway 5/3/93 Laurie Beechman Liz Callaway Linda Balgord
Jellylorum	Bonnie Simmons Nina Hennessey 6/22/92 Jean Arbeiter
Jennyandots	Anna McNeely Carol Dilley 8/22/94 Sharon Wheatley 6/21/99

Mistoffeles	Timothy Scott Gen Horiuchi 3/18/95 Jacob Brent Christopher Gattelli Jacob Brent 9/27/99 Julius Sermonia 12/28/99
Mungojerrie	Rene Clemente Roger Kachel 5/11/92
Munkustrap	Harry Groener Michael Gruber Matt Farnsworth Michael Gruber Abe Sylvia Michael Gruber 5/10/99 Jeffry Denman 9/13/99
Old Deuteronomy	Ken Page Jimmy Lockett Ken Prymus Jimmy Lockett
Plato/Macavity	Kenneth Ard Karl Wahl Rick Gonzalez Jim T. Ruttman Jaymes Hodges Karl Wahl Philip Michael Baskerville Steve Geary Keith Wilson 5/17/99
Pouncival	Herman W. Sebek Jacob Brent 10/24/94 Christopher Gattelli Joey Gyondla Jon-Eric Goldberg 1/17/00
Rum Tum Tugger	Terrence Mann David Hibbard 9/20/93 Stephen M. Reed Ron DeVito Abe Sylvia David Hibbard Stephen Bienskie
Rumpleteazer	Christine Langner Maria Jo Ralabate 4/1/96 Tesha Buss Maria Jo Ralabate 6/10/00
Sillabub	Whitney Kershaw Bethany Samuelson 8/8/94 Alaine Kashian Bethany Samuelson Maria Jo Ralabate Jessica Dillan 6/10/00

Skimbleshanks	Reed Jones
	Eric Scott Kincaid 6/3/94
	Owen Taylor
	J.P. Christensen 6/28/99
	James Hadley 3/27/00
Tumblebrutus	Robert Hoshour
	Levensky Smith 8/29/94
	Randy Bettis
	Andrew Hubbard
	Patrick Mullaney
Victoria	Cynthia Onrubia
	Nadine Isnegger 7/25/94
	Missy Lay Zimmer
	Melissa Hathaway 6/10/00

CHICAGO

	New York 11/14/96	*#1 Cincinnati 3/25/97*
		#2 Ft. Myers, FL 12/12/97
Roxie Hart	Ann Reinking	#1 Charlotte d'Amboise
	Marilu Henner	Belle Calaway
	Karen Ziemba	Ann Reinking 4/22/99
	Belle Calaway	Belle Calaway 5/18/99
	Charlotte d'Amboise	Sandy Duncan 4/22/99
	Sandy Duncan 8/12/99	Ann Reinking 5/1/99
	Belle Calaway 1/18/00	Belle Calaway 6/1/99
	Charlotte d'Amboise 3/24/00	Sandy Duncan 7/13/99
	Belle Calaway	Belle Calaway 8/3/99
	Nana Visitor	Nana Visitor 11/16/99
		Tracy Shane 1/4/00
		#2 Karen Ziemba
		Nancy Hess
		Charlotte d'Amboise
		Amy Spanger 11/10/98
		Charlotte d'Amboise 11/24/98
		Amy Spanger 12/1/98
		Chita Rivera 2/2/99
		Marilu Henner 7/6/99
		Charlotte d'Amboise 8/24/99
		Marilu Henner 12/22/99
		Nana Visitor 1/3/00
Velma Kelly	Bebe Neuwirth	#1 Jasmine Guy
	Nancy Hess	Janine LaManna
	Ute Lemper	Jasmine Guy
	Bebe Neuwirth	Donna Marie Asbury
	Ruthie Henshall 5/25/99	Stephanie Pope
	Mamie Duncan-Gibbs 10/26/99	Jasmine Guy 7/7/98
	Bebe Neuwirth 1/18/00	Stephanie Pope 7/14/98
	Donna Marie Asbury 3/23/00	Mamie Duncan-Gibbs 1/12/99
	Sharon Lawrence 4/11/00	Deidre Goodwin 2/16/99
	Vicki Lewis	Ruthie Henshall 4/22/99
	Jasmine Guy	Deidre Goodwin 5/18/99
	Bebe Neuwirth	Ruthie Henshall 4/22/99

	Donna Marie Asbury	Deidre Goodwin 6/1/99
	Deidre Goodwin	Donna Marie Asbury 10/12/99
	Vicki Lewis	Vicki Lewis 11/16/99
		Roxanne Carrasco 1/4/00
		Vicki Lewis 3/14/00
		Roxanne Carrasco 3/21/00
		#2 Stephanie Pope
		Jasmine Guy
		Stephanie Pope
		Khandi Alexander 8/4/98
		Donna Marie Asbury 9/29/98
		Stephanie Pope 2/2/98
		Ute Lemper 2/19/99
		Stephanie Pope 4/5/99
		Mamie Duncan-Gibbs 8/3/99
		Jasmine Guy 8/24/99
		Marianne McCord 12/22/99
		Vicki Lewis 1/3/00
Billy Flynn	James Naughton	#1 Obba Babatunde
	Gregory Jbara	Alan Thicke
	Hinton Battle	Michael Berresse 8/18/98
	Alan Thicke	Alan Thicke 8/25/98
	Michael Berresse	Destin Owens 10/13/98
	Brent Barrett	Alan Thicke 10/27/98
	Robert Urich 1/11/00	Destin Owens 1/26/99
	Clarke Peters 2/1/00	Adrian Zmed 2/16/99
	Brent Barrett 2/15/00	Hal Linden 8/6/99
	Chuck Cooper	Gregory Jbara 8/17/99
		Robert Urich 10/19/99
		Lloyd Culbreath 1/4/00
		Alan Thicke 1/18/00
		Lloyd Culbreath 2/29/00
		Alan Thicke 3/14/00
		Clarke Peters 3/21/00
		#2 Brent Barrett
		Michael Berresse 11/3/98
		Brent Barrett 11/24/98
		Michael Berresse 12/1/98
		Ben Vereen 2/19/99
		Hal Linden 8/31/99
		Gregory Jbara 1/3/00
		Clarke Peters
Amos Hart	Joel Grey	#1 Ron Orbach
	Ernie Sabella	Michael Tucci
	Tom McGowan	Bruce Winant 12/22/98
	P.J. Benjamin	Ray Bokhour 10/19/99
	Ernie Sabella 11/23/99	P.J. Benjamin 4/4/00
	P.J. Benjamin	#2 Ernie Sabella
	Tom McGowan	Ron Orbach
		Tom McGowan
		Ron Orbach
		P.J. Benjamin 11/10/98
		Joel Grey 12/1/98
		P.J. Benjamin 12/29/98
		Ernie Sabella 2/2/99
		Michael Tucci 8/24/99
		P.J. Benjamin 1/3/00

Matron "Mama" Morton	Marcia Lewis Roz Ryan Marcia Lewis Roz Ryan Marcia Lewis Roz Ryan 7/27/99	#1 Carol Woods Lea DeLaria Carol Woods 8/4/98 #2 Avery Sommers Marcia Lewis 2/2/99
Mary Sunshine	D. Sabella J. Loeffelholz R. Bean A. Saunders J. Maldonado R. Bean	#1 M.E. Spencer D.C. Levine M.E. Spencer 7/7/98 R. Bean 7/28/98 A. Saunders 10/13/98 R. Bean 10/20/98 J. Maldonado 10/27/98 J. Roberson 2/9/99 M. Von Essen 5/12/99 J. Maldonado 10/12/99 M. Agnes 1/4/00 #2 D.C. Levine M.E. Spencer 2/2/99 D. Sabella 9/7/99

CONTACT

	New York 3/30/00
Girl in Swing	Stephanie Michaels
Servant	Seán Martin Hingston
Aristocrat	Scott Taylor
Wife	Karen Ziemba
Husband	Jason Antoon Danny Mastrogiorgio 3/9/01
Head Waiter	David McGillivray
Michael Wiley	Boyd Gaines
Girl in Yellow Dress	Deborah Yates

DINNER WITH FRIENDS

	New York 11/4/99
Gabe	Matthew Arkin
Karen	Lisa Emery Sophie Hayden Lisa Emery
Beth	Julie White Carolyn McCormick
Tom	Kevin Kilner John Hillner

DIRTY BLONDE

	New York 5/1/00
Jo;Mae	Claudia Shear Kathy Najimy 1/9/01
Charlie;Others	Kevin Chamberlin Tom Riis Farrell
Frank; Ed; Others	Bob Stillman

FOSSE

New York 1/14/99
Stephanie Pope
Ben Vereen 1/26/01
Bebe Neuwirth 4/2/01
Ann Reinking 3/2/01
Ken Alan
Brad Anderson†
Mark Arvin
Ashley Bachner
Bill Burns†
Lynne Calamia
Marc Calamia†
J.P. Christensen
Angel Creeks
Dylis Croman
Bryon Easley
Parker Esse
Eugene Fleming†
Meg Gillentine
Greg Graham
Francesca Harper
Suzanne Harrer
Anne Hawthorne
Scott Jovovich†
James Kinney
Dede LaBarre†
Susan Lamontagne†
Lorin Latarro
Robin Lewis
Edwaard Liang
Julio Monge
Dana Moore†
Sharon Moore
Jill Nicklaus
Rachelle Rak†
Mark C. Reis
Christopher Windom

Chicago 9/22/99
Linda Bowen
Mark Burrell
Tina Cannon
Lamae Caparas
Janice Cronkite
Lloyd Culbreath
Rick Delancy
Aaron Feiske
Laura Haney Gomez
Amy Hall
Tyler Hanes
Curtis Holbrook
Sarah Jayne Jensen
Terace Jones
Gelan Lambert Jr.
Krisha Marcano
Cassel Miles
Kathryn Mowat Murphy
Steve Ochoa
Josef Patrick Pescetto
Reva Rice
Vincent Sandoval
Jennifer Savelli
Lynn Sterling
Mark Swanhart
Estelle Tomasovic
Steve Wenslawski
Chryssie Whitehead

† *original cast member*

I LOVE YOU, YOU'RE PERFECT, NOW CHANGE

New York 8/1/96
Jordan Leeds
  Danny Burstein 10/1/96
  Adam Grupper 8/22/97
  Gary Imhoff 2/9/98
  Adam Grupper 4/1/98
  Jordan Leeds 3/17/99
  Bob Walton 10/27/00
  Jordan Leeds 1/30/01

Robert Roznowski
  Kevin Pariseau 5/25/98
  Adam Hunter 4/20/01

Jennifer Simard
  Erin Leigh Peck 5/25/98
  Kelly Anne Clark 1/10/00

Andrea Chamberlin 3/13/00
Lori Hammel 11/04/00
Andrea Chamberlin 1/29/01

Melissa Weil
Cheryl Stern 2/16/98
Mylinda Hull 9/17/00
Melissa Weil 2/09/01
Evy O'Rourke 3/13/01
Marylee Graffeo 6/11/01

JEKYLL & HYDE

	New York 4/28/97
Sir Danvers Carew	Barrie Ingham
Dr. Henry Jekyll; Edward Hyde	Robert Cuccioli Robert Evan (alt.) Robert Evan Joseph Mahowald (alt.) Jack Wagner 1/25/00 Sebastian Bach 6/13/00 David Hasselhoff 10/18/00
Emma Carew	Christiane Noll Anastasia Barzee Andrea Rivette 1/25/00
Lucy	Linda Eder Luba Mason Coleen Sexton 1/25/00

KISS ME, KATE

	New York 11/18/99
Fred; Petruchio	Brian Stokes Mitchell Burke Moses 1/30/01
Kate; Katherine	Marin Mazzie Carolee Carmello 3/29/01
Lois Lane; Bianca	Amy Spanger JoAnn Hunter 4/24/01
Bill Calhoun; Lucentio	Michael Berresse David Elder 9/19/00 Michael Berresse 12/19/00
Hattie	Adriane Lenox Mamie Duncan-Gibbs 2/20/01

LES MISÉRABLES

	New York 3/12/87	*Tampa 11/28/88*
Jean Valjean	Colm Wilkinson Robert Marien 3/12/97 Ivan Rutherford 9/9/97 Robert Marien 12/12/97 Craig Schulman 3/3/98 Fred Inkley 9/8/98 Tim Shaw 9/7/99 J. Mark McVey 3/7/00 Ivan Rutherford 4/23/01	Gary Barker Gregory Calvin Stone 3/3/97 Colm Wilkinson 7/15/98 Ivan Rutherford 1/19/99 Randal Keith

Javert	Terrence Mann Christopher Innvar 10/15/96 Robert Gallagher 12/6/97 Philip Hernandez 10/27/98 Greg Edelman 9/7/99 Shuler Hensley 11/14/01	Peter Samuel Todd Alan Johnson 3/31/97 Stephen Bishop 8/3/99
Fantine	Randy Graff Juliet Lambert 3/12/97 Lisa Capps 4/15/98 Alice Ripley 9/8/98 Susan Gilmour 3/9/99 Alice Ripley 3/23/99 Jane Bodle 9/7/99 Jacquelyn Piro 4/23/01	Hollis Resnik Lisa Capps 3/24/97 Holly Jo Crane Susan Gilmour 6/2/98 Joan Almedilla 3/2/99 Thursday Farrar
Enjolras	Michael Maguire Stephen R. Buntrock 3/12/97 Gary Mauer 12/8/98 Stephen R. Buntrock 4/6/99 Christopher Mark Peterson 6/21/99	Greg Zerkle Brian Herriott Kurt Kovalenko Michael Todd Cressman Matthew Shepard 12/8/98 Kevin Earley 1/19/99 Stephen Tewksbury 2/15/00
Marius	David Bryant Peter Lockyer 3/12/97	Matthew Porretta Rich Affannato 8/12/96 Steve Scott Springer Tim Howar Stephen Brian Patterson
Cosette	Judy Kuhn Cristeena Michelle Riggs 3/12/97 Tobi Foster 11/6/98 Sandra Turley 2/5/01	Jacquelyn Piro Kate Fisher 9/9/96 Regan Thiel Stephanie Waters
Eponine	Frances Ruffelle Sarah Uriarte Berry 3/12/97 Megan Lawrence 6/19/98 Kerry Butler 12/11/98 Megan Lawrence 2/25/99 Rona Figueroa 6/3/99 Megan Lawrence 6/24/99 Jessica-Snow Wilson 8/31/99 Rona Figueroa 9/14/99 Jessica Boevers 12/7/00 Catherine Brunell 8/10/00	Michele Maika Rona Figueroa 3/31/97 Jessica-Snow Wilson 5/19/99 Sutton Foster 1/19/99 Diana Kaarina 3/21/00

MISS SAIGON

	New York 4/11/91	*Seattle 3/16/95*
The Engineer	Jonathan Pryce Luoyong Wang 10/2/95 Joseph Anthony Foronda 8/7/00 Luoyong Wang 8/21/00 Joseph Anthony Foronda 1/14/01 Luoyong Wang 1/24/01	Thom Sesma Joseph Anthony Foronda 4/22/97

Kim	Lea Salonga Joan Almedilla Deedee Lynn Magno 7/21/97 Lea Salonga 1/18/99 Deedee Lynn Magno 6/14/99 Melinda Chua 5/22/00 Deedee Lynn Magno 6/19/00 Melinda Chua 7/17/00 Lea Salonga 12/31/00	Deedee Lynn Magno Elizabeth Paw Kristine Remigio Kim Hoy 1/19/99 Mika Nishida 7/21/99
Chris	Willy Falk Matt Bogart 1/12/98 Will Chase 7/20/98 Michael Flanigan 7/3/00 Will Chase 12/31/00	Matt Bogart Will Chase 4/16/96 Steven Pasquale 6/30/97 Greg Stone 1/19/99 Will Swenson 12/22/99
John	Hinton Battle C.C. Brown 1/3/00 Charles E. Wallace 5/2/00	C.C. Brown Eugene Barry-Hill 10/22/98
Ellen	Liz Callaway Margaret Ann Gates 10/26/98 Jacquelyn Piro 11/21/00 Ruthie Henshall 12/31/00	Anastasia Barzee Jacquelyn Piro 4/27/99 Christine Allocca 1/28/00
Thuy	Barry K. Bernal Edmund Nalzaro 1/24/99 Michael K. Lee 12/31/00	Michael K. Lee Johnny Fernandez 7/20/99
Kim (alternate)	Kam Cheng Elizabeth Paw 11/22/99 Melinda Chua 12/31/00	Christina Paras Michelle Nigalan

NAKED BOYS SINGING!

New York 7/22/99

Glenn Steven Allen
Trevor Richardson 10/22/99
Eric Dean Davis 3/8/00

Jonathan Brody
Richard Lear 2/2/00
Steve Spraragen 9/8/00

Tim Burke
Kristopher Kelly 3/10/01

Tom Gualieri

Daniel C. Levine
George Livengood 2/9/00

Sean McNally
Luis Villabon 3/1/00

Adam Michaels
Glenn Steven Allen 11/1/99
Patrick Herwood 3/10/01

Trance Thompson
Dennis Stowe 2/5/00
Ralph Cole Jr. 5/22/00
Stephan Alexander 7/4/00
Eric Potter 9/8/00

RENT

	New York 4/29/96	*#1 Boston 11/18/96* *closed 9/5/99* *#2 La Jolla 7/1/97*
Roger Davis	Adam Pascal Norbert Leo Butz Richard H. Blake (alt) Manley Pope	#1 Sean Keller Manley Pope 3/14/97 Christian Anderson Dean Balkwill #2 Christian Mena Cary Shields Christian Mena Cary Shields Jeremy Kushnier 3/8/01
Mark Cohen	Anthony Rapp Jim Poulos Trey Ellett	#1 Luther Creek Christian Anderson Trey Ellett #2 Neil Patrick Harris Kirk McDonald Scott Hunt Matt Caplan 2/1/00
Tom Collins	Jesse L. Martin Michael McElroy Rufus Bonds Jr. 9/7/99 Alan Mingo Jr. 4/10/00 Mark Leroy Jackson 1/15/01	#1 C.C. Brown Mark Leroy Jackson #2 Mark Leroy Jackson Dwayne Clark Horace V. Rogers Mark Ford 6/13/99
Benjamin Coffin III	Taye Diggs Jacques C. Smith Stu James 3/13/00	#1 James Rich Dwayne Clark Brian Love #2 D'Monroe Brian Love Carl Thornton Stu James Brian Love 2/29/00
Joanne Jefferson	Fredi Walker Gwen Stewart Alia León Kenna J. Ramsey Danielle Lee Greaves 10/4/99 Natalie Venetia Belcon 10/2/00	#1 Sylvia MacCalla Kamilah Martin #2 Kenna J. Ramsey Monique Daniels Danielle Lee Greaves Jacqueline B. Arnold

Angel Schunard	Wilson Jermaine Heredia	#1 Stephan Alexander
	Wilson Cruz	Shaun Earl
	Shaun Earl	Evan D'Angeles
	Jose Llana	Shaun Earl
	Jai Rodriguez	#2 Wilson Cruz
	Andy Senor 1/31/00	Andy Senor
		Pierre Bayuga
		Shuan Earl 11/23/99
Mimi Marquez	Daphne Rubin-Vega	#1 Simone
	Marcy Harriell 4/5/97	Laura Dias
	Krysten Cummings	Daphne Rubin-Vega
	Maya Days	Sharon Leal
	Loraine Velez 2/28/00	#2 Julia Santana
		Saycon Sengbloh 11/30/99
		Dominique Roy 12/5/00
Maureen Johnson	Idina Menzel	#1 Carrie Hamilton
	Sherrie Scott	Amy Spanger 6/5/97
	Kristen Lee Kelly	Erin Keaney
	Tamara Podemski	#2 Leigh Hetherington
	Cristina Fadale 10/4/99	Carla Bianco
		Leigh Hetherington
		Cristina Fadale
		Michelle Joan Smith 9/28/99
		Erin Keaney 4/7/00
		Maggie Benjamin 9/12/00

RIVERDANCE ON BROADWAY

	New York 3/16/00
Principal Dancers	Pat Roddy
	Eileen Martin
Featured Singers	Tsidii Le Loka
	Michel Bell 12/10/01
	Brian Kennedy
	Michael Londra 12/5/00
Soloist	Sara Clancy
	Kira Deegan 5/23/01
Flamenco	Maria Pagés
Riverdance Tappers	Walter "Sundance" Freeman
	Channing Cook Holmes
	Karen Callaway Williams
	Parris Mann 3/2/01
	Van "The Man" Porter 3/2/01

SATURDAY NIGHT FEVER

	New York 10/21/99	*Chicago 03/06/01*
Tony Manero	James Carpinello	Richard H. Blake
	Sean Palmer	
Stephanie Mangano	Paige Price	Jeanine Meyers
Annette	Orfeh	Aileen Quinn

Bobby C	Paul Castree	Jim Ambler
Joey	Sean Palmer	Andy Karl
Double J	Andy Blankenbuehler	Joey Calveri
Gus	Richard H. Blake	Daniel Jerod Brown
Monty	Bryan Batt Michael Paternostro	Joseph Ricci

THE LION KING

	New York 11/13/97	*Los Angeles, CA 10/19/00*
Rafiki	Tsidii Le Loka Thuli Dumakude 11/11/98 Shelia Gibbs	Fuschia
Mufasa	Samuel E. Wright	Rufus Bonds Jr.
Sarabi	Gina Breedlove Meena T. Jahi 8/4/98 Denise Marie Williams	Marvette Williams
Zazu	Geoff Hoyle Bill Bowers 10/21/98 Robert Dorfman Tony Freeman	William Akey
Scar	John Vickery Tom Hewitt 10/21/98 Derek Smith	John Vickery
Banzai	Stanley Wayne Mathis Keith Bennett 9/30/98 Leonard Joseph	Jeffrey Polk
Shenzi	Tracy Nicole Chapman Vanessa S. Jones Lana Gordon	Carla Renata Williams
Ed	Kevin Cahoon Jeff Skowron 10/21/98 Jeff Gurner Timothy Gulan	Price Waldman
Timon	Max Casella Danny Rutigliano 6/16/98 John E. Brady	Danny Rutigliano
Pumba	Tom Alan Robbins	Bob Bouchard
Simba	Jason Raize Christopher Jackson	Clifton Oliver
Nala	Heather Headley Mary Randle 7/7/98 Heather Headley 12/8/98 Bashirrah Creswell Sharon L. Young	Moe Daniels

MEREDITH WILLSON'S THE MUSIC MAN

	New York 4/27/00
Harold Hill	Craig Bierko
Marian Paroo	Rebecca Luker
Marcellus	Max Casella Joel Blum 1/5/01
Mayor Shinn	Paul Benedict Kenneth Kimmins 4/10/01
Eulalie Shinn	Ruth Williamson Ruth Gottschall 8/17/00
Tommy Djilas	Clyde Alves Manuel Herrera 4/10/01
Zaneeta Shinn	Kate Levering Cameron Adams 2/20/01

THE PHANTOM OF THE OPERA

	New York 1/26/88	*#1 Los Angeles 5/31/90* *#2 Chicago 5/24/90* *#3 Seattle 12/13/92*
The Phantom	Michael Crawford Thomas James O'Leary 10/11/96 Hugh Panaro 2/1/99 Howard McGillin 8/23/99	#1 Michael Crawford Franc D'Ambrosio 3/28/94 #2 Mark Jacoby Rick Hilsabeck Craig Schulman 1/30/97 Ron Bohmer 9/97 Davis Gaines 8/98 #3 Franc D'Ambrosio Brad Little 9/28/96 Ted Keegan 3/31/99 Brad Little 6/28/22 Ted Keegan 2/28/00
Christine Daae	Sarah Brightman Sandra Joseph 1/29/98 Adrienne McEwan (alt.) 4/21/97 Adrienne McEwan 8/2/99 Sarah Pfisterer (alt.) Sarah Pfisterer 1/17/00 Adrienne McEwan (alt.) Sandra Joseph 10/30/00 Lisa Vroman (alt.) 10/30/00	#1 Dale Kristien Lisa Vroman 12/2/93 Cristin Mortenson (alt.) Karen Culliver (alt.) 6/3/97 #2 Karen Culliver Sandra Joseph 3/26/96 Marie Danvers 1/13/98 Teri Bibb 4/98 Susan Owen (alt.) 9/24/96 Rita Harvey (alt.) 3/98 Marie Danvers 6/98 Susan Facer (alt.) 6/98 #3 Tracy Shane Kimilee Bryant Amy Jo Arrington Tamra Hayden (alt.)11/1/96 Marie Danvers (alt.) Megan Starr-Levitt (alt.) 1/21/98 Rebecca Pitcher 3/31/99 Kathy Voytko (alt.)
Raoul	Steve Barton Gary Mauer 4/19/99 Jim Weitzer 4/23/01	#1 Reece Holland Christopher Carl 7/2/96 #2 Keith Buterbaugh Lawrence Anderson

Jason Pebworth 1/13/98
Lawrence Anderson 7/98
#3 Ciaran Sheehan
Jason Pebworth 1/29/97
Jim Weitzer
Jason Pebworth 7/22/98
Richard Todd Adams 3/31/99
Jim Weitzer 1/12/00
John Cudia

FIRST CLASS NATIONAL TOURS

THE BEST LITTLE WHOREHOUSE IN TEXAS

Wallingford, CT 2/13/01

Mona Stangley	Ann-Margret
Sheriff Dodd	Gary Sandy
Jewel	Avery Sommers
Governor	Ed Dixon
Angel	Terri Dixon
Doatsey Mae	Roxie Lucas
Shy	Jan Celene Little
Mayor Poindexter; Senator Wingwoah	Matt Landers

BLAST!

Boston, MA 08/22/00

Trey Alligood III
Rachel J. Anderson
Nicholas E. Angelis
Matthew A. Banks
Kimberly Beth Baron
Wesley Bullock
Mark Burroughs 10/3/00
Jesus Cantu Jr.
Jodina Rosario Carey
Alan "Otto" Compton
Dayne Delahoussaye
Karen Duggan
John Elrod 10/3/00
Brandon J. Epperson
Kenneth Frisby
J. Derek Gipson
Trevor Lee Gooch
Casey Marshall Gooding
Bradley Kerr Green
Benjamin Taber Griffin
Benjamin Raymond Hardel
Benjamin W. Harloff
Joe Hayworth
Darren M. Hazlett
Tim Heasley
Freddy Hernandez Jr.
George Hester
Jeremiah Todd Huber
Martin A. Hughes
Naoki Ishikawa
Stacy J. Johnson
Sanford R. Jones
Ray Linkous
Jean Marie Mallicoat
Jack Mansager
Brian Mayle
Jim Moore
Westley Morehead
David Nash
David Newcomb
Jeffrey A. Queen
Douglas Raines
Chris Rasmussen
Joseph J. Reinhart
Jamie L. Roscoe
Jennifer Ross
Christopher Eric Rutt
Christopher J. Schletter
Jonathan L. Schwartz
Greg Seale
Andy Smart
Radiah Y. Stewart
Bryan Anthony Sutton
Sean Terrell
Andrew James Toth
Joni Paige Viertel
Kristin Whiting

CINDERELLA

Tampa Bay, FL 11/28/00

Cinderella	Deborah Gibson Jamie-Lynn Sigler 3/6/01
Prince	Paolo Montalban
Fairy Godmother	Eartha Kitt
King	Ken Prymus

Queen	Leslie Becker
Stepmother	Everett Quinton
Grace	NaTasha Yvette Williams
Joy	Alexandra Kolb
Lionel	Victor Trent Cook
	Brooks Ashmanskas 5/8/01

BARRY MANILOW'S COPACABANA

Pittsburgh, PA 6/17/00

Tony	Franc D'Ambrosio
Lola	Darcie Roberts
Rico	Philip Hernandez
Sam	Gavin MacLeod
	Dale Radunz 11/00
Gladys	Beth McVey

FIDDLER ON THE ROOF

Detroit, MI 10/24/00

Tevye	Theodore Bikel
Golde	Susan Cella
Lazar Wolf	John Preece
Yente	Miriam Babin
Chava	Dana Lynn Caruso
	Sara Schmidt 4/17/01
Perchik	Daniel Cooney
Fyedka	Brad Drummer
	Justin Patterson 5/28/01
Hodel	Tamra Hayden
Motel	Michael Innucci
Tzeitel	Eileen Tepper

LEADER OF THE PACK

Wilmington, DE 3/16/01

Shoshana Bean
Dianna Bush
Brenda Braxton
Todd DuBail
Duane Martin Foster
Angela Garrison
Amy Goldberg
David Josefberg
Joe Machota
Ric Ryder
Denise Summerford
Jewel Thomkins
  Mary Wilson 4/14/01
  Jewel Thomkins 5/2/01
Ashley Howard Wilkinson

MAMMA MIA!

San Francisco, CA 11/14/00

Donna Sheridan	Louise Pitre
Sam Charmichael	Gary P. Lynch
Sophie Sheridan	Tina Maddigan
Sky	Adam Brazier
Rosie	Gabrielle Jones
Tanya	Mary Ellen Mahoney
Harry Bright	Lee MacDougal
Bill Austin	David Mucci

PROMISES, PROMISES

Wilmington, DE 2/23/01

C.C. Baxter	Evan Pappas
Fran Kueblick	Kelli Rabke
J.D. Sheldrake	Paul Schoeffler
Miss Olson	Brenda Braxton
Marge McDougal	Beth Glover
Dr. Dreyfuss	Gordon Stanley
Karl Kueblick	A.J. Irvin
Sylvia Gilhooley	Carol Schuberg
Ginger Wong	Pauline A. Locsin
Vivien Della Hoya	Krissy Richmond

RAGTIME

Washington, D.C. 4/29/98

Father	Chris Groenendaal Stephen Zinnato 7/31/99 Joseph Dellgar 10/31/00
Mother	Rebecca Eichenberger Cathy Wydner 7/31/99 Victoria Strong 2/20/00
Mother's Younger Brother	Aloysius Gigl Adam Hunter 2/14/00 John Frenzer 2/8/00 Sam Samuelson 8/8/00
Coalhouse Walker Jr.	Alton Fitzgerald White Lawrence Hamilton 12/28/98
Sarah	Darlesia Cearcy Lovena Fox 7/31/99
Tateh	Michael Rupert Jim Corti 7/31/99
Harry Houdini	Bernie Yvon Eric Olson 7/31/99
Henry Ford	Larry Cahn Jay Bodin 7/31/99
Emma Goldman	Theresa Tova Cyndi Neal 7/31/99 Mary Gutzi 8/8/00
Evelyn Nesbit	Melissa Dye Michele Ragusa 7/31/99 Jacqueline Bayne 11/9/99

RIVERDANCE

Vancouver, CN 1/9/98	
Principal Dancers	Michael Patrick Gallagher
	Niamh Roddy
	Tara Barry
Singers	Sara Clancy
	Caitriona Fallon
	Lisa Kelly
	Michael Londra
	Aidan Conway
Flamenco	Rosa Manzano Jimenez
	Nelida Tirado
Riverdance Tappers	Walter "Sundance" Freeman
	Karen Callaway Williams
	Aaron Tolson
	Ronald "Cadet" Bastine
	Jason E. Bernard

THE SCARLET PIMPERNEL

New Haven, CT 2/20/00	
Percy Blakeney	Douglas Sills
	Robert Patteri 6/27/00
	Ron Bohmer 12/12/00
Chauvelin	William Paul Michals
Marguerite St. Just	Amy Bodner

SWING!	*Los Angeles, CA 11/20/00*
	Ann Crumb
	Alan H. Green
	Charlie Marcus
	Scott Fowler
	Jeb Bounds 12/20/00

THE SEASON OFF OFF BROADWAY

THE SEASON OFF OFF BROADWAY

○○○○○ *By Mel Gussow* ○○○○○

WITH A SHIFT IN BODY COATING from chocolate to honey, Karen Finley's *Shut Up and Love Me* may have been the most representative of the theatrical events presented Off Off Broadway this season. A fringe artist famous for confrontation, in her new show Finley was in an audience-friendly mode. On this and other stages, the entertainment quotient was high, as pretension took a back seat to clarity. Such experimental artists as Mac Wellman and Richard Foreman introduced new plays that were for them more accessible than previous work without vitiating their gift for innovation and idiosyncrasy.

At the same time, in what might be called the Karaoke Syndrome, theatergoers were eagerly participatory—at *Shut Up and Love Me* and other shows. Lines continued to form outside the Off Broadway production of *De La Guarda*, the Blue Man Group threatened to run as long as *The Fantasticks* (and in makeup who would know if these were the original or new blue men?) and a revival of *The Rocky Horror Show* became a long-run on Broadway. Taking advantage of the trend, interactive shows sprouted Off Off Broadway.

In Avery Crozier's *Eat the Runt*, produced by the Mefisto Theatre Company, theatergoers determined the course of a play by drawing lots and assigning roles to actors. As its title indicated, *Game Show*, created by Jeffrey Finn and Bob Walton, was the theatrical equivalent of a television game show at 45 Bleecker. In it—or rather on it—audience members became contestants and won prizes. An apex of a sort was reached with *Lifegame*. The latest venture of Britain's Improbable Theater Company at the Jane Street Theatre, this play solicited volunteers from the audience to offer autobiographical stories that then became the subject of improvisations by actors. All of these shows seemed to appeal to a young audience, those who had grown up with rock and rap and playing video and computer games. The performances were totally dependent on the responsiveness of theatergoers. Naturally, questions were raised. What if nobody showed up

Melville musicale: Composer Rinde Eckert and Nora Cole in And God Created Great Whales. *Photo: Carol Rosegg*

for the performance or if those who did show up were dull? Was this live theater's response to reality television—and if so, could it compete? Or was it just a new millennial response to improvisational theater of the 1960s or Anne Hamburger's En Garde Arts troupe of the 1990s?

But, back to Karen Finley, whose new show merits a citation as an outstanding OOB production. A pioneer in body language, the leader of the uncensorable NEA Four, an artist who fought her cause all the way to the United States Supreme Court, Finley has forged new freedoms from the firing line. Having survived assault from the decency brigade in and out of the US Congress, she returned to New York this season with a zestful comedy of self exposure. Years ago when she covered her naked body with chocolate in a public performance, that substance was meant to symbolize human feces and the show was a compelling commentary on the abuse of women in our society. In *Shut Up and Love Me*, she covered her naked body with honey, which stood, simply, for honey. For all of the nudity and outspoken language, the show had a kind of sweetness (the honey effect) and innocence.

A woman bereft of inhibitions, a confirmed exhibitionist, Finley began by flirting outrageously with the audience. Then she told a long story of seduction and incest, and finally, in the *pièce de résistance* (who could resist?), she did her honey number. At her final performance at Performance Space 122 (the show later returned for an extended engagement), she asked for volunteers, and people rushed onstage to join her. Following her instructions, they squirted and sloshed honey on a plastic-covered mattress. After the volunteers reluctantly returned to their seats, Finley stripped to the buff, rolled ecstatically on the mattress and then dashed into a delirious pas de honey. Her body glistened with a golden glow and she danced for joy. In this show, Finley revealed herself as a 21st-century Mae West doing her own version of *The Full Monty*.

It must be underscored that this is performance art, and it has to be seen live. One could not imagine reading a script of *Shut Up and Love Me*—if one existed—and having any notion of how it would look on stage. And no other actress could stand in for the author and do her act. Finley continues to be one of a kind. On other stages, actors performed solo—often to great effect. Leslie Ayvazian, who is both an actress and a playwright, crafted a one-woman show called *High Dive*. Standing on an imaginary high diving board over a pool at a resort in Greece, she spoke about her fears—and other family matters such as disaster-filled vacations, leading the audience on a comic tour of her mind and memory. Setting a record for audience participation, she stood by the entrance to the MCC Theater before the performance and enlisted scores of people to join in the narrative, not simply as helpmates but as actors. They were all given lines to speak and cues about when to speak them. Such an approach, of course, has pitfalls galore, but at least at one performance, the theatergoers, perhaps accustomed to audience participation, were flawless. As charmingly presented by Ayvazian, the show went, well, swimmingly. In common with *Shut Up and Love Me*, this would be an easy work to tour. In Finley's case all she needs is honey, with Ayvazian all she needs is an acting audience.

That masterly clown Bill Irwin returned with a new version of Samuel Beckett's *Texts for Nothing* at Classic Stage Company, cited as an outstanding OOB production. Joseph Chaikin had acted in an adaptation of the prose piece in 1981, then returned as director in 1991 with Irwin as the performer. This season Irwin was solely responsible—as adapter and director as well as performer. On the page, *Texts* is a haunting interior monologue, which critic Hugh Kenner characterized as "fantasies of nonbeing." Irwin gave those fantasies visceral life onstage. Looking as gaunt as a Beckett tramp, the actor entered by sliding down a hill into an end-of-the-world environment. While pratfalling—but limiting his clown moves—he conjured a stream of consciousness about a Beckettian man in limbo. He can't stay; he can't go. He can only wonder, "Let's see what happens next."

The Irish playwright Conor McPherson specializes in monologues, as in *The Weir* and *This Lime Tree Bower*. Both of those plays are multi-character tapestries. In *The Good Thief*, which was first staged in Dublin in 1994, there is only one voice, that of a killer, in his own words, "a paid thug," caught in a web of violence. This tough, abrasive monologue, cited as an outstanding OOB production, was given a pungent performance by Brian d'Arcy James (as directed by Carl Forsman on a bare stage). The production, which opened at the Jose Quintero Theatre, transferred to 45 Bleecker for an eight-week Off Broadway run. In contrast to Mark Rowe's *Howie the Rookie* at PS 122, a related piece of underworld adventure that was so vernacular as to be nearly indecipherable, *The Good Thief* was straightforward. Trying to explain why his girlfriend had left him for his boss, the protagonist says, "Power attracts women," and adds quickly, "also I had been beating her up."

And God Created Great Whales was almost a one-man show, written, directed, composed and acted by Rinde Eckert (with the onstage assistance of Nora Cole as muse and singer). First produced by Foundry Theatre at Dance Theatre Workshop, the Obie Award-winning production later ran at 45 Bleecker. In this complex, convoluted performance piece, a composer is trying to create an impossible opera, drawn from *Moby Dick*. Occasionally there were bursts of Melvillean music. With stops and starts and moments of theatrical anarchy, Eckert traced an artist's downward spiral into madness and catatonia.

Masterly tramp: Bill Irwin in Samuel Beckett's Texts for Nothing *at Classic Stage Company. Photo: Dixie Sheridan*

The prolific Mac Wellman had two new shows of note Off Off Broadway, *Cat's Paw* (an outstanding OOB production) and the musical

Jennie Richee. In *Cat's Paw* at Soho Rep, mothers and daughters are in conflict in high public places: the top of the Empire State building, the World Trade Center, the hand of the Statue of Liberty. With witty, literate dialogue, Wellman explored "the weather of the word." This time, there was also a clear line of narrative within the wordplay, as the author moved into the mind-set of women, with a subtext about Don Juan. Nancy Franklin was offhandedly amusing as the mother and Alicia Goranson quirkily captivating as a daughter. Credit should also go to Daniel Aukin as director and Kyle Chepulis for his deep focus, diminishing-perspective setting, which gave the appearance of height while remaining on level ground.

Jennie Richee (written by Wellman, with music by Julia Wolfe and direction by Bob McGrath) was a musical descent into the strange world of Henry Darger, that mad artist-author. An outsider and self-styled "protector of children," Darger was a kind of cross between Lewis Carroll and Joe Gould—that denizen of Greenwich Village who never did write the history of the world as promised. In his hermit-like life, Darger wrote, among other works, a 15,000 page manuscript called *The Story of the Vivian Girls, in What Is Known as the Realms of the Unreal of the Glandico-Angelinian Wars, as Caused by the Child Slave Rebellion*. This collaborative Ridge Theater production at The Kitchen was a plunge down Darger's rabbit-hole into his wonderland. The musical was visually striking, using adaptations of the artist's own drawings of the Vivian girls, a gaggle of Bo Peeps battling an Evil Empire. Some of the pictures were pretty, others bizarre (with penises attached to a chorus of angels). Abstract and difficult to follow, *Jennie Richee* was a venturesome theatrical expedition.

With *Now That Communism Is Dead My Life Feels Empty!*, Richard Foreman's Ontological-Hysteric Theater ascended (or descended) into politics. Or did he? In his program notes, he wrote, "This is, obviously, not a play of political analysis, but a theatrical event that would echo the anguish of a world inside the head and heart. . . ." Having said that, he took his audience on a trip littered with detritus both worldly and insular, as a pair of alter egos (Tony Torn and Jay Smith) posed threats and counterthreats. As usual, Foreman's universe was black and white, but this time splashed with red (for Russia? for blood?). Offstage, we heard Foreman's sepulchral voice intoning such messages as "Red Communism is dead." As he acknowledged in an interview, "My plays have always been political." Throughout his work there are battles for control, as the empowered confronts the powerless. In that sense, there is a side to Foreman that mirrors Harold Pinter.

Theodora Skipitares was at La MaMa Annex with *Optic Fever*, moving from science, her favored area of expertise, into art (with a touch of science). This was a miniaturist view of the birth of painting, with the emphasis on the Renaissance and Leonardo da Vinci and Paolo Uccello, in particular. The show was highlighted by a vignette of five Freuds sitting around talking, in this case amusingly analyzing Leonardo. At another point, the *Mona Lisa* was projected on the head of a huge puppet. Other puppeteer tricks and treats dotted what must be considered a work in progress. Robert Lepage's *The Far Side of the Moon*, a one-man, two character play about divisive brothers (both played by the author) and rockets to the moon, seemed out of place in the Henson International Festival of Puppet Theater at the Joseph Papp Public Theater. There was minimal puppetry, but inventive images: Lepage riding an ironing board/bicycle as the world slid by on a moving canvas.

Robert Wilson was in residence at the Brooklyn Academy of Music with *A Dream Play* by August Strindberg, who speaks of "dissolving views," meaning "transforming pictures." This should have been a natural subject for the imaginative director, who typically forges his own path into dreams. At first, there were silent still pictures and a seesaw-like ramp for Indra to descend. The production was slow and hypnotic and not always clear. At moments it seemed to contradict the text. Or was that intended as a parallel vision, or universe? For one thing, Strindberg's castle, a centerpiece of the play, was absent.

In its 10th anniversary season, the Signature Theatre Company featured new plays by three of its celebrated playwrights. Romulus Linney offered his stageworthy adaptation of Ernest J. Gaines's novel, *A Lesson Before Dying* about a prisoner on death row; Lee Blessing was represented by *Thief River*, a sprawling, multi-generational study of two gay men (with evocative performances by Remak Ramsay and Frank Converse as the oldest versions of the characters).

The most memorable play in the Signature series was *The Last of the Thorntons* written by Horton Foote and directed by James Houghton. An outstanding OOB production, this was an affectionate and poignant look at limited but not lesser lives. In a quiet nursing home in Harrison, Texas, residents and visitors reflect on the past—not always with fondness, and often with rue—as they tell overlapping tales about absent people, most of them dead. The characters on stage are colorful survivors: Hallie Foote as the last of the Thornton family, a woman now submerged in delusions; Estelle Parsons as an outsider who still has her wits and her vigorous opinions. Artfully, Foote gathered the characters into a litany of remembrance and repetition.

Rob Ackerman's *Tabletop*, which moved into an Off Broadway run after playing at Dance Theatre Workshop, was a small, marginal play on a very specialized subject, people who film commercials on tabletops—not an auspicious dramatic idea and an evening not marked by surprises. The play had its amusing moments and was reasonably well acted, especially by Jeremy Webb as a kind of troublesome genius of this still-life tabletop art. *The Road Home*, written by James Lecesne and directed by Lawrence Sacharow, an earnest collage about children of war, played briefly at the Kaye Playhouse at Hunter College before embarking on tour.

The Jean Cocteau Repertory, a long running, highly productive home for classics, offered a full season of classic and contemporary plays, including, unfortunately, a misguided revival of Tom Stoppard's *Night and Day*, an astute view of front-line journalism in the days before everything was computerized and digitalized. The play was just too demanding for the artistic resources of this pocketsize theater.

In *Force Continuum* at Atlantic Theater Company, Kia Corthron took an interesting subject—three generations of a family of black policemen and a question of police brutality—and confused the issue with too many scenes and fuzzy flashbacks. Coming after *One Woman Shoe* and other shows, *The Book of Liz* promised a great deal of humor and delivered little. This comedy by the brother and sister team of David and Amy Sedaris, produced by the Drama Dept., was a limp spoof of religious fanaticism and the wayward on the road.

No estimation of the season Off Off Broadway would be complete without recognition of the remarkable contribution of Lyn Austin. In October of 2000, she was struck by a taxicab and died. She was 78 and in the midst of another active season. As the founder and driving force behind the Music-Theatre Group, she was responsible for the discovery and encouragement of many major talents in the American theater. Her artists included Martha Clarke, Julie Taymor (who with Elliot Goldenthal as composer made her theatrical breakthrough with *Juan Darien* under Austin's guidance), Richard Foreman, Stanley Silverman, Anne Bogart and Eve Ensler. Austin's primary accomplishment was in linking theater, music, dance and the visual arts.

Having abandoned her successful career as a Broadway producer, she found a rewarding niche in the experimental theater, where for 30 years she was an innovator, both Off Off Broadway and in her company's country home in Lenox, in the Berkshire area of Massachusetts. Clarke, who did *The Garden of Earthly Delights* and *Vienna: Lusthaus* among other shows for Austin, compared her to Diaghilev, adding that she was "the key person in my creative life up to now." As Ensler said, "The Music-Theatre Group believes in young artists before the artists believe in themselves," adding that Austin had "nurtured and produced some of the most original, outrageous and groundbreaking artists of our time."

In other words, Lyn Austin represented the boldness and fearlessness characteristic of the best of Off Off Broadway. The plays she produced were created by inventive writers, directors and actors for the edification of theatergoers who remained in their seats. This was active—not interactive—theater, pure theater, in which audiences were moved and sometimes transfixed by new and exciting artistic experiences.

PLAYS PRODUCED OFF OFF BROADWAY AND ADDITIONAL NYC PRESENTATIONS

Compiled by Vivian Cary Jenkins
(assisted by Joshua Crouthamel)

BELOW IS A COMPREHENSIVE SAMPLING of 2000–01 Off Off Broadway productions in New York. There is no definitive "Off Off Broadway" area or qualification. To try to define or regiment it would be untrue to its fluid, exploratory purpose. The listing below of hundreds of works produced by more than 130 OOB groups and others is as inclusive as reliable sources will allow, however, and takes into account all leading Manhattan-based, new-play producing, English-language organizations.

The more active and established producing groups are identified in **bold face type**, in alphabetical order, with artistic policies and the names of its leaders given whenever these are a matter of record. Each group's 2000–01 schedule, with emphasis on new plays and with revivals of classics usually omitted, is listed with play titles in CAPITAL LETTERS. Often these are works-in-progress with changing scripts, casts and directors, sometimes without an engagement of record (but an opening or early performance date is included when available).

Many of these Off Off Broadway groups have long since outgrown a merely experimental status and offer programs that are the equal in professionalism and quality (and in some cases the superior) of anything in the New York theater. These listings include special contractual arrangements such as the showcase code, letters of agreement (allowing for longer runs and higher admission prices than usual) and, closer to the edge of the commercial theater, so-called "mini-contracts." In the list below, available data has been provided by press representatives and company managers.

A large selection of lesser-known groups and other shows that made appearances Off Off Broadway during the season appears under the "Miscellaneous" heading at the end of this listing.

Amas Musical Theatre. Dedicated to bringing people of all races, creeds, colors, religious and national origins together through the performing arts. Rosetta LeNoire founder, Donna Trinkoff producing director.

STARMITES, Musical with book by Stuart Ross and Barry Keating; music and lyrics by Barry Keating. March 22, 2001. Directed by Barry Keating; puppet design, Ritchard Druther and Jeffrey Wallach; scenery Beowulf Boritt; lighting; Aaron Spivey; costumes, John Russell.

Boys in blue: Chris McGarry and Chad L. Coleman in Kia Corthron's Force Continuum. *Photo: Carol Rosegg*

With Craig Bonacorsi, Chaundra Cameron, Kim Cea, Adam Fleming, Darlene Bel Grayson, Nicole Leach, Eric Millegan, Larry Purifory, Gwen Stewart, Pegg Winter, Jason Wooten.

American Place Theatre. Issue-oriented and community-focused plays. Wynn Handman artistic director, Carl Jaynes general manager.

FOR COLORED GIRLS WHO HAVE CONSIDERED SUICIDE/WHEN THE RAINBOW IS ENUF. By Ntozake Shange. June 11, 2000. Directed and choreographed by George Faison; scenery, Walt Spangler; costumes, Ann Hould-Ward; lighting, Robert Perry; sound, Janet Kalas. With Eleanor McCoy, Novella Nelson, Lizan Mitchell, Jackée, Carol-Jean Lewis, Katherine J. Smith, J. Ieasha Prime.

LIVING IN THE WIND. By Michael Bradford. October 29, 2000. Directed by Regge Life; scenery, Beowulf Boritt; lighting, Chad McArver; costumes, Helen L. Simmons; sound, David D. Wright. With Nathan Hinton, Keesha Sharp, Arthur French, Lizan Mitchell, Cheryl Freeman, Chad L. Coleman.

I LOVE AMERICA. Written and performed by Lidia Ramirez. May 30, 2001. Directed by Elise Thoron; choreography, Marlies Yearby; scenery, Beowulf Boritt; costumes, Mimi O'Donnell; lighting, Jane Cox; sound, David Lawson.

Atlantic Theater Company. Produces new plays or reinterpretations of classics that speak to audiences in a contemporary voice on issues reflecting today's society. Neil Pepe artistic director, Hilary Hinckle managing director.

JOE FEARLESS (A FAN DANCE). By Liz Tuccillo. June 19, 2000. Directed by Craig Carlisle; choreography, Taro Alexander; Fearless Fly Girls choreography, Danielle Flora, Laura Sheehy; scenery and lighting; Michael Brown; costumes, Mattie Ullrich; music, Keith Middleton. With Fred Benjamin, Michael Leydon Campbell, Jessica Castro, Charlotte Colavin, Matthew Dawson, Nathan Dean, Julie Dretzin, Michael Ealy, Dan Fogler, Danielle Flora, Eric Ingram, Robert Manning, Matthew McMurray, Sundra Oakley, Blake Robbins, Randy Ryan, Laura Sheehy, Callie Thorne, Keith Tisdell.

THE BEGINNING OF AUGUST. By Tom Donaghy. October 11, 2000. Directed by Neil Pepe; scenery, Scott Pask; costumes, Ilona Somogyi; lighting, Christopher Akerlind; sound,

Summer hijinks: Mary Steenburgen in Tom Donaghy's The Beginning of August. *Photo: Carol Rosegg*

Janet Kalas. With Mary Steenburgen, Garrett Dillahunt, Mary McCann, Ray Anthony Thomas, Jason Ritter.

MOMMA. Written and performed by Siobhan Fallon. January 22, 2001. Directed by Alysa Wishingrad; lighting, Kirk Bookman; sound, Raymond D. Schilke, original music, Nancy Hower, Kevin Holmes.

FORCE CONTINUUM. By Kia Corthron. February 8, 2001. Directed by Michael John Garcés; scenery, Alexander Dodge; costumes, Mimi O'Donnell; lighting, Kirk Bookman; sound, Raymond D. Schilke; fight direction, Rick Sordelet. With Chad L. Coleman, Caroline S. Clay, David Fonteno, Jordan Lage, Chris McGarry, Donovan Hunter McNight, Sean Squire, Myra Lucretia Taylor, Ray Anthony Thomas.

Blue Light Theater Company. Produces a wide range of plays and strives to give young working actors the opportunity to grow by working with established theater artists. Greg Naughton actor-manager, Mandy Greenfield producing manager, Peter Manning artistic director.

PRINCESS TURANDOT. Written and directed by Darko Tresnjak. December 7, 2000. Scenery, David P. Gordon, costumes, Linda Cho; lighting Christopher J. Landy; sound, Robert Murphy. With Jeffrey Binder, Crispin Freeman, Roxanna Hope, Christopher K. Morgan, Gregor Paslawsky, Susan Pourfar, Maria Elena Ramirez, Josh Radnor, James Stanley, Andrew Weems.

Brooklyn Academy of Music Next Wave Festival. Since 1981, this annual three-month festival has presented over 200 events, including more than 50 world premieres. Featuring leading international artists, it is one of the world's largest festivals of contemporary performing arts. Joseph V. Melillo executive producer.

WAR OF THE WORLDS. Conceived and directed by Anne Bogart, written by Naomi Iizuka. October 4, 2000. Scenery, Neil Patel; costumes, James Schuette; lighting, Mimi Jordan Sherin; sound, Darron L. West. With Akiko Aizawa, J. Ed Araiza, Will Bond, Tom Nelis, Ellen Lauren, Barney O'Hanlon, Stephen Webber.

MÁQUINA HAMLET. By Heiner Müller. October 18, 2000. Translated by Gabriela Massuh, Dieter Welke. Directed by Daniel Veronese, Emilio García Wehbi, Ana Alvarado; costumes and construction, Rosna Barcena; lighting, Jorge Doliszniak, Alejandro Le Roux and Mariano Dobrysz; original music and sound, Cecilia Candia.

UTTAR-PRIYADARSHI (THE FINAL BEATITUDE). Music, design and direction by Ratan Thiyam. October 25, 2000. From a verse poem by Ajneya. Translated by Shri A. Krishnamohan Sharma. Scenery, Sbrata, N. Tomba, Ningthembir; costumes, Somo, Chingkheinganbi, Sushma; lighting, Mr. Thiyam, Kanishka Sen. With R.K. Bhogen, Ibomcha Sorok, Robindro, Somo, Premananda, Subrata, Ningthembir, Ibochouba Meetei.

REQUIEM FOR SREBRENICA. Conceived and directed by Olivier Py. November 8, 2000. Scenery and costumes, Pierre-André Weitz. With Anne Bellec, Irina Dalle, Frédérique Ruchaud.

A DREAM PLAY. By August Strindberg. November 28, 2000. Direction, design and lighting, Robert Wilson; costumes, Jacques Reynaud; lighting Andreas Fuchs, Mr. Wilson; sound, Ronald Hallgren; music Michael Galasso. With Jessica Liedberg, Henrik Rafaelsen, Gerhard Hoberstorfer, Andreas Liljeholm, Lasse Petterson, Åke Lundqvist, Anita Ekström, Kajsa Reingardt, Axelle Axell, Christer Banck, Robert Panzenböck, Thomas Wijkmark, Bo Samuelson, Per-Olov Gerhard Larsson, Cecilia Nilsson, Ulricha Johnson, Anna Rydgren.

Classic Stage Company. Reinventing and revitalizing the classics for contemporary audiences. Barry Edelstein artistic director, Beth Emelson producing director.

TEXTS FOR NOTHING. By Samuel Beckett. October 15, 2000. Directed by Bill Irwin; scenery, Douglas Stein; costumes, Anita Yavich; lighting, Nancy Schertler; sound, Aural Fixation. With Bill Irwin.

RACE. By Ferdinand Bruckner. February 18, 2001. Adapted and directed by Barry Edelstein; scenery, Neil Patel; costumes, Angela Wendt; lighting, Russell H. Champa; sound, Robert Murphy. With Jenny Bacon, Colleen Corbett, Robert L. Devaney, Mark H. Dold, Ron Guttman, Gregory Porter Miller, Tom Nolan, Aaron Nutter, Duncan Nutter, Marc Palmieri, Tommy Schrider, Kirsten Sahs, Jeremy Shamos, Chris Stewart, Stephen Barker Turner, C.J. Wilson.

I WILL BEAR WITNESS. By Victor Klemperer. March 11, 2001. Directed by Karen Malpede. Adapted and directed by George Bartenieff, Karen Malpede. Translated by Martin Chalmers. Scenery, Neil Patel; costumes, Angela Wendt; lighting, Tony Giovannetti. With George Bartenieff.

Drama Dept. A collective of actors, directors, designers, stage managers, writers and producers who collaborate to create new works and revive neglected classics. Douglas Carter Beane artistic director, Michael S. Rosenberg managing director.

LES MIZRAHI. Written and performed by Isaac Mizrahi. October 19, 2000. Directed by Richard Move; visual director, Wendall K. Harrington; lighting, Kirk Bookman; sound, Laura Grace Brown. With the Ben Waltzer Trio.

THE BOOK OF LIZ. Written by David and Amy Sedaris. March 26, 2001. Directed and scenery by Hugh Hamrick; costumes, Victoria Farrell; lighting, Kirk Bookman; sound, Laura Grace Brown; music, Mark Levenson. With Amy Sedaris, Chuck Coggins, David Rakoff and Jackie Hoffman.

Ensemble Studio Theatre. Membership organization of playwrights, actors, directors and designers dedicated to supporting individual theater artists and developing new works for the stage. More than 200 projects each season, ranging from readings to fully-mounted productions. Curt Dempster artistic director, Jamie Richards executive producer, Eliza Beckwith managing director.

OCTOBERFEST 2000. Twentieth annual month-long celebration of comedy, drama, music, poetry and storytelling on Ensemble Studio Theatre's two stages. October 1–November 5, 2000.

THE SHANEEQUA CHRONICLES. Written and performed by Stephanie Berry. November 9, 2000. Directed by Talvin Wilks; choreography, Amparo Santiago; scenery, Evan Alexander; costumes, Sydney Kai Inis; sound, Robert Gould.

ARMONK. By Sean Sutherland. November 14, 2000. Directed by Eileen Myers; with Paul Bartholomew, Derrick McGinty, Heather Robinson, Sonya Rokes, Sarah Rose, Eric Scott, Kevin Shinick, Sean Sutherland.

SUMMER CYCLONE. By Amy Fox. March 7, 2000. Directed by Nela Wagman; scenery, George Xenos and Dorothea Brunialti; costumes, Amela Baksic; lighting, Greg MacPherson;

Truth teller: George Bartenieff in Victor Klemperer's I Will Bear Witness. *Photo: Dixie Sheridan*

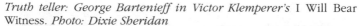

sound, Dean Gray; composer, David Rothenberg. With Jenna Stern, Christine Farrell, Chris Ceraso, Johnny Giacalone, William Wise, Amy Staats.

LOUIS SLOTIN SONATA. By Paul Mullin. April 10, 2000. Directed by David P. Moore; choreography, Kathryn Gayner; scenery, Rachel Hauck; lighting, Greg MacPherson; costumes, Amela Baksic; sound, Robert Gould. With Bill Salyers, Ezra Knight, Bill Cwikowski, Joel Rooks, Allyn Burrows, Matthew Lawler, Richard Hoxie, Amy Love.

MARATHON 2001 SERIES A. May 24, 2001. Scenery, Charles Kirby; costumes, Jacqueline Firkins; lighting Greg MacPherson; sound, Robert Gould.

ARABIAN NIGHTS. By David Ives. Directed by Jason McConnell Buzas; with Anne O'Sullivan, Melinda Page Hamilton, Christopher Duva.

UKIMWI. By Tom Coash. Directed by Eliza Beckwith; with Nicole Leach, Holter Graham.

NIGHT RULES. By Billy Aronson. Directed by Jamie Richards; with Thomas Lyons, Katherine Leask, Joe Uria, Geneva Carr.

BROWN. By Cherie Vogelstein. Directed by Jamie Richards; with Sam Freed, Susan Greenhill, Grant Shaud, Zach Shaffer.

INTAR. Identifies, develops and presents the talents of gifted Hispanic-American theater artists and multicultural visual artists. Max Ferra artistic director.

TIGHT EMBRACE. By Jorge Ignacio Cortiñas. June 8, 2000. Directed by Ruben Polendo.

SAN DIEGO STREET PADRES. By Janis Astor del Valle. June 15, 2000. Directed by Daniel Jáquez.

AIRE/ARENA. Written and directed by David Anzuelo. June 22, 2000.

GENERIC LATINA. By Teatro Luna. June 29, 2000. Directed by Alexandra Lopez.

NUYORICAN VOICES. Directed by Max Ferra. March 13–April 22, 2001. Miriam's Flowers. By Migdalia Cruz. Giants Have Us in Their Books. By José Rivera. Unmerciful Good Fortune. By Edwin Sanchez. With David Anzuelo, Liza Colón Zayas, Melissa Delaney DelValle, Michael Ray Escamilla, Yetta Gottesman, Alvaro Heinig, Carlos Molina, Jezabel Montero, Rolando Morales, Michelle Rios, Nicolás Salgado, Liam Torres.

KING LEAR. By William Shakespeare. September 28, 2000. Directed by Bernice Rohret; scenery, Mary Houston, lighting, Aaron Spivey; fight direction, Samantha Phillips. With Natily Blair, Julie Campbell, David Logan Rankin, Ashton Crosby, Kathryn Graybill, Joe Hickey, Samuel Frederick Reynolds, Shirley Roeca, Dale Soules, Suanne Savoy, Christi Spain-Savage, Gregory Ivan Smith, Todd Weldon.

Irish Repertory Theatre. Aims to bring works by Irish and Irish-American masters and contemporary playwrights to a wider audience and to develop new works focusing on a wide range of cultural experiences. Charlotte Moore artistic director, Ciaran O'Reilly producing director.

DON JUAN IN HELL. By George Bernard Shaw. August 20, 2000. Directed by Charlotte Moore; costumes, David Toser; lighting, Jason A. Cina; sound, Murmod, Inc. With Celeste Holm, Fritz Weaver, James A. Stephens, Donal Donnelly.

THE HOSTAGE. By Brendan Behan. October 29, 2000. Directed by Charlotte Moore; scenery, Eugene Lee, N. Joseph DeTullio; costumes, Linda Fisher; lighting, Gregory Cohen; sound, Murmod, Inc. With Terry Donnelly, Anto Nolan, Ciaran O'Reilly, Derdriu Ring, Erik Singer, James A. Stephens.

THE PICTURE OF DORIAN GRAY. By Oscar Wilde. March 22, 2001. Adapted for the stage and directed by Joe O'Byrne. Scenery, Akira Yoshimura, Rebecca Vary; costumes, David Toser; lighting, Brian Nason; sound, Murmod, Inc. With Crispin Freeman, Paul Vincent Black, Nick Hetherington, Tertia Lynch, Colleen Madden, Paul Anthony McGrane, Daniel Pearce, Angela Pierce, Andrew Seear, Timothy Smallwood, Alan Campbell.

Jewish Repertory Theatre. Presents plays in English relating to the Jewish experience. Ran Avni artistic director, Steven Anderson managing director.

BIG POTATO. By Arthur Laurents. November 5, 2000. Directed by Richard Sabellico; scenery James Noone; costumes, Carrie Robbins; lighting, Richard Latta. With Dylan Chalfy, Elizbieta Czyzewska, David Margulies, Joanna Glushak, Paul Hecht.

EXCUSE ME, I'M TALKING. Words and music by Annie Korzen. February 11, 2001. Directed by Judy Chaikin; scenery, Michelle Malavet; lighting, Richard Latta; musical arrangements, Beth Ertz, Jackie O'Neill. With Annie Korzen.

THE GARDENS OF FRAU HESS. By Milton Frederick Marcus. April 29, 2001. Directed by Rhoda R. Herrick; scenery, Richard Ellis; costumes, Gail Cooper-Hecht; lighting, Richard Latta; sound, Steve Shapiro. With Lisa Bostnar, Joel Leffert.

The Joseph Papp Public Theater/New York Shakespeare Festival. Schedule of special projects, in addition to its regular Off Broadway productions. George C. Wolfe producer, Fran Reiter executive director, Rosemarie Tichler artistic producer, Mark Litvin managing director, Michael Hurst general manager.

New Work Now! Eighth Annual Festival of New Play Readings at the Anspacher Theater.

AS YOU LIKE IT. By William Shakespeare. May 7, 2001. Adapted and directed by Erica Schmidt.

SHE STOOPS TO COMEDY. By David Greenspan. May 7, 2001.

STONE COLD DEAD SERIOUS. By Adam Rapp. May 8, 2001

MONSTER. By Derek Nguyen. May 9, 2001

DULCE DE LECHE. By Daniel Goldfarb. May 10, 2001

BETHLEHEM. By Octavio Solis. May 11, 2001

MONKEY IN THE MIDDLE. By Brighde Mullins. May 12, 2001

THE CLOUDS, THE OCEAN AND EVERYTHING IN BETWEEN. By Michael P. Premsrirat

GOOD THING. By Jessica Goldberg. May 14, 2001

BREAKFAST, LUNCH & DINNER. By Luis Alfaro. May 15, 2001

BEL CANTO. By Daniel Alexander Jones. May 16, 2001

MOVIES. Written and directed by Christopher Walken. May 17, 2001

THE SUPERFRIENDS OF FLUSHING QUEENS. By Ji Hyun Lee. May 18, 2001

THE DINOSAUR WITHIN. By John S. Walch. May 19, 2001.

THE STORY. By Tracey S. Wilson. May 20, 2001.

La MaMa Experimental Theatre Club (ETC). A busy workshop for experimental theater of all kinds. Ellen Stewart founder and director.

THE SEAGULL. By Anton Chekhov, in Italian with English subtitles. October 19, 2000. Directed by Giancarlo Nanni.

FAME TAKES A HOLIDAY. By Cassandra Danz, Mary Fulham, Warren Leight. October 26, 2000. Directed by Mary Fulham; choroeography, Barbara Allen; music, Tracy Berg, Dick Gallagher, Cliff Korman, Marc Shaiman; scenery, Gregory John Mercurio; costumes, Ramona Poce; lighting, David Adams; sound, Tim Schellenbaum. With Abigail Gampel, Deborah LaCoy, Susan Murphy, Mary Purdy.

FRANKENSTEIN: THE ROCK MUSICAL. Book, music and direction by William Electric Black. October 26, 2000.

OPTIC FEVER. Conceived, designed and directed by Theodora Skipitares. January 4, 2001. Music, David First; lighting, Pat Digman. With Preston Foerder, Chris Maresca, Neil McNally, Alissa Mello, Michael Moran, Sarah Provost, Dara Steinberg.

FIDDLER SUB-TERRAIN. By Oren Safdie. January 4, 2001. Music and lyrics by Ronnie Cohen. Directed by Anthony Patellis, Oren Safdie. With Anthony Patellis, Mary Ann Conk,

Michelle Solomon, Amy Shure, Michael Gargani, Ali Anderson, Sean Power, Janine Molinari, Nick Locilento, Sean Devine.

HYMN TO THE RISING SUN. By Paul Green. February 5, 2001. Directed by Barbara Montgomery; costumes, Francia Maldonaldo; scenery and lighting, David Adams. With Charley Hayward, Charles Weldon, Kevin Lee, Gian Marco Lo Forte, Steven Pizzano.

SEVEN AGAINST THEBES. By Aeschylus. May 7, 2001. Adapted and directed by Ellen Stewart; music by Elizabeth Swados, Michael Sirotta, Genji Ito. With Emanuele Ancolrini, Billy Clark, Arthur Adair, Cary Gant, Omni Johnson, Julia Martin, Valois Mickens, Mitsunari Sakamoto.

Lincoln Center Festival. An annual international summer arts festival offering classic and contemporary works. Nigel Redden festival director. July 2000.

FILAO. July 11, 2000. Directed by Laszlo Hudi; composer, Carl Schlosser; costumes, Cissou Winling; lighting, Michael Serejnikoff; sound, Grégoire Chomel. Performed by the French Troupe, Les Colporteurs. With Kathleen Reynolds, David Dimitri, Sophie Kantorowicz, Xavier Martin, Thiery Suty, Miquel de la Rocha, Linda Peterson.

INNOCENT AS CHARGED. By Aleksandr Ostrovksy. July 21, 2000. Directed by Pyotr Fomenko; scenery, Tatyana Selvinskaya; costumes, Olga Akhmatovakaya; lighting, Vladmir Amelin. With Yuliya Borisova, Lyudmila Maksakova, Yuri Yakovlev, Vyacheslav Shalevich, Yevgeny Knyazev, Viktor Zozulin, Mikhail Uliyano, Inna Alabina, Alla Kazanskaya, Anatoly Menshchikov, Yelena Sotnikova, Nonna Grishayeva, Yuri Kraskov, Olga Gavrilyuk.

BROTHERS AND SISTERS. By Lev Dodin, Sergei Bekhterev and Arkady Katsman; based on the trilogy of novels by Fyodor Abramov. July 11, 2000.

MCC Theater. Dedicated to the promotion of emerging writers, actors, directors and theatrical designers. Robert LuPone and Bernard Telsey artistic directors, William Cantler associate artistic director.

A PLACE AT THE TABLE. By Simon Block. October 25, 2000. Directed by Michael Sexton; scenery, James Noone; costumes, David Zinn; lighting, John-Paul Szczepanski; music and sound, David Van Tieghem. With Jen Drohan, Zak Orth, Jesse Pennington, Robin Weigert.

HIGH DIVE. Written and performed by Leslie Ayvazian. February 26, 2001. Directed by David Warren; scenery, Neil Patel; lighting, Brian MacDevitt; sound, Robert Murphy.

THE DEAD EYE BOY. By Angus MacLachlan. April 27, 2001. Directed by Susan Fenichell; scenery, Christine Jones; costumes, David Zinn; lighting, Russell H. Champa; fight direction, Rick Sordelet. With Joseph Murphy, Lilli Taylor, Aaron Himelstein.

Melting Pot Theatre Company. Presents multicultural theater in an effort to reflect the ethnic diversity of the city. Larry Hirschhorn, artistic director.

A CHILD'S GARDEN. Musical with book by Louis Rosen, Arthur Perlman, Charlotte Maier; based on the autobiographical writings of Robert Louis Stevenson. December 10, 2000. Directed by Lori Steinberg; choreography, Robert La Fosse; scenery, Kris Stone; costumes, Sue Gandy; lighting, Michael Lincoln; music, Louis Rosen. With Aloysius Gigl, Tony Speciale, Thomas Scott Parker, Jessica Walling, Rebecca Bellingham.

THE DEVIL'S MUSIC: THE LIFE AND BLUES OF BESSIE SMITH. By Angelo Parra. February 3, 2001. Directed by Joe Brancato; scenery, Matthew Maraffi; lighting, Jeff Nellis; costumes, Curtis Hay; musical arrangements, Miche Braden. With Miche Braden, Terry Walker, Jimmy Hankins, Pierre Andrè.

Mint Theater Company. Committed to bringing new vitality to worthy but neglected plays. Jonathan Bank artistic director.

JULIUS CAESAR. By William Shakespeare. July 1, 2000. Directed by Joanne Zipay; with Jennifer Chudy, Jane Titus, Alice M Gatling, Richard Simon, Antonio del Rosario.

THE COMEDY OF ERRORS. By William Shakespeare. July 1, 2000. Directed by Joanne Zipay; with Kevin LeCaon, Leese Walker, James Pinkowski, Susan Beyer, Ginny Hack, Kelli Cruz.

WELCOME TO OUR CITY. By Thomas Wolfe. September 8, 2000. Directed by Jonathan Bank; scenery, Vicki R. Davis; costumes, Elly Van Horne; lighting, Randy Glickman; music and sound, Ellen Mandel; fight choreography, Michael Chin. With John Lyndsay Hall, Haakon Jepsen, Michael LiDondici, Michael McLernon, Bergin Michaels, Gregory Mikell, Lee Moore, Michael Moore, Erick R. Moreland, Robyne Parrish, Brocton Pierce, Patrick Riviere, Larry Swansen, Frank Swingler, Jonathan Tindle, Colleen Smith Wallnau, T.D. White, Don Clark Williams, David Winton.

FAREWELL TO THEATRE. By Harley Granville-Barker. THE FLATTERING WORD. By George Kelly. (Two One Acts). November 10, 2000. Directed by Gus Kaikkonen; scenery, Sarah Lambert; costumes, Henry Shaffer; lighting, William Armstrong. With Sara Barnett, Allyn Burrows, Sally Kemp, Sioux Madden, George Morfogen, Michael Stebbins, Colleen Smith Wallnau.

CODE OF THE WEST. Written and Directed by Mark R. Giesser. January 18, 2001. Scenery, John C. Scheffler; costumes, Melanie Ann Schmidt; lighting, Aaron Meadow. With Bradley Cole, Mark McDonough, Linda Ewing, Jordan Charney, Elisabeth Ziambetti. Transferred to McGinn/Cazale Theatre March 24, 2001.

DOUBLE BASS. By Patrick Süskind. February 15, 2001. Directed by Jonathan Bank; scenery, Katerina Fiore; lighting, Randy Glickman. With Michael W. Connors.

DIANA OF DOBSON'S. By Cicely Hamilton. May 4, 2001. Directed by Eleanor Reissa; scenery, Sarah Lambert; costumes, Tracy Christensen; lighting, Jeff Nellis; sound, Ray Leslee. With Sara Barnett, Glynis Bell, Caren Browning, Deborah Cresswell, Maitreya Friedman, Karl Kenzler, Mikel Sarah Lambert, David Marantz, Jina Oh, John Plumpis, Rachel Sled.

New Dramatists. An organization devoted to playwrights. Member writers may use the facilities for anything from private cold readings of their material to public script-in-hand readings. Todd London artistic director, Joel Ruark director of administration and finance, Paul A. Slee executive director.

Readings and Workshops:
FLAPPERJAKKY. By Mark Bazzone. September 7, 2000.

LEFT ON CHURCH STREET.Written and directed by Nathan Parker. September 7, 2000.

New Member Event, September 11, 2000:
A LAST SUPPER. Written and directed by Karl Gajdusek. With Ed Vassallo, Anne Dudek. SANTA CONCEPCION. By Anne García-Romero. Directed by Leah C. Gardiner. With Mercedes Herrero, Zabryna Guevara. ST. JOAN AND THE DANCING SICKNESS. By Julie Hébert. Directed by Michael John Garcés. With Timothy Douglas, Jan Leslie Harding, Kwana Martinez, Mike Hodge, Dale Soules, Gareth Saxe. CRACKSKULL ROW. By Honour Kane. Directed by Timothy Douglas. With Caroline Winterson, Fergus Loughnane. SWEATY PALMS. Written and directed by Alejandro Morales. With Jennifer Cohn, Eduardo Vega, Mario Prado. TORCH. By Caridad Svich. Directed by Debbie Saivetz. With Gretchen Lee Krich. HYPE HERO. Written and directed by Dominic Taylor. With Stacey Robinson, Ron Brice, Joanna Rhinehart, Kelly Taffee. [SIC]. By Melissa James Gibson. Directed by Melissa Kievman. With James Urbaniak, Jan Leslie Harding, Jeremy Shamos.

STEAL BACK LIGHT FROM THE VIRTUAL. By Caridad Svich. September 15, 2000. Directed by Anne Kauffman. With Todd Cerveris, Carla Harting, TR Knight, Carolyn Baeumler, John McAdams, Mercedes Herrero.

MARY & MYRA. By Catherine Filloux. September 18, 2000. Directed by Lou Jacob. With Rosemary Knower, Babo Harrison.

CHILD OF THE DARK SUN. By Justin Flemming. September 22, 2000. Directed by Susan Fenichell. With Joanna P. Adler, Tom Barbour, Matthew Maguire, Bill Camp, Heather Gillespie.

BURNT PIANO. By Justin Fleming. September 28, 2000. Directed by M. Burke Walker. With Chet Baker, Babo Harrison, Roger Hendricks Simon, Celia Howard, Paul Iacono, Robert MacMickan.

MY CHEKHOV LIGHT. Written, directed and performed by Frank Gagliano. October 2, 2000.

RECONSTRUCTION. By Herman Daniel Farrell III. October 2, 2000 Directed by John Steber. With Laurie Kennedy, Jon Krupp, Mark LaMura, Tracey A. Leigh, Novella Jackson, Charles Parnell.

ALL THE CHILDREN SING. By Eli Bolin, Sam Forman and Jamie Salka. October 4, 2000. Directed by Jamie Salka. With David Ayers, Meredith Zeitlin, Billy Eichner, Josh Radnor, Rachel Stern.

DEUX MARIAGES. By Lynne Alvarez. October 5, 2000. Directed by Timothy Douglas. With Thomas Christopher Nieto, Christina Ross, John Seitz, Maria Tucci, Christa Scott-Reed, Neal Lerner, Pascale Armand, Amanda Diaz.

Six-Pack Graduation Festival:
THE LEGACY CODES. By Cherylene Lee. October 16, 2000. Directed by Ron Nakahara. With Tom Lee, Les J.N. Mau, Wai-Ching Ho, Scott Kalvin, Rhea Seehorn, Janet Zarish. JOE AND STEW'S THEATRE. By Jacquelyn Reingold. October 17, 2000. Directed by Ethan Silverman. With Matthew Cowles, David Eigenberg, Nancy Giles, Wendy Hoopes, Jodi Long, Mark Nelson, Angelina Phillips, Larry Pine, Martha Plimpton, Joseph Siravo, Frank Wood. MAYHEM. By Kelly Stuart. October 18, 2000. Directed by Jeff Teare. With Adam Davidson, Tatyana Yassukovich, Sherri Grabert, Jack Weatherall. DUSK. By Lenora Champagne. October 19, 2000. Directed by Rachel Dickstein. With Ellen McLaughlin. WAITING FOR GODOT TO LEAVE. By Oana Maria Hock. October 20, 2000. Directed by David Levine. With Paul Savas, Mary Shultz, Dale Soules, Paul Zimet, T. Ryder Smith. A BEAUTIFUL WHITE ROOM. By Barry Jay Kaplan. October 23, 2000. Directed by Jean Randich. With Starla Benford, Lynn Cohen, Mark H. Dold, Kathryn Foster, Babo Harrison, Joel Garland, JoJo Gonzalez, Ken Marks, Kate Rigg, Michael B. Washington.

THE SILENT CONCERTO. By Alejandro Morales. October 26, 2000. Directed by Eduardo Vega. With Randy Reyes, Jennifer Cohn, Sean McNall, Scott Ebersold, Steve Cuiffo.

CRACKSKULL ROW. By Honour Kane.October 30, 2000. Directed by Eve Beglarian. With Caroline Winterson, Yvonne Molloy, Fergus Loughnane, Jarlath Conroy, Terasa Livingstone.

EASTWEST. By Mark Bazzone. November 6, 2000. Directed by David Levine. With Lazaro Perez, Charlie Kevin, Todd Woodard, Steve Cuiffo.

LOVE MINUS. By Mary Gallagher. November 7, 2000. Directed by Garrett Bligh Eisler. With Maggie Lacey, Chris Henry Coffey, Kate Adams, Christa Scott-Reed, Jefferies Thaiss.

STEEPLECHASE (1). By John Pielmeier and Matty Selman. November 14, 2000.

STEEPLECHASE (2). By John Pielmeier and Matty Selman. November 15, 2000.

A VERY OLD MAN WITH ENORMOUS WINGS. By Nilo Cruz. December 1, 2000. Directed by Graciela Daniele. With Caleb Archer, Gemini Quintos, Ron Crawford, Saundra Santiago, Shawn Elliot, Marva Hicks, George de la Pena, Gary Perez, Tracey A. Leigh, Adriana Sevan.

CHINA CALLS. By Lonnie Carter. December 4, 2000. Directed by Loy Arcenas. With David Strathairn, Tanya Selvaratnam, Glen Cruz, Randall Duk Kim, Sharon Scruggs, Robin Shorr.

Yale Graduation Festival:
VELVET ROPES. By Joshua Scher. Directed by Anne Kauffman. With Glenn Kessler, Jeremy Shamos, Peter Russo. COLD WATER COMING. By Colleen Picket. Directed by Loretta Greco. With Stacey Karen Robinson, Vanessa Aspillaga. GOD HATES THE IRISH PLAYWRIGHT. By Sean Cunningham. Directed by Susan Fenichell. With Pete Simpson, Pete Starrett, Patrick Brinker, Liam Craig, Anne O'Sullivan, Julia Prud'homme, Heather Goldenhersh, Robert MacMickan. Friday, December 8, 2000

I REGRET SHE'S MADE OF SUGAR. By Rogelio Martinez. December 15, 2000. Directed by Bill Hart. With K.J. Sanchez, Antonio Suarez, Shawn Elliott, J. Ed Araiza, Raúl Esparza.

LIFE IN A WIND TUNNEL. By Mark Bazzone. December 18, 2000. Directed by Hayley Finn. With Molly Powell, Kathryn Foster, Gary Brownlee, Ed Vassallo, Liz Douglas.

WOMEN OF LOCKERBIE. January 17, 2001. By Debbie Brevoort. January 17, 2001. Directed by Liz Diamond. With Chris W. Bamonte, Caitlin O'Connell, Mark LaMura, Helen Jean Arthur, Anne O'Sullivan, Jurian Hughes, Sam Tsoutsouvas, Rosemary Fine.

I REGRET SHE'S MADE OF SUGAR (second reading). By Rogelio Martinez. January 19, 2001. Directed by Bill Hart. With K.J. Sanchez, Tony Gillian, Shawn Elliot, George de la Pena, Gilbert Cruz.

KATE CRACKERNUTS. By Sheila Callaghan (2000 Princess Grace Award Winner). February 7, 2001. Directed by Hayley Finn. With Rhea Seehorn, Shannon Burkett, Hank Jacobs, Lisa Gillan, Brent Popolizio, Fiona Jones, Jason Howard, Luther Creek, Joanna Liao, Catherine Brown.

Brown Festival of Readings:
THE IMPROVIDENCE OF MR. POE. By Stacia Saint Owens. February 21, 2001. Directed by Amy Lynn Budd. With Julie McGetrick, Joe Ouellette, Gary Brownlee, Rebecca Nelson, Erica N. Tazel, Joanna P. Adler, David Carson, Sharon Freedman. XOXOXOXO. February 22, 2001. By Laura Zam. February 21, 2001. Directed by Ruben Polendo. With Charles Smith, Darren Petit, Yetta Gottesman.

EURYDICE. By Sarah Ruhl. February 23, 2001. Directed by Rebecca Brown. With Meg Gibson, Jenny Weaver, Caroline McMahon, Paul Savas, Dominic Fumusa.

DIOSA. By Edwin Sanchez. March 2, 2001. Directed by John Steber; choreography,Willie Rosario. With Larry Block, David Grillo, Nancy Ticotin, Marcy Harriell, Robert Montano.

AUGUST IS A THIN GIRL. By Julie Myatt. March 5, 2001. Directed by Loretta Greco. With Clare Joyce, Wendy Hoopes, Paul Sparks, Les J.N. Mau, Joanie Ellen, Randy Reyes, Mandy Wolfson.

THE MOTHERLINE. By Chantal Bilodeau. March 9, 2001. Directed by Emily Morse. With Michelle Federer, Jenny Bacon, Barbara Pitts, Gareth Saxe, Larry Block, Jessica Colley.

THE WAITING ROOM. By Tanika Gupta. April 2, 2001. Directed by Liz Diamond. With Ajay Naidu, Sean T. Krishnan, Aparna Sen, Kalyan Ray, Rita Wolf, Hany Kamal.

SHE STOOPS TO COMEDY. Written and directed by David Greenspan. April 2, 2001. With Marissa Copeland, Mia Barron, Sharon Scruggs, Jeremy Shamos, T. Scott Cunningham.

GUTTED & TORNADO. By Beau Willimon. April 4, 2001. Directed by Emily Morse. With Joanna Liao, Gilbert Cruz, Florence Galperin, Paden Fallis, Barbara Wengerd, David Salper, Jessica Colley, Matthew Korahais, Livia Newman, Steve Cuiffo, Matt Benjamin.

BRINGING DOWN THE HOUSE. By Eve Sawyer. April 11, 2001. Directed by Tony Walton.

I REGRET SHE'S MADE OF SUGAR (third reading). By Rogelio Martinez. April 16, 2001. Directed by Bill Hart. With Greta Sanchez-Raminez, Raúl Esparza, Gary Perez, Christopher McCann, Antonio Suarez, Laura D. Hernandez.

XRDZK. By Mark Druck. April 17, 2001. With Christie Klein, Jay Stuart, J. Everett Sherman, Kate Lunsford, Rebecca Roberts, Charles Karel, Christine Kelly Karel, Mel Boudrot, Howard Ross.

THE WORLD SPEED CARNIVAL. By Stephanie Fleischmann. April 18, 2001. Directed by Rachel Dickstein. With Babo Harrison, Jenny Bacon, Phyllis Somerville, David Patrick Kelly, Melody Cooper, Laura-Jo Anderson, Paul Sparks, Lauren Ruggiero, Laura D. Hernandez, Robin Taylor.

THE DEW POINT. By Neena Beber. April 19, 2001. Directed by Simon Hammerstein

BITTEROOT. By Paul Zimet. April 20, 2001. Composer, Peter Gordon; Musical Director, Allison Sniffin. With Jeffrey Reynolds, Randy Reyes, Michelle Rios, Tina Shepard, Ellen Maddow, Isaac Maddow-Zimet, Michael Lofton, Hyunyup Lee, Ryan Deitz.

PORTRAIT OF A PRESIDENT. By Herman Daniel Farrell III. May 3, 2001. Directed by Emily Morse. With Babo Harrison, Kate Skinner, Tom Lee, John Daggett, Arthur French, Anita Hollander, Kwana Martinez, Ron Riley, Zachary Knower.

COARSE MAJEURE. By Gordon Dahlquist. May 7, 2001. With Gary Brownlee, Molly Powell, Annie McAdams, Alana Jerins, Lars Hanson, Emily Morse.

THE BREAKING LIGHT. By Sander Hicks. May 25, 2001. Directed by Peter Hawkins. With Cheryl Lynn Bowers, Michael Cannis, John Gregorio, Jeffrey Bender, Dan O'Brien, Brendan Toner, Lars Hanson, Catherine Mueller, Michael B. Washington.

LUSCIOUS MUSIC. By Matthew Maguire. May 31, 2001. Directed by Michael John Garcés. With Adriana Sevan, Paula Pizzi, Rocco Sisto, Edwin Lee Gibson, Jeff Barry.

New Federal Theatre. Dedicated to integrating minorities and women into the mainstream of American theater by training artists and by presenting plays by minorities and women to integrated, multicultural audiences. Woodie King Jr. producing director.

THE DANCE ON WIDOWS' ROW. Written and directed by Samm-Art Williams. July 3, 2000. Scenery, Felix E. Cochren; costumes, Evelyn Nelson; lighting, Shirley Prendergast; sound, Sean O'Halloran. With Barbara Montgomery, Marie Thomas, Elizabeth Van Dyke, Elain Graham, Adam Wade, Jack Landron, Ed Wheeler.

CONFLICT OF INTEREST. Writtten and directed by Jay Broad. October 27, 2000. Scenery, Robert Joel Schwartz; lighting, David Segal.

THE CONJURE MAN DIES: A MYSTERY TALE OF DARK HARLEM. By Rudolph Fisher. January 11, 2001. Directed by Clinton Turner Davis; scenery, Kent Hoffman; lighting, Shirley Prendergast; costumes, Evelyn Nelson; sound, Sean O'Halloran. With Peggy Alston, Christine Campell, Kevin. R. Free, Marcuis Harris, Cat Jagar, Everton Lawrence, Eric McLendon, Curtis McClarin, Esau Pritchett, Justice Pratt, Edward Washington, Tee C. Williams.

The New Group. Provides an artistic home for artists by launching fresh acting, writing and design talent. Committed to cultivating a young and diverse theater-going audience by providing accessible ticket prices. Scott Elliott artistic director, Elizabeth Timperman producing director.

WHAT THE BUTLER SAW. By Joe Orton. November 12, 2000. Directed by Scott Elliott; scenery, Derek McLane; costumes, Mattie Ullrich; lighting, James Vermeulen; sound, Ken Travis. With Dylan Baker, Chloë Sevigny. Lisa Emery, Karl Geary, Peter Frechette, Max Baker.

PARADISE ISLAND. By Benjie Aerenson. January 23, 2001. Directed by Andy Goldberg; scenery, Rob Odorisio; costumes, Mimi O'Donnell; lighting, Russell H. Champa; sound, Ken Travis. With Lynn Cohen, Adrienne Shelly.

SERVICEMEN. By Evan Smith. March 25, 2001. Directed by Sean Mathias; scenery, Derek McLane; costumes, Catherine Zuber, Alejo Vietti; lighting, Jeff Croiter; sound, Fabian Obispo. With Eric Martin Brown, Olivia Birkelund, William Westenberg, Anthony Veneziale, Steven Polito, Heather Matarazzo.

The New Victory Theater. Mission is to introduce young people and families, reflective of New York City's diverse communities, to live performances. Cora Cahan president.

ARABIAN NIGHTS. Adapted and directed by Dominic Cooke. September 29, 2000. Scenery, Georgia Sion; lighting, Johanna Town; choreography, Liz Ranken; composer, Gary Yershon; sound, Crispian Covel. With Paul Bhattacharjee, Paul Chahidi, Priyanga Elan, Natasha Gordon, Nizwar Karanj, Richard Katz, Martina Laird, Tristan Sharps, Yasmin Wilde.

KWAIDAN. Conceived, adapted and directed by Ping Chong; based on a book by Lafcadio Hearn. October 27, 2000. Art direction and production design, Mitsuru Ishii; lighting, Liz Lee; sound, David Meschter. With David Ige, Pamella O'Connor, Lee Randall, Fred C. Riley III, Don Smith.

CIRCUS. By Dick Feld and Theo Terra. March 2, 2001. Directed by Theo Terra; scenery and costumes, Karen Beens; composed, Feico De Leeuw; lighting, Geldof and Den Ottolander. With Dick Feld, Eric Jan Lens, Marcelle Van Der Velden.

THE POST MAN DELIVERS. Written and performed by Robert Post. May 4, 2001. Directed by Tony Montanaro; scenery, Steve Quinn; costumes, Wendy Goldstein; lighting, Brian Ferguson; sound, Tom Boyer, Great Big Spanking Records.

Ontological-Hysteric Theater. Avant garde productions designed by Richard Foreman. Richard Foreman artistic director, Judson Kniffen associate artistic director.

PAGEANT. Devised, designed and directed by Ken Nintzel. June 18, 2000. Lighting, Owen Hughes. With Darren Anderson, Stacy Dawson, Ruthie Epstein, Jesse Hawley, Beth Kurkjian, David Neumann, Beth Portnoy, Holly Twining, Bryan Webster.

BAAL. By Bertolt Brecht. July 20, 2000. Directed by Josh Chambers. With Noel Allain, Jason Berenstein, Alec Brewster, Ethan Cole, Clayton Dowty, Timothy Fannon, Justin Fayne, Bob Hendren, Sue Kessler, Dara Lewis, Coleman O'Toole, Kara Martinez-Weilding.

THE BLUEPRINT SERIES. Curated by Owen Hughes and Judson Kniffen. August 9, 2000. Kaspar. By Jyana S. Gregory; The Baddest Natashas. By Tony Torn; Cold Pole, or Boxed Compass in the Yellow Sea. By Ryan Brown, Franklin Laviola and Brian Walsh.

NOW THAT COMMUNISM IS DEAD MY LIFE FEELS EMPTY! Written, directed, designed and scored by Richard Foreman. January 4, 2001. Costumes, Sarah Beadle, Laura Angotti. With Jay Smith, Tony Torn.

THE SEVEN MINUTE SERIES. Curated by Owen Hughes and Brian PJ Cronin. May 24, 2001. With works by Jillian Mcdonald, Evan Cabnet, Jonas Oppenheim, Ryan Bronz, Jonathan Jacobs, Brian PJ Cronin, Padraic Lillis, Beth Kurkjian.

Pan Asian Repertory Theatre. Celebrates and provides opportunities for Asian American artists to perform under the highest professional standards and to create and promote plays by and about Asians and Asian Americans. Tisa Chang artistic/producing director.

RASHOMON. Written by Fay and Michael Kanin, based on novellas by Ryunosuke Akutagawa. March 15, 2001. Directed by Tisa Chang; scenery, Kaori Akazawa; costumes, Molly Reynolds; lighting, Victor En Yu Tan; sound, Shigeko Suga, Tom Matsusaka; fight choreography, Michael G. Chin. With Orville Mendoza, Ron Nakahara, Les J.N. Mau, Tom Matsusaka, Ken Park, Marcus Ho, Rosanne Ma, Shigeko Suga.

Performance Space 122. Exists to give artists of a wide range of experience a chance to develop their work and find an audience. Mark Russell executive/artistic director.

SURFACE TRANSIT. Written and performed by Sarah Jones. July 28, 2000. Directed by Gloria Feliciano; lighting, Frank DenDanto III; sound, Sarah Jones and Jimmie Lee.

HOWIE THE ROOKIE. By Mark O'Rowe. January 5, 2001. Directed by Mike Bradwell; scenery, Es Devlin; lighting, Simon Bennison. With Aidin Kelly, Karl Shiels.

THREE SECONDS IN THE KEY. By Deb Margolin. February 22, 2001. Directed by Lee Gundersheimer; choreography, Stormy Brandenberger; scenery, Samuel C. Tresler; costumes, Elizabeth Goodman; lighting, Frank DenDanto III; sound, Michael Kraskin. With Deb Margolin, Bennett Kirshner, E.L. Gibson, Chadwick Aharon Boseman, Ben Fox, Lee Gundersheimer, Christopher Goodrich, Aole T. Miller, Rocco Turso.

SHUT UP AND LOVE ME. Written and performed by Karen Finley. May 22, 2001. Lighting, Frank DenDanto III.

Playwrights Horizons New Theater Wing. Full productions of new works, in addition to the regular Off Broadway productions. Tim Sanford artistic director, Leslie Marcus managing director.

OTHER PEOPLE. By Christopher Shinn. October 22, 2000. Directed by Tim Farrell; scenery, Kyle Chepulis; costumes, Mimi O'Donnell; lighting, Andrew Hill; sound, Ken Travis. With Kate Blumberg, Neal Huff, Austin Lysy, Victor Slezak, Pete Starrett, Philip Tabor.

Primary Stages. Dedicated to new American plays by new American playwrights. Casey Childs artistic director, Margaret Chandler managing director, Janet Reed associate artistic director.

STRAIGHT AS A LINE. By Luis Alfaro. October 2, 2000. Directed by Jon Lawrence Rivera; scenery, Bob Phillips; lighting, Deborah Constantine; sound, Eric Shim. With James Sie, Natsuko Ohama.

KRISIT. By Y York. January 29, 2001. Directed by Melia Bensussen; scenery, James Noone, costumes, Claudia Stephens; lighting, Jeff Croiter; sound, Charles T. Brastow. With Scotty Bloch, Jessica Stone, Larry Pine.

NO NIGGERS, NO JEWS, NO DOGS. By John Henry Redwood. April 2, 2001. Directed by Israel Hicks; scenery, Michael Brown; costumes, Christine Field; lighting, Ann G. Wrightson; sound Eileen Tague. With Charis M. Wilson, Rayme Cornell, Elizabeth Van Dyke, Marcus Naylor, Jack Aaron, Adrienne Carter.

Signature Theatre Company. Dedicated to the exploration of a playwright's body of work. James Houghton founding artistic director, Bruce E. Whitacre managing director.

A LESSON BEFORE DYING. By Romulus Linney based on the novel by Ernest J. Gaines. September 18, 2000. Directed by Kent Thompson; scenery, Marjorie Bradley Kellogg; costumes, Alvin B. Perry; lighting, Jane Cox; sound, Don Tindall. With Stephen Bradbury,

Love and death: Andrew Weems in Peter Hall's version of William Shakespeare's Troilus and Cressida. *Photo: Ken Howard*

Signature Theatre Company 2000–2001 Season

Top: Estelle Parsons and Hallie Foote in The Last of the Thorntons. *Photo: Susan Johann*

Right: Isiah Whitlock Jr., Jamahl Marsh and Aaron Harpold in A Lesson Before Dying. *Photo: Susan Johann*

Right: Frank Converse, Gregg Edelman and Jeffrey Carlson in Thief River. *Photo: Susan Johann*

Left: Regina Taylor in Urban Zulu Mambo. *Photo: Susan Johann*

Aaron Harpold, Tracey A. Leigh, Jamahl Marsh, John Henry Redwood, Isiah Whitlock Jr., Beatrice Winde.

URBAN ZULU MAMBO. Conceived and performed by Regina Taylor; a collection of short works written by Kia Corthron, Suzan-Lori Parks, Ntozake Shange and Ms. Taylor. February 25, 2001. Directed by Henry Godinez; scenery, G.W. Mercier; costumes, Brenda Rousseau; lighting, Jane Cox; sound, Robert Kaplowitz; original music composed by Loren Toolajian.

THE LAST OF THE THORNTONS. By Horton Foote. December 3, 2000. Directed by James Houghton; scenery, Christine Jones; costumes, Elizabeth Hope Clancy; lighting, Michael Chybowski; sound, Kurt B. Kellenberger. With Mason Adams; Timothy Altmeyer, Hallie Foote, Mary Catherine Garrison, Michael Hadge, Jen Jones, Alice McLane, Estelle Parsons, Anne Pitoniak, Cherene Snow.

THIEF RIVER. By Lee Blessing. May 20, 2001. Directed by Mark Lamos; scenery, Marjorie Bradley Kellogg; costumes, Jess Goldstein; lighting, Pat Collins; music and sound, John Gromada; fight direction, B.H. Barry. With Jeffrey Carlson, Erik Sorensen, Neil Maffin, Greg Edelman, Remak Ramsay, Frank Converse.

Soho Rep. Dedicated to new American playwrights with a focus on works outside the mainstream. Daniel Aukin artistic director, Alexandra Conley executive director.

Summer Camp 6: GET IN. By Brad Fetzer. FAMILY, GENUS, SPECIES. By Emily Jenkins. VISIONS OF APOCALYPTIC DOOM. By Josh Ben Friedman. July 13–15, 2000. THE WORLD SPEED CARNIVAL. By Stephanie Fleischmann, directed by Will Pomerantz. July 20, 2000. MARGE. By Peter Morris, directed by Steve Cosson. July 27, 2000. DEAD RECKONING. By Amy Rebecca Boyce, directed by Jesse Berger. August 3, 2000. NEW CREATIONS. By teenage theater artists. August 6, 2000. ARCHIPELAGO. Conceived, written and performed by The Flying Machine. July 13–August 11, 2000.

CAT'S PAW. By Mac Wellman. December 21, 2000. Directed by Daniel Aukin; scenery and lighting, Kyle Chepulis; costumes, Robin Shane; additional lighting, Michael O'Connor; sound, Colin Hodges; music, Cynthia Hopkins. With Alicia Goranson, Ann Talman, Nancy Franklin, Laurie Williams.

STARS. By Francine Volpe. March 7, 2001. Directed by Linsay Firman; scenery, Blythe R. D. Quinlan; costumes, Meredith Benson; lighting, Matt Frey; sound, Eric Shim.

CAVEMAN. Written and directed by Richard Maxwell. April 25, 2001. Scenery and costumes, Stephanie Nelson; lighting, Eric Dyer; choreography/fight direction, Johanna S. Meyer. With Tory Vazquez, Lakpa Bhutia, Jim Fletcher.

BOXING 2000. Written and directed by Richard Maxwell. May 1, 2001. Scenery and costumes, Stephanie Nelson; lighting, Eric Dyer. With Lakpa Bhutia, Jim Fletcher, Gladys Pérez, Candido "Pito" Rivera, Alexander Ruiz, Chris Sullivan, Benjamin Tejeda, Robert Torres, Gary Wilmes.

Theatre for a New Audience (TFANA). Develops new productions of Shakespeare and classic drama. Jeffrey Horowitz artistic director, Theodore C. Rogers chairman of the board, M. Edgar Rosenblum executive director.

SAVED. By Edward Bond. February 25, 2001. Directed by Robert Woodruff; scenery, Douglas Stein; costumes, Catherine Zuber; lighting, David Weiner; sound, Leah Gelpe; composer, Douglas Wieselman. With Pete Starrett, Norbert Leo Butz, Terence Rigby, Amy Ryan, Randy Danson, Joey Kern, David Barlow.

TROILUS AND CRESSIDA. By William Shakespeare. April 15, 2001. Directed by Peter Hall; scenery, Douglas Stein; costumes, Martin Pakledinaz; lighting, Scott Zielinski; fight director, B.H. Barry; composer, Herschel Garfein. With Vivienne Benesch, Jordan Charney, Tony Church, David Conrad, Idris Elba, Philip Goodwin, Thomas M. Hammond, Earl Hindman, Cindy Katz, Nicholas Kepros, Joey Kern, Luke Kirby, Andrew Elvis Miller, Tricia Paoluccio, Lorenzo Pisoni, Frank Raiter, Terence Rigby, Michael Rogers, Tari Signor, Andrew Weems.

Theater for the New City. Developmental theater and new American experimental works. Crystal Field executive director.

BIOTECH. Written and directed by Crystal Field. August 5, 2000. Lyrics by Ms. Field; music composed and arranged by Joseph Vernon Banks; scenery, Walter Gurbo; sound, Joy Linscheid, David Nolan; costumes, Alessandra Nichols. With Alex Bartenieff, Luz Caban, Mary Cunningham, Steve DeLorenzo, Crystal Field, Cheryl Gadsden, Michael-David Gordon, Kishiko Hasegawa, Ashley Hymson, Jerry Jaffe, Terry Lee King, Jose "Pito" Luzunaris, Mark Marcante, Craig Meade, Jane Needleman, Flora Ortiz, Jessy Ortiz, Primy Rivera, Johanna Rhyns, Ofrit Shiran, Tiffany Smoak, Harmony S'On, Elizabeth Speck, Spondee, Angel Vasquez, Michael Vasquez, Venus Velazquez.

BRECHT ON BRECHT. Adapted by George Tabori from the writings of Bertolt Brecht. December 6, 2000. Directed by Jim Niesen and Jacques Levy; choreography, Sarah Adams; scenery, Ken Rothchild; costumes, Christianne Myers; lighting, Randy Glickman;. With Christian Brandjes, Heidi K. Eklund, Carolyn Fischer, Michael-David Gordon, Terry Greiss, Jack Lush, Barbara Mackenzie-Wood, Sven Miller, Patrena Murray, Damon Scranton..

SKETCHING UTOPIA. By Laurel Hessing. January 25, 2001. Directed by Crystal Field; scenery, Donald L. Brooks; lighting, Jon Andreakis; costumes, Terry Leong; music, Arthur Abrams. With Anthony Ames, Miles Angerson, India Blake, Kathryn Chilson, Carmine De Betta, Crystal Field, Enzo Gentile, Ian Gordon, Philip Hackett, Kishiko Hasegawa, Samara Kanegis, Terry Lee King, Timothy Lawrence, Victoria Linchon, Kevin Martin, Carmen Mathis, Craig Meade, Jane Needleman, Primy Rivera, Julian Rozzell, Bina Sharif, Elizabeth Speck, Angel Vasquez, Michael Vasquez.

IN THE JUNGLE OF THE CITY. By Bertolt Brecht, translated by Philip Boehm. May 2, 2001. Directed by Jim Niesen; choreography, Sarah Adams; scenery, Ken Rothchild; costumes, Christianne Myers, Matthew Gregory; lighting, Randy Glickman. With Christian Brandjes, Sven Miller, Terry Greiss, Patrena Murray, Michael-David Gordon, Jack Lush, Carolyn Fischer, Sarah Adams.

GLORIA. By Peter Hilton. October 5, 2000. Directed by Alexandra Ornitz; costumes, Christianne Myers; original music and sound, Robert Kaplowitz; lighting, Diane D. Fairchild; fight choreographer, David Dean Hastings. With Carrie Brewer, Kittson O'Neill, Bevin Kaye,

Et tu, Brute?: Alex Webb, Robert Richmond and Shirleyann Kaladjian in the Aquila Theatre Company's version of William Shakespeare's Julius Caesar. *Photo: Ken Howard*

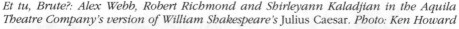

Judy Lewis, Barbara J. Spence, Jennifer Loia Alexander, Denise Alessandria Hurd, Alexandra Ornitz, Danya Steinfeld, Carey Van Driest.

The Vineyard Theatre. Multi-art chamber theater dedicated to the development of new plays and musicals, music-theater collaborations and innovative revivals. Douglas Aibel artistic director, Barbara Zinn Krieger executive director, Jeffrey Solis managing director.

STRANGER. By Craig Lucas. October 17, 2000. Directed by Mark Brokaw; scenery, Neil Patel; costumes, Jess Goldstein; lighting, Mark McCullough; music and sound, David Van Tieghem, Jill B.C. DuBoff. With Kyra Sedgwick, David Strathairn, David Harbour, Julianne Nicholson.

MORE LIES ABOUT JERZY. By Davey Holmes. January 21, 2001. Directed by Darko Tresnjak; scenery, Derek McLane; costumes, Linda Cho; lighting, Frances Aronson; sound, Laura Grace Brown. With Gretchen Egolf, Jared Harris, Daniel London, Lizbeth Mackay, Boris McGiver, Betty Miller, Portia Reiners, Martin Shakar, Adam Stein, Gary Wilmes.

ELI'S COMIN'. Music and Lyrics by Laura Nyro; created by Bruce Buschel and Diane Paulus. May 3, 2001. Directed by Diane Paulus; scenery, G.W. Mercier; costumes, Linda Cho; lighting, Jane Cox; sound, Brett Jarvis; orchestral arrangements, Diedre Murray. With Judy Kuhn, Mandy Gonzalez, Anika Noni Rose, Ronnell Bey, Wilson Jermaine Heredia.

The Women's Project and Productions. Nurtures, develops and produces plays written and directed by women. Julia Miles artistic director, Patricia Taylor managing director.

HARD FEELINGS. By Neena Beber. October 11, 2000. Directed by Maria Mileaf; scenery, Neil Patel; costumes, Katherine Roth; lighting, Russell H. Champa; sound, Eileen Tague. With Seana Kofoed, Guy Boyd, Kate Jennings Grant, Mary Fogarty, Pamela J. Gray.

LEAVING QUEENS. Book and lyrics by Kate Moira Ryan; music by Kim D. Sherman. March 1, 2001. Directed by Allison Narver; scenery Anita Stewart; costumes, Louisa Thompson; lighting, Jennifer Tipton. With Alexander Bonnin, Sean Dooley, Jim Jacobsen, Paul Niebanck, Cynthia Sophiea, Barbara Terrill, Alice Vienneau.

SAINT LUCY'S EYES. By Bridgette A. Wimberly. April 5, 2001. Directed by Billie Allen; scenery Beowulf Boritt; costumes, Alvin B. Perry; lighting, Jane Reisman; original music and sound, Michael Wimberly. With Ruby Dee, Toks Olagundoye, Willis Burks II, Sally A. Stewart.

O PIONEERS! By Willa Cather. Adaption and lyrics by Darrah Cloud. May 2, 2001. Directed by Richard Corley; music by Kim D. Sherman; scenery, Loy Arcenas; costumes, Murell Dean Horton; lighting, Dennis Parichy; sound, David A. Arnold. With Beth Barley, Corey Behnke, Todd Cerveris, Elliot Dash, Joe Domencic, Michael Thomas Holmes, Matt Hoverman, Grace Hsu, Gregory Jackson, Royden Mills, Evan Robertson, Erika Rolfsrud, Michele Tauber, Johnathan Uffelman.

Miscellaneous

IN THE ADDITIONAL LISTING of 2000–01 Off Off Broadway productions below, the names of the producing groups or theaters appear in CAPITAL LETTERS and the titles of the works in *italics*. This list consists largely of new or reconstituted works. It includes a few productions staged by groups that rented space from the more established organizations listed previously.

ABINGDON THEATRE COMPANY. *Little Fishes* by Steven Haworth. February 28, 2001. Directed by Kim T. Sharp; with Paul Barry, Frank J. O'Donnell, Nicholas Piper, John Tardibuono.

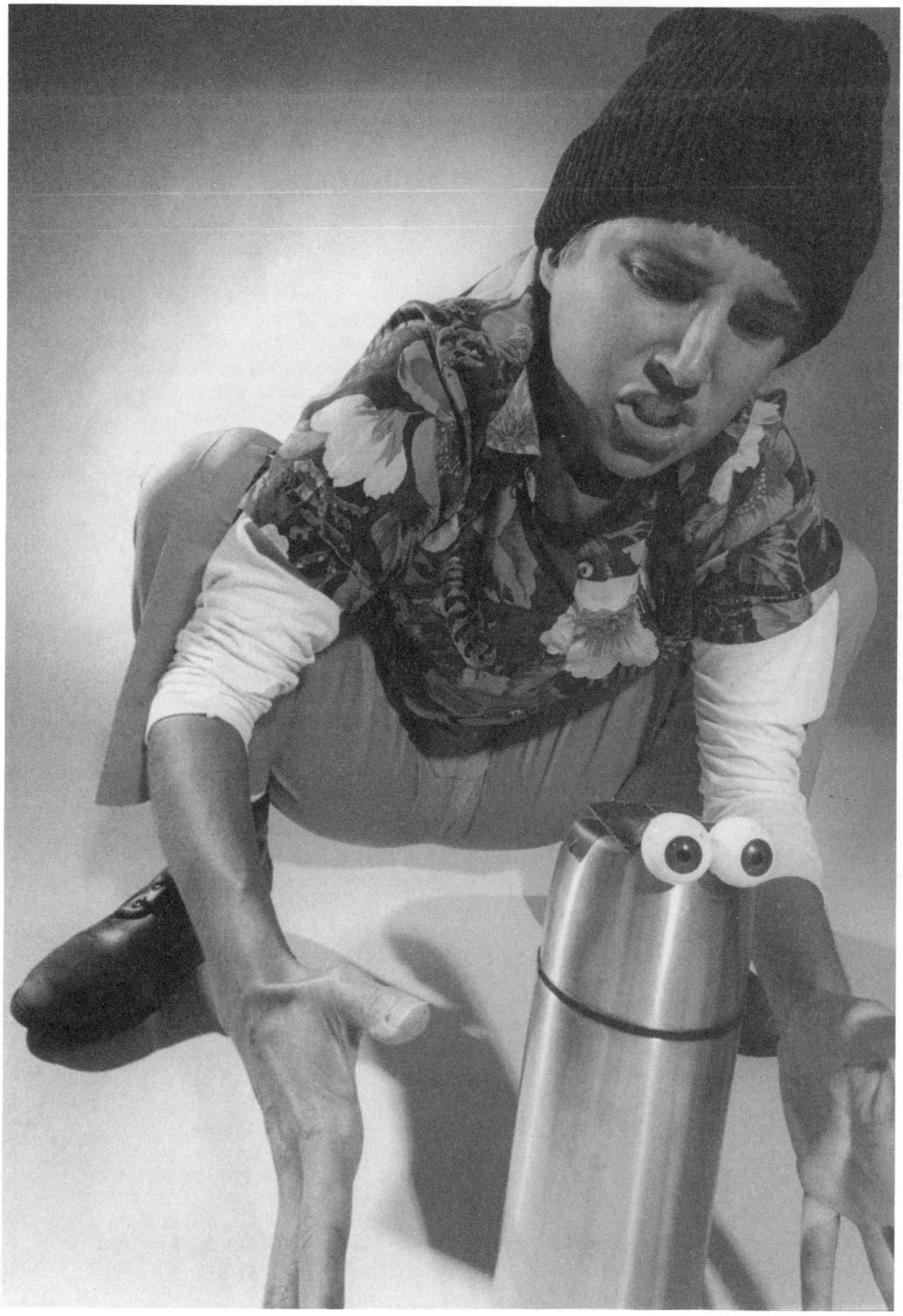

Going up: Susie Sokol in Elevator Repair Service's Highway to Tomorrow. *Photo: Greg Weiner*

THE ACTORS COMPANY THEATRE (TACT). *First Lady* by Katharine Dayton and George S. Kaufman. October 13, 2000. *The Admirable Crichton* by J.M. Barrie. January 12, 2001. *A Family Affair* adapted by Nick Dear. *The Apollo of Bellac* by Jean Giraudoux and *The Bald Soprano* by Eugene Ionesco. March 23, 2001. *Separate Tables* by Terence Rattigan. May 4, 2001.

ADOBE THEATRE COMPANY. *Orpheus and Eurydice* written and directed by Jeremy Dobrish. October 23, 2000. With Arthur Aulisi, Jeremy Brisiel, Vin Knight, Kathryn Langwell, Andrew Elvis Miller, Erin Quinn Purcell, Adam Smith, Jennifer Ward. *Hooray for Iceboy*. Created by Adobe Theatre Company. April 7, 2000. Directed by Jeremy Dobrish; with Arthur Aulisi, Frank Ensenberger, Arthur Halpern, Vin Knight, Erin Quinn Purcell, David Slivken.

AMERICAN GLOBE THEATRE. *Hamlet* by William Shakespeare. November 5, 2000. Directed by John Basil; with Michael Bachmann, Robert Chaney, Tim Cooper, Jonathan Dewberry, Kathleen Early, Scott Eck, Stanley Harrison, Elizabeth Keefe, Justin Lewis, Dan Matisa, H.T. Snowday, Graham Stevens, Rusty Tennant, Dennis Turney. *Hedda Gabler* by Henrik Ibsen. March 17, 2001. Directed by John Basil; with Richard Fay, Maureen Hayes, Melissa Hill, Elizabeth Keefe, Kelley McKinnon, David Munnell, Charles Tucker. *The Importance of Being Earnest* by Oscar Wilde. March 26, 2001. Directed by Nataniel Merchant; with Rick Forstmann, Peter Parks Husovsky, Julia Levo, Julia McLaughlin, Philip "Pip" Rogers, Kathryn Savannah, Anna Stone, David Wilcox.

AQUILA THEATRE COMPANY. *The Iliad: Book One* by Homer, translated by Stanley Lombardo. June 30, 2000. Directed by Robert Richmond; with Louis Butelli, Lisa Carter, David Caron, Anthony Cochrane, Mira Kingsley, Mark Pow, Lindsay Rae Taylor, Alex Web. *The Comedy of Errors* by William Shakespeare. June 29, 2000. Adapted and directed by Robert Richmond; with Marci Adilman, Louis Butelli, Lisa Carter, David Caron, Mira Kingsley, William Kwapy, Alex Web. *Cyrano de Bergerac* by Edmond Rostand. August 20, 2000. Directed and adapted by Robert Richmond; with Lisa Carter, Anthony Cochrane, Sean Fri, Alvaro Heinig, Jennie Israel, William Kwapy, Daniel Rappaport, Noah Trepanier. *Julius Caesar* by William Shakespeare. November 28, 2000. Directed by Robert Richmond; with Robert Richmond, Alex Webb, Shirleyann Kaladjian, David Caron, Jessica Perlmeter, Anthony Cochrane, Lisa Carter, Louis Butelli, Noah Trepanier.

ARCLIGHT THEATRE. *Bobbi Boland* by Nancy Hasty. March 1, 2001. Directed by Evan Bergman; with Nancy Hasty, Gregg Henry, Tanya Clarke, Holiday Segal, Byron Loyd, David Little, Rose McGuire.

AXIS COMPANY. *Crave* by Sarah Kane. November 11, 2000. Directed by Randy Sharp; with Brian Barnhart, David Guion, Kristin DiSpaltro, Deborah Harry.

BANK STREET THEATRE. UNITY FEST (PROGRAM B). June 24, 2000. *Cherry Reds* by Gary Garrison. Directed by Maggie Lally; with Lorna Ventura. *Hiding the Pink* by Mrinalini Kamath. Directed by Eddie Lew; with James Hay, Matthew Gorrek. *Something Akin to a Restoration* by Jim Fitzmorris. Directed by Dennis Smith; with Ian O'Donnell, Ivan Davila, Joanie Ellen, Gisele Richardson. *Red Wait* by Amy A. Kirk. Directed by Donna Jean Fogel; with Jenny Pringle, Bilgin Turker. *Too Much of Me* by James Magruder. Directed by Dennis Smith; with C. Richard Cranwell Jr., Ann Chandler, Tony Hamilton. *Beggar on Horseback* by George S. Kaufman and Marc Connelly. August 5, 2000. Directed by Dan Wackerman; with Ernesto Altamirano, Todd Allen Durkin, Alicia Minshew, Tara Sands, Robert Tyree. *Icarus* by Edwin Sanchez. December 3, 2000. Directed by Dennis Smith; with Ann Chandler, Ivan Davila, Matthew Gorrek, Tony Hamilton, Marlène Ramírez-Cancio. *Jig Saw* by Dawn Powell. March 31, 2001. Directed by Dan Wackerman; with Jeffrey Paul Bobrick, Diane Bradley, Terence Goodman, Jozie Hill, Prudence Wright Holmes, Mark Irish, Susan Jeffries, Constance Kane, Jessica Chandlee Smith, Fred Velde.

BAT THEATER COMPANY. *Baal* by Bertolt Brecht, translated by Peter Mellencamp. August 12, 2000. Directed by Jim Simpson; with Kate Benson, Joanie Ellen, Michael J.X.Gladis, Gordon Holmes, Andrew Ledyard, Alfredo Narciso, Jack O'Neill, Meredith Perlman, Tamar Schoenberg, Paul Siemens, Leah Smith, Kristin Steward, Siobhan Towey, Irene Walsh. *Sincerity Forever* (April 26, 2001) and *Cleveland* (May 10, 2001) by Mac Wellman. Directed by Laramie Dennis; with Kate Benson, Louis Cancelmi, Tim Cummings, Jeffrey Emerson, Daniel Gurian, Greg Keller, Nicole Kovacs, J.J. Lind, Lisa Louttit, Seleena Marie Harkness, Sam Marks, Cori Clark Nelson, Kristin Stewart, Beth Tapper, Siobhan Towey, Angela Tweed, Irene Walsh. *Ajax (por nobody)* by Alice Tuan. May 3, 2001. Directed by Jim Simpson; with Joanie Ellen, Sam Marks, Alfredo Narciso, Kristin Stewart, Siobhan Towey.

B.B. KING BLUES CLUB. *It Ain't Nothin' But The Blues* by Charles Bevel, Lita Gaithers, Randal Myler, Ron Taylor, Dan Wheetman based on an original idea by Ron Taylor. August 28, 2000. Directed by Randal Myler; with Cheryl Alexander, Charles Bevel, Carter Calvert, Debra Law, Michael Mandell, Gregory Porter, Charles Weldon.

BLUE HERON THEATRE. *Kings* by Christopher Logue based on Homer's *Iliad*. June 7, 2000. Directed by James Milton; with James Doherty, Michael T. Ringer. *Sacred Journey* by Matt Witten. October 5, 2000. Directed by Michael Warren Powell; with Gregory Zaragoza. *Autoeroticism in Detroit* by Steven Somkin. January 10, 2001. Directed by James B. Nicola; with Ariane Brandt, Colleen Clinton, Peter Parks Husovsky, Dennis Jordan, Jill Kotler, Stu Richel, J.R. Robinson. *The London Cuckolds* by Edward Ravenscroft. March 5, 2001. Adapted by John Byrne. Directed by Owen Thompson; with Jeff Gurner, Michael Daly, Eva Kaminsky, Jenny Deller, Michael Cone, Jerry Jerger. *Blood Orange* by David Wiener. April 11, 2001. Directed by Anders Cato; with Jonathan Hova, Julienne Hanzelka Kim, Ilene Kristen, Susan Pellegrino, Brian Sacca, Pablo T. Schreiber, Wendy vanden Heuvel. *Concertina's Rainbow* by Glyn O'Malley. May 9, 2001. Directed by Bob Gasper; with Mia Dillon, Jeffrey Plunkett. *The Shoebox of Ebbets Field* by Ross M. Berger. May 23, 2001. Directed by Hayley Finn.

CAP 21 THEATER. *The Immigrant* by Mark Harelik. September 19, 2000. Directed by Randal Myler; with Evan Pappas, Cass Morgan, Walter Charles, Jacqueline Antaramian. *Six Goumbas and a Wannabe* by Vincent M. Gogliormella. March 27, 2001. Directed by Thomas G. Waites; with George Bamford, David Cera, Dan Grimaldi, Sian Heder, Joe Iacovino, Tara Kapoor, Joe Maruzzo, Annie McGovern, Ernest Mingione, Kathrine Narducci, Sal Petraccione, Howard Spiegel, Charles E. Wallace.

CENTURY CENTER FOR THE PERFORMING ARTS. *Rosmersholm* by Henrik Ibsen. February 24, 2001. Directed by J.C. Compton; with William Broderick, Tamara Daniel, Bruce Edward Barton, Dean Harrison, David Jones, Kelly Overton. *The Lady From the Sea* by Henrik Ibsen. November 2, 2000. Directed by Alfred Christie; with Laurena Mullins, Jay Gould, Larry Petersen, Tina Jones, Steve Witting, Christopher Burns, Eleanor Madrinan. SUMMER FESTIVAL: OH, SHAW, DON'T BE A COWARD, GO WILDE! IBSEN'S WATCHING. *Heartbreak House* by George Bernard Shaw; directed by Alfred Christie; with Keir Dullea, Mia Dillon. *Major Barbara* by George Bernard Shaw. June 6, 2000. Directed by Marco Capalbo. *Mrs. Warren's Profession* by George Bernard Shaw. June 12, 2000. Directed by Sue Lawless; with Tammy Grimes. *Blithe Spirit* by Noël Coward. June 13, 2000. Directed by Alfred Christie; with Tammy Grimes. *Peer Gynt* (part I) by Henrik Ibsen. June 14, 2000. Directed by Alex Lippard. *Look After Lulu* by Noël Coward. June 19, 2000. Directed by Steve Ramshur. *Present Laughter* by Noël Coward. Directed by Emily Hill. *Peer Gynt* (part 2) by Henrik Ibsen. June 21, 2000. Directed by Alex Lippard. *Lady Windermere's Fan* by Oscar Wilde. June 26, 2000. Directed by Alex Lippard. *Salome* by Oscar Wilde. June 27, 2000. Directed by Joel Friedman. WOMEN WONDERS: A FESTIVAL OF PLAYS BY AMERICAN WOMEN PLAYWRIGHTS. June 6–28, 2000. Directed by Alfred Christie. *The Autumn Garden* by Lillian Hellman; with Carolyn Younger, Sylvia Gassell, Clement Fowler, Reno Roop. *Look Homeward, Angel* by Ketti Frings, based on a novel by Thomas Wolfe; with Marilyn Rockafellow, Bo Foxworth, Lea Tolub, Serna Berne, Christian Thom. *A Raisin in the Sun* by Lorraine Hansberry; with Gerre Samuels, Ato Essandoh, Donovan McKnight. *Trifles* and *Suppressed Desires* by Susan Glaspell; with Judith Light, Peter Von Berg, Julia Prud'homme, Mark Hofmaier, Bo Foxworth.

CHASHAMA THEATER. *As You Like It* by William Shakespeare. October 24, 2000. Directed and designed by Erica Schmidt; with Johnny Giacalone, Angela Goethals, Lethia Nall, Lorenzo Pisoni, Drew Cortese, Molly Ward. *Resistance* by Hanon Rezikov. March 10, 2001. Directed by Judith Malina; with Johnson Anthony, Joanie Fritz-Zosike, Jerry Goralnick, Robert Hieger, Mattias Kraemer, Judith Malina, Lois Kagan Mingus, Craig Pertiz, Rob Schmidt, Tom Walker.

CHERRY LANE ALTERNATIVE MENTOR PROJECT. *Blood Orange* by David Wiener (David Henry Hwang, mentor). April 11–21, 2001. Directed by Anders Cato; with Matt Bohmer and Wendy vanden Heuvel. *Concertina's Rainbow* by Glyn O'Malley (Alfred Uhry, mentor). May 9–19, 2001. Directed by Bob Gasper; with Mia Dillon and Jeffrey Plunkett. *The Shoebox of Ebbets Field* by Ross M. Berger (Michael Weller, mentor). May 23–June 2, 2001 Directed by Hayley Finn.

CHERRY LANE THEATRE. *Dead Reckoning* by Gary Winter. Directed by Hayley Finn; with Rosemarie DeWitt, Kevin Patrick Dowling, Crispin Freeman, Margaret Ritchie, Daniel Serafini-Sauli, Chime Serra. *50 Minutes With Harriet & Phillis* created and performed by Margo Jefferson and Francesca Harper. February 15, 2001. *Freedom*. Written and directed by Chime Serra. August

30, 2001. With Ron Faber, Erika Malone, Robert Mobley, Chime Serra. *When It's Cocktail Time in Cuba* by Rogelio Martinez. November 30, 2001. Directed by Michael John Garcés; with Gerry Bamman, Maggie Bofill, Chris De Oni, Erin Hill, Oscar Isaac, Lourdes Martin, Yul Vazquez.

CLARK STUDIO THEATRE. *The St. Nicola Cycle: Pusong Babae* by Linda Faigao-Hall; directed by Gail Noppe-Brandon; with Lydia Gaston, Arthur T. Acuna, Roxanne Baisas, Ron Trenouth. *Double-Cross* written and directed Gail Noppe-Brandon. November 5, 2000. With Susan Peters, June Squibb, Jose M. Aviles.

CLEMENTE SOTO VELEZ CULTURAL CENTER. *Henry IV* by William Shakespeare. October 27, 2000. Directed by Bradford Brown; with Ben Killberg, Michael Poignand. *Theater of Light.* Conceived and directed by Rudi Stern. February 6, 2001. *The Queen of the Silver Screen.* Book, music and lyrics by Daniel Lanning. April 12, 2001. Directed by Bill Gile; with Holly Faris.

COMMON BASIS THEATRE. *Will Mr. Merriwether Return From Memphis?* By Tennessee Williams. May 5, 2001. Directed by Dan Isaac; with Marcia Haufrecht, Miranda Black, Janet Ward, Linda Creamer, Janet Girardeau, Marie Vassallo.

CONNELLY THEATRE. *Romeo and Juliet* by William Shakespeare. June 11, 2000. Directed by Gregory Wolfe; with Gregory Sherman, Monique Vukovic, Mason Pettit, Tom Shillue, Anna Cody, Jennifer Carta, Gary Desbien. *When Real Life Begins.* By Karen Sunde. September 13, 2000. Directed by Ken Marini; with Raye Lankford. *What You Will* score by Rusty Magee and Andrew Sherman. April 5, 2001. Directed by Gregory Wolfe; with Mason Pettit, Margaret Nichols, Rusty Magee, Tom Shillue, Jason Cicci, Brandy Zarle, Ron McClary, John Roque, Craig Pearlberg, Julie Dingman. *The Elephant Man* by Bernard Pomerance. October 11, 2000. Directed by David Travis; with Timothy McCracken, Tony Ward, Jamie Jones, Jeff Burchfield, Nina Hellman, Danny Dyer, Glenn Peters, Angus Hepburn, Hillary Keegin. CHEKHOV NOW FESTIVAL: November 1–16, 2000. *The Madman* by Anton Chekhov; adapted by Ron Fitzgerald; directed by Peter Campbell. *Revolution to Disillusionment: Russian Music After Chekhov*, Alan Moverman and friends featuring Catherine Gallant. *The Foulest of All Creatures* by Anton Chekhov; adapted and directed by David Gochfeld. *Salesman* an original work by Dmitry Lipkin; directed by Adam Melnick. *In the Widow's Garden* adapted from *The Student* by Courtney Baron; directed by Carl Forsman. *The Three Sisters* by Anton Chekhov; directed by Steven McElroy. *The Beginning of No* adapted from *Anna on the Neck* by Cusi Cram; directed by Shilarna Stokes. *The Enemies* by Anton Chekhov; adapted and directed by Alla Kigel. *Gull* adapted from *The Seagull* by Anton Chekhov; created and directed by Ellen Beckerman and company. *Hello Meatman* adapted from *Murder* by Leah Ryan; directed by Tim Moore. *How to Insult Your True Love* music and lyrics by Burton Sternthal; directed by Howard Berkowitz. *Ionych* by Anton Chekhov; adapted and directed by Lise Liepman. *To Kill Charlotte* adapted from *Ivanov*; directed by Slava Stepnov.

CURRICAN THEATER. *Big Cactus* by David T. King. September 21, 2000. Directed by Victoria Pero; with Anthony DiMaria, Irene Glezos, Nick Gomez, Fred Burrell, Mark Hofmaier. *Roberto Zucco* by Bernard Marie Koltes. October 13, 2000. Directed by Daniel Safer; original musical score, Douglas Wagner; with Peter Bisgaier, Emmitt George, Wendy Allegant, Laura Avery, Justin Barrett, Jessman Evans, John McCausland, Cecil Mackinnon, Kevin Mambo, Fred Tietz, Raina Von Waldenberg.

DANCE THEATRE WORKSHOP. *Tabletop* by Rob Ackerman. Directed by Constance Grappo; with Harvy Blanks, Jeremy Webb, Dean Nolen, Jack Koenig, Elizabeth Hanly Rice, Rob Bartlett. July 11, 2000. (See listing in Plays Produced Off Broadway section.)

DIXON PLACE. *Hot! Celebration of Queer Culture.* Festival of lesbian and gay arts and entertainment. July 5–31, 2000. *The Propaganda Plays* by Micah Schraft. September 9, 2000. Directed by Trip Cullman; with Sheri Graubert, David Hornsby, Adrian La Tourelle, Tatyana Yassukovich. *Party Devil* written and performed by Ken Bullock. October 13, 2000. Directed by Eric Silberman. Original music by Roger Pauletta. *Breaker: An Aerial Fairie Tale* written, directed and choreographed by Chelsea Bacon. March 9, 2001. Additional direction, Patricia Buckley; with Katie Baldwin, K. Olness, Sabine Lathrop, Britt Nhi Sarah, Aurelia Thierree, Carla Van Vechten. *Tender: An Evening Of Songs, Situations and Shoes* written and performed by Scott Heron with original score by Chris Cochrane. April 12, 2000.

DON'T TELL MAMA. *Let Me Say This About That!* By Theresa Wozunk, CaSandra Brooks, Wende O'Reilly. October 3, 2000. Directed by Eliza Beckwith; with CaSandra Brooks, Wende O'Reilly.

DOUGLAS FAIRBANKS THEATRE. *It Ain't Over Till the First Lady Sings!* Conceived, written and directed by Bill Strauss and Elaina Newport. July 1, 2000. With the comedy troupe Capital Steps (Mike Carruthers, Andy Clemence, Janet Davidson Gordon, Toby Kemper, Mike Loomis, Elaina Newport, Linda Rose Payne, Ann Schmitt, Walter T. Smith, Bill Strauss, Mike Thornton, Mike Tilford, Brad Van Grack, Delores Williams, James Zemarel).

DUKE THEATER. *The In-Gathering* a musical by John Henry Redmond; music by Daryl Waters. September 21, 2000. Directed and choreographed by Hope Clarke; with Ann Duquesnay, Frederick Owens, Kimberly JaJuan, Dathan Williams, Janice Lorraine, Daryl Hall, Nancy Ringham, Rudy Robertson, Vinson German, Richard White, Ronald Wyche, Stacie Precia. *Excuse Me, I'm Talking* written and performed by Annie Korzen. Directed by Judy Chaikin. February 11, 2001.

DUPLEX CABARET THEATER. *The Glass Mendacity* (spoof of Tennessee Williams's best-known plays). October 26, 2000. Directed by Thomas Morrissey; with John Ellis, Harold Slazer, Jennifer Doctorovich, Tom Huston, Roslyn Cohn, Jessica Calvello, Joey Landwehr.

ELEVATOR REPAIR SERVICE. *Highway to Tomorrow*. Created by Elevator Repair Service. November 1, 2000. Directed by John Collins, Steve Bodow; with Paul Boocock, Rinne Groff, James Hannaham, Randolph Curtis Rand, Susie Sokol.

EXPANDED ARTS. *Poor Superman* by Brad Fraser. February 25, 2001. Directed by Joe Tantalo; with Ryan Harrington, Rob Iulo, Christina Wollerman, Ivy Cates, Anthony Cerbins, Rob Maitner.

FLATIRON PLAYHOUSE. *Auto-Trains, Fire Ants and Lesbians* written and performed by Michael Garin. November 8, 2000. Directed by Jeremy Dobrish.

FLORENCE GOULD HALL. *How To Explain The History Of Communism To Mental Patients* by Matéi Visniec. October 20, 2000. Directed by Florinel Fatulescu.

45 BLEECKER. *Game Show* by Jeffrey Finn and Bob Walton, based on an idea by Jeffrey Finn. October 25, 2000. Directed by Mark Waldrop; with Jeremy Ellison-Gladstone, Joel Blum, Brandon Williams, Cheryl Stern, Jeb Brown, Michael McGrath, Dana Lynn Mauro. *An Idiot Divine*. Written, composed and performed by Rinde Eckert. January 16, 2001. Directed by Ellen McLaughlin. *Cartas: Love Letters of a Portuguese Nun* a play based on *Les Lettres d'une Religieuse Portugaise*, translated and performed by Myriam Cyr. March 4, 2001. Directed by Lisa Forrell.

47TH STREET THEATRE. *The Flame Keeper* by Amos Kamil. July 6, 2000. Directed by Charles Goforth; with Lenny Mandel, Paul Whelihan.

FOUNDRY THEATRE. *And God Created Great Whales* conceived, composed and performed by Rinde Eckert. Directed by David Schweizer; with Nora Cole. June 8, 2000 (Dance Theatre Workshop); September 6, 2000 (45 Bleecker). *Lipstick Traces: A Secret History of the 20th Century* conceived and directed by Shawn Sides. May 10, 2001. Adapted by Kirk Lynn based on the book by Greil Marcus. Created by Rude Mechs.With Ean Sheehy, David Greenspan, Lana Lesley, James Urbaniak, T. Ryder Smith, Jason Liebrecht.

GERSHWIN HOTEL. *Why We Don't Bomb the Amish* written and performed by Casey Fraser. July 22, 2000. Directed by Darren Press.

GLORIA MADDOX THEATRE. *Sweeney Todd: The Demon Barber Of Fleet Street* by C.G. Bond. September 20, 2000. Directed by Marc Geller; with Edwin Sean Patterson, Zoey O'Toole, David Paterson, J.M. McDonough, Charlie Romanelli, Ellen Lindsay, Tom Kulesa, Mary Beth Twisdale, Mike Murphy, Gabe Hernandez. *Barking Sharks* by Israel Horovitz. February 1, 2001. Directed by Terry Schreiber; with Dennis Anderson, Alexandra Westmore, Rob Dodd, Bob Rogerson, J.M. McDonough, Quinn Lemley, Jerry Rago, Mary Beth Kowalski-Twisdale, Jason Starr, Gib Von Bach.

GORILLA REPERTORY THEATRE. *Twelfth Night* by William Shakespeare. June 23, 2000. Directed and designed by Christopher Carter Sanderson; with Michael Colby Jones, Katherine Gooch, Nick Janik, Doron Toister, Julie Thaxter-Gourlay, Brian Olsen, Bruce Edward Barton, Russell Marcel. *Story of an Unknown Man* by Anton Chekhov. Adapted by Anthony Pennino. October 26, 2000. Directed by Christopher Carter Sanderson; with Tracy Appleton, Kina Bermudez, Michael Colby Jones, Sean Elias-Reyes, Matt Freeman, Clayton Hodges, Lynda Kennedy, Brian O'Sullivan, Greg Petroff, Tom Staggs, John Walsh. *Ubu is King!* Adapted and directed by Christopher Carter Sanderson from Alfred Jarry's *Ubu Roi*. *Macbeth* by William Shakespeare. May 13, 2001. Directed by Christopher Carter Sanderson.

GREENWICH STREET THEATER. *Syria, America* by Lance Crowfoot-Suede. June 8, 2000. Directed by Derek Jamison; with Bob Bucci, Dan Fotou, Josh Jonas, Peter Macklin, J.T. Patton, Matthew Rashid, Max Ryan, Michael Silva. *The "A" Word* by Latife Mardin. February 4, 2001. Directed by Melanie Martin Long; with Defne Halman, Becky London, Lara Agar Stoby, Jennifer Dorr White, Babs Winn.

GROVE STREET PLAYHOUSE. *Happy Anniversary* written and directed by Lou Reda. June 1, 2000. With Brett Berkeley, Alan Cove, Craig Cullinane, Joe Gulla, Carey Hyde, Darren Kendrick, Paul Stancato. *Dahling* by Nan Schmid. October 28, 2000. Directed by Gareth Hendee; with Nan Schmid, Elizabeth London, Janice O'Rourke, Lee Blair, Tracey Gilbert, Andrew Oswald, Andy Rapoport, Kathy Schmidt.

HEARTBEAT PRODUCTIONS. *W.E.B. Dubois, Prophet In Limbo* by Dan Snow and Alexa Kelly. February 22, 2001. Directed by Alexa Kelly; with Dan Snow, Brian Richardson.

HENRY STREET SETTLEMENT. GREAT BLACK ONE-ACTS 2000. July 5–August 6, 2000. Schedule included *Sugar Mouth Sam Don't Dance No More* by Don Evans; *Mojo* by Alice Childress; *First Militant Preacher* by Ben Caldwell; *Soul Gone Home* by Langston Hughes. Directed by Anderson Johnson; *The Past Is the Past* by Richard Wesley; *When The Chickens Came Home to Roost* by Laurence Holder; *Happy Ending* by Douglas Turner Ward; *Andrew* by Clay Goss. Directed by Clinton Turner Davis; *Pain In My Heart* by Rob Penny; *Meditation: A Family Affair* by Martie-Evans Charles; *Skin Trouble* by Amiri Baraka. Directed by Chuck Patterson. *Chain* by Pearl Cleage; *Fallen Angels* by Elois Beasly; *Every Goodbye Aint Gone* by Bill Harris. Directed by Imani. *A Son Come Home* by Ed Bullins; *A Message in Our Music* by James Gillard; *Sara Love, Sara Love* by Charles Fuller; *Life Agony* by Ron Milner. Directed by Ed Smith, Kenneth Green. With Alvin Alexis, Peggy Alston, Karamuu Kush, Kenneth Green, Ron Himes, Phillip Chance, Anderson Johnson, Ramon Moses, Lamman Rucker, Kim Yancy, Trazana Beverely, Claire Dorsey, Kim Weston-Moran, E. Patric, Andre Mtumi, Marjorie Johnson, Michael Chenevert, Perri Gaffney, Joyce Lee, Karen Malina White, Justin Lord, Ken Atkins, Shalinthia Miles, Kim Sullivan. *Beautiful Things* written and directed by Selaelo Maredi. April 27, 2001. With Selaelo Maredi, Ramadumetja Rasebotsa.

HENSON INTERNATIONAL FESTIVAL OF PUPPET THEATER. *The Far Side of the Moon* (Canada) written, directed and performed by Robert Lepage. September 7, 2001 at the Public Theater (Newman). *Street of Blood* (Canada) by Ronnie Burket. September 6, 2001 at New York Theatre Workshop. *Stowaways* (France) by Philippe Genty. September 19, 2001 at the Joyce Theater. *Gustaf and His Ensemble* (Germany) by Albrecht Roser. September 6, 2001 at the Public Theater (Shiva). *Snuffhouse Dustlouse* (United Kingdom) by Faulty Optic. September 6, 2001 at PS 122. *Salome* (New York) by Hanne Tierney. September 7, 2001 at Danspace Project. *A Prelude to Faust* (Minneapolis) by Michael Sommers. September 6, 2001 at Here Arts Center (Mainstage). *Women's Songs* (Russia) by White Goat, Victor Plotnikov, Natasha Tsvetkova. September 7, 2001 at Here Arts Center. *Psyche* (New York) by Ralph Lee and the Mettawee River Theatre Company. September 6, 2001 at the Kitchen. *Hunchback* (Chicago) by Redmoon Theater. September 12, 2001 at the Public Theater (Newman). *Hand Shadows/Short Stories* (India/Peru) by Prasanna Rad/Teatro Hugo and Ines. September 13, 2001 at the Public Theater (Shiva). *Night Behind the Windows* (Los Angeles/New York) by Janie Greiser & Co. September 12, 2001 at La MaMa ETC (Annex). *Assemblage of Souls* (New York) by the Cosmic Bicycle Theatre, Jonathan Edward Cross. September 13, 2001 at Here Arts Center (Mainstage). *Two Tales From Japan* (Japan) by Otome Bunraku. September 13, 2001 at Japan Society. *Theater of the Ears* (France/United States) by Valère Novarina/ Allen S. Weiss/Zaven Paré. September 13, 2001 at La MaMa ETC (Little Theater). *Echo Trace* (Orlando) by Heather Henson. September 21, 2001 at Here Arts Center (Mainstage). *Millennium Autopsy* (Hong Kong) by Tang Shu-Wing. September 20, 2001 at the Public Theater (Newman). *The Girl Who Waters Basil and the Nosy Prince* (Cuba) by Teatro De Las Estaciones. September 20, 2001 at the Public Theater (Shiva). *Everyday Uses for Sight: Nos. 3 and 7* (New York) by Dan Hurlin. September 20, 2001 at The Kitchen. *Three Tales by Poe/Der Signal* (New Haven) by Puppetsweat. September 19, 2001 at La Mama, E.T.C. *Theater of Light* (New York) by Rudi Stern. September 12, 2001 at La MaMa, ETC (Annex). *Showcase Artists* (United States and International) by Late Night Cabaret. September 8, 2001 at P.S. 122.

HERE ARTS CENTER. *Stage Door* by Edna Ferber and George S. Kaufman. February 8, 2001. Directed by Emma Griffin; with Maria Striar, Linda Donald, Tonya Canada, Christina Kirk, Sheila Mitchell, Billie James, Ryan Shogren, Liissa Yonker, Suzi Takahashi, Yuri Skujins. *Possessed* by

Fyodor Dostoevsky, adapted by Robert Lyons and Kristin Marting. April 1, 2001. Directed and choreographed by Kristin Marting; with Paul Boocock, Mariana Newhard, Thomas Shaw, Richard Toth, Molly Ward, Cezar Williams. *Communications from a Cockroach: Archy and the Underside* by Don Marquis, adapted, directed and designed by Ralph Lee. May 6, 2001. With George Drance, Tom Marion, Margi Sharp, Sam Zuckerman. *The Right Way to Sue* by Ellen Melaver. May 21, 2001. Directed by Anne Kauffman; with Kelly AuCoin, Stephanie Brooke, Robert English, TR Knight, Caitlin Miller, Jennifer Morris. *Orestes* by Euripides, adapted by Charles L. Mee. May 27, 2001. Directed by Ellen Beckerman; with Josh Conklin, James Saidy, Margot Ebling and the voices of C. Andrew Bauer, Shawn Fagan, Bray Poor.

HOMEGROWN THEATRE. *Memorial Days* by John Attanas. August 12, 2000. Directed by John Gaines; with Kate Downing, Glen Williamson, Cory Bonvillain, Karen Krantz, T.J. Mannix, Brian Patrick Mooney, Melissa Wolff, Jensen Wheeler. *The First Jewish Boy in the Ku Klux Klan* written and directed by Lionel Kranitz. January 29, 2001. With Mary Round, Richard Springle, Peter Stadlen, Brad Surosky.

HUDSON GUILD THEATRE. *Off The Meter* by Peter Zablotsky. June 22, 2000. Directed by John Ahlers; with David Blackman, Kent C. Jackman, Gary Lowery, Tim Miller. *That Ilk* by Nancy Dean. September 17, 2000. Directed by Jere Jacob; with Kathleen Garrett, Steven Gibbons, Susan Izatt, Sandra Kazan, Annie Montgomery, James Nugent, Loria Parker, Jennifer Sternberg.

HYPOTHETICAL THEATRE COMPANY. *Buying Time* by Michael Weller. November 5, 2000. Directed by Amy Feinberg; with Patrick Boll, Mark H. Dold, Tibor Feldman, Monique Fowler, Jennifer Gibbs, Jeff Kronson, Lee Sellars, Evan Thompson, Jennifer Trimble, Chuck Montgomery. *Sitting Pretty* by Amy Rosenthal. February 14, 2001. Directed by Amy Feinberg; with Lina Roessler, Jo Hanney, Aviva Jane Carlin, Tanny McDonald, Nora Brown, John O'Creagh, Mark Jacoby, Dannah Chaifetz, Marilyn Bernard.

IRISH ARTS CENTER. *Red Roses and Petrol* by Joseph O'Connor. October 30, 2000. Directed by Neal Jones; with Dara Coleman, David Costelloe, Fiona Gallagher, Julie Hale, Aideen O'Kelly, Frank McCourt. *An Evening with Niall Toibin*. March 7–24, 2001. *Apres Match*. March 22–31, 2001. With Barry Murphy, Risteard Cooper, Gary Cooke. *Once a Man, Twice a Boy* written and performed by Joe Lucas. April 11, 2001. Directed by Mark W. Travis.

JANE STREET THEATRE. *Lifegame* created by Keith Johnstone and the Improbable Theater Company. September 28, 2000. Directed by Phelim McDermott, Lee Simpson, Julian Crouch; with Niall Ashdown, Angela Clerkin, Guy Dartnell, Stella Duffy, Phelim McDermott, Toby Park, Lee Simpson. *The Love Machine*. One-woman show with Sandra Bernhard. January 16, 2001. Mitch Kaplan musical director.

JEAN COCTEAU REPERTORY. *The Cradle Will Rock* by Marc Blitzstein. August 18, 2000. Directed by David Fuller; with Craig Smith, Harris Berlinsky, Elise Stone, Jason Crowl, Christopher Black, Angela Madden, Jolie Garrett, Tim Deak, Michael Sarabian, Kyra Himmelbaum, Taylor Bowyer, Jennifer Herzog. *The Merchant of Venice* by William Shakespeare. October 6, 2000. Directed by Eve Adamson. *Night and Day* by Tom Stoppard. December 1, 2000. Directed by Ernest Johns. *The Country Girl* by Clifford Odets. February 9, 2001. Directed by David Fuller. *The Misanthrope* by Molière. April 6, 2001. Translated and directed by Rod McLucas.

JEWISH THEATER OF NEW YORK. *The Diary of Adolf Eichmann* from the writings of Adolf Eichmann and other Nazi materials and documents of Josef Löwenerz. December 14, 2000. Adapted and directed by Tuvia Tenenbom; with Ron Paolillo.

JOHN HOUSEMAN STUDIO. *Michigan Impossible* written and performed by Robert Christophe. June 21, 2000. Directed Kim Waldauer.

JOHN MONTGOMERY THEATRE. *Icons and Outcasts* written and directed Suzanne Bachner. August 15, 2000. With Rebecca Doerr, Barbara Hentscher, Alex McCord, Trish Minskoff, Cara Pontillo, Felicia Scarangello, Liz Sullivan, Stacey Tomassone. *Circle* by Suzanne Bachner. March 15, 2001. Adaptation of Arthur Schnitzler's *La Ronde*. Directed by Trish Minskoff; with Bob Celli, Thaddeus Daniels, Felicia Scarangello, Judy Turkisher.

JOSE QUINTERO THEATRE. *Ernest* musical based on Oscar Wilde's *The Importance of Being Earnest* with book and lyrics by Gayden Wren. June 30. 2000. Directed by Gayden Wren; with Brian Bartley, Chris Bock, Simon Chaussé, Lorraine DeMan, Jay Haddad, Sara Elizabeth Holliday, Kathleen

McClafferty, Randy Noak, Annette Triquére. *The Good Thief* by Conor McPherson. March 11, 2001. Director, Carl Forsman; with Brian d'Arcy James. *Eula Mae's Beauty, Bait & Tackle* by Frank Blocker and Chuck Richards. April 9, 2001. Directed by Linda A. Patton; with Frank Blocker, Helen Bessette, Chuck Richards.

KEY THEATRE. *Boston Proper* by Edward Musto. October 12, 2000. Directed by Nathan Halvorson; with Angie Den Adel, Steven Camarillo, Tiffany May, Matt Mullin, Brian Ach.

THE KITCHEN. *Jennie Richee* by Mac Wellman. Directed by Bob McGrath; with Kati Agocs, Laura Avery, Melody Bates, Natily Blair, Jeff Breland, Helena Gronberg, Phoebe Jonas, Aris Mejias, Esra Padgett, Pamela Samuelson, Stephanie Sanditz, Fred Tietz, David Turley, Malinda Walford, Daniel Zippi.

KRAINE THEATER. *Work=Pain=Success* written and performed by Harry Prichett. September 27, 2000. Directed by Anna Ivara.

LABYRINTH THEATER COMPANY. *The Trail of Her Inner Thigh* by Erin Cressida Wilson. April 3, 2001. Directed by John Gould Rubin; with Quincy Tyler Bernstine, Jennifer Hall, Laura Hughes, Gina Maria Paoli, Johnny Sánchez.

MANHATTAN ENSEMBLE THEATER. *The Idiot* by Fyodor Dostoevsky. February 22, 2001. Adapted and directed by David Fishelson; with Carl Bradford, Christian Conn, Gibson Frazier, Peter Goldfarb, Karl Herlinger, Roxanna Hope, John Kinsherf, Jerusha Klemperer, John Lenarz, Abigail Lopez, Tricia Norris, Kevin Orton, Triney Sandoval, April Sweeney, Angela Vitale.

MAP PENTHOUSE. *Psycho/Dramas* conceived and directed by Chuck Noell. November 29, 2000. With Jay Alvarez, Alex Bond, Lawrence C. Daly, Susan J. Jacks, Nancy Lipner, Dominic Marcus, Bill Tatum.

MA-YI THEATER COMPANY. *Middle Finger* by Han Ong. September 14, 2000. Directed by Loy Arcenas; with Michi Barall, Ramon De Ocampo, JoJo Gonzalez, Mia Katigbak, Seth Michael May, Orlando Pabatoy, Harvey Parr, Shawn Randall, Brian Webster, B. Martin Williams, Rebecca Wisocky, Ching Valdes-Aran, Marty Zentz.

MAZER THEATER. *Mamaleh!* Book, lyrics by Mitchell Uscher; music by Roy Singer. May 15, 2001. Directed by Mr. Uscher; with Sandra Hartman, Molly Stark, Jeanne Goodman, Diane Houghton, Deborah Boily.

MCGINN/CAZALE THEATRE. *Tamicanfly* by Scott Marshall Taylor. January 17, 2001. Directed by Ethan McSweeny; with Robert Walden, Chris Messina, Erica Leehrsen, Betsey Aidem, Michael Mastro. *The Tempest Project: An Experiment in Non-Traditional Casting* by William Shakespeare. March 7, 2001. Directed by Thomas A. Abbey, Alexandra Lopez, Keith Oncale, Rusty Tennant and Joanne Zipay; with Naomi Barr, Susan Beyer, Joyia D. Bradley, Milena Davila, Antonio del Rosario, Terre L. Holmes, Robert M. Jimenez, Abena Koomson, Lawrence Merritt, Jennifer Nadeau, Drucilla O'Brien, Jane Titus, Virginia Wing. *Code of the West.* Written and directed by Mark R. Giesser. March 24, 2001; with Linda Ewing, Mark McDonough, Elisabeth Zambetti. Transferred from Mint Theater.

MEFISTO THEATRE COMPANY. *Eat the Runt* by Avery Crozier. June 12, 2000. Directed by Peter Hawkins; with Kelli K. Barnett, Lora Chio, La Keith Hoskin, Katrishka King, Myles O'Connor, Weil Richmond, Curtis Mark Williams, Jama Williamson. *Miscast* by J.S. Staniloff. August 17, 2000. Directed by Jaret Christopher; with Kelli K. Barnett, Katrishka King, Andrew Robbins.

METROPOLITAN PLAYHOUSE. *The Woman* by William C. deMille. Adapted and directed by David Zarko; with Kristin Stewart, Russell Hamilton, David Heckel, Leo Bertelsen, Annette Previti, Tod Mason, Tom Staggs, Sam Kitchin, Ken Bolden, Mike Nowak.

MIDTOWN INTERNATIONAL THEATER FESTIVAL. August 9, 2000–September 3, 2000. Dozens of shows brought to New York from around the world. Shows were staged at the following locations: Common Basis Theatre, New Perspectives Theatre, Pantheon Theatre and Raw Space. *American Story* by Laurel Vartabedian, Bill Evans. *Barstool Words* by Josh Ben Friedman. *Cognomen* by Peter Galman. *Cultural Refugee* by Wednesday Kennedy. *Durang by the Dozen: No Guns, No Sofas*. Twelve short plays by Christopher Durang. *I Took Your Name* written and performed by Michael Howard Nathanson. *Icons and Outcasts* by Suzanne Bachner. *Java Jive* by Hank Meyerson. *Jihad* by Ann Chamberlin. Little Delusions: Three one-act plays. *The Lover* by Harold Pinter. *Marat/*

Sade by Peter Weiss. *A Memory Play* by Bob Stewart. *Pericles* by William Shakespeare. A SELECTION OF PLAYS BY GEORGE BERNARD SHAW: *How He Lied to Her Husband* and *The Music Cure*. Splash! 2000. Eight new short plays. *sTop-Less Go-Go Girls at the Troll Hole* by Charles Battersby. Three plays by Samuel Beckett: *A Piece of Monologue*, *Act Without Words II* and *Not I*. *The Women in My Soul* by Owen Robertson, Michael David Brown.

MINT SPACE. *Macbeth* by William Shakespeare. July 31, 2000. Directed by Rebecca Patterson; with Virginia Baeta, Sheila Lynn Buckley, Aysan Çekik, Heather Grayson, Jacqueline Gregg, Stacie Hirsch, Lisette Merenciana, Jina Oh, Karen Pruis, Ami Skukla, Katlan Walker, DeeAnn Weir, Tessa Zugmeyer. She Keeps Time (two one-act plays): *Come to Leave* by Allison Eve Zell; with Lethia Nall. *Pickling* by Suzan-Lori Parks; with Jaye Austin-Williams. Directed by Allison Eve Zell.

MUSICALS TONIGHT! *I Married an Angel*. Book by Lorenz Hart, music by Richard Rodgers. September 23, 2000. Director, Thomas Mills; musical director, Mark Hartman.

NADA SHOW WORLD. *When You Try to Save Your Life You Lose It* written and performed by Rahti Gorfien. June 15, 2000.

NATIONAL ASIAN AMERICAN THEATRE COMPANY. *The House of Bernarda Alba* by Federico García Lorca. December 1, 2000. Adapted and directed by Chay Yew; with Ching Valdes-Aran, Natsuko Ohama, Michi Barall, Eunice Wong, Kati Kuroda, Gusti Bogard, Jo Yang, Sophia Morae, Julienne Hanzelka Kim, Julyana Soelistyo.

NEW DIRECTIONS THEATER. *F-Stop* by Olga Humphrey. June 10, 2000. Directed by Eliza Beckwith; with Patricia Randell, Christopher Burns, Rebekka Grella, Vincent D'Arbouze, Heland Lee. *Random Harvest* by Richard Willett. June 25, 2000. Directed by Eliza Beckwith; with Patrick Welsh, Patricia Randell, Ann Talman, Jay Alvarez, Kate Downing, Jonathan Kandel. *Memorial Days* by John Attanas. August 21, 2000. Directed by John Gaines; with Kate Downing, Glen Williamson, Cory Bonvillain, Karen Krantz, T.J. Mannix, Brian Patrick Mooney, Melissa Wolff, Jensen Wheeler.

NEW 42ND STREET THEATER. *The Trials of Martin Guerre* by Frank Cossa. November 24, 2000. Directed by Mark Bloom; with Jeff Berry, Peter J. Coriaty, Eric Hanson, Joseph Kamal, H. Clark Kee, Rachael Lyerla, Susan Matus, Thomas McCann, Dudley Stone, Christopher Todd, Lorree True. *Antigravity's Crash Test Dummies*.Original concept by Duncan Pettigrew. May 18, 2001. Directed and choreographed by Christopher Harrison.

NEW YORK PERFORMANCE WORKS. *Where Everything is Everything* written and directed by Stephen Spoonamore. September 7, 2000. With Daisy Eagan, Paul Sparks. *Wrong Way Up* book, music and lyrics by Robert Whaley, Tom Grimaldi. October 26, 2000. Directed by Trent Jones.

OHIO THEATRE. *Eloise & Ray* by Stephanie Fleischmann. September 10, 2000. Directed Alexandra Aron; with Black-Eyed Susan, Chris Payne Gilbert, Maria Thayer. *Secret History* conceived and directed by Ping Chong. December 6, 2000. With Trinket Monsod, Vaimoana Niumeitolu, Hiromi Sakamoto, Tania Salmen, Patrick Ssenjovu, Cherry Lou Sy. *Machinal* by Sophie Treadwell. March 7, 2001. Directed by Ginevra Bull; with Jessica Claire, Richard Kohn, Alison Cimmet, Jacqueline Sydney, Jerry Della Salla, David Lapkin, Michael Doyle, Jack O'Neill, David B. Martin, Dina Comolli.

135. 3 (SHORT PLAYS) October 21, 2000. *Before Breakfast* by Eugene O'Neill, directed by Rip Torn; with Danae Torn. *Box* by Juliana Francis, directed by Tony Torn; with Funda Duyal. *Pandora's Box of Sweets* by Chay Costello, directed by Tony Torn; with Susan Tierney. *Funbox Times Square* conceived and directed by Mark Greenfield. February 21, 2001. With Corey Carthew, Lamar Davenport, Tom Day, Josh Dibb, Emily Doubilet, Don Downie, Carrie DuBois, Brie Eley, Layna Fisher, Mark Frankos, Jenni Graham, Lisa Hargus, Sue Hyon, Cerris Morgan-Moyer, Brian Simons, Nakia Savonne, Constance Tarbox, Mike Urdaneta, Ben Wilson, Jennifer Wineman.

PEARL THEATRE COMPANY. *Blithe Spirit* by Noël Coward. September 11, 2000. Directed by Stephen Hollis; with Elizabeth Ureneck, Joanne Camp, Doug Stender, Dominic Cuskern, Glynis Bell, Delphi Harrington, Hope Chernov. *Richard III* by William Shakespeare. November 13, 2000. Directed by Shepard Sobel; with Glynis Bell, Rachel Botchan, Matthew J. Cody, Dominic Cuskern, Dan Daily, Matthew Gray, Grant Hand, Robert Hand, Brent Harris, Albert Jones, Anna Minot, Christopher Moore, Paul Niebanck, Jonathan Earl Peck, Judith Roberts, Edward Seamon, David Toney. *The Cherry Orchard* by Anton Chekhov, translated by John Murrell. January 22, 2001. Directed by Joseph Hardy; with Joanne Camp, Rachel Botchan, Robert Hock, Dan Daily, Mimi Bilinski, Edward Seamon, John Wylie, Arnie Burton, Jennifer Lynn Thomas, Robin Leslie Brown,

Dominic Cuskern, Christopher Moore, Alex Roc. *A Will of His Own* by Jean-François Regnard. Translated by Michael Feingold. April 9, 2001. Directed by Russell Treyz; with Celeste Ciulla, Arnie Burton, Christopher Moore, John Wylie, Dominic Cuskern, Andrew Firda. *Andromache* by Jean Racine, translated by Earle Edgerton. May 7, 2001. Directed by Shepard Sobel.

PHIL BOSAKOWSKI THEATRE. *Spine* by Jessie McCormack. November 16, 2000. Directed by Craig Carlisle; with Jessie McCormack, Aliza Waksal. *The Doctor in Spite of Himself* by Molière. December 18, 2000. Adapted and directed by Owen Thompson. Translated by Guylaine Laperriere. With Gregory Couba, Lisa Ann Goldsmith, John Grace, David H. Hamilton.

PLAYERS THEATRE. *Boys Don't Wear Lipstick* written and perfomed by Brian Belovitch. October 22, 2000. Directed by Keith Greer.

PLAYHOUSE 91. *Straight-Jacket* written and directed by Richard Day. June 18, 2000. With Ron Matthews, John Littlefield, Jackie Hoffman, Carrie Preston, Mal Z. Lawrence, Adam Greer, Stevie Ray Dallimore.

PRESENT COMPANY THEATORIUM. *Valerie Shoots Andy* by Carson Kreitzer. March 1, 2001 . Directed by Randy White; with Lynne McCollough, Heather Grayson, Walter Magnuson, Jeff Burchfield. *Two Girls From Vermont* by John Kaufman. May 23, 2001. Directed by Liesl Tommy; with Harvey Bogen, Andy Bichler, Doug Brandt, Stephanie Goldman, Nathan Halvorson, Carolyn Humphrey, Tiffany May, Molly Mullin, Branden Joy Pospisil, Bob Casey, Richard Kent Green, Brent Smith.

PRODUCERS CLUB. *Michael's #1 Fan* written and directed by Frank J. Avella. November 8, 2000. With Kristi Elan Caplinger, Michael P. Ciminera, Jami Coogan, Jessica Faller, Christian W. Macchio, Jeanine Tolve, Brian Townes, Greta Thyssen. A Tandem of One-Acts: *Down the Loft* and *The Tanning Salon* by Patrick Hurley. February 17, 2001. Directed by Glyn O'Malley; with Donna Svennevick, Tony Moore, Ryohi Hirochi, Scott Miller, Courtney Bunch.

PROVINCETOWN PLAYHOUSE. *The Personal Equation* by Eugene O'Neill. August 10, 2000. Directed by Stephen Kennedy Murphy; with Ralph Waite, Daniel McDonald.

PULSE ENSEMBLE THEATRE. *Misalliance* by George Bernard Shaw. December 1, 2000. Directed by Ann Bowen; with Michael Gilpin, Maureen Hayes, Natalie Wilder, Bryan Grosbauer, Stephen Aloi, Juliehera DeStefano, Steve Abbruscato. *Towards Zero* by Agatha Christie. February 16, 2001. Directed by Alexa Kelly; with Juliehera DeStefano, Stephen Aloi, Marianne Matthews, Steve Abbruscato, Jo Ann Tolassi, Mar McClain Wilson, Adam Green. *King Lear* by William Shakespeare. May 25, 2001. Directed by Alexa Kelly. With Ed Schiff, Hanna Hayes, Michael Gilpin, Adam Green, Frank Episale, Carl Danielsen, Danielle Stilli, Francesca Marrone, Melanie McCarthy, Carlie McCarthy, Brian Linden, Glenn Stoops.

RATTLESTICK THEATRE. *See Bob Run* by Daniel MacIvor. May 24, 2001. Directed by Timothy P. Jones; with Susan O'Connor. *The Crumple Zone* by Buddy Thomas. June 28, 2000. Directed by Jason Moore; with Mario Cantone, Joshua Biton, Steve Mateo, Gerald Downey, Paul Pecorino. *Saved or Destroyed* by Harry Kondoleon. November 20, 2000. Directed by Craig Lucas; with Michi Barall, Scotty Bloch, Michael Doyle, David Greenspan, Julie Halston, Larry Pine, Ray Anthony Thomas. *Killers and Other Family* by Lucy Thurber. January 20, 2001. Directed by John Lawler; with Ana Reeder, Tessa Auberjonois, Dan Snook, Jason Weinberg.

SANFORD MEISNER THEATRE. *Wanderers* by Michael Rhodes. September 13, 2000. Directed by Keith Teller; with Mike Campion, Heather Dilly, Martha Millan, Paul Molnar, Elissa Piszel, Michael Rhodes, Caise Rode.

SANDE SHURIN THEATRE. *Last of the Red Hot Lovers* by Neil Simon. Directed by Christopher L. Bellis; with Dennis Paladino, Alicia Sedwick, Stacie Renna, Bobbi Michelle, Caryn Rosenthal. *A Moment Too Soon* by Paul Weinstein. September 15, 2000. Directed by Chris Pelzer.

78TH STREET THEATRE LAB. *Man in the Flying Lawn Chair* created and directed by Eric Nightengale. July 20, 2000. With Toby Wherry, Carey Cromelin, Monica Read, Kimberly Reiss, Troy W. Taber. *Wyoming* by Catherine Gillet. September 14, 2000. Directed by Eric Nightengale; with Marylouise Burke, Rosalyn Coleman, Camilla Enders, George R. Sheffrey. *Deer Season* by Pamela Cuming. October 19, 2000. Directed by Del Matthew Bigtree; with Debra Kay Anderson, Abra Bigham, George Brouillette, Delyn Hall, Keith Perry. *Boss Grady's Boys* by Sebastian Barry. March 25, 2001. Directed by Ina Marlowe; with William H. Andrews, Tom Toner, Margo Skinner, Kay Michaels, Alfred Cherry, Bob Sonderskov, Corliss Preston, Meghan Wolf. *Historic Times* by Andrew Case. May 13, 2001. Directed by Carolyn Rendell; with Richarda Abrams, Kate Cordero,

Livia Newman, Christian Pedersen, Scott C. Reeves, Jeremy Alan Richards, Keri Setaro, Zander Teller, Evan Zes. *Just As If* by Shelly Berc and Andrei Belgrader. May 15, 2001. Directed by Andrei Belgrader; with Joanna Glushak, Walker Jones, Michael Mags, Caroline Hall, Sergei Dreznin.

STORM THEATER COMPANY. *Money* by Edward Bulwer-Lytton. October 6, 2000. Directed by John S. Davies; with Peter Dobbins, Colleen Crawford, Laurence Drozd, Stephen Longan Day, Elizabeth Robey, Roger DeWitt, Ray Friedeck.

STUDIO THEATRE. *Santos & Santos* by Octavio Solis. July 18, 2000. Directed by Michael John Garcés; with Dacyl Acevedo, Arthur Acuña, David Anzuelo, Maite Bonilla, Jose Febus, Dorothea Harahan, Yvonne Jung, Jesse Ontiveros, Kaipo Schwab, Don Silva, Nilaja Sun, Manuel Terrón, Sturgis Warner.

TARGET MARGIN THEATRE. *Dido, Queen of Carthage*. By Christopher Marlowe. January 25, 2001. Directed by David Herskovits; with Nicole Halmos, Adrian LaTourelle, Greig Sargeant, Rinne Groff, William Badgett, Mary Neufeld, Abigail Savage, Rizwan Manji, Steven Rattazzi, Douglass Stewart. *Tamburlaine* by Christopher Marlowe. April 4, 2001. Presented in five parts. Evening 1: *Tamburlaine the Great* (Acts 1 & 2). Directed by James Hannaham. Evening 2: *Hexachlorapbene*. Directed by Yuri Skujins. Evening 3: *More Bloody Tales of Ruth*. Directed by James Rattazzi, Steven Rattazzi. Evening 4: *Three Fold World*. Directed by Susannah Gellert. Evening 5: *Pluto's Belles*. Directed by Hillary Specter.

THEATRE AT ST. CLEMENT'S. *Bloomer Girl* book by Sig Herzig and Fred Saidy; lyrics, E.Y. Harburg; music, Harold Arlen. August 31, 2000. Directed by Alisa Roost; with April Allen, John Anthony, Chris Boldon, MaryEllen Conroy, Mimi Ferraro, Heidi Flanagan, Jane Guyer, Meghan Maguire, Lenore Manzella, Amy McAlexander, David McMullin, Andrew Michalski, Kofi Mills, Greg Mills, Mary Murphy, PJ Nelson, David Reinhart, Tonianne Robinson, Amy Shure, Frank Stellato, Geoff Sullivan, Lee Winston, Leah Zimmerman. *The Vocal Lords* by Eric Winick. May 31, 2001. Directed by Floyd Rumohr; with Joseph Ragno, Philip Levy, Ethan James Duff, Fred Berman.

THEATER AT ST. PETER'S CHURCH. *Embers* by Catherine Gropper. January 22, 2001. Directed by Mark Bloom; with Salome Jens.

THEATRE 3. *Two From Ireland* by J.M. Synge. June 15, 2000. Directed by David Leidhold. *The Soul of an Intruder* by Steve Braunstein. August 22, 2000. Directed by Frank Cento; with Stephen Beach, Cliff Diamond, Sylvia Kelegian. *Rain From Heaven* by S.N. Behrman. November 9, 2000. Directed by Julie Hamberg; with Donna Jean Fogel, Jon Krupp, Wendell Laurent, Andrea Maulella, Nell Mooney, Bruce Ross, Jane Shepard, Richard Swan. *The Tempest* by William Shakepeare. May 5, 2001. Directed by Joanne Zipay; with Jane Titus, Hilary Ward, Antonio del Rosario, Dacyl Acevedo, Steven Fales, Michael Shattner, Suzanne Hayes, Peter Zazzali, Ivanna Cullinan, Bill Galarno, Joseph Primavera, Laurie Bannister-Colon, Christiana Blain, Lea C. Franklin, Jennifer Jonassen, Richard Kass, Michelle Kovacs, Angie Moore, Kevin Till.

30TH STREET THEATRE. *The Four Corners of Suburbia* by Elizabeth Puccini. September 22, 2000. Directed by Alan Langdon; with Emily Brannen, Danielle Langolis, Brian Letscher, Rick Silverman, Jamie Watkins, and Eddie Weiss.

TRIBECA PLAYHOUSE. *Dance Like a Man* by Mahesh Dattani. July 21, 2000. Directed by Lillete Dubey; with Suchitra Pillai, Joy Sengupta, Vijay Crishna, Lillete Dubey.

TRILOGY THEATRE. *Night Maneuver* by Howard Korder. June 4, 2000. Directed by Greg O'Donovan; with Brian Flanagan, Ed Nattenberg.

29TH STREET REP. *Charles Bukowski's South of No North* adapted and directed by Leo Farley and Jonathan Powers. September 20, 2000. With Stephen Payne, Tim Corcoran, Elizabeth Elkins, Moira MacDonald, Paula Ewin, Gordon Holmes, Charles Willey.

URBAN STAGES. *Mother Lolita* by Guillermo Reyes. November 21, 2000. Directed by T.L. Reilly; with Piter Fatttouche, Rana Kazkaz, Carlos Molina, Debora Rabbai, Caesar Samayoa, Matt Skollar, Brigitte Viellieu-Davis.

WESTBETH THEATRE CENTER. *Circle*. June 23, 3000. A one-man show with Eddie Izzard. *Jerusalem Syndrome* July 27, 2000. Written and performed by Marc Maron. Directed and developed by Kirsten Ames. *Lypsinka! The Boxed Set*. Created and performed by John Epperson. September 20, 2001. Directed by Kevin Malony.

WEST END THEATRE. *Stop Kiss* by Diana Son. May 3, 2001. Directed by Lee Brock, Michael Connors; with Polly Adams, Christina Denziger, Donna Jean Fogel, Jeremy Folmer, K. Lorrel Manning, Emory Van Cleve.

WINGS THEATRE COMPANY. *Cowboys!* book and lyrics by Clint Jefferies, music Paul L. Johnson. September 28, 2000. Directed by Jeffery Corrick; with John Lavin, Steve Hasley, Steven Baker, Andrew Phelps, Judy Kranz, Stephen Cabral, Daniel Carlton, Laura Sechelski, Jim Gaddis, Winnie the Wonder Horse. *Strange Bedfellows* by Clint Jefferies. May 3, 2001. Directed by Jeffery Corrick; with Daniel Carlton, Carol Nelson, Karen Stanion, Jym Winner.

WOMEN'S SHAKESPEARE COMPANY. *Rosencrantz and Guildenstern Are Dead* by Tom Stoppard. October 30, 2000. Directed by Brian PJ Cronin; with Missy Bonaguide, Cheryl Dennis, Gwyneth Dobson, Clayton Dowty, Sarah Gifford, Ginny Hack, Ellen Lee, Heather Mieko, Diane Neal, Kate Sandberg, Kelly Ann Sharman.

WORTH STREET THEATER COMPANY. *Isn't It Romantic* by Wendy Wasserstein. February 14, 2001. Directed by Jeff Cohen; with Maddie Corman, Susie Cover, Hillel Meltzer, Barbara Spiegel, Peter Van Wagner, Jennifer Bassey, Tom Wiggin, Adam Hirsch.

THE SEASON AROUND THE UNITED STATES

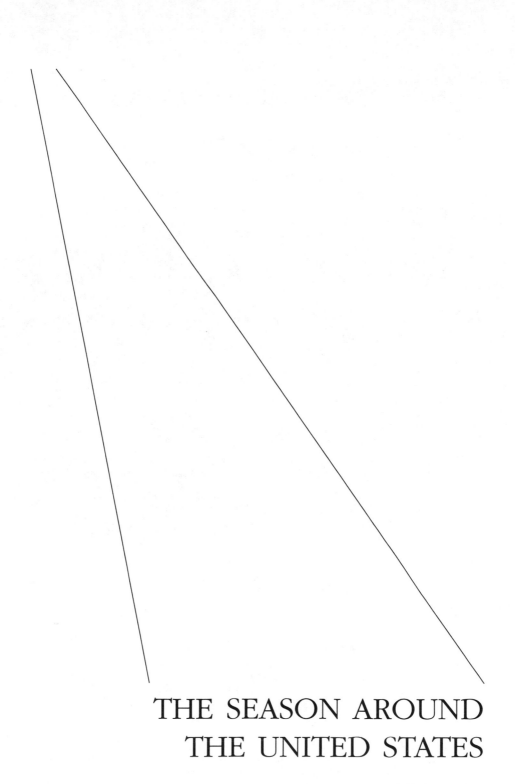

AMERICAN THEATRE CRITICS/STEINBERG NEW PLAY AWARD AND CITATIONS

○○○○○

A DIRECTORY OF NEW-PLAY PRODUCTIONS IN THE UNITED STATES

THE AMERICAN THEATRE CRITICS ASSOCIATION (ATCA) is the organization of drama critics in all media throughout the United States. One of the group's stated purposes is "To increase public awareness of the theater as a national resource." To this end, ATCA has annually cited outstanding new plays produced around the US, which were excerpted in our series beginning with the 1976–77 volume. As we begin our new policy of celebrating playwrights and playwriting in *Best Plays* essays, we offer essays on the recipients of the 2001 American Theatre Critics/Steinberg New Play Award and Citations. The ATCA/Steinberg New Play Award of $15,000 was awarded to Jane Martin for her play *Anton in Show Business*. ATCA/Steinberg New Play Citations were given to Charles L. Mee for *Big Love* and to August Wilson for *King Hedley II*. Citation honorees receive prizes of $5,000 each. The ATCA awards are funded by the Harold and Mimi Steinberg Charitable Trust, which supports theater throughout the United States with its charitable giving. The ATCA/Steinberg New Play Award and Citations are given in a ceremony at Actors Theatre of Louisville.

Two of the honored plays—*Big Love* and *Anton in Show Business*—premiered at the 2000 Humana Festival of New American Plays at Actors Theatre of Louisville. *King Hedley II* premiered in a co-production of the Pittsburgh Public Theater and the Seattle Repertory Theatre. Essays on *Anton in Show Business* and *Big Love*, by Michael Sommers (Newark *Star-Ledger*) and Michael Grossberg (Columbus *Dispatch*), respectively, follow this introduction. An essay on *King Hedley II*, by Christopher Rawson (*Pittsburgh Post-Gazette*), appears in the Best Plays of 2000–01 section of this volume—the play was honored by the editor for its Broadway production.

ATCA's eighth annual M. Elizabeth Osborn Award for an emerging playwright was voted to S.M. Shephard-Massat for *Waiting to be Invited*, produced by the Denver Center Theatre Company. Ms. Shephard-Massat received her award in a February luncheon at Sardi's in New York.

Of the new scripts nominated by ATCA members for the ATCA/Steinberg prizes, six were selected as finalists by the 2000–01 ATCA New Plays Committee before making their final citations. Other finalists included: *Fall* by Bridget Carpenter, produced by Trinity Repertory Company of Providence and the Playwrights Center of Minneapolis; *Glimmer, Glimmer and Shine* by Warren Leight, produced by Ensemble Theatre of Cincinnati; and *The Dead Eye Boy* by Angus MacLachlan, produced by Cincinnati Playhouse in the Park.

The process of selecting these outstanding plays is as follows: any American Theatre Critics Association member may nominate the first full professional production of a finished play (not a reading or an airing as a play-in-progress) during the calendar year under consideration. Nominated 2000 scripts were studied and discussed by the New Plays Committee chaired by Lawrence Bommer (*Chicago Tribune* and *Chicago Reader*) and comprising assistant chairman Alec Harvey (*Birmingham News*), Jackie Demaline (*Cincinnati Enquirer*), Marianne Evett (Cleveland *Plain Dealer*, retired), Ellen Foreman (*Theater News London*), Barbara Gross (freelance, *Washington Post*), Robert Hurwitt (*San Francisco Chronicle*), Elizabeth Maupin (*Orlando Sentinel*) and Herb Simpson (Rochester, N.Y., *City Newspaper*). These committee members made their choices on the basis of script rather than production. If the timing of nominations and openings prevents some works from being considered in any given year, they may be eligible for consideration the following year if they haven't since moved to New York.

2001 ATCA/Steinberg New Play Award

ANTON IN SHOW BUSINESS

By Jane Martin

○○○○○

Essay by Michael Sommers

> T-ANNE: Something called "regional theater" [. . .] once showed a lot of promise but has since degenerated into dying medieval fiefdoms and arrogant baronies producing small-cast comedies, cabaret musicals, mean-spirited new plays and the occasional deconstructed classic, which everybody hates.

A SATIRICAL FARCE that's playful in ways far beyond just the frisky sense of the word, Jane Martin's *Anton in Show Business* paints a colorful yet sharply edged canvas of the regional theater scene.

Rooting the comedy in an Anton Chekhov classic that practically everyone involved in the theater knows (let's hope!), Martin mocks the artistic bankruptcy of the current American stage while reflecting sympathetically upon the individual artist's desire for self-fulfillment.

The story is straightforward: Contrasting actresses—Lisabette, a sunny novice, Casey, a sardonic Off Off Broadway survivor, and Holly, a sexy TV power player—are respectively cast as Irina, Olga and Masha in a regional production of *The Three Sisters*.

Their subsequent experiences with successive directors, a hapless producer and a blandly idiotic corporate fund giver, among others, only mildly stretch the daily vicissitudes of making professional theater in America's regions today.

Martin's comedy provides plentiful laughter as the artists scramble along a rocky road towards their opening night. Yet it also offers up some thoughtful commentary regarding doing theater on the cusp of the millennium when other forms of entertainment have long since usurped its once dominant place in society.

Is it simply that television, film, video, sports and the internet are more accessible to a broader range of people than theater, or have its authors and producers lost touch with popular concerns?

Arts funning: Annette Helde and Saidah Errika Ekulona in Jane Martin's Anton in Show Business. *Photo: Richard Trigg*

One unwilling patron of the Texas theater company in the play bitterly complains of its artistic priorities, griping,

> JOE BOB MATTINGLY: Half the time, that stuff doesn't have a story, and it's been five years since you done one takes place in a kitchen, which is the kind all of us like. The rest of the time it's about how rich people is bad and Democrats is good and white people is stupid and homosexuals have more fun an' we should get rid of corporations an' eat grass an' then, by God, you wonder why you don't have a big audience!

Another character even questions the very essence of *Anton in Show Business*:

> JOBY: If doing plays doesn't speak to the culture, then examining why, or satirizing why, is kind of beating a dead horse—from the inside.

Perhaps so, but insiders will find Martin's comedy irresistible. Everyone toiling in the business loves plays about theater folk whether it's the Victorian troupers of *Trelawney of the "Wells"*, the flamboyant clan of *The Royal Family* or the backstage back-stabbers of *Noises Off*. Even weaker examples of the genre such as *Light Up the Sky* and *Moon Over Buffalo* provide some sense of the mad comradeship among artists that at times is the only thing getting the curtain up.

By design as well as content, *Anton in Show Business* is a deliciously theatrical play. In the first place, it is meant to happen upon a virtually bare stage with scenic bits brought on and costumes changed in whirlwind view of spectators. The unique magic of theater is invoked even as its relevance is questioned.

Secondly, apart from the sororal trio, a dozen other roles—male and female alike—are shared by another four actresses. That makes for more bravura theatricality and also speaks to regional theater's constant budget crunch. "We all have to play a lot of parts to make the whole thing economically viable," explains an omnipresent stage manager who annotates and abridges the story in an affectionate, effective Thornton Wilder homage.

Spanning the audience-performer gap, Martin even seats a would-be drama critic out in the auditorium, a prickly know-nothing who intermittently crashes through the fourth wall with unwelcome comments like the aforementioned "dead horse" remark.

Highlighting the fact that men still overwhelmingly hold down the majority of theater jobs, Martin's stage notes decree that all performers and avista scene changers/dressers must be women. That's an appropriate choice for a play aligned with *The Three Sisters*, whose protagonists embody the dependent status of women at the beginning of the last century.

Not incidentally, issues relating to women and power are central to *Anton in Show Business*. Directors are dismissed and artistic concepts are dictated by Holly, whose box office clout and personal financing outrank every other consideration in the forthcoming show. "I'm going to play Masha because it's the best part, and the most powerful person plays the best part," she explains. "That's one of Hollywood's Ten Commandments."

Holly's power, however, is derived from her bankable good looks, a "completely natural beauty" she has achieved after 17 separate surgical procedures. Later, when the three are fiercely exercising and one of them wonders why all actors constantly go to the gym, Holly replies, "Because it's a beauty contest, not a profession."

So there's a lot more going on here than a simple "bad theater" burlesque of Chekhov, although Martin fashions many a parallel between the Russian author's sisters and the actresses who portray them.

Like Irina, Lisabette is a clueless innocent who slowly wises up to life. Self-sacrificing Olga is essayed by Casey, a genuine artist who devotes herself to the stage at huge personal expense. And sitcom siren Holly not only seduces Masha's adulterous lover Vershinin offstage (with devastating results for that married actor) but at the comedy's end finds herself unable to get to the longed-for destination she so desperately desires—Hollywood.

Grounded at the airport by bad weather, a high school band performing in the terminal's distance, the three are inspired to enact Chekhov's concluding speeches for the sisters: "Meantime we must live; we must work, only work!" It's a lovely moment, an isolated bit of tenderness for people who can realize themselves only when they are acting.

With all those gears smoothly meshing together to create laughter and provoke thought, it's little wonder that *Anton in Show Business* proved such a hit at Actors Theatre of Louisville's Humana Festival of New American Plays in the spring of 2000. Nicely suited to the Bingham Theatre's in-the-round circumstances (a configuration once conceived as a blessing but is now often considered a curse of many regional houses), the premiere was confidently staged in a light-handed manner by Jon Jory.

The show marked Jory's swan song as longtime producing director of Actors Theatre of Louisville before departing for a university post. Commentators often speculate that Jory is closely related to the mysteriously pseudonymous author Jane Martin; possibly writing her stuff in league with different and varied collaborators. If so, the mordant wit that infuses this comedy suggests that ATL veteran Marsha Norman may have had her wicked hand in it.

Whether he wrote *Anton in Show Business* or simply staged its premiere in a delightfully breezy production, this stage-wise comedy certainly represents a devilish farewell gesture to the constitutional monarchy in Louisville that Jory governed so admirably for more than 30 years.

2001 ATCA/Steinberg New Play Citation

BIG LOVE

By Charles L. Mee

○○○○○

Essay by Michael Grossberg

> LYDIA: Why can't a man / be more like a woman? / Plainspoken and forthright, / honest and clear. / Able to process, / to deal with his feelings. / To speak from the heart / to say what he means. / Because if he can / I don't have a grudge / or something against him / we couldn't work out. / I think it's wrong / to make sweeping judgments / write off a whole sex / the way men do to women / we could talk to each other / person to person / get along with each other / then we could go deep / to what a man or a woman / really can be / deep down to the mysteries / of being alive / of knowing ourselves / to know what it is / to live life on earth

A SLAPSTICK FOOD FIGHT becomes a Dionysian bloodbath. A mass wedding prompts mass murder—but true love survives. Three sisters repeatedly throw themselves to the ground, while shouting their frustrations about the opposite sex. Later, their suitors similarly shout and leap, driven by urges as primordial as salmon swimming upstream to spawn.

What's not to love about *Big Love*? The war between the sexes is an age-old story. Yet, in updating one of the oldest extant Greek tragedies, Charles L. Mee has fashioned one of the freshest, funniest and wisest modern plays about sex, violence, gender, power, liberty and love.

Commissioned by Actors Theatre of Louisville to write a play about the millennium for the 24th Humana Festival of New American Plays, Mee was drawn to the roots of Western civilization—and to the first great tragic dramatist. He found his inspiration in Aeschylus's *The Suppliants*, the first part of a trilogy. Written 2,500 years ago, *The Suppliants* (also known as *The Suppliant Women*) focuses on the flight of the 50 daughters of Danaüs from arranged marriages and ends with them being granted asylum.

With the other two parts of the trilogy lost—of Aeschylus's 90 plays, only seven survive—Mee had ample license to imagine how the tale reached its legendary violent climax and how a contemporary update might shed new light on today's male-female relationships.

Mad love: Karenjune Sanchez (now K.J. Sanchez) and Carolyn Baeumler in Charles L. Mee's Big Love. *Photo: Richard Trigg*

Mee condenses the trilogy into a brisk 90-minute one-act set at a seaside Italian villa. Fleeing Greece by boat, the 50 sisters send three wedding-gowned representatives ashore to seek sanctuary. Three of their Greco-American suitors later arrive by helicopter, wearing jump suits over their tuxedos—projecting the aura of a military invasion from an imperial power. After impassioned debate, the sisters agree among themselves to kill the suitors on their wedding night.

Such a savagely contemporary work demands a nimble cast capable of expressing strong ideas and emotions while blending comedy and tragedy. At the Humana Festival, Actors Theatre's top-notch ensemble met the challenge with panache. Director Les Waters achieved the script's specified "over-the-top extremity," while leavening the manic energy with piercing moments of tenderness, wistfulness, hopelessness and hopefulness.

Karenjune Sanchez's (now known as K.J. Sanchez) spirited Thyona takes the lead in arguing that arranged marriage is the equivalent of rape. Carolyn Baeumler's Lydia balances Thyona's vengefulness with a sweet vulnerability and romantic optimism. Aimée Guillot played submissive Olympia, torn between her loyalty to her sisters and her desire for men.

Mark Zeisler's Constantine, T. Ryder Smith's Nikos and Jeff Jenkins's (now known as J. Matthew Jenkins) Oed were full of brio and swagger, later dropping their macho fronts to reveal touching primal doubts about their expected masculine roles. Humana veteran Fred Major played Piero, the wealthy villa owner, with ambivalent hospitality, while Broadway's Lauren Klein exhibited stoic wisdom and wry humor as Bella, Piero's mother.

Big Love couldn't have been bigger in the intimate Victor Jory Theatre, with the audience on three sides of the explosive action. Resident scenic designer Paul Owen painted the padded floor in a bright blue extending up the white-clouded back wall to suggest a surreal Mediterranean landscape. The major set piece was an antique bathtub filled with soapy water. From its opening image of Lydia stripping away her wedding dress to plunge into the tub, the Actors Theatre production seduced the audience and established a mood of emotional nakedness.

When Bella's gay grandson Giuliano (Tony Speciale) comes in with an armload of wedding gifts and begins talking about his elaborate Barbie and Ken collection, his libertarian affirmation that "everyone should be free to choose for themselves" broadens the theme to include same-sex relationships.

The wedding scene, the giddy peak of Jean Isaacs's brilliant choreography, fuses horror and hilarity. As globs of wedding cake fly, the ceremony disintegrates into a bacchanalian orgy. The women seduce the men to the floor—only to make war, not love.

All of the sisters carry out their pact except for Lydia, who makes love with Nikos until morning. Because of her refusal to kill her beloved, Lydia is put on trial, with Bella as the judge. In a merciful verdict that weighs justice against social harmony, Bella affirms that love is the highest law.

One of four full-length plays about sexual violence at the Humana Festival, *Big Love* tackles all of the big questions raised in recent decades about shifting gender roles and the difficulty of overcoming genetic programming or social conditioning. Without falling into today's instantly dated traps of male-bashing or political correctness, Mee honors the best arguments on both sides.

The playwright's reconstruction of Aeschylus doubles as a vaudeville-style deconstruction of modern feminist discourse. If the women's speeches give angry voice to our contemporary unease over lingering gender inequality, the men's speeches express a wounded self-esteem about a masculinity caught between ancient imperatives and modern ideals.

Given such speechifying, *Big Love* might well have come across as too wordy and didactic if Mee hadn't balanced it with such delightful physicality and striking imagery.

Just as Aeschylus's classic has endured because it found a core of human feelings about fundamental issues of conflict and community, *Big Love* fuses dramatic excitement, emotional intensity and a timeless spirit of philosophic inquiry.

With vivid scenes of body-slamming, dish-smashing, tomato-splatting and circular-saw-blade-throwing, the physical actions are as important to the comedy and drama as the poetic dialogue. Mee finds deft ways to ground even his wildest flights of verbal fancy in physicality. In a delightful early scene, Bella sorts a basket of tomatoes into good and (splat!) bad—a hilariously passive-aggressive metaphor for her monologue weighing the merits of her 13 sons (and, by extension, all men).

In its full-bodied embrace of the physical, the emotional and the intellectual, *Big Love* points the way to a 21st century American theater in which movement is as pivotal as words.

Mee also finds fresh ways to recast the bloody drama, philosophic monologues and choruses of Greek tragedy, while incorporating the stylish romantic comedy of Noël Coward, the slapstick seriousness of Samuel Beckett and his own collage style into a ruefully modern meditation on romantic relationships.

The playful theatricality, slapstick physicality, rhapsodic speeches, vaudeville shtik and musical interludes (from Felix Mendelssohn and Richard Wagner to Lesley Gore's "You Don't Own Me") make it easy to embrace the seriocomic piece—even with its bloodshed. To quote from the script instructions about what kind of music to choose to accompany an early scene, here is truly "a contemporary song about freedom and making one's own life."

Although only one couple survive the slaughter, that's enough for Mee to cautiously reaffirm the power of love and the possibility of community. Like Lydia, Mee hopes for a world "where people care for one another, where men are good to women, and there is not a men's history and a separate women's history but a human history where we are all together."

Just as in his adaptations of Aeschylus's *Agamemnon* and Euripides's *Orestes*, *The Bacchae* and *The Trojan Women*, Mee updates Greek tragedy with contemporary pop culture, an absurd sense of humor and a romanticism informed by historical realism. Through the archetypal prism of Greek drama, Mee filters his mournful awareness of the excesses of a refugee-strewn 20th century that gave in too easily to the totalitarian temptation to use force as a means to an end.

Big Love is an especially accessible example of recent reinterpretations of the classics, such as Peter Hall's 10-play adaptation of John Barton's *Tantalus* at the Denver Center Theatre Company. Perhaps the fracturing of modern mythologies—about masculinity, femininity, patriarchy and the authority of the nation-state—has prompted more thoughtful looks at the oldest Western plays for new answers.

A DIRECTORY OF NEW-PLAY PRODUCTIONS

○○○○○

Compiled by Joshua Crouthamel

PROFESSIONAL PRODUCTIONS JUNE 1, 2000–MAY 31, 2001 of new plays by a variety of resident companies around the United States. The companies supplied information on casts and credits, which are listed here in alphabetical order, by state, of 45 producing organizations. Date given is opening date. Most League of Resident Theatres (LORT) and other regularly producing Actors Equity groups were queried for this comprehensive directory. Active United States theater companies not included in this list either did not present new (or newly revised) scripts during the year under review or had not responded to our query by press time. Productions listed below are world premieres, United States premieres or new revisions. Theaters in the United States are encouraged to submit proposed listings of new works and new adaptations, in addition to the premieres indicated above, to the editor of the *Best Plays* series.

ALABAMA

Alabama Shakespeare Festival, Montgomery

Kent Thompson artistic director; Kevin K. Maifeld managing director

THE NEGRO OF PETER THE GREAT. By Carlyle Brown. March 6, 2001. Director, Kent Gash; scenery, Emily Beck; costumes, Elizabeth Novak; lighting, Liz Lee; sound, Bethany Tucker; dramaturg, Gwen Orel; fight choreography, John Paul Sheidler.

Ibrahim Petrovich Hannibal .... Johnny Lee Davenport
Korsakov .... Brian Kurlander
The French Officer .... John Triana
A French Soldier .... Michael J. Reilly
Countess Leonora .... Greta Lambert
Marquis Merville .... Paul Hebron
Count L. .... John Rensenhouse
Madame Dubois .... Sonja Lanzener
A Servant Maid .... Jen Faith Brown
The Servant, Ivan .... Scott Mann
The Czar, Peter the Great .... Philip Pleasants
Prince Alexander Menshikov .... Rodney Clark
Liza .... Susan Wands
Natalya Gavrilovna .... Jenny Wales
Gustav Adamych .... Jenny Wales
Gustav Afanasyevitch Rzhevsky .... John Rensenhouse
Tatyana Afanasyevna .... Sonja Lanzener
Valeryan .... Michael J. Reilly

Place: France; Saint Petersburg, Russia

ARIZONA

Arizona Theatre Company, Tucson

David Ira Goldstein artistic director; Jessica Andrews managing director

INVENTING VAN GOGH. By Steven Dietz. April 13, 2001. Director, David Ira Goldstein; scenery, Scott Weldin; costumes, Laura Crow; lighting, Rick Paulsen; sound, Brian Jerome Peterson; composer, Roberta Cason; dramaturg, Jennifer LeCarrell.

Dr. Jonas Miller;
Dr. Paul Gachet .... Peter Van Norden
Patrick Stone .... Lee Sellars
Rene Bouchard;
Paul Gauguin .... Tom Ramirez
Hallie Miller;
Marguerite Gachet .... Jennifer Erin Roberts
Vincent van Gogh .... Dan Donohue

Scene: The present, an abandoned warehouse in a large American city; and various moments from the late 1800s, France. One intermission.

California

American Conservatory Theater, San Francisco

Carey Perloff artistic director; Heather Kitchen managing director

HANS CHRISTIAN ANDERSEN. Music and lyrics by Frank Loesser, book by Sebastian Barry, based on the motion picture. August 31, 2000. Director and choreographer, Martha Clarke; music director and conductor, Constantine Kitsopoulos; orchestrations, Michael Starobin; music adaptor and arranger, Richard Peaslee; scenery, Robert Israel; costumes, Jane Greenwood; lighting, Paul Gallo; sound, Garth Hemphill; puppet creator, Roman Paska; dramaturg, Paul Walsh.

Hans Christian Andersen .... John Glover
Shadow .... Rob Besserer
Grandpappy .... George Hall
Father .... Jarlath Conroy
Mother; Farmer's Wife .... Karen Trott
Schoolmaster .... John Christopher Jones
Witch .... Jenny Sterlin
Young Lover; Jenny Lind;
the Nightingale .... Teri Dale Hansen
Ballerina .... Galina Alexandrova
Drummer Boy; Deacon;
Condemned Man .... Dashiell Eaves
Children .... Joey Browne Contreras, Katie Green, Julia Mattison, Ian Wolff
The Dog .... Hedley

Ensemble of Mermaids, Acrobats, Chimney Sweeps, Courtiers, and Townspeople: Felix Blaska, Marie-Christine Mouis, Alexandre Proia, Erica Stuart, Paola Styron, Shen Wei.

Vocal Ensemble: Lucinda Hitchcock Cone, Jackson Davis, Stephen Klum, Ian Knauer, Kathy McMillan.

THE MISANTHROPE. A new verse version by Constance Congdon of the original text by Molière. October 19, 2000. Director, Carey Perloff; scenery, Kate Edmunds; costumes, Beaver Bauer; lighting, Rui Rita; sound, Garth Hemphill; choreography, Francine Landes; dramaturg, Paul Walsh.

Alceste .... David Adkins
Philinte .... Gregory Wallace
Oronte .... Anthony Fusco
Célimène .... René Augesen
Eliante .... Kathleen Kaefer
Arsinoé .... Kimberly King
Acaste .... Patrick McNulty
Clitandre .... Chris Ferry
Basque .... Steven Anthony Jones
DuBois; Guard .... David Mendelsohn

Ensemble: Darrick Clayton, Tom Clyde, Meridith Crosley, Ian McConnel, Eryka Raines, Paul Silverman

Place: Célimène's house in Paris. One intermission.

ENRICO IV. A new adaptation by Richard Nelson of original text by Luigi Pirandello. March 29, 2001. Director, Carey Perloff; original music, David Lang; scenery, Ralph Funicello; costumes, Deborah Dryden; lighting, Peter Maradudin; sound, Garth Hemphill; fight choreography, Gregory Hoffman; dramaturg, Paul Walsh.

Young Servants .... Scott Asti
Samuel R. Gates
Harold .... Douglas Nolan
Ordulph .... Benton Greene
Berthold .... Chris Ferry
Landolph .... Tommy A. Gomez
John .... Tom Blair
Charles Di Nolli .... David Mendelsohn

Tito Belcredi .... Anthony Fusco
Doctor Dionysus Genoni .... Charles Lanyer
Donna Matilda .... Felicity Jones
Frida .... Claire Winters
Enrico IV .... Marco Barricelli

Time: 1922. Place: An isolated villa in Italy.

Berkeley Repertory Theatre, Berkeley

Tony Taccone artistic director; Susan Medak managing director

SUNDIATA. By Edward Mast. October 9, 2000. Director, Colman Domingo; scenery, Andrea Bechert; costumes, Allison Connor; sound, Matthew Spiro; fight choreography, Gendell Hernandez.

CAST: Selana Allen, Cyril Jamal Cooper, Dawn Elin-Fraser, Benton Greene.

East West Players, Los Angeles

Tim Dang producing artistic director; Al Choy managing director

THE THEORY OF EVERYTHING. By Prince Gomolvilas. November 8, 2000. Director, Tim Dang; scenery, Victoria Petrovich; costumes, Joyce Kim Lee; lighting, Jose Lopez; sound, Joel Iwataki; produced in association with the Singapore Repertory Theatre, artistic director, Tony Petito.

Shimmy .... Melody Butiu
Lana .... Michelle Chong
Nef .... Brendon Marc Fernandez
Gilbert .... Kennedy Kabasares
Patty .... Emily Kuroda
Hiro .... Ken Narasaki
May .... Marilyn Tokuda

Time: The month of May; Act I, Saturday; Act II, Sunday. Place: The rooftop of the Chapel of Love in Las Vegas, Nevada.

La Jolla Playhouse, La Jolla

Anne Hamburger artistic director; Terrence Dwyer managing director

LIFEGAME. By Keith Johnstone. June 11, 2000 (United States premiere). Directors, Phelim McDermott and Lee Simpson; design, Julian Crouch; lighting, Colin Grenfell; featuring the Improbable Theater Company.

CAST: Niall Ashdown, Angela Clerkin, Julian Crouch, Guy Dartnell, Stella Duffy, Phelim McDermott, Toby Park, Lee Simpson and guests.

One intermission.

SHERIDAN; OR, SCHOOLED IN SCANDAL. By David Grimm. July 23, 2000. Director, Mark Brokaw; scenery, Mark Wendland; costumes, Annie Smart; lighting, Mark McCullough; sound, John Gromada; dramaturg, Elizabeth Bennett.

Lord Byron .... Jeremy Shamos
Duchess of Devonshire .... Sandra Shipley
Hopkins .... Christopher Burris
Richard Brinsley Sheridan ... Sherman Howard
Perdita Robinson .... Francesca Faridany
Miss Pope .... Bairbre Dowling
Charles James Fox .... Robert Machray
William Pitt .... Charles Janasz
Mrs. Crewe .... Maria Dizzia
George III .... Ray Reinhardt
Prince George .... Trey Lyford
Mrs. Fitzherbert .... Alison Weller
Eliza Sheridan .... Francesca Faridany
Father Rammage .... Ray Reinhardt
Justice McKeye .... Robert Machray

Time: The end of the 18th century. Place: London. One intermission.

THE COSMONAUT'S LAST MESSAGE TO THE WOMAN HE ONCE LOVED IN THE FORMER SOVIET UNION. By David Greig. August 6, 2000 (United States premiere). Director, Neel Keller; scenery, Mark Wendland; costumes, Christal Weatherly; lighting, Geoff Korf; sound, Darron L. West.

Oleg .... Jan Triska
Casimir .... Kurt Fuller
Vivienne .... Gretchen Lee Krich
Keith .... Mark Nelson
Nastassja .... Irina Björklund
Proprietor of a Heathrow Airport Café .... John Feltch
Claire .... Irina Björklund
Eric .... John Feltch
Sylvia .... Gretchen Lee Krich
Bernard .... Mark Nelson
Proprietor of a French Bar .... John Feltch
Patient .... Neil Vipond
Proprietor of a Scottish Pub .... John Feltch

Time: The present. Place: Various locations in Scotland, England, France, Norway and Outer Space. One intermission.

THOROUGHLY MODERN MILLIE. Book by Richard Morris and Dick Scanlan; additional music by Jeanine Tesori; additional lyrics by Dick Scanlan; based on Richard Morris's original story and screenplay. October 10, 2000. Director, Michael Mayer; choreography, Rob Ashford; scenery, David Gallo; costumes, Robert Perdziola; lighting, Donald Holder; sound, Otts Munderloh; musical direction, Michael Rafter; orchestrations, Ralph Burns; vocal arrangements and incidental music, Jeanine Tesori; dance music arrangements, David Krane.

Millie Dillmount .... Sutton Foster
Miss Dorothy Brown .... Sarah Uriarte Berry
Ching Ho .... Stephen Sable
Bun Foo .... Francis Jue
Jimmy Smith .... Jim Stanek
Mrs. Meers .... Pat Carroll
Taxi Driver .... Randl Ask
Miss Flannery .... Anne L. Nathan
Trevor Graydon .... Marc Kudisch
Muzzy .... Tonya Pinkins
Dorothy Parker .... Julie Connors
Maitre 'd .... Yusef Miller
Anniversary Couple .... Chane't Johnson, Randl Ask
Ladies' Lounge Attendant .... Zina Camblin

Moderns: Randl Ask, Kate Baldwin, Joshua Bergasse, Zina Camblin, Julie Connors, David Eggers, Nicole Foret, Matthew Gasper, Gregg Goodbrod, Susan Haefner, Chane't Johnson, Matt Lashey, Michael Malone, Yusef Miller, Anne L. Nathan, Tina Ou, Noah Racey, Megan Sikora, Leigh-Anne Wencker.

One intermission.

Mark Taper Forum, Los Angeles

Gordon Davidson artistic director and producer; Charles Dillingham managing director

FOR HERE OR TO GO. By Alison Carey; inspired by Francis Beaumont's *The Knight of the Burning Pestle*. December 15, 2001. Director, Bill Rauch; composers, Michael Abels and Shishir Kurup; music direction, Michael Abels; scenery, Lynn Jeffries; costumes, Christopher Acebo; lighting, Geoff Korf; sound, Paul James; choreography, Jessica Wallenfels; fight direction, Randy Kovitz; produced by Cornerstone Theater Company.

Cast of the "Interrupted" Production
Ms. Chen .... Page Leong
June .... Emily Hong
Nabil .... Ahmad Enani
Jiddu .... George Haddad
Mr. Merchant .... Larry Dozier
Mrs. Merchant .... Theodora Hardie
Luce Merchant .... Gracy Brown
Mr. Garcia .... Armando Molina
Mr. Humphrey .... Peter Howard
MC .... Marcenus Earl
Harris .... Harris Craig Jr.
Nancy .... Nancy Yee
Tamadhur .... Tamadhur Al-Aqeel
Nickole .... Nickole K. Ivory
Quentin .... Quentin Drew
Rob .... Rob Kadivar
Gezel .... Gezel Nehmadi
Al Miller .... Alpheus Merchant
Infant Son .... Liam Tyrese Rauch-Moore
Critic .... Rob Kendt

Cast Portraying Audience Members
Bruce .... Bruce Friedman
Loraine .... Loraine Shields
Rafa .... Omar Gómez
Daniel .... Daniel Chacón

Cast Portraying CTG and Performing Arts Center Employees
House Manager .... Keith Chaffee
Assistant Stage Manager .... Regina Menez

IATSE Crew Member .... Bernie Hatt
Usher .... Christopher Liam Moore
Wardrobe Crew Member ..... Lorraine Lucero
Security Guard .... Fred A. Fluker
Parking Attendant .... Rosalio Mendiola

Cast of Police Officers
Officer Jon .... Jon Greene
Officer Eric .... Eric Peterson
Officer Don .... Don Wynne
Officer Jim .... Jim Montoya
Officer Ramona .... Ramona Beaty

Cast Portraying Other People from the Real World
Pizza Delivery Gal .... Frances Armijos
Homeless Woman .... Irma Ashe
Dolly .... Emma Carey Cobb
Atlanta .... JoAnn Charles Smith

Musicians: Michael Abels, Dave Brown, Kerry Morris, Ryo Okumoto
Time: Present. Place: Mark Taper Forum. One intermission.

QED. By Peter Parnell, inspired by the writings of Richard Feynman and Ralph Leighton's *Tuva or Bust!*. March 10, 2001. Director, Gordon Davidson; scenery, Ralph Funicello; costumes, Marianna Elliott; lighting, D. Martyn Bookwalter; sound, Jon Gottlieb; choreography, Donald McKayle; drumming consultant, Tom Rutishauser; creative consulting, Ralph Leighton.

Richard Feynman .... Alan Alda
Miriam Field .... Allison Smith

Time: June 1986. Place: California Institute of Technology, Pasadena, California. One intermission.

THE BODY OF BOURNE. By John Belluso. May 27, 2001. Director, Lisa Peterson; scenery, Rachel Hauck; costumes, Candice Cain; lighting, Geoff Korf; sound, Darron L. West; projections, Christopher Komuro; wigs and hair, Carol F. Doran.

Randolph Bourne .... Clark Middleton
Sara Bourne; Landlady; Max Eastman; Another of Them #1; Chorus .... Jenny O'Hara
Ruth Bourne; Lilla; Esther Cornell; Chorus .... Jodi Thelen
Uncle Halsey; Professor; John Erskine; Nonna; Albert Bristol; Ellery Sedgwick; Chorus .... Nicolas Coster
Helen Hummel; Emmy; Another of Them #2; Chorus .... Ann Stocking
Beulah Amidon; Yvonne; Agnes de Lima; Jane Addams; Chorus .... Heather Ehlers
Frederick Hoschke; Carl Zigrosser; Eugene Debs; Chorus .... Stephen Caffrey

Chorus: Mitchell Edmonds, Lisa Lovett-Mann, Michelle Marsh, Jill Remez, Michael Eric Strickland, Christopher Thornton.

Time: 1886-1918. Place: America. One intermission.

The Globe Theatres, San Diego

Jack O'Brien artistic director

THE FULL MONTY. By Terrence McNally, music and lyrics by David Yazbek. June 1, 2000. Director, Jack O'Brien; scenery, John Arnone; costumes, Robert Morgan; lighting Howell Binkley; sound, Jeff Ladman; choreography, Jerry Mitchell; music director, Ted Sperling; orchestrations, Harold Wheeler; dance music arranger, Zane Mark.

Dave Bukatinski .... John Ellison Conlee
Nathan Lukowski .... Adam Covalt
Thomas Michael Fiss
Malcolm Macgregor .... Jason Danieley
Pam Lukowski .... Lisa Datz
Noah "Horse" T. Simmons .... André De Shields
Minister .... Jay Douglas
Susan Hershey .... Laura Marie Duncan
Teddy Slaughter .... Angelo Fraboni
Jeanette Burmeister .... Kathleen Freeman
Ethan Girard .... Romain Frugé
Georgie Bukatinski .... Annie Golden
Buddy "Keno" Walsh .... Denis Jones
Joanie Lish .... Jannie Jones
Harold Nichols .... Marcus Neville
Molly Macgregor .... Patti Perkins
Vicki Nichols .... Emily Skinner

Tony Giordano .... Jimmy Smagula
Police Sergeant/Moving Man .... C.E. Smith
Reg Willoughby .... Todd Weeks
Jerry Lukowski .... Patrick Wilson

Time: the Present. Place: Buffalo, New York. One intermission.

MUSICAL NUMBERS, ACT I: Overture, "Scrap," "It's a Woman's World," "Man," "Big-Ass Rock," "Life with Harold," "Big Black Man," "You Rule My World," "Michael Jordan's Ball." ACT II: Entr'acte, "Jeanette's Showbiz Number," "Breeze Off the River," "The Goods," "You Walk with Me," "You Rule My World" (Reprise), "Let it Go."

GOD'S MAN IN TEXAS. By David Rambo. July 22, 2000 (West Coast premiere, revised by playwright). Director, Leonard Foglia; scenery, Robin Sanford Roberts; costumes, Lewis Brown; lighting, Ann Archbold; sound, Jeff Ladman.

Reverend Jeremiah Mears .... Robert Pescovitz
Dr. Philip Gottschall .... Robert Symonds
Hugo Taney .... Andy Taylor

ORSON'S SHADOW. By Austin Pendleton. September 16, 2000 (West Coast premiere, with rewrites made by playwright). Director, Kyle Donnelly; scenery, David Ledsinger; costumes, Ann Hould-Ward; lighting, Ann Archbold; sound, Paul Peterson.

Joan Plowright .... Alexandra Boyd
Vivien Leigh .... Judith Chapman
Orson Welles .... Jonathan Fried
Laurence Olivier .... Nicholas Hormann
Kenneth Tynan .... Adam Stein
Sean .... Scott Wood

THE TROJAN WOMEN. A new translation by Marianne McDonald of the original text by Euripides. September 9, 2000. Director, Seret Scott; scenery, Ralph Funicello; costumes, Ann Hould-Ward; lighting, Peter Maradudin; sound, Chris Walker; composer, Larry Delinger.

Menelaus .... John Campion
Cassandra .... Rayme Cornell
Helen .... Celeste Ciulla
Hecuba .... Randy Danson
Astyanax .... Nick Fowler
Nick Navarro
Talthybius .... Michael James Reed
Andromache .... Jennifer Regan
Chorus Leader .... Rosina Reynolds

Chorus: D'Vorah Bailey, Brian Ibsen, Michael Kary, Tami Mansfield, Eleanor O'Brien, Glen Pannell, Lucas Rooney, Michele Vasquez.

Pasadena Playhouse, Pasadena

Sheldon Epps artistic director; Tom Ware producing director

IKEBANA (LIVING FLOWERS). By Velina Hasu Houston. September 17, 2000. Director, Shirley Jo Finney; scenery, Andrei Both; costumes, Lydia Tanji; lighting, Victor En Yu Tan; sound and original music, Mitch Greenhill.

Ayame .... June Angela
Itamura .... Dana Lee
Hanako .... Lina Patel
Kitayama .... Francisco Viana
Nakamura .... Gedde Watanabe

South Coast Repertory, Costa Mesa

David Emmes producing artistic director; Martin Benson artistic director

EVERETT BEEKIN. By Richard Greenberg. September 8, 2000. Director, Evan Yionoulis; composer, Mike Yionoulis; scenery, Chris Barreca; costumes, Candice Cain; lighting, Donald Holder; sound, Mike Yionoulis.

Ma; Waitress .... Carole Goldman
Sophie; Celia .... Kandis Chappell
Anna; Nell .... Nike Doukas
Jack; Bee .... Jeff Allin
Miri; Laurel .... Tessa Auberjonois
Jimmy; Ev .... Adam Scott

KIMBERLY AKIMBO. By David Lindsay-Abaire. April 13, 2001. Director, David Petraca; composer, Jason Robert Brown; scenery, Robert Brill; costumes, Martin Pakledinaz; lighting, Brian MacDevitt; sound, Bruce Ellman.

Debra .... Joanna P. Adler
Kimberly .... Marylouise Burke
Pattie .... Ann Dowd
Buddy .... Steven Flynn
Jeff .... John Gallagher Jr.

COLORADO

Denver Center Theatre Company, Denver

Donovan Marley artistic director

TANTALUS: AN EPIC MYTH FOR A NEW MILLENNIUM. An adaptation of the original 10-play cycle by John Barton, additional text by Colin Teevan. October 21, 2000. Director, Peter Hall and Edward Hall; associate directors, Anthony Powell and Colin Teevan; composer and musical director, Mike Sands; scenery and costumes, Dionysis Fotopoulos; lighting, Sumio Yoshii; sound, David R. White; in association with the Royal Shakespeare Company, Adrian Noble, artistic director.

Thetis; Cassandra; Pythoness .... Alyssa Bresnahan
Odysseus; Calchas .... Alan Dobie
Agamemnon; Priam; Menelaus .... Greg Hicks
Clytemnestra; Andromache; Ilione; Helen .... Annalee Jefferies
Hecuba; Nurse; Aethra .... Ann Mitchell
Achilles; Aegisthus; Neoptolemus; Orestes .... Robert Petkoff
Poet; Tyndareus; Peleus; Telephus; Palamedes; Polymestor .... David Ryall
Leda; Deidamia; Electra; Hermione; Iphigenia; Polyxena .... Mia Yoo

Chorus: Francesca Carlin, Joy Jones, Tess Lina, Jeanne Paulsen, Christina Pawl, Nicole Poole, Juliet Smith, Mia Tagano, Vickie Tanner, Robin Terry.

Ensemble: Elijah Alexander, Joshua Coomer, Pierre-Marc Diennet, Morgan Hallett, Steve Hughes, Tif Luckenbill, David McCann, Randy Moore, Matt Pepper.

1933. Adapted from the John Fanté novel *1933 Was a Bad Year* by Randal Myler and Brockman Seawell. January 18, 2001. Director, Randal Myler; scenery, G.W. Mercier; costumes, Andrew V. Yelusich; lighting, Charles R. MacLeod; sound, Craig Breitenbach; projection, Jan Hartley.

The Writer .... Yusef Bulos
The Writer's Wife .... Kathleen M. Brady
Dom .... Bryant Richards
Grandma Bettina .... Irma St. Paule
Mary .... Jacqueline Antaramian
Peter .... Mike Genovese
August .... Daniel E. James
Clara .... Aaryn Smith
Ken Parrish .... Michael Twist
Dorothy Parrish .... Stina Nielsen
Mr. Parrish .... Mark Rubald
Mrs. Parrish .... Kathleen M. Brady
Students .... Steve Hughes, Dan O'Neill
Bartender .... Mark Rubald
Woman in the Bar .... Kathleen M. Brady
Art .... Steve Hughes
Newsies .... Steve Hughes, Dan O'Neill, Daniel E. James
Chicago Cubs Coach .... Mark Rubald
Chicago Cubs Players .... Steve Hughes, Dan O'Neill
Chicago Cubs Bat Boy .... Daniel E. James

INNA BEGINING. Conceived by Gary Leon Hill, Jamie Horton and Lee Stametz; written by Gary Leon Hill. April 5, 2001. Director, Jamie Horton; music, Lee Stametz; scenery, Michael Ganio; costumes, Kevin Copenhaver; lighting, Don Darnutzer; sound, David R. White.

Dodge .... Paul Michael Valley
Flo .... Dovora Millman
Tsubo .... Keith L. Hatten
Skella .... Shannon Koob
Ramona .... Michelle Shay
Rupert .... Rodney Lizcano
Dewey Headlong .... William Denis
Female Ensemble .... Gabriella Cavallero
Musician .... Neil Haverstick

PORK PIE: A MYTHIC JAZZ FABLE. By Michael Genet. May 24, 2001. Director, Israel Hicks; music orchestration, arrangement and direction, Coleridge-Taylor Perkinson; assistant musical direction, Eli Fountain; costumes, David Kay Mickelsen; lighting, Allen Lee Hughes; sound, David R. White.

The Storyteller	Roger Robinson	Maggie	Kimberly JaJuan
The Devil's Wife	Vivian Reed	Protean	Glenn Turner
The Champion	Alton Fitzgerald White	Keyboard	George Caldwell
Charlie	Ron Cephas Jones	Saxophone	Lawrence A. Clark
Mahaley	Kim Staunton	Drums	Eli Fountain
Mable	Ora Jones	Bass	Billy Johnson
Volcy	Bobby Daye	Saxophone	Anthony E. Nelson Jr.

Ensemble: Billöah Greene, Janice Guy-Sayles, Keith L. Hatten, January Murelli.

Connecticut

Eugene O'Neill Theater Center, Waterford

George C. White founder; Howard Sherman executive director; Thomas Viertel chairman of the board; James Houghton artistic director of O'Neill Playwright's Conference, Beth Whitaker artistic associate of O'Neill Playwright's Conference; Paulette Haupt artistic director of O'Neill Music Theater Conference

National Playwrights Conference (Staged Readings, July 7–29)

THIEF RIVER. By Lee Blessing.

PAVANE. By Alexandra Cunningham.

MADININA. By Sarah C. Diamond.

PARTS UNKNOWN. By Ron Fitzgerald.

THE HAND OF GOD. By Daisy Foote.

A.M. SUNDAY. By Jerome Hairston.

ROAD RAGE: A LOVE STORY. By Wendy Hammond.

THE HOME LIFE OF POLAR BEARS. By Hilly Hicks Jr.

WHERE IT CAME FROM. By Susan Kim.

KIMBERLY AKIMBO. By David Lindsay-Abaire.

SKITALETZ ("THE WANDERER"). By Dmitry Lipkin.

THE SQUARE ROOT OF MINUS ONE. By Peter Morris.

NO NIGGERS, NO JEWS, NO DOGS. By John Henry Redwood.

Directors: Jessica Bauman, Timothy Douglas, Michael Engler, David Esbjornson, Susan Fenichell, Michael John Garcés, Loretta Greco, Michael Greif, Judy Minor, Mark Rucker, Mel Shapiro, Steven Williford, Evan Yionoulis.

National Music Theater Conference (Staged Concert Readings, August 9–12)

THE SCREAMS OF KITTY GENOVESE. Libretto by David Simpatico, music by Will Todd.

THE HIGHWAYMEN. Book, lyrics and music by Kirsten Childs, based on the poem by Alfred Noyes.

Director: Eleanor Reissa.

Goodspeed Musicals, Chester

Michael P. Price executive director; Sue Frost associate producer; Michael O'Flaherty music director

SUMMER OF '42. Book by Hunter Foster, music and lyrics by David Kirshenbaum, based on the novel and motion picture by Herman Raucher. August 10, 2000. Director, Gabriel Barre; musical director, orchestration, vocal arrangements, Lynne Shankel; scenery, James Youmans; costumes, Pamela Scofield; lighting, Tim Hunter; sound, J.W. Hilton Jr.

Hermie .... Ryan Driscoll
Dorothy .... Idina Menzel
Miriam .... Megan Walker
Aggie .... Celia Keenan-Bolger
Gloria .... Jeanne Goodman
Oscy .... Brett Tabisel
Benjie .... Jason Marcus
Mr. Sanders; Walter Winchell .... Bill Kux
Pete .... Matt Farnsworth

MUSICAL NUMBERS, ACT I: Opening, "The Terrible Trio," "Little Did I Dream," "Will That Ever Happen to Me?," "Unfinished Business," "You're Gonna Miss Me," "Less Than Perfect," "The Walk," "I Always Wanted," "I Think I Like Her," "The Good Guy Polka," "The Movies," "Someone to Dance With Me." ACT II: "The Heat," "Less Than Perfect" (Reprise), "The Drugstore," "The Campfire," "Losing Track of Time," "Oh Gee, I Love My G.I.," "The Dance," Finale. One intermission.

THE NEW RED, HOT AND BLUE. Adaptation by Michael Leeds of original music and lyrics by Cole Porter, original book by Howard Lindsay and Russel Crouse. October 13, 2000. Director, Michael Leeds; musical director and arranger, Michael O'Flaherty; choreography, Andy Blankenbuehler; orchestrations, Dan DeLange; dance music arrangements and additional vocal arrangements, David Loud; assistant music director, F. Wade Russo; scenery, Kenneth Foy; costumes, Ann Hould-Ward; lighting, Ken Billington.

Nails O'Reilly Duquesne .... Debbie Gravitte
Bob Hale .... Peter Reardon
Policy Pinkle .... Ben Lipitz
Grace .... Jessica Kostival
Fingers .... Billy Hartung
Peaches .... Robin Baxter

The Convicts
Rats Dugan .... Brian Barry
Bugs Metelli .... Randy Bobish
Eagle-Eye O'Roarke .... Steve Luker
Coyote Johnson .... Matt Williams
Leonard .... Kevin Covert

The Debutantes
Vivian .... Trish Reidy
Olive .... Dianna Bush
Barbara .... Darlene Wilson
Jane .... Stephanie Kurtzuba
Helen .... Kristin Maloney

The Senators
Senator Craig .... Paul Carlin
Senator Johnson .... Beth Glover
Senator O'Shaughnessy .... Vince Trani
Senator Del Grasso .... Lesley Blumenthal

And a Cast of Thousands
Sergeant-at-Arms;
Servant; Minister .... Jody Madaras
Warden .... Paul Carlin
Guard .... Vince Trani
Woman One .... Lesley Blumenthal
Woman Two .... Beth Glover

MUSICAL NUMBERS, ACT I: Overture, "It Ain't Etiquette," "Perennial Debutantes," "You've Got That Thing/You Do Something to Me," "Down in the Depths," "Carry On," "Five Hundred Million," "It's De-Lovely," "Ridin' High," "Ridin' High" (Reprise). ACT II: Entr'acte, "I'm Throwing a Ball Tonight," "Just One of Those Things," "Most Gentlemen Don't Like Love," "Goodbye, Little Dream, Goodbye," "The Ozarks are Callin' Me Home," "I've Got You Under My Skin," "Hymn to Hymen," "Red, Hot and Blue." One intermission.

DEAR WORLD. Adaptation by David Thompson of original music and lyrics by Jerry Herman, original book by Jerome Lawrence and Robert E. Lee, based on *The Madwoman of Chaillot* by Jean Giraudoux. November 16, 2000. Director, Richard Sabellico; music direction and arrangements, Darren R. Cohen; choreography, Jennifer Paulson Lee; orchestrations and additional arrangements, Christopher Jahnke; scenery, James Morgan; costumes, Suzy Benzinger; lighting, Mary Jo Dondlinger; sound, Jay Hilton.

Countess Aurelia (Madwoman of Chaillot) ... Sally Ann Howes
Deaf Mute ... Adam Barruch
Waiter ... Frank Moran
Nina ... Kristin Carbone
The Prospector ... Kirby Ward
President La Farge ... Richard Bell
President La Frec ... Warren Kelley
President La France ... Jeff Talbott
Julian ... Ben Sheaffer
Sergeant ... Jon Vandertholen
Sewer Man ... Guy Stroman
Constance (Madwoman of the Flea Market) ... Diane J. Findlay
Gabrielle (Madwoman of Montmarte) ... Georgia Engel

MUSICAL NUMBERS, ACT I: "A Sensible Woman," "Just a Little Bit More," "Tomorrow Morning," "Garbage," "I Don't Want to Know," "I've Never Said I Love You," "Dear World," "The Spring of Next Year," "The Tea Party," "And I Was Beautiful," "It's Really Rather Rugged to be Rich," "Kiss Her Now," "Tomorrow Morning" (Reprise). Time: 1945. Place: Paris.

DOUBLE TROUBLE. Book, music and lyrics by Bob Walton and Jim Walton. May 17, 2001. Director, Ray Roderick; music director, John Glaudini; choreography, Darlene Wilson; scenery, Edward Gianfrancesco; costumes, Martha Bromelmeier; lighting, Eric Haugen; sound, Tony Meola.

CAST: Bob Walton and Jim Walton.

Hartford Stage, Hartford

Michael Wilson artistic director

DOLLHOUSE. New adaptation by Theresa Rebeck of original text by Henrik Ibsen. February 28, 2001. Director, Tracy Brigden; scenery, Walt Spangler; costumes, Elizabeth Hope Clancy; lighting, Robert Perry; original music and sound, John Gromada.

Nora ... Shelley Williams
Evan ... Frank Converse
Christine ... Gretchen Lee Krich
Damian Rank ... Christopher McCann
Neil Fitzpatrick ... Glenn Fleshler
Julianna ... Andi Jackson Ali
Children (alternating) ... Christian Dinello and Kaylee Dinello; Luke Murphy and Lillian Rigling

BAPTISTE: THE LIFE OF MOLIÈRE. By William Luce. May 30, 2001. Director, David Warren; scenery, James Youmans; costumes, Toni Leslie-James; lighting, Peter Maradudin; music and sound, John Gromada, choreography, Mark Dendy.

Molière ... Sam Tsoutsouvas
Player I ... Jeremy Shamos
Player II ... Mary Lou Rosato

Long Wharf Theatre, New Haven

Doug Hughes artistic director; Michael Ross managing director

THE BUNGLER. New translation by Richard Wilbur of original work by Molière. September 20, 2000 (United States premiere). Director, Doug Hughes; original music, Louis Rosen; scenery, Neil Patel; costumes, Linda Fisher; lighting, Pat Collins; sound, Matthew Mezick; wigs, Paul Huntley; dramaturg, Mark Bly.

Lélie ... Jeremy Shamos
Mascarille ... Jeff Weiss
Célie ... Heidi Dippold
Trufaldin ... Frank Raiter
Anselme ... J.R. Horne
Pandolfe ... Christopher Wynkoop
Hippolyte ... Tari Signor
Léandre ... Danyon Davis
A Messenger ... Dan Snook
Ergaste ... Paul Blankenship
Andrès ... Dan Snook

MODERN ORTHODOX. By Daniel Goldfarb. October 11, 2000. Director, John Pasquin; scenery, Walt Spangler; costumes, Linda Fisher; lighting, Peter Maradudin; sound, Matthew Mezick.

Hershel Klein .... Michael Goldstrom
Ben Jacobson .... Matthew Rauch
Hannah Ziggelstein .... Julie Lauren
Rachel Feinberger .... Rebecka Ray

GOLDEN BOY. New adaptation by Keith Glover of original book by Clifford Odets and William Gibson, lyrics by Lee Adams; music, new songs and additional lyrics by Charles Strouse. November 8, 2000. Director, Keith Glover; choreography, Willie Rosario; scenery, David Gallo; costumes, Paul Tazewell; lighting, Robert Wierzel; sound, David B. Smith; music director, George Caldwell; arrangements, Charles Strouse, George Caldwell; fight technician, Michael Olajide Jr.; fight captain, Noah Tuleja; wigs, Paul Huntley, Cynthia Demand.

Tom Moody .... Michael Rupert
Lorna Moon .... Nana Visitor
Joe Bonaparte .... Rodney Hicks
Eddie Sateen .... Peter Jay Fernandez
Tokio .... Frank Mastrone
Mr. Bonaparte .... Doug Eskew
Ronnie Jefferson .... Milton Craig Nealy
Annie Jefferson .... Harriett D. Foy
Frank Lane .... David St. Louis
Downsey .... Marc Damon Johnson

Ensemble: Iona Alfonso, John D. Baker, Angela Brydon, Alison Cramer, Mark Myars, Karine Newborn.

MUSICAL NUMBERS, ACT I: "Workout Song," "Everything's Great," "Stick Around," "Stick Around" (Reprise), "Nightsong," "Gimme Some," "Playing the Game," "Natural African Man," "Don't Forget 127th Street," "No Big Deal," "Winners," "The Road Tour," "Butterfly," "Yes, Yes, Yes," "This is the Life," "Yes I Can." ACT II: Entr'acte, "Golden Boy," "Everybody's Got a Price," "He's a Jolly Good Fellow," "Colorful," "I Wanna Be With You," "What am I Gonna Do Without You?," "Can't You See It," "Lorna's Here," "Butterfly" (Reprise), "No More," "Lane's Lament," "Everything Can Be Lovely in the Morning." One intermission.

THE THIRD ARMY. By Joe Sutton. January 10, 2001. Director, Greg Leaming; original music, Fabian Obispo; scenery, Christine Jones; costumes, David Zinn; lighting, Dan Kotlowitz.

Pavel Marek .... Neil Maffin
Diane Brodsky .... Meg Gibson
Lubo Brodsky .... Jan Triska
Barry Axelrod .... Patrick Husted
Alison Crawford .... Carla Bianco

THE MANDRAKE ROOT. By Lynn Redgrave. January 31, 2001. Director, Warner Shook; original music, Dan Moses Schreier; scenery, Michael Olich; costumes, Frances Kenny; lighting, Rui Rita; sound, Dan Moses Schreier; dramaturg, Tom Bryant; fight choreography, Noah Tuleja.

Rose Randall .... Lynn Redgrave
Sally Randall .... Pippa Pearthree
Kate Randall; Young Man ..... Angela Goethals
Robert Randall .... Henry Stram
Alistair McKay .... Mark Chamberlin
A Vicar; A Nurse; Sophie; Sister Felicity; Ruby .... Jeanne Paulsen
Child Sally (alternating) .... Francesca Smith, Miranda Valerio

Seven Angels Theatre, Waterbury

Semina De Laurentis artistic director

THE MAN WHO COULD SEE THROUGH TIME. By Terri Wagener. February 3, 2001. Director, Dennis Delaney; scenery, Adam Huggard; costumes, Jessica D. Grover; lighting, David O'Connor; sound, Asa Wember; in association with Playwright's Kitchen Ensemble, a Los Angeles-based theater company.

Professor Mordecai Bates .... Dimitry Christy
Ellen Brock .... Mary Proctor

Time: The present. Place: A shared studio space, a lecture hall.

Yale Repertory Theatre, New Haven

Stan Wojewodski Jr. artistic director; Victoria Nolan managing director

RICE BOY. By Sunil Kuruvilla. October 19, 2000. Director, Liz Diamond; scenery, Tobin Ross Ost; costumes, Cameron Lee Roberts; lighting, Matthew Richardo; sound, David Budries; fight direction, Rick Sordelet; dramaturg, Claudia Wilsch.

Tommy .... Wayne Kasserman
Tina .... Angel Desai
Father .... Sean T. Krishnan
Uncle .... Sanjiv Jhaveri
Auntie .... Shaheen Vaaz
Granny .... Yolande Bavan
Servant Girl .... Anita Gandhi
Fish Seller; Sari Clerk;
Umbrella Man; Nut Seller .... Ajay Naidu
Mr. Harris; Farmer .... Colin Lane

BIG NIGHT. By Dawn Powell. May 1, 2001. Director, Stan Wojewodski Jr.; scenery, Stuart Polasky; costumes, Tammy Elizabeth McBride; lighting, Stephen Strawbridge; sound, Mimi Epstein; dramaturgs, Catherine Sheehy, Linda Bartholomai and Amy Rogoway.

Ed Bonney .... Matthew Mabe
Myra Bonney .... Katie MacNichol
Vera Murphy .... Jennifer Frankel
Bob Tuttle .... William Theodore Thompson II
Bill Fargo .... Graham Winton
Lucille Fargo .... Susan Marie Brecht
Bert Jones .... Jay Patterson
Chet Davies .... Frank Vlastnik
Miss Zoom .... Bess Wohl
Miss Zumph .... Anne Worden
Delicatessen Boy;
Policemen ..... William Theodore Thompson II

Time: 1931. Place: New York City. One intermission.

FLORIDA

Coconut Grove Playhouse, Miami

Arnold Mittelman producing artistic director

KAREN. By Leonard David Berkowitz. March 6, 2001. Director, Barbara Lowery; scenery, Steve Lambert; costumes, Ellis Tillman; lighting, Eric Nelson; sound, Steve Shapiro.

David Ross .... Christopher Bishop
Karen Wyndam .... Maureen Silliman
John Wyndam .... Arland Russell

Time: The present and the near future. Place: John Wyndam's home in Cornwall, England. Two intermissions.

ILLINOIS

Court Theatre, Chicago

Charles Newell artistic director; Diane Claussen managing director

IN THE PENAL COLONY. By Philip Glass; an opera theatre work based on the original story by Franz Kafka. November 1, 2000. Produced in collaboration with A Contemporary Theatre in Seattle; see production details under A Contemporary Theatre.

PIANO. By Trevor Griffiths. Based on the film *Unfinished Piece for Mechanical Piano* by A. Adabashyan and N. Mikhalkov. April 22, 2001 (United States premiere). Director, Charles Newell; scenery, John Culbert; lighting, Christopher Akerlind; costumes, Nan Cibula-Jenkins; sound, Andre Pluess, Ben Sussman.

Sergei .... Guy Adkins
Sashenka .... Kate Fry
Shcherbuk .... Bradley Mott
Porfiry .... John Reeger
Anna .... Barbara Robertson
Petrin .... Lance Baker
As Cast .... Jennifer Barclay
Zakhar .... Aaron Cedolia

Colonel .... Maury Cooper
Gorokhov .... John Bryce Fischer
Platonov .... Christian Kohn
Yasha .... Matthew Krause
Radish .... Larry Neumann Jr.
Sophia .... Carey Peters
Triletksi .... Yasen Peyankov
Servant .... Dana Wise

Goodman Theatre, Chicago

Robert Falls artistic director; Roche Schulfer executive director

HOUSE AND GARDEN. By Alan Ayckbourn. February 5, 2001 (United States premiere). Director, Robert Falls; scenery, Linda Buchanan; costumes, Mara Blumenfeld; lighting, James F. Ingalls; music, sound, Richard Woodbury; dramaturg, Tom Creamer.

Giles Mace .... Donald Brearley
Lucille Cadeau .... Christina Carrera
Barry Love .... William Dick
Trish Platt .... Susan Hart
Teddy Platt .... Joel Hatch
Gavin Ryng-Mayne .... B.J. Jones
Pearl Truce .... Rebecca Jordan
Fran Biggs .... Maia Madison
Sally Platt .... Liesel Matthews
Izzie Truce .... Susan Osborne-Mott
Joanna Mace .... Barbara Robertson
Jake Mace .... Joe Sikora
Lindy Love .... Natalie West
Warn Coucher .... Ray Wild

Townspeople: Brian Deneen, Judy Blue, Melanie Dix, Tony Dobrowolski, Michelle Hensley, Eric Kramer, Karen Pratt.

Dancers: Katrina Atkin, Claire Alrich, Emily Berkson, Molly Berkson, Jennifer Gaughan Bostrom, Laura Drake, Lena Guerriero, Marina Karver, Elizabeth Kelly, Erika Kuhn, Elizabeth Larsen, Anna Navin, Sara Navin, Jessica Perlman, Rachel Perlman, Ally Reiser, Meahgan Wallace, Mia Weinberger.

Steppenwolf Theatre Company, Chicago

Martha Lavey artistic director; Michael Gennaro executive director

THE BALLAD OF LITTLE JO. By Mike Reid and Sarah Schlesinger. September 14, 2000. Director, Tina Landau; musical director, Patrick Vaccariello; orchestrations, Don Sebesky; vocal arrangements, Patrick Vaccariello, Mike Reid; scenery, G.W. Mercier; costumes, Birgit Rattenborg Wise; lighting, Scott Zielinski; sound, Michael Bodeen, Rob Milburn; choreography, Marc Robin; fight choreography, Robin H. McFarquhar; dramaturg, Julie Felise Dubiner.

Thomas Harrison; Ensemble .... D.C. Anderson
Sarah Stewart Ellis .... Jessica Boevers
Lawrence Monaghan; Ensemble .... Daniel Bogart
Photographer's Wife; Ensemble .... Sandy Borglum
Photographer; Ensemble (Nov. 7-11) .... Jack Donahue
Josephine Monaghan; Jo Monaghan .... Judy Kuhn
Tin Man Wong (older) .... José Llana
Caroline; Ensemble .... Iris Lieberman
Lee Gibbs; Ensemble .... James Moye
Jordan Ellis .... David New
Tin Man Wong (younger) .... Kyle Paek
Traveling Salesman; Ensemble .... Ron Rains
Marian Cummings; Ensemble .... Rondi Reed
James Monaghan; Ensemble .... John Reeger
Percy Corcoran; Ensemble .... Andrew Rothenberg
Kate Monaghan; Ensemble .... Paula Scrofano
Photographer; Ensemble .... Paul Slade Smith
Elvira; Ensemble .... Kate Staiger
Horner Burns; Ensemble .... Daniel Tater

MUSICAL NUMBERS, ACT I: "Hand in the River," "Train to San Francisco," "I See Heaven," "Everything That Touched Her," "Far From Home," "Grab That Handle," "Hi-Lo-Hi," "There is This Man," "To Winter," "I See Heaven" (Reprise), "New Beginning." ACT II: "Independence!," "There's No One Here," "Hi-Lo-Hi" (Reprise), "Where Would I Be?," "Idaho!," "All Around Us," "Listen to the Rain," "Do You Love Me?/There is This Man," "Unbuttoning the Buttons," "All Around Us (the Gathering Storm)," Finale. Time: Between 1867 and 1883. Place: Boston, Massachusetts and Silver City Idaho, Idaho. One intermission.

THE DUEL. Frank Galati's adaptation of Anton Chekhov's short story. October 21, 2000. Director, Luda Lopatina; scenery, Joey Wade; lighting, Jaymi Lee Smith; costumes, Ann Kessler; original music, Moses Moe; sound, Chris Johnson; choreography, Katerina Levitan; produced in association with the European Repertory Company.

Samoylenko .... Robert Breuler
Ivan Layevsky .... Kurt Brocker
Nadezhda .... Amy Landecker
Von Koren .... Yasen Peyankov

THE ORDINARY YEARNING OF MIRIAM BUDDWING. By Alexandra Gersten-Vassilaros. January 20, 2001. Director, Anna D. Shapiro; scenery, Geoffrey Curley; lighting, Jaymi Lee Smith; costumes, Janice Pytel; sound, Andre Pluess, Ben Sussman; dramaturg, Sarah Gubbins.

Miriam Buddwing .... Mary Ann Thebus
Sannie Buddwing .... Brett Korn
William Buddwing .... John G. Connolly
Doug Buddwing .... David Matthew Warren
Serita Moya .... Charin Alvarez
Julius Burger .... Mike Nussbaum

Place: the Buddwing house, a middle class home in Upper Pelham Manor, New York. Act I, Scene 1: Early evening; Scene 2: The next morning. Act II: Noon, three days later. One intermission.

DAVID COPPERFIELD. New adaptation by Giles Havergal of the novel by Charles Dickens. February 1, 2001. Director, Giles Havergal; scenery, Kate Edmunds; costumes, Virgil C. Johnson; lighting, Peter Maradudin; composer, Joe Cerqua; dramaturg, Julie Felise Dubiner.

David Copperfield .... Jim True-Frost
Young David .... Ryan Rentmeester
Betsey Trotwood .... Molly Regan
Mrs. Copperfield; Agnes ..... Mariann Mayberry
Mr. Murdstone .... Christian Kohn
Peggotty .... Maureen Gallagher
Dan Peggotty .... Rick Snyder
Ham .... Christian Stolte
Emily .... Julie Marie Paparella
James Steerforth .... James Houton
Mr. Micawber .... Troy West
Mrs. Micawber .... Rondi Reed
Mr. Wickfield .... Robert Breuler
Uriah Heep .... Jay Whittaker
Dora Spenlow .... Krista Lally

Children: Lacie Goff, Zach Gray, Max Kirsch, Majid Nolley, Dennis Olsen, Miranda Pettengill. One intermission.

THE HOUSE OF LILY. By Lydia Stryk. March 11, 2001. Director, Curt Columbus; scenery, David Wolf; costumes, Natasha Djukich; lighting, J.R. Lederle; dramaturg, Edward Sobel; assistant director, Elizabeth Birnkrant.

Lily .... Martha Lavey
Gina .... Amy Warren
Zig .... Gary Wingert

Time: The present. Place: A living room, a café, a bank.

Victory Gardens Theater, Chicago

Dennis Zacek artistic director; Marcelle McVay managing director

NO ONE AS NASTY. By Susan Nussbaum. June 2, 2000. Director, Susan V. Booth; scenery, Kevin Hagan; costumes, Frances Maggio; lighting, Joe Appelt; sound, Lindsay Jones.

Lois .... Patricia Pierre-Antoine
Ken .... Phil Ridarelli
Janet .... Janelle Snow
Janet .... Lusia Strus
Actress One (Lucy; Lois' Friend; Message 1 Voice; Message 4 Voice; PA) .... Penelope Walker
Actress Two (PA; Joanne; Gloria; Message 2 Voice; Janet's Friend; Wheelchair Pusher; PA 3) .... Kerry Cox
Male Actor (Boyfriend; Edwin the Doorman; Christopher Reeve; Buster the Cat; Message 3 Voice; Clark Gable) .... Jesse Weaver

Time: Now. Place: Here. No intermission.

BLISSFIELD. By Douglas Post. September 25, 2000. Director, Dennis Zacek; scenery, Jack Magaw; costumes, Judith Lundberg; lighting, Todd Hensley; sound, Andre Pluess.

Sally Oglesby .... Jane Blass
Ben Oglesby .... Patrick Bresnyan
Carter Bartosek .... Kevin Gudahl
Beth McAlister Harper .... Kelley Hazen
Zoe Harper .... Beth O'Grady
Reverand Roy McAlister .... Tom Roland
Dexter Defillipis .... Patrick Thornton
Ernie Noodleman .... Jeff Still
Lois Garrity .... Mary Ann Thebus

HELLO DALI: FROM THE SUBLIME TO THE SURREAL. By Jamie O'Reilly and Michael Smith. November 20, 2000. Director, Paul Amandes; music direction, Michael Smith; design, Sam Ball.

CAST: Jamie O'Reilly, Michael Smith and Beau O'Reilly.

THE ACTION AGAINST SOL SCHUMANN. By Jeffrey Sweet. March 26, 2001. Director, Dennis Zacek; scenery, Mary Griswold; costumes, Judith Lundberg; lighting, Jaymi Lee Smith; sound, Andre Pluess and Ben Sussman.

Mrs. Shapiro; Rivka; Nurse .... Roslyn Alexander
Diane .... Kati Brazda
Kate .... Melissa Carlson
Paul .... Anthony Fleming III
Michael .... Eli Goodman
Holgate; Frieder; Reiner; Felix .... Richard Henzel
Aaron .... Robert K. Johansen
Sol .... Bernie Landis
Leah .... Amy Ludwig

JONATHAN WILD. By Stuart Flack. April 8, 2001. Director, Sandy Shinner; scenery, Mark Lohman; costumes and sound, Lisa Lewandowski; lighting, John Rodriguez.

Dave .... Joe Dempsey
Larry .... Phil Ridarelli
Dex .... Kelly Van Kirk

FOSSILS. By Claudia Allen. May 21, 2001. Director, Sandy Shinner; scenery, Jeff Bauer; costumes, Karen Weglarz Klein; lighting, Todd Hensley; sound, Andre Pluess and Ben Sussman.

Carrie .... Julie Harris
Abigail .... Ann Whitney

KENTUCKY

Actors Theatre of Louisville, Louisville

Marc Masterson artistic director; Alexander Speer executive director

QUAKE. By Melanie Marnich. February 27, 2001. Director, Susan V. Booth; scenery, Paul Owen; costumes, Linda Roethke; lighting, Tony Penna; sound, Martin R. Desjardins; dramaturg, Amy Wegener.

Lucy .... Tracey Maloney
Guy; Jock; Roger; Angel Bruce .... David New
Brian; Cooper Trooper; Auto Repair Man .... David Wilson-Barnes
That Woman .... Lusia Strus
Dr. Psychiatrist; Store Clerk; Pilot; Priest .... Allison Briner
Nice Man; Flight Attendant; Drilled Guy; Park Janitor .... Joey Williamson

Time: the present. Place: Constant migration around the United States, ending up in San Francisco. No intermission.

WHEN THE SEA DROWNS IN SAND. By Eduardo Machado. March 3, 2001. Director, Michael John Garcés; scenery, Paul Owen; costumes, Lindsay W. Davis; lighting, Tony Penna; sound, Martin R. Desjardins; dramaturg, Michael Bigelow Dixon.

Federico .... Joseph Urla
Fred .... Ed Vassallo
Ernesto .... Felix Solis
Percussionist .... Hugh "Fuma" Petersen

Time: December of 1999. Place: Act I, New York and Havana; Act II, Havana. One intermission.

FLAMING GUNS OF THE PURPLE SAGE. By Jane Martin. March 8, 2001. Director, Jon Jory; scenery, Paul Owen; costumes, Lindsay W. Davis; lighting, Amy Appleyard; sound, Kurt B. Kellenberger; dramaturg, Michael Bigelow Dixon.

Big 8 .... Phyllis Somerville
Rob Bob .... Leo Kittay
Shedevil .... Monica Koskey
Shirl .... Peggity Price
Black Dog .... Mark Mineart
Baxter Blue .... William McNulty
Memphis Donnie Pride .... Atticus Rowe

Time: the present. Place: a house on a small ranch near Casper, Wyoming. One intermission.

DESCRIPTION BEGGARED; OR THE ALLEGORY OF WHITENESS. By Mac Wellman, music by Michael Roth. March 11, 2001. Director, Lisa Peterson; scenery, Paul Owen; costumes, Linda Roethke; lighting, Tony Penna; sound, Martin R. Desjardins; dramaturg, Amy Wegener.

The Ring Family
Cousin Julia, called "the Eraser" because of a wicked habit .... Adale O'Brien
Aunt Bianca, a sort of human Blank, perhaps a parrot .... Anne O'Sullivan
Uncle Fraser, Fraser Outermost Ring, a damnable marplot .... Edwin C. Owens
Moth, an elegant older person .... Eleanor Glockner
Louisa, something of a ninny (not really) .... Lia Aprile

The Others
The White Dwarf .... Claire Anne Longest
Disputant .... Lia Aprile

Time: Late summer at the turn of this century, or perhaps the last. Place: A vast, metaphysical Rhode Island. No intermission.

WONDERFUL WORLD. By Richard Dresser. March 16, 2001. Director, Marc Masterson; scenery, Paul Owen; costumes, Linda Roethke; lighting, Amy Appleyard; sound, Kurt B. Kellenberger; dramaturg, Tanya Palmer.

Jennifer .... Babo Harrison
Max .... Chris Hietikko
Barry .... Jim Saltouros
Patty .... Barbara Gulan
Lydia .... Rosemary Prinz

Time: The present. Place: Various locations throughout New England. One intermission.

BOBRAUSCHENBERGAMERICA. By Charles L. Mee, created by the SITI Company. March 22, 2001. Director, Anne Bogart; scenery and costumes, James Schuette; lighting, Brian Scott; sound, Darron L. West; dramaturg, Tanya Palmer.

Bob's Mom .... Kelly Maurer
Susan .... Ellen Lauren
Phil's Girl .... Akiko Aizawa
Phil Trucker .... Leon Pauli
Becker .... J. Ed Araiza
Allen .... Will Bond
Carl .... Barney O'Hanlon
Wilson .... Danyon Davis
Bob, the Pizza Boy .... Gian-Murray Gianino
Girl .... Jennifer Taher

No intermission.

HEAVEN AND HELL (ON EARTH): A DIVINE COMEDY. A comic anthology. March 24, 2001. Directors, Sullivan Canady White and Meredith McDonough; scenery, Paul Owen; costumes, Kevin McLeod; lighting, Tony Penna; sound, Jason A. Tratta with Martin R. Desjardins; dramaturgs, Amy Wegener, Tanya Palmer, Michael Bigelow Dixon.

THE VICTIMLESS CRIME. By Deborah Lynn Frockt. With Maesie Speer.

SAINTS AT THE RAVE. By Guillermo Reyes. With Matt Ryan Whitesel, Gian-Murray Gianino.

COCO PUFFS. By Alice Tuan. With Misty Dawn Jordan.

2001 Humana Festival of New American Plays

Leon Pauli and Ellen Lauren in Charles L. Mee's bobrauschenbergamerica *(left).*
Photo: Richard Trigg

Tracey Maloney and David New in Melanie Marnich's Quake *(above).*
Photo: Richard Trigg

Monica Koskey and Leo Kittay in Jane Martin's Flaming Guns of the Purple Sage *(right).*
Photo: Richard Trigg

2001 Humana Festival of New American Plays

Barbara Gulan, Jim Saltouros, Babo Harrison and Rosemary Prinz in Richard Dresser's Wonderful World *(left). Photo: Richard Trigg*

Felix Solis, Joseph Urla and Ed Vassallo in Eduardo Machado's When the Sea Drowns in Sand—*later retitled* Waiting for Havana *(right). Photo: Richard Trigg*

Edwin C. Owens and Lia Aprile in Mac Wellman's Description Beggared; or the Allegory of WHITENESS. *Photo: Richard Trigg*

JUST HOLD ME. By William Mastrosimone. With Brad Abner, Jessica Browne-White.

ROBIN. By Sarah Schulman. With Star Xaviera Little.

I-KISSANDTELL. By Michael Kassin. With Travis Horseman.

VIRTUAL VIRTUE. By Elizabeth Dewberry. With Andrew Jackson, Pauline Yasuda.

YOUNG MAN PRAYING. By Karen Hines. With Nehal Joshi.

CAPITALISM 101. By Rebecca Gilman. With Peter Stone, Atticus Rowe.

WHITE ELEPHANTS. By Jane Martin. With Nastaran Ahmadi.

SWIRLING WITH MERLIN. By Keith Glover. With Breton Nicholson.

WORLDNESS. By Jenny Lyn Bader. With Shoshona Currier, Rebecca Brooksher.

RIOT GRRRRRL GUITAR. By Robert Alexander. With Lia Aprile.

NOTE TO SELF. By Hilly Hicks Jr. With Joey Williamson, Emera Felice Krauss.

ROSA'S EULOGY. By Richard Strand. With Jennifer Taher.

BAD-ASS OF THE RIP ETERNAL. By Elizabeth Wong. With Alex Finch.

CHAD CURTISS, LOST AGAIN. By Arthur Kopit. March 30, 2001. Director, Constance Grappo; scenery, Paul Owen; costumes, Kevin McLeod; lighting, Paul Werner; sound, Jason A. Tratta, dramaturg, Michael Bigelow Dixon.

CAST: Rebecca Brooksher, Luke Glaser, Chris Hietikko, Sarah Keyes, Leo Kittay, Monica Koskey, William McNulty, Mark Mineart, David New, Jim Saltouros, Lusia Strus, David Wilson-Barnes.

Phone Plays Series:

CLICK. Written and directed by Brighde Mullins; produced by Thick Description with Amy Resnick, Warren David Keith.

Message Sent. By Sterling Houston; director, Felice Garcia; produced by Jump-Start Performance Company; with Debbie Basham-Burns, Steve Bailey, Lisa Suarez, Paul Bonin-Rodriguez.

SOMEBODY CALL 911. Written and directed by Jennifer L. Nelson; produced by the African Continuum Theatre Company; with Deidra LaWan Starnes, KenYatta Rogers, Jennifer L. Nelson.

OWLS. By Erin Courtney; director, Pam MacKinnon; produced by Clubbed Thumb; with Dan Illian, Colleen Werthman.

SUBLIMINABLE. Writen, directed and performed by Greg Allen; produced by the Neo-Futurists.

CALL WAITING. Writen, directed and performed by Rachael Claff; produced by the Neo-Futurists.

HYPE-R-CONNECTIVITY. Writen, directed and performed by Andy Bayiates; produced by the Neo-Futurists.

Maryland

Center Stage, Baltimore

Irene Lewis artistic director; Thomas Pecher managing director

FALL. By Bridget Carpenter. November 16, 2000 (Major revision). Director, Lisa Peterson; choreography, Peter Pucci; scenery, Andrew Jackness; costumes, Ann Hould-Ward; lighting, Scott Zielinski; sound, John Gromada; dramaturg, Charlotte Stoudt; co-produced with Berkeley Repertory Theatre, Berkeley, California.

Lydia .... Megan Austin Oberle
Jill .... Nancy Bell
Dog .... Andy Murray
Gopal .... Donnie Keshawarz
Mr. Gonzales .... Thomas Christopher Nieto
Lead .... Chad Kubo
Follow .... Niloufar Talebi

MASSACHUSETTS

American Repertory Theatre, Cambridge

Robert Brustein artistic director; Robert J. Orchard managing director

NOCTURNE. By Adam Rapp. October 13, 2000. Director, Marcus Stern; scenery, Christine Jones; costumes, Viola Mackenthun; lighting, John Ambrosone; sound, David Remedios.

The Son .... Dallas Roberts
The Father .... Will LeBow
The Mother .... Candice Brown
The Sister .... Nicole Pasquale
The Red-Headed Girl with the Grey-Green Eyes .... Marin Ireland

ANIMALS AND PLANTS. By Adam Rapp. March 30, 2001. Director, Scott Zigler; scenery, J. Michael Griggs; costumes, Jane Stein; lighting, John Ambrosone; sound, David Remedios.

Burris .... Benjamin Evett
Dantley .... Will LeBow
A Man with a Plant .... Scott Albert
Cassandra .... Frances Chewning

One intermission.

Berkshire Theatre Festival, Stockbridge

Kate Maguire producing director

THE SHADOW OF GREATNESS. By Gary Socol. July 26, 2000. Director, Martin Rabbett; scenery, Rob Odorisio; costumes, David Murin; lighting, Fabrice Kebour; sound, Rich Dionne.

Alan Perry .... Richard Chamberlain
Elle .... Kellie Overbey
Roxanne .... Jan Maxwell
Scott .... Ross Gibby
Voice of Naomi .... Lady Eleanore Kooke

One intermission.

SAY YES! Book and lyrics by Sherman Yellen, music by Wally Harper. August 16, 2000. Director, Jay Binder; dance and musical staging, Thommie Walsh; musical direction, Steven Freeman; scenery, Kenneth Foy; costumes, Ann Hould-Ward; lighting, Ken Billington; sound, Denise Eberly.

Grover Whelan; Helmut Bertelsman .... John Deyle
Hirshy .... Nicholas Cutro
Josef Hirsh .... Mitchell Greenberg
Lenore Hirsh .... Christianne Tisdale
Peaches O'Grady .... Denny Dillon
Baroness .... Linda Thorson
Gloria Host .... Meredith Patterson
Hurricane Murphy .... Timothy Warmen
Barnaby Cross .... J. Robert Spencer

MUSICAL NUMBERS: "Life," "Say Yes," "Guys Like You," "So Whaddaya Do," "This World's Fair," "Blessed are the Chic," "Rumbleseat Blues," "Isn't She," "Stay Tuned," "This World's Fair" (Reprise), "The Future is You," "Matterhorn Waltz," "Sob, Sister, Sob," "Doesn't Mean a Thing," "Spies," "I Lied," "Say Yes" (Reprise). One intermission.

MICHIGAN

Purple Rose Theatre, Chelsea

Jeff Daniels executive director; Guy Sanville artistic director; Alan Ribant managing director

RAIN DANCE. By Lanford Wilson. January 11, 2001. Director, Guy Sanville; scenery, Vince Mountain; lighting, Dana White; costumes, Rebecca Ann Valentino; sound, Suzi Regan; props, Dana Segrest.

Hank .... Matt Letscher
Tony .... Billy Merasty
Irene .... Suzi Regan
Peter .... Paul Hopper

ORPHAN TRAIN: AN AMERICAN MELODRAMA. By Dennis E. North. April 12, 2001. Director, Guy Sanville; scenery, Andrew Gorney; lighting, Rob Murphy; costumes, Colleen Ryan-Peters; props, Dana Segrest.

Grace .... Maggie Smith
Angel Chorus .... Jessica Foley, Pamela Lehman, Christine Purchis, Tracy Spada, Beth Watson
Nettie MacCleary .... Inga Wilson
Tyler MacCleary .... John Lepard
J.C. MacCleary .... Will Young
Rufus .... Lynch R. Travis
Hypacia .... Rhonda Freya English
Conrad Strachen .... Tom Whalen
Gladys Strachen .... Mila Govich
Willis .... Aaron Toronto
Reverend .... Jeffrey Nash
Harlan .... Tobin Hissong
Emmett .... Paul Hopper
Tom Mason .... Gary McKenzie
Dorene .... Shirley Perich
Maylene .... Tonya Beckman
Douglas .... Aaron Toronto
Porter .... Gary McKenzie
Mrs. Leech .... Michelle Mountain
Mr. Leech .... Jim Porterfield
Miss Baxter .... Tonya Beckman
Orphan .... Theodore Eyster, Kenneth Gerald Sutton
Various Townsfolk .... The Cast

MINNESOTA

Guthrie Theater, Minneapolis

Joe Dowling artistic director; David Hawkanson managing director

TO FOOL THE EYE. By Jeffrey Hatcher. Based on a literal translation by Stephanie L. Debner of Jean Anouilh's *Leocadia* . October 7, 2000. Director, John Miller-Stephany; scenery, John Lee Beatty; lighting, Kenneth Posner; costumes, Matthew J. LeFebvre; composer and music director, Andrew Cooke; dramaturg, Michael Lupu.

Bela; Valet .... Joey Babay
Duchess .... Barbara Bryne
Butler .... Steven Epp
Prince Albert .... Scott Ferrara
Inn Proprietor; Valet .... Dan Foss
Amanda .... Melinda Page Hamilton
Hector .... Denis Holmes
Flagel; Valet .... Michael Kissin
Head Waiter .... Jim Lichtscheidl
Nikos .... Richard Long
Maria .... Molly Sue McDonald
Taxi Driver .... Kris L. Nelson
Ice Cream Vendor .... Dudley Riggs
Hunting Aide .... Mark Rosenwinkel
Peshke; Valet .... Peter Vitale

Scene 1: Late afternoon, the solarium of a French chateau; Scene 2: Soon thereafter, a clearing on the estate grounds; Scene 3: The following morning, the solarium; Scene 4: The next evening, a café in another part of the estate; Scene 5: The following morning, at dawn, the grounds of the chateau and an outside inn. One intermission.

BLOOD WEDDING. A newly commisioned translation by Lillian Garrett-Groag of Federico García Lorca's *Blood Wedding*. January 31, 2001. Director and choreographer, Marcela Lorca; scenery, Christine Jones; lighting, Jeff Bartlett; costumes, Paul Tazewell; sound, Scott W. Edwards; Flamenco composer and musical director, Pedro Cortés; composer and musical director, Victor Zupanc; dramaturg, Michael Lupu.

Mother .... Brenda Thomas
Groom .... Drew Cortese
Leonardo's Wife .... Nadia Bowers
Leonardo's Mother-in-Law .... Marquette Senters
Leonardo .... René Millán
Young Girl .... Elizabeth Peterson
Bride .... Morena Baccarin
Maid .... Maria Elena Ramirez
Father of the Bride .... Richard Ooms
Death (as a beggar woman) .... Susana di Palma
Moon .... Nadia Bowers
Young Women .... Veronica Alvarado, Rachel Leslie, Jada D. Odom
Woodcutters .... Joey Babay, Gavin Lawrence, Marcus Quiniones
Musician .... Pedro Cortés

Blood Wedding was inspired by a newspaper account of actual events in the town of Níjar, Almería province, Spain, in 1928. The action of the play unfolds in a small village in Andalusia. Scene 1: The mother's house; Scene 2: Next morning, Leonardo's house; Scene 3: Next day, Bride's *cueva*; Scene 4: Wedding day, dawn, front porch of Bride's *cueva*; Scene 5: Same; Scene 6: Later that day; Scene 7: Night, the woods; Scene 8: Next morning.

NEW JERSEY

Playwrights Theatre of New Jersey, Madison

John Pietrowski artistic director; Elizabeth Murphy producing director

Dance With Me: A New Musical Revue Celebrating the Songs of John and Johanna Hall and Jonell Mosser. Conceived by Elisabeth Lewis Corley and Joseph Megel. November 30, 2000. Director, Joseph Megel; vocal and musical arrangements, Margaret Dorn and Dennis Deal; scenery, E. David Cosier; lighting, Christopher Gorzelnik; costumes, Cindy Caparo; choreography, Dennis Deal.

Man Two .... Justin Bank
Woman One .... E. Alyssa Claar
Woman Two .... Kathy Deitch
Woman Three .... Connie Pachl
Man One .... Tom Stuart

CRIMINAL ACTS. By Kim Merrill. February 1, 2001. Director, Susan Fenichell; scenery, Sarah Edkins; lighting, Christopher Gorzelnik; costumes, Danielle Castronovo.

Crane .... Tina Frantz
Moot .... John McCarthy
Topper .... Derek Richardson
Julie .... Sarah Knapp
Brian .... Patrick Brinker

Scene 1: the Upper East Side, Scene 2: the Upper West Side, Epilogue: a video-rental store. No intermission.

Concert Readings

THE LAST SEDER. By Jennifer Maisel. October 28, 2000. Director, Joseph Megel.

A SIMPLE GIFT. By T. Cat Ford. January 5, 2001. Director, Joseph Megel.

NEW YORK

Arena Players Repertory Theatre, East Farmingdale

Frederic DeFeis producer

ATLANTIC CITY RENDEZVOUS. By Robert Karmon. February 8, 2001. Director, Frederic DeFeis; scenery, Fred Sprauer; lighting, Al Davis; costumes, Lois Lockwood.

Susan .... Gail Merzer Behrens
Sam .... Martin Edmond
Smirnoff .... John F. Anderson
Ann .... Judith Anderson
Carlos .... Joe Gulotta
Willard .... Vernon Gravdal

Time: The 1970s, evening. Act I: Scene 1, winter in an Atlantic City hotel about to be torn down, a room on the 20th floor; Scene 2, a half hour later. Act II: Scene 1, Immediatly after; Scene 2, The next day, early morning; Scene 3, The next day. One intermission.

Bay Street Theatre, Sag Harbor

Sybil Christopher and Emma Walton artistic directors; Stephen Hamilton executive director

HEDDA GABLER. A new version by Jon Robin Baitz of the classic text by Henrik Ibsen. June 21, 2000. Director, Nicholas Martin; scenery, Alexander Dodge; costumes, Michael Krass; lighting, Kevin Adams; sound, Randall Freed.

Berta .... Kathryn Hahn
Miss Julia Tesman .... Angela Thornton
George Tesman .... Michael Emerson
Hedda .... Kate Burton
Judge Brack .... Harris Yulin
Mrs. Elvsted .... Katie Finneran
Eilert Lovborg .... David Lansbury

Place: The home of George and Hedda Tesman, Christiana, Norway. Near the turn of the 20th century. Time: Act I, morning; Act II, afternoon; Act III, early the next day; Act IV, evening. One intermission.

Staged Readings

HOW I FELL IN LOVE. By Joal Fields. October 21, 2000.
GROSS POINTS. By Ira Lewis. October 22, 2000.
THE TWO OF US. By Brad Desch. April 28, 2001.
INEXPRESSIBLE ISLAND. By David S. Young. April 29, 2001.

Helen Hayes Performing Arts Center, Nyack

Tony Stimac executive producer; Rod Kaats artistic director

A TALE OF TWO CITIES. Adapted from the classic text by Charles Dickens by Joseph P. McDonald, music and lyrics by Robert Hoover. March 17, 2001. Director and choreographer, Richard Sabellico; scenery, J. Branson; costumes, Gail Baldoni; lighting, John-Paul Szczepanski; sound, Rafe Carlotto; orchestrations, Yaron Gershovsky; musical director and arrangements, Vincent Trovato.

Marquis Evremonde	Wayne Schroder
The Count	Mark Aldrich
The Countess	Robin Manning
Lady Celestine	Maren Montalbano
Philip Damiens	Bram Heidinger
Nancy Damiens	Elizabeth Inghram
The Rag Man	Wayne Schroder
The Fish Monger	Bram Heidinger
The Cobbler	Mark Aldrich
The Prostitute	Robin Manning
Mister Lorry	Tom Henry
Lucie Manette	Sarah Uriarte Berry
Miss Pross	Marilyn Farina
Monsieur Defarge	Ken McMullen
Madame Defarge	Jan Nemberger
Doctor Manette	Mark Jacoby
Bursar Harper	Mark Aldrich
John Barsad	Ray DeMantis
Charles Darnay	Peter Flynn
Monsieur Gabelle	Bram Heidinger
Sidney Carton	Tom Zemon
Man at the Bar	William Thomas Evans
Woman at the Bar	Elizabeth Inghram
Second Man at the Bar	Mark Aldrich
Attorney General	Wayne Schroder
Constable One	Mark Aldrich
Constable Two	Tom Henry
Waiter	Bram Heidinger
Court Clerk	Bram Heidinger
Judge at the Old Bailey	Mark Aldrich
Jerry Cruncher	Patrick Garner
Jury Foreman	Ken McMullen
Sheila	Andrea Bianchi
Sheila's Man	William Thomas Evans
Vengeance	Robin Manning
Knife	Andrea Bianchi
Breeder	Lenora Eve
Jacques One	Bram Heidinger
Jacques Two	Mark Aldrich
Jacques Three	William Thomas Evans
A Nobleman	Bram Heidinger
President of the Citizens' Tribunal	Wayne Schroder
Public Prosecutor	William Thomas Evans
Citizen Jury Foreman	Mark Aldrich
Cholat, a Bastille Guard	Bram Heidinger
Sentry	William Thomas Evans

MUSICAL NUMBERS, ACT I: "Nobility," "The Best of Times," "Someone, But Who?," "Lullaby," "My Name is Charles Darnay," "Independence," "What's on Your Mind," "A Touch of Larceny," "Justice in England," "This is Not Like Me at All," "More Than Just a Lifetime," "Let's Wait and See," "More Than Just a Lifetime" (Reprise), "I Love You Now," "And Nothing More," "It is So!" ACT II: "Lullaby" (Reprise), "Sleep, Little Evremonde," "I am a Patriot," "There's No Home Without You," "A Touch of Larceny" (Reprise), "My Name is Evremonde," "I'll Build a Rainbow." One intermission.

Syracuse Stage, Syracuse

Robert Moss artistic director; James A. Clark producing director

New Play Festival

MAP OF HEAVEN. By Michele Lowe. January 8, 2001. Director, Robert Moss.

BOURBON AT THE BORDER. By Pearl Cleage. January 15, 2001. Director, Timothy Douglas.

MAN IN MOTION. By Kenneth Pressman. January 23, 2001. Director, Robert Moss.

Ohio

The Cleveland Play House, Cleveland

Peter Hackett artistic director; Dean R. Gladden managing director

JERUSALEM. By Seth Greenland. March 16, 2001. Director, Peter Hackett; composer, Lewis Flinn; scenery, Michael Ganio; costumes, David Kay Mickelsen; lighting, Richard Winkler; sound, Robin Heath.

Will	Stephen Kunken
Meg	Sue-Anne Morrow
Glory	Susan Ericksen
Bing	Steve McCue
Mary	Ann Guilbert
Yitz; Saladin; Cop Voice; Fisher	David Alan Novak
Guberman	Ben Lipitz

Great Lakes Theater Festival, Cleveland

James Bundy artistic director

PETER PAN. Adaptation by Alison Carey of original text by J.M. Barrie. May 5, 2001. Director, Bill Rauch; composer, Paul James; scenery, Lynn Jeffries; costumes, Christopher Acebo; lighting, Geoff Korf; sound, Stan Kozak; fight choreography, Ken Roht.

12 to 18 Months	Jon Jon Adams
Peter Pan	Richard Augustine
Tailpipe	Bob Henry Baber
Browns	Cody Troy Baber
Mrs. Darling; Tiger Lilly	Monica Bell
Ravenous Ruby	Bernice A. Bolek
Buckeye Bell; Adult Wendy	Gracy Brown
John	Paul Carlson
Wells Fargo	Tracey Evans
Twin	Sean Fitzgerald
Parent; Fairy; Merman	Felipe Gonzalez
Pothole	Charles Hancock
Romeo	Larry Hancock
Wendy	Betsy Hogg
Mustang Sally	Karin Hess-Hopkins
No Name	Arnalesa Jenkins
Jane	Caitlin Kelley
Diapers	Jay Kim
Twinner	Corey Mach
Nanny; Crocodile	Sandi McCree
Parent; Fairy; Mermaid	Vashon Renée McIntrye
Dakota	Robin Pease
Michael	Denzale Reese
Hops	Carl Schanz
Tinkerbell	Ashby Semple
Smee	Noble Shropshire
Wendy	Brittany Spicer
Bruiser	Hannah Stofan
Parent; Fairy; Merman	Josh Theilan
Captain Hook; Mr. Darling	Jeffrey V. Thompson
Parent; Fairy; Mermaid; Adult Wendy	Anne Tofflemire

Playhouse in the Park, Cincinnati

Edward Stern producing artistic director; Buzz Ward executive director

DARK PARADISE: THE LEGEND OF THE FIVE POINTED STAR. By Keith Glover. February 1, 2001. Director, Keith Glover; scenery, David Gallo; costumes, Ann Hould-Ward; lighting, Thomas C. Hase; sound, David B. Smith; fight choreography, Drew Fracher; special effects direction, Jim Steinmeyer; dramaturg, Maxine Kern.

Chiron	Tony Todd
Colonel Jeddadiah Crate	Sean Haberle
William LaRue, Ty LaRue	Leland Gantt
Sura Rise	Kim Brockington
Wyatt Earp	James Horan
John Henry Holliday	Gary Sloan
Bessatura	Elena Aaron
Cole Regert	Ron Riley
Packard Tate	Mike Hartman

Time: 1878. Place: The towns of Arkan City and Paraiso Oscuro. One intermission.

PENNSYLVANIA

Philadelphia Theatre Company, Philadelphia

Sarah Garonzik producing artistic director; Ada Coppock general manager

COMPLEAT FEMALE STAGE BEAUTY. By Jeffrey Hatcher. October 25, 2000 (newly revised production). Director, Walter Bobbie; scenery, John Lee Beatty; lighting, Peter Kaczorowski; costumes, Catherine Zuber; music, Stanley Silverman; dramaturg, Michele Volansky.

Kynaston .... Brandon Demery
Margaret Hughes .... Jenny Bacon
Villiars, Duke of Buckingham .... Glenn Howerton
Pepys; Hyde; Revels .... Stephen DeRosa
Charles II .... Robert Stanton
Thomas Betterton .... Steven Skybell
Sir Charles Sedley .... Tom Nelis
Maria .... Lauren Ward
Lady Meresvale .... Laura Knight
Ensemble .... Leo Neiderriter, Mark Buettler, John Zak
Miss Frayne .... Brea Bee

NO NIGGERS, NO JEWS, NO DOGS. By John Henry Redwood. January 31, 2001. Director, Israel Hicks; scenery, Michael Brown; lighting, Ann G. Wrightson; costumes, Christine Field; sound, Eileen Tague.

Mattie Cheeks .... Elizabeth Van Dyke
Rawl .... Marcus Naylor
Aunt Cora .... Rayme Cornell
Joyce .... Adrienne Carter
Matoka .... Charis M. Wilson
Yaveni .... Jack Aaron

Time: 1949. Place: Rural Halifax, North Carolina

Walnut Street Theater, Philadelphia

Bernard Havard producing artistic director; Mark D. Sylvester managing director

EYE OF THE STORY. A one-man show written by, starring and directed by Will Stutts. March 28, 2001. Scenery, Michelle Burnworth; costumes, Naomi Katz; lighting, Tim Ashby.

Judge Johnson .... Will Stutts

RHODE ISLAND

Trinity Repertory Company, Providence

Oskar Eustis artistic director; William P. Wingate managing director

HENRY FLAMENTHROWA. By John Belluso. January 5, 2001. Director, Lisa Peterson; scenery, Rachel Hauck; costumes, William Lane; lighting, Mimi Jordan Sherin; sound, Darron L. West.

Beth Parker .... Joanna P. Adler
Peter Rhamelower .... Fred Sullivan Jr.
Henry Rhamelower .... Michael Esper

Time: The present. No intermission.

THE NEW ENGLAND SONATA. By Eliza Anderson. March 16, 2001. Director, Amanda Dehnert; scenery, David Jenkins; costumes, William Lane; lighting, Deb Sullivan; sound, Peter Sasha Hurowitz.

Wallace .... Timothy Crowe
Clara .... Amy Van Nostrand
Eleanor .... Barbara Meek
Pip .... Andy MacDonald
Charlie .... Benjamin E.M. Lovejoy

One intermission.

TEXAS

Alley Theatre, Houston

Gregory Boyd artistic director; Paul R. Tetreault managing director

SYNERGY. By Keith Reddin. February 2, 2001. Director, Karen Kohlhaas; choreography, Brian Byrnes; scenery, Kevin Rigdon; costumes, Karyl Newman; lighting, Michael Lincoln; sound, Malcolm Nicholls; dramaturg, Travis Mader.

Deb .... Jenny Maguire
Marc .... Eric Sheffer Stevens
Devil .... Edmond Genest
Roland .... Christopher Duva
Otto .... Callum Keith-King
Jade; Michelle .... Fay Ann Lee
Sidney .... Reathel Bean

One intermission.

UTAH

Utah Shakespearean Festival, Cedar City

Fred C. Adams founder and executive producer

New Plays-in-Progress Readings

WHISTLER V. RUSKIN. By L.L. West. August 3, 2000. Director, Sylvie Drake.

TEARS OF TIME. By Stuart Boyce. August 10, 2000. Director, George Judy.

MEMORABILIA. By Red Shuttleworth. August 17, 2000. Director, Bruce K. Sevy.

LITTLE RED WAGON PAINTED BLUE. By Don Monaco. August 24, 2000. Director, Davey Marlin-Jones.

WASHINGTON

A Contemporary Theatre, Seattle

Gordon Edelstein artistic director; Jim Loder managing director

A SKULL IN CONNEMARA. By Martin McDonagh. July 27, 2000 (United States premiere). Director, Gordon Edelstein; scenery, David Gallo; costumes, Susan Hilferty; lighting, Michael Chybowski; composer/arranger, Martin Hayes and Dennis Cahill; sound, Stephen LeGrand; dramaturg, Liz Engelman; fight direction, Geoffrey Alm.

Mick Dowd .... Kevin Tighe
Maryjohnny Rafferty .... Zoaunne LeRoy
Mairtin Hanlon .... Andrew McGinn
Thomas Hanlon .... Christopher Evan Welch

Place: Rural Galway. One intermission.

IN THE PENAL COLONY. By Philip Glass; an opera theatre work based on the original story by Franz Kafka. August 31, 2000. Director, JoAnne Akalaitis; libretto, Rudolph Wurlitzer; conductor and music director, Alan Johnson; scenery, John Conklin; lighting, Jennifer Tipton; costumes, Susan Hilferty; sound, Dominic Kramers; choreography, Pat Graney. Produced in collaboration with Court Theatre in Chicago, Ill.

Visitor .... John Duykers
Officer (alt.) .... Herbert Perry
Kafka .... José J. Gonzales
Condemned Man .... Matt Seidman
Officer (alt.) .... Eugene Perry
Soldier .... Steven M. Levine

Time: 1907. Place: A penal colony, off the coast of Africa. No intermission.

Workshop Production:

MOSCOW NIGHTS. By Dmitry Lipkin. December 10, 2000. Director, Gordon Edelstein; dramaturg, Liz Engelman.

Evelina .... Marjorie Nelson
Tamara .... Marianne Owen
Victor .... Anthony DeFonte
Alyosha .... Laurence Ballard
Nonna .... Suzanne Bouchard
Natalia .... Anne Ludlum
Yefim .... R. Hamilton Wright
Zoya .... Katie Tomlinson

Act I: Evelina Naumovna's apartment, Brighton Beach, Brooklyn. The present. Act II: The boardwalk on Brighton Beach. Later that night. One intermission.

New Play Reading Series:

GREENSWARD. By R. Hamilton Wright. February 22, 2001. Director, Steven Dietz; dramaturg, Liz Engelman.

Timothy Hay .... Jeff Cummings
Arden Flemhorn; French Ambassador; Lothar; Joe .... Wesley Rice
Dr. Douglas Fletchley; Curtis; Kemp; A Waiter .... Jerry McGarity
T. Scott Jacobsen; Chairman .... Tom Spiller
Audrey Mays; Daisy Rainbow; Snail Lady .... Liz McCarthy
Jennifer de Lancy .... Molly Robinson

One intermission.

TALES FROM THE SALT MINES. By Mary Lathrop. February 22, 2001. Director, Rita Giomi; dramaturg, Liz Engelman.

Martha .... Alyson Bedford
Pepper .... Maria Glanz
Chris .... Deb Fialkow
Mr. Gruber .... Robert Shampain
Rayelle; Margo; Meter Maid .... Kit Harris
Roy .... José J. Gonzales

One intermission.

THE BUMPY SUTRA. By Kurt Beattie. February 22, 2001. Director, Victor Pappas; dramaturg, Liz Engelman.

Jim .... Jeff Cummings
Carolyn .... Liz McCarthy
Trinity .... Mari Nelson
Oscar, Sebastian .... Bill terKuile
Son, Sam, Guzman, et al. .... Robert Shampain
Lori, Old Woman, Joyce, et al. .... Kit Harris

One intermission.

New Play Reading Series, produced in collaboration with Hedgebrook Writers' Retreat:

VISIBLE/INVISIBLE. By Jamie Pachino. May 11, 2001. Director, Victor Pappas; dramaturg, Liz Engelman.

Leigh .... Laura Ann Worthen
Saul .... Frank Corrado
Robbie .... Paul Morgan Stetler
Mrs. Leonard .... Cynthia Lauren Tewes
Young Saul .... Galen Joseph Osier
Young Leigh .... Alexis Chamow

THE BELLS. By Theresa Rebeck. May 11, 2001. Director, Bartlett Sher; dramaturg, Christine Sumption.

Xuifei .... Chil Kong
Sally .... Julie Briskman
Jim .... Tom Spiller
Charley .... Clayton Corzatte
Annette .... Monica Appleby
Baptiste .... Jason Cottle
Matthias .... Frank Corrado

LEAVE ME IN LIMBO. By Valetta Anderson. May 11, 2001. Director, Valerie Curtis-Newton; dramaturg, Christine Sumption.

Daisy; Ifeoma .... Shawntina Vernon
Aunt Emma; Omu .... Demene Hall
Chuck .... David Scully
Sally .... Lanise Shelley
Mike .... Gael To'mas Jones

LADY LAY. By Lydia Stryk. May 11, 2001. Director, Leslie Swackhamer; dramaturg, Liz Engelman.

Herr K; Seth Wheatfield .... E. Ray Anderson
Frau L; Frau Y; Sara James .... Laura Kenny
Frau M; Frau H; Frau F .... Liz McCarthy
MariAnne .... Jayne Muirhead
Herr D; Bob Dylan .... David Silverman

Intiman Theatre, Seattle

Bartlett Sher artistic director; Laura Penn Managing Director

THE CHAIRS. A new translation by Jim Lewis of the text by Eugene Ionesco. August 11, 2000. Director, Kate Whoriskey; scenery, Christine Jones; costumes, Frances Kenny; lighting, Robert Perry; sound, Eric Chappelle; dramaturg, Mame Hunt.

Old Man .... Larry Block
Old Woman .... Anne O'Sullivan
The Orator .... Myra Platt

Seattle Repertory Theatre, Seattle

Sharon Ott artistic director

NEW PATAGONIA. By Elizabeth Heffron. November 13, 2000. Director, Sharon Ott; scenery, Karen Gjelsteen; costumes, Frances Kenny; lighting, M.L. Gieger; sound, Stephen LeGrand; videography, Nikki Appino; dramaturg, Christine Sumption.

Karl .... John Seitz
Tank .... Charles Dean
Angel .... Cynthia Jones
Jesse .... Quentin Mare
Roxie .... Lori Larsen
John-John .... Jesse Lee Thomas

IN REAL LIFE. Written and performed by Charlayne Woodard. December 4, 2000. Director, Daniel Sullivan; composer, Daryl Waters; scenery, John Lee Beatty; costumes, James Berton Harris; lighting, Kathy A. Perkins; sound, Chris Walker.

New Play Workshops

WHEN GRACE COMES IN. By Heather McDonald. July 8, 2000. Director, Sharon Ott.

TEMPLE. Book and lyrics by Silvia Peto, music by Norman Durkee. December 15, 2000. Director, Gabriel Barre.

OKRA. By Anne Galjour. April 8, 2001. Director, Sharon Ott.

INMAN. By Lorenzo di Stephano. April 26, 2001. Director, Jonathan Miller.

WISCONSIN

Milwaukee Repertory Theater, Milwaukee

Joseph Hanreddy artistic director; Timothy J. Shields managing director

WORK SONG. By Eric Simonson and Jeffrey Hatcher. September 8, 2000. Director, Eric Simonson; scenery, Kent Dorsey; costumes, Karen Kopischke; lighting, Chris Parry; sound, Barry G. Funderburg.

Frank Lloyd Wright .... Lee E. Ernst
Edwin Cheny; Overton .... Ron Frazier
Louis Sullivan; Otto Freundlich .... James Pickering
George Brodell; Grant; William Brooks .... Torrey Hanson
Riley; Reporter; Sheriff; Stout .... Chris Mangels
Eisner; Farmer; Reporter; Farris .... Christopher Prentice
Anna Wright; Grace .... Rose Pickering
Catherine Wright; Britta; Carolyn Brooks .... Kirsten Potter
Mamah Cheney; Ayn Rand .... Laura Gordon
Juian Carlton; Leelai ...... Leon Addison Brown
Daniel Burnham; Alexander Woollcott .... Richard Halverson

John Wright;
Wes Peters .... Andrew Morris
Farmer's Wife;
Olgivanna Wright .... Angela Iannone

Others: Andy Gladbach, Andrew Groble, Ian Alderman, Heather René Corallo, Jeff Ehren, Lisa C. Jones, Sarah Patterson Malkin, Trina Nance, Robert P. Reeves III, Molly Rhode, Leon Satchell-Page, Charles Schoenherr.

SOUNDING THE RIVER (HUCK FINN REVISITED). By Edward Morgan, based on *The Adventures of Huckleberry Finn* by Mark Twain. February 23, 2001. Director, Edward Morgan; music arrangement and director, Chic Street Man; scenery, Bill Clarke; costumes, Martha Hally; lighting, Bob Jared; sound, Stephen LeGrand; fight choreography, Lee E. Ernst.

Old Huck .... Jim Baker
Duke; Doc Penrod .... Mark Corkins
Silas; Blake ....Jonathan G. Daly
Miss Watson; Liza .... Laura Gordon
King; Hopkins ....Paul Bentzen
Jennie .... Olivia D. Dawson
Old Jim .... Charles Dumas
Huck .... Sean McNall
Parker; Burton .... Carl Palmer
Jim .... Raphael Peacock
Singer ....Cedric Turner
Singer; Actor .... Scott Wakefield
Fiddler .... L.J. Slavin
Pap; Sam .... Jim Pickering
Widow; Aunt Sally .... Rose Pickering

Others: Leslie Anderson, La Shawn Banks, Heather Corallo, Darin Doms, Ben Fitch, Sarah Malkin, Chris Mangels, Chris Mayse, Leon Satchell-Page, Charles Schoenherr.

FACTS AND FIGURES

LONG RUNS ON BROADWAY

○○○○○

THE FOLLOWING SHOWS HAVE RUN 500 or more continuous performances in a single production, usually the first, not including previews or extra non-profit performances, allowing for vacation layoffs and special one-booking engagements, but not including return engagements after a show has gone on tour. In all cases, the numbers were obtained directly from the show's production offices. Where there are title similarities, the production is identified as follows: (p) straight play version, (m) musical version, (r) revival, (tr) transfer.

THROUGH MAY 31, 2001

(PLAYS MARKED WITH ASTERISK WERE STILL PLAYING JUNE 1, 2001)

Plays	*Performances*
Cats	7,485
A Chorus Line	6,137
Oh! Calcutta! (r)	5,959
*Les Misérables	5,859
*The Phantom of the Opera	5,570
Miss Saigon	4,097
42nd Street	3,486
Grease	3,388
Fiddler on the Roof	3,242
Life With Father	3,224
Tobacco Road	3,182
*Beauty and the Beast	2,891
Hello, Dolly!	2,844
My Fair Lady	2,717
Annie	2,377
Man of La Mancha	2,328
Abie's Irish Rose	2,327
Oklahoma!	2,212
*Rent	2,125
Smokey Joe's Cafe	2,036
Pippin	1,944
South Pacific	1,925
The Magic Show	1,920
*Chicago (m)(r)	1,894
Deathtrap	1,793
Gemini	1,788
Harvey	1,775
Dancin'	1,774
La Cage aux Folles	1,761
Hair	1,750
The Wiz	1,672
Born Yesterday	1,642
The Best Little Whorehouse in Texas	1,639

Plays	*Performances*
Crazy for You	1,622
Ain't Misbehavin'	1,604
Mary, Mary	1,572
Evita	1,567
The Voice of the Turtle	1,557
Jekyll & Hyde	1,543
Barefoot in the Park	1,530
Brighton Beach Memoirs	1,530
Dreamgirls	1,522
Mame (m)	1,508
Grease (r)	1,503
*The Lion King	1,482
Same Time, Next Year	1,453
Arsenic and Old Lace	1,444
The Sound of Music	1,443
Me and My Girl	1,420
How to Succeed in Business Without Really Trying	1,417
Hellzapoppin'	1,404
The Music Man	1,375
Funny Girl	1,348
Mummenschanz	1,326
Angel Street	1,295
*Cabaret (r)	1,292
Lightnin'	1,291
Promises, Promises	1,281
The King and I	1,246
Cactus Flower	1,234
Sleuth	1,222
Torch Song Trilogy	1,222
1776	1,217
Equus	1,209
Sugar Babies	1,208

Plays	Performances
Guys and Dolls	1,200
Amadeus	1,181
Cabaret	1,165
Mister Roberts	1,157
Annie Get Your Gun	1,147
Guys and Dolls (r)	1,144
The Seven Year Itch	1,141
Bring in 'da Noise, Bring in 'da Funk	1,130
Butterflies Are Free	1,128
Pins and Needles	1,108
Plaza Suite	1,097
They're Playing Our Song	1,082
Grand Hotel (m)	1,077
Kiss Me, Kate	1,070
Don't Bother Me, I Can't Cope	1,065
The Pajama Game	1,063
Shenandoah	1,050
The Teahouse of the August Moon	1,027
Damn Yankees	1,019
Never Too Late	1,007
Big River	1,005
*Fosse	1,001
The Will Rogers Follies	983
Any Wednesday	982
Sunset Boulevard	977
A Funny Thing Happened on the Way to the Forum	964
The Odd Couple	964
Anna Lucasta	957
Kiss and Tell	956
Show Boat (r)	949
*Annie Get Your Gun (r)	938
Dracula (r)	925
Bells Are Ringing	924
The Moon Is Blue	924
Beatlemania	920
The Elephant Man	916
Kiss of the Spider Woman	906
Luv	901
The Who's Tommy	900
Chicago (m)	898
Applause	896
Can-Can	892
Carousel	890
I'm Not Rappaport	890
Hats Off to Ice	889
Fanny	888
Children of a Lesser God	887
Follow the Girls	882
City of Angels	878
Camelot	873
I Love My Wife	872
The Bat	867
My Sister Eileen	864
No, No, Nanette (r)	861
Ragtime	861
Song of Norway	860

Plays	Performances
Chapter Two	857
A Streetcar Named Desire	855
Barnum	854
Comedy in Music	849
Raisin	847
Blood Brothers	839
You Can't Take It With You	837
La Plume de Ma Tante	835
Three Men on a Horse	835
The Subject Was Roses	832
Black and Blue	824
The King and I (r)	807
Inherit the Wind	806
Anything Goes (r)	804
Titanic	804
No Time for Sergeants	796
Fiorello!	795
Where's Charley?	792
The Ladder	789
Forty Carats	780
Lost in Yonkers	780
The Prisoner of SecondAvenue	780
M. Butterfly	777
Oliver!	774
The Pirates of Penzance (1980 r)	772
Woman of the Year	770
My One and Only	767
Sophisticated Ladies	767
Bubbling Brown Sugar	766
Into the Woods	765
State of the Union	765
Starlight Express	761
The First Year	760
Broadway Bound	756
You Know I Can't Hear You When the Water's Running	755
Two for the Seesaw	750
Joseph and the Amazing Technicolor Dreamcoat (r)	747
Death of a Salesman	742
For Colored Girls . . .	742
Sons o' Fun	742
Candide (m, r)	740
Gentlemen Prefer Blondes	740
The Man Who Came to Dinner	739
Nine	739
Call Me Mister	734
Victor/Victoria	734
West Side Story	732
High Button Shoes	727
Finian's Rainbow	725
Claudia	722
The Gold Diggers	720
Jesus Christ Superstar	720
Carnival	719
The Diary of Anne Frank	717

Plays	*Performances*
A Funny Thing Happened on the Way to the Forum (r)	715
I Remember Mama	714
Tea and Sympathy	712
Junior Miss	710
Footloose	708
Last of the Red Hot Lovers	706
The Secret Garden	706
Company	705
Seventh Heaven	704
Gypsy (m)	702
The Miracle Worker	700
That Championship Season	700
Da	697
Cat on a Hot Tin Roof	694
Li'l Abner	693
The Children's Hour	691
Purlie	688
Dead End	687
The Lion and the Mouse	686
White Cargo	686
Dear Ruth	683
East Is West	680
Come Blow Your Horn	677
The Most Happy Fella	676
Defending the Caveman	671
The Doughgirls	671
The Impossible Years	670
Irene	670
Boy Meets Girl	669
The Tap Dance Kid	669
Beyond the Fringe	667
Who's Afraid of Virginia Woolf?	664
Blithe Spirit	657
A Trip to Chinatown	657
The Women	657
Bloomer Girl	654
The Fifth Season	654
Rain	648
Witness for the Prosecution	645
Call Me Madam	644
Janie	642
*Kiss Me, Kate	640
The Green Pastures	640
Auntie Mame (p)	639
A Man for All Seasons	637
Jerome Robbins' Broadway	634
The Fourposter	632
The Music Master	627
Two Gentlemen of Verona (m)	627
The Tenth Man	623
The Heidi Chronicles	621
Is Zat So?	618
Anniversary Waltz	615
The Happy Time (p)	614
Separate Rooms	613
Affairs of State	610

Plays	*Performances*
Oh! Calcutta! (tr)	610
Star and Garter	609
The Mystery of Edwin Drood	608
The Student Prince	608
Sweet Charity	608
Bye Bye Birdie	607
Irene (r)	604
Sunday in the Park With George	604
Adonis	603
Broadway	603
Peg o' My Heart	603
Master Class	601
Street Scene (p)	601
Flower Drum Song	600
Kiki	600
A Little Night Music	600
Art	600
Agnes of God	599
Don't Drink the Water	598
Wish You Were Here	598
Sarafina!	597
A Society Circus	596
Absurd Person Singular	592
A Day in Hollywood/ A Night in the Ukraine	588
The Me Nobody Knows	586
The Two Mrs. Carrolls	585
Kismet (m)	583
Gypsy (m, r)	582
Brigadoon	581
Letective Story	581
No Strings	580
Brother Rat	577
Blossom Time	576
Pump Boys and Dinettes	573
Show Boat	572
The Show-Off	571
Sally	570
Jelly's Last Jam	569
Golden Boy (m)	568
One Touch of Venus	567
The Real Thing	566
Happy Birthday	564
Look Homeward, Angel	564
Morning's at Seven (r)	564
The Glass Menagerie	561
I Do! I Do!	560
Wonderful Town	559
The Last Night of Ballyhoo	557
Rose Marie	557
Strictly Dishonorable	557
Sweeney Todd, the Demon Barber of Fleet Street	557
The Great White Hope	556
A Majority of One	556
The Sisters Rosensweig	556
Sunrise at Campobello	556

Plays	*Performances*
Toys in the Attic	556
Jamaica	555
Stop the World—I Want to Get Off	555
Florodora	553
Noises Off	553
Ziegfeld Follies (1943)	553
Dial "M" for Murder	552
Good News	551
Peter Pan (r)	551
How to Succeed in Business Without Really Trying (r)	548
Let's Face It	547
Milk and Honey	543
Within the Law	541
Pal Joey (r)	540
The Sound of Music (r)	540
What Makes Sammy Run?	540
The Sunshine Boys	538
What a Life	538
Crimes of the Heart	535
Damn Yankees (r)	533
The Unsinkable Molly Brown	532
The Red Mill (r)	531
Rumors	531
A Raisin in the Sun	530
Godspell (tr)	527
Fences	526
The Solid Gold Cadillac	526
Biloxi Blues	524
Irma La Douce	524
The Boomerang	522
Follies	521
Rosalinda	521
The Best Man	520
Chauve-Souris	520
Blackbirds of 1928	518
The Gin Game	517
Sunny	517
Victoria Regina	517
*Riverdance on Broadway	515
Fifth of July	511
Half a Sixpence	511
The Vagabond King	511
The New Moon	509
The World of Suzie Wong	508
The Rothschilds	507
On Your Toes (r)	505
Sugar	505
Shuffle Along	504
Up in Central Park	504
Carmen Jones	503
Saturday Night Fever	502
The Member of the Wedding	501
Panama Hattie	501
Personal Appearance	501
Bird in Hand	500
Room Service	500
Sailor, Beware!	500
Tomorrow the World	500

LONG RUNS OFF BROADWAY

Plays	*Performances*
*The Fantasticks	16,907
*Perfect Crime	5,837
*Tubes	4,621
*Tony 'n' Tina's Wedding	4,168
Nunsense	3,672
*Stomp	3,048
The Threepenny Opera	2,611
Forbidden Broadway 1982-87	2,332
Little Shop of Horrors	2,209
Godspell	2,124
*I Love You, You're Perfect, Now Change	2,032
Vampire Lesbians of Sodom	2,024
Jacques Brel	1,847
Forever Plaid	1,811
Vanities	1,785
You're a Good Man, Charlie Brown	1,597
The Blacks	1,408
One Mo' Time	1,372
Grandma Sylvia's Funeral	1,360
Let My People Come	1,327
Driving Miss Daisy	1,195
The Hot l Baltimore	1,166
I'm Getting My Act Together and Taking It on the Road	1,165
*De La Guarda	1,144
Little Mary Sunshine	1,143
Steel Magnolias	1,126
El Grande de Coca-Cola	1,114
The Proposition	1,109
Beau Jest	1,069
Tamara	1,036
One Flew Over the Cuckoo's Nest (r)	1,025
The Boys in the Band	1,000
Fool for Love	1,000
Other People's Money	990
Cloud 9	971
*Late Nite Catechism	962

Plays	*Performances*
Secrets Every Smart Traveler Should Know	953
Sister Mary Ignatius Explains It All for You & The Actor's Nightmare	947
Your Own Thing	933
Curley McDimple	931
Leave It to Jane (r)	928
Hedwig and the Angry Inch	857
Forbidden Broadway Strikes Back	850
When Pigs Fly	840
The Mad Show	871
Scrambled Feet	831
The Effect of Gamma Rays on Man-in-the-Moon Marigolds	819
Over the River and Through the Woods	800
*Naked Boys Singing!	792
A View From the Bridge (r)	780
The Boy Friend (r)	763
True West	762
Forbidden Broadway Cleans Up Its Act!	754
Isn't It Romantic	733
Dime a Dozen	728
The Pocket Watch	725
The Connection	722
The Passion of Dracula	714
Adaptation & Next	707
Oh! Calcutta!	704
Scuba Duba	692
*The Vagina Monologues	687
The Foreigner	686
The Knack	685
Fully Committed	675
The Club	674
The Balcony	672
Penn & Teller	666

Plays	*Performances*
Dinner With Friends	654
America Hurrah	634
Oil City Symphony	626
The Countess	618
*Our Sinatra	613
Hogan's Goat	607
Beehive	600
The Trojan Women	600
The Dining Room	583
Krapp's Last Tape & The Zoo Story	582
Three Tall Women	582
The Dumbwaiter & The Collection	578
Forbidden Broadway 1990	576
Dames at Sea	575
The Crucible (r)	571
The Iceman Cometh (r)	565
*The Donkey Show	554
The Hostage (r)	545
Wit	545
What's a Nice Country Like You Doing in a State Like This?	543
Forbidden Broadway 1988	534
Gross Indecency: The Three Trials of Oscar Wilde	534
Frankie and Johnny in the Clair de Lune	533
Six Characters in Search of an Author (r)	529
All in the Timing	526
Oleanna	513
Making Porn	511
The Dirtiest Show in Town	509
Happy Ending & Day of Absence	504
Greater Tuna	501
A Shayna Maidel	501
The Boys From Syracuse (r)	500

NEW YORK DRAMA CRITICS CIRCLE 1935–1936 TO 2000–2001

○○○○○

LISTED BELOW ARE THE NEW YORK Drama Critics Circle Awards from 1935–1936 through 2000–2001 classified as follows: (1) Best American Play, (2) Best Foreign Play, (3) Best Musical, (4) Best, Regardless of Category (this category was established by new voting rules in 1962–63 and did not exist prior to that year).

1935–36 (1) *Winterset*
1936–37 (1) *High Tor*
1937–38 (1) *Of Mice and Men*, (2) *Shadow and Substance*
1938–39 (1) No award, (2) *The White Steed*
1939–40 (1) *The Time of Your Life*
1940–41 (1) *Watch on the Rhine*, (2) *The Corn Is Green*
1941–42 (1) No award, (2) *Blithe Spirit*
1942–43 (1) *The Patriots*
1943–44 (2) *Jacobowsky and the Colonel*
1944–45 (1) *The Glass Menagerie*
1945–46 (3) *Carousel*
1946–47 (1) *All My Sons*, (2) *No Exit*, (3) *Brigadoon*
1947–48 (1) *A Streetcar Named Desire*, (2) *The Winslow Boy*
1948–49 (1) *Death of a Salesman*, (2) *The Madwoman of Chaillot*, (3) *South Pacific*
1949–50 (1) *The Member of the Wedding*, (2) *The Cocktail Party*, (3) *The Consul*
1950–51 (1) *Darkness at Noon*, (2) *The Lady's Not for Burning*, (3) *Guys and Dolls*
1951–52 (1) *I Am a Camera*, (2) *Venus Observed*, (3) *Pal Joey* (Special citation to *Don Juan in Hell*)
1952–53 (1) *Picnic*, (2) *The Love of Four Colonels*, (3) *Wonderful Town*
1953–54 (1) *The Teahouse of the August Moon*, (2) *Ondine*, (3) *The Golden Apple*
1954–55 (1) *Cat on a Hot Tin Roof*, (2) *Witness for the Prosecution*, (3) *The Saint of Bleecker Street*
1955–56 (1) *The Diary of Anne Frank*, (2) *Tiger at the Gates*, (3) *My Fair Lady*
1956–57 (1) *Long Day's Journey Into Night*, (2) *The Waltz of the Toreadors*, (3) *The Most Happy Fella*
1957–58 (1) *Look Homeward, Angel*, (2) *Look Back in Anger*, (3) *The Music Man*
1958–59 (1) *A Raisin in the Sun*, (2) *The Visit*, (3) *La Plume de Ma Tante*
1959–60 (1) *Toys in the Attic*, (2) *Five Finger Exercise*, (3) *Fiorello!*
1960–61 (1) *All the Way Home*, (2) *A Taste of Honey*, (3) *Carnival*
1961–62 (1) *The Night of the Iguana*, (2) *A Man for All Seasons*, (3) *How to Succeed in Business Without Really Trying*
1962–63 (4) *Who's Afraid of Virginia Woolf?* (Special citation to *Beyond the Fringe*)
1963–64 (4) *Luther*, (3) *Hello, Dolly!* (Special citation to *The Trojan Women*)
1964–65 (4) *The Subject Was Roses*, (3) *Fiddler on the Roof*
1965–66 (4) *The Persecution and Assassination of Marat as Performed by the Inmates of the Asylum of Charenton Under the Direction of the Marquis de Sade*, (3) *Man of La Mancha*
1966–67 (4) *The Homecoming*, (3) *Cabaret*
1967–68 (4) *Rosencrantz and Guildenstern Are Dead*, (3) *Your Own Thing*
1968–69 (4) *The Great White Hope*, (3) *1776*
1969–70 (4) *Borstal Boy*, (1) *The Effect of Gamma Rays on Man-in-the-Moon Marigolds*, (3) *Company*
1970–71 (4) *Home*, (1) *The House of Blue Leaves*, (3) *Follies*
1971–72 (4) *That Championship Season*, (2) *The Screens* (3) *Two Gentlemen of Verona* (Special citations to *Sticks and Bones* and *Old Times*)
1972–73 (4) *The Changing Room*, (1) *The Hot l Baltimore*, (3) *A Little Night Music*
1973–74 (4) *The Contractor*, (1) *Short Eyes*, (3) *Candide*
1974–75 (4) *Equus* (1) *The Taking of Miss Janie*, (3) *A Chorus Line*

1975–76 (4) *Travesties*, (1) *Streamers*, (3) *Pacific Overtures*
1976–77 (4) *Otherwise Engaged*, (1) *American Buffalo*, (3) *Annie*
1977–78 (4) *Da*, (3) *Ain't Misbehavin'*
1978–79 (4) *The Elephant Man*, (3) *Sweeney Todd, the Demon Barber of Fleet Street*
1979–80 (4) *Talley's Folly*, (2) *Betrayal*, (3) *Evita* (Special citation to Peter Brook's Le Centre International de Créations Théâtrales for its repertory)
1980–81 (4) *A Lesson From Aloes*, (1) *Crimes of the Heart* (Special citations to *Lena Horne: The Lady and Her Music* and the New York Shakespeare Festival production of *The Pirates of Penzance*)
1981–82 (4) *The Life & Adventures of Nicholas Nickleby*, (1) *A Soldier's Play*
1982–83 (4) *Brighton Beach Memoirs*, (2) *Plenty*, (3) *Little Shop of Horrors* (Special citation to Young Playwrights Festival)
1983–84 (4) *The Real Thing*, (1) *Glengarry Glen Ross*, (3) *Sunday in the Park With George* (Special citation to Samuel Beckett for the body of his work)
1984–85 (4) *Ma Rainey's Black Bottom*
1985–86 (4) *A Lie of the Mind*, (2) *Benefactors* (Special citation to *The Search for Signs of Intelligent Life in the Universe*)
1986–87 (4) *Fences*, (2) *Les Liaisons Dangereuses*, (3) *Les Misérables*
1987–88 (4) *Joe Turner's Come and Gone*, (2) *The Road to Mecca*, (3) *Into the Woods*
1988–89 (4) *The Heidi Chronicles*, (2) *Aristocrats* (Special citation to Bill Irwin for *Largely New York*)
1989–90 (4) *The Piano Lesson*, (2) *Privates on Parade*, (3) *City of Angels*
1990–91 (4) *Six Degrees of Separation*, (2) *Our Country's Good*, (3) *The Will Rogers Follies* (Special citation to Eileen Atkins for her portrayal of Virginia Woolf in *A Room of One's Own*)
1991–92 (4) *Dancing at Lughnasa*, (1) *Two Trains Running*
1992–93 (4) *Angels in America: Millennium Approaches*, (2) *Someone Who'll Watch Over Me*, (3) *Kiss of the Spider Woman*
1993–94 (4) *Three Tall Women* (Special citation to Anna Deavere Smith for her unique contribution to theatrical form)
1994–95 (4) *Arcadia*, (1) *Love! Valour! Compassion!* (Special citation to Signature Theatre Company for outstanding artistic achievement)
1995–96 (4) *Seven Guitars*, (2) *Molly Sweeney*, (3) *Rent*
1996–97 (4) *How I Learned to Drive*, (2) *Skylight*, (3) *Violet* (Special citation to *Chicago*)
1997–98 (4) *Art*, (1) *Pride's Crossing*, (3) *The Lion King* (Special citation to the revival production of *Cabaret*)
1998–99 (4) *Wit*, (3) *Parade*, (2) *Closer* (Special citation to David Hare for his contributions to the 1998–99 theater season: *Amy's View*, *Via Dolorosa* and *The Blue Room*)
1999–00 (4) *Jitney*, (3) *James Joyce's The Dead*, (2) *Copenhagen*
2000–01 (4) *The Invention of Love*, (1) *Proof*, (3) *The Producers*

NEW YORK DRAMA CRITICS CIRCLE VOTING 2000–2001
Michael Sommers (*Star-Ledger*, Newark), President

AT ITS MAY 8, 2001 MEETING the New York Drama Critics Circle reversed its recent practice of giving top honors to an Off Broadway production when it named Broadway's *The Invention of Love* best play of the 2000–2001 season. The group also honored *Proof* as best American play following that work's strong showing both off and on Broadway. It took two ballots to name the best play, but the best American play category required four ballots. The fierce competition for best American play reflected staunch support for *Proof*, *The Play About the Baby* and *King Hedley II*—all of which also contended for the best-of-bests award received by *The Invention of Love*. In a vote that was easy to predict, *The Producers* was named best musical on the first ballot.

Eighteen members of the Circle were present, and two (Ben Brantley of the *New York Times* and Elysa Gardner of *USA Today)* voted by proxy. The first ballot voting for best-of-bests was divided as follows: *The Invention of Love* 8 (Clive Barnes, *New York Post*; Brantley; Amy Gamerman, *Wall Street Journal*; John Heilpern, *New York Observer*; Howard Kissel, *Daily News*; Jacques le Sourd, Gannett *Journal-News*; Donald Lyons, *New York Post*; Linda Winer, *Newsday*), *The Play About the Baby* 3 (Charles Isherwood, *Variety*; Michael Kuchwara, Associated Press; Michael Sommers, *Star-Ledger*/Newhouse newspapers), *Proof* 3 (Robert Feldberg, *Bergen Record*; Ken Mandelbaum, Broadway.com; John Simon, *New York*), *Lobby Hero* 2 (Frank Scheck, *Hollywood Reporter*; David Sheward, *Back Stage*), *Boy Gets Girl* 1 (Richard Zoglin, *Time*), *The Designated Mourner* 1 (Bruce Weber, *New York Times*), *Force Continuum* 1 (Michael Feingold, *Village Voice*), *King Hedley II* 1 (Gardner).

No play received a majority of votes on the first ballot, so the Circle went to a weighted system for the second round, which allowed voters to select first, second and third choices. Following the election of *The Invention of Love*, the critics slogged through four rounds of voting for best American play. For the final round, proxy ballots were not included and the competition was head-to-head between top vote-getters *Proof* and *The Play About the Baby*. With 18 members present for this round of voting, *Proof* received 11 votes to *The Play About the Baby*'s 7.

The Producers won on the first ballot by receiving the votes of all critics present—or voting by proxy—except Weber and Lyons (*Urinetown*), Feingold (*And God Created Great Whales*), Mandelbaum (*The Full Monty*) and Simon (abstained).

It is worth noting that the 2000–2001 Critics Circle awards mark the first time that the group has failed to honor a New York production of an August Wilson play.

CHOICES OF SOME OTHER CRITICS

Critic	Best Play	Best Musical
Sherry Eaker *Back Stage*	*Proof*	*The Producers*
Ralph Howard WINS Radio	*The Invention of Love*	*The Producers*
Alvin Klein *New York Times* Suburban	*Proof*	*The Producers*
Dick Schaap ABC *World News Tonight*	*Proof*	*The Producers*

PULITZER PRIZE WINNERS 1916–1917 TO 2000–2001

1916–17 No award
1917–18 *Why Marry?* by Jesse Lynch Williams
1918–19 No award
1919–20 *Beyond the Horizon* by Eugene O'Neill
1920–21 *Miss Lulu Bett* by Zona Gale
1921–22 *Anna Christie* by Eugene O'Neill
1922–23 *Icebound* by Owen Davis
1923–24 *Hell-Bent fer Heaven* by Hatcher Hughes
1924–25 *They Knew What They Wanted* by Sidney Howard
1925–26 *Craig's Wife* by George Kelly
1926–27 *In Abraham's Bosom* by Paul Green
1927–28 *Strange Interlude* by Eugene O'Neill
1928–29 *Street Scene* by Elmer Rice
1929–30 *The Green Pastures* by Marc Connelly
1930–31 *Alison's House* by Susan Glaspell
1931–32 *Of Thee I Sing* by George S. Kaufman, Morrie Ryskind, Ira and George Gershwin
1932–33 *Both Your Houses* by Maxwell Anderson
1933–34 *Men in White* by Sidney Kingsley
1934–35 *The Old Maid* by Zoe Akins
1935–36 *Idiot's Delight* by Robert E. Sherwood
1936–37 *You Can't Take It With You* by Moss Hart and George S. Kaufman
1937–38 *Our Town* by Thornton Wilder
1938–39 *Abe Lincoln in Illinois* by Robert E. Sherwood
1939–40 *The Time of Your Life* by William Saroyan
1940–41 *There Shall Be No Night* by Robert E. Sherwood
1941–42 No award
1942–43 *The Skin of Our Teeth* by Thornton Wilder
1943–44 No award
1944–45 *Harvey* by Mary Chase
1945–46 *State of the Union* by Howard Lindsay and Russel Crouse
1946–47 No award
1947–48 *A Streetcar Named Desire* by Tennessee Williams
1948–49 *Death of a Salesman* by Arthur Miller
1949–50 *South Pacific* by Richard Rodgers, Oscar Hammerstein II and Joshua Logan
1950–51 No award
1951–52 *The Shrike*, by Joseph Kramm
1952–53 *Picnic* by William Inge
1953–54 *The Teahouse of the August Moon* by John Patrick
1954–55 *Cat on a Hot Tin Roof* by Tennessee Williams
1955–56 *The Diary of Anne Frank* by Frances Goodrich and Albert Hackett
1956–57 *Long Day's Journey Into Night* by Eugene O'Neill
1957–58 *Look Homeward, Angel* by Ketti Frings
1958–59 *J.B.* by Archibald MacLeish
1959–60 *Fiorello!* by Jerome Weidman, George Abbott, Sheldon Harnick and Jerry Bock
1960–61 *All the Way Home* by Tad Mosel
1961–62 *How to Succeed in Business Without Really Trying* by Abe Burrows, Willie Gilbert, Jack Weinstock and Frank Loesser
1962–63 No award
1963–64 No award
1964–65 *The Subject Was Roses* by Frank D. Gilroy
1965–66 No award
1966–67 *A Delicate Balance* by Edward Albee
1967–68 No award
1968–69 *The Great White Hope* by Howard Sackler
1969–70 *No Place To Be Somebody* by Charles Gordone
1970–71 *The Effect of Gamma Rays on Man-in-the-Moon Marigolds* by Paul Zindel
1971–72 No award
1972–73 *That Championship Season* by Jason Miller
1973–74 No award
1974–75 *Seascape* by Edward Albee
1975–76 *A Chorus Line* by Michael Bennett, James Kirkwood, Nicholas Dante, Marvin Hamlisch and Edward Kleban
1976–77 *The Shadow Box* by Michael Cristofer
1977–78 *The Gin Game* by D.L. Coburn
1978–79 *Buried Child* by Sam Shepard
1979–80 *Talley's Folly* by Lanford Wilson
1980–81 *Crimes of the Heart* by Beth Henley
1981–82 *A Soldier's Play* by Charles Fuller
1982–83 *'night, Mother* by Marsha Norman
1983–84 *Glengarry Glen Ross* by David Mamet
1984–85 *Sunday in the Park With George* by James Lapine and Stephen Sondheim
1985–86 No award

1986–87 *Fences* by August Wilson
1987–88 *Driving Miss Daisy* by Alfred Uhry
1988–89 *The Heidi Chronicles* by Wendy Wasserstein
1989–90 *The Piano Lesson* by August Wilson
1990–91 *Lost in Yonkers* by Neil Simon
1991–92 *The Kentucky Cycle* by Robert Schenkkan
1992–93 *Angels in America: Millennium Approaches* by Tony Kushner
1993–94 *Three Tall Women* by Edward Albee
1994–95 *The Young Man From Atlanta* by Horton Foote
1995–96 *Rent* by Jonathan Larson
1996–97 No award
1997–98 *How I Learned to Drive* by Paula Vogel
1998–99 *Wit* by Margaret Edson
1999–00 *Dinner With Friends* by Donald Margulies
2000–01 *Proof* by David Auburn

TONY AWARDS 2001

○○○○○

THE AMERICAN THEATRE WING'S 55th annual Tony Awards, named for Antoinette Perry, are presented in recognition of distinguished achievement in the Broadway theater. The League of American Theatres and Producers and the American Theatre Wing present these awards, founded by the Wing in 1947. Legitimate theater productions opening in 40 eligible Broadway theaters during the present Tony season—May 4, 2000 to May 2, 2001—were considered by the Tony Awards Nominating Committee (appointed by the Tony Awards Administration Committee) for the awards in 21 competitive and several special categories. The 2000–2001 Nominating Committee included Lisa Aronson, scenic designer; Price Berkley, publisher; Kate Burton, actor; Robert Callely, administrator; Mary Schmidt Campbell, educator; Merle Debuskey, publicist; Jerry Dominus, executive; Henry Guettel, administrator; Carol Hall, composer and lyricist; Geraldine Hammerstein, actor and writer; Jay Harnick, artistic director; Sheldon Harnick, lyricist; Robert Kamlot, general manager; Louise Kerz, historian; Stuart Little, writer and editor; Joanna Merlin, actor and casting director; Theodore Mann, producer and director; Peter Neufeld, general manager; Estelle Parsons, actor; Shirley Rich, casting director; Aubrey Reuben, photographer; Arthur Rubin, producer; Meg Simon, casting director; Arnold Weinstein, educator, and George C. White, artistic director.

The Tony Awards are voted from the list of nominees by members of the theater and journalism professions: the governing boards of the five theater artists' organizations—Actors' Equity Association, the Dramatists Guild, the Society of Stage Directors and Choreographers, the United Scenic Artists and the Casting Society of America—the members of the designated first night theater press, the board of directors of the American Theatre Wing and the membership of the League of American Theatres and Producers. Because of fluctuation in these groups, the size of the Tony electorate varies from year to year. For the 2000–2001 season there were 705 qualified Tony voters.

The list of 2000–2001 nominees follows, with winners in each category listed in **bold face type**.

BEST PLAY (award goes to both author and producer). *The Invention of Love* by Tom Stoppard, produced by Lincoln Center Theater under the direction of André Bishop and Bernard Gersten. *King Hedley II* by August Wilson, produced by Sageworks, Benjamin Mordecai, Jujamcyn Theaters, 52nd Street Productions, Spring Sirkin, Peggy Hill, Manhattan Theatre Club, Kardana-Swinsky Productions. ***Proof* by David Auburn**, produced by **Manhattan Theatre Club, Roger Berlind, Carole Shorenstein Hays, Jujamcyn Theaters, Ostar Enterprises, Daryl Roth, Stuart Thompson**. *The Tale of the Allergist's Wife* by Charles Busch, produced by Manhattan Theatre Club, Lynne Meadow, Barry Grove, Carole Shorenstein Hays, Daryl Roth, Stuart Thompson, Douglas S. Cramer.

BEST MUSICAL (award goes to the producer). *A Class Act* produced by Marty Bell, Chase Mishkin, Arielle Tepper, Manhattan Theatre Club. *The Full Monty* produced by Fox Searchlight Pictures, Lindsay Law, Thomas Hall. *Jane Eyre* produced by Annette Niemtzow, Janet Robinson, Pamela Koslow, Margaret McFeeley Golden, Jennifer Manocherian, Carolyn Kim McCarthy. ***The Producers*** produced by **Rocco Landesman, SFX Theatrical Group, The Frankel-Baruch-Viertel-Routh Group, Bob and Harvey Weinstein, Rick Steiner, Robert F.X. Sillerman, Mel Brooks, James D. Stern/Douglas Meyer**.

BEST BOOK OF A MUSICAL. *A Class Act* by Linda Kline and Lonny Price, *The Full Monty* by Terrence McNally, *Jane Eyre* by John Caird, ***The Producers* by Mel Brooks and Thomas Meehan**.

BEST ORIGINAL SCORE (music & lyrics). *A Class Act*, music and lyrics by Edward Kleban; *The Full Monty*, music and lyrics by David Yazbek; *Jane Eyre*, music by Paul Gordon, lyrics by Paul Gordon and John Caird; ***The Producers*, music and lyrics by Mel Brooks**.

BEST REVIVAL OF A PLAY (award goes to the producer). *Betrayal* produced by Roundabout Theatre Company, Todd Haimes, Ellen Richard, Julia C. Levy. *Gore Vidal's The Best Man* produced by Jeffrey Richards/Michael B. Rothfeld, Raymond J. Greenwald, Jerry Frankel, Darren Bagert. ***One Flew Over the Cuckoo's Nest*** produced by **Michael Leavitt, Fox Theatricals, Anita Waxman, Elizabeth Williams, John York Noble, Randall L. Wreghitt, Dori Berinstein, The Steppenwolf Theatre Company**. *The Search for Signs of Intelligent Life in the Universe* produced by Tomlin and Wagner Theatricalz.

BEST REVIVAL OF A MUSICAL (award goes to the producer). *Bells Are Ringing* produced by Mitchell Maxwell, Mark Balsam, Victoria Maxwell, Robert Barandes, Mark Goldberg, Anthony R. Russo, James L. Simon, Fred H. Krones, Allen M. Shore, Momentum Productions, Inc. *Follies* produced by Roundabout Theatre Company, Todd Haimes, Ellen Richard, Julia C. Levy. ***42nd Street*** produced by **Dodger Theatricals, Joop van den Ende, Stage Holding**. *The Rocky Horror Show* produced by Jordan Roth, Christopher Malcolm, Howard Panter, Richard O'Brien, The Rocky Horror Company Ltd.

BEST PERFORMANCE BY A LEADING ACTOR IN A PLAY. Seán Campion in *Stones in His Pockets*, **Richard Easton in *The Invention of Love***, Conleth Hill in *Stones in His Pockets*, Brian Stokes Mitchell in *King Hedley II*, Gary Sinise in *One Flew Over the Cuckoo's Nest*.

BEST PERFORMANCE BY A LEADING ACTRESS IN A PLAY. Juliette Binoche in *Betrayal*, Linda Lavin in *The Tale of the Allergist's Wife*, **Mary-Louise Parker in *Proof***, Jean Smart in *The Man Who Came to Dinner*, Leslie Uggams in *King Hedley II*.

BEST PERFORMANCE BY A LEADING ACTOR IN A MUSICAL. Matthew

Broderick in *The Producers*, Kevin Chamberlin in *Seussical*, Tom Hewitt in *The Rocky Horror Show*, **Nathan Lane in *The Producers***, Patrick Wilson in *The Full Monty*.

BEST PERFORMANCE BY A LEADING ACTRESS IN A MUSICAL. Blythe Danner in *Follies*, **Christine Ebersole in *42nd Street***, Randy Graff in *A Class Act*, Faith Prince in *Bells Are Ringing*, Marla Schaffel in *Jane Eyre*.

BEST PERFORMANCE BY A FEATURED ACTOR IN A PLAY. Charles Brown in *King Hedley II*, Larry Bryggman in *Proof*, Michael Hayden in *Judgment at Nuremberg*, **Robert Sean Leonard in The Invention of Love**, Ben Shenkman in *Proof*.

BEST PERFORMANCE BY A FEATURED ACTRESS IN A PLAY. **Viola Davis in *King Hedley II***, Johanna Day in *Proof*, Penny Fuller in *The Dinner Party*, Marthe Keller in *Judgment at Nuremberg*, Michele Lee in *The Tale of the Allergist's Wife*.

BEST PERFORMANCE BY A FEATURED ACTOR IN A MUSICAL. Roger Bart in *The Producers*, **Gary Beach in *The Producers***, John Ellison Conlee in *The Full Monty*, André De Shields in *The Full Monty*, Brad Oscar in *The Producers*.

BEST PERFORMANCE BY A FEATURED ACTRESS IN A MUSICAL. Polly Bergen in *Follies*, Kathleen Freeman in *The Full Monty*, **Cady Huffman in *The Producers***, Kate Levering in *42nd Street*, Mary Testa in *42nd Street*.

BEST DIRECTION OF A PLAY. Marion McClinton for *King Hedley II*, Ian McElhinney for *Stones in His Pockets*, Jack O'Brien for *The Invention of Love*, **Daniel Sullivan for *Proof***.

BEST DIRECTION OF A MUSICAL. Christopher Ashley for *The Rocky Horror Show*, Mark Bramble for *42nd Street*, Jack O'Brien for *The Full Monty*, **Susan Stroman for *The Producers***.

BEST SCENIC DESIGN. Bob Crowley for *The Invention of Love*, Heidi Ettinger for *The Adventures of Tom Sawyer*, Douglas W. Schmidt for *42nd Street*, **Robin Wagner for *The Producers***.

BEST COSTUME DESIGN. Theoni V. Aldredge for *Follies*, Roger Kirk for *42nd Street*, **William Ivey Long for *The Producers***, David C. Woolard for *The Rocky Horror Show*.

BEST LIGHTING DESIGN. Jules Fisher and Peggy Eisenhauer for *Jane Eyre*, Paul Gallo for *42nd Street*, **Peter Kaczorowski for *The Producers***, Kenneth Posner for *The Adventures of Tom Sawyer*.

BEST CHOREOGRAPHY. Jerry Mitchell for *The Full Monty*, Jim Morgan, George Pinney and John Vanderkloff for *Blast!*, Randy Skinner for *42nd Street*, **Susan Stroman for *The Producers***.

BEST ORCHESTRATIONS. **Doug Besterman for *The Producers***, Larry Hochman for *A Class Act*, Jonathan Tunick for *Follies*, Harold Wheeler for *The Full Monty*.

SPECIAL TONY AWARDS. Special theatrical event: ***Blast!*** Lifetime achievement in the theater: **Paul Gemignani**, musical director.

TONY HONORS. For excellence in theater. **Betty Corwin** and the **Theatre on Film and Tape Archive at the New York Public Library for the Performing Arts at Lincoln Center**. **New Dramatists**, playwright's workshop. ***Theatre World***.

REGIONAL THEATRE. To a regional theater company that has displayed a continuous level of artistic achievement contributing to the growth of the theater nationally, recommended by the American Theatre Critics Association: **Victory Gardens Theater, Chicago Illinois**.

TONY AWARD WINNERS, 1947–2001

LISTED BELOW ARE THE ANTOINETTE PERRY (Tony) Award winners in the catgories of Best Play and Best Musical from the time these awards were established until the present.

1947—No play or musical award
1948—*Mister Roberts*; no musical award
1949—*Death of a Salesman*; *Kiss Me, Kate*
1950—*The Cocktail Party*; *South Pacific*
1951—*The Rose Tattoo*; *Guys and Dolls*
1952—*The Fourposter*; *The King and I*
1953—*The Crucible*; *Wonderful Town*
1954—*The Teahouse of the August Moon*; *Kismet*
1955—*The Desperate Hours*; *The Pajama Game*
1956—*The Diary of Anne Frank*; *Damn Yankees*
1957—*Long Day's Journey Into Night*; *My Fair Lady*
1958—*Sunrise at Campobello*; *The Music Man*
1959—*J.B.*; *Redhead*
1960—*The Miracle Worker*; *Fiorello!* and *The Sound of Music* (tie)
1961—*Becket*; *Bye Bye Birdie*
1962—*A Man for All Seasons*; *How to Succeed in Business Without Really Trying*
1963—*Who's Afraid of Virginia Woolf?*; *A Funny Thing Happened on the Way to the Forum*
1964—*Luther*; *Hello, Dolly!*
1965—*The Subject Was Roses*; *Fiddler on the Roof*
1966—*The Persecution and Assassination of Marat as Performed by the Inmates of the Asylum of Charenton Under the Direction of the Marquis de Sade*; *Man of La Mancha*
1967—*The Homecoming*; *Cabaret*
1968—*Rosencrantz and Guildenstern Are Dead*; *Hallelujah, Baby!*
1969—*The Great White Hope*; *1776*
1970—*Borstal Boy*; *Applause*
1971—*Sleuth*; *Company*
1972—*Sticks and Bones*; *Two Gentlemen of Verona*
1973—*That Championship Season*; *A Little Night Music*
1974—*The River Niger*; *Raisin*
1975—*Equus*; *The Wiz*
1976—*Travesties*; *A Chorus Line*
1977—*The Shadow Box*; *Annie*
1978—*Da*; *Ain't Misbehavin'*
1979—*The Elephant Man*; *Sweeney Todd, the Demon Barber of Fleet Street*
1980—*Children of a Lesser God*; *Evita*
1981—*Amadeus*; *42nd Street*
1982—*The Life & Adventures of Nicholas Nickleby*; *Nine*
1983—*Torch Song Trilogy*; *Cats*
1984—*The Real Thing*; *La Cage aux Folles*
1985—*Biloxi Blues*; *Big River*
1986—*I'm Not Rappaport*; *The Mystery of Edwin Drood*
1987—*Fences*; *Les Misérables*
1988—*M. Butterfly*; *The Phantom of the Opera*
1989—*The Heidi Chronicles*; *Jerome Robbins' Broadway*
1990—*The Grapes of Wrath*; *City of Angels*
1991—*Lost in Yonkers*; *The Will Rogers Follies*
1992—*Dancing at Lughnasa*; *Crazy for You*
1993—*Angels in America, Part I: Millennium Approaches*; *Kiss of the Spider Woman*
1994—*Angels in America, Part II: Perestroika*; *Passion*
1995—*Love! Valour! Compassion!*; *Sunset Boulevard*
1996—*Master Class*; *Rent*
1997—*The Last Night of Ballyhoo*; *Titanic*
1998—*Art*; *The Lion King*
1999—*Side Man*; *Fosse*
2000—*Copenhagen*; *Contact*
2001—*Proof*; *The Producers*

LUCILLE LORTEL AWARDS 2001

THE LUCILLE LORTEL AWARDS for outstanding Off Broadway achievement were established in 1985 by a resolution of the League of Off Broadway Theatres and Producers, which administers them and has presented them annually since 1986. Eligible for the 16th annual awards in 2001 were all Off Broadway productions that opened between April 1, 2000 and March 31, 2001. Winners were selected by a committee comprising Clive Barnes, Maria DiDia, Susan Einhorn, Beverly Emmons, Bruce Ferguson, George Forbes, David Marshall Grant, Barbara Hauptman, Gerald Rabkin, Marc Routh, Donald Saddler, David Stone, Anna Strasberg, Carol Waaser and Linda Winer.

PLAY. ***Proof*** by David Auburn.

MUSICAL. ***Bat Boy: The Musical*** book by Keythe Farley and Brian Flemming, music. and lyrics by Laurence O'Keefe.

REVIVAL. ***Tiny Alice*** by Edward Albee, produced by Second Stage Theatre.

ACTOR. **Alan Bates** in *The Unexpected Man*.

ACTRESS. **Mary-Louise Parker** in *Proof*.

FEATURED ACTOR. **Justin Kirk** in *Ten Unknowns*.

FEATURED ACTRESS. **Julianna Margulies** in *Ten Unknowns*.

DIRECTION. **Daniel Sullivan** for *Proof*.

CHOREOGRAPHY. **Christopher Gatelli** for *Bat Boy: The Musical*.

SCENERY. **David Gallo** for *Jitney*.

COSTUMES. **Jane Greenwood** for *Old Money*.

LIGHTING. **Paul Anderson** for *Mnemonic*.

SOUND. **Christopher Shutt** for *Mnemonic*.

BODY OF WORK. **Eileen Heckart**.

LIFETIME ACHIEVEMENT. **Kitty Carlisle Hart**.

EDITH OLIVER AWARD. **Lanford Wilson**.

UNIQUE THEATRICAL EXPERIENCE. ***Mnemonic***.

BODY OF WORK. **New York Theatre Workshop**.

LORTEL AWARD WINNERS, 1986–2001

LISTED BELOW ARE THE LUCILLE LORTEL Award winners in the categories of Outstanding Play and Outstanding Musical from the time these awards were established until the present.

1986—*Woza Africa!*; no musical award
1987—*The Common Pursuit*; no musical award
1988—No play or musical award
1989—*The Cocktail Hour*; no musical award
1990—No play or musical award
1991—*Aristocrats*; *Falsettoland*
1992—*Lips Together, Teeth Apart*; *And the World Goes 'Round*
1993—*The Destiny of Me*; *Forbidden Broadway*
1994—*Three Tall Women*; *Wings*
1995—*Camping With Henry & Tom*; *Jelly Roll!*
1996—*Molly Sweeney*; *Floyd Collins*
1997—*How I Learned to Drive*; *Violet*
1998—*Gross Indecency*, and *The Beauty Queen of Leenane* (tie); no musical award
1999—*Wit*; no musical award
2000—*Dinner With Friends*; *James Joyce's The Dead*
2001—*Proof*; *Bat Boy: The Musical*

AMERICAN THEATRE CRITICS/STEINBERG NEW PLAY AWARDS AND CITATIONS

○○○○○

INCLUDING PRINCIPAL CITATIONS AND NEW PLAY AWARD WINNERS, 1977–2001

BEGINNING WITH THE SEASON of 1976–77, the American Theatre Critics Association (ATCA) has cited one or more outstanding new plays in United States theater. The principal honorees have been included in *Best Plays* since the first year. In 1986 the ATCA New Play Award was given for the first time, along with a $1,000 prize. The award and citations were renamed the **American Theatre Critics/Steinberg New Play Award and Citations** in 2000 (see essays on the 2001 ATCA/Steinberg honorees in the Plays Produced On Broadway and Season Around the United States sections of this volume). The award dates have been renumbered beginning with this volume to correctly reflect the year in which ATCA conferred the honor.

NEW PLAY CITATIONS, 1977–1985

1977—*And the Soul Shall Dance* by Wakako Yamauchi
1978—*Getting Out* by Marsha Norman
1979—*Loose Ends* by Michael Weller
1980—*Custer* by Robert E. Ingham
1981—*Chekhov in Yalta* by John Driver and Jeffrey Haddow
1982—*Talking With* by Jane Martin
1983—*Closely Related* by Bruce MacDonald
1984—*Wasted* by Fred Gamel
1985—*Scheherazade* by Marisha Chamberlain

NEW PLAY AWARD 1986–1999

1986—*Fences* by August Wilson
1987—*A Walk in the Woods* by Lee Blessing
1988—*Heathen Valley* by Romulus Linney
1989—*The Piano Lesson* by August Wilson
1990—*2* by Romulus Linney
1991—*Two Trains Running* by August Wilson
1992—*Could I Have This Dance?* by Doug Haverty
1993—*Children of Paradise: Shooting a Dream* by Steven Epp, Felicity Jones, Dominique Serrand and Paul Walsh
1994—*Keely and Du* by Jane Martin
1995—*The Nanjing Race* by Reggie Cheong-Leen
1996—*Amazing Grace* by Michael Cristofer
1997—*Jack and Jill* by Jane Martin
1998—*The Cider House Rules, Part II* by Peter Parnell
1999—*Book of Days* by Lanford Wilson.

ATCA/STEINBERG NEW PLAY AWARD AND CITATIONS

2000—*Oo-Bla-Dee* by Regina Taylor
Citations: *Compleat Female Stage Beauty* by Jeffrey Hatcher; *Syncopation* by Allan Knee
2001—*Anton in Show Business* by Jane Martin
Citations: *Big Love* by Charles L. Mee; *King Hedley II* by August Wilson

ADDITIONAL PRIZES AND AWARDS, 2000–2001

THE FOLLOWING IS A LIST of major awards for achievement in the theater this season. The names of honorees appear in **bold face type**.

1999–2000 GEORGE JEAN NATHAN AWARD. For dramatic criticism. **Albert Williams**.

20th ANNUAL WILLIAM INGE FESTIVAL AWARD. For distinguished achievement in American theater. **Lanford Wilson.** New voice: **Mark St. Germain**.

2001 M. ELIZABETH OSBORN AWARD. Presented by the American Theatre Critics Association to an emerging playwright. **S.M. Shephard-Massat** for *Waiting to be Invited.*

23rd ANNUAL KENNEDY CENTER HONORS. For distinguished achievement by individuals who have made significant contributions to American culture through the arts. **Mikhail Baryshnikov**, **Chuck Berry**, **Plácido Domingo**, **Clint Eastwood**, **Angela Lansbury**.

4th ANNUAL KENNEDY CENTER–MARK TWAIN PRIZE. For American humor. **Whoopi Goldberg**.

2000 NATIONAL MEDALS OF THE ARTS. For individuals and organizations who have made outstanding contributions to the excellence, growth, support and availability of the arts in the United States, selected by the President from nominees presented by the National Endowment. **Maya Angelou**, **Eddy Arnold**, **Mikhail Baryshnikov**, **Benny Carter**, **Chuck Close**, **Horton Foote**, **Lewis Manilow**, **National Public Radio**, **Claes Oldenburg**, **Itzhak Perlman**, **Harold Prince**, **Barbra Streisand**.

2000 ELIZABETH HULL–KATE WARRINER AWARD. To the playwright whose work deals with social, political or religious mores of the time, selected by the Dramatists Guild Council. **David Auburn** for *Proof.*

2001 HEWES DESIGN AWARDS (formerly American Theatre Wing Design Awards). For design originating in the U.S., selected by a committee comprising Tish Dace (chairman), Glenda Frank, Mario Fratti, Randy Gener, Mel Gussow, Henry Hewes, Jeffrey Eric Jenkins and Joan Ungaro. Scenic design: **John Moran**, *Book of the Dead (Second Avenue).* Costume design (tie): **David C. Woolard**, *The Rocky Horror Show*, and **Roger Kirk**, *42nd Street.* Lighting design: **Brian MacDevitt**, *The Invention of Love.* Noteworthy Unusual Effects: **Rudi Stern**, *Theater of Light.*

21st KESSELRING PRIZE FOR PLAYWRITING. To a playwright who shows exceptional promise but has not achieved prominent national recognition. **David Lindsay-Abaire** for *Kimberly Akimbo.* Honorable Mention: **Dael Orlandersmith**.

23rd ANNUAL SUSAN SMITH BLACKBURN PRIZE. For women who have written works of outstanding quality for the English-speaking theater. **Charlotte Jones** for *Humble Boy.*

2000 GEORGE FREEDLEY MEMORIAL AWARD. For the best book about live theater published in the United States the previous year. ***The Economics of the British Stage: 1800–1914*** by **Tracy C. Davis**.

20th ANNUAL ASTAIRE AWARDS. For excellence in dance and choreography, administered by the Theatre Development Fund and selected by a committee comprising Douglas Watt, Clive Barnes, Howard Kissel, Michael Kuchwara, Donald McDonagh, Richard Philp, Charles L. Reinhart and Linda Winer. Choreography: **Susan Stroman** for *The Producers.* Female dancer: **Kate Levering** in *42nd Street.* Male dancer: **Michael Arnold** in *42nd Street.* Lifetime Achievement: **Donald Saddler**.

2001 RICHARD RODGERS AWARDS. For production and staged reading of musicals in nonprofit theaters, administered by the American Academy of Arts and Letters and selected by a jury of its musical theater members comprising Stephen Sondheim (chairman), Lynn Ahrens, Jack Beeson, John Guare, Sheldon Harnick, R.W.B. Lewis, Richard Maltby Jr. and Robert Ward. Richard Rodgers Production Award: ***The Spitfire Grill*** by Fred Alley and James Valcq. Richard Rodgers Development Award: ***Heading East*** by Leon Ko and Robert Lee.

67th ANNUAL DRAMA LEAGUE AWARDS. For distinguished achievement in the American theater. Play: ***Proof***. Musical: ***The Producers***. Revival of a play or musical: ***One Flew Over the Cuckoo's Nest***. Distinguished performance: **Mary-Louise Parker** in *Proof* and **Gary Sinise** in *One Flew Over the Cuckoo's Nest*. Julia Hansen Award for excellence in directing: **Jack O'Brien**. Achievement in Musical Theatre: **Susan Stroman**. Outstanding contribution to theater: **Steppenwolf Theatre Company**.

2001 GEORGE OPPENHEIMER AWARD. To the best new American playwright, presented by *Newsday*. **Chris Burns** for *My Mother's a Baby Boy*.

2001 NEW DRAMATISTS LIFETIME ACHIEVEMENT AWARD. To an individual who has made an outstanding artistic contribution to the American theater. **Arthur Miller**.

12th ANNUAL OSCAR HAMMERSTEIN AWARD. For lifetime achievement in musical theater. **Terrence McNally**.

2001 *THEATRE WORLD* AWARDS. For outstanding debut performers in Broadway or Off Broadway theater during the 2000–2001 season, selected by a committee comprising John Willis, Clive Barnes, Peter Filichia, Alexis Greene, Harry Haun, Frank Scheck, Michael Sommers, Douglas Watt and Linda Winer. **Juliette Binoche** in *Betrayal*, **Macaulay Culkin** in *Madame Melville*, **Janie Dee** in *Comic Potential*, **Raúl Esparza** in *The Rocky Horror Show*, **Kathleen Freeman** in *The Full Monty*, **Deven May** in *Bat Boy: The Musical*, **Reba McEntire** in *Annie Get Your Gun*, **Chris Noth** in *Gore Vidal's The Best Man*, **Joshua Park** in *The Adventures of Tom Sawyer*, **Rosie Perez** in *References to Salvador Dalí Make Me Hot*, **Joely Richardson** in *Madame Melville* and **John Ritter** in *The Dinner Party*. Special award: **Seán Campion** and **Conleth Hill** in *Stones in His Pockets*.

46th ANNUAL DRAMA DESK AWARDS. For outstanding achievement in the 2000–2001 season, voted by an association of New York drama reporters, editors and critics from nominations made by a committee. New play: ***Proof***. New musical: ***The Producers***. Revival of a play: ***Gore Vidal's The Best Man***. Revival of a musical: ***42nd Street***. Book: **Mel Brooks** and **Thomas Meehan** for ***The Producers***. Composer: **David Yazbek** for ***The Full Monty***. Lyricist: **Mel Brooks** for ***The Producers***. Actor in a play: **Richard Easton** in *The Invention of Love*. Actress in a play: **Mary-Louise Parker** in *Proof*. Featured actor in a play: **Charles Brown** in *King Hedley II*. Featured actress in a play: **Viola Davis** in *King Hedley II*. Actor in a musical: **Nathan Lane** in *The Producers*. Actress in a musical: **Marla Schaffel** in *Jane Eyre*. Featured actor in a musical: **Gary Beach** in *The Producers*. Featured actress in a musical: **Cady Huffman** in *The Producers*. Solo performance: **Pamela Gien** in *The Syringa Tree*. Director of a play: **Jack O'Brien** for *The Invention of Love*. Director of a musical: **Susan Stroman** for *The Producers*. Choreography: **Susan Stroman** for *The Producers*. Orchestrations: **Doug Besterman** for *The Producers*. Set design of a play: **Bob Crowley** for *The Invention of Love*. Set design of a musical: **Robin Wagner** for *The Producers*. Costume design: **William Ivey Long** for *The Producers*. Lighting design: **Paul Anderson** for *Mnemonic*. Sound design: **Christopher Shutt** for *Mnemonic*. Outstanding Musical Revue: ***Forbidden Broadway 2001: A Spoof Odyssey***. Unique theatrical experience: ***Mnemonic***. Special awards: **Reba McEntire** for *Annie Get Your Gun*; **Seán Campion** and **Conleth Hill** for *Stones in His Pockets*. Ensemble Performance: ***Cobb*** (**Michael Cullen**, **Clark Jackson**, **Matthew Mabe**, **Michael Sabatino**); ***Tabletop*** (**Rob Bartlett**, **Harvy Blanks**, **Jack Koenig**, **Dean Nolen**, **Elizabeth Hanly Rice**, **Jeremy Webb**).

51st ANNUAL OUTER CRITICS CIRCLE AWARDS. For outstanding achievement in the 2000–2001 season, voted by critics on out-of-town periodicals and media.

Broadway play: ***Proof***. Off-Broadway play: ***Jitney***. Revival of a play (tie): ***Gore Vidal's The Best Man***; ***One Flew Over the Cuckoo's Nest***. Actor in a play: **Richard Easton** in *The Invention of Love*. Actress in a play: **Mary-Louise Parker** in *Proof*. Featured actor in a play: **Robert Sean Leonard** in *The Invention of Love*. Featured actress in a play: **Viola Davis** in *King Hedley II*. Director of a play: **Jack O'Brien** for *The Invention of Love*. Broadway musical: ***The Producers***. Off-Broadway musical: ***Bat Boy: The Musical***. Revival of a musical: ***42nd Street***. Actor in a musical: **Nathan Lane** in *The Producers*. Actress in a musical (tie): **Christine Ebersole** in *42nd Street*; **Marla Schaffel** in *Jane Eyre*. Featured actor in a musical (tie): **Gary Beach** in *The Producers*; **André De Shields** in *The Full Monty*. Featured actress in a musical: **Cady Huffman** in *The Producers*. Director of a musical: **Susan Stroman** for *The Producers*. Choreography: **Susan Stroman** for *The Producers*. Scenic design: **Robin Wagner** for *The Producers*. Costume design: **William Ivey Long** for *The Producers*. Lighting design: **Brian MacDevitt** for *The Invention of Love*. Solo performance: **Pamela Gien** in *The Syringa Tree*. John Gassner Playwriting Award: **David Auburn** for *Proof*. Special Achievement Award: **Seán Campion** and **Conleth Hill** in *Stones in His Pockets*; **Henry Winkler**, **John Ritter**, **Len Cariou**, **Penny Fuller**, **Veanne Cox** and **Jan Maxwell** in *The Dinner Party*; **Reba McEntire** in *Annie Get Your Gun*.

46th ANNUAL *VILLAGE VOICE* OBIE AWARDS. For outstanding achievement in Off and Off-Off Broadway theater. Performance: **George Bartenieff** in *I Will Bear Witness*; **Stephanie Berry** in *The Shaneequa Chronicles*; **Ronnell Bey**, **Mandy Gonzalez**, **Judy Kuhn** and **Anika Noni Rose** in *Eli's Comin'*; **Bette Bourne** in *Resident Alien*; **Brian d'Arcy James** in *The Good Thief*; **Janie Dee** in *Comic Potential*; **Jackie Hoffman** in *The Book of Liz*; **Pamela Isaacs** in *Newyorkers*; **Brian Murray** in *The Play About the Baby*; **John Ortiz** in *References to Salvador Dalí Make Me Hot*; **Mary-Louise Parker** in *Proof*. Direction: **Michael Greif** for *Dogeaters*; **Craig Lucas** for *Saved or Destroyed*; **Bob McGrath** for *Jennie Richee*. Set design: **Neil Patel** for *I Will Bear Witness*, *Race*, *Resident Alien* and *War of the Worlds*; **Douglas Stein** *Saved* and *Texts for Nothing*. Music: **Diedre Murray** *Eli's Comin'*; **Bill Sims Jr**. *Lackawanna Blues*. Choreography: **John Carrafa** for *Urinetown*. Playwriting: **José Rivera** *References to Salvador Dalí Make Me Hot*. Best Play: **Pamela Gien** for *The Syringa Tree*. Sustained achievement: **Marian Seldes**.

Special Citations: **Justin Bond** and **Kenny Mellman** for *Kiki and Herb: Jesus Wept*; **Kirsten Childs** for *The Bubbly Black Girl Sheds Her Chameleon Skin*; **Rinde Eckert** *And God Created Great Whales*; **Mark Hollmann** and **Greg Kotis** for *Urinetown: The Musical*; **Edward Kleban** for *A Class Act*; **Cynthia Hopkins**, **Pilar Limosner**, **Bill Morrison**, **Laurie Olinder**, **Ruth Pongstaphone**, **Tim Schellenbaum**, **Howard S. Thies**, **Matthew Tierney**, **Fred Tietz** and **Julia Wolfe** for *Jennie Richee*; **Ruben Santiago-Hudson** for *Lackawanna Blues*. Grants: **Classical Theatre of Harlem**, **Clubbed Thumb**, **Mint Theater Company**, **Soho Rep**. Ross Wetzsteon Award: **Theatre for a New Audience**.

11th ANNUAL CONNECTICUT CRITICS CIRCLE AWARDS. For outstanding achievement in Connecticut theater during the 2000–2001 season. Production of a play: **Long Wharf Theatre** for *Big Love*. Production of a musical: **Goodspeed Musicals** for *Brigadoon*. Actress in a play (tie): **Anne Dudek** in *The Glass Menagerie*; **Lauren Klein** in *Big Love*. Actor in a play: **Jeremy Shamos** in *Baptiste: The Life of Molière*. Actress in a musical: **Kristen Howe** in *Joseph and the Amazing Technicolor Dreamcoat*. Actor in a musical: **John Scherer** in *George M*. Direction of a play: **Les Waters** for *Big Love*. Direction of a musical: **Greg Ganakas** for *Brigadoon*. Choreography: **Peggy Hickey** for *Brigadoon*. Set design: **Adam Huggard** for *The Man Who Could See Through Time*. Lighting design: **Hugh Hallinan** for *Joseph and the Amazing Technicolor Dreamcoat*. Costume design: **Toni-Leslie James** for *Baptiste: The Life of Molière*. Sound design: **David Budries** for *Heaven*. Ensemble performance: **Jane Curtin**, **Sam Freed**, **Neil Patrick Harris**, **Fritz Weaver** and **Elizabeth Wilson** in *Ancestral Voices*. Roadshow: **International Festival of Arts and Ideas**, presenter of the Royal Shakespeare Company's *Macbeth*.

Debut Award: **M. Neko Parham** in *Tamer of Horses*. Tom Killen Memorial Award: **George C. White**, Founder of Eugene O'Neill Theater Center. Special award: **Irene M. Backalenick** and **David A. Rosenberg**, co-founders of the Connecticut Critics Circle.

19th ANNUAL ELLIOT NORTON AWARDS. For outstanding contribution to the theater in Boston, voted by a Boston Theater Critics Association Selections Committee comprising Terry Byrne, Carolyn Clay, Iris Fanger, Arthur Friedman, Joyce Kulhawik, Jon Lehman, Bill Marx, Ed Siegel and Caldwell Titcomb. New play: **Adam Rapp** for *Nocturne*. Norton Prize: **Tina Packer**. Productions—Visiting company: ***Death of a Salesman***; Large resident company: ***Hedda Gabler*** produced by Huntington Theatre Company; Small resident company: ***Stonewall Jackson's House*** produced by New Repertory Theatre; Local fringe company: ***Not About Nightingales*** produced by Boston Theatre Works. Solo performance: **Eve Ensler** in *The Vagina Monologues*. Musical production: ***Honk!*** produced by North Shore Music Theatre. Actor—Large company: **Dallas Roberts** in *Nocturne*; Small company: **Phillip Patrone** in *Side Man* and *Inspecting Carol*. Actress—Large company: **Elizabeth Franz** in *Death of a Salesman*; Small company: **Bobbie Steinbach** in *Stonewall Jackson's House*, *Sailing Down the Amazon* and *Over the River and Through the Woods*. Director—Large company: **Amanda Dehnert** for *My Fair Lady* and *Who's Afraid of Virginia Woolf?*; Small company: **Carmel O'Reilly** for *This Lime Tree Bower*. Design—Large company: **Csaba Antal**, **Edit Szücs**, **John Ambrosone**, and **David Remedios** for *Mother Courage*; Small company: **Laura McPherson** for *Not About Nightingales*.

Special citation: **Wellfleet Harbor Actors Theater** for establishing a beachhead for serious theater on Cape Cod.

16th ANNUAL HELEN HAYES AWARDS. In recognition of excellence in Washington, D.C. theater, presented by the Washington Theatre Awards Society.

Resident productions—Play: ***The Glass Menagerie*** produced by Round House Theatre and Everyman Theatre. Musical: ***Side Show*** produced by Signature Theatre (Arlington). Lead actress, musical: **Sherri L. Edelen** in *Side Show*. Lead actor, musical: **Dwayne Nitz** in *Sing Down the Moon: Appalachian Wonder Tales*. Lead actress, play: **Lee Mikeska Gardner** in *A House in the Country*. Lead actor, play: **Philip Goodwin** in *Timon of Athens*. Supporting performer, musical: **Eric Jordan Young** in *Side Show*. Supporting actress, play: **Jewell Robinson** in *Blue*. Supporting actor, play: **Ted van Griethuysen** in *Timon of Athens*. Director, play: **Donald Hicken** for *The Glass Menagerie*. Director, musical: **Joe Calarco** for *Side Show*. Set design, play or musical: **Tony Cisek** for *Leaving the Summer Land*. Costume design, play or musical: **Robert Perdziola** for *The Country Wife*. Lighting design, play or musical: **Dan Covey** for *The Tempest*. Sound design, play or musical: **Scott Burgess** for *The Tempest*. Musical direction, play or musical: **Jason Robert Brown** and **William Knowles** for *Dinah Was*. Choreography: **Irina Tsikurishvili** for *Faust*.

Non-resident productions—Production: ***James Joyce's The Dead*** produced by the Kennedy Center. Lead actress: **Judith Light** in *Wit*. Lead actor: **Marc Wolf** in *Another American: Asking and Telling*. Supporting performer: **Alice Cannon** in *James Joyce's The Dead*.

Charles MacArthur Award for outstanding new play: ***A House in the Country*** by Peter Coy.

32nd ANNUAL JOSEPH JEFFERSON AWARDS. For achievement in Chicago theater during the 1999–2000 season, given by the Jefferson Awards Committee in 27 competitive categories. Twenty-six producing organizations were nominated for various awards. The Goodman Theatre topped all other companies by winning 6 of the 10 for which it was nominated.

Resident productions—New work: *Boy Gets Girl* by **Rebecca Gilman.** New Adaptation: *The Odyssey* by **Mary Zimmerman.** Production of a play: **Famous Door Theatre's** *Ghetto*. Production of a musical: **Drury Lane Oakbrook's** *1776*. Michael Maggio Award of direction of a play: **Calvin MacLean** for *Ghetto*. Director of a musical: **Ray Frewen** and **Gary Griffin** for *1776*. Actor in a principal role, play: **William Brown** in *Nixon's Nixon*. Actress in a principal role, play: **Irma P. Hall** in *A Raisin in the Sun*. Actor in a supporting role, play: **Roy Dotrice** in *A Moon for the Misbegotten*. Actress in a supporting role, play: **Julia Neary** in *Ghetto*. Actor in a principal role, musical: **Andrew J. Lupp** in *My One and Only*. Actress in a principal role, musical: **E. Faye Butler** in *Dinah Was*. Actor in a supporting role, musical: **Nikkieli DeMone** in *Side Show*. Actress in a supporting role, musical: **Kelly Anne Clark** in *Victor/Victoria*. Actor in a revue: **Chester Gregory II** in *The Jackie Wilson Story*. Actress in a revue: **La Tonya Beacham** in *Mahalia*. Ensemble: ***Among the Thugs*** produced by Next Theatre. Scenic design: **Geoffrey Curley** for *[sic]*. Costume design: **Paul Tazewell** for *A Midsummer Night's Dream*. Lighting design: **T.J. Gerckens** for *The Odyssey*. Sound design: **Lindsay Jones** for *Among the Thugs*. Choreography: **Tammy Mader** for *My One and Only*. Original music: **Michael Bodeen** and **Willie Schwarz** for *The Odyssey*. Musical direction: **Tom Murray** for *Once on This Island*.

Non-resident productions—Production: **Fosse Touring LLC's** *Fosse*. Actor in a principal role: **Joseph Anthony Foronda** in *Miss Saigon*. Actress in a principal role: **Heather Headley** in *Aida*.

Special Awards—**Joyce and Byrne Piven** for creating a legacy of theater and providing fertile training ground for some of today's finest young actors and actresses. **Kary M. Walker** for his role as producer, visionary and advocate of musical theater.

28th ANNUAL JOSEPH JEFFERSON CITATIONS WING AWARDS. For outstanding achievement in professional productions during the 2000–2001 season of Chicago area theaters not operating under union contracts. Productions: *Another Part of the Forest* produced by **Eclipse Theatre Company**; *Not About Nightingales* produced by **TimeLine Theatre Company**. Ensembles: ***Another Part of the Forest***, ***Not About Nightingales***, ***Porcelain***. Directors: **Nick Bowling** for *Another Part of the Forest*, **William Brown** for *Not About Nightingales*. New work: **Luther Goins** for *Love Child*, **G. Riley Mills** and **Ralph Covert** for *Streeterville*. New adaptation: **Christina Calvit** for *Pistols for Two*. Actress in a principal role: **Marlene Flood** in *Passion*; **Jenifer Tyler Key** in *Jane Eyre*. Actor in a principal role: **Steve Key** in *Coyote on a Fence*. Actress in a supporting role: **Jenny McKnight** in *Watch on the Rhine*; **Linda Reiter** in *Invitation to a March*; **Ann Wakefield** in *Another Part of the Forest*. Actor in a supporting role: **John Cabrera** in *Refuge*, **David Parkes** in *Not About Nightingales*, **Marco Verna** in *Not About Nightingales*. Scenic design: **Alan Donahue** for *Jane Eyre*; **Jim Lasko** and **Shoshanna Utchenik** for *Hunchback*. Costume design: **Jeffrey Kelly** for *Triumph of Love*. Lighting design: **Kevin Gawley** for *Jane Eyre*; **Joe Kazmierski** for *Not About Nightingales*. Sound design: **Bob Rokos** and **Dave Bell** for *Coyote on a Fence*. Choreography: **Kevin Bellie** for *The Life*. Original music: **Michael Zerang** for *Hunchback*. Musical direction: **Eugene Dizon** for *Into the Woods*.

THE THEATER HALL OF FAME

○○○○○

THE THEATER HALL OF FAME was created in 1971 to honor those who have made outstanding contributions to the American theater in a career spanning at least 25 years, with at least five major credits. Honorees are elected annually by members of the American Theatre Critics Association, members of the Theater Hall of Fame and theater historians. Names of those elected in 2000 and inducted January 29, 2001 appear in ***bold face italics***.

George Abbott
Maude Adams
Viola Adams
Stella Adler
Edward Albee
Theoni V. Aldredge
Ira Aldridge
Jane Alexander
Mary Alice
Winthrop Ames
Judith Anderson
Maxwell Anderson
Robert Anderson
Julie Andrews
Margaret Anglin
Jean Anouilh
Harold Arlen
George Arliss
Boris Aronson
Adele Astaire
Fred Astaire
Eileen Atkins
Brooks Atkinson
Lauren Bacall
Pearl Bailey
George Balanchine
William Ball
Anne Bancroft
Tallulah Bankhead
Richard Barr
Philip Barry
Ethel Barrymore
John Barrymore
Lionel Barrymore
Nora Bayes
Samuel Beckett
Brian Bedford
S.N. Behrman
Norman Bel Geddes
David Belasco
Michael Bennett
Richard Bennett
Robert Russell Bennett
Eric Bentley
Irving Berlin
Sarah Bernhardt
Leonard Bernstein
Earl Blackwell
Kermit Bloomgarden
Jerry Bock
Ray Bolger
Edwin Booth
Junius Brutus Booth
Shirley Booth
Philip Bosco
Alice Brady
Bertolt Brecht
Fannie Brice
Peter Brook
John Mason Brown
Billie Burke
Abe Burrows
Richard Burton
Mrs. Patrick Campbell
Zoe Caldwell
Eddie Cantor
Morris Carnovsky
Mrs. Leslie Carter
Gower Champion
Frank Chanfrau
Carol Channing
Ruth Chatterton
Paddy Chayefsky
Anton Chekhov
Ina Claire
Bobby Clark
Harold Clurman
Lee J. Cobb
Richard L. Coe
George M. Cohan
Alexander H. Cohen
Jack Cole
Cy Coleman
Constance Collier
Betty Comden
Marc Connelly
Barbara Cook
Katharine Cornell
Noel Coward
Jane Cowl
Lotta Crabtree
Cheryl Crawford
Hume Cronyn
Russel Crouse
Charlotte Cushman
Jean Dalrymple

Augustin Daly
E.L. Davenport
Gordon Davidson
Ossie Davis
Ruby Dee
Alfred de Liagre Jr.
Agnes DeMille
Colleen Dewhurst
Howard Dietz
Dudley Digges
Melvyn Douglas
Eddie Dowling
Alfred Drake
Marie Dressler
John Drew
Mrs. John Drew
William Dunlap
Mildred Dunnock
Charles Durning
Eleanora Duse
Jeanne Eagels
Fred Ebb
Florence Eldridge
Lehman Engel
Maurice Evans
Abe Feder
Jose Ferrer
Cy Feuer
Zelda Fichandler
Dorothy Fields
Herbert Fields
Lewis Fields
W.C. Fields
Jules Fisher
Minnie Maddern Fiske
Clyde Fitch
Geraldine Fitzgerald
Henry Fonda
Lynn Fontanne
Horton Foote
Edwin Forrest
Bob Fosse
Rudolf Friml
Charles Frohman
Robert Fryer
Athol Fugard
John Gassner
Grace George
George Gershwin
Ira Gershwin
John Gielgud
W.S. Gilbert
Jack Gilford
William Gillette
Charles Gilpin
Lillian Gish
John Golden
Max Gordon
Ruth Gordon
Adolph Green
Paul Green
Charlotte Greenwood
Joel Grey
John Guare
Otis L. Guernsey Jr.
Tyrone Guthrie
Uta Hagen
Lewis Hallam
Oscar Hammerstein II
Walter Hampden
Otto Harbach
E.Y. Harburg
Sheldon Harnick
Edward Harrigan
Jed Harris
Julie Harris
Rosemary Harris
Sam H. Harris
Rex Harrison
Kitty Carlisle Hart
Lorenz Hart
Moss Hart
Tony Hart
June Havoc
Helen Hayes
Leland Hayward
Ben Hecht
Eileen Heckart
Theresa Helburn
Lillian Hellman
Katharine Hepburn
Victor Herbert
Jerry Herman
James A. Herne
Al Hirschfeld
Raymond Hitchcock
Hal Holbrook
Celeste Holm
Hanya Holm
Arthur Hopkins
De Wolf Hopper
John Houseman
Eugene Howard
Leslie Howard
Sidney Howard
Willie Howard
Barnard Hughes
Henry Hull
Josephine Hull
Walter Huston
Earle Hyman
Henrik Ibsen
William Inge
Bernard B. Jacobs
Elsie Janis
Joseph Jefferson
Al Jolson
James Earl Jones
Margo Jones
Robert Edmond Jones
Tom Jones
Jon Jory
Raul Julia

John Kander
Garson Kanin
George S. Kaufman
Danny Kaye
Elia Kazan
Gene Kelly
George Kelly
Fanny Kemble
Jerome Kern
Walter Kerr
Michael Kidd
Richard Kiley
Sidney Kingsley
Florence Klotz
Joseph Wood Krutch
Bert Lahr
Burton Lane
Lawrence Langner
Lillie Langtry
Angela Lansbury
Charles Laughton
Arthur Laurents
Gertrude Lawrence
Jerome Lawrence
Eva Le Gallienne
Ming Cho Lee
Robert E. Lee
Lotte Lenya
Alan Jay Lerner
Sam Levene
Robert Lewis
Beatrice Lillie
Howard Lindsay
Frank Loesser
Frederick Loewe
Joshua Logan
Pauline Lord
Lucille Lortel
Alfred Lunt
Charles MacArthur
Steele MacKaye
Rouben Mamoulian
Richard Mansfield
Robert B. Mantell
Fredric March
Nancy Marchand
Julia Marlowe
Ernest H. Martin
Mary Martin
Raymond Massey
Siobhan McKenna
Terrence McNally
Helen Menken
Burgess Meredith
Ethel Merman
David Merrick
Jo Mielziner
Arthur Miller
Marilyn Miller
Liza Minnelli
Helena Modjeska
Ferenc Molnar
Lola Montez
Victor Moore
Robert Morse
Zero Mostel
Anna Cora Mowatt
Paul Muni
Tharon Musser
George Jean Nathan
Mildred Natwick
Nazimova
James M. Nederlander
Mike Nichols
Elliot Norton
Sean O'Casey
Clifford Odets
Donald Oenslager
Laurence Olivier
Eugene O'Neill
Jerry Orbach
Geraldine Page
Joseph Papp
Osgood Perkins
Bernadette Peters
Molly Picon
Harold Pinter
Luigi Pirandello
Christopher Plummer
Cole Porter
Robert Preston
Harold Prince
Jose Quintero
Ellis Rabb
John Raitt
Tony Randall
Michael Redgrave
Ada Rehan
Elmer Rice
Lloyd Richards
Ralph Richardson
Chita Rivera
Jason Robards
Jerome Robbins
Paul Robeson
Richard Rodgers
Will Rogers
Sigmund Romberg
Harold Rome
Lillian Russell
Donald Saddler
Gene Saks
William Saroyan
Joseph Schildkraut
Harvey Schmidt
Alan Schneider
Gerald Schoenfeld
Arthur Schwartz
George C. Scott
Marian Seldes
Irene Sharaff
George Bernard Shaw
Sam Shepard

Robert E. Sherwood
J.J. Shubert
Lee Shubert
Herman Shumlin
Neil Simon
Lee Simonson
Edmund Simpson
Otis Skinner
Maggie Smith
Oliver Smith
Stephen Sondheim
E.H. Sothern
Kim Stanley
Maureen Stapleton
Frances Sternhagen
Roger L. Stevens
Ellen Stewart
Dorothy Stickney
Fred Stone
Tom Stoppard
Lee Strasberg
August Strindberg
Elaine Stritch
Jule Styne
Margaret Sullavan
Arthur Sullivan
Jessica Tandy
Laurette Taylor
Ellen Terry
Tommy Tune
Gwen Verdon
Robin Wagner
Nancy Walker
Eli Wallach
James Wallack
Lester Wallack
Tony Walton
Douglas Turner Ward
David Warfield
Ethel Waters
Clifton Webb
Joseph Weber
Margaret Webster
Kurt Weill
Orson Welles
Mae West
Robert Whitehead
Oscar Wilde
Thornton Wilder
Bert Williams
Tennessee Williams
Lanford Wilson
P.G. Wodehouse
Peggy Wood
Alexander Woollcott
Irene Worth
Teresa Wright
Ed Wynn
Vincent Youmans
Stark Young
Florenz Ziegfeld
Patricia Zipprodt

THE THEATER HALL OF FAME FOUNDERS AWARD

ESTABLISHED IN 1993 in honor of Earl Blackwell, James M. Nederlander, Gerard Oestreicher and Arnold Weissberger, The Theater Hall of Fame Founders Award is voted by the Hall's board of directors to an individual for his or her outstanding contribution to the theater.

1993 James M. Nederlander
1994 Kitty Carlisle Hart
1995 Harvey Sabinson
1996 Henry Hewes
1997 Otis L. Guernsey Jr.
1998 Edward Colton
1999 No Award
2000 Gerard Oestreicher
Arnold Weissberger

MARGO JONES CITIZEN OF THE THEATER MEDAL

PRESENTED ANNUALLY TO A CITIZEN of the theater who has made a lifetime commitment to theater in the United States and has demonstrated an understanding and affirmation of the craft of playwriting.

1961 Lucille Lortel
1962 Michael Ellis
1963 Judith Rutherford Marechal
George Savage (University Award)
1964 Richard Barr, Edward Albee & Clinton Wilder
Richard A. Duprey (University Award)
1965 Wynn Handman
Marston Balch (University Award)
1966 Jon Jory
Arthur Ballet (University Award)
1967 Paul Baker
George C. White (Workshop Award)
1968 Davey Marlin-Jones
Ellen Stewart (Workshop Award)
1969 Adrian Hall
Edward Parone & Gordon Davidson (Workshop Award)
1970 Joseph Papp
1971 Zelda Fichandler
1972 Jules Irving
1973 Douglas Turner Ward
1974 Paul Weidner
1975 Robert Kalfin
1976 Gordon Davidson
1977 Marshall W. Mason
1978 Jon Jory
1979 Ellen Stewart
1980 John Clark Donahue
1981 Lynne Meadow
1982 Andre Bishop
1983 Bill Bushnell
1984 Gregory Mosher
1985 John Lion
1986 Lloyd Richards
1987 Gerald Chapman
1988 No Award
1989 Margaret Goheen
1990 Richard Coe
1991 Otis L. Guernsey Jr.
1992 Abbot Van Nostrand
1993 Henry Hewes
1994 Jane Alexander
1995 Robert Whitehead
1996 Al Hirschfeld
1997 George C. White
1998 James Houghton
1999 George Keathley
2000 Eileen Heckart

MUSICAL THEATRE HALL OF FAME

THIS ORGANIZATION WAS ESTABLISHED at New York University on November 10, 1993.

Harold Arlen
Irving Berlin
Leonard Bernstein
Eubie Blake
Abe Burrows
George M. Cohan
Dorothy Fields
George Gershwin
Ira Gershwin
Oscar Hammerstein II
E.Y. Harburg
Larry Hart
Jerome Kern
Burton Lane
Alan Jay Lerner
Frank Loesser
Frederick Loewe
Cole Porter
Ethel Merman
Jerome Robbins
Richard Rodgers
Harold Rome

2000-2001 PUBLICATION OF NEW PLAYS, ANTHOLOGIES, ADAPTATIONS AND TRANSLATIONS

○○○○○

Compiled by Rue E. Canvin

Adaptations of Shakespeare. Ed. Daniel Fischlin and Mark Fortier. Routledge. (paper)
Ain't Nothing But a Thang. Marlin T. Tazewell. Dramatic Publishing. (acting ed.)
Ajax. Sophocles. Trans. Shomit Dutta. Cambridge. (paper)
Albert Speer. David Edgar. Nick Hern. (paper)
All My Sons. Arthur Miller. Penguin. (paper)
America Hurrah & Other Plays. Jean-Claude Van Itallie. Grove. (paper)
All Powers Necessary and Convenient. Mark F. Jenkins. University of Washington. (paper)
Anna Karenina. Leo Tolstoy. Adapt. Helen Edmundson. Nick Hern. (paper)
Antigone. Sophocles. Trans. Marianne McDonald. Nick Hern. (paper)
Antigone. Jean Anouilh. Trans. Barbara Bray. Methuen. (paper)
Antigone. Sophocles. Adapt. Declan Donnellan. Absolute. (paper)
Antiphon, The. Djuna Barnes. Green Integer. (paper)
Antipodes, The. Richard Brome. Theatre Arts. (paper)
Anton in Show Business. Jane Martin. Samuel French. (acting ed.)
A.R. Gurney, Volume III. A. R. Gurney. Smith & Kraus. (paper)
A.R. Gurney, Volume IV. A. R. Gurney. Smith & Kraus. (paper)
Auschwitz Lullaby. James C. Wall. Dramatic. (acting ed.)
Back Story. Joan Ackermann. Dramatic. (acting ed.)
Barefoot Boy with Shoes On. Edwin Sanchez. Broadway Play Publishing. (paper)
Beauty's Daughter, Monster, The Gimmick. Dael Orlandersmith. Random House/Vintage. (paper)
Beggar's Opera, The. Vaclav Havel. Trans. Paul Wilson. Cornell.
Beginning of August, The. Tom Donaghy. Dramatists Play Service. (acting ed.)
Beginning of August & Other Plays. Tom Donaghy. Grove. (paper)
Best Plays of the Early American Theatre, 1787-1911. Ed. John Gassner. Dover. (paper)
Best Student One Acts, Volume 6. Ed. Lauren Friesen. Dramatic Publishing. (paper)
Beth Henley: Collected Plays, Volume 1. Beth Henley. Smith & Kraus. (paper)
Betty's Summer Vacation. Christopher Durang. Grove. (paper)
Bible: The Complete Word of God, The. Adam Long, Reed Martin, Austin Tichenor and Matthew Croke. Broadway Play Publishing. (paper)
Black and Asian Plays: Anthology. Cheryl Robson. Aurora Metro Plays. (paper)
Book of Days. Lanford Wilson. Grove. (paper)
Bourgeois Gentleman, The. Molière. Trans. Bernard Sahlins. Ivan R. Dee/Plays for Performance. (paper)
Bow-Wow Club. Levy (Lee) Simon. Dramatic Publishing Co. (acting ed.)

Brooding and Dangerous. Daniel Fenton. Dramatic. (acting ed.)
Cairn Stones, The. Anne V. McGravie. Dramatic. (acting ed.)
Carlo Gozzi: Translations of The Love of Three Oranges, Turandot, *and* The Snake Lady. John Louis Di Gaetani. Greenwood.
Celebration and The Room. Harold Pinter. Grove. (paper)
Chaim's Love Song. Marvin Chernoff. Samuel French. (acting ed.)
Chesapeake. Lee Blessing. Broadway Play Publishing. (paper)
Cider House Rules-Part 1: Here in St. Cloud's, The. Dramatists. (acting ed.)
Cider House Rules-Part 2: In Other Parts of the World. Dramatists. (acting ed.)
Complete Plays. Sophocles. Trans. Paul Roche. Signet. (paper)
Contemporary German Plays I. Ed. Margaret Herzfeld-Sander. Continuum. (paper)
Conversations After a Burial. Yasmina Reza. Trans. Christopher Hampton. Faber & Faber. (paper)
Cooking with Elvis & Bollocks: Two Plays. Lee Hall. Methuen. (paper)
Copenhagen: Revised. Michael Frayn. Methuen. (paper)
Country Club, The. Douglas Carter Beane. Dramatists Play Service. (acting ed.)
Crime of the Twenty-First Century, The. Edward Bond. Methuen. (paper)
Cyclops. Euripides. Trans. Heather McHugh. Oxford. (paper)
Death & Taxes: Hydriotaphia & Other Plays. Tony Kushner. TCG. (paper)
Devil Inside, A. David Lindsay-Abaire. Dramatists. (acting ed.)
Dinner With Friends. Donald Margulies. TCG. (paper)
Doctor Faustus. Christopher Marlowe. Ed. Sylvan Barnet. New American Library/ Signet. (paper)
Emperor and Galilean. Henrik Ibsen. Trans. Brian Johnston. Smith & Kraus. (paper)
Ensemble Studio Theatre Marathon 2000. Ed. Ensemble Studio Theatre. Faber & Faber. (paper)
Estrogenius 2000. Ed. Fiona Jones and Claire Sommers. Smith & Kraus. (paper)
Euripides: Plays 1. Euripides. Methuen. (paper)
Exact Center of the Universe, The. Joan Vail Thorne. Dramatists. (acting ed.)
Experiment with an Air Pump. Shelagh Stephenson. Methuen. (paper)
Faust Part One. Goethe. Trans. Randall Jarrell. Farrar Straus Giroux.
Federico Garcia Lorca: Impossible Theater. Federico Lorca. Trans. Caridad Svich. (paper)
Five Lesbian Brothers (Four Plays). The Five Lesbian Brothers. TCG. (paper)
4.48 Psychosis. Sarah Kane. Methuen. (paper)
Four Major Plays. Federico Garcia Lorca. Trans. John Edmunds. Oxford World Classics. (paper)
Fuddy Meers. David Lindsay-Abaire. Dramatists Play Service. (acting ed.)
Fugitive Kind. Tennessee Williams. New Directions. (paper)
Fully Committed. Becky Mode. Dramatists. (acting ed.)
Getting In & Contact with the Enemy. Frank D. Gilroy. Samuel French. (acting ed.)
Glass Mendacity, The. Illegitmate Players. Broadway Play Publishing. (paper)
Hazing the Monkey. Marcus A. Hennessy. Samuel French. (acting ed.)
Heart of Art, The. Michael Weller. Samuel French. (acting ed.)
Hedda Gabler. Henrik Ibsen. Adapt. Jon Robin Baitz. Grove. (paper)
Hedwig and the Angry Inch. John Cameron Mitchell and Stephen Trask. Libretto. Overlook.
Heinrich von Kleist: Three Major Plays. Heinrich von Kleist. Trans. Carl R. Mueller. Smith & Kraus. (paper)
Herb Gardner: The Collected Plays. Herb Gardner. Applause. (paper)
Hotel on Marvin Gardens, A. Nagle Jackson. Dramatists. (acting ed.)

House & Garden. Alan Ayckbourn. Faber & Faber. (paper)
Humana Festival 2000: The Complete Plays. Ed. Michael Bigelow Dixon and Amy Wegener. Smith & Kraus. (paper)
Iceman Cometh, The. Eugene O'Neill. Random House. (paper)
Importance of Being Earnest, & Other Plays, The. Oscar Wilde. Ed. Richard Allen Cave. Penguin. (paper)
In the Blood. Suzan-Lori Parks. Dramatists. (acting ed.)
International Plays for Young Audiences. Ed. Roger Ellis. Meriwether. (paper)
Job, The. Shem Bitterman. Samuel French. (acting ed.)
Johan Padan and the Discovery of the Americas. Dario Fo. Publishers Group West/ Grove. (paper)
Lake Hollywood. John Guare. Dramatists. (acting ed.)
Language of Angels. Naomi Iizuka. TheatreForum.
Last Lists of My Mad Mother. Julie Jensen. Dramatic. (acting ed.)
Last of the Thorntons, The. Horton Foote. Overlook. (paper)
Latino Plays from South Coast Repertory. Ed. Christopher Gould. Broadway Play Publishing. (paper)
Lesson Before Dying, A. Romulus Linney. Dramatists. (acting ed.)
Lives of the Saints: Seven One-Act Plays. David Ives. Dramatists Play Service. (acting ed.)
Lot's Daughters. Rebecca Basham. Samuel French. (acting ed.)
Mary Stuart. Friedrich Schiller. Trans. Charles E. Passage. Dover Thrift. (paper)
Men in Suits. Jason Milligan. Samuel French. (acting ed.)
Merry Devil of Edmonton, The. Ed. Nicola Bennett. Theatre Arts. (paper)
Message to Aztlan: Selected Writings. Rodolfo "Corky" Gonzales. Arte Publico. (paper)
Michael Frayn: Plays 3. Michael Frayn. Methuen. (paper)
Mnemonic. Complicite. Methuen. (paper)
My Zinc Bed. David Hare. Faber & Faber. (paper)
Navy Pier. John Corwin. Oberon. (paper)
Night Thoreau Spent in Jail, The. Jerome Lawrence and Robert E. Lee. Hill & Wang. (paper)
Nine Adaptations for the American Stage. Romulus Linney. Smith & Kraus. (paper)
Nineteenth Century American Plays. Ed. Myron Matlaw. Applause. (paper)
Of Grapes and Nuts. Illegitimate Players. Broadway Play Publishing. (paper)
Old Glory: Three Plays, The. Robert Lowell. Farrar Straus. (paper)
Osborne: Four Plays. John Osborne. Oberon. (paper)
Oscar Wilde: The Major Works. Oscar Wilde. Oxford. (paper)
Other Shore: Plays by Gao Xingjian, The. Trans. Gilbert C. F. Fong. Chinese University. (paper)
Plays and Playwrights 2001. Ed. Martin Denton. N.Y. Theatre Experience. (paper)
Plays by Jeffrey M. Jones. Jeffrey M. Jones. Broadway Play Publishing. (paper)
Plays by Eugene O'Neill: Early Full-Length Plays. Eugene O'Neill. Broadway Play Publishing. (paper)
Plays by Eric Overmyer. Eric Overmyer. Broadway Play Publishing. (paper)
Plays by Megan Terry. Megan Terry. Broadway Play Publishing. (paper)
Plays by Y York. Y York. Broadway Play Publishing. (paper)
Plays One: Horvath. Odon Von Horvath. Trans. Penny Black. Oberon. (paper)
Plays Two: Horvath. Odon Von Horvath. Oberon. (paper)
Playwriting Master Class. Michael Wright. Heinemann. (paper)
Postcolonial Plays: An Anthology. Ed. Helen Gilbert. Routledge. (paper)
Proof. David Auburn. Faber & Faber. (paper)

Pygmalion: Penguin Classics. Bernard Shaw. Ed. Dan H. Laurence. Penguin. (paper)
Quake. Melanie Marnich. TheatreForum.
Recruiting Officer, The. George Farquhar. Nick Hern. (paper)
Romance in D. James Sherman. Dramatists. (acting ed.)
Saint Joan: Penguin Classics. Bernard Shaw. Penguin. (paper)
Sarah Kane: Complete Plays. Sarah Kane. Methuen. (papeback).
Shakespeare for My Father. Lynn Redgrave. Samuel French. (acting ed.)
Seattle Children's Theatre: Six Plays for Young Audiences. Volume II. Ed. Deborah Lynn Frockt. Smith & Kraus. (paper)
Sophokles: The Complete Plays. Sophocles. Trans. Carl R. Mueller and Anna Krajewska-Wieczorek. Smith & Kraus. (paper)
Spinning into Butter. Rebecca Gilman. Dramatic Publishing. (acting ed.)
Spinning into Butter. Rebecca Gilman. Faber & Faber. (paper)
Steven Berkoff: Plays 3. Steven Berkoff. Faber & Faber. (paper)
Stones in His Pockets. Marie Jones. Applause. (paper)
Taking Leave. Nagle Jackson. Dramatists. (acting ed.)
Tale of the Allergist's Wife and Other Plays, The. Charles Busch. Grove. (paper)
Tantalus: Ten New Plays on Greek Myths. John Barton. Oberon.
Tennessee Williams: Plays 1937-1955. Tennessee Williams. Library of America.
Tennessee Williams: Plays 1957-1980. Tennessee Williams. Library of America.
Theater of the Avant-Garde 1890-1950. Ed. Bert Cardullo and Robert Knopf. Yale. (paper)
This Day and Age. Nagle Jackson. Dramatists. (acting ed.)
Three Masterpieces of Cuban Drama. Ed. Luis F. Gonzalez-Cruz and Ann Waggoner Aken. Green Integer. (paper)
Three Musketeers: Youth Theatre Version, The. Max Bush. Dramatic Publishing. (acting ed.)
Tom Stoppard: Plays 4. Tom Stoppard. Faber & Faber. (paper)
Trestle at Pope Lick Creek, The. Naomi Wallace. Broadway Play Publishing. (paper)
Trying to Find Chinatown: The Selected Plays of David Henry Hwang. David Henry Hwang. TCG. (paper)
Various Voices: Prose, Poetry, Politics. Harold Pinter. Grove.
Vieux Carré. Tennessee Williams. New Directions. (paper)
Village Fable, A. James Still and Michael Keck. Dramatic Publishing. (acting ed.)
Waverly Gallery, The. Kenneth Lonergan. Grove. (paper)
Wedekind: Four Major Plays. Frank Wedekind. Smith & Kraus. (paper)
Wesker: Plays 1 – The Wesker Trilogy. Arnold Wesker. Methuen. (paper)
Where the Pavement Ends. William S. Yellow-Robe. University of Oklahoma.

IN MEMORIAM

MAY 2000–MAY 2001

○○○○○

PERFORMERS

Allen, Steve (78) – October 30, 2000
Arquette, Lewis (65) – December 10, 2000
Barnes, Rayford K. (80) – November 11, 2000
Baron, Sandy (64) – January 21, 2001
Barton, Anne (72) – November 27, 2000
Barty, Billy (76) – December 23, 2000
Bernier, Peggy (Wilson) (93) – March 5, 2001
Blain, Gerard (70) – December 17, 2000
Borge, Victor (91) – December 23, 2000
Bowker, Irma (89) – June 9, 2000
Boyer, Sully (77) – March 23, 2000
Brenner, Dori (53) – September 16, 2000
Cardriche, Jaime (32) – July 28, 2000
Chandler, Rita (84) – June 14, 2000
Church, George L. (88) – November 23, 2000
Como, Perry (88) – May 12, 2001
Converse, Peggy (95) – March 2, 2001
Cuccione, Michael (16) – January 20, 2001
DeCamp, Rosemary (90) – February 20, 2001
Devlin, Don (70) – December 11, 2000
Downey, Morton Jr. (68) – March 12, 2001
Dukes, David (55) – October 9, 2000
Edmonds, Louis (77) – March 3, 2001
Enright, Erica (52) – July 16, 2000
Evans, Dale (88) – January 31, 2001
Farnsworth, Richard (80) – October 6, 2000
Fisher, Gail (65) – December 2, 2000
Francis, Arlene (93) – May 31, 2001
Friedman, Arthur (81) – January 23, 2001
Garry, William J. (56) – June 29, 2000
Gassman, Vittorio (77) – June 29, 2000
Glasser, Dick (67) – July 10, 2000
Gordon, Leo (78) – December 26, 2000
Gottlied, Theodore (94) – April 5, 2001
Graf, David (50) – April 7, 2001
Greco, Jose (82) – January 2, 2001
Guinness, Sir Alec (86) – August 5, 2000
Harris, Erich Leon (35) – July 5, 2000
Haskell, David M. (52) – August 30, 2000
Hitchens, Neal (43) – July 17, 2000
Hobard, Rose (94) – August 29, 2000
Howard, Jean Speegle (73) – September 2, 2000
Hughes, Glenn (50) – March 4, 2001
Jarrett, Jerry (82) – May 16, 2000
Jason, Rich (74) – October 17, 2000
Kahane, Jackie (79) – March 26, 2001
Karnilova, Maria (80) – April 20, 2001
Kerner, Jeannette (85) – May 25, 2001
King, Carl (79) – January 16, 2001
Klemperer, Werner (80) – December 6, 2000
Lancaster, Stuart (80) – December 22, 2000
Leon, Joseph (82) – March 25, 2001
Lewis, David (84) – December 11, 2000
Lockwood, Vera (82) – July 28, 2000
London, Julie (74) – October 18, 2000
MacColl, Kirsty (41) – December 18, 2000
MacRae, Meredith (56) – July 14, 2000
Macmillan, Norma (79) – March 16, 2001
Mansfield, Virginia (96) – February 16, 2001
Marchand, Nancy (71) – June 18, 2000
Marcus, Bea (88) – September 18, 2000
Marquand, Christian (73) – November 22, 2000
Matthau, Walter (79) – July 1, 2000
Whitman, Mayo (70) – May 22, 2001
McCorkle, Susannah (55) – May 19, 2001
Milford, John (73) – August 14, 2000
Miller, Jason (62) – May 13, 2001
Montgomery, George (84) – December 12, 2000
Moore, Anita (51) – April 28, 2001
Mulligan, Richard (67) – September 26, 2000
Nicholas, Harold (79) – July 3, 2000
O'Brien, Virginia (81) – January 18, 2001
O'Rear, James (86) – June 14, 2000
Orin, Renee (73) – August 26, 2000
Parsons, Nancy (58) – January 5, 2001
Perrine, Winifred "Renee" (92) – January 9, 2001

Peters, Jean (73) – October 13, 2000
Premice, Josephine (74) – April 13, 2001
Ramsey, Logan (79) – June 26, 2000
Redglare, Rockets (52) – May 28, 2001
Richards, Beah (74) – September 14, 2000
Robards, Jason Jr. (78) – December 26, 2000
Robinson, Joan (72) – January 5, 2001
Rodway, Norman (72) – March 13, 2001
Ruivivar, Francis (40) – May 23, 2001
Rutherford, Maude Russell (104) – March 8, 2001
Schumacher, Clarke M. (53) – January 30, 2001
Secombe, Harry (79) – April 11, 2001
Sinclair, Mary (78) – November 5, 2000
Sothern, Ann (92) – March 15, 2001
Steel, Anthony (80) – March 21, 2001
Steele, Lou (72) – February 25, 2001
Stewart, Nick "Nicodemus" (90) – December 18, 2000
Straight, Beatrice (86) – April 7, 2001
Tabakin, Ralph (79) – May 13, 2001
Tovey, Arthur Roland (95) – October 20, 2000
Townes, Harry (86) – May 23, 2001
Verdon, Gwen (75) – October 18, 2000
Walker, Randolph (71) – May 22, 2001
Walley, Deborah (57) – May 10, 2001
Walston, Ray (86) – January 1, 2001
Wayland, Len (80) – February 5, 2001
Williams, Michael (65) – January 12, 2001
Wilson, Peggy Bernier (93) – March 5, 2001
Windsor, Marie (86) – December 10, 2000
Wing, Toby (85) – March 23, 2001
Winter, Edward (63) – March 8, 2001
Wood, G. (George) (80) – July 24, 2000
Woods, Richards (77) – January 16, 2001
Yadin, Yossi (81) – May 17, 2001
Young, Loretta (87) – August 12, 2000

PRODUCERS, DIRECTORS, CHOREOGRAPHERS

Austin, Lyn (78) – October 29, 2000
Bartel, Paul (61) – May 13, 2000
Cantor, Arthur (81) – April 9, 2001
de Maat, Martin (52) – February 15, 2001
Dougherty, Frances Ann Cannon (82) – April 25, 2001
Epstein, Arthur J. (57) – November 1, 2000
FitzSimons, Charles B. (76) – February 14, 2001
Florea, John T. (84) – August 25, 2000
Fryer, Robert (71) – May 28, 2000
Gennaro, Peter (80) – September 28, 2000
Haley, Jack Jr. (67) – April 21, 2001
Hammerstein, William (82) – March 9, 2001
Johnston, Alexander Jennette "Sandy" (41) – November 27, 2000
Koch, Howard W. (84) – February 16, 2001
Kramer, Stanley (87) – February 19, 2001
Ludlum, Edward (80) – November 21, 2000
Maggio, Michael (49) – August 19, 2000
Peskin, Randy (48) – October 14, 2000
Ritchie, Michael (62) – April 16, 2001
Stone, Andrew L. (96) – June 1999
Tucker, Larry (67) – April 1, 2001
Weis, Don (78) – July 25, 2000
Wiesenthal, Sam (92) – February 11, 2001
Wolf, Mary Hunter (95) – November 3, 2000

PLAYWRIGHTS

Abel, Lionel (90) – April 19, 2001
Adams, Douglas (42) – May 11, 2001
Babe, Thomas (59) – December 6, 2000
Dunkel, John (86) – February 22, 2001
Epstein, Julius J. (91) – December 30, 2000
Ettlinger, Don (86) – August 7, 2000
Gomberg, Sy (82) – February 11, 2001
Hepburn, Richard (89) – October 20, 2000
Hunter, Kermit (90) – April 11, 2001
Kennedy, Burt (78) – February 14, 2001
Kramer, Anne Pearce (74) – December 3, 2000
Lardner, Ring Jr. (85) – October 31, 2000
Miller, Jason (62) – May 13, 2001
Mitchell, Loften (82) – May 14, 2001
Nash, N. Richard (87) – December 1, 2000
Phillips , Irving W. (95) – October 28, 2000
Taylor, Samuel (87) – May 26, 2000
Thompson, Gene (76) – April 14, 2001
Ulmer, Shirley Kassler (86) – July 6, 2000

COMPOSERS, LYRICISTS, SONG WRITERS

Allen, Robert (73) – October 1, 2000
Alley, Fred (38) – May 1, 2001
Curtin, Hoyt (78) – December 3, 2000

Hazlewood, Michael (59) – May 6, 2001
Nitzsche, Jack (63) – August 25, 2000
Phillips, John (65) – March 18, 2001

DESIGNERS

Bixby, Jonathan (41) – April 29, 2001
Dever, Sean (32) – April 13, 2001
Heschong, Albert "Hesch" (82) – March 1, 2001
Huebner, Mentor (83) – March 19, 2001
Kuri, Emile (93) – October 10, 2000
Weiner, Roberta (52) – November 14, 2000

CRITICS

Ardoin, John (66) – March 18, 2001
Canby, Vincent (76) – October 15, 2000
Curtiss, Thomas (85) – November 27, 2000
Guernsey, Otis L., Jr. (82) – May 2, 2001
Hulbert, Dan (46) – September 26, 2000
Koda, Michael "Cub" (51) – July 1, 2000
Kroll, Jack (74) – June 8, 2000
Kupferberg, Herbert (83) – February 22, 2001
Whitney, Dwight (82) – February 12, 2001

MUSICIANS

Buck, Rob (42) – December 19, 2000
Bull, Sandy (60) – April 11, 2001
Carle, Frankie (97) – March 7, 2001
Cole, Isaac "Ike" (73) – April 22, 2001
Foster, Willie (79) – May 20, 2001
Glazer, David (87) – March 4, 2001
Golub, David (50) – October 16, 2000
Gregory, Bryan (46) – January 10, 2001
Higgins, Billy (64) – May 4, 2001
C, Joe "Joseph Calleja" (26) – November 16, 2000
Jones, Herbie (74) – March 19, 2001
Koffman, Moe (72) – March 28, 2001
Krakauer, Barbara (69) – April 30, 2001
Lewis, John (80) – March 29, 2001
Levy, Lou (72) – January 23, 2001
McMichael, Ted (92) – February 27, 2001
Mitchell, Billy (74) – April 18, 2001
Mulieri-Dagort, Aida (82) – June 9, 2000
Pearl, Hal (92) – November 23, 2000
Rascher, Sigurd (94) – February 25, 2001
Reed, Israel (20) – March 17, 2001
Schuman, Henry (69) – May 8, 2001
Stern, Mitchell (45) – April 9, 2001
Sterne, Teresa (73) – December 10, 2000

CONDUCTORS

Brown, Les (88) – January 4, 2001
Frisina, David (86) – November 1, 2000
Maag, Peter (81) – April 20, 2001
Sinopoli, Giuseppe (54) – April 20, 2001

OTHERS

Gerard, Margaret Burns Mantle (80) – January 10, 2001
Daughter of Burns Mantle

Harris, Radie (96) – February 22, 2001
Entertainment journalist for *Hollywood Reporter*

Ketcham, Hank (81) – June 1, 2001
Creator of *Dennis the Menace*

LeRoy, Warner (65) – March 22, 2001
Entrepreneur

Littman, Robert (63) – January 29, 2001
Agent and film executive

Ludlum, Robert (73) – March 12, 2001
Writer, actor on Broadway and daytime television dramas

Mangum, Edward (87) – January 10, 2001
Co-founder of Arena Stage in Washington, D.C.

McGuire, Al (72) – January 26, 2001
Broadcaster and former Marquette University basketball coach

Schier, Walter C. (75) – January 3, 2001
Theatrical attorney

THE BEST PLAYS AND MAJOR PRIZEWINNERS 1894–2001

○○○○○

LISTED IN ALPHABETICAL ORDER below are all works selected as Best Plays in previous volumes of the *Best Plays* series through 1995–96 and beginning again with this volume. Also listed are the major prizewinners and special *Best Plays* citations for the four editions of 1996–97 through 1999–2000. Opposite each title is given the volume in which the play appears, its opening date and its total number of performances. Two separate opening-date and performance-number entries signify two separate engagements when the original production transferred. Plays marked with an asterisk (*) were still playing on June 1, 2001 and their number of performances was figured through May 31, 2001. Adaptors and translators are indicated by (ad) and (tr), the symbols (b), (m) and (l) stand for the author of the book, music and lyrics in the case of musicals and (c) signifies the credit for the show's conception, (i) for its inspiration. Entries identified as 94–99 and 99–09 are late 19th and early 20th century plays from one of the retrospective volumes. 94–95, 95–96, 96–97, 97–98, 98–99 and 99–00 are late-20th century plays.

PLAY	VOLUME	OPENED	PERFS
ABE LINCOLN IN ILLINOIS—Robert E. Sherwood	38-39	Oct. 15, 1938	472
ABRAHAM LINCOLN—John Drinkwater	19-20	Dec. 15, 1919	193
ACCENT ON YOUTH—Samson Raphaelson	34-35	Dec. 25, 1934	229
ADAM AND EVA—Guy Bolton, George Middleton	19-20	Sept. 13, 1919	312
ADAPTATION—Elaine May; and NEXT—Terrence McNally	68-69	Feb. 10, 1969	707
AFFAIRS OF STATE—Louis Verneuil	50-51	Sept. 25, 1950	610
AFTER THE FALL—Arthur Miller	63-64	Jan. 23, 1964	208
AFTER THE RAIN—John Bowen	67-68	Oct. 9, 1967	64
AFTER-PLAY—Anne Meara	94-95	Jan. 31, 1995	400
AGNES OF GOD—John Pielmeier	81-82	Mar. 30, 1982	599
AH, WILDERNESS!—Eugene O'Neill	33-34	Oct. 2, 1933	289
AIN'T SUPPOSED TO DIE A NATURAL DEATH—(b, m, l) Melvin Van Peebles	71-72	Oct. 20, 1971	325
ALIEN CORN—Sidney Howard	32-33	Feb. 20, 1933	98
Alison's House—Susan Glaspell	30-31	Dec. 1, 1930	41
ALL MY SONS—Arthur Miller	46-47	Jan. 29, 1947	328
ALL IN THE TIMING—David Ives	93-94	Feb. 17, 1994	526
ALL OVER TOWN—Murray Schisgal	74-75	Dec. 29, 1974	233
ALL THE WAY HOME—Tad Mosel, based on James Agee's novel *A Death in the Family*	60-61	Nov. 30, 1960	333
ALLEGRO—(b, l) Oscar Hammerstein II, (m) Richard Rodgers	47-48	Oct. 10, 1947	315
AMADEUS—Peter Shaffer	80-81	Dec. 17, 1980	1,181

Ambush—Arthur Richman	21-22	Oct. 10, 1921	98
America Hurrah—Jean-Claude van Itallie	66-67	Nov. 6, 1966	634
American Buffalo—David Mamet	76-77	Feb. 16, 1977	135
American Enterprise—Jeffrey Sweet (special citation)	93-94	Apr. 13, 1994	15
American Plan, The—Richard Greenberg	90-91	Dec. 16, 1990	37
American Way, The—George S. Kaufman, Moss Hart	38-39	Jan. 21, 1939	164
Amphitryon 38—Jean Giraudoux, (ad) S.N. Behrman	37-38	Nov. 1, 1937	153
And a Nightingale Sang—C.P. Taylor	83-84	Nov. 27, 1983	177
Andersonville Trial, The—Saul Levitt	59-60	Dec. 29, 1959	179
Andorra—Max Frisch, (ad) George Tabori	62-63	Feb. 9, 1963	9
Angel Street—Patrick Hamilton	41-42	Dec. 5, 1941	1,295
Angels Fall—Lanford Wilson	82-83	Oct. 17, 1982	65
	82-83	Jan. 22, 1983	64
Angels in America, Part I: Millennium Approaches—Tony Kushner	92-93	May 4, 1993	367
Angels in America, Part II: Perestroika—Tony Kushner	93-94	Nov. 23, 1994	216
Animal Kingdom, The—Philip Barry	31-32	Jan. 12, 1932	183
Anna Christie—Eugene O'Neill	21-22	Nov. 2, 1921	177
Anna Lucasta—Philip Yordan	44-45	Aug. 30, 1944	957
Anne of the Thousand Days—Maxwell Anderson	48-49	Dec. 8, 1948	286
Annie—(b) Thomas Meehan, (m) Charles Strouse, (l) Martin Charnin, based on Harold Gray's comic strip *Little Orphan Annie*	76-77	Apr. 21, 1977	2,377
Another Language—Rose Franken	31-32	Apr. 25, 1932	344
Another Part of the Forest—Lillian Hellman	46-47	Nov. 20, 1946	182
Antigone—Jean Anouilh, (ad) Lewis Galantiere	45-46	Feb. 18, 1946	64
Applause—(b) Betty Comden and Adolph Green, (m) Charles Strouse, (l) Lee Adams, based on the film *All About Eve* and the original story by Mary Orr	69-70	Mar. 30, 1970	896
Apple Tree, The—(b, l) Sheldon Harnick, (b, m) Jerry Bock, (add'l b) Jerome Coopersmith, based on stories by Mark Twain, Frank R. Stockton and Jules Feiffer	66-67	Oct. 18, 1966	463
Arcadia—Tom Stoppard	94-95	Mar. 30, 1995	173
Aristocrats—Brian Friel	88-89	Apr. 25, 1989	186
Arsenic and Old Lace—Joseph Kesselring	40-41	Jan. 10, 1941	1,444
Art—Yasmina Reza	97-98	Mar. 1, 1998	600
As Husbands Go—Rachel Crothers	30-31	Mar. 5, 1931	148
As Is—William M. Hoffman	84-85	Mar. 10, 1985	49
	84-85	May 1, 1985	285
Ashes—David Rudkin	76-77	Jan. 25, 1977	167
Aunt Dan and Lemon—Wallace Shawn	85-86	Oct. 1, 1985	191
Autumn Garden, The—Lillian Hellman	50-51	Mar. 7, 1951	101
Awake and Sing—Clifford Odets	34-35	Feb. 19, 1935	209
Bad Man, The—Porter Emerson Browne	20-21	Aug. 30, 1920	350

Broadway—Philip Dunning, George Abbott	26-27	Sept. 16, 1926	603
Broadway Bound—Neil Simon	86-87	Dec. 4, 1986	756
Burlesque—George Manker Watters, Arthur Hopkins	27-28	Sept. 1, 1927	372
Bus Stop—William Inge	54-55	Mar. 2, 1955	478
Butley—Simon Gray	72-73	Oct. 31, 1972	135
Butter and Egg Man, The—George S. Kaufman	25-26	Sept. 23, 1925	243
Butterflies Are Free—Leonard Gershe	69-70	Oct. 21, 1969	1,128
Cabaret—(b) Joe Masteroff, (m) John Kander, (l) Fred Ebb, based on John van Druten's play *I Am a Camera* and stories by Christopher Isherwood	66-67	Nov. 20, 1966	1,165
Cactus Flower—Abe Burrows, based on a play by Pierre Barillet and Jean-Pierre Gredy	65-66	Dec. 8, 1965	1,234
Caine Mutiny Court-Martial, The—Herman Wouk, based on his novel	53-54	Jan. 20, 1954	415
California Suite—Neil Simon	76-77	June 10, 1976	445
Caligula—Albert Camus, (ad) Justin O'Brien	59-60	Feb. 16, 1960	38
Call It a Day—Dodie Smith	35-36	Jan. 28, 1936	194
Camping with Henry & Tom—Mark St. Germain	94-95	Feb. 20, 1995	88
Candide—(b) Lillian Hellman, based on Voltaire's satire, (l) Richard Wilbur, John Latouche, Dorothy Parker, (m) Leonard Bernstein	56-57	Dec. 1, 1956	73
Candle in the Wind—Maxwell Anderson	41-42	Oct. 22, 1941	95
Caretaker, The—Harold Pinter	61-62	Oct. 4, 1961	165
Case of Rebellious Susan, The—Henry Arthur Jones	94-99	Dec. 20, 1894	80
Cat on a Hot Tin Roof—Tennessee Williams	54-55	Mar. 24, 1955	694
Cats—(m) Andrew Lloyd Webber, based on T.S. Eliot's *Old Possum's Book of Practical Cats,* (add'l l) Trevor Nunn, Richard Stilgoe	82-83	Oct. 7, 1982	7,485
Celebration—(b, l) Tom Jones, (m) Harvey Schmidt	68-69	Jan. 22, 1969	109
Chalk Garden, The—Enid Bagnold	55-56	Oct. 26, 1955	182
Changelings, The—Lee Wilson Dodd	23-24	Sept. 17, 1923	128
Changing Room, The—David Storey	72-73	Mar. 6, 1973	192
Chapter Two—Neil Simon	77-78	Dec. 4, 1977	857
Chicago—Maurine Dallas Watkins	26-27	Dec. 30, 1926	172
Chicago—(b) Fred Ebb, Bob Fosse, (m) John Kander, (l) Fred Ebb,based on the play by Maurine Dallas Watkins	75-76	June 3, 1975	898
Chicken Feed—Guy Bolton	23-24	Sept. 24, 1923	144
Children of a Lesser God—Mark Medoff	79-80	Mar. 30, 1980	887
Children's Hour, The—Lillian Hellman	34-35	Nov. 20, 1934	691
Child's Play—Robert Marasco	69-70	Feb. 17, 1970	342
Chips With Everything—Arnold Wesker	63-64	Oct. 1, 1963	149
Chorus Line, A—(c) Michael Bennett, (b) James Kirkwood, Nicholas Dante, (m) Marvin Hamlisch, (l) Edward Kleban	74-75	Apr. 15, 1975	101
	75-76	July 25, 1975	6,137

Criminal Code, The—Martin Flavin	29-30	Oct. 2, 1929	173
Crucible, The—Arthur Miller	52-53	Jan. 22, 1953	197
Cryptogram, The—David Mamet	94-95	Apr. 13, 1995	62
Curtains—Stephen Bill	95-96	May 21, 1996	64
Cynara—H.M. Harwood, R.F. Gore-Browne	31-32	Nov. 2, 1931	210
Da—Hugh Leonard	77-78	May 1, 1978	697
Daisy Mayme—George Kelly	26-27	Oct. 25, 1926	112
Damask Cheek, The—John van Druten, Lloyd Morris	42-43	Oct 22, 1942	93
Dance and the Railroad, The—David Henry Hwang	81-82	July 16, 1981	181
Dancing at Lughnasa—Brian Friel	91-92	Oct. 24, 1991	421
Dancing Mothers—Edgar Selwyn, Edmund Goulding	24-25	Aug. 11, 1924	312
Dark at the Top of the Stairs, The—William Inge	57-58	Dec. 5, 1957	468
Dark Is Light Enough, The—Christopher Fry	54-55	Feb. 23, 1955	69
Darkness at Noon—Sidney Kingsley, based on Arthur Koestler's novel	50-51	Jan. 13, 1951	186
Darling of the Gods, The—David Belasco, John Luther Long	99-09	Dec. 3, 1902	182
Daughters of Atreus—Robert Turney	36-37	Oct. 14, 1936	13
Day in the Death of Joe Egg, A—Peter Nichols	67-68	Feb. 1, 1968	154
Dead End—Sidney Kingsley	35-36	Oct. 28, 1935	687
Deadly Game, The—James Yaffe, based on Friedrich Duerrenmatt's novel	59-60	Feb. 2, 1960	39
Dear Ruth—Norman Krasna	44-45	Dec. 13, 1944	683
Death of a Salesman—Arthur Miller	48-49	Feb. 10, 1949	742
Death Takes a Holiday—Alberto Casella, (ad) Walter Ferris	29-30	Dec. 26, 1929	180
Deathtrap—Ira Levin	77-78	Feb. 26, 1978	1,793
Deburau—Sacha Guitry, (ad) Harley Granville Barker	20-21	Dec. 23, 1920	189
Decision—Edward Chodorov	43-44	Feb. 2, 1944	160
Déclassée—Zoë Akins	19-20	Oct. 6, 1919	257
Deep Are the Roots—Arnaud d'Usseau, James Gow	45-46	Sept. 26, 1945	477
Delicate Balance, A—Edward Albee	66-67	Sept. 22, 1966	132
Deputy, The—Rolf Hochhuth, (ad) Jerome Rothenberg	63-64	Feb. 26, 1964	109
Design for Living—Noël Coward	32-33	Jan. 24, 1933	135
Designated Mourner, The—Wallace Shawn (special citation)	99-00	May 13, 2000	30+
Desire Under the Elms—Eugene O'Neill	24-25	Nov. 11, 1924	208
Desperate Hours, The—Joseph Hayes, based on his novel	54-55	Feb. 10, 1955	212
Destiny of Me, The—Larry Kramer	92-93	Oct. 20, 1992	175
Detective Story—Sidney Kingsley	48-49	Mar. 23, 1949	581
Devil Passes, The—Benn W. Levy	31-32	Jan. 4, 1932	96
Devil's Advocate, The—Dore Schary, based on Morris L. West's novel	60-61	Mar. 9, 1961	116
Dial "M" for Murder—Frederick Knott	52-53	Oct. 29, 1952	552

EPITAPH FOR GEORGE DILLON—John Osborne, Anthony Creighton	58-59	Nov. 4, 1958	23
EQUUS—Peter Shaffer	74-75	Oct. 24, 1974	1,209
ESCAPE—John Galsworthy	27-28	Oct. 26, 1927	173
ETHAN FROME—Owen and Donald Davis, based on Edith Wharton's novel	35-36	Jan. 21, 1936	120
EVE OF ST. MARK, THE—Maxwell Anderson	42-43	Oct. 7, 1942	307
EXCURSION—Victor Wolfson	36-37	Apr. 9, 1937	116
EXECUTION OF JUSTICE—Emily Mann	85-86	Mar. 13, 1986	12
EXTRA MAN, THE—Richard Greenberg	91-92	May 19, 1992	39
EXTREMITIES—William Mastrosimone	82-83	Dec. 22, 1982	325
FAIR COUNTRY, A—Jon Robin Baitz	95-96	Oct. 29, 1995	153
FALL GUY, THE—James Gleason, George Abbott	24-25	Mar. 10, 1925	176
FALSETTOLAND—William Finn, James Lapine	90-91	June 28, 1990	215
FAMILY BUSINESS—Dick Goldberg	77-78	Apr. 12, 1978	438
FAMILY PORTRAIT—Lenore Coffee, William Joyce Cowen	38-39	May 8, 1939	111
FAMOUS MRS. FAIR, THE—James Forbes	19-20	Dec. 22, 1919	344
FAR COUNTRY, A—Henry Denker	60-61	Apr. 4, 1961	271
FARMER TAKES A WIFE, THE—Frank B. Elser, Marc Connelly, based on Walter D. Edmonds's novel *Rome Haul*	34-35	Oct. 30, 1934	104
FATAL WEAKNESS, THE—George Kelly	46-47	Nov. 19, 1946	119
FENCES—August Wilson	86-87	Mar. 26, 1987	526
FIDDLER ON THE ROOF—(b) Joseph Stein, (l) Sheldon Harnick, (m) Jerry Bock, based on Sholom Aleichem's stories	64-65	Sept. 22, 1964	3,242
5TH OF JULY, THE—Lanford Wilson	77-78	Apr. 27, 1978	159
FIND YOUR WAY HOME—John Hopkins	73-74	Jan. 2, 1974	135
FINISHING TOUCHES—Jean Kerr	72-73	Feb. 8, 1973	164
FIORELLO!—(b) Jerome Weidman, George Abbott, (l) Sheldon Harnick, (m) Jerry Bock	59-60	Nov. 23, 1959	795
FIREBRAND, THE—Edwin Justus Mayer	24-25	Oct. 15, 1924	269
FIRES IN THE MIRROR—Anna Deavere Smith	91-92	May 12, 1992	109
FIRST LADY—Katherine Dayton, George S. Kaufman	35-36	Nov. 26, 1935	246
FIRST MONDAY IN OCTOBER—Jerome Lawrence, Robert E. Lee	78-79	Oct. 3, 1978	79
FIRST MRS. FRASER, THE—St. John Ervine	29-30	Dec. 28, 1929	352
FIRST YEAR, THE—Frank Craven	20-21	Oct. 20, 1920	760
FIVE FINGER EXERCISE—Peter Shaffer	59-60	Dec. 2, 1959	337
FIVE-STAR FINAL—Louis Weitzenkorn	30-31	Dec. 30, 1930	175
FLIGHT TO THE WEST—Elmer Rice	40-41	Dec. 30, 1940	136
FLOATING LIGHT BULB, THE—Woody Allen	80-81	Apr. 27, 1981	65
FLOWERING PEACH, THE—Clifford Odets	54-55	Dec. 28, 1954	135
FOLLIES—(b) James Goldman, (m, l) Stephen Sondheim	70-71	Apr. 4, 1971	521
FOOL, THE—Channing Pollock	22-23	Oct. 23, 1922	373
FOOL FOR LOVE—Sam Shepard	83-84	May 26, 1983	1,000

Grapes of Wrath, The—(ad) Frank Galati from the novel by John Steinbeck	89-90	Mar. 22, 1990	188
Great Divide, The—William Vaughn Moody	99-09	Oct. 3, 1906	238
Great God Brown, The—Eugene O'Neill	25-26	Jan. 23, 1926	271
Great White Hope, The—Howard Sackler	68-69	Oct. 3, 1968	556
Green Bay Tree, The—Mordaunt Shairp	33-34	Oct. 20, 1933	166
Green Goddess, The—William Archer	20-21	Jan. 18, 1921	440
Green Grow the Lilacs—Lynn Riggs	30-31	Jan. 26, 1931	64
Green Hat, The—Michael Arlen	25-26	Sept. 15, 1925	231
Green Julia—Paul Abelman	72-73	Nov. 16, 1972	147
Green Pastures, The—Marc Connelly, based on Roark Bradford's *Ol' Man Adam and His Chillun*	29-30	Feb. 26, 1930	640
Gross Indecency: The Three Trials of Oscar Wilde—Moisés Kaufman	97-98	June 5, 1997	534
Gus and Al—Albert Innaurato	88-89	Feb. 27, 1989	25
Guys and Dolls—(b) Jo Swerling, Abe Burrows, based on a story and characters by Damon Runyon, (m, l) Frank Loesser	50-51	Nov. 24, 1950	1,200
Gypsy—Maxwell Anderson	28-29	Jan. 14, 1929	64
Hadrian VII—Peter Luke, based on works by Fr. Rolfe	68-69	Jan. 8, 1969	359
Hamp—John Wilson, based on an episode from a novel by J.L. Hodson	66-67	Mar. 9, 1967	101
Hapgood—Tom Stoppard	94-95	Dec. 4, 1994	129
Happy Time, The—Samuel Taylor, based on Robert Fontaine's book	49-50	Jan. 24, 1950	614
Harriet—Florence Ryerson, Colin Clements	42-43	Mar. 3, 1943	377
Harvey—Mary Chase	44-45	Nov. 1, 1944	1,775
Hasty Heart, The—John Patrick	44-45	Jan. 3, 1945	207
He Who Gets Slapped—Leonid Andreyev, (ad) Gregory Zilboorg	21-22	Jan. 9, 1922	308
Heart of Maryland, The—David Belasco	94-99	Oct. 22, 1895	240
Heidi Chronicles, The—Wendy Wasserstein	88-89	Dec. 11, 1988	81
	88-89	Mar. 9, 1989	621
Heiress, The—Ruth and Augustus Goetz, suggested by Henry James's novel *Washington Square*	47-48	Sept. 29, 1947	410
Hell-Bent fer Heaven—Hatcher Hughes	23-24	Jan. 4, 1924	122
Hello, Dolly!—(b) Michael Stewart, (m, l) Jerry Herman, based on Thornton Wilder's *The Matchmaker*	63-64	Jan. 16, 1964	2,844
Her Master's Voice—Clare Kummer	33-34	Oct. 23, 1933	224
Here Come the Clowns—Philip Barry	38-39	Dec. 7, 1938	88
Hero, The—Gilbert Emery	21-22	Sept. 5, 1921	80
High Tor—Maxwell Anderson	36-37	Jan. 9, 1937	171
Hogan's Goat—William Alfred	65-66	Nov. 11, 1965	607
Holiday—Philip Barry	28-29	Nov. 26, 1928	229
Home—David Storey	70-71	Nov. 17, 1970	110

Life in the Theatre, A—David Mamet	77-78	Oct. 20, 1977	288
Life With Father—Howard Lindsay, Russel Crouse, based on Clarence Day's book	39-40	Nov. 8, 1939	3,224
Life With Mother—Howard Lindsay, Russel Crouse, based on Clarence Day's book	48-49	Oct. 20, 1948	265
Light Up the Sky—Moss Hart	48-49	Nov. 18, 1948	216
Liliom—Ferenc Molnar, (ad) Benjamin Glazer	20-21	Apr. 20, 1921	300
Lion in Winter, The—James Goldman	65-66	Mar. 3, 1966	92
*Lion King, The—(b) Roger Allers, Irene Mecchi, (m, l) Elton John, Tim Rice, (add'l m, l) Lebo M, Mark Mancina, Jay Rifkin, Julie Taymor, Hans Zimmer	97-98	Nov. 13, 1997	1,482
Lips Together, Teeth Apart—Terrence McNally	91-92	June 25, 1991	406
Little Accident—Floyd Dell, Thomas Mitchell	28-29	Oct. 9, 1928	303
Little Foxes, The—Lillian Hellman	38-39	Feb. 15, 1939	410
Little Minister, The—James M. Barrie	94-99	Sept. 27, 1897	300
Little Night Music, A—(b) Hugh Wheeler, (m, l) Stephen Sondheim, suggested by Ingmar Bergman's film *Smiles of a Summer Night*	72-73	Feb. 25, 1973	600
Living Room, The—Graham Greene	54-55	Nov. 17, 1954	22
Living Together—Alan Ayckbourn	75-76	Dec. 7, 1975	76
*Lobby Hero—Kenneth Lonergan	00-01	Mar. 13, 2001	40
	00-01	May 8, 2001	27
Loman Family Picnic, The—Donald Margulies	89-90	June 20, 1989	16
Long Day's Journey Into Night—Eugene O'Neill	56-57	Nov. 7, 1956	390
Look Back in Anger—John Osborne	57-58	Oct. 1, 1957	407
Look Homeward, Angel—Ketti Frings, based on Thomas Wolfe's novel	57-58	Nov. 28, 1957	564
Loose Ends—Michael Weller	79-80	June 6, 1979	284
Lost Horizons—Harry Segall, revised by John Hayden	34-35	Oct. 15, 1934	56
Lost in the Stars—(b, l) Maxwell Anderson, based on Alan Paton's novel *Cry, the Beloved Country,* (m) Kurt Weill	49-50	Oct. 30, 1949	273
Lost in Yonkers—Neil Simon	90-91	Feb. 21, 1991	780
Love Letters—A.R. Gurney	89-90	Aug. 22, 1989	64
	89-90	Oct. 31, 1989	96
Love of Four Colonels, The—Peter Ustinov	52-53	Jan. 15, 1953	141
Love! Valour! Compassion!—Terrence McNally	94-95	Nov. 1, 1994	72
	94-95	Feb. 14, 1995	249
Lovers—Brian Friel	68-69	July 25, 1968	148
Loyalties—John Galsworthy	22-23	Sept. 27, 1922	220
Lunch Hour—Jean Kerr	80-81	Nov. 12, 1980	262
Lute Song—(b) Sidney Howard, Will Irwin from the Chinese classic *Pi-Pa-Ki,* (l) Bernard Hanighen, (m) Raymond Scott	45-46	Feb. 6, 1946	385
Luther—John Osborne	63-64	Sept. 25, 1963	211
Luv—Murray Schisgal	64-65	Nov. 11, 1964	901

Once in a Lifetime—Moss Hart, George S. Kaufman	30-31	Sept. 24, 1930	406
Once on This Island—(b, l) Lynn Ahrens, (m) Stephen Flaherty, based on the novel *My Love My Love* by Rosa Guy	89-90	May 6, 1990	24
	90-91	Oct. 18, 1990	469
One Sunday Afternoon—James Hagan	32-33	Feb. 15, 1933	322
Orpheus Descending—Tennessee Williams	56-57	Mar. 21, 1957	68
Other People's Money—Jerry Sterner	88-89	Feb. 16, 1989	990
Otherwise Engaged—Simon Gray	76-77	Feb. 2, 1977	309
Our Country's Good—Timberlake Wertenbaker	90-91	Apr. 29, 1991	48
Outrageous Fortune—Rose Franken	43-44	Nov. 3, 1943	77
Our Town—Thornton Wilder	37-38	Feb. 4, 1938	336
Outward Bound—Sutton Vane	23-24	Jan. 7, 1924	144
Over 21—Ruth Gordon	43-44	Jan. 3, 1944	221
Overture—William Bolitho	30-31	Dec. 5, 1930	41
P.S. 193—David Rayfiel	62-63	Oct. 30, 1962	48
Pacific Overtures—(b) John Weidman, (m, l) Stephen Sondheim, (add'l material) Hugh Wheeler	75-76	Jan. 11, 1976	193
Pack of Lies—Hugh Whitemore	84-85	Feb. 11, 1985	120
Painting Churches—Tina Howe	83-84	Nov. 22, 1983	206
Parade—(b) Alfred Uhry, (m,l) Jason Robert Brown	98-99	Dec. 17, 1998	85
Paris Bound—Philip Barry	27-28	Dec. 27, 1927	234
Passion—(b) James Lapine, (m) Stephen Sondheim, based on the film *Passione D'Amore*	93-94	May 9, 1994	280
Passion of Joseph D., The—Paddy Chayevsky	63-64	Feb. 11, 1964	15
Patriots, The—Sidney Kingsley	42-43	Jan. 29, 1943	173
Perfect Ganesh, A—Terrence McNally	93-94	June 27, 1993	124
Perfect Party, The—A.R. Gurney	85-86	Apr. 2, 1986	238
Period of Adjustment—Tennessee Williams	60-61	Nov. 10, 1960	132
Persecution and Assassination of Marat as Performed by the Inmates of the Asylum of Charenton Under the Direction of the Marquis de Sade, The—Peter Weiss, English version by Geoffrey Skelton, verse (ad) Adrian Mitchell	65-66	Dec. 27, 1965	144
Petrified Forest, The—Robert E. Sherwood	34-35	Jan. 7, 1935	197
*Phantom of the Opera, The—(b) Richard Stilgoe, Andrew Lloyd Webber, (m) Andrew Lloyd Webber, (l) Charles Hart, (add'l l) Richard Stilgoe, adapted from the novel by Gaston Leroux (special citation)	87-88	Jan. 26, 1988	5,570
Philadelphia, Here I Come!—Brian Friel	65-66	Feb. 16, 1966	326
Philadelphia Story, The—Philip Barry	38-39	Mar. 28, 1939	417
Philanthropist, The—Christopher Hampton	70-71	Mar. 15, 1971	72
Physicists, The—Friedrich Dürrenmatt, (ad) James Kirkup	64-65	Oct. 13, 1964	55
Piano Lesson, The—August Wilson	89-90	Apr. 16, 1990	329

Red Diaper Baby—Josh Kornbluth .... 92-93 ..... June 12, 1992 59

Rehearsal, The—Jean Anouilh, (ad) Pamela Hansford Johnson, Kitty Black .... 63-64 ..... Sept. 23, 1963 110

Remains To Be Seen—Howard Lindsay, Russel Crouse ...... 51-52 ..... Oct. 3, 1951 199

*Rent—(b,m,l) Jonathan Larson .... 95-96 ..... Feb. 13, 1996 56

95-96 ..... Apr. 29, 1996 2,125

Requiem for a Nun—Ruth Ford, William Faulkner, adapted from William Faulkner's novel .... 58-59 ..... Jan. 30, 1959 43

Reunion in Vienna—Robert E. Sherwood .... 31-32 ..... Nov. 16, 1931 264

Rhinoceros—Eugene Ionesco, (tr) Derek Prouse .... 60-61 ..... Jan. 9, 1961 240

Ritz, The—Terrence McNally .... 74-75 ..... Jan. 20, 1975 400

River Niger, The—Joseph A. Walker .... 72-73 ..... Dec. 5, 1972 120

72-73 ..... Mar. 27, 1973 280

Road—Jim Cartwright .... 88-89 ..... July 28, 1988 62

Road to Mecca, The—Athol Fugard .... 87-88 ..... Apr. 12, 1988 172

Road to Rome, The—Robert E. Sherwood .... 26-27 ..... Jan. 31, 1927 392

Rockaby—(see *Enough, Footfalls* and *Rockaby*)

Rocket to the Moon—Clifford Odets .... 38-39 ..... Nov. 24, 1938 131

Romance—Edward Sheldon .... 09-19 ..... Feb. 10, 1913 160

Rope Dancers, The—Morton Wishengrad .... 57-58 ..... Nov. 20, 1957 189

Rose Tattoo, The—Tennessee Williams .... 50-51 ..... Feb. 3, 1951 306

Rosencrantz and Guildenstern Are Dead—Tom Stoppard .. 67-68 ..... Oct. 16, 1967 420

Round and Round the Garden—Alan Ayckbourn .... 75-76 ..... Dec. 7, 1975 76

Royal Family, The—George S. Kaufman, Edna Ferber ...... 27-28 ..... Dec. 28, 1927 345

Royal Hunt of the Sun—Peter Shaffer .... 65-66 ..... Oct. 26, 1965 261

Rugged Path, The—Robert E. Sherwood .... 45-46 ..... Nov. 10, 1945 81

Runner Stumbles, The—Milan Stitt .... 75-76 ..... May 18, 1976 191

St. Helena—R.C. Sheriff, Jeanne de Casalis .... 36-37 ..... Oct. 6, 1936 63

Same Time, Next Year—Bernard Slade .... 74-75 ..... Mar. 13, 1975 1,453

Saturday's Children—Maxwell Anderson .... 26-27 ..... Jan. 26, 1927 310

Screens, The—Jean Genet, (tr) Minos Volanakis .... 71-72 ..... Nov. 30, 1971 28

Scuba Duba—Bruce Jay Friedman .... 67-68 ..... Oct. 10, 1967 692

Sea Horse, The—Edward J. Moore (James Irwin) .... 73-74 ..... Apr. 15, 1974 128

Searching Wind, The—Lillian Hellman .... 43-44 ..... Apr. 12, 1944 318

Seascape—Edward Albee .... 74-75 ..... Jan. 26, 1975 65

Season in the Sun—Wolcott Gibbs .... 50-51 ..... Sept. 28, 1950 367

Season's Greetings—Alan Ayckbourn .... 85-86 ..... July 11, 1985 20

Second Threshold—Philip Barry, revisions by Robert E. Sherwood .... 50-51 ..... Jan. 2, 1951 126

Secret Service—William Gillette .... 94-99 ..... Oct. 5, 1896 176

Separate Tables—Terence Rattigan .... 56-57 ..... Oct. 25, 1956 332

Serenading Louie—Lanford Wilson .... 75-76 ..... May 2, 1976 33

Serpent: A Ceremony, The—Jean-Claude van Itallie .... 69-70 ..... May 29, 1973 3

Seven Guitars—August Wilson .... 95-96 ..... Mar. 28, 1996 187

Staircase—Charles Dyer	67-68	Jan. 10, 1968	61
Star-Wagon, The—Maxwell Anderson	37-38	Sept. 29, 1937	223
State of the Union—Howard Lindsay, Russel Crouse	45-46	Nov. 14, 1945	765
Steambath—Bruce Jay Friedman	70-71	June 30, 1970	128
Steel Magnolias—Robert Harling	87-88	June 19, 1987	1,126
Sticks and Bones—David Rabe	71-72	Nov. 7, 1971	121
	71-72	Mar. 1, 1972	245
Stone and Star—Robert Ardrey (also called *Shadow of Heroes*)	61-62	Dec. 5, 1961	20
Stop the World–I Want to Get Off—(b, m, l) Leslie Bricusse, Anthony Newley	62-63	Oct. 3, 1962	555
Storm Operation—Maxwell Anderson	43-44	Jan. 11, 1944	23
Story of Mary Surratt, The—John Patrick	46-47	Feb. 8, 1947	11
Strange Interlude—Eugene O'Neill	27-28	Jan. 30, 1928	426
Streamers—David Rabe	75-76	Apr. 21, 1976	478
Street Scene—Elmer Rice	28-29	Jan. 10, 1929	601
Streetcar Named Desire, A—Tennessee Williams	47-48	Dec. 3, 1947	855
Strictly Dishonorable—Preston Sturges	29-30	Sept. 18, 1929	557
Subject Was Roses, The—Frank D. Gilroy	64-65	May 25, 1964	832
Substance of Fire, The—Jon Robin Baitz	90-91	Mar. 17, 1991	120
SubUrbia—Eric Bogosian	93-94	May 22, 1994	113
Sugar Babies—(ad) Ralph G. Allen from traditional material (special citation)	79-80	Oct. 8, 1979	1,208
Sum of Us, The—David Stevens	90-91	Oct. 16, 1990	335
Summer of the 17th Doll—Ray Lawler	57-58	Jan. 22, 1958	29
Sunday in the Park with George—(b) James Lapine, (m, l) Stephen Sondheim	83-84	May 2, 1984	604
Sunrise at Campobello—Dore Schary	57-58	Jan. 30, 1958	556
Sunset Boulevard—(b, l) Don Black, Christopher Hampton, (m) Andrew Lloyd Webber, based on the film by Billy Wilder	94-95	Nov. 17, 1994	977
Sunshine Boys, The—Neil Simon	72-73	Dec. 20, 1972	538
Sun-Up—Lula Vollmer	22-23	May 25, 1923	356
Susan and God—Rachel Crothers	37-38	Oct. 7, 1937	288
Swan, The—Ferenc Molnar, (tr) Melville Baker	23-24	Oct. 23, 1923	255
Sweeney Todd, the Demon Barber of Fleet Street—(b) Hugh Wheeler, (m, l) Stephen Sondheim, based on a version of *Sweeney Todd* by Christopher Bond	78-79	Mar. 1, 1979	557
Sweet Bird of Youth—Tennessee Williams	58-59	Mar. 10, 1959	375
Table Manners—Alan Ayckbourn	75-76	Dec. 7, 1975	76
Table Settings—James Lapine	79-80	Jan. 14, 1980	264
Take a Giant Step—Louis Peterson	53-54	Sept. 24, 1953	76
Taking of Miss Janie, The—Ed Bullins	74-75	May 4, 1975	42
Talley's Folley—Lanford Wilson	78-79	May 1, 1979	44
	79-80	Feb. 20, 1980	277
Tarnish—Gilbert Emery	23-24	Oct. 1, 1923	248

Tribute—Bernard Slade	77-78	June 1, 1978	212
Tuna Christmas, A—Jaston Williams, Joe Sears, Ed Howard	94-95	Dec. 15, 1994	20
Twilight: Los Angeles, 1992—Anna Deavere Smith	93-94	Mar. 23, 1994	13
	93-94	Apr. 17, 1994	72
Two Blind Mice—Samuel Spewack	48-49	Mar. 2, 1949	157
Two Trains Running—August Wilson	91-92	Apr. 13, 1992	160
Unchastened Woman, The—Louis Kaufman Anspacher	09-19	Oct. 9, 1915	193
Uncle Harry—Thomas Job	41-42	May 20, 1942	430
Under Milk Wood—Dylan Thomas	57-58	Oct. 15, 1957	39
*Urinetown—(b) Greg Kotis, (m) Mark Hollmann, (l) Greg Kotis, Mark Hollmann	00-01	May 6, 2001	28
Valley Forge—Maxwell Anderson	34-35	Dec. 10, 1934	58
Valley Song—Athol Fugard	95-96	Dec. 12, 1995	96
Venus Observed—Christopher Fry	51-52	Feb. 13, 1952	86
Very Special Baby, A—Robert Alan Aurthur	56-57	Nov. 14, 1956	5
Victoria Regina—Laurence Housman	35-36	Dec. 26, 1935	517
View From the Bridge, A—Arthur Miller	55-56	Sept. 29, 1955	149
Violet—(b,1) Brian Crawley, (m) Jeanine Tesori, based on *The Ugliest Pilgrim* by Doris Betts	96-97	Mar. 11, 1997	32
Visit, The—Friedrich Dürrenmatt, (ad) Maurice Valency	57-58	May 5, 1958	189
Visit to a Small Planet—Gore Vidal	56-57	Feb. 7, 1957	388
Vivat! Vivat Regina!—Robert Bolt	71-72	Jan. 20, 1972	116
Voice of the Turtle, The—John van Druten	43-44	Dec. 8, 1943	1,557
Wager, The—Mark Medoff	74-75	Oct. 21, 1974	104
Waiting for Godot—Samuel Beckett	55-56	Apr. 19, 1956	59
Walk in the Woods, A—Lee Blessing	87-88	Feb. 28, 1988	136
Waltz of the Toreadors, The—Jean Anouilh, (tr) Lucienne Hill	56-57	Jan. 17, 1957	132
Watch on the Rhine—Lillian Hellman	40-41	Apr. 1, 1941	378
We, the People—Elmer Rice	32-33	Jan. 21, 1933	49
Wedding Bells—Salisbury Field	19-20	Nov. 12, 1919	168
Wednesday's Child—Leopold Atlas	33-34	Jan. 16, 1934	56
Wenceslas Square—Larry Shue	87-88	Mar. 2, 1988	55
What a Life—Clifford Goldsmith	37-38	Apr. 13, 1938	538
What Price Glory?—Maxwell Anderson, Laurence Stallings	24-25	Sept. 3, 1924	433
What the Butler Saw—Joe Orton	69-70	May 4, 1970	224
When Ladies Meet—Rachel Crothers	32-33	Oct. 6, 1932	191
When You Comin' Back, Red Ryder?—Mark Medoff	73-74	Dec. 6, 1973	302
Where Has Tommy Flowers Gone?—Terrence McNally	71-72	Oct. 7, 1971	78
White House Murder Case, The—Jules Feiffer	69-70	Feb. 18, 1970	119
White Steed, The—Paul Vincent Carroll	38-39	Jan. 10, 1939	136

YOU'RE A GOOD MAN CHARLIE BROWN—(b, m, l) Clark Gesner, based on the comic strip *Peanuts* by Charles M. Schulz .... 66-67 ..... Mar. 7, 1967 1,597

ZOOMAN AND THE SIGN—Charles Fuller .... 80-81 ..... Dec. 7, 1980 33

CONTRIBUTORS TO *BEST PLAYS*

○○○○○

Robert Brustein is the author of twelve books on theater and society, including *The Theatre of Revolt* and *Making Scenes*, a memoir of his Yale years when he was Dean of the Drama School. He has received two George Jean Nathan Awards for dramatic criticism. Brustein is also Professor of English at Harvard University and drama critic for *The New Republic*. As founding director of the Yale Repertory Theatre and American Repertory Theatre, Brustein has supervised more than 200 productions, as well as acting, directing and writing for them. His direction and adaptation of *Six Characters in Search of an Author* won the Boston Theatre Award for Best Production of 1996. His play *Demons*, which was broadcast on WGBH radio in 1993, had its stage world premiere as part of ART New Stages. His play *Nobody Dies on Friday* was given its world premiere in the spring of 1998 and was presented at the Singapore Festival of Arts that summer. It was published in *New Playwrights: The Best Plays of 1998*, and premiered in Russia at the Pushkin Theatre in Moscow. His short play *Chekhov on Ice* became part of his adaptation of three plays by Anton Chekhov, *Three Farces and a Funeral*. He recently completed a new play called *The Face-Lift* and a new book, *The Siege of the Arts*. Brustein is a member of the American Academy of Arts and was recently inducted into the Theater Hall of Fame.

Rue E. Canvin worked at the *New York Herald Tribune*, first as a secretary in the advertising department and then as an editorial assistant in the drama department for 15 years where she worked with the editors and the drama, movie, dance, music, television critics until the demise of the newspaper in 1966. She also worked at the *World Journal Tribune* until its demise the following year. Canvin has served as an assistant editor of the *Best Plays* series since 1963. She has also transcribed taped interviews for the Dramatists Guild and Authors League.

Joshua Crouthamel has worked on two editions of the *Best Plays* series. In addition to editing, he performs in New York City and is a freelance travel writer. He hopes to publish a collection of his travel writing in the near future.

Tish Dace, Chancellor Professor of English at the University of Massachusetts Dartmouth and winner of that university's 1997 Scholar of the Year Award, has published 200 essays, articles and book chapters; reviews of several thousand plays; and several books, most recently *Langston Hughes: The Contemporary Reviews*. She has chaired the Maharam Foundation/American Theatre Wing/Hewes Design Awards in New York since 1984 and served six years as a member of the Executive Committee of the American Theatre Critics Association. She currently serves on the Executive Commitee of the International Association of Theatre Critics and is the New York critic for *Plays International* in London.

Christine Dolen has been the *Miami Herald*'s theater critic since 1979. She holds bachelor's and master's degrees in journalism from Ohio State University and was a John S. Knight Journalism Fellow at Stanford University in 1984–85. In 1997, she was a member of the Pulitzer Prize drama jury; in 1999, she was a senior fellow in the National Arts Journalism Program at Columbia University. Currently, she is on the advisory council of the American Theatre Critics Association and is president of the South Florida Critics Circle, which gives the annual Carbonell Awards for theater excellence. She is working on a biography of George Abbott with Mr. Abbott's widow, Joy. Dolen began her career as a copy editor and freelance film/theater reviewer for the Columbus, Ohio, *Dispatch*. She was rock music critic and an arts copy editor at the *Detroit Free Press* before joining the *Herald* staff in 1976. Before becoming the *Herald*'s theater critic, she was arts editor and pop music critic. Her awards include the Green Eyeshade in criticism from the Atlanta Chapter of the Society of Professional Journalists and first place in arts writing in the Missouri Lifestyle Journalism Awards. Dolen received the George Abbott Award for Outstanding Achievement in the Arts at the 2001 Carbonell Awards. She is the daughter of an actor, the late Carbonell and Abbott Award-winner William Hindman.

Michael Grossberg has served since 1985 as theater critic at *The Dispatch* newspaper in Columbus, Ohio. He is vice chairman of the American Theatre Critics Association, and served for six years as chair of ATCA's New Plays Committee and four years as chair of ATCA's Regional Theatre Award committee. He has written articles for *Reason* and *Libertarian Review* magazines. He is a frequent contributor to *Best Plays*.

Mel Gussow, a cultural writer for the *New York Times*, is the author of the biography, *Edward Albee: A Singular Journey*, and of books about Harold Pinter, Tom Stoppard and Samuel Beckett. A past winner of the George Jean Nathan Award for Dramatic Criticism, he also wrote *Theater on the Edge: New Visions, New Voices*, and is the co-editor of the Library of America's two-volume edition of the plays of Tennessee Williams.

Hirschfeld has virtually been synonymous with Broadway since his first theatrical drawing was published in December 1926. A stay in Bali in 1932 convinced Hirschfeld of the graphic possibilities of line. He says, "It was in Bali that my attraction to drawing blossomed into an enduring love affair with line." He returned to America to record the American theater in distinct line drawings for New York newspapers. His work has appeared in virtually every publication of the last 80 years, including a 74-year relationship with the *New York Times*. In 1951, he wrote and illustrated *Show Business is No Business*, a satirical primer on the mechanics of Broadway production. He is the subject of the Academy Award-nominated documentary, *The Line King*. Among his many awards, he has won two Tonys for lifetime achievement and been designated a "Living Landmark" in New York. Hirschfeld has appeared in *Best Plays* since the 1952–53 edition.

John Istel has written about the theater for many publications, including the *Atlantic Monthly*, *Elle*, the *Village Voice*, *Newsday*, *New York*, *Mother Jones* and *American Theatre*. He has served as contributing editor at *American Theatre* and editor-in-chief at *Stagebill*. He has contributed entries to several reference books, including the *Reference Guide to American Literature* and *Contemporary Dramatists*, for which he was also an adviser, and has taught at New York University and City University's Medgar Evers College.

Jeffrey Eric Jenkins is the sixth editor of the *Best Plays* series founded by drama critic Burns Mantle in 1920. He has written more than 300 articles about theatre and culture for a variety of publications in the past decade. He is a faculty member in the Drama Department at New York University's Tisch School of the Arts, where he has taught theatre studies—with an emphasis in United States drama and theatre—since 1998. Jenkins has also taught at Carnegie Mellon University, the University of Washington, and SUNY–Stony Brook. Jenkins received degrees in drama and theatre arts from Carnegie Mellon University and San Francisco State University, and he has directed more than two dozen productions in professional and educational theaters across the United States. Jenkins is a former board member of the American Theatre Critics Association (1995–2001) and served as the association's chairman from 1999 to 2001. He is a board member of the American Theatre and Drama Society and the Theater Hall of Fame.

Vivian Cary Jenkins spent more than 20 years working as a healthcare administrator in both the public and private sectors. Prior to her work in healthcare, she was a student at the School of the American Ballet, a dancer and a Peace Corps volunteer in Honduras. Over the past decade, she has also begun to develop her skills as a theater producer, with productions of Sam Shepard's *True West* and Slawomir Mrozek's *The Emigrants*.

Jeffrey Finn Productions is an entertainment and production management company. JFP credits include *Game Show* (US and International productions) for which Jeffrey Finn is also a co-author, and Broadway National Tours including *The Who's Tommy*, *Leader of the Pack*, *Promises, Promises*, *Company*, *Chess*, Diahann Carroll in *Almost Like Being in Love*, Marilyn McCoo & Billy Davis Jr. in *Hit Me With a Hot Note!*, *A Swell Party*, *Puttin' on the Ritz* and *A Slice of Saturday Night*. JFP also features a Special Events Division customizing Broadway corporate entertainment.

Julius Novick, author of *Beyond Broadway: The Quest for Permanent Theaters*, has been a theater critic at the *Village Voice*, Channel 13, the *New York Observer* and *New York Newsday*, and has written for *American Theatre*, *Harper's Magazine*, *The Threepenny Review*, *The Nation*, the *Los Angeles Times* and the *New York Times*. He is a recipient of the George Jean Nathan Award for Dramatic Criticism, and has served as chairman of the Pulitzer Prize Drama Jury. He has taught at New York University, Juilliard, Columbia, Harvard and Purchase College, SUNY.

Christopher Rawson has been drama critic at the *Pittsburgh Post-Gazette* since 1983 and drama editor since 1990; also reviewing regularly in New York and London. A former chairman of the American Theatre Critics Association, he serves on the board of directors of the Theater Hall of Fame. His BA is from Harvard, and MA and PhD (English literature) from the University of Washington. A member of the University of Pittsburgh English Department since 1968, he teaches Shakespeare, satire and criticism.

Michael Sommers is the New York theater reviewer for the *Star-Ledger* of New Jersey, the *Staten Island Advance* and other Newhouse News publications. He is the president of the New York Drama Critics Circle.

Jeffrey Sweet is the author of three books on theatre, *Something Wonderful Right Away* (about Second City), *The Dramatist's Toolkit* and *Solving Your Script*, and for eleven years was associate editor to Otis L. Guernsey Jr. of the *Best Plays* series. He is a widely-produced playwright and television writer, teaches playwriting for the Actors Studio MFA program and serves on the Council of the Dramatists Guild of America.

Bruce Weber, a theater critic for the *New York Times*, has been on staff at the newspaper, as an editor, reporter and writer, since 1986. A former fiction editor for *Esquire* magazine, he was the editor of the collection *Look Who's Talking: An Anthology of Voices in the Modern American Short Story*, and he is the author, with the dancer Savion Glover, of *Savion! My Life in Tap*.

Charles Wright grew up in eastern Tennessee and attended Vanderbilt University, where he studied with English poet Donald Davie. Subsequently, he earned degrees at Oxford and the University of Pennsylvania. For the past decade, he has covered theater and books for *Biography Magazine* and its predecessor, *A&E Monthly*. A resident of New York City, he writes for a variety of publications and serves on the board of directors of the Drama Desk.

Index

Titles in bold are play titles.
Page numbers in italic indicate essay citations.
Page numbers in bold italic indicate Broadway and Off Broadway listings.